PERTURBED SPIRIT

The Life and Personality

of Samuel Taylor Coleridge

2

DOUGHTY, Oswald. **Perturbed spirit: the life and personality of Samuel Taylor Coleridge. Fairleigh Dickinson, 1981. 565p index 78-66792. 35.00 ISBN 0-8386-2353-0. CIP**
One of the most comprehensive to date, Doughty's biography of Coleridge covers every aspect of his life: indolence; self-pity; illness and opium addiction; unsatisfactory marriage; love for Sarah Hutchinson; travels; impecuniousness; loss of inspiration; plagiarism; ill treatment of friends; and fame as poet, critic, lecturer, and talker. It provides what is perhaps the most detailed account of the great quarrel between Coleridge and Wordsworth. Though ·Doughty relies heavily on Coleridge's letters and notebooks (the publisher claims "ample use of material that had previously been unpublished") and on writings of Coleridge's acquaintances, he offers exceedingly sparse documentation. Despite the absence of bibliography or acknowledgements, this book obviously contains monumental research. It does, however, also contain numerous speculative statements of how Coleridge "probably" felt or acted in given situations. Despite the book's continual negative revelations, readers will emerge with sympathetic appreciation of Coleridge's genius as poet, critic, and thinker.

Thus Doughty has captured the enigma that is Coleridge. Although an inexcusably large number of typographical and punctuation errors mar this work, it represents a major achievement by an eminent scholar. Well indexed. An essential for all Coleridge collections.

OTHER BOOKS BY OSWALD DOUGHTY

Author:
English Lyric in the Age of Reason
Forgotten Lyrics of the Eighteenth Century
A Victorian Romantic: Dante Gabriel Rossetti
Dante Gabriel Rossetti
*Early Diamond Days: The Opening of the Diamond Fields
 in South Africa*
William Collins

Editor:
The Beggar's Opera by John Gay
Polly. An Opera by John Gay
The Vicar of Wakefield by Oliver Goldsmith
The Castle of Otranto by Horace Walpole
*The Letters of D. G. Rossetti to His Publisher,
 F. S. Ellis*
The Poems of Dante Gabriel Rossetti
The Letters of D. G. Rossetti (coeditor)

Perturbed Spirit

The Life and Personality of Samuel Taylor Coleridge

Oswald Doughty

Rutherford • Madison • Teaneck
Fairleigh Dickinson University Press
London and Toronto: Associated University Presses

© 1981 by Associated University Presses, Inc.

Associated University Presses, Inc.
4 Cornwall Drive
East Brunswick, New Jersey 08816

Associated University Presses Ltd.
69 Fleet Street
London EC4Y 1EU, England

Associated University Presses
Toronto, Ontario, Canada M5E 1A7

Library of Congress Cataloging in Publication Data

Doughty, Oswald.
　Perturbed spirit.

　Includes index.
　1. Coleridge, Samuel Taylor, 1772–1834—Biography.
2. Poets, English—19th century—Biography. 3. Critics
—England—Biography.　I. Title.
PR4483.D6　1981　　　821'.7　　　78-66792
ISBN 0-8386-2353-0　　　　　　　AACR2

Printed in the United States of America

Publisher's Note

The late Oswald Doughty was born July 4, 1889, in Yorkshire, England. He was graduated from both Durham and Oxford Universities. After holding a Senior Lectureship in English at London University, he was appointed to the Arderne Chair of English Literature at Capetown University, which he occupied until his retirement.

After editing a number of eighteenth-century classics and writing two books on the eighteenth-century English lyric, Professor Doughty turned his attention to Dante Gabriel Rossetti, in connection with which his most celebrated work was a life of Rossetti entitled *A Victorian Romantic*.

After his retirement Professor Doughty devoted his life entirely to writing. *Perturbed Spirit*, which he considered to be his best work, was completed only shortly before his death on April 8, 1975, in Capetown. The manuscript was subsequently submitted for publication by the author's daughter, Mrs. Odile Sophia Pittman of London.

Perturbed Spirit contains only a few notes, no bibliography, and no acknowledgments. However, the Editorial Committee of Fairleigh Dickinson University Press felt it desirable to make available the work of a renowned scholar with an impeccable reputation in his field. This book is the result of careful study and research, and is eminently worthy of posthumous publication, even without more extensive documentation.

It is for the biographer, not the Poet, to give the accidents of individual life.

> —Coleridge to William Wordsworth, May 30, 1815

Facts—stubborn facts! none of your theory!

> —Coleridge, *Anima Poetae* (1805)

Truth! Truth! but yet Charity! Charity!

> —Coleridge's *Notebook*, December 23, 1804

Contents

Preface

On February 6, 1797, Samuel Taylor Coleridge, then only twenty-four years of age, sent Poole the following plan for his own autobiography:

> I could inform the dullest author how he might write an interesting book—let him relate the events of his own Life with honesty, not disguising the feelings that accompanied them. . . .As to my Life, it has all the charms of variety: high Life, and low Life, Vices and Virtues, great Folly and some Wisdom. However what I am depends on what I have been; and you, my best Friend! have a right to the narration.—To me the task will be a useful one; it will renew and deepen *my* reflections on the past; and it will perhaps make you behold with no unforgiving or Impatient eye those weaknesses and defects in my character, which so many untoward circumstances have concurred to plant there.

Although Coleridge never wrote his autobiography, on various occasions his thoughts again turned to biography and biographers. On May 30, 1815, he told Wordsworth: "It is for the biographer, not the poet, to give the accidents of individual life." Ten years before, Coleridge told his nephew Henry Nelson Coleridge: "Facts—stubborn facts! None of your theory!" In a similarly realistic mood, though particularly conscious of his weaknesses, Coleridge in his *Notebook*, on December 23, 1804, implored his imaginary critics: "Truth! Truth! but yet Charity! Charity!"

In the following pages, in accordance with Coleridge's excellent suggestions for an autobiography, the reader will find Coleridge himself, self-revealed in his own words and actions, as he lived his life in this world. But Coleridge's own words are here supplemented by the words and actions of his most intimate friends and relatives—and, occasionally, of his enemies. In this way the reader may learn how to know Coleridge as one learns to know people in real life.

When the eulogistic Dr. Gillman published the first and only volume of his never completed *Life of Coleridge*—four years after Coleridge's death—Wordsworth remarked: "Of idolatrous biography I think very lightly."

Coleridge's friend Joseph Cottle clearly defined what should be the biographer's aim, when in his *Early Recollections*, published the year after the publication of Gillman's *Life of Coleridge*, he wrote: "Neither to clothe the subject of biography with undeserved applause, nor unmerited censure, but to present an exact portraiture, is the object which ought scrupulously to be aimed at by every impartial writer.'' Perhaps indeed Coleridge's own warning ''Truth! Truth! but yet Charity! Charity!'' is the best advice for his biographers.

Coleridge, whose vices and virtues are inextricably mingled, presents an unusually difficult subject for the impartial biographer. But fortunately, he has unintentionally provided in his voluminous and often self-revealing correspondence and private notebooks the most intimate biographical material.

Thus it is that in the following pages I attempt an intimate presentation of ''the living Coleridge'' on his stormy voyage through life. In this way I trust I may attain not only detachment and impartiality, but also freedom from idolatry or denigration, without excluding the interest of Coleridge's intense, self-contradictory personality.

O.D.

Introduction

Samuel Taylor Coleridge's self-contradictory temperament is too complex for summary treatment. For such a person, self-conflict and conflict with the world about him were almost inevitable, at least for one so egotistical and so lacking in emotional self-control as himself. Hence came frustrations and disappointments. Haunted by the loss of his poetic inspiration, he attempted to find compensation in purely abstract intellectual studies— metaphysics, philosophy, and theology. But unable to concentrate amid such varied interests, Coleridge, in despair, increasingly resorted to opium and brandy for relief from his depression. Nor was this all. Other sources of his unhappiness were his failure in a first love, an unhappy marriage, and a later idealized, probably unrealized, passion. In these circumstances, Coleridge came to see himself as doomed to complete frustration, failure, and disappointment in all his undertakings. His keen consciousness of the real world about him, and his realization of his temperamental inability to cope with it, his letters and private memoranda continually reveal. Coleridge might well have said, like the modern poet:

I a stranger, and afraid
In a world I never made.

Despite the unemotional factuality of this biography of Coleridge, no intelligent reader can fail to perceive the essential tragedy of Coleridge's existence. His inadequacy to meet the ordinary daily demands of life has been imputed by previous biographers—perhaps too readily—to weakness of will. The modern psychologist would doubtless regard it as primarily due to "anxiety hysteria." Coleridge once rightly denounced as facile and false the literary criticism in which the critic substitutes himself for the character he is criticizing. But when Coleridge did this in the case of Hamlet, he had some excuse: for Hamlet's temperament was like Coleridge's, basically hysterical and contemplative. Both shared the same "anxiety hysteria" arising from conflicting demands upon their emotional personalities, and opposed to their natural tendencies and desires.

Perhaps the sudden death of his father in the night, in Coleridge's eighth year, affected the little boy's development. At any rate, clear signs of Coleridge's hyperemotional state soon appeared in his life and continued, though more discreetly, almost to the end. Thus, while still a child, Coleridge, quarreling with his brother, angrily rushed out into the surrounding country and remained there all night, until found by searchers, asleep and half frozen. Similarly, when disappointed in his passion for Mary Evans, Coleridge rushed from his Cambridge studies into the army as a refuge and then was glad to be saved again by his friends.

Although in later life Coleridge gained more self-control amid increasing disappointments and frustrations, he was never entirely master of this impulse to escape from any duty or environment that irked him. It was thus that to escape from his marriage he fled to Malta; and even to the end under the influence of real or imaginary grievances, he fled at times from his benefactors, the Morgans and the Gillmans. Throughout his life this almost uncontrollable impulse to escape from unpleasant realities occurs, not only in his relations with friends, but also and continually in those with his publishers. In all these disappointments, self-contradictions, and such, Coleridge's chief means of escape—opium (partly the cause and partly the consequence of his misfortunes)—was always at hand, and was never entirely rejected to the end of his life.

For Coleridge the hysteric, the only truth of things was his own mood at the time of writing, and this from moment to moment may have completely changed but inevitably found expression. This, too, largely explains the frequent self-contradictions (sometimes apparently direct falsehoods) in his correspondence written about one person to another. This Southey rightly condemned even to Coleridge himself. It was this that made poor Coleridge so often an uncertain friend or a positive enemy.

Although Coleridge sought detachment from unhappy realities in abstract subjects, they proved but inadequate compensations for the many disappointments that life brought him. Nevertheless, these abstractions seemed to him entities that could not disappoint, and they gave him many opportunities for the supersubtle argumentation that he loved. Such argumentation was more important to Coleridge than the final results of his work in these subjects. Even so sympathetic an expositor of Coleridge's philosophy as Muirhead declared: "The philosophical development of a mind like Coleridge's, omnivorous, sensitive, growing to the last, is necessarily a tangled tale; in his case rendered more tangled still by apparently contradictory accounts of it in his own writings and conversations."[1] And Elton writes: "His great renovated scheme of metaphysics, ethics and aesthetics remained in splinters, which flaw far and pierced deep; and his disciples tried, with little success, to piece it out after he had gone."[2] Sampson's opinion of Coleridge's metaphysics is even more incisive: "For a year or two Coleridge spoke in poetry as mortal man had never spoken before; and then having wandered into his metaphysical Venusberg he could never get out, and his song was lost to men."[3]

If one turns from these subjects to Coleridge's political writings, the result is the same. "Coleridge gave no systematic form to his political thought," says one of Coleridge's critics:

> What he called his "omni-pregnant nihil-parturient genius" shrank from so intensive an effort; and when he did bring forth, it was, as he said, after the manner of Surinam toads—"as they crawl on, little toads vegetate out from back and sides, grow quickly, and draw off the attention from the mother toad!" So his ideas have to be gathered from newspaper articles, scattered comments and digressions, and it is difficult to know how closely any pattern formed from these sources corresponds to the true design of his thought.[4]

That Coleridge's writings are thus fragmentary was the almost inevitable result of his bewilderment; when he sat down to write, such a great variety of interests and ideas pressed for his attention. The frustration, disappointment, anxiety, and a distaste for writing that he expressed from time to time were the consequence. Coleridge often proclaimed himself a "genius," but real genius almost always concentrates upon material that offers the fullest expression for the individual's talent and does not dissipate its energy amid rival claims for attention. The surprising range of Coleridge's interests and knowledge was remarked on by his contemporaries and led the satirical Peacock to present him in *Headlong Hall* as "Mr. Panscope: the chemical, botanical, geological, astronomical, mathematical, metaphysical, meteorological, anatomical, physiological, galvanistical, musical, pictorial, bibliographical, critical philosopher who had run through the whole circle of the sciences, and understood them all equally well." The effect of opium upon intellectuals, the experts state, is to suggest impossibly grandiose plans for intellectual works. In Coleridge's hundred dream volumes on impossibly grandiose subjects one finds confirmation of the opium experts' opinion, and additional reasons for Coleridge's disappointments.

Perhaps the bitterest disappointment, one that dogged Coleridge throughout his life, was the failure of his early poetic inspiration. Coleridge's highest achievement in essential poetry was undoubtedly "Dejection," the ode inspired by his unhappy love for Sara Hutchinson; it would seem also in part to have been inspired by the proximity of Wordsworth, who was then writing his great "Ode: Intimations of Immortality from Recollections of Early Childhood."

It is significant that Coleridge's three most famous poems are not self-expression like his "Dejection," but were largely inspired by the then fashionable *Tales of Terror*, which in fact he disliked. If one accepts, at least for the moment, Coleridge's sometimes suggestive but unpsychological distinction between fancy and imagination, one must surely regard these three poems as basically the product of fancy. Of Coleridge's later poems—some inspired by his need of money and written for magazines—many do not rise above the level of competent verse, while some come perilously near to doggerel. Although disappointment in love is Coleridge's occasional theme to the end, he never again rose to the height of his "Dejection" ode of 1802.

Disappointment in prose as well as in poetry haunted Coleridge to the last. The *Logosophia*, which he intended to be his greatest work, remained in fragments. Coleridge emphasized to various friends throughout his life his dislike of writing. "I compose very little," he told Thelwall in 1796, "and I absolutely hate composition." Twenty-nine years later, describing to his nephew, John Taylor Coleridge, the miseries of authorship, Coleridge wrote: "I had time out of mind given it up as a lost cause, given myself over, I mean, as a predestined author, tho' without a drop of true *Author* Blood in my veins."

In the journalistic articles of his earlier years, Coleridge wrote in a style of admirable directness and brevity. The very condition of such writing, the speed that such articles in the daily press demanded—much as he disliked it—prevented the wanderings of his subtle and hesitating mind in a maze of possibilities, probabilities, qualifications, modifications, and doubts. Stuart, the newspaper editor, clearly saw this when he said of Coleridge that he could never write but with the printer's devil at his elbow.

Coleridge's later style in prose, so strangely contrasting with his early journalistic writings, was well described by Southey when he told his friend Miss Barker in 1810: "It is not a little extraordinary that Coleridge, who is fond of logic and who has actual love and passion for close hard thinking, should write in so rambling and inconclusive a manner;. . .and he goes to work like a hound, nosing his way, turning, and twisting, and winding, and doubling, till you get weary with following the mazy movements." This style, indeed, was an unconscious mirror of Coleridge's temperamental development. Amid his incessant proliferation of ideas and his intense desire for extreme accuracy in expression, his later writing followed a serpentine course such as Southey described. Coleridge himself was unhappily aware of this, but he sometimes consoled himself with the belief that the "serpentine" was a characteristic of "genius." In these circumstances, the almost inevitable consequence was—as Elton remarks—"Coleridge. . .hardly wrote anything in prose that can be called a book."

In the final period of his life, at ease with the Gillmans, Coleridge found some compensation for his disappointed ambitions and vanity in his famous weekly "conversations," which were monologues, streams of subconsciousness. To these, delivered in a room of the Gillmans' house, a few interested persons, sometimes socially distinguished, eagerly came and increased by their account of the experience Coleridge's reputation as poet, writer, and thinker. That this was to be his destiny Coleridge almost foresaw in 1817 when he told Thomas Curtis: "Such is *my nature*, i.e. that which from complex causes, partly constitutional, partly inflicted or acquired *ab extra*—to my own unhappiness and detriment—that I can do nothing well by *effort*. Hence it is that I often converse better than I can compose. . .[*sic*].''

It is not strange that at one period of his life Coleridge was interested in "animal magnetism"—then a popular subject of discussion—for Coleridge possessed it in various forms. As this quality finds but little open expression in his correspondence, it is well to describe it in some detail here, and to emphasize its importance throughout Coleridge's life. By his external geniality and charm, Coleridge created everywhere friends and helpers, and throughout the last eighteen years of his life he completely enslaved his benefactors, the fascinated Gillmans. How early he became aware of his power he revealed when he was only thirty-one years of age, in a letter to his wife. "You know," he wrote, "it is no new thing for people to take sudden and hot likings for me.''

Well aware of this power, Coleridge sometimes consciously employed it for his own advantage. Some he fascinated by his "natural gladness"—as Dr. Gillman described it. This in favorable circumstances might develop into Bohemian gaiety. Coleridge's nature, wrote Dr. Gillman, "was remarkably joyous.'' With this Wordsworth would have agreed, for as early as 1802 he described Coleridge, in stanzas written in the *Castle of Indolence*, thus: "Noisy he was, and gamesome as a boy.'' One of Coleridge's manuscript notes in a copy of the *Friend* shows that he considered the continuation of this boyish spirit into manhood an essential quality of genius. "I define Genius," he wrote, "as originality in intellectual construction: the moral accompaniment and actuating principle of which consists perhaps in the carrying on of the freshness and feelings of childhood into the powers of manhood." How strongly this quality in Coleridge appealed to Wordsworth, the latter again reveals in his poem "A Character," a description of his friend, which concludes:

This picture from nature may seem to depart,
Yet the Man would at once run away with your heart;
And I for five centuries right gladly would be
Such an odd such a kind happy creature as he.

Coleridge's moods of happiness, kindness, playfulness, and geniality were not, however, the only sources of his charm. Many, including Wordsworth, found the chief source of Coleridge's attraction in his intellectual and critical powers, and those who thus regarded him with reverent miscomprehension were often even more attracted than those who understood him.

The list of Coleridge's friends and acquaintances who were fascinated by his charm in one way or another is a long one. It includes Poole, Southey, Stuart, De Quincey, Hazlitt, Lamb, Morgan, Allsop, and many others. For women, Coleridge's appeal was generally, though of course unconsciously, to their maternal instinct to protect the weak, which his appearance of

being lost and hopeless in the world particularly stimulated. Of such were
Mrs. Clarkson and above all Mrs. Gillman, who, even after Coleridge's
death, mourned him to the end of her life. For some women, however,
Coleridge's chief attraction was rather his personality as a whole,
particularly his intellectual and literary abilities. Among these were
Dorothy Wordsworth and Sara Hutchinson, who at different periods of their
lives were for some years in love with Coleridge. But Coleridge's continual
literary unproductiveness and his demands upon the admirers who
advanced money to meet his debts too often created disillusion and
disappointment among them; and some, like Josiah Wedgwood, withdrew
their support when the great poems and works that they had expected from
Coleridge failed to appear. Beyond doubt Coleridge was in Hazlitt's mind
when, in a lecture on the English poets, he wrote: "Poets are not ideal
beings; they have their prose sides, like the commonest of the people."

For the first time, Mrs. Coleridge takes here her rightful place among the
dramatis personae of Coleridge's life. Her essentially eighteenth-century
nature—realistic, patient when not provoked—presents a striking contrast
to her husband's emotional, imaginative, and vacillating temperament. This
contrast of temperaments must sometimes have oppressed Coleridge with
the unhappy consciousness of his own inadequacy amid realities. In later
life, after revolting against Wordsworth's moral domination, Coleridge
described himself, with relief, "a free man." The same sense of escape to
freedom must have been Coleridge's after his separation from his wife.
Certainly, Southey's reference to his own occasional playful, irritating
teasing of Mrs. Coleridge suggests less self-control in her than appears in
her admirable letters to Poole. Even daughter Sara Coleridge, despite her
admiration for her mother, admitted the occasional hastiness of her
temper, though as a small fault far outweighed by great virtues: "Hasty she
was at the moment of provocation, but never was anyone more just to all
mankind, as far as her knowledge and insight extended, less swayed by
peevish resentments in her deliberate judgments."

A letter written by Sara Coleridge to Aubrey de Vere in 1849 shows that
Mrs. Coleridge by 1817, long after the separation from her husband, had
developed at the age of forty-seven a touch of eccentricity that was at the same
time characteristically economical. "I remember," wrote Sara,

> Mama at my age put on quite the old woman, and the Keswick people
> called her "auld Mrs. Cauldridge," though her complexion was a hundred
> times clearer and rosier than mine is now, and her cheeks rounder. As for
> her hair, she cut it all off and wore a wig when she was quite a young
> woman, and her every-day front (a sort of semi-wig or wig to wear with a
> cap) for she was too economical to wear the glossy one in common, was
> as dry and rough and dull as a piece of stubble, and as short and stumpy!

Then, overcome by intimate memories of her dear, dead mother, Sara
continued: "Dear mother! what an honest, simple, lively-minded, affectionate

woman she was, how free from disguise and artifice, how much less she played tricks with herself, and tried to be and seem more and better than she was, than the generality of the world!"

Poole's friendship and evident occasional support of Mrs. Coleridge after the separation clearly show his sympathy with her. Nor was Poole Mrs. Coleridge's only sympathizer at Stowey. So too was a young naturalist there, a Mr. Baker. "Mrs. Coleridge," he said, "struck him as 'a quiet, unaffected, pleasant lady' whom he was a little inclined to pity for being 'made uncomfortable by the habits of a man of learning,' who not only 'sat up late,' but was even capable of getting up 'after he had retired to rest, when a bright idea came to his mind.' "[5] Coleridge's biographer, Campbell, speaks sympathetically of Mrs. Coleridge's unhappy marriage. "Coleridge," he wrote, "was a difficult man to manage, and. . .his wife was unequal to the task. It is doubtless a correct view, but it does not go deep enough. Coleridge's many faults as a husband have been made patent enough, perhaps more than enough; of Mrs. Coleridge as a wife, I have heard of none save that sometimes she was 'fretful.' Had she not fretted, and often, it would have been a miracle, for she had provocation in abundance."[6]

It is Chambers, who in the introduction to his biography of Coleridge, solemnly warns his readers of the darker aspects of their impending fate: "He who walks with Coleridge must thread thorny ways and pass through valleys of humiliation."[7] The truth of this no one who reads the present work can fail to appreciate. But, as Charles Lamb well knew, humor, conscious and unconscious, is often present to lighten the occasional gloom.

NOTES TO INTRODUCTION

1. J. H. Muirhead, *Coleridge as Philosopher* (London, 1930), p. 35.
2. Oliver Elton, *A Survey of English Literature* (London, 1920), 2:102.
3. George Sampson, *The Concise Cambridge History of English Literature* (Cambridge, 1841), p. 180.
4. Harold Beeley, "The Political Thought of Coleridge," in *Coleridge Studies*, ed. Edmund Blunden and Earl Leslie Briggs (London, 1934), p. 151.
5. Mrs. Henry Sandford, *Thomas Poole and His Friends* (London, 1888), p. 291.
6. J. Dykes Campbell, *Samuel Taylor Coleridge: A Narrative of the Events in His Life* (London, 1894), p. 131.
7. E. K. Chambers, *Samuel Taylor Coleridge* (Oxford, 1938), p. viii.

PERTURBED SPIRIT

The Life and Personality
of Samuel Taylor Coleridge

PART I

1772-1806: Birth-33 Years. Hopes and Disappointments— Escape to Opium and Malta.

1 "Mother's Darling" (1772-82)

"I was my mother's darling. . . "
—*Coleridge to Poole, October 9, 1797*

On October 4, 1781, the Reverend John Coleridge, vicar and schoolmaster of Ottery Saint Mary in Devon, returned home "in high health and good spirits." He had been to Plymouth to enter his son Francis as a midshipman in the navy, and having been fortunate enough to place him "under a religious captain," he was particularly pleased. Refreshed by a bowl of punch, the vicar related to his family the chief incidents of his journey, including an unusually vivid dream in which "Death appeared and touched him with his dart." Soon afterward Mr. Coleridge went to bed, but in the night died suddenly and without warning. Little Samuel, his youngest son, then only eight years old, was sleeping, unaware of his father's return. Awakened by his mother's scream, he cried instinctively: "Papa is dead!" That was a turning point in Samuel Taylor Coleridge's life.

The good vicar, of humble parentage, had made his own way in a life of sixty-two years, which had not been without its vicissitudes. His father had been a weaver or wool dealer in a Devonshire village. Samuel, when twenty-four and romantically enthusiastic for the French Revolution and sansculottism, delightedly asserted a plebeian origin for himself, declaring his father to have been a workhouse bastard. Two years later he claimed a similar distinction for his great-grandfather, telling a friend, after meeting an "old boy" of his father's school: "*My* Great-grandfather was his Great-great-grandfather's Bastard"—a relationship he thought "tender and interesting."

Whatever the truth or otherwise in Samuel's assertions, dull, unromantic, verifiable records merely inform one that the weaver sent his son John to the local grammar school until, falling on evil days, he gladly accepted a friend's generosity to complete his son's school course.

Young John in time became schoolteacher, curate, and husband, and when twenty-eight years old, having saved sufficient funds for his purpose, entered Sidney-Sussex College, Cambridge. Despite, or perhaps because of, his scholarly interests, he took no degree. In 1754, three years a widower and with four daughters, he married Ann Bowden, daughter of a solid farming family. Here, too, Samuel later found a politically satisfactory humble origin. The

Bowdens, he said, "inherited a house-style and a pigstye in the Exmore
Country in the reign of Elizabeth, and nothing better since that time." Within
eighteen years of her marriage, Ann presented her husband with one daughter
and nine sons, one of whom died in infancy. The others were: John, born in
1754; William, in 1758; James, in 1759; Edward, in 1760; George, in 1764;
Luke, in 1765; Ann, in 1767; Francis ("Frank"), in 1770, and Samuel, in 1772.

In 1760, after a long experience as schoolmaster and curate elsewhere, the
Reverend John Coleridge became vicar of Ottery and master of its ancient
grammar school. And there he remained until his death.

Samuel loved and honored the memory of his "revered" father, his
companion in his earliest years, to the end of his life. "I confess," he wrote in
middle age, "I have a feeling one third pride and two thirds tenderness, in
being told that I strongly resemble him in person and mind." The father, who
was fifty-three when Samuel was born, fully returned his son's affection,
loving him "as the child of his old age."

In later years Samuel loved to recall how his father used to take him on his
knee for "long conversations," and at night point out to him the stars by
name, "worlds rolling round them," and "Jupiter, a thousand times larger
than our world." To all, little Samuel listened "with a profound delight and
admiration; but without the least mixture of wonder or incredulity. For from
my early reading of faery tales and Genii, etc., my mind had been habituated
to the Vast, and I never regarded *my senses* in any way as the criteria of my
belief. I regulated all my creeds by my conceptions not by my *sight* even at that
age."

But Samuel's affection did not blind him to the touch of eccentricity in his
father, at times even of unconscious comedy. The memory of it occasionally
provoked in the son an undertone, sometimes indeed an overtone, of kindly
amusement as he recalled early days. Then, to intimate friends, he would tell
tales of his father's endearing peculiarities until tears of laughter ran down his
cheeks. "The truth is," he once summarily remarked, "my father was not a
first-rate genius; he was, however, a first-rate Christian. In general good-
heartedness, absentness of mind and excessive ignorance of the world, he was
a perfect Parson Adams." On another occasion Samuel described him
similarly as "an Israelite without guile; simple, generous and, taking some
scripture texts in their literal sense, conscientiously indifferent to the good or
evil of this world." The distinguished son was to inherit several of his
undistinguished father's characteristics, including one not yet mentioned: the
good vicar's tendency, "under the stimulus of society and eager
conversation," to be affected by wine.

Unlike her husband, Samuel's mother was far from "indifferent to the good
and evil of this world." On the contrary, she was wisely ambitious for the
welfare of her sons, and when the unworldly—perhaps also somewhat
lethargic—vicar would have let them become tradesmen ("blacksmiths," said
Samuel, sardonically in later years), she intervened to such effect that three of
them, including the "midshipman," became army officers, another became a

doctor, and three more adopted their father's profession of parson-school-master. The early deaths of five of her nine sons and of her only daughter must have deeply grieved her.

Mrs. Coleridge's family pride and practicality gained Samuel admittance into the distinguished London orphanage school, Christ's Hospital. But characteristically, she disliked the school uniform of blue coat and yellow stocking, advertising, it seemed to her, the stigma of charity. For that reason she would have preferred the Charterhouse. In youth Samuel regarded his mother's pride and ambition with a sardonic eye. When a pompous neighbor —a nobody whose son-in-law's sister's husband had just been made governor general of India—happened to meet Mrs. Coleridge, Samuel enjoyed the comedy of the situation and described it to his brother George: "What a puffed-up creature! What pomposity! Our mother positively drinks in his long-winded speeches, and dreams of the most wonderful prospects." Mrs. Coleridge was, however, an unconsciously pathetic figure; for this attempt to advance the career of her son Francis in the Indian Army came too late. John, his brother and brother officer, had died five years before; and now, although Mrs. Coleridge had not yet learned it, Francis, too, was dead.

Despite the romantic tendency of Mrs. Coleridge's ambitions in domestic matters, she was severely practical. "An admirable economist and managed exclusively," said Samuel. It is thus one sees her, as in a domestic interior of the Dutch School, "mending stockings" in the evenings while little Samuel sits on his stool beside her and reads the *Arabian Nights*. A widow with grown sons, she evidently maintained strict authority in the home for their good. Doubtless her memory of her good husband's little weakness, perhaps even of that last possibly fatal bowl of punch, explains the message that Samuel, aged twenty and visiting his mother, sent to his brother George: "As to wine, not a single drop. I must not get out our Caecuban;* that is mother's fixed ruling."

Mrs. Coleridge's affection for her late husband is revealed in one or two glimpses of her after his death. Young Samuel temporarily attending the Ottery School under his father's successor, and amusing his mother with tales of the new master's mistakes in Latin grammar, observed that her pleasure in his tales were increased by the fact that "every detraction" from the master's merits seemed to her "an oblation to the memory of my father." Southey, calling on the family in September 1799, during one of Samuel's short and rare visits home, described to a friend an amusing scene that he had just witnessed, in which the old lady showed the same characteristic: "We were all a good deal amused by the old lady. She could not hear what was going on, but seeing Samuel arguing with his brothers, took it for granted that he must have been wrong, and cried out 'Ah! if your poor father had been alive, he'd soon have convinced you.' "

---

* *Caecuban*: A district in Latium famed for its wine; also the wine itself.

That despite her practicality and self-control Mrs. Coleridge was fundamentally emotional appears from Samuel's occasional references to her in his letters, particularly from his reminiscences of infancy. "I was my mother's darling," he declared. When after a childlike quarrel with a brother he ran away and hid, she was "almost distracted"; when he was found, she was "outrageous with joy." When after a long absence from home he returned as a young man, she received him "with transport." Such were Samuel's recollections of her. Yet there were no signs of a close relationship between her and her gifted but erratic son after he left home for school.

The "darling" of both parents, Samuel incurred the jealousy of his brothers, particularly of "Frank," who was influenced, said Samuel, by a jealous nurse. Because of this he told James Gillman, the friend and protector of his last years,

> I was in earliest childhood huffed away from the enjoyment of muscular activity from play, to take refuge at my mother's side, on my little stool, to read my little book, and to listen to the talk of my elders. I was driven from life in motion to life in thought and sensation. I never played except by myself, and then only acting over what I had been reading or fancying, or half one, half the other, with a stick cutting down weeds and nettles, as one of the seven champions of Christendom.

His brothers' destructive jealousy Samuel attributed to the favoritism accorded himself by his parents, and at least once in later life he evidently regretted it when he wrote: "our best loves and solicitudes may be in excess, and assuredly are so when they are exclusively confined to one object, or so attached as to distract from the love and care due to others, even as the anxious love of a mother for a favourite child."

The picture that Samuel painted in later years of his early childhood at home is in general unhappy, although in his poems and letters it occasionally appears in brighter colors. In brief, he came to see himself as a child petted by doting parents, disliked by jealous elder brothers and consequently timid, a tell-tale, hypersensitive, solitary, fascinated by fairy tales and the world of his own imagination, aloof from sports and games, an incessant reader, precocious, witty, satirical, and vain. Such qualities (without his brothers' "jealousy") were sufficient to set not only his brothers but "normal" schoolmates against him—as they did. "Alas!" he declared near the end of his life, "I had all the simplicity, all the docility of the little child, but none of the child's habits. I never thought as a child, never had the language of a child."

It is as such that one sees him in the few but vivid pictures that Coleridge later made of himself in these earliest days. Handsome Frank, his brother, only two years older than himself, was evidently a leading influence upon him until he left home. Frank, the contrary of himself, the handsomest of all the brothers, all of whom but Samuel were handsome: Frank so vital, so active, climbing, fighting, playing, robbing orchards, hating books, hating, beating, and tormenting Samuel too—"in a strange mixture of admiration and contempt," said Samuel. One sees Frank creeping upstairs, though forbidden, during Samuel's illness, to read Pope's *Homer* to him, despite Frank's hatred of reading. The moral and emotional disturbance, the feeling of inferiority that Frank by contrast created in Samuel, made his departure for the navy before Samuel was nine years old a blessing, although it left Samuel brotherless at home.

How deeply his relations with Frank affected Samuel is clearly and very consciously revealed in his longest, most detailed reminiscence of these years. How long that influence remained with Samuel the vividness of the memory itself clearly shows. In brief, little Samuel, annoyed by one of Frank's irritating practical jokes played upon him, struck him and was at once terrified and agonized by Frank's shamming dead, before suddenly jumping up and attacking Samuel, who seized a knife in his rage, only to have it snatched from his hand by his mother. Desperate, Samuel ran to the river and stayed hidden all night, gratified by the thought of his mother's distress and the shouts of the search parties he evaded. Not until the next morning was he found, asleep, cold, and stiff, and with the first germs of the rheumatic illness that was said to haunt him throughout life. For such a child as Coleridge, this permanent, intimate environment of tense unhappy emotions—anger, inferiority, frustration, anxiety, and instinctive escape—was almost the worst that could be found.

Rejected by his brothers and schoolmates in their games, Samuel found compensations in the world of imagination: in reading fairytales incessantly, and with such absorption that the world of *Jack-the-Giant Killer, Robinson Crusoe,* and the *Arabian Nights* became more real to him than the external world. His father, concerned, burned his books, for Samuel was now haunted by specters. As he lay in bed in the dark he saw "armies of ugly Things bursting in upon me, and four angels keeping them off." Similar experiences in the daytime he described later as "moping": "I used to lie by the wall and *mope*; and my spirits used to come upon me suddenly, and in a flood. And then I was accustomed to run up and down the churchyard, and act over all I had been reading, on the docks and nettles and the rank grass." Thus, through the churchyard, the child entered the road to Xanadu.

But when as a man of twenty-four he looked back upon himself in childhood, the vision gave him little satisfaction. "I became a dreamer," he wrote,

and acquired an indisposition to all bodily activity. And I was fretful, and inordinately passionate, and as I could not play at anything, and was slothful, I was despised and hated by the boys. And because I could read and spell, and had, I may truly say, a memory and understanding forced into an almost unnatural ripeness, I was flattered and wondered at by all the old women; and so I became very vain, and despised most of the boys that were at all near my own age. And before I was eight years old I was a *character*. Sensibility, imagination, vanity, sloth, and feelings of deep and bitter contempt for almost all who traversed the orbit of my understanding, were even then prominent and manifest.

How unfortunate the loss of his loved and revered father must have been at this critical stage of Samuel's development is only too obvious. Not less obvious were the effects of this childhood upon Coleridge's later life.

Coleridge well knew that, for him, the child remained in the man. "What I am," he wrote long afterward, "depends upon what I have been," and in his prose and verse from time to time one finds buried like fossils unconscious memories of childhood. Thus in his "Monody on the Death of Chatterton," the memory of his mother's anxious search for him after his quarrel with Frank lurks behind the lines describing

a seeking Mother's anxious call,
Return, poor Child! Home, weary Truant, home!

And again is it not his ambitious mother who inspires, in memory, the following passage from the *Friend*: "Transfer yourself in fancy to an English cottage,

Where o'er the cradled infant bending
Hope has fixed her wishful gaze

and the fond mother dreams of her child's future fortunes—who knows but he may come home a rich merchant, like such a one? or be a bishop or a judge?" Doubtless, too, below the experiences inspiring such reminiscent passages, lay an experience deeper than all, moral and emotional, the sense of guilt at having disappointed his mother by his failure to actualize the material hopes and ambitions that she had centered upon him.

The one other early feminine influence upon Coleridge was that of his only sister, Ann, five years older than himself. For her his affection was real and deep and sometimes passionately expressed. Sweet, kind, and good he thought her, and for him, perhaps most important of all, beautiful. When she was only twenty-one, Ann died of tuberculosis. Ten years after her death Samuel, writing of her to a friend, concluded:

Rest, gentle Shade, and wait thy Maker's will;
Then rise *unchang'd*, and be an Angel still!

Two of Coleridge's brothers—James, the British soldier, and Edward, parson and teacher—inspired in him little affection. His account of his relation to them is as significant in its way, though brief, as that relating to Frank, of whom he wrote to a friend in 1793 on hearing of his death: "Within this last month I have lost a Brother and a Friend! But I struggle for cheerfulness—and sometimes, when the sun shines out, I succeed in the effort."

On the preceding day, however, he had written of Francis more intimately to his brother George, who now took the place of his father for Samuel: "Poor Francis! I have shed the tear of natural affection over him. He was the only one of my family, whom similarity of ages made more peculiarly my Brother—he was the hero of all the little tales that make the remembrance of my earliest days interesting! Yet his death filled me rather with Melancholy than Anguish." Under the emotion of the moment Samuel wrote to George with unusual frankness and critical insight an account of his attitude toward his brothers, which was also, unconsciously, a defense and an apologia:

> Of the state of my feelings with regard to my brothers, James and Edward, how shall I speak with truth yet delicacy? I will open my whole heart to you. Fraternal affection is the offspring of long habit and of reflection. But when I first went into the country (to school) I had scarcely seen either James or Edward—they had neither been the companions or the guardians of my childhood. To love them therefore was a sensation yet to be learnt:—to be learnt at an age when my best affections had been forestalled; and when long wont to admire and esteem the few I loved, I deemed admiration and esteem necessary parts in the constitution of affection.

And not only were these "necessary parts" missing in these brothers; "both the one and the other exacted a deference which, conscious of few obligations to *them*, aware of no *real* inferiority, and laughing at the artificial claims of primogeniture, I felt myself little inclined to pay." He concluded, "however, I will write to them. I will assume the semblance of affection. Perhaps by persevering in appearing, I shall learn to be—a Brother."

"Aware of no *real* inferiority": in those words Coleridge unconsciously reveals the deepest source of his later, lifelong anger with his family, particularly with his brothers. Aware of no *mental* inferiority he could have said; but he was only too well aware in childhood of his inferiority in games and sports, and in facial beauty. This last, in one so sensitive to beauty in all its forms, not only increased his bitterness but also made him self-consciously exaggerate the defects in his appearance in these later years. But this he did in the hopes of contradiction by friends. At times attempting insensibility and the relief of semihysteria, he would relapse into ironical laughter in the mistaken belief of personal ugliness. This belief was intensified during his school life in London by the sneer of a sadistic schoolmaster who, when caning him, would give him "an extra cut, because you are such an ugly fellow." As time passed, his resentment against his brothers created by his sense of inferiority, for which his mental superiority failed to provide adequate compensation, was increased by their failure to recognize his "genius," a "genius" of which he was too early convinced, and too early advertised.

This feeling of resentment of which his family was the target became fixated in him as time passed. "My family! What claims have I on my family!" he cried almost hysterically, in a letter to a friend, Thomas Poole, when almost twenty-nine years old:

A name and nothing but a name. . . .My family! I have wholly neglected them. I do not love them; their ways are not my ways, nor their thoughts my thoughts. I have no recollections of childhood connected with them, none but painful thoughts in my after years. At present I think of them habitually as commonplace rich men, bigots from ignorance, and ignorant from bigotry. To me they have always behaved unexceptionally. I have a little to thank them for, and nothing to complain of.

Yet he did complain, often, haunted by his feeling not only of inferiority, unsuccess, but also and poignantly by his sense of loneliness, of intellectual remoteness, of barriers between himself and his family that could never be crossed.

How fundamentally emotional and irrational this attitude was is shown in the way it spread beyond his family, his home, and even his village to include the whole of his native county, Devonshire, although in fact he saw little of Devonshire after leaving for school when nine years old. His occasional visits in later life were few, short, and at long, distant intervals. He attacked the county and its inhabitants with a generalizing bitterness that outstripped his indictments of his family. When twenty years old, he wrote: "When at last I revisited Devon, the manners of the inhabitants annihilated whatever tender ideas of pleasure my fancy rather than my memory had pictured to my expectation. I found them (almost universally) to be gross without openness and cunning without refinement."

At thirty-six Coleridge was even more bitter, and he extended his dislike at his own face to those of Devonians in general. "Of his abilities I know nothing," he wrote undiplomatically, recommending one Devonian in London to employment by another, "but his countenance is far more intelligent than ordinarily falls to the lot of *us* Devonshire Dumplins; for, on my conscience, I believe that both in morals and intellect, Devonshire is the Sink, the common Sewer, of England. But really, judging from outward looks, this young man might have belonged to another county without dishonouring it." The lovely Devonshire scenery he dismissed on another occasion as "tame" compared with the Somerset Quantocks—a ridiculous comparison—and the Devonshire people, as they did not sympathize with his transient revolutionary sentiments, were "bigots, unalphabeted in the first feelings of liberality."

These, however, were the rancid feelings of later years. Now, when his earliest dame's school had been followed by the years at the Ottery Grammar School, and these were also ended, as the time for his departure for London and Christ's Hospital drew near, his feelings were those natural to all children at such times: a sense of lost happiness, of the sadness of parting from a fond mother, and some fear of a strange, unknown future. When in later years the mood of self-pity, so strong in him, was in the ascendant, he lamented in verse his sad fate:

my weeping childhood, torn
By early sorrow from my native seat,
Mingled its tears with hers—my widowed parent torn.

Yet in a different more usual frame of mind he was able to write: "I quitted Ottery when I was so young that most of those endearing circumstances that are wont to render the scenes and companions of our childhood delightful in the recollection, I have associated with the place of my education." But in yet another mood, he saw Christ's Hospital, too, as an unhappy experience, a wearisome and hateful prison. The common denominator in the three moods was however, Coleridge's basic mood of self-pity. So doubtless amid tears and fears, little Samuel set out for London and Christ's Hospital.

2 "A Deserted Orphan" (1782-91)

"To a deserted Orphan every kindness appeared great."
—*Coleridge to George Coleridge, May 11, 1808*

Upon Samuel's arrival in London, his talented but too convivial uncle Charles Bowden, a widower who was an underwriter's clerk and tobacconist, received him affectionately in his home. The home was managed by a daughter Betsy and also occupied by Bowden's married sister, her children, and Betsy's friend Miss Cabriere. There Samuel was much petted. Proud of the boy's precociousness, his uncle took him on a round of coffeehouses and taverns, to meet his friends and hear Samuel discuss and dispute like a man. "Most completely spoilt and pampered, both mind and body" was Samuel's terse and ungrateful verdict in later years upon the ten weeks passed under his uncle's care.

On July 18 Samuel entered the Preparatory School of Christ's Hospital at Hertford, and for the first time "donned the blue coat and yellow stockings" that were the historic uniform of the great school. Throughout his life eating was ever an important consideration for Coleridge, who at home had rejoicingly "wallowed in a beef and pudding dinner" and never found anything that surpassed a dish of beans and bacon. At Hertford among his 300 schoolmates he was "very happy on the whole," with "plenty to eat and drink, and pudding and vegetables almost every day." But after only six weeks in this prandial paradise he was transferred to the main school in London.

His advent on that September day of 1782, as he described it years afterward, was inauspicious. It suggests no such compensation for home miseries as in another mood he later asserted. "O! what a change!" he exclaimed; "Depressed, moping, friendless, poor orphan, half starved." The food he found "cruelly insufficient," which is not surprising if the tale of another blue-coat boy—Charles Lamb—is true that "one out of two of every hot joint" was stolen by women servants. The meals apparently consisted of little but dry bread supplemented on alternate days with a little boiled beef. Except for one day in the week, Samuel complained, "I never had a bellyfull. Our appetites were *damped*, never satisfied—and we had no vegetables." The coarse food upset his sensitive stomach, the heavy regulation shoes hurt his feet, and the never-forgotten smell from the shoe cupboard hurt his nose, which was as sensitive as his stomach. And as a climax to these experiences he got "the itch." It was thus that little Samuel, not yet ten years old, began his nine years' education at Christ's Hospital.

Samuel's entry into the school brought him into contact with some 700 boys of all classes and of all ages. "A nursery of tradesmen, of merchants, of naval officers and of scholars," said Leigh Hunt, who entered Christ's Hospital two years after Coleridge had left. The only discrimination recognized there was intellectual ability; "the cleverest was the highest in rank," Hunt declared. Otherwise, all were equals: the sons of servants, of "poor gentry," of merchants, even an occasional aristocrat.

So heterogeneous an assemblage demands different departments to meet their different needs. Leigh Hunt, in his autobiography, well describes the organization of Christ's Hospital at his and Coleridge's time:

> There were five schools; a grammar-school, a mathematical or navigation-school. . .a writing, a drawing, and a reading school. Those who could not read when they came on the foundation went into the last. There were few in the last-but-one, and I scarcely know what they did, or for what object. The writing-school was for those who were intended for trade and commerce; the mathematical, for boys who went as midshipmen into the naval and East India service; and the grammar-school for such as were designed for the Church, and to go to the University.

The brief list of these departments that Coleridge sent to Poole in 1798 is identical with Leigh Hunt's.

The "Grecians," the best classical scholars, were lordly beings, dignified, aloof, superior, awaiting their scholarships to Oxford or Cambridge. The navigation-school instilled mathematics, stoicism, hardihood in its members, partly by ill treatment, blows, and other toughening methods. "Hardy, brutal and often wicked," said Lamb, who though two years younger than Coleridge had entered Christ's Hospital a few months before him. "They were," he added, "the most graceless lump in the whole mass." They were certainly the terror of the smaller fry.

Originally a Franciscan monastery—with tombs of historic aristocrats in its cloisters—Christ's Hospital, despite its egalitarian atmosphere, absorbed something of the dignity and piety of the ancient order. This occasional formal memorial dinners in the Great Hall, with its paintings by Antonio Verrio and Sir Peter Lely, helped to sustain. Less appreciated was the almost monastic routine of chapels, prayers, and Bible readings before all meals and at bedtime, a superabundance that overburdened and bored the boys. Hunt asserted, "Although the morals of the school were in the main excellent and exemplary, we all felt, without knowing it, that it was the orderliness and example of the general system that kept us so, and not the religious part of it, which seldom entered our heads at all, and only tired us when it did." Indeed, judging by such later republicans as Coleridge and Hunt, it would seem that the egalitarian system at Christ's Hospital exerted a much greater influence upon some of the boys than their devotional exercises.

Almost monastic, too, were other aspects of the daily discipline: the waking bell at 6:00 A.M. in the summer, an hour for washing and breakfast (baths not mentioned), lessons from 7:00 to 11:00, an hour's play before the midday dinner, then lessons again from 1:00 to 5:00, followed by another hour's play until 6:00 supper, and then more play until the 8:00 bedtime. In winter the only changes were to rise an hour later, at 7:00, and immediately after the 6:00 supper the boys went to bed.

In the lower school under the mild and gentlemanly master, the Reverend Matthew Field, Samuel, like the rest of his class, enjoyed several years of dreaming, idleness, and play, for Field troubled neither to teach nor to persecute. Thus, what Coleridge had been at home in infancy he still largely remained: "a playless daydreamer, a helluo librorum," as he afterward said. He remained in a "continual low fever," which combined with hunger to create for him a compensatory, imaginary world as he lay reading, "crumpled up in a sunny corner," fancying himself on Robinson Crusoe's island—finding a mountain of plum cake, and eating a room for himself, then eating it into the shapes of tables and chairs—hunger and fancy. It was certainly a very materialistic dream related perhaps to the earliest known letter by him in which, on February 4, 1785 he acknowledged to his mother, with gratitude, several small gifts from various friends at home, and was evidently anxious at not hearing "a word of the plumb [sic] cake."

This very practical letter from the twelve-year-old schoolboy gives no hint of the nostalgic youth, the pining blue-coat prisoner that he later described himself in both poetry and prose, and impressed upon his nearest friends. As early as 1798, in "Frost at Midnight," in a lovely passage, he appears as a schoolboy, longing for home:

With unclosed lids already had I dreamt
Of my sweet birth-place, and the old church-tower,
Whose bells, the poor man's only music, rang
From morn to evening, all the hot Fair-day,
So sweetly, that they stirred and haunted me
With a wild pleasure, felling on mine ear
Most like articulate sounds of things to come!
So gazed I, till the soothing things I dreamt,
Lulled me to sleep, and sleep prolonged my dreams,
And so I brooded all the following morn,
Awed by the stern preceptor's face, mine eye
Fixed with meek study on my swimming book.

When those lines were written Coleridge had fallen under Wordsworth's influence, and had even for a moment in the seventh line caught one of Wordsworth's most personal and exquisite combinations of rhythmical and verbal music. And Wordsworth caught from Coleridge the vision of him as the pathetically nostalgic schoolboy:

Who, yet a liveried schoolboy, in the depths
Of that huge city, on the leaded roof
Of that wide edifice, thy school and home,
Wert used to lie and gaze upon the clouds
Moving in heavens; or, of that pleasure tired,
To shut thine eyes, and by internal light
See trees, and meadows, and thy native stream,
Far distant, thus beheld from year to year
Of a long exile.

As late as 1802, in verses to Sara Hutchinson, Coleridge again described himself as the imprisoned schoolboy longing for home:

In my first Dawn of Youth that Fancy stole
With many secret Yearnings on my Soul.
At eve, sky-gazing in ecstatic fit
(Alas! for cloister'd in a city School
The Sky was all I knew of Beautiful).
At the barr'd window often did I sit,
And oft upon the leaded School-roof lay

Upon the imagination of Lamb as upon Wordsworth Coleridge's picture of himself as a schoolboy made a strong impression.

Coleridge drew another pathetic picture of his situation on the occasional "leave-days," when the children willy-nilly were forced out into the streets to pass the day as best they could. "Friendless wanderings," Coleridge described them; "friendless holidays of gloom haunting his memory," wrote Lamb.

Yet the reality was far different. By 1785 Samuel's two favorite brothers were in London and in close touch with him. Luke was training to be a doctor, and Samuel for a time visited him every Saturday in a London hospital. Fascinated by what he saw, medicine became one of his sudden, overwhelming enthusiasms: "O the bliss if I was permitted to hold the plasters or to attend the dressings!" He "became wild to be apprenticed to a surgeon," and he studied all the medical works he could find. Fortunately perhaps for his potential patients, his enthusiasm turned away in an opposite direction, to find inspiration in metaphysics and theology. Besides his brothers, the uncle who had received him so kindly was still there with his diverse household, and all made Samuel welcome. They treated him, he told Luke in 1787, "more kindly than I can express. I dine there every Saturday." For a time also he dined on Sundays with the patron who had secured his admission to the school, Sir Francis Buller, baronet and High Court Judge. But when because of press of company he was once placed at the second table, his inferiority feeling took offense, and he went there no more.

Doubtless like most children in similar circumstances, Coleridge knew moods of nostalgia at times and was pathetically (and very poetically) conscious of them. But that they were deep and permanent there is no solid evidence to suggest. Coleridge's later deep and lifelong nostalgia was not primarily due to his separation from home, but to his already awakening sense of being solitary and unprotected in a different and indifferent world. Coleridge was ever ready to blame others for his own ills, and despite the evident momentary sincerity of his emotional indictments of home and family in his letters, he could in poetic mood imagine them as sources of happiness and virtue from which he had been shamefully excluded:

> Too soon transplanted, ere my soul had fix'd
> Its first domestic loves; and hence through life
> Chasing chance-started friendships. . .

>   . . .at times
> My soul is sad, that I have roam'd through life
> Still most a stranger, most with naked heart
> At mine own home and birthplace. . . .

>   For I was reared
> In the great city, pent 'mid cloisters dim,
> And saw nought lovely but the sky and stars.

The picture and the pathos soothed him throughout life—became indeed an *idée fixe*. An annual summer vacation of three weeks was the only opportunity given to the school children to return to their homes. Thus but two visits to Ottery made by Samuel during his school years are known. The first occurred in the summer of 1789, the second during the interval between his leaving Christ's Hospital in 1791 and entering Cambridge the following October.

Coleridge's moral and, indeed, physical dependence upon others in life began in his early school years. Luke's departure from London to start a medical practice near Exeter saddened Samuel. He wrote, "I have now no one to whom I can open my heart in full confidence," yet in the same letter he described his brother George as "father, brother and everything to me." For George was the first of the surrogate fathers the so self-conscious "orphan" was to seek throughout his life. Soon in the school he found another: a "Grecian," Thomas Fanshaw Middleton, who, surprised at seeing little Samuel sitting on a step in the cloisters reading Virgil "for pleasure," recommended him for promotion to the upper school.

Although one can learn little of school friends during Samuel's earliest years at Christ's Hospital, Coleridge's almost hypnotic power of attracting others already appeared. Characteristically dreaming, even in the Strand, that he was Leander swimming the Hellespont, and suiting his actions to his dream, he accidentally touched the pocket of a passer-by, who mistaking him for a pickpocket seized him exclaiming: "What! so young and so wicked?" But Samuel's tearful explanation so impressed the man that he presented the boy with a ticket for a local library, so assisting his omnivorous reading. Coleridge's stories about himself generally owed much to his creative imagination, but in essentials the tale may be true. "I read through the catalogue," he declared, "folios and all, whether I understood them, or did not understand them, running all risks in skulking out to get the two volumes which I was entitled to have daily." Henceforth he was to be found during play hours often with the knees of his breeches unbuttoned, and his shoes down at the heel, walking to and fro, or sitting on a step, or in a corner, deeply engaged in some book.

Sometime in 1787 apparently, Coleridge entered the upper school where Field gave place to the Reverend James Boyer. According to Coleridge in later years, his promotion was "against my will." He had neither "ambition" nor "emulation," but knew that "my talents, not any wish to excel" had placed him at the top of his class. But he was also very conscious of the "measureless difference between me and them in the wide, wild wilderness of useless, unarranged book knowledge and book thoughts."

Passing to the upper school under Boyer was to pass from dreaming idleness into frantic nightmare. For Boyer was a sadistic scoundrel and neurotic bully, a disgrace to the church and to education. Lamb (never actually under him), Hunt, and Coleridge, who were his victims, all painted the same revolting picture of the man, though Coleridge's public praise of him almost completely contradicted his more veracious, private estimate. Hunt mercifully summarized Coleridge's two opinions of Boyer as "exoterical" and "esoterical." But from these three critical minded, gifted schoolboys there came when they were leading writers of the age, closely similar, independent and evidently truthful descriptions of Boyer's revolting nature and personality.

Boyer's appearance, as Hunt saw him, was expressive of the man:

a short, stout man, inclining to paunchiness with large face and hands, an aquiline nose, long upper lip, and a sharp mouth. His eye was close and cruel. The spectacles which he wore threw a balm over it. Being a clergyman, he dressed in black, with a powdered wig. His clothes were cut short; his hands hung out of the sleeves, with tight wristbands, as if ready for execution; and as he generally wore gray worsted stockings, very tight, with a little balustrade leg, his whole appearance presented something formidably succinct, hard and mechanical. In fact his weak side, and undoubtedly his natural destination, lay in carpentry; and he accordingly carried in a side pocket made on purpose, a carpenter's rule.

So wrote Hunt.

Coleridge, like Hunt, saw a mechanistic quality in the man, unconsciously intuiting the automatism of his sadistic practices. Three years after leaving the school Coleridge wrote to one of Boyer's present victims: "I condole with you on the unpleasant motions, to which a certain Uncouth Automation has been mechanized."

The perfection with which Lamb's account of Boyer dovetails with Hunt's is

a measure of their veracity. The psychological significance of Boyer's wigs
particularly impressed Lamb, who could observe Boyer minutely and in safety,
from the junior school:

> His two wigs, both pedantic but of differing omen. The one serene,
> smiling, fresh powdered, betokening a mild day. The other, an old, dis-
> coloured, unkempt, angry caxon, denoting frequent and bloody execution.
> Woe to the school when he made his appearance in his *passy*, or *passionate*
> wig. No comet expounded surer. J. B. had a heavy hand. I have known him
> double his knotty fist at a poor trembling child (the maternal milk hardly
> dry upon its lips) with a "Sirrah, do you presume to set your wits at
> me?"

As Lamb proceeds, the image of a man on the verge of insanity—if not
indeed over it—appears.

> Nothing was more common than to see him make a headlong entry into
> the schoolroom, from his inner recess or library, and with turbulent eye,
> singling out a lad, roar out: "Od's my life, Sirrah" (his favourite
> adjuration), "I have a great mind to whip you," then with sudden retracting
> impulse, fling back into his lair—and, after a cooling lapse of some minutes
> (during which all but the culprit had totally forgotten the context) drive
> headlong out again, piecing out his imperfect sense, as if it had been some
> Devil's Litany, with the expletory yell—"*and I will, too.*"

In his gentler moods, when the rabidus furor was assuaged, he had resort to an
ingenious method, peculiar to himself, of whipping the boy, and reading the
Debates at the same time; a paragraph, and a lash between.

In this, even more if possible than in the passionate outbursts in this cold
calculated infliction of pain, one sees the sadist. His desire was not only to
inflict physical pain, but also among these helpless orphans fear and anxiety,
which created for some, certainly, a permanent disability. "I should have
pitied him," said Hunt, "if he had taught us to do anything but fear."
Coleridge said, "I was hardly used from infancy to boyhood and from
boyhood to youth most cruelly." And on another occasion Coleridge
confessed: "I have been always preyed upon by some dread"—in other words
a state of anxiety. Nor should we forget that Lamb and Hunt stammered. It
would be interesting to know how many of Boyer's other victims were in the
same state. Hunt asserted that this "infirmity used to get me into terrible
trouble with Boyer," but when temporarily in the hands of a kind and
sympathetic master he improved.

Nor for Boyer was simple beating sufficient to satisfy his sadistic nature. In
other ways, too, he had to torment his victims. "When you were out in your
lesson," wrote Hunt, "he turned upon you a round, staring eye like a fish; and
he had a trick of pinching you under the chin, and by the lobes of the ears, till
he would make the blood come. He has many times lifted a boy off the ground
in this way. He was indeed a proper tyrant, passionate and capricious: he
would take violent likes and dislikes to the same boys; fondle some without

any apparent reason." Servile to the sons of rich and important people, he would help them like a nurse with an infant. "Others he would persecute in a manner truly frightful." Hunt saw him "beat a sickly-looking, melancholy boy about the head and ears, till the poor fellow, hot, dry-eyed, and confused, seemed lost in bewilderment." Shortly afterward the boy became a parson, but he soon died insane.

Boyer the bully was also a coward, afraid of his wife and of any big boy who dared to stand up to him. Although Coleridge appears to have suffered *comparatively* little at his hands, there are available one or two glimpses of their mutual relationship. "Boy! the school is your father! Boy! the school is your mother!" Boyer shouted at little Samuel, finding him in tears after a visit home. "The discipline at Christ's Hospital," said Coleridge "was ultra-Spartan; all domestic ties were to be put aside." He also told Gillman that when fifteen years old, "from the little comfort he experienced, he was very desirous of quitting the school."

This desire to escape, as well as to find human sympathy, combined with Samuel's unambitious nature to persuade a friendly shoemaker and his wife to take him as apprentice. When the shoemaker requested Boyer's permission, Boyer's reply was to push the shoemaker out of the room and knock Coleridge down. But it was when Coleridge turned Voltairian skeptic that Boyer, shouting "I'll flog your infidelity out of you," gave him the worst beating of all. For Boyer was "very orthodox and of rigid morals." Coleridge's fatuous remark in later years that this was the only just flogging that he ever received from Boyer, was obviously made for show, while its devastating significance for Boyer was unobserved. Nor did the beating, in fact, end Coleridge's infidelity.

An atmosphere of blows, kicks, and scuffles is hardly conducive to serious study, and there was little enthusiasm for it among Boyer's victims. "Few of us cared for any of the books that were taught," said Hunt,

and no pains were taken to make us do so. The boys had no helps to information, bad or good, except what the master afforded them respecting manufactures, which was the only point on which he was enthusiastic and gratuitous. It was the only one on which he volunteered any assistance. In this he took evident delight. I remember, in explaining pigs of iron or lead to us, he made a point of crossing one of his legs with the other, and cherishing it up and down with great satisfaction, saying, "A pig, children, is about the thickness of my leg." Upon which, with a slavish pretence of novelty, we all looked at it, as if he had not told us so a hundred times.

What a perfect picture of the inferior, bullying teacher and his vicious influence upon his pupils, one of whom was Coleridge, as should often be recalled when reading incidents of Coleridge's later life.

One would hardly expect in such a man as Boyer any refinement of culture; nor according to both Lamb and Hunt did he possess any. A "rabid pedant," Lamb described him, possessing nothing beyond some verbal accuracy of memory. "He had not," said Hunt, "imagination of any sort." Lamb exactly described Boyer's pedantic substitute for a vital sense of humor: "He would laugh, ay, and heartily, but then it must be at Flaccus's quibble about *Rex*—or at the *tristis severitas in vultu* or *inspicere in patinas*, of Terence— thin jests, which at their first broaching could hardly have had vis enough to move a Roman muscle."

What little one learns of Boyer's cultural guidance—apart from his punitive exercises—is unimpressive, except to Coleridge long afterward in "exoterical" mood. Then, Coleridge imputed to him wide, vague, general poetical critical principles, which in fact bear the stamp of Coleridge's own authorship. He taught, said Coleridge, "that poetry, even that of the loftiest and, seemingly, that of the wildest odes, had a logic of its own, as severe as that of science and more difficult, because more subtle, more complex, and dependent on more and more fugitive causes," and that "in the truly great poets, there is a reason assignable, not only for every word, but for the position of every word." Such a general statement required a multitude of detailed examples and expositions, which if miraculously forthcoming would have been far beyond most of the boys' comprehension, or otherwise remain as meaningless and pretentious as its reference to "science."

At any rate, whatever the value of Boyer's poetical principles, his practice in both poetry and prose was unfortunate. "His English style was cramped to barbarism," wrote Lamb. "His Easter anthems (for his duty obliged him to those periodical flights) were grating as scrannel pipes." Hunt, like Lamb, was far from confirming Coleridge's praise of Boyer's teaching. Upon Coleridge's commendation of Boyer's alleged objection to hackneyed phrases, Hunt remarked: "But I do not think the master saw through them, out of a perception of anything further. His objection to a commonplace must have been itself commonplace." And Hunt very definitely contradicted Coleridge's praise of Boyer as one who had so admirably "moulded" his taste in poetry. "Coleridge," Hunt replied, "has praised Boyer for teaching us to laugh at 'muses' and 'Castalian streams,' but he ought rather to have lamented that he did not teach us how to love them wisely, as he might have done had he known anything about poetry, or loved Spenser and the old poets. . . .Even Coleridge's juvenile poems were none the better for Boyer's training." Nor did Hunt forget that Boyer's assistance to himself in the appreciation of poetry was limited to suggesting Ruffhead's *Life of Pope* and Johnson's poems.

To all this Hunt might have added that, despite Coleridge's eulogy of Boyer in his *Biographia Literaria* and elsewhere, Boyer's teaching did not prevent the young Coleridge from immediately hailing the contemporary minor poet Bowles as the greatest of all English poets and an obscure, undistinguished Baptist minister of the day as the finest of prose writers. The best that Hunt could say of Boyer as teacher was: "a good verbal scholar and conscientiously acting up to the letter of time and attention. . . .We had to hunt out our own knowledge. He would not help us with a word till he had ascertained that we had done all we could to learn the meaning of it ourselves." Many years later with the charity of age and distance, Hunt added: "Boyer was a severe, nay a cruel master but age and reflection have made me sensible that I ought always to add my testimony to his being a laborious and conscientious one." It was praise that any hack teacher could claim.

Boyer could have claimed no such extensive interest here but for Coleridge's misleading praise of him and his outstanding importance in Coleridge's development and later life. What Coleridge really thought of him appears in his "esoterical" comments, and these closely resemble those of Lamb and Hunt, save for a touch of characteristic Coleridgian bravado at times. This led Coleridge to such flamboyancies as: "Thank Heaven! I was flogged instead of being flattered. However, as I climbed up the school, my lot was somewhat alleviated." Indeed, Coleridge's private notebooks show far worse effects of Boyer's cruelty upon him than is found in either Lamb or Hunt. Throughout his life he was pursued by Boyer in hideous nightmares from which he would wake himself and those near him by his screams. Hunt also reported Coleridge as saying that "he dreamt of the master all his life, and that his dreams were horrible." To Boyer, as mentioned above, Coleridge also owed a lifelong anxiety about his appearance.

Yet in his *Biographia*, Coleridge not only made light of his ill treatment, but also unduly praised Boyer's teaching and moral influence. "At school," he wrote,

> I enjoyed the inestimable advantage of a very sensible, though at the same time a very severe master, the Reverend James Boyer. . . .a man whose severities, even now, not seldom furnish the dreams, by which the blind fancy would fain interpret to the mind the painful sensations of distempered sleep; but neither lessen nor dim the deep sense of my moral and intellectual obligations. . . .Our classical knowledge was the least of the good gifts which we derived from his zealous and conscientious tutorage. He is now gone to his final reward full of years and full of honours.

Thus, with more to the same effect! But privately (on hearing of Boyer's death) Coleridge dismissed him with a weak jest, expressing a wish that Boyer had been carried to heaven by celestial cherubs anatomically immune from chastisement.

It is difficult to believe that Coleridge, who so often asserted his own "genius" and declared "sensibility, both quick and deep" to be "a component part of genius," was not permanently harmed by his long subjection, not only to Boyer, but also to the "ultra-Spartan discipline" of the Christ's Hospital of his day, with its dungeons and public scourgings for serious offenses, particularly in the face of Coleridge's own "esoterical" revelations. But Lamb, very conscious that the children of Christ's Hospital were not bodiless cherubs, remarked that we may well believe that their "sense of right and wrong was peculiarly tender and sensitive."

Despite these adverse influences, "alleviated" as he "climbed up the school," Coleridge developed rapidly during his last years in Christ's Hospital. In his fifteenth year, he said long afterward, he showed "talent only, but great talent." Of his weak poem "Dura Navis," written when he was fifteen, he said: "it does not contain a line that any schoolboy might not have written, and like most school poetry, there is a putting of thoughts into verse. Yet such verses, as a striving of mind and struggles after the intense and vivid, are a promise of better things."

At the same time he asserted that his interest in such abstractions as metaphysics and theology had destroyed his taste for literature: "History and particular facts, lost all interest in my mind—poetry itself, yea novels and romances became insipid to me." But to Gillman, near the close of his life, he said that at this time, "his sixteenth year, although he began to indulge in metaphysical speculations, he was wedded to verse, and many of his early poems were planned." Gillman also has related, in words of grave dignity, that about this time Coleridge "first developed genius"; that henceforth "his mind was incessantly toiling in the pursuit of knowledge," and "his love of reading seemed to have increased in proportion to his acquirements which were equally great." But his two available prose essays, far from suggesting either personal genius or good teaching, are wooden and stilted oratorical exercises on such impossible "themes" as Virtue and Vice. They are impersonal, of course, pompous, and they read like bad translations from a foreign language. They are obviously the fine fruit of Boyer's training; for they were written in the last two years of Coleridge's school life.

Lamb's famous description of Coleridge at this time as "Logician, Metaphysician, Bard!" holding forth in the school cloisters on "the mysteries of Iamblichus, or Plotinus, or reciting Homer in his Greek, or Pindar," to the admiration of passers-by, may perhaps be somewhat larger than life, or affected unconsciously by the fame and qualities of the later Coleridge. For the touch of exhibitionism is characteristic of the boy. It led him when swimming with the school boys in the New River to swim across fully clothed and again provoke a rheumatic illness that kept him in the school hospital for some weeks.

Inspired, it is said, by the nurse's daughter, he wrote the poem "Genevieve" —a name he evidently mispronounced à l'anglaise, so gaining him a special entry in a modern phonetic dictionary. To the nurse herself he showed unusual gratitude, not a common quality with Coleridge, a gratitude that found practical expression twenty years later when the nurse was a widow in extreme poverty. Not only did he help her with money—almost a unique event in his own impecunious existence—but he also canvassed a member of Parliament to obtain her admission into an almshouse. "From her," he wrote, "I obtained the greatest tenderness, which God knows! I had never received before, even from my own family."

Adolescence brought Coleridge conflict between, on the one hand, his rational intellectual interests and, on the other, his emotions and imagination.

He rejected mathematics because "though Reason is feasted, Imagination is starved." For a time Neoplatonism and theology lost their charms for him as he entered "a long and blessed interval, during which my natural faculties were allowed to expand, and my original tendencies to develop themselves:— my fancy, and the love of nature, and the sense of beauty in forms and sounds." That his previous abstract interests revived later, he once acknowledged with regret: "Well would it have been for me, perhaps, had I never relapsed into the same mental disease."

Coleridge's human emotions were now, in fact, being stimulated by the two great polarities of love and death. In 1790 Coleridge's beloved brother Luke died. Immediately afterward, Coleridge heard that all hope for his sister, Ann, was abandoned. In March of the following year, she too died. Coleridge's misery during these months found expression in two sonnets chiefly inspired by his love for Ann, while in one of them he also sees himself with characteristic self-pity—

> Fated to rove thro' Life's wide cheerless plain,
> No Father, Brother, Sister. . .
> Better to die, than live and not be loved!

—an expression of his deep, permanent longing for a love that was essentially affection. His sister Ann he thought beautiful and kind—he had loved her:

> I too a Sister had—an only Sister—
> She loved me dearly—and I doted on her—
> On her soft bosom I reposed my cares
> And gained for every wound an healing tear,
> O! I have woke at midnight, and have wept
> Because she was not!

His sister's death, like his father's, was to leave a permanent impression upon Coleridge's development.

The influence of the poet Bowles upon these poems is very evident. Like Coleridge, Bowles was primarily inspired by the themes of love and death— the death of a lady he was about to marry. The prevailing mood of Bowles's sonnets, *Elegiac and Descriptive*, first published in 1798, combining sad and sentimental emotions with appreciation of picturesque nature, aroused such enthusiasm in Coleridge that he had made and distributed forty copies of them among his school friends—he declared later.

With a critical independence unconsciously opposed to Boyer's belauded teaching, Coleridge admirably described the effects of Bowles's sonnets upon him:

> The great works of past ages seem to a young man things of another race, in respect to which his faculties must remain passive and submiss, even as to the stars and mountains. But the writings of a contemporary, perhaps not many years older than himself, surrounded by the same circumstances,

and disciplined by the same manner, possess a reality for him, and inspire an actual friendship as of a man for a man. His very admiration is the wind which fans and feeds his hope. The poems themselves assume the properties of flesh and blood.

How great were the many and varied influences of Christ's Hospital upon so sensitive a child as Coleridge is impossible to assess with nicety, though their existence is beyond all doubt. That the school's influence was both important and lifelong was definitely stated, though in but general terms, by Lamb: "The very compass and magnitude of the school, its thousand bearings, the space it takes up in the imagination beyond the ordinary schools, impresses a remembrance, accompanied with an elevation of mind, that attends him (the blue-coat boy) through life. It is too big, too affecting an object, to pass away quickly from the mind." That Coleridge clearly realized the importance of all these early influences upon himself is evident in his remark in 1797 that, after he was three years old, "the remaining years *all* assisted to form *my particular mind.*" Nor were those first three years insignificant, as he believed.

One bad effect of the school upon him, as he admitted, was a permanent sense of inferiority to persons of social importance because of their titles or wealth. "In regard to worldly rank," he told his young friend Allsop, a stockbroker, in 1822,

from eight years old to nineteen, I was habituated, nay, naturalized, to look up to men circumstanced as you are, as my superiors—a large number of our governors, and almost *all* of those whom we regarded as greater men still, and whom we saw most of, viz. our committee governors, were such—and as neither awake nor asleep have I any other feelings than what I had at Christ's Hospital, I distinctly remember that I felt a little flush of pride and consequence. . .when I first heard who you were, and laughed at myself for it, with that pleasurable sensation that, spite of my sufferings at that school, still accompanies any sudden reawakening of our school-boy feelings and notions.

When later one reads Coleridge's servile and ingratiating letters to Lord and Lady Beaumont and other socially distinguished persons, that confession must come to mind.

The sense of loneliness created by the early death of his loved father, later intensified by the deaths of his brothers and sister, and at school by solitariness amid a crowd—a crowd of *orphans* of which he was one—was impressed upon him in daily school prayers, imploring the pity of heaven upon "us poor orphans." So in Coleridge's early tragedy, *Osorio* (and in its revised form, *Remorse*), Maria (Dona Teresa) is "an orphan heiress," and throughout his life, whether in quarrels with his brothers or to extract sympathy and help from friends, he exploited his "orphan" state to the utmost. "For I was an orphan," he wrote in his *Biographia*, and when he was thirty-five, he told his brother George, during a quarrel: "When brothers can exert themselves against an Orphan Brother, the latter must be either a mere monster, or the former must be warped by some improper passion.'' The fact that if he were an orphan so too were his brothers and half-sisters did not apparently enter his mind.

The final effect of all these influences, that of self-pity, worked permanent detriment upon Coleridge's life. It furnished moral support for his parasitic qualities, made them, indeed, virtues. "Providence," he declared, "gave me the first intimation [by his father's death] that it was my lot, and that it was best for me, to make or find my way of life a detached individual, a *terrae filius*, who was to ask love or a service of no one on any more specific relation than that of being a man, and as such to take my chance for the free charities of humanity." This last, literally, he certainly did, and with no small success! But one cannot follow Coleridge's life without realizing his sense of being "lost" in the world—like his Ancient Mariner.

Despite the darker aspects of life in Christ's Hospital, the final note, even of its most outspoken critics, is one of large approval, even of gratitude. Hunt appreciated the education it gave him, and also "for its having secured to me, on the whole, a well-trained and cheerful boyhood." He praised it for having pressed no superstition on his mind, and for leaving him free to roam at will over all reputable literature without any prohibition or inquisition.

And now, at the close of the summer term of 1791, new vistas were opening for Coleridge as the time for his entry into Cambridge approached.

3 Cambridge and First Love (1791-94)

"With faery wand O bid my Love arise,
The dewy brilliance dancing in her eyes"
—Coleridge, "An Effusion at Evening" (1792)

At the opening of the October term in 1791, Coleridge arrived in Cambridge furnished with a seven years' scholarship for Jesus College. He also had several small additional benefactions, and a promise of further help from his brothers if required. Like his father and two of his brothers, Samuel was to be a clergyman (a profession in which Jesus College specialized), and the bishop of Exeter had promised him a "title," when the time was ripe.

Samuel's first impressions were critical. After the discipline of Christ's Hospital the freedom of Cambridge shocked him. The master of Jesus was away, and "still more extraordinary and rather shameful," so were his two tutors. Besides, he continued his complaint to his brother George, "neither lectures, or chapel—or anything is begun." The college was still "very thin," and the only member he had been introduced to was "a very blackguardly fellow, whose physiog I do not like." Samuel's introducer was his old friend and protector Middleton, now at Pembroke, whom he had called on before daring to enter Jesus alone. In the silent dining hall the only sound he heard was "the noise of suction which accompanies my eating." The meal finished, he again joined Middleton in his room at Pembroke.

From the first he complained of the impecuniosity—which was to haunt him throughout life; without cash, he must pay more for furnishing his rooms, and besides, "one feels cold and naked and shivering, and gelid and chilly and such like synonyms without a little money in one's pocket." By November, however, he was settled, and college life was proceeding normally. Twice a day he had to attend chapel or pay a fine of two pence for every absence—four pence on Sundays and Saints' Days. "I am," he said, "remarkably religious upon an economical plan." With Middleton helping, he read mathematics three hours a day and classics from teatime to his eleven-o'clock bedtime, besides attending a daily mathematical lecture. The lectures in classics were poor, and he decided not to "be often *bored* with them." But he read Pindar, translated Anacreon, and, hoping for the prize offered, went on composing Greek verse "like a mad dog." If he continued like this, he felt sure that he would be "a Classical Medallist and a very high Wrangler"; but, he prophetically remarked, *"Freshmen* always *begin* very *furiously."*

The climate of Cambridge he found detestable, and his rooms were so damp that they first gave him a bad cold in the head, and then a recurrence of his rheumatic illness. Bedridden, he moaned: "Cambridge is a damp place—the very palace of the winds!" He took the common remedy, opium, doubtless used before when he was ill at school. "Opium," he said, "never used to have any disagreeable effects on me—but it has upon many." He was, then, forewarned.

So the first term passed. Finding new friends and constantly companioned by Middleton, Samuel apparently settled down to the regular life of the good student. He prided himself, indeed, that despite his illness he was not behind in his work. When his brother George, whether instinctively suspicious of Samuel's weakness or moved by disturbing rumors, wrote in late November for reassurance as to his mode of life, Samuel meekly replied: "My dear Brother,—I assure you I am an Economist. I keep no company—that is, I neither give or receive invitations to wine parties; because in our college there is no end of them. I eat no suppers." Soon came the end of term and the Christmas vacation brightened by an invitation from a friend, Mrs. Evans, and her family to stay with them.

Before leaving Christ's Hospital, Coleridge had formed a new and growing intimacy with the Evans family, a Welsh family living in London. The family consisted of Mrs. Evans, a widow, her three attractive daughters, and her young son, whom Coleridge had befriended at school. The Welsh spontaneity of the family had charmed Coleridge from the first. Soon he was another son to the widowed mother, and "brother Coly" to her daughters. Mrs. Evans, Coleridge said long afterward, "taught me what it was to have a mother. I loved her as such. She had three daughters and of course I fell in love with the eldest. From this time to my nineteenth year, when I quitted school for Jesus, Cambridge, was the era of poetry and love." But in fact, this "era" continued long afterward.

Even before he left Christ's Hospital, "brother Coly's" affection for Mary Evans had passed beyond the fraternal stage. Some thirty years later he recalled with pleasure the happiness and exaltation of this, his first love.

Oh, from sixteen to nineteen, what hours of Paradise had Allen [a school friend] and I in escorting the Miss Evanses home on a Saturday, who were then at a milliner's whom I used to think, and who I believe really was, such a nice lady;—and we used to carry thither, of a summer morning, the pillage of the flower gardens within six miles of town, with sonnet or love rhyme wrapped round the nosegay. To be feminine, kind, and genteely (what I should now call neatly) dressed, these were the only things to which my head, heart, or imagination had any polarity, and what I was then, I still am.

Doubtless Mary Evans is the inspiration of several poems of idealistic love that Samuel composed during these last years at school, and perhaps also at home during his last vacation before entering Cambridge. "The Evening Star" speaks to him of Mary:

> O first and fairest of the starry choir,
> O loveliest 'mid the daughters of the night,
> Must not the maid I love like thee inspire
> *Pure* joy and *calm* delight?

His idealistic, reverent, romantic attitude toward Mary was intensified by his inferiority feeling, especially by his dissatisfaction about his own appearance:

> Ah! doubly blest, if Love supply
> Lustre to this now heavy eye,
> And with unwonted Spirit grave
> That fat vacuity of face.
> Or if e'en Love, the mighty Love
> Shall find this change his power above;
> Some lovely maid perchance thou'lt find
> To read thy visage in thy mind.

But in "Absence" idealism yields to disappointment and sadness. Whereupon he recalls those idyllic Saturday afternoons when he and his friend conducted the Evans sisters home:

> cease, fond Heart! this bootless moan:
> Those Hours on rapid Pinions flown
> Shall yet return, by Absence crowned,
> And scatter livelier roses round.

So now, as the first term ended and Mrs. Evans's invitation arrived, Samuel's hope in "Absence" was to be realized.

Samuel, in high hopes, joined the Evans family and was soon greatly improved in health and spirits. He presented Mrs. Evans with a copy of Fielding's *Amelia*, with his complimentary verses to her, "the parent of a race so sweet," who will learn from the story

> Maternal hope, that her loved progeny
> In all but sorrows shall Amelias be!

The "maternal hope" that was, in fact, then rising in the breast of Mrs. Evans for "her loved progeny," was to capture the simple but brilliant Cambridge undergraduate for one of her poor working daughters. Whatever Mary may have thought of it, the plan was certainly successful so far. For after Coleridge spent a fortnight at Christmas with the family, his affection for them had greatly increased. From Cambridge at the end of January he expatiated to George upon the great benefits he now owed to Mrs. Evans's "solicitude of maternal affection" for him. Indeed "the relaxation from study, co-operating with the cheerfulness and attention" he had met there had proved so "potently medicinal" that his "own corporealities were in a state of better health" than at any time he could remember. Besides, good Mrs. Evans's generosity would welcome George, too, if he would drop in to tea or dinner when passing their home on Villiers Street. "And I *too*," Samuel added, "have made a half promise that you would. I assure you, you will find them not only a very amiable, but a very sensible family."

By mid-February 1792 Samuel was telling "My very dear" Mrs. Evans, "What word shall I add sufficiently expressive of the warmth which I feel? You covet to be near my heart. Believe me that You and my Sisters have the very first row in the front box of my Heart's little theatre," in which they, his "dear Spectators," should see him without disguise: "Farce, Comedy, and Tragedy"; his "Laughter, Cheerfulness and Melancholy"; his "Joys and Sorrows, Hopes and Fears, Good Tempers and Peevishnesses."

These five letters, written in the latter half of February, are all that we have from Samuel to his friends throughout the whole year. They make slightly painful yet comic reading, as Mrs. Evans leads him into a clumsy, explorative flirtation with Mary. She remains aloof and enigmatic despite Samuel's posturing from crude jests to self-vaunting, from apologetic references to his unaesthetic appearance to reproaches that Mary's letters are cold and remote. His references to Mary's physical reaction when annoyed suggest muscularity and temper as conspicuous among Mary's endowments, and remind one of Lamb's description of her four years later as "the Miss Evans whom Coleridge so narrowly escaped marrying." But the "escape" was due to Mary. Both her hint that a long letter with three poems he feared too long *was* too long and her indifference to his verses annoyed him. His final letters to her and to her mother show an unaccustomed coldness.

Whatever their further relations, Samuel was certainly far from happy in the spring of the year 1792. Nor was Mary's aloofness the sole reason. Mounting debts at Cambridge worried him, and his friend and protector, Middleton, failing to obtain a fellowship, left the university for a country curacy, remarking: "I am Middleton, which is another name for misfortune." Misfortune was also Samuel's name, as the changes in his mode of life after Middleton's departure soon showed.

George, ever uneasy about Samuel's behavior at Cambridge, despite his blameless existence as described by Samuel, still continued to ask awkward questions, and now suspected "indolence." But Samuel denied the suggestion. In "ordinary business" he was not "indolent," he said. He had been "writing for all the prizes," the Greek and Latin odes and epigrams, though with "little expectation of success." But he was in very low spirits, "most villainously vapoured." At Easter, however, he would spend a week in London—and of course see the Evanses as he had promised.

Meanwhile, Cambridge with its academic round was dull—even duller now that his hated mathematical studies were unassisted by Middleton. His spleen found relief in verse:

Where deep in mud Cam rolls his slumbrous stream
And Bog and Desolation reign supreme,
Where all Boeotia clouds the misty brain,
The Owl Mathesis pipes her loathsome strain.
Far, far aloof the frighted Muses fly,
Indignant Genius scowls and passes by:
The frolic Pleasures start amid their dance,
And wit congealed stands fixed in Wintry trance.
But to the sounds with duteous haste repair
Cold Industry, and wary-footed Care,
And Dullness, dosing on a couch of lead,
Pleased with the song uplifts her heavy head,
The sympathetic numbers lists awhile,
Then yawns propitiously a frosty smile. . .
    (Caetera desunt.)

That Coleridge inherited something of his father's simplicity and eccentricity is beyond doubt. "Coleridge's peculiarities," wrote Gillman, doubtless as usual quoting Coleridge himself, "were sometimes construed into irregularities; but through his whole life, attracting notice by his splendid genius, he fell too often under the observation of men who busied themselves in magnifying small things, and minifying large ones." The indifference of an original mind to accepted conventions was, of course, the basic cause of Coleridge's "peculiarities." One such was his carelessness in dress, which along with his self-absorption led mischievous students surreptitiously to cut off pieces from the tail of his gown as he sat at lectures. When thus so shortened as to be ridiculous, it was noticed by the master of Jesus, who called out: "Mr. Coleridge! Mr. Coleridge! When will you get rid of that shameful gown?" To which Samuel, turning his head and glancing over his shoulder at the remnant, replied with whimsical courtesy: "Why, Sir, I think I've got rid of the greatest part of it already!"

Misfortune dogged his footsteps. His first party on the river ended in a capsized boat and a swim ashore in his clothes, as once before in his schooldays. He was also "cashless"; he needed five pounds from George, or better, ten. And he had grown fat. Then he heard that his school friend Allen, at Oxford, was despised there for taking a Bible clerkship in the university. Samuel was hoping for the same post at Cambridge, and the news alarmed him. Surely they would behave better at Cambridge! "Oxford! 'Tis a childish university. Thank God I am at Cambridge!" That was hardly in tone with his recent verses, but Coleridge was ever superior to consistency in personal concerns.

What happened to Samuel in London at Easter 1792 is not known. When the veil of obscurity lifts it is the summer vacation, and he is visiting his home and various relatives in Devonshire, after a short stay with his brother Edward at Salisbury on the way. He thought little of Edward, who in several ways most resembled him. So Samuel went on to his mother at Ottery, then to his brother

James at Tiverton and to his half-sister Elizabeth (now Mrs. Phillips) at Exeter. There he was "very happy and comfortable." He was much looking forward to George's arrival, "for I have promised myself a vast deal of snug comfortability with you." He also sent George a set of satirical verses on the vicar of Ottery and his wife, which must have pleased Samuel's mother. More pleased she must have been to learn that he had won a gold medal for a Greek ode on the slave trade, which he had publicly recited at the Cambridge Encaenia in July. Porson, the distinguished professor of Greek, found 134 mistakes in Coleridge's ode, which was evidently more admirable morally than linguistically.

However bright, satirical, and amusing Samuel appeared during this vacation, his private thoughts and feelings were increasingly disturbed by the memory of Mary. In August, in "An Effusion at Evening," they found expression in romantic verse in which, after invoking

Imagination, Mistress of my Love!

he describes the visions of Mary that haunt him:

The absent Maiden flashes on mine eye!
When first the matin bird with startling song
Salutes the sun his veiling clouds among.
I trace her footsteps on the steaming lawn,
I view her glancing in the gleams of dawn!
When the bent flower beneath the night-dew weeps
And on the lake the silver lustre sleeps,
Amid the paly radiance soft and sad
She meets my lonely path in moonbeams clad.
With her along the streamlet's brink I rove;
With her I list the warblings of the grove;
And seems in each low wind *her* voice to float,
Lone-whispering Pity in each soothing note!

So the summer vaction of 1792 passed.

Samuel's dejection still haunted him when he returned to Cambridge for the opening of the new academic year. "Too worried and tired out," and with his prospects for winning the approaching Craven Scholarship "quite hopeless," he evaded a discussion of his debts with George, though "a brother to me in kindness, and a father in wisdom." On hearing of his failure, he described himself as "perfectly satisfied." As compensation he was appointed librarian and chapel clerk—worth thirty-three pounds a year. Unfortunately, it meant getting up in the mornings, as he could not cut chapel more than three or four times a week: "but all good things have their contingencies of evil."

Other contingencies of evil were also now accumulating for him. Without a near "father-substitute," Coleridge was ever like a drifting ship without an anchor. George was, of course, his permanent "father." But George was in London and could not supply the place of the now-absent Middleton.

"Middleton," wrote Gillman, "loving Coleridge so much, and being his senior in years, as well as in studies, was to him, while at school and at college, what the Polar Star is to the mariner on the wide sea without compass,—his guide, and his influential friend and companion." Without Middleton working beside him and guiding, Coleridge drifted into erratic and aimless reading, and whatever offered distraction from anxiety and boredom, social and political sprees, consequent expenses, debts, and general disorder.

His debts, he told George, when at last in mid-January 1793 he condescended to discuss them, "have corroded my spirits greatly for some time past." But the profits from a volume of translations of Greek and Latin lyrics that he was making would not only pay them but also establish his reputation. Those translations, of which more was often to be heard, was the first of his hundred dream volumes. To George, too, he had to show repentance: "I have been lessoned by the wholesome discipline of experience, that *Nemo felix qui debet*—and I hope I shall be the happier man for it."

Similarly tactful now was Coleridge's correspondence with Mrs. Evans. His attempt a year before to impress Mary with a description of a wine party that brought two of his friends sprawling in the gutter had failed in its object. Now his goodness was to be revealed instead. His concern for Mrs. Evans was excessive. He found her "too apt to go far beyond her strength, if by any means she may alleviate the sufferings of others." He pointed out to her how far she was above the vile herd: "a set of little, dirty pimping, pettyfogging, ambidextrous fellows, who would set your house on fire, tho' it were but to roast an egg for themselves!" A little too strong he must have thought it, for he lowered the note of moral indignation to a quieter, more religious tone: "Yet surely—considering it even in a selfish view, the pleasures that arise from whispering peace to those who are in trouble, and healing the broken in heart are far superior to all the unfeeling can enjoy!" And in his mood of religious exaltation he sent her "a little work of that great and good man, Archdeacon Paley, entitled *Motives of Contentment*, addressed to the poorer part of our fellow men." He even pointed out pages twelve and twenty for her special attention, as "the reasoning has been of some service to *me*—who am of the Race of Grumbletonians." Eight years later he included Paley's writings among "the corrupters and poisoners of all moral sense and dignity."

Samuel, fearing the possible effect of mere riches upon Mary—not without reason as events proved—lamented to her mother his "cashlessness"—a lament apparently beyond the reach of Paley's *Motives of Contentment*—the misery of not having a rich father. But Mrs. Evans must "excuse the wanderings of my castle-building imagination." He has not a thought that he conceals from her. "I *write* to others, but my pen talks to you. . . .Your grateful and affectionate boy, S.T. Coleridge." Evidently, it seemed to him that the way to Mary was through her mother, and the mother was on his side.

When two days later he wrote to Mary, she was no longer "Dear Mary" as before; "My dear Miss Evans" introduced a dull, joyless, perfunctory letter, in which he tells her that he is learning to play the violin since music is "the sweetest assuager of cares,'' and that he also wants to drown the noise made by neighboring violinists and flautists. He tries with little success to brighten his letter. Mary has reproved him for indolence, and he reminds her of it: '' 'Nothing makes the temper so fretful as Indolence,' said a young lady, who beneath the soft surface of feminine delicacy possesses a mind acute by Nature, and strengthened by habits of reflection—'pon my word, Miss Evans, I beg your pardon a thousand times for bepraising you to your face—but really I have written so long, that I had forgot to whom I was writing.''

It is all very naive, even childish, and he has really nothing to say but cannot break off—''there is an old proverb of a river of words and a spoonful of sense, and I think this letter has been a pretty good proof of it. But as nonsense is better than blank paper, I will fill this side with a song I wrote lately.'' Then follow the five stanzas of ''The Complaint of Ninathoma,'' romantic, Ossianic, in which he finds a new rhythmic freedom, and in at least one stanza a hint of Mary:

A Ghost! by my cavern it darted!
In moon-beams the Spirit was drest—
For lovely appear the departed,
When they visit the dreams of my rest.

''Are you asleep my dear Mary?'' he concluded, and continued with an unconsciously sinister reference: ''I have administered rather a strong dose of opium. However, if in the course of your nap you should chance to dream that I am with the ardour of fraternal friendship, Your affectionate S. T. Coleridge, you will never have dreamt a truer dream in all your born days.'' Evidently Mary allowed nothing more than ''fraternal friendship,'' and Samuel was feeling increasing frustration.

To George, ever more uneasy about Samuel's doings, he sent thanks in a Latin letter for banknotes (*pecuniam chartaceam*), and appeared a model of behavior. He would spend the summer in Cambridge, working hard, for ''I love classical studies more every day: they are my delight and in them I find both my serious and my lighter occupations.'' A relapse into the Boyeresque cant of his pious school essays followed: ''I know—how well I know—that the pleasure obtained from lower pursuits rapidly vanishes; but the regret they leave behind is long-lasting. But labour expended on worth-while subjects is quickly past, yet the memory which it leaves in the mind is a source of most enduring pleasure.'' Surely, unless this antithetical see-saw sent him to sleep, George should have been reassured, especially as Samuel was sending him sermons to preach at his school. Neither of the brothers appeared to have had moral qualms when Samuel wrote: ''I have sent you a sermon metamorphosed from an obscure publication by vamping transposition; if you like it, I can send you two more of the same kidney.''

One cause of George's anxiety was the rumors he heard of Samuel's politicoreligious sympathies. A year ago he had been alarmed to hear that

Samuel was friendly with a fellow of Jesus College, William Frend, notorious for his horrible Unitarian views and sympathy with the French Revolution. Samuel had attempted to calm his brother's fears: "Mr. Frend's company is by no means invidious." On the contrary, "the Master of Jesus was very intimate with him. No! Tho' I am not an *Alderman*, I have yet *prudence* enough to *respect* that *gluttony of Faith* waggishly yclept Orthodoxy." This from the man who later boasted that Boyer had thrashed him back into orthodoxy!

Whatever George's feeling about the matter a year previous, he certainly had good reason to fear when Frend became the center of a political storm in Cambridge, and pro- and anti-French sentiment ran high. Samuel's sympathy with the French revolutionists had led him, four years before, upon the fall of the Bastille on July 14, 1789, to celebrate the event in an ode, though he was only sixteen years old at the time. Freedom, he cried, was not for France alone, but for the whole world:

Shall France alone a Despot spurn?
Shall she alone, O Freedom, boast thy care?
Lo, round the standard Belgia's heroes burn,
Tho' Power's blood-stain'd streamers fire the air,
And wider yet thy influence spread,
Nor e'er recline thy weary head,
Till every land from pole to pole
Shall boast one independent soul!
And still, as erst, let favour'd Britain be
First ever of the first and freest of the free!

Since writing that, Samuel had enthusiastically followed the tremendous events across the Channel and their great impact upon English life: the September Massacres and the execution of Louis XVI, and war between France and England with her continental allies. Pro-Revolution societies in England had roused Burke to write his famous *Reflections on the Revolution in France and on the Proceedings in Certain Societies in London, Relative to that Event*, and just before Samuel first entered Cambridge, anti-French feeling was so strong in Birmingham that the mob there destroyed the house and belongings of the distinguished dissenting minister and scientist, Joseph Priestley.

Early in 1793, when the French declaration of war against England was embarrassing Pitt, Frend, who had already been dismissed from his tutorship for his Unitarianism, published a pamphlet, *Peace and Union*, against the war. It aroused much enthusiasm among the Cambridge students but the opposite feeling among the university authorities. The authorities attacked it on both theological and political grounds, and after trying Frend in the Vice-Chancellor's Court, they dismissed him from the university. During the trial, excitement among Frend's supporters rose to fever pitch, and conspicuous among the leaders were Samuel Coleridge and a student of Trinity (afterward Lord Lyndhurst). They scrawled "Frend for Ever" on college walls, and wrote

"Liberty and Equality" on the smooth lawns of Trinity in a train of gunpowder and set it alight. In short, they enjoyed themselves vastly, as students always will when such an opportunity occurs.

Samuel's former school friend, Charles Le Grice, who was also a contemporary of Coleridge at Cambridge, has left the best external glimpse of Samuel throughout the whole of his undergraduate career:

> He did not bend to that discipline which was to qualify him for the whole course (of study). He took little exercise merely for the sake of exercise; but he was ready at any time to unbend his mind in conversation, and for the sake of this, his room was a constant rendezvous of conversation-loving friends; I will not call them loungers, for they did not call to kill time, but to enjoy it. What evenings have I spent in those rooms! What little suppers, or "sizings," as they were called, have I enjoyed; when Aeschylus, and Plato, and Thucydides, were pushed aside, with a pile of lexicons, etc., to discuss the pamphlets of the day. Ever and anon, a pamphlet issued from the pen of Burke. There was no need of having the book before us. Coleridge had read it in the morning; and in the evening, with our negus, we had them viva voce, gloriously.

For Samuel from first to last was never a remote, purely academic scholar. A social environment was a necessity to him. His "genius" was no less evident in the friendships that he attracted by his "natural gladness" than in his purely intellectual pursuits. At Cambridge such social temptations were ever present. And soon the departure of Middleton and Coleridge's increasing anxiety about Mary and his debts distracted him from study.

When the summer term of 1793 ended, Samuel, instead of keeping his promise to remain in Cambridge and work, set off again for the West country and visited his relatives as before. At his brother Edward's in Salisbury they fell to arguing again, disputing and drinking from four o'clock in the afternoon until ten at night with a friend as umpire, who "by decision more embroiled the fray." Yet at the end, all "arose as cool as three undressed cucumbers!" Edward's wife, twenty years older than Edward's own mother, he found "well and merry, and by all the Cupids, a very worthy old lady."

During the vacation, in revolt against his bondage to an indifferent Mary, he philandered with the local beauties, getting "no small kudos among the young belles," he said, "by complimentary effusions in the poetic way." These poems' sole interest is not their poetic inspiration but their poetic economy. By merely altering names, he made them serve various flirtatious occasions, including Mary, and later the lady whom he ultimately married.

But Mary's image could not be thus erased, and when memories of her became poignant, he wrote poems of a sincerity absent from the complimentary verses of his casual encounters. In such a mood he rewrote his previous poem to Mary, "An Effusion at Evening," renaming it "Lines on an Autumnal Evening." Some of the changes he made in it strongly suggest phases of his relation with Mary during the preceding year, particularly the following passage, which surely alludes to a proposal from Samuel and an uncertain reply from Mary:

> when from the "Muses" calm abode
> I came, with Learning's meed not unbestowed;
> When as she twined a laurel round my brow,
> And met my kiss, and half returned my vow,
> O'er all my frame shot rapid my thrilled heart,
> And every nerve confessed the electric dart.

As imagination brings the radiant Mary before him the verse acquires, despite hackneyed epithets and imagery, a passionate note seldom repeated in Coleridge's verse.

Despite his philanderings Samuel was unhappy. Like Bowles he saw Nature's beauty through a veil of sorrow—sorrow for a lost sister, a lost brother, and, he feared, a lost love. His poetic memories of these early days were widely different from those he recorded in prose.

The summer vacation of 1793 was also darkened by Samuel's increasing anxiety about his debts, now much larger than he had pretended. This, shortly before leaving for the West country, he had been forced to admit to George, and although at home later he had sent George a witty and amusing letter about his flirtations, George did not reply. Overcome by anxiety, he wrote to George penitently, fearing his displeasure and promising reform. Whatever scolding George gave Samuel, he also gave him his fare to Cambridge and money to pay his debts. Already Samuel's lifelong inability to manage money had shown itself. Now it was to be yet more evident: for on his way to Cambridge he inadvertently spent all the money, and on arrival, almost penniless, was horrified to find his debts still awaiting him.

It was an inauspicious opening for the first term of his third undergraduate year. Panic seized him. Probably, too, Mary on his passage through London was still unkind. To escape his debts, and perhaps with fears of a debtor's prison haunting his excitable imagination, he joined a spree-party to London. There, desperately hoping to win money to pay his debts and to enable him to marry Mary, he bought a lottery ticket that inspired a poem that should have been entitled "Love's Lottery." In it (a fact curiously overlooked by Coleridge's biographers, who treat the verses as a prayer for luck in the lottery), Coleridge rejects mere money as the cause of his venture, which is due to a nobler aim—Love:

> Let the little bosom cold
> Melt only at the sunbeam ray of gold—
> My pale cheeks glow—the big drops start—
> The rebel Feeling riots at my heart!

But oh! if ever song thine ear
Might soothe, O haste with fostering hand to rear
One Flower of Hope! At Love's behest.
Trembling, I placed it in my secret breast.

In those lines Samuel recapitulated the course of his three years' passion for Mary (who, as time revealed, acquired a rich husband).

After three hysterical days in London, Samuel returned to Cambridge. Despite his later exaggerated account of it, he spent a week there in which, at least to the outer world, he appeared quite normal, reading his poems to the Cambridge literary society. Suddenly he dashed to London again, probably to plead once more with Mary. The lottery ticket also proved disappointing; even the debts at Cambridge could not be paid. Panic again seized him, and he looked for any means of escape.

Wandering miserable and moneyless down Chancery Lane, he noticed a recruiting poster that offered money—and escape—and on December 2 he enlisted as a common soldier. He would be lost to all relatives and friends, to all whom he now feared above everything to meet. On December 4, two days after seeing the poster, wanting "a few smart lads" for the army, he presented himself under the assumed name of Silas Tomkyn Comberbache at the regimental headquarters at Reading, as one "smart lad." After some natural doubt on the part of the responsible officer, he was accepted as a dragoon. From the first Coleridge was disappointed. He complained later that even "the King's Bounty" of six and one-half guineas was all absorbed in the expense of his military outfit as a trooper in the 15th Light Dragoons.

Later, to his friend Cottle the Bristol publisher, Samuel related this event, clearly stating that its main cause was his rejection by Mary. "He said," wrote Cottle in both his *Reminiscences* and *Recollections*, "that he had paid his addresses to Mary Evans, who rejecting his offer, he took it so much in dudgeon, that he withdrew from the University to London, when, in a reckless state of mind he enlisted in the 15th Elliot's Light Dragoons." Indeed, Coleridge confirmed this later. Speaking of Charles Lloyd's novel *Edmund Oliver*, which was said to be a malignant travesty of Coleridge's life, he told Charles Lamb that he would be "cautious not too hastily to affirm the falsehood of an assertion of Lloyd's that in Edmund Oliver's love-fit, debaucheries, leaving college, and going into the army, he had no sort of allusion to, or recollection of my love-fit, debaucheries, leaving college and going into the army."

In his new role as trooper, Samuel was, of course, a complete failure. If, as he asserted in later life, he joined the army to get rid of an inhibition—saying to himself, "Well, I have had all my life a violent antipathy to soldiers and horses; the sooner I can cure myself of these absurd prejudices the better, and I will enlist in this regiment"—the experiment was a complete failure. He could not keep on his horse, could not groom it, did not keep his musket clean, and gained prominence as a soldier solely in being the worst of the awkward squad.

The sergeant, in ironical allusion to Samuel's clumsy maneuvers, would shout to the rest: "Take care of that Comberbache, take care of him, for he will ride over you!"—adding similar sarcastic comments. "Mr. Coleridge," wrote Cottle, "in the midst of all his deficiencies, it appeared, was liked by the men, although he was the butt of the whole company; being esteemed by them as next kin to a natural, though of a peculiar kind—a talking natural."

If Coleridge's later assertion that he wrote the soldiers' love letters for them is true, that, as well as his "natural gladness," would explain their liking for him, despite his eccentricities and social and intellectual superiority. But it is difficult to disentangle fact from fiction in Coleridge's accounts of his military experiences. It *may* have been true that the recruiting sergeant to whom Samuel first went thought him too good for the army, gave him half a guinea to go to the theater, provided bed and breakfast, and then, upon Coleridge's insistence on being a recruit, burst into tears. It *may* be that the sergeants who fought Napoleon were like that but there have been none such since!

It *may* be true that Samuel overheard an officer misquote Sophocles as Aeschylus—it was more likely then to hear Sophocles or Aeschylus quoted or misquoted anywhere than today; but that the officer should have been so charmed at being corrected by a private suggests the same army as the weeping sergeants. Nor was the Greek classicist enough. Coleridge's other remarkable classical experience among the dragoons at Reading was due to his proclaiming in Latin on a stable wall the depth of his misery—"*Eheu! quam infortunil miserrimum est fuisse felicem.*" This so gained the respect of an officer that he insisted on Samuel's walking by his side when not in town, thus attracting the jealousy of the other privates. One need not doubt the tale of the ironical sergeant, but the rest of these tales told to Gillman many years afterward recall Cottle's warning of "that playful and ebullient imagination for which Mr. Coleridge was distinguished. Subjects high and low received the same embellishment. Figure crowded on figure, and image on image, in new and perpetual variety."

In January 1794 the regiment moved to Henley. By this time, through horse riding, Samuel was so ill with skin eruptions that sitting, whether on a horse or a chair, was almost impossible. He was, therefore, sent to nurse a smallpox patient isolated in Henley workhouse. This unpleasant and dangerous task he apparently completed satisfactorily, although worn out through lack of sleep, sickened by the putrid smell, and wearied by fatiguing struggles with the delirious man. The man appears to have recovered, and Samuel did not take the infection. Neither, one hopes, did the two friends whom Samuel escorted about Henley—one a "beautiful girl," the other "the handsome daughter of a musician."

His antipathy toward the army, instead of being destroyed, was by this time immensely increased. Almost as soon as he had joined, his overwhelming desire was to escape. But he soon found that it was easier to get in than to get out. To conceal from his friends his eagerness to be discharged, and doubtless afraid of informing his brothers whom he had left in ignorance, he wrote to friends at Christ's Hospital informing them of his situation—under a seal of secrecy that he knew they would not keep, and did not want them to keep. The news spread to Cambridge, and then to his anxious brothers.

For the next two months, while attempts to obtain his release were being made, Coleridge poured forth in letter after letter to his brothers George and James rhetorical cant like his school essays. In these Coleridge appears over-burdened with repentance, humility, shame, gratitude, religious revival, and conversion. Only occasionally does an intelligent and intelligible remark occur in this apparently emotional but obviously calculated flood of contrition, intended to expedite his brothers' attempts at his release. "I have been a fool even to madness," he tells George. "I laugh almost like an insane person." The religious effects of the mess he was in were immediate and very obvious. He repeatedly begged George to pray for him, and as the time for his deliverance approached, he regained belief in a future state—previously, it would seem, lost.

Meanwhile his brothers sent him generous, kind, practical letters, with money, which he needed as badly as ever. They paid his £150 or more of debts, as well as small sums requiring much involved, unintelligible explanation. He was already in this time of bitter misery turning to opium for relief.

However genuine was his repentance, his love of creating an impression, even by exaggerating his misdeeds and penitence, could not be restrained. His life, he told George, had been "a gloomy huddle of eccentric actions and dim-discovered motives," ever since he received his tutor's first bill. Instead of study, he had dreamed of ways of evading his debts, he "became a proverb in the University for idleness. . . .better for me if my imagination had been less vivid. I fled to debauchery." That, on various occasions later, he both repeated and indignantly denied. Again, he told George: "for the whole six weeks that preceded the examination [for the Craven Scholarship] I was almost constantly intoxicated!" In writing he felt the "painful blush" on his cheek. "My brother: you shudder as you read." Despite his learning and sophistication, the naïveté he had inherited from his father was ineradicable. But his desire to thrill his reader is evident. So we went on, in letter after letter, as he waited in increasing anxiety for release. Nor was spiritual misery his sole interest: "Within this week I have been thrown three times from my horse, and run away with to the no small perturbation of my nervous system almost every day. I ride an horse young and as undisciplined as myself." Later, back in Cambridge, he wrote: "my soul sickens at its own guilt." Indeed, he had contemplated suicide, but avoided the word—"I will not shock your religious feelings." The week for this suicide in Cambridge was, in fact, the one of his reading to the literary society, a week with unusually reliable external evidence as to his normal state of mind and activity.

As release came nearer, Samuel's gratitude and self-abasement increased. To James, who as an officer could now best help him, he wrote:

In a mind which Vice has not utterly divested of sensibility, few occurrences can inflict a more acute pang than the receiving proofs of tenderness and love, where only resentment and reproach were expected and deserved. The gentle Voice of Conscience, which had incessantly murmured within the soul, then raises its tone, and speaks with the tongue of thunder. My conduct towards you and towards my other brothers has displayed a strange combination of Madness, Ingratitude, and Dishonesty. But you forgive me. May my Maker forgive me! May the time arrive when I shall have forgiven myself!

"God bless him!" he fervently exclaimed a week later, on hearing that difficulties were being overcome by James and that his release was imminent.

In these brighter circumstances, as March drew to a close, Samuel's spirits markedly rose, and his moral and spiritual interests similarly declined. But there were mysterious complications about Samuel's army pay, which, he said, had gone "in the additional comforts I so much wanted"—probably including opium. George also scraped enough money to pay, by installments, Samuel's debt to his tutor.

Meanwhile, Samuel turned to writing Cambridge odes, which amused him. He had also sent his old school friend Robert Allen at Oxford, he told George, a dissertation on "The Comparative Good and Evil of Novels," and would blush to tell George how great was the credit that Allen had gained by it: "All the Fellows have got copies—and they meditate having it printed and dispersing it through the University." Samuel had also met, in a "pot house," an extraordinary person with strangely original "theories of Heaven and Hell," which provoked his satirical comments.

At last, after long hanging fire, matters moved. A substitute for Samuel would cost twenty-five guineas, and was beyond possibility. Nor could James by influence procure his discharge. But perhaps he did so by other means, for on April 8, 1794, the delighted Samuel was given his discharge as "insane"— a verdict that many of his fellow troopers had long since given. So upon the regimental muster roll was inscribed: "Discharged, S. T. Comberbache, insane, 10 April, 1794." Thus ended Samuel's five months as a trooper in the Light Dragoons.

4 Pantisocracy and Love's Entanglements (1794)

It is good to be merry and wise,
It is good to be honest and true,
It is best to be off with the old love,
Before you are on with the new.
—Old Song (Anonymous)

Back in Cambridge, Samuel was sternly rebuked by the master of Jesus, "gated" for a month, and given some pages of "Demetrius Phalereus" to translate as a punishment.

Now full of good intentions, Coleridge avoided his wicked friends and was grateful for the kind reception given him by the others. He also made virtuous resolutions: He would rise every morning at six o'clock; he would work hard for "all the prizes"; he would cultivate "correctness and perspicuity, not genius." Nor were Samuel's debts at Cambridge only those to his tutor. What remained, he informed George, could be deferred "for this year at least, as mere trifles." "Every enjoyment—except of *necessary* comforts, I look upon as criminal," he added. For him to neglect economy, he said, would prove him "a monster." So, matching words with deeds, he advertised in a local paper the impending publication of his never-written *Translations*. Samuel's economies, however, did not exclude a walking tour in June to Wales—Mary's ancestral land—with another student, Joseph Hucks.

Calling on Allen at Oxford, they met Robert Southey, an undergraduate of Balliol, who had been dismissed from Westminster School for denouncing flogging there. Coleridge and Southey were at once drawn together by a mutual attraction. "Coleridge," wrote Southey's son long afterward, "was seized with the most lively admiration for my father's person and conversation." Southey at the time of their meeting told a friend, "Coleridge is of most uncommon merit,—of the strongest genius, the clearest judgement, the best heart. My friend he already is, and must hereafter be yours."

Inspired by French ideas and ideals of *Liberté, Egalité et Fraternité*, Coleridge and Southey planned an ideal society of romantic dream, where all would be free and equal, where virtuous toil—of an hour or two daily—would provide a comfortable existence, leaving the rest of the day for the

61

cultivation of poetry and other intellectual pursuits. During these short hours of labor the women would do the housework and attend to the children. Lack of money had deeply afflicted both Coleridge and Southey—so money they agreed in despising. Indeed, it seemed to Coleridge that money had thwarted his passion for Mary Evans. In their new society, Mr. Godwin's aim, "the perfectibility of Man," prevented in Europe, it appeared, merely by a sordid social system, would be achieved—without money. And where better than in America, the land of moral idealism, where perfect Man existed in freedom and equality, unperverted by greed of gold or by sordid European commercialism? So to America they would go.

Coleridge, with his love of resounding words, named their ideal society "pantisocracy"—the equality of all; everybody should be free to do as he liked, and general freedom and happiness would be inevitable. In Oxford for the next three weeks Coleridge and Southey planned and preached and made converts to pantisocracy, with great enthusiasm; until on July 5, 1794, Coleridge and Hucks resumed their tour.

From Gloucester the next day, Samuel wrote to Southey, anxious for his "Health and Republicanism," but disgusted with Oxford and its inhabitants who were doubtless lethargic to pantisocracy. Among such people, Coleridge wrote, Southey was "a nightingale among owls." Before leaving Gloucester, Coleridge noticed and recorded an incident: a young girl sailing down the Severn, who, passing some thirty naked bathers, returned their jeers with interest. Another sight, that of a poor girl nursing her baby as she begged for food, disgusted him: "when the pure system of Pantisocracy arrives, these things will not be so." Of such was Coleridge's letter to Southey, which concluded with "Fraternity and civic remembrances" to a new convert at Oxford, and closed finally: "Farewell, sturdy Republican!"

A week later at Wrexham—where Mary's sister and grandmother lived, a fact that Coleridge said, surprisingly, "had entirely escaped my memory"—he wrote to Southey in a mood of deep depression. He had accidentally caught sight of Mary Evans there—Mary Evans "quam efflictim et perdite amabam." The shock was so great that he "turned sick and all but fainted away." Describing the same incident shortly afterward to a Cambridge friend, Samuel heightened the dramatic tension: "As I was standing at the window of the inn she passed by, and with her to my utter astonishment her sister, Mary Evans—quam efflictim et perdite amabam—yea, even to anguish. They both started—and gave a short cry—almost a faint shriek—I sickened and well nigh fainted—but instantly retired. Had I appeared to recognize her, my Fortitude would not have supported me."

The sight of Mary brought Coleridge a day of fasting and a sleepless night. The next day, sixteen miles from Wrexham, Coleridge began to feel better—"praised be God!" He now realized that "Love is a local anguish." At this distance he was "not half so miserable." Indeed, he would "endeavour to forget it amid the terrible Graces of the Wildwood scenery that surrounds me."

Nevertheless, the "local anguish" was not readily destroyed by distance or scenery; and to Southey, Samuel's distress again found characteristic expression. "I never durst even in a whisper avow my passion, though I knew she loved me," he cried: "Where were my Fortunes? And why should I make her miserable? Almighty God bless her! Her image is in the sanctuary of my Heart, and never can it be torn away but with the strings that grapple it to life. —Southey! There are few men of whose delicacy I think so highly as to have written all this. I am glad I have so deemed of you. We are soothed by communication."

The best antidote to Mary was, it seemed, pantisocracy; so Samuel went with Hucks through Wales preaching pantisocracy everywhere as their cure for all the ills of humanity, much enjoying the excitement that they caused amid jeers and plaudits from the yokels, and occasional bizarre incidents that Samuel delightedly observed. It was thus when "two great huge fellows, of butcher-like appearance, danced about the room in enthusiastic agitation, and one of them of his own accord called for a large glass of brandy, and drank it off to this, his own toast—'God save the King—and may he be the last!' " But even amid such stirring scenes Coleridge's poetical instinct, revived by the sight of Mary, could not be entirely suppressed. He had bought "a little blank book and portable inkhorn," and, as he told Southey, "As I journey onward I ever and anon pluck the wild Flowers of Poesy—'inhale their odours awhile'— then throw they away and think no more of them;" But now, "will I not do so!"

From the very day of Coleridge's meeting with Mary Evans, a note of personal, very self-conscious sadness crept into his verse, whatever its ostensible inspiration. Thus in the hotel at Ross he cries to an imaginary traveler:

If, like me, through Life's distressful scene
Lonely and sad thy pilgrimage hath been;

and so continues. Even "A Beautiful Spring in a Village" only prolongs the note of personal sadness:

Unboastful Stream! thy fount with pebbled falls
The faded form of past delight recalls

A month after leaving Oxford, Coleridge came to Bristol to again join Southey and two recent converts to pantisocracy, George Burnett and Robert Lovell. Other circumstances in common besides political opinions cemented the friendship of Coleridge and Southey. He, too, was a "poor orphan," having lost his father in early life. The boy's upbringing had been chiefly due to an aunt, Elizabeth Tyler, who now lived in Bristol. At Oxford Southey had been supported by a clerical uncle-chaplain to the English community at Lisbon—on the understanding that his nephew would enter the church. But as with Coleridge, Southey's opinions had made the church unattractive, and he had continued at Oxford intending to study law. Southey, too, was a poet; he was indeed already beginning his long series of epics with a republican *Joan of Arc*. The church was, however, still a possibility for Southey, for law was even less palatable. Into Southey's struggles with conscience Samuel threw himself with urgent advice and warning: a man he knew who against his conscience took a government post "threw himself in agony out of a two pair of stairs' window." To become a parson would prevent Southey's leaving for America with the other pantisocrats. Besides, Southey could easily become a "clerk in a compting house" in America, and "beyond all doubt, by the creative powers of your Genius you might supply whatever the stern simplicity of Republican Wants could require." Thus sagely advised, Southey decided to devote his "genius" to literature and pantisocracy instead of returning to Oxford.

So, united in a single aim, the two friends and their disciples spread the gospel of pantisocracy in Bristol and, at the same time, advisedly, clarified their own ideas as to what "pantisocracy" really meant. To the brother of one convert, Samuel now optimistically explained that the pantisocrats "vanity apart. . .have each a sufficient strength of head to make the virtues of the heart respectable; and. . .are all highly charged with that enthusiasm which results from strong perceptions of moral rectitude, called into life and action by ardent feelings."

As for "pecuniary matters," if, as he expected, a dozen men and their families emigrated to America "on this system"—next March, as he hoped—the "aggregate of their contributions" should be £2,000. "But infer not from hence that each man's quota is to be settled with the littleness of arithmetical accuracy. No; *all* strain *every* nerve, and then I trust the surplus money of some will supply the deficiencies of others." However, no detail was overlooked:

> The minutiae of topographical information we are daily endeavouring to acquire; but at present our plan is, to settle. . .on the banks of the Susquehannah. This however will be the subject of future investigation. . . .
> In the course of the winter those of us whose bodies, from habits of sedentary study or academic indolence, have not acquired their full tone and strength, intend to learn the theory and practice of agriculture and carpentry, according as situation and circumstance make one or the other convenient.

It was all as simple as that. But instead of going to the Susquehannah—which Samuel was said to have chosen for its "Poetical" name—Samuel's correspondent remained to become twice mayor of Monmouth.

The home and center of pantisocracy in Bristol was the house of a widowed lady, a Mrs. Fricker, who ran a private school, while her five daughters supplemented the slender family income by assisting friends with their family sewing. Southey was already engaged to one of the daughters, Edith; another, Mary, was about to marry Lovell, and George Burnett was in love with another sister, Martha. The eldest sister, Sarah, was said to be the prettiest. Before going on to see Burnett at his father's Somersetshire farm, Southey and Coleridge, *en passant*, converted Southey's mother at Bath to pantisocracy.

On August 18 the two friends reached the little village of Nether Stowey and made the acquaintance of a leading inhabitant, Tom Poole, a well-to-do tanner, who not long afterward became one of Samuel's closest friends. Flaunting their republican sympathies, Southey and Coleridge shocked the villagers and delighted Poole, who, though never a pantisocrat, held liberal views.

It is Poole who has left the one clear, concise account of the pantisocratic scheme:

Twelve gentlemen of good education and liberal principles are to embark with twelve ladies in April next. Previous to their leaving this country they are to have as much intercourse as possible, in order to ascertain each other's dispositions, and firmly to settle every regulation for the government of their future conduct. Their opinion was that they should fix themselves. . .somewhere in a delightful part of the new back settlements; that each man should labour two or three hours in a day, the produce of which labour would, they imagine, be more than sufficient to support the colony. . . .The produce of their industry is to be laid up in common for the use of all; and a good library of books is to be collected, and their leisure hours to be spent in study, liberal discussions, and the education of their children. . . .The regulations relating to the females strike them as the most difficult; whether the marriage contract shall be dissolved if agreeable to one or both parties, and many other circumstances, are not yet determined. The employments of the women are to be the care of infant children, and other occupations suited to their strength; at the same time the greatest attention is to be paid to the cultivation of their minds. Every one is to enjoy his own religious and political opinions, provided they do not encroach on the rules previously made. . . .They calculate that each gentleman providing £125 will be sufficient to carry the scheme into execution. Finally every individual is at liberty, whenever he pleases to withdraw from the society.

So having happily destroyed their reputations in Stowey, and leaving democratic Tom Poole similarly under a cloud, Coleridge and Southey set out on their return journey to Bristol. On their way they again stopped at Bath for a moment, and there, suddenly and for no apparent reason, Samuel engaged himself to Sarah Fricker: "not a little to my astonishment," wrote Southey; "for he had talked of being deeply in love with a certain Mary Evans." Enthusiasm for pantisocracy, a reaction against the indifference of Mary Evans, and probably a promise that Samuel had made to Poole to be "sober and rational," in other words practical—all had combined to thrust Samuel into this impulsive and irrational engagement. The other pantisocrats had already chosen their feminine partners for the voyage to America, and Coleridge felt the need of one for himself. Besides, a pantisocratic engagement was not necessarily binding; for the free-love theory of William Godwin, recently expressed in his *Political Justice*, had attracted at least some of the pantisocrats.

In London on September 1, Samuel wrote to Southey, "in melancholy mood." He had completed the first act of a blank verse drama, *The Fall of Robespierre*, of which Southey was writing the remaining two acts. It was a topical theme, for Robespierre had been executed only five weeks before. To Lovell and his new wife, Mary Fricker, Samuel sent via Southey "my fraternal love," and to Sarah anxiously awaiting some message from her fiancé he sent by the same route merely "much more." In the meantime Samuel resisted his depression by convivial evenings at The Salutation and Cat, near Christ's Hospital. There with his friend Charles Lamb, an old blue-coat boy, he discussed pantisocracy, philosophy, literature, and metaphysics as they sat "drinking egg-hot and smoking Oronooko," as Lamb described the occasions.

Ten days later Samuel was still in London, though "detesting this vile city." His discussions at The Salutation and Cat had left him "heavy of head, turbulent of bowel and inappetent." However, he had got "two Bishops and four Lords" to subscribe to his forthcoming dream—*Translations*. He had also been delighted to meet a young land agent from America, an old blue-coat boy who had doubtless heard of Samuel and pantisocracy at the school. The land agent consequently appeared at The Salutation and Cat—quite accidentally, of course! There, nightly, Samuel listened to the agent's most encouraging reports of America, which Coleridge retailed to Southey. Two thousand pounds would be sufficient. Twelve men could "easily" clear 300 acres of ground in four or five months. And the wily agent recommended the "Susquehannah" for its "excessive beauty, security from hostile Indians," and a ten years' allowance of credit for the land. Nor was this all—at the "Susquehannah," "literary characters made money there." Who could resist going to the "Susquehannah?" Yet more tempting—for Samuel seems to have foreseen all possible dangers—bisons were so rare that the agent had never seen one; and even if you met some by chance, they were "quite backwards." As for the mosquitoes, they too must have been "quite backwards," for they were far less troublesome than English gnats. No wonder Samuel's pantisocratic enthusiasm for the "Susquehannah" intensified!

Indeed, the land agent's roseate picture of America inspired Samuel to write a sonnet, "On the Prospect of Establishing a Pantisocracy in America." In this he contrasted his gloomy vision of England with his golden dream of the "Susquehannah"—

> In other climes
> Where dawns, with hope serene, a brighter day
>   Than e'er saw Albion in her happiest times,
> With mental eye exulting now explore,
>   And soon with kindred minds shall haste to enjoy
> (Free from the ills which here our peace destroy)
>   Content and Bliss on Transatlantic shore.

The hysterical impulse that haunted Coleridge throughout his life, to escape from frustrations instead of overcoming them, appears in these verses.

Back in Cambridge, in mid-September, Coleridge enthusiastically proclaimed to fellow undergraduates his new pantisocratic gospel. "I have drawn up my arguments in battle array," he told Southey in his first letter since his return. "They shall have the *Tactician* Excellence of the Mathematician with the Enthusiasm of the Poet—The Head shall be the Mass—the Heart the fiery Spirit, that fills, informs, and agitates the whole." It was all wonderfully exciting for Samuel, and he must give Southey full details. When one friend laughed at him, "Up I arose terrible in Reasoning—he fled from me—because 'he could not answer for his own sanity sitting so near a madman of Genius!' He told me that the Strength of my imagination had intoxicated my Reason—and that the acuteness of my Reason had given a directing influence to my Imagination.—Four months ago the remark would not have been more elegant than just.—Now it is nothing."

But to a vulgar, stupid, and hostile world the pantisocrats would present a united front of human love and sympathy, of superior virtues, which must in time confound their opponents. All the pantisocrats would be as brothers and sisters. "Make Edith my Sister," Coleridge exhorted Southey: "she must therefore be more emphatically my Sister." Indeed, on the preceding day Samuel had sent Edith Fricker a similar exhortation of unusual warmth, although she was Southey's fianceé. "I had a Sister—an only Sister," he told her.

Most tenderly did I love her! Yea, I have woke at midnight and wept—because *she was not*. There is no attachment under heaven so pure, so endearing. The Brother who is blessed with it, I have envied him! Let whatsoever discompose him, he has still a gentle Friend, in whose soft Bosom he may repose his Sorrows, and receive for every wound of affliction the Balm of a Sigh. My Sister, like you, was beautiful and accomplished—like you she was lowly at Heart. Her Eye beamed with meekest Sensibility. I know, and *feel* that I am *your Brother*. I would that you would say to me "I *will* be your Sister—your *favourite* Sister in the Family of Soul."

What, if anything, Coleridge wrote to Sarah at this time is not known but probably neither Sarah nor Southey was unduly appreciative of Samuel's effusion to Edith. However, perhaps by way of reassurance, Coleridge the next day cried to Southey: "My God! how tumultuous are the movements of my Heart. Since I quitted this room what and how important Events have been evolved! America! Southey! Miss Fricker!—Yes—Southey—you are right—Even Love is the creature of strong Motive—I certainly love her. I think of her incessantly and with unspeakable tenderness—with that inward melting away of Soul that symptomatizes it."

Samuel complimented Southey on his sonnets, "the best of any I have yet seen." Nevertheless, he corrected them and sent one of his own, apologetically, in return: "I am almost ashamed to write the following—it is so inferior. Ashamed! No Southey—God knows my heart—I am *delighted* to feel you superior to me in Genius as in Virtue." The sonnet, far superior to Southey's, clearly reveals Coleridge's inner dream of "pantisocracy," and equally clearly shows how compensatory it was to the loss of Mary:

> No more my visionary soul shall dwell
> On Joys that were; no more endure to weigh
> The shame and anguish of the evil day
> Wisely forgetful! O'er the ocean swell
> Sublime of Hope, I seek the cottag'd dell
> Where Virtue calm with careless step may stray,
> And dancing to the moonlight roundelay,
> The wizard Passions weave an holy spell.
> Eyes that have ach'd with Sorrow! Ye shall weep
> Tears of doubt-mingled joy, like theirs who start
> From Precipices of distemper'd sleep
> On which the fierce-eyed Fiends their revels keep,
> And see the rising Sun, and feel it dart
> New rays of pleasance trembling to the heart.

Whatever enmity toward Samuel his letter to Edith may or may not have created in Sarah or Southey, his benevolent attempt to console them by praise of Sarah failed in its effect. Unfortunately, his letter was crossed on its way to Southey by an angry one from Southey himself, which reproached him for not having written to Sarah since quitting Bristol, thus leaving her prey to doubt and anxiety. Immediately on its arrival, Samuel replied, characteristically defending himself with unconvincing excuses, unctuously presented in a spirit of Christian forgiveness—a technique that he was to refine with much practice throughout the rest of his life. Sorrow for Southey's weakness was now his keynote. "Angry, no! I esteem and confide in you the more; but it *did* make me sorrowful. I was blameless; it was therefore only 'a passing cloud empictured on the breast.' " He was evidently proud of the image and phrase, which he had used recently in his verses "To a Beautiful Spring in a Village."

How differently he would have acted, he said, had he been in Southey's place, and Southey in his. "Surely had I written to you the *first* letter you directed to *me* at Cambridge, I *would* not have believed that you *could* have received it without immediately answering it. Still less that you *could* have given a momentary pain to her that loved you. If I could have imagined no *rational* excuse for you, I would have peopled the vacancy with events of impossibility." Have so turned the table on his correspondent, Samuel then entered upon a detailed but similarly unconvincing apologia. He had arrived in Cambridge only on the preceding day, and "perhaps the very hour you were writing in the severity of offended friendship, was I pouring forth the heart to Sarah Fricker. . . .I saw no one. On the moment of arrival I shut my door, and wrote to her. But why not before? In the first place Miss F. did not authorize me to direct immediately to her"—with a long rigmarole to the same effect.

This however, was not enough for Samuel; he must heap coals of fire upon his adversary's bowed head. He had been ill—"very ill. I exhausted my finances, and ill as I was, I sat down and scrawled a few guineas' worth of nonsense for the booksellers. . . .Languid, sick at heart, in the back room of an inn! Lofty conjunction of circumstances for me to write to Miss F. . . .If you are satisfied, tell Miss F. that *you* are *so* but assign no reasons. I ought not to have been *suspected*." The last reproach was evidently for "Miss F."

At the tail end of the letter Samuel's hidden feelings suddenly burst through all his pretenses, when, evidently alluding to his engagement, he suddenly cried: "Southey! Precipitance is wrong. . . .I have been the slave of impulse, the child of imbecility. . . .My heart is very heavy much more than when I began to write." He was already discovering that having engaged himself in haste he was now repenting at leisure.

Immediately after sending off his letter, Samuel heard from a common friend that Southey had also complained to him of Samuel's conduct, and his next reply to Southey suddenly exploded in a collapse of patience and self-restraint. He had just sent a second letter to Sarah, he said, directed to Mrs. Southey's in Bath: "Perhaps you have not heard from Bath—damn perhapses." And he did not hesitate to tell Southey that he was now finding new feminine consolation in the society of the daughter of a local theater proprietor and owner of a theatrical company. This was a Mr. Brunton, who sent Samuel a free ticket for the theatrical season. Samuel pretended that he was the victim of an unsought attachment, which Miss Brunton—"said to be the most literary of the beautiful and the most beautiful of the literatae"— felt for him.

Within a fortnight, however, Samuel told a friend: "Instead of being the wizard I am the bewitched. I have indeed incautiously drank too deeply from the bowl of the blameless Circe—the sweet intoxication that makes the heart forget its duties and its cares. The Bruntons left us yesterday morning—since which time Caldwell [his friend whom Samuel thought she favored more than himself] and I have chaunted a love-duet most pathetically." Under the spell of Miss Brunton's witchery he wrote and presented to her various amorous and complimentary poems, as well as a copy of the just-published *Fall of Robespierre*. In the verses that accompanied the present, Samuel's feelings toward Miss Brunton found their most gallant conventional expression. After this, Miss Brunton disappears.

Shortly after her departure an unsigned letter came to Samuel, which doubtless drove the memory of Ann Brunton out of his mind, and was perhaps so intended. The writer was the elusive Mary Evans. Samuel's reference to himself in his verses to Ann Brunton as "the love-wilder'd maniac" was not all poetry. It was, indeed, suggested by unpleasant reality. Samuel's dismissal from the army as officially "insane" had combined with his actions both before and since to appear to his alarmed brothers not unnaturally as a simple statement of fact. Nor were his brothers the only persons to believe it. The rumor had doubtless spread among his Cambridge acquaintances; his best friend had called him, laughingly, "a madman of genius," and Mary, who had other friends at Cambridge, had certainly heard it—whether from them alone or perhaps also from Samuel's brothers is not certain.

Whatever the reason, Mary now appeared upon the scene melodramatically enough and with obvious enjoyment of her part, which also seemingly included keeping Samuel on a string. That pantisocracy and the engagement to Sarah were intimately associated may not have been beyond the range of her knowledge. "Is this handwriting," she melodramatically began,

altogether erased from your memory? To whom am I addressing myself? For whom am I now violating the rules of female delicacy? Is it for the same Coleridge whom I once regarded as a sister her best-beloved Brother? Or for one who will *ridicule* that advice from me, which he has *rejected* as offered by his family? I will hazard the attempt. I have no right, nor do I feel myself inclined to reproach you for the Past. God forbid! You have already suffered too much from self-accusation. But I conjure you, Coleridge, earnestly and solemnly conjure you to consider long and deeply before you enter into any rash schemes.

There is an eagerness in your Nature, which is ever hurrying you in the sad Extreme. I have heard that you mean to leave England, and on a plan so absurd and extravagant that were I for a moment to imagine it *true*, I should be obliged to listen with a more patient ear to suggestions which I have rejected a thousand times with scorn and anger. Yes! whatever Pain I might suffer, I should be forced to exclaim, "O what a noble mind is here *o'er-thrown*, Blasted with ecstasy." You have a country, does it demand nothing of you? You have doting Friends! Will you break their Hearts! There is a God—Coleridge! Though I have been told (indeed I do not believe it) that you doubt of his existence and disbelieve a hereafter. No! you have too much sensibility to be an Infidel. You know I was never rigid in my opinions concerning Religion—and have always thought *Faith* to be only Reason applied to a particular subject. [Surely from Coleridge, who often proclaimed it.] In short I am the same being as when you used to say, "We thought in all things alike." I often reflect on the happy hours we spent together and regret the loss of your Society. I cannot easily forget those whom I once loved—nor can I easily form new Friendships. I find women in general vain—all of the same trifle, and therefore little and envious, and (I am afraid) without sincerity; and of the other sex those who are offered and held up to my esteem are very prudent, and very worldly. If you value my peace of mind, you must *on no account* answer this letter, or take the least notice of it. I *would* not for the world *any part* of my Family should suspect that I have written to you. My mind is sadly harassed by being perpetually obliged to resist the solicitations of those whom I love. I need not explain myself. Farewell, Coleridge! I shall always feel that I have been your *Sister.*

Whether the virtuous Mary consciously or unconsciously desired it, her final injunction against a reply was, of course, in its context a particular incentive to Coleridge to answer it. But for some time he refrained, plunged into renewed misery by the reawakening of his frustrated desire. At last, three weeks after receiving it, he copied Mary's epistle in a letter to Southey, written at Cambridge on October 21, 1794.

"I loved her, Southey, almost to madness," he continued.

> Her image was never absent from me for three years; for *more* than three years. My resolution has never faltered, but I want a comforter. I have done nothing. I have gone into company. I was constantly at the theatre here till they left us. I endeavoured to be perpetually with Miss Brunton. I even hoped that her exquisite beauty and uncommon accomplishments might have cured one passion by another. The latter I could easily have dissipated in her absence. [i.e., Ann Brunton's absence] and so have restored my affections to her whom I do not love [Sarah Fricker]. I should have detested myself, if after my first letter I had written coldly—how could I write *as warmly*?

Inspired by very conscious self-pity, Coleridge appended to his letter a sonnet beginning: "Thou bleedest, my poor Heart!" in which he hints that "Jealousy" has caused the ruin of his love for Mary, and he should not have so easily abandoned hope. The original title, "To My Heart," he later changed to "On a Discovery Made too Late." In a postscript he suddenly recalled that "yesterday" he was "twenty-two years old." In fact, his birthday was that very day, October 21; but throughout life he mistook its date as the 20th. He had also just heard "from my Brothers—from him particularly who has been Friend, Brother, Father—'Twas all remonstrance, and Anguish, and suggestions that I am deranged!! Let me receive from you a letter of Consolation—for believe me! I am most completely wretched!" Three days later he sent the sonnet "To My Heart" to his friend Wrangham, with throbbing head and in low spirits, "occasioned by a letter which I lately received from a young lady, whom for five years I loved almost to madness, dissuasive from my American scheme—but where Justice leads I will follow, though her path be through thorns and roughness."

Throughout October Samuel found some relief from his purely personal miseries in increasing discussions of pantisocracy with Southey, and in preaching it at Cambridge in all its Platonist, idealistic purity. For six hours he debated with two leading Cambridge intellectuals, including "one of the most powerful and Briarean intellect," and they finally admitted that the system was "impregnable, supposing the assigned quantum of virtue and genius in the first individuals." At one in the morning Samuel returned to his rooms, "exulting in the honest consciousness of having exhibited closer argument in more elegant and appropriate language, than I had ever conceived myself capable of."

But a letter from the prudent and practical Southey suggesting that servants be brought to America caught Samuel's eye, and his spirits fell. Servants meant the end of the ideal egalitarian principle. Samuel was horrified at the suggestion. *Servants* was only another name for slaves. The married women could prepare "the food of simplicity" for all, and look after the pregnant women, and nurse the sick. "Let the husbands do *all* the rest—and what will that all be?—washing with a machine and cleaning the house; one hour's addition to our daily labour." Samuel showed that he could be as practical, as detailed, in planning as Southey. "That the greater part of our Female Companions [*N.B.* not "wives"] should have the task of Maternal exertion at the same time, is very *improbable*. But though it were to happen, an infant is almost always sleeping—and during its slumbers the Mother may in the same room perform the little offices of ironing clothes or making shirts. But," he added, "the hearts of the women are not *all* with us."

Nor were these the sole problems caused by the presence of women in pantisocracy that worried Samuel. Would they not instill religious and other prejudices into their children? "How can we ensure their silence concerning God &c? Is it possible *they* should enter our *motives* for this silence? If not, we must produce their *obedience* by *Terror*. Obedience? Terror? The repetition is sufficient!" The warning of one of his Cambridge disputants still haunted him. "Your system, Coleridge," he had said, "appears strong to the head and lovely to the heart; but depend upon it, you will never give your *women* sufficient strength of mind, liberality of heart, or vigilance of attention. They will spoil it." Samuel now told Southey he wished "that the two mothers were not to go, and that the children stayed with them." Mrs. Fricker, whom Samuel detested, must at all costs be left behind; "*That* Mrs. Fricker—we shall have her teaching the infants Christianity, I mean that mongrel whelp that goes under its name—teaching them by stealth in some ague-fit of superstition."

All these questions in so logical a mind as Samuel's simply led away from mere details to fundamental principles. "The more perfect our System is—supposing the necessary Premises—the more eager in anxiety am I—that the necessary Premises should exist." And as had been clearly established in his six hours' debate, the necessary premise was the "assigned quantum of virtue and genius" in the first pantisocrats. Had they all got it? he asked himself, especially the women? Were not the women, in fact, attracted to pantisocracy rather by the "novelty" of the idea than by a "generous enthusiasm for Benevolence" such as inspired himself, who evidently had the "quantum?" Could women sacrifice "individual comforts" as he could? Were they "saturated with the Divinity of truth, sufficiently?" He could not allay his doubts and fears on these matters. "Men *can* be vicious, some *will* be," he knew. But "the leading idea of Pantisocracy is to make men necessarily virtuous by removing all motives to evil—all possible temptations."

Despite his practical attitude toward servants, Southey's visionary enthusiasm for pantisocracy was at times almost as greast as that of Coleridge. His aims and expectations he clearly explained to a friend a few days after first meeting Coleridge in Oxford: "Many of my friends will blame me for so bold a step, but as many encourage me; and I want to raise money enough to settle myself across the Atlantic. If I have leisure to write there, my stock of imagery will be much increased. . . .Methinks my name will look well in print. I expect a host of petty critics will buzz about my ears but I must brush them off."

Evidently influenced by Samuel's excited optimism, Southey wrote a few days later, on August 1:

> Everything smiles upon me; my mother is fully convinced of the propriety of our resolution; she admires the plan; she goes with us: never did so delightful a prospect of happiness open my view before; to go with all I love; to go with all my friends. . .to live with them in the most agreeable and most honourable employment, to eat the fruits I have raised, and see every face happy around me; my mother sheltered in the declining years from the anxieties which have pursued her; my brothers educated to be useful and virtuous.

By mid-October, however, this "delightful prospect" no longer "smiled" upon Southey. For the rich aunt who now supported him, vexed by his pantisocracy and his engagement to the impecunious Edith Fricker, turned him out of the house on a stormy night—penniless and disinherited. In her anger she vowed never to see his face again or open one of his letters. This vow she kept unbroken to the end of her life.

"It was late in the evening," Southey told his brother, a naval midshipman:

> The wind blew and the rain fell and I had walked from Bath in the morning. Luckily my father's old great-coat was at Lovell's, I clapped it on, swallowed a glass of brandy, and set off; I met an old drunken man three miles off, and was obliged to drag him all the way to Bath, nine miles! Oh, Patience, Patience, thou hast often helped poor Robert Southey, but never didst thou stand by him in more need than on Friday the 17th of October, 1794!!! I do my duty, and will continue to do it, be the consequences what they may. You are unpleasantly situated, so is my mother, so were we all till this grand scheme of Pantisocracy flashed upon our minds, and now all is perfectly delightful. . . .But of all the catalogue of enormities, nothing enrages my aunt so much as my intended marriage with Mrs. Lovell's sister Edith.

Samuel, too, found little to cheer him except his pantisocratic dream. His brother George was very troublesome: he sent him advice, "affected coldness, an assumed alienation, mixed with involuntary bursts of ANGUISH and disappointed affection." However, George's fears for Samuel's sanity were apparently subsiding, and, consequently, Samuel's own worries about them diminished. By November 3 he was able to write: "There is little danger of my being confined." When George questioned Samuel as to how his mother had best be informed of his way of life he cried, "These are the daggers which are plunged into my Peace! Enough!"

Yet Samuel's youth occasionally reveals itself in a touch of unconscious comedy amid his woes: "A lady of fashionable rank and most fashionable ideas" had told one of his friends, "I was a man of the *most courtly* and polished manners, of the most *gentlemanly* address,—she had ever met with. But I will not crow." Samuel's apparent vanity was largely compensatory, to counteract his lifelong uneasiness about his appearance. Nor did Samuel's naïve pantisocratic republicanism know any limitations except those of superior social position. All compliments he now abjured (except, apparently, those of the fashionable lady) as "cold, aristocratic inanities." But short of the aristocratic, his love was unbounded: "If there be any whom I deem worthy of remembrance—I am their Brother. In the Fraternity of universal Nature," he would even call his cat "Sister." Owls he respected, and jackasses he loved, but he had no "particular partiality" for aldermen, hogs, and bishops, whom he would admit by courtesy as cousin; "but Kings, Tygers, Generals, Ministers and Hyaenas, I renounce them all. May the Almighty Pantisocratizer of Souls pantisocratize the Earth."

Yet Samuel's youthful self-conscious misery over Mary was, of its kind, real enough. When amid his pantisocratic anxieties his underlying memories of her break out in words of simple sincerity, the depth and strength of his frustrated feeling is very evident: "She was VERY lovely, Southey! We formed each other's minds; our ideas were blended. Heaven bless her! I cannot forget her; everyday her memory sinks deeper into my heart."

For Coleridge lacked the stoic's temperament; and all his sources of consolation—political, literary, rhetorical, philosophical, metaphysical, religious, and skeptical, which with sublime impartiality he tried in turn—proved unavailing when his too vivid imagination re-created the lovely image of Mary, and for a moment he relived the golden hours. Again he played with the thought of suicide, and, remembering the death of another poet by his own hand, began another "Monody on the Death of Chatterton," four years after writing the first one in Boyer's book at school. This last version was as expressive of his own misery and death-wish as of Chatterton's:

> When faint and sad o'er Sorrow's desert wild
> Slow journeys onward, poor Misfortune's child,
> When fades each lovely form by Fancy drest,
> And inly pines the self-consuming breast,
> (No scourge of scorpions in thy right arm dread,
> No helmed terrors nodding o'er thy head,)
> Assume O DEATH! the cherub wings of PEACE,
> And bid the heartsick Wanderer's Anguish cease.
> . . . .
> And oft, in Fancy's saddest hour, my soul
> Averted shudders at the poison'd bowl.

November brought Samuel yet more disturbing news of Mary; a rumor reached him that she was engaged. His last faint hope died, or rather remained dying until confirmation of the report came. Again in his anxiety he turned to verse, writing "The Sigh," a short lyric in which he traced the course of his unfortunate passion, and described truly enough his proposed settlement in America as due to his desire to escape from such unhappy memories, for hope was then dead:

> And though in distant climes to roam
> A wanderer from my native home,

I fain would soothe the sense of care,
And lull to sleep the Joys that were!
Thy image may not banished be—
Still Mary! still I sigh for thee.

Southey, meanwhile, though not at heart unsympathetic, continued to exhort Samuel to abandon his attachment to a hopeless love and follow the path of duty, which led back to Sarah Fricker, his pantisocratic partner. In these exhortations Southey rose to sublime heights of imaginary self-sacrifice, which poor Samuel vainly strove to attain, but then, Hamlet-like, fell to pondering his own state instead. "Whatever of mind we *will* to do we *can* do. What then palsies the will? The Joy of Grief!"

The confusion into which Samuel's affairs had fallen, including his Cambridge studies, left him dazed and lethargic when not panic-stricken by fears. He complained of the "feverish distemperature of brain during which some horrible phantom threatens our eyes in every corner, until, emboldened by terror, we rush on it, and then—why then we return, the heart indignant at its own palpitation!" It was evidently thus, when, in this same letter to Southey of November 3, he described the effect upon him of reading Schiller's *Robbers* after midnight. He had read "chill and trembling" for an hour, and then was so excited that "I could read no more. My God! Southey! Who is this Schiller? This convulser of the Heart? Did he write this Tragedy amid the yelling of Fiends? I tremble like an Aspen Leaf. I should not like to be able to describe such Characters. Upon my Soul, I write to you because I am frightened. I had better go to bed." On November 8, with the rumor of Mary's engagement ever in his ears, Coleridge set off for London again.

By this time the anxiety and distress occasioned by Mary's letter, intensified by the rumor of her engagement, dissipated Coleridge's lethargy for a moment and drove him to action. Despite her prohibition he sent her a despairing letter asking to know the worst. If Mary would write in the high romantic vein so, too, could he:

Too long has my heart been the torture house of Suspense. After infinite struggles of Irresolution I will at last dare to request of you, Mary! that you will communicate to me whether or no you are engaged to Mr—— [Fryer Todd, a man of "good fortune," who married Mary on October 13, 1795]. I conjure you not to consider this request as presumptious indelicacy. Upon mine Honor, I have made it with no other Design or Expectation than that of arming my fortitude by total hopelessness. Read this letter with benevolence—and consign it to Oblivion. For four years I have endeavoured to smother a very ardent attachment—in what degree I have succeeded, you must know better than I can. With quick perceptions of moral Beauty it was impossible not to admire in you your sensibility regulated by Judgement, your Gaiety proceeding from a cheerful Heart acting on the stores of a strong understanding. At first I voluntarily invited the recollection of these qualities into my mind. I made them the perpetual Objects of my Reveries. Yet I entertained no one Sentiment beyond that of the immediate Pleasure annexed to the thinking of you. At length it became an Habit. I awoke from the Delusion, and found that I had unwittingly harboured a Passion which I felt neither the power or the courage to subdue. My associations were irrevocably formed, and your Image was blended with every idea. I thought of you incessantly: yet that Spirit (if Spirit there be that condescends to record the lonely Beatings of my heart) that Spirit knows, that I thought of you with the purity of a Brother. Happy were I, had I been with no more than a Brother's ardor! The Man of dependent fortunes while he fosters an attachment commits an act of suicide on his happiness. I possessed no Establishment—my views were very distant—I saw that you regarded me merely with the kindness of a Sister. What expectations *could* I form? I formed no expectations. I was ever resolving to subdue the disquieting Passion: still some inexplicable Suggestion palsied my Efforts, and I clung with desperate fondness to this Phantom of Love, its mysterious attractions and hopeless Prospects. It was a faint and rayless Hope! Yet it soothed my Solitude with many a delightful day-dream. It was a faint and rayless Hope! Yet I nursed it in my Bosom with an Agony of Affection, even as a Mother her sickly infant.*

But these are the poisoned Luxuries of a diseased Fancy! Indulge, Mary! this my first, my last request—and restore me to *Reality*, however gloomy. Sad and full of heaviness will the Intelligence be—my heart will die within me—I shall receive it however with steadier resignation from yourself, than were it announced to me (haply on your marriage Day!) by a Stranger! Indulge my request. I will not disturb your Peace by even a *Look* of Discontent—still less will I offend your Ear by the Whine of selfish Sensibility. In a few months I shall enter at the Temple—and there seek forgetful Calmness, where only it can be found, in incessant and useful Activity. Were you not possessed of a Mind and of a Heart above the usual Lot of Women I should not have written you sentiments that would be unintelligible to three fourths of your Sex. But our Feelings are congenial, though your (my?) attachment is doomed not to be reciprocal. You will not deem so meanly of me as to believe that I shall regard Mr.——[Todd] with the jaundiced Eye of disappointed Passion. God forbid! He, whom you honor with your affections, becomes sacred to me. I shall love him for *your* Sake. The time may perhaps come, when I shall be philosopher enough—not to envy him for *his own*.

The next day Coleridge returned for the last time to Cambridge, where a few days later he addressed a letter to the editor of the London *Morning Chronicle*, offering to write a series of sonnets on eminent contemporaries. Soon they began to appear in the paper, attracting a good deal of attention in literary and political circles. Then, restlessly awaiting Mary's reply, he returned to town.

---

*　Faint was that Hope and rayless: yet 'twas fair
And sooth'd with many a dream the Hour of Rest!
Thou should'st have lov'd it most when most opprest,
An nurs'd it with an Agony of Care,
Even as a mother her sweet infant heir
That pale and sickly droops upon her Breast.
　　　"To My Heart"—later entitled "On a Discovery Made Too Late."

There, with Lamb, heartbroken like himself over a love affair, he resumed the genially melancholy evenings at The Salutation and Cat. Lamb never forgot the happiness of those evenings and often reminded Samuel of them in later years. He recalled the pleasure of listening "when you were repeating one of Bowles's sweetest sonnets, in your sweet manner, while we two were indulging sympathy, a solitary luxury, by the fire-side at the Salutation. Yet have I no higher ideas of Heaven."

Meanwhile, Southey had become almost certain of Coleridge's treachery to Sarah, whose defender he now openly became, insistently summoning the reluctant Samuel to Sarah's side. Samuel's reply to Southey's nagging and coolness was his customary one of assuming a pose of Christian humility and benevolence in the face of unjust detraction. "My very virtues are of the slothful order—God forbid my vices should be otherwise. I never feel anger, still less retain resentment. But I should be a monster, if there had risen in my heart even a *propensity* to either, towards you, whose conduct has been regulated by *affection*."

Throughout December this debate between Southey and Coleridge on Sarah and on pantisocracy continued with increasing disaffection into the following year. At the very beginning Samuel openly admitted that his engagement to Sarah was merely part of his scheme for pantisocracy (to have a female partner like the others) and not the result of affection. But, he argued, Southey's "accusations" of neglect of Sarah were "unjust." He had written four or five letters to her since leaving Bristol in August and had received only one in return. "I am not conscious," he told Southey,

> of having injured her otherwise than by having mistaken the ebullience of *schematism* for affection, which a moment's reflection might have told me is not a plant of so mushroom a growth—had it even not been counteracted by a prior attachment. But my whole life has been a series of blunders! God have mercy upon me—for I am a most miserable Dog. The most criminal action of my life was the "first letter I wrote to Sarah." I had worked myself to such a pitch, that I scarcely knew I was writing like a hypocrite. However it still remains for me to be externally just, though my heart is withered within me—and life seems now to give me disgust rather than pain.

After this he sent his love to Southey's mother and to Edith Fricker, "and to whomever it is right or convenient."

Sarah, however, was not the only subject of contention between the two friends. Southey, more prudent and practical when not infected by Samuel's visionary enthusiasm, now suggested a preliminary experiment in pantisocracy in Wales before launching out on so expensive and reckless an expedition as that to America. But the suggestion was summarily rejected: "As to the Welsh scheme—pardon me—it is nonsense. We must go to America, if we can get Money enough." Money, or rather the lack of it, he had gently informed Southey (still insistent on Coleridge's return to Sarah), prevented his return to Bristol, and when Southey sent him his verse instead of his purse, Samuel brusquely replied: "I received your poetry which will be of no pecuniary service to me." Already Samuel was beginning to practice his lifelong habit of "touching" his friends for money, generally with success. However, on this occasion, he was, he said, expecting a remittance from Cambridge, "and then I will set off for Bristol." But he did not come.

He was still waiting for the reply from Mary, which also did not come. He wondered whether he would ever write his dream book on pantisocracy, which could only be done if the system were perfect. Southey, he found to his regret, was dubious about the visionary perfection. He feared that in Southey, "the *Feelings* prevailed over the Dea optima maxima"; which they doubtless had. But writing to Southey, he found "a relief," even without "any particular thing to say," and poetry was also a relief as well as a bond between them. "Your *Poems* (just published) and Bowles are my only morning companions," Samuel wrote. Disappointment had now, he said, made him "a complete Necessitarian." He informed his friend, "By way of a detached truth, when I am unhappy, a sigh or a groan does not feel sufficient to relieve the oppression of my heart; I give a long whistle."

Despite his unhappiness Samuel did not isolate himself in London but gave rein to his strong social instincts, dining with the proprietors and editors of the *Morning Chronicle*, which was now publishing his sonnets on "eminent contemporaries." Samuel was writing them daily and reading them nightly to Lamb at the Salutation. Lamb reminded him long afterward of "the time when you wrote those on Bowles, Priestley, Burke, in that nice little smoky room at the Salutation, which is even now continually presenting itself to my recollection, with all its associated train of pipes, tobacco, egg-hot, welsh-rabbit, metaphysics and poetry. I have never yet met with anyone—never shall meet with anyone—who could or can compensate me for the loss of your society." Coleridge, too, was evidently happy there with Lamb, happier than anywhere else, very unlike the pathetic picture he had drawn of himself to Southey, to excuse his neglect of Sarah.

One of Samuel's sonnets composed at the Salutation was inspired by Mary and by the influence of the poet Bowles:

> O gentle Look, that didst my Soul beguile,
> Why hast thou left me? Still in some fond dream
> Revisit my sad Heart, auspicious Smile!
> As falls on closing Flowers the lunar Beam.

In Bowles's honor he wrote two sonnets; the first, like one to Southey, was included among those to "eminent contemporaries" published in the *Morning Chronicle*.

At last, on Christmas Eve 1794, Mary's reply reached Coleridge and evidently left him no hope. He replied with a dramatic, self-conscious nobleness such as Mary had displayed in her earlier letter, and doubtless also in her last:

I have this moment received your letter, Mary Evans! Its firmness does honour to your understanding, its gentleness to your humanity. You condecend [*sic*] to accuse yourself—most unjustly! You have been altogether blameless. In my wildest day-dream of Vanity I never supposed that you entertained for me any other than a common friendship. To love you Habit has made unalterable. This passion however, divested, as it now is, of all Shadow of Hope, will lose its disquieting power. Far distant from you I shall journey thro' the vale of Men in calmness. He cannot long be wretched, who dares be actively virtuous. I have burnt your Letters—forget mine—and that I have pained you, forgive me! May God infinitely love you! S. T. Coleridge.

So ended this very poetical passion of youth, of such mixed elements, pain and folly, pathos and absurdity, but leaving in Samuel a deep and bitter, if also poetical, pain. Nor was this quite the end. His love episode now ended; but there was an epilogue thirteen years later when for a moment Mary's path in life crossed his own.

5 Sarah Fricker (1794-95)

My Sara—best beloved of human kind!
When breathing the pure soul of tenderness,
She thrills me with the husband's promis'd name!
—Coleridge, "The Nightingale" (1795)

The final separation from Mary made these last days of the year 1794 painful indeed for Samuel. To Southey he relieved his overburdened heart of all the emotion and rhetoric with which it was afflicted, not without evident self-satisfaction in his own sensibility, and even more in the sentimental language of its expression: "I am calm, dear Southey, as an Autumnal day when the sky is covered with grey moveless clouds. To *love her*, habit has made unalterable: I had placed her in the sanctuary of my Heart, nor can she be torn from thence but with the strings that grapple it to life. This Passion however, divested as it now is of all Shadow of Hope, seems to lose its disquieting Power. Far distant, and never more to behold or hear of her, I shall sojourn in the Vale of Men, sad and in loneliness, yet not unhappy." Next, as in his last letter to Mary herself, he continues with the parrot cant of his school exercises: "He cannot be long wretched who dares be actively virtuous."

Even worse than the loss of his beloved Mary was the thought of his affianced bride, Sarah Fricker, waiting for him in Bristol. He again expressed to Southey his emotions at the loss of Mary and the thought of marriage to another. "To lose her! I can rise above that selfish pang. But to marry another—O Southey! bear with my weakness. Love makes all things pure and heavenly like itself. But to marry a woman whom I do *not* love—to degrade her whom I call my wife, by making her the instrument of low Desire, and on the removal of a desultory appetite, to be perhaps not displeased with her absence! Enough! These refinements are the wild wildering fires that lead me into Vice. Mark you, Southey!—I will do my Duty."

Southey at this very time was insistently urging that his duty was to return to Sarah and that he should do so without delay. Samuel, irritated, began to point out newly discovered flaws in Southey's otherwise "perfect character": particularly his "indignation at weakness." But he promised to return and to meet Southey at Bath, "whatever be the consequences." He informed Sarah of his intention to return, speaking "indefinitely that I might not disappoint."

And he assured Southey that he was all eagerness to leave London, and that Southey was quite wrong in thinking otherwise.

Poetry was a solace, and the friends exchanged sonnets. Samuel's were still appearing in the *Morning Chronicle*. Just now, however, he wanted his poems to express his personal sorrows. "Your sonnet is a noble burst of poetry," he told Southey, "but my mind is weakened and I turn with selfishness of thought to those milder songs that develop my lonely feelings. Sonnets," he considered, "scarcely for the hard gaze of the public. Manly yet gentle egotism is perhaps the only conversation which pleases from these melancholy children of the Muse." The soleful egotism that now permeated his sonnets to Bowles, Godwin, and others in the *Morning Chronicle* was, however, less "manly" than "gentle." His misery found a different form of poetic consolation when on Christmas Eve, the very day of his final letter to Mary, he began that huddle of biblical and religious sentiment, political feeling, ethical, metaphysical, and philosophical elements, named *Religious Musings*. This was preceded by a significant epigraph, an adaptation from Akenside's *Pleasures of the Imagination*.

> Who tho' first,
> In years unseason'd, I attun'd the lay
> To idle Passion and unreal Woe?
> Yet serious Truth her empire o'er my song
> Hath now asserted; Falsehood's evil brood,
> Vice and deceitful Pleasure, she at once
> Excluded, and my Fancy's careless toil
> Drew to the better cause!

Nevertheless, "manly yet gentle egotism" as well as various appetizing concoctions he still continued to enjoy nightly with Lamb in The Salutation and Cat. These he naturally found more alluring than Bath or Bristol with Sarah and the increasingly indignant Southey. So, despite his promises to return, at The Salutation and Cat he remained, until, leaving most of his clothes behind as surety for his unpaid bill (which Lamb ultimately discharged), he had to seek the humbler shelter of the well-named Angel Inn nearby.

Fear and anxiety, which had driven him from Cambridge on several occasions and which were later to appear in some of his finest poetry, were again shaping Samuel's career. While Sarah despaired and Southey grew angrily impatient, Coleridge lay low in London, unable to move by his own volition. As the new year 1795 dawned, he sent them new assurances couched in the tone of semihysterical humor that his misery sometimes assumed. He would return immediately, he said, despite the dangers of the road, the fear of colds and rheumatism: "I will dash through the towns and helter-skelter it into Bath in the Flying Waggon!" With much more to the same effect. At any rate he would be with them "on Wednesday I suppose."

On receiving the message Southey and Lovell walked to Marlborough to meet the coach, but Samuel was not on it. On January 9, a week after Samuel's letter, Southey's exasperation found vent in a note to Sarah: "Friday night—no Coleridge. This state of expectation totally unfits me for anything. When I attempt to employ myself, the first knock at the door wakes all my hopes again and again disappoints them. I am kept in exercise by walking to meet the coaches. Did he say Wednesday positively to you? I told you about the middle of the week. Why will he ever fix a day if he cannot abide by it?" Time passed, but still no Coleridge appeared. Southey, like Samuel's family and his late comrades-in-arms, and like Mary, began to fear that he was insane and had been "placed somewhere in confinement" by his relations.

So, unable to bear further suspense, Southey hastened to London, determined to bring Samuel back by main force if necessary. Hearing of his arrival, Samuel sent him a brusque note: "My dearest Southey, Come to me at the 'Angel Inn', Angel Street, St. Martin's le Grand, Newgate Street. I am not glad that you are come to town—and yet I am glad. It was total want of cash that prevented my expedition.—Coleridge."

In Southey's presence Samuel could no longer disobey the call of "Duty," and his triumphant friend carried him sagely back to the waiting Sarah without further delay. "Coleridge," Southey complained later, "did not come back to Bristol till January 1795, *nor would he, I believe, have come back at all*, if I had not gone to London to look for him." Yet a month later Samuel could tell his friend, George Dyer, that Sarah's devotion to him had overcome all obstacles.

Coleridge openly admitted to his friend that poor Sarah Fricker had originally been intended as a sacrifice to pantisocracy. The pantisocrats' departure, he explained, had unfortunately been delayed by unforeseen circumstances. Their plans, he now saw, had been made "with precipitance that did credit to our hearts rather than heads." So for the present their plans were dissolved.

"But," he told Dyer, "there are other engagements not so dissoluble," and of these was his engagement to Sarah Fricker.

Independently of the Love and Esteem which her Person and polished understanding may be supposed to have inspired into a young Man, I consider myself as under particular Ties of Gratitude to her—since in confidence of my Affection she has rejected the Addresses of two Men, one of them of large Fortune—and by her perseverant Attachment to me, disobliged her Relations in a very uncomfortable Degree. Perpetually obliged to resist the entreaties and to endure the reproachful admonitions of her Uncle etc., she vainly endeavours to conceal from me how heavy her heart is with anxiety, how disquieted by Suspense. To leave her for two or three years would, I fear, be sacrificing her health and happiness. In short, why should I write circuitously to you? So commanding are the requests of her Relations, that a short Time must decide whether she marries me whom she loves with an affection to the ardour of which my Deserts bear no proportion—or a man whom she strongly dislikes, in spite of his fortune and solicitous attentions to her. These peculiar circumstances she has with her usual Delicacy concealed from me till my arrival at Bristol.

Doubtless, Sarah had heard from Southey of Mary Evans's rejection of Coleridge for, as Samuel believed, a wealthier rival.

On leaving London Samuel had intended to return within a few days and perhaps to accept an offer to be tutor to two youths, relatives of the Earl of Buchan. But both Sarah and Southey did not mean to let him escape again, and indeed gratitude for such undeserved excellence as that for which he had been selected made another departure from Sarah and Bristol impossible. Yet Mary's ghost still haunted him, as the verses from a contemporary poet, William Preston, which he now entered into a new notebook, clearly showed:

> I mix in life, and labour to seem free
>> With common persons pleased and common things,
> While every thought and action tends to thee,
>> And every impulse from thy influence springs.

It is not surprising that, considering all circumstances—the pantisocrats' postponement of their plans, their declining faith, and Coleridge's rising anger against Southey for making him return to Sarah—dissensions now broke out among the pantisocratic fraternity. Southey's defection from America to Wales, even if only as a preliminary experiment, gave Samuel the chance to vent his personal anger against his friend. Forgetting his own voluntary engagement to Sarah in the first place, Samuel now saw himself as Southey's victim. Instead of pantisocracy and Sarah, which he had expected at the worst, he was now left without pantisocracy, which he *did* want, but *with* Sarah, whom he did not!

In this mood, Samuel toward the close of January turned the tables on his friend. Southey, who had so nagged at him about "duty," should now have his own duty urged upon him. Why was Southey cool toward him? Samuel asked. Did he suspect Samuel of being "alienated from the System? On what could you build so injurious a suspicion? Wherein when roused to a recollection of my duty have I shrunk from the performance of it? I hold my life and my feebler feelings as ready sacrifice to Justice." Southey, he pontificated, must not weary of the world because it was not perfect; such "sentiments look like the sickly offspring of disgusted pride. Why do you say I- I- I will do so and so, instead of saying as you were wont to do:—'it is all *our Duty* to do so and so, for such and such reasons?' " And with the ever wandering spirit that was one of Coleridge's anxiety effects, he would "walk to Bath to-morrow morning and return in the evening"—to discuss the matter in person with Southey, who was then living in his mother's boardinghouse at Bath. The difference between the friends was soon—at least superficially— smoothed over, and shortly afterward Southey returned to Bristol and joined Burnett and Samuel in their rooms on College Street.

For both Burnett and Coleridge, the need of money was urgent. Both had ceased attendance at their respective universities, and in June the Cambridge authorities finally removed Samuel's name from their records. Like Southey, he abandoned whatever vague intention he had ever had of entering the church and, also like his friend, decided to live by literature. By this time Samuel had lost all touch with his wearied family, and Southey, disinherited by his aunt, was no longer supported by his uncle since his precipitate departure from Oxford and his rejection of a clerical career.

In later life Coleridge greatly exaggerated the effect upon himself of his final exclusion from his university. "In an inauspicious hour," he wrote in the *Biographia*, "I left the friendly cloisters and the happy grove of quiet, ever honoured Jesus College, Cambridge." "Making a row about me at Jesus" was his less dignified but truer comment at the time. Coleridge, as both his friends' evidence and his own conduct revealed, was ill adapted to the restrictive discipline of set university courses. He particularly disliked mathematical studies, as shown above. Although as a friend said, "eagerly ambitious of classical honours," his own frequent assertion that he lacked ambition and took no pleasure in trying to outstrip competitors was true enough. When Middleton was no longer at Cambridge to keep him at work, he had left study for promiscuous reading, the excitement of political rowdyism, and social amusements; and when his final association with Cambridge came to an end, he evidently felt it, if anything, a relief. As a student he never showed any real affection for his university and sometimes wrote of it, as noted, in a very depreciatory spirit. Of course it was natural for Coleridge, when looking back nearly a quarter of a century later, after years of parasitic dependence upon others, to feel how much pleasanter than his own irregular way of life a snug fellowship at Jesus would have been. Gillman doubtless accurately expressed Coleridge's own feelings when he wrote: "However excellent for the many, the system adopted by our Universities was ill suited for a mind like Coleridge's, and there were some who felt that a College routine was not the kind of education which would best evolve, cultivate, and bring into training powers so *unique*."

At no time, in fact, was Coleridge the remote, concentrated scholar, permanently and above everything devoted to solitary study. He was ever the most sociable of men. The interests of the day, especially in politics and literature, were his interests—whatever purely intellectual questions also engaged his private thoughts. Upon the outbreak of war with France and the trial of Frend, heightening political tension in Cambridge had inevitably absorbed him.

At Bristol, meanwhile, Coleridge and Southey, looking for a means of subsistence, could find only the unpromising possibilities of journalism, lecturing, and poetry. For a beginning they considered producing an ill-named *Provincial Magazine*, which never appeared. "Coleridge," wrote Southey to a friend on February 8, 1795, "is writing at the same table; our names are written in the book of Destiny, on the same page." Samuel's love of rhetoric had evidently affected his friend.

But Samuel was not mistaken in suspecting Southey of faintheartedness toward pantisocracy. For this, Southey was not without reasons. By this time, although still pretending belief in the system, Southey saw that the scheme was impossible. Apart from the need of money and of knowledge and skill to settle successfully on virgin soil in a distant and strange land, he also saw that the necessary quantum of virtue would be lacking in the pantisocrats themselves. So now, with his beloved Edith Fricker awaiting him, Southey wanted above everything to adopt a settled means of livelihood, marry Edith, and live with her the life of an ordinary, cultured, middle-class person, instead of embarking on harebrained adventures impossible to succeed.

In his anxiety, Southey fell into a mood like that Coleridge had so recently experienced: "peace and domestic life are the highest blessings I could implore. Enough! this state of suspense must soon be over: I am worn and wasted with anxiety; and if not at rest in a short time shall be disabled from exertion, and sink in a long repose. Poor Edith! Almighty God protect her." For Southey's hopes of the reversion to himself of a family estate had also just been disappointed. Perhaps it was seeing his friend as despondent as himself that changed Samuel's feeling toward Southey from anger to sympathy and the old affection. "You will esteem and love him," he told Dyer. "His Genius and acquirements are uncommonly great—yet they bear no proportion to his moral Excellence. He is truly a man of *perpendicular Virtue*—a downright upright Republican! He is Christianizing apace. I doubt not that I shall present him to you right orthodox in the heterodoxy of Unitarianism."

With Southey to introduce him, and his own "natural gladness" (aided by equally natural astuteness) to charm, Coleridge soon had a crowd of admiring friends about him in Bristol. Some, indeed, for many years, despite his frequent demands upon their purse, remained true to him. Republican and Unitarian sympathies, one or the other or both, appealed to most of his circle of friends in Bristol. To this environment he accommodated himself as happily, fascinatingly, and instinctively as he had done to that of The Salutation and Cat.

Chief among these friends were John Prior Estlin, Unitarian minister and schoolmaster, and his wife; an assistant master (the Reverend Mr. Hort); a well-to-do tradesman, Josiah Wade; and a Mrs. Morgan, widow of a wealthy husband, and her son John. There was also a distinguished physician, Thomas Beddoes; a Mr. Jardine, a minister of the Unitarian Chapel at Bath; and Charles Danvers, the friend of Southey. Above all, there was Joseph Cottle, Evangelical bookseller, small publisher, and very small but self-satisfied poetaster. There was Cottle's brother Amos, also in the family business.

Robert Lovell, Quaker, poetaster, and pantisocrat, recently married to Mary Fricker, had introduced Southey and Coleridge to Cottle, who in turn had introduced them to many more of their Bristol friends. Cottle was attracted by their reputation as poets, but not at all by that as pantisocrats. He found Southey "tall, dignified, possessing great dignity of manners; an eye, piercing, with a countenance full of genius, kindliness and intelligence. I gave him at once the right hand of fellowship." Coleridge he found more impressive: "I instantly described his intellectual character; exhibiting as he did, an eye, a brow and a forehead, indicative of commanding genius."

Cottle, quickly learning that his two friends' chief need was money, at once organized a series of lectures to be given by them to the Bristol intelligentsia. Coleridge began with three political lectures against the wartime restrictions of the Pitt government.*These, in such a time of political excitement, naturally attracted more attention than Southey's on safe historical subjects and in a less attractive style. Coleridge's previous experience in public speaking during his Welsh tour now stood him in good stead, and as the rows he now provoked excelled those formerly occasioned by his pantisocracy, he was proportionately delighted with them. Several he printed and published as much to disprove accusations of treason as to disseminate his antigovernmental opinions. Coleridge's innate tendency to exaggerate doubtless falsified his epistolary descriptions of the strength and virulence of his opponents. But the September Massacres and the execution of the French king only two years before were still associated with the present war fever, and democratic movements among the English lower classes were being punished with the extreme severity of the law. Fears and tempers ran high and made the expression of democratic opinions dangerous. To express such was to be thought a "Jacobin"—to be a traitor.

Perhaps, therefore, one need not so heavily discount Coleridge's complaisant descriptions of his activities:

> Since I have been in Bristol I have endeavoured to disseminate Truth by three political lectures. I believe I shall give a fourth. But the opposition of the Aristocrats is so furious and determined that I begin to fear that the good I do is not proportionate to the evil I occasion. Mobs and Mayors, Blockheads and Brickbats, Placards and Pressgangs have leagued in horrible conspiracy against me. The Democrats are as sturdy in support of me—but their number is comparatively small. Two or three uncouth and unbrained automata have threatened my life, and in the last lecture the *Genius Infimum* was scarcely restrained from attacking the house in which the "damned Jacobin was jawing away."

Since it was still February, Samuel must have begun his political lecturing almost immediately after his return to Bristol. Whether Sarah appeared at all in these exciting scenes is not known.

Nor did Coleridge confine his lectures to definitely political subjects. Now a Unitarian, he touched upon religious questions, but so discreetly as to win great approval from Mr. Estlin and other Unitarians in his audience. Even these lectures at times touched on politics, because the Dissenters, led by Unitarians, were then demanding Parliamentary reform to get civil rights. Some, like the famous preacher and scientist Joseph Priestley of Birmingham, had had their houses and chapels attacked by the mob, and had been forced to find an asylum in America. Coleridge's discussions on politics included the

---

* A very full list of Coleridge's lectures (and subjects) given between 1795 and 1819 appears with comments in *Coleridge the Talker*, ed. R. W. Armour and R. F. Howes (New York and London, 1940), pp. 412-14.

slave trade, the Corn Laws, and even the Hair Powder Tax. By mid-November 1795 Coleridge claimed to have given eleven lectures, to have written half of Southey's, and to have contributed "all the Tug of Brain" in them. So he told Southey!

The description of Coleridge's lecturing now, left by one journalist-critic, shows that he still presented the shabby appearance of Christ's Hospital and Cambridge days. His speech was described as "perfect monotonism," his "person" as "slovenly." "Mr. C.," the critic concluded, "would therefore do well to appear with cleaner stockings in public, and if his hair were combed out every time he appeared in public, it would not depreciate him in the esteem of his friends."

But the proceeds of these lectures by no means met all the needs of the lecturers. Samuel, therefore, lost no time in using the fascinated Cottle as a favored "friend." Frank and eminently friendly, Samuel's little note to Cottle in the first days of March did not beat about the bush: "My dear Sir,—Can you conveniently lend me five pounds, as we want a little more than four pounds to make up our lodging bill, which is indeed much higher than we expected; seven weeks and Burnett's lodging for twelve weeks, amounting to eleven pounds! Yours affectionately, S.T. Coleridge." From his friend Dyer in London, he was also extracting money, but in letters long and elaborate, recognizing that "the finely fibred heart, like the statue of Memnon, trembles into melody on the sunbeam touch of Benevolence." This led to a pathetic line: "Not to be poor would make me very rich." As for his lectures, "I was soon obliged by the persecutions of Darkness, to discontinue them."

Cottle, though a bad poet, was a good friend to Samuel and Southey. Soon made well aware of their penniless state, he at once offered each poet thirty guineas in advance for his poems, with an additional fifty for Southey's republican epic, *Joan of Arc*. As the best offer Coleridge had been able to extract from lukewarm London publishers was six guineas, Cottle's offer was immediately accepted. The poets and their genial publisher were on the very best of terms. The poets' hopes for prosperity so encouraged, soared again, and they planned to write, save, marry, and farm in Wales, until able to live ideally on the banks of the Susquehannah. Cottle, in his own inimitable style, described Samuel's state at this time. "There was, in Mr. Coleridge's mind an interior spring of action. He wanted to 'build up' a provision for his speedy marriage: and with those grand combined objects before him, no effort appeared too vast to be accomplished by his invigorated faculties."

In fact, Samuel's passion for pantisocracy and Sarah rose and fell with the mood of the hour. His emotional vicissitudes left their mark upon his verse. Sarah, too, appears to have diligently fanned the often feebly fluttering flame of his affection with whatever she could muster of feminine charm and wiles. Indeed, he now presented her with those earlier amatory verses from which, surreptitiously no doubt, the original names—Mary, Ann Brunton, and others—had been removed. These were almost all the poetical tributes that Sarah was destined to receive: for seldom indeed did she inspire even a few lines of his verse.

   Yet almost all knowledge of Sarah at this time comes from the poems that
Coleridge now wrote, attempting with whatever strength of the poetic
imagination he could exert, to create his erotic illusion. Thus, when Sarah,
under the soft emotions of the hour, took to singing while the assistant schoolmaster, the Reverend Mr. Hort, accompanied her on the flute, Samuel,
momentarily inspired by the twofold influence of music and love, exhorted the
clerical accompanist:

> O skill'd with magic to spell to roll
> The thrilling tones that concentrate the soul!
> Breathe through thy flute those tender notes again,
> While near thee sits the chaste-eyed Maiden mild;
> And bid her raise the poet's kindred strain
> In soft impassion'd voice, correctly wild.

He went on to imagine himself listening to her "correctly wild" notes as they
wander amid the sylvan beauties of their pantisocratic American paradise, and
also remembers Mr. Hort, Sarah's teacher:

> In Freedom's UNDIVIDED dell,
> Where Toil and Health with mellow'd Love shall dwell,
> Far from folly, far from men,
> In the rude romantic glen,
> Up the cliff and through the glade,
> Wandering with the dear-lov'd maid,
> I shall listen to the lay,
> And ponder on thee far away
> Still, as she bids those thrilling notes aspire
> (Making my fond attuned heart her lyre)

In Sarah, Samuel now found hitherto unsuspected virtues, including pity and
tenderness. These virtues, as Sarah soon must have discovered, Samuel
particularly desired in women, and so, in a sonnet of superabundant pity for
an old man, not only will Coleridge in some unspecified way "melt the frozen
dews"

> That hang from thy white beard and numb thy breast,

but

> My Sarah too shall tend thee, like a child.

Inevitably, as Sarah's virtues become more obvious, Coleridge's affection
grows:

> all thy soft diversities of tone,

he tells the nightingale, in another sonnet,

Are not so sweet as is the voice of her,
My Sara—best beloved of human kind!
When breathing the pure soul of tenderness,
She thrills me with the Husband's promis'd name!

Thus Sarah became "Sara" henceforth.

Nevertheless, even in Samuel's poetry, Sarah's chief fault, impatience, soon appears—but in annoying circumstances. In "In Lines in the Manner of Spenser," Samuel tells how, instead of meeting Sarah at some early hour as arranged, he has remained in bed dreaming of her (but evidently, in fact, of Mary) and now fears her anger when they meet:

For O! I wish my Sarah's frowns to flee,
And fain to her some soothing song would write,
Lest she resent my rude discourtesy,
Who vow'd to meet her ere the morning light,
But broke my plighted word—Ah! false and recreant wight!
. . . .
Too long, our Slave the Damsel's *smiles* hath seen:
To-morrow shall he ken her altered mien!

The situation was prophetic of their future: Samuel's fault, indolence, which would have exasperated a saint, and Sarah's impatience—two absolute incompatibles. Even the Spenserian stanza could hardly make such a situation romantic. As the vision of Mary fades into the more real memory of Sarah, so does the poetry become artificial and conventional—an unconscious expression of his own deeper reality.

Outside the pale of love, Samuel's life in Bristol went on as usual. Cottle would be asked to "lend" money or to come to tea—or both—and would vainly attempt to extract from Coleridge the poems that—now that they had been paid for—Samuel was too indolent to produce. The "quantum of virtue" among the pantisocrats was proving inadequate, even in Bristol, and quarrels spread. Cottle tried to make peace among them. Lovell, momentarily perceptive, observed that Coleridge and Sarah were unlikely to make a happy married life, and from supporting their union he turned to oppose it. "Lovell, you are a villain," said Samuel; but Cottle with smooth words reconciled them.

Cottle, generous and peaceful, invited the two poets and their fiancées to a two days' excursion to Tintern Abbey hoping to promote unity. For, cooped up on College Street, Southey and Coleridge had become unhappily aware of profound temperamental differences, and were again growing estranged. But Cottle's plan proved unfortunate. Southey, now wanting no companionship but that of Edith, was reluctant to accept Cottle's invitation. Samuel, observing Southey's declining interest in pantisocracy— and conveniently forgetting that, for Mary, he too would have left it for law—was condemnatory and quarrelsome.

Poor Cottle, unaware of such smoldering fires, set out lightheartedly for Tintern Abbey with his friends. At Chepstow they dined, and presumably

wined. The two poets certainly quarreled, each stoutly supported, despite their
sisterhood, by his betrothed. The quarrel began when Southey rebuked
Coleridge for having been absent on the previous day, instead of taking
Southey's place at a lecture as he had promised. The audience, disappointed,
had complained and gone home, and Southey's reputation had suffered. The
complaint was well founded, but Samuel turned it into a general squabble,
accusing Southey of intending to desert the pantisocrats when they began their
experiment in Wales, until, overcome by virtuous emotion, Samuel began to
cry. When, the following day, Southey convinced him of his loyalty to the
Welsh scheme—never executed—Samuel was "glad and satisfied," and his
heart "leapt back to esteem and love." After this, it is hardly surprising to
learn that the party lost its way and never reached Tintern Abbey!

Soon, however, another cause of division arose and a new quarrel burst out:
this time at a "Strawberry Party." Coleridge, penniless as usual, heard from
Burnett that Southey, who now expected money from several sources, did not
mean to divide it among the pantisocrats, as pantisocratic theory demanded;
but since so far there had been no money among them to divide, division
remained purely theoretical. Coleridge was overwhelmed at the news when
Burnett told him: "It scorched my throat. Your private resources were to
remain your individual property, and everything to be separate except on five
or six acres. In short we were to commence partners in a petty farming trade.
This was the mouse of which the mountain Pantisocracy was at last safely
delivered! I received the account with Indignation and Loathings of unutterable Contempt." Southey's "quantum of virtue" was evidently lacking, and
Coleridge was disgusted.

The strained relations between them continued. Coleridge, resenting
Southey's "heart-chilling sentiments," asked him "*solemnly*, whether you
disapproved of anything in *my* conduct." To this Southey replied: "Nothing, I
like you better now than at the commencement of our friendship."
Whereupon the indignant Sarah, throwing herself again into the fray,
"affronted Southey into an angry silence by exclaiming: 'What a Story!' "
Next, hearing that Southey under pressure from his uncle, was considering
returning to Oxford to become a parson, Samuel fervently urged him to reject
the temptation—not for pantisocracy—"Pantisocracy is not the question. Its
realization is distant—perhaps a miraculous Millenium. What you have seen,
or think that you have seen of the human heart, may render the formation
even of a Pantisocratic *seminary* improbable to you; but this is not the
question." The question was (to summarize much of Samuel's exhortation and
rhetoric), simply, in his view, "perjury." Southey, with his opinions, could
not enter the church without "perjuring" himself. And Southey, at last
persuaded, reluctantly rejected his uncle's suggestion of the church.

The devil's temptations to Southey, it seemed to Coleridge, were endless.
For now a friend of Southey's offered him an annuity of £160 to take up law.
But Samuel, who a year before was willing to take to law in order to marry
Mary, now found law for Southey "a wicked profession," even worse than the

church; and again, not on pantisocratic but on moral grounds: "Even if you had persisted in your design of taking Orders, your motives would have been weak and shadowy and vile; but when you changed your ground for the law, they were annihilated."

The impregnable moral integrity with which each of the poets rejected the other's temptations was impressive, but it hardly led to mutual friendship. Southey as much detested Samuel's interference in his affairs as Samuel had recently detested Southey's. Southey left College Street and returned to his mother in Bath, and the poets passed each other in the street "unsaluting and unsaluted." "You are lost to *me* because you are lost to Virtue," Coleridge reproached Southey in mid-November, adding: "This will probably be the last time I shall have occasion to address you."

When all Samuel's arguments for sharing Southey's £160 pantisocratically, or rejecting it and the law, entirely failed, Samuel sent Cottle the news of his friend's apostasy and was too deeply moved even for the expression of emotion or the relief of extensive rhetoric: "Dear Cottle—I congratulate Virtue and her friends, that Robert Southey has relinquished all intention of taking Orders. He leaves our party however, and means, he thinks, to study the Law.—Yours, S. T. Coleridge."

By this time Southey's opinion of Coleridge was as little complimentary as Samuel's of him. "My opinion of Coleridge was not what it had been," Southey told a friend, "for by long living with him I know much of his character now." He had discovered Samuel's bad habit of denigrating friends behind their backs while preserving an unchanging appearance of friendship to their faces, and was disgusted. "I discovered," he said, "that he had been employing every possible calumny against me, and representing me as a villain." Southey had also wearied of Samuel's "inordinate love of talking," not only in private, when often, as Southey readily admitted, original, valuable, and interesting ideas would emerge, but particularly his continual repetition of the same remarks to every new listener, "repeated to every fresh company, seven times in the week if we were in seven parties." Above all other of Southey's grievances, no doubt, was the sudden realization that pantiso-cratic egalitariansim meant his sharing everything with a man who contributed nothing to be shared in return. He had noted with increasing contempt Samuel's sponging on Cottle, and on himself. "I went to Bristol to Coleridge," Southey wrote two years later, "and supported myself and almost him, I may say, for what my labours earned were as four to one." Coleridge's reply to such reproaches was: "The truth is, you sat down and wrote. I used to saunter about and think what I should write." However true, this did not meet Southey's complaint. Only too often Samuel's sublime thoughts did not find expression on paper at all.

Although Southey's defection had sent the depressed Burnett back to the parental farm, and Samuel to another house on College Street, Coleridge's Bohemian buoyancy was unaffected. From his new dwelling he sent Cottle (who had just settled the pantisocrats' debts with a check for twenty pounds) a genial note showing no sign of the sorrowing moralist who had written to Southey. "Dear Cottle—By the thick smokes that precede the volcanic eruptions of Etna, Vesuvius and Hecla, I feel an impulse to fumigate, at 25, College Street, one pair of stairs room; yea with our Oronoco [sic], and if thou wilt send me by the bearer four pipes, I will write a panegyrical epic poem upon thee, with as many books as there are letters in thy name. Moreover, if thou wilt send me 'the copy book,' I hereby bind myself, by tomorrow morning, to write out enough copy for a sheet and a half.—God bless you! S.T.C."

This dissolution of the coterie must have brought Coleridge to a closer contemplation of marriage to Sarah, and a widening of the distance between himself and his prospective mother-in-law—"that Mrs. Fricker." Thus, about mid-August, Samuel rented a cottage at Clevedon near Bristol. There he and Sarah, Martha Fricker, and Burnett all lived together after Coleridge's marriage—and, as his poem "The Eolian Harp" and Godwinian pantisocratic principles suggest, before marriage also—though quite probably sexually apart. Certainly the house was to be run on the egalitarian system of labor. With marriage in the air, poor Burnett proposed to Martha Fricker, who refused him with the inspired comment that he wanted not her, "but a wife in a hurry."

The Clevedon cottage with Sarah and her harp in it inspired Coleridge on August 20, 1795, to begin one of his happiest poems, "The Eolian Harp." For once Coleridge and his environment blended into a single, harmonious, idyllic mood, and the "blank verse" poem is permeated with a rare fusion of reflective thought and sensitivity to peaceful, natural beauty:

My pensive Sara! thy soft cheek reclined
Thus on my arm, how soothing sweet it is
Beside our cot to sit, out cot o'ergrown
With white-flowered jasmin, and the blossomed myrtle,
(Meet emblems they of Innocence and Love!)
And watch the clouds, that late were rich with light,
Slow-saddening round, and mark the star of eve
Serenely brilliant, like thy polished sense,
Shine opposite! What snatches of perfume
The noiseless gale from yonder bean-field wafts!

The stilly murmur of the far-off Sea
Tells us of Silence! and behold, my love!
In the half-closed window we will place the Harp,
Which by the desultory breeze caressed,
Like some coy maid half willing to be wooed,
Utters such sweet upbraidings as, perforce,
Tempt to repeat the wrong!

This "coy maid" with her "sweet upbraidings," yet "halfwilling to be wooed," provides one of the very few glimpses to be gained of Sarah at this time.

Ever wandering, Samuel in September was on his way to visit Poole at Stowey, and in reply to a gloomy letter from Sarah, who was left behind, he sent her cheering verses, of which she was apparently in need. Her observation of Samuel's indolence and poverty can no more have pleased her than it did Southey. To cheer Sarah, Coleridge sent her the following verses:

> I see you all oppressed with gloom
> Sit lonely in that cheerless room—
> Ah me! You are in tears!
> . . . .
> With cruel weight these trifles press
> A temper sore with tenderness,
> When aches the void within.

So he recalls how in the past he would rejoice in watching the fury of the storm-tossed sea, lightning-rent sky and "tempest-shattered bark," as he sat

> in black soul-jaundiced fit
> A sad gloom-pampered man. . . .
> Ere Peace with Sara came.

But the ending strikes the apparently happy note:

> How oft my Love! with shapings sweet
> I paint the moment we shall meet!
> With eager speed I dart—
> I seize you in the vacant air,
> And fancy, with a husband's care
> I press you to my heart!
> 'Tis said, in Summer's evening hour
> Flashes the golden-coloured flower
> A fair electric flame:
> And so shall flash my love-charg'd eye
> When all the heart's big ecstasy
> Shoots rapid through the frame!

At Nether Stowey Samuel, who had just lost one father substitute in Southey, was happily finding another in Tom Poole, the wealthy, intellectual, self-taught tanner. The mutual attraction that they had felt during Coleridge's first visit had increased with growing intimacy during the intervening year. Poole had not only come to Bristol to hear some of Coleridge's lectures but had also prepared material for them, suggested subjects, made critical comments, and had assisted (probably suggested) the lecture on the Hair Powder Tax, a subject particularly interesting to Poole who detested hair powder and refused to use it.

So to Stowey Samuel took six printed proof sheets of the poems he was preparing for Cottle, and left them with Poole for criticism when he returned home. Poole, inspired by Samuel's companionship and the poetic environment, burst into unwonted song, and on September 12 produced a bad poem of nine stanzas in praise of Coleridge, which clearly reveals the deep impression made upon Poole, this strong-minded, strong-willed, alert businessman, almost thirty years of age. The poem also shows that Coleridge had poured out his grievances against Southey, and had also described Sarah as a solace to him in his misery. But Poole, like other friends of Samuel at this time, strangely calls him "Coldridge," a mistake perhaps due to Samuel's known bad pronounciation, a mixture of Devonshire dialect and adenoidal obstruction.

Despite its technical inadequacy, Poole's solitary poem gives too rare and clear a picture of the impression Samuel made upon such a friend, for abbreviation:

Hail to thee, Coleridge, youth of various powers!
I love to hear thy soul pour forth the line,
I hear it sing of love and liberty
As if fresh breathing from the hand divine.
As if on earth it never yet had dwelt!
As if from heaven it now had wing'd its way;
And brought us tidings how, in argent fields,
In love and liberty blest spirits stray.
I love to mark that soul-pervaded clay,
To see the passions in thine eyeballs roll—
Their quick succession on thy weighty brow—
Thy trembling lips express their very soul.
I love to view the abstracted gaze which speaks
Thy soul to heavenwards towering—then I say,
He's gone—for us to cull celestial sweets
Amid the flowerets of the milky way.
And now at home, within its mortal cage,
I see thy spirit pent—Ah me!—and mourn
The Sorrow sad, that weighs it down to earth,
As if the Cherub Hope would ne'er return,
And then I mark the starting tear that steals
adown thy cheek, when of a friend thou speak'st,
Who erst, as thou dost say, was wondrous kind,
And now, unkind, forgets—I feel and weep.
I hear thee speak indignant of the world,
Th'unfeeling world crowded with folly's train;
I hear thy fervent eloquence dispel
The murky mists of error's mazy reign.
Anon thy Sarah's image cheers thy soul,
When sickening at the world, thy spirits faint;
Soft balm it brings—thou hail'st the lovely maid
Paint'st her dear form as Love alone can paint!
And thou, Religion, white-robed Maid of Peace,
Who smil'st to hear him raise his voice on high
To fix thy image on the Patriot's breast—
Remove the bitter tear, the fearful sigh.
Sept. 12, 1795   T.P.

Probably Poole provided Samuel with consolation more substantial than the merely poetic. Exactly seven days after Poole's effusion, his critical, clear-minded cousin Charlotte commemorated Samuel's visit in prose in her diary: "a young man of brilliant understanding, great eloquence, desperate fortune, democratic principles, and entirely led away by the feelings of the moment." So Samuel had left Poole in no doubt as to his "desperate fortune."

Charlotte's succinct account of Samuel is a fitting prelude to his marriage to Sarah a fortnight later. A rumor in Bristol, which reached the ears of Charlotte and of her family, and continued at least until the close of the century, asserted "that the marriage was believed to have been rather hurried on in consequence of some hostile breath of rumour that had arisen in connection with the Misses Fricker. This was caused partly by the unconventional manner in which they were to be seen constantly walking about Bristol with two such remarkable and well-known young men as Coleridge and Southey, and partly from the impression that pantisocracy meant a system of things which dispensed with the marriage tie. When this disagreeable gossip came round to the ears of those most nearly concerned, the result was a general impatience for immediate marriage on the part of the two poets."

Coleridge and Sarah (with Martha Fricker and Josiah Wade as witnesses) stood before the altar in Chatterton's church, St. Mary's Redcliffe, in Bristol, and were made man and wife—while Samuel pondered Chatterton's suicide. "On Sunday morning," he informed Poole a day or two later, "I was *married* at St. Mary's Redcliff [*sic*], poor Chatterton's church! The thought gave a tinge of melancholy to the Solemn joy which I felt, united to the woman whom I love best of all created beings." Nor was his "solemn joy" disturbed by fears of poverty. Cottle had just offered him a guinea and a half for every hundred lines of verse he could turn out; so, when a solicitous friend asked Samuel how he would keep the pot boiling, he airily replied: "Mr. Cottle has made me such an offer, that I feel no solicitude on that subject!"

6 Married Life and *The Watchman* (1795-96)

"I love and I am beloved, and I am happy."
—Coleridge to Southey, November 13, 1795

"We are settled, nay, quite domesticated at Clevedon, our comfortable cot!! Mrs. Coleridge—MRS. COLERIDGE!! I like to *write* the name. . .Mrs. Coleridge desires her affectionate regards to you." So wrote Samuel in his first postmarital letter to Poole. Continuing, he increased the note of affectionate intimacy: "I talked of you on my wedding night. God bless you. Your affectionate and mindful *Friend*—shall I soon dare to say? Believe me, my *heart* prompts it."

No sooner had husband and wife returned to their cottage than they discovered the lack of many domestic necessities overlooked, ranging from a dustpan and teakettle to a keg of porter and a Bible. These the faithful Cottle—urgently summoned—hastened to bring. He found their cottage ideal, beautifully situated on the outskirts of the village, with a small pretty garden, no taxes, and a rent of only five pounds a year: "everything the heart could desire." But he sent them "a few pieces of sprightly paper" to cover the whitewashed parlor walls, which displeased him.

Coleridge was certainly happy during these early days of married life. He delighted in his cottage and in the views from its windows—"the prospect more *various* than any in the kingdom. Mine eye gluttonizes. The sea!—the distant islands! The opposite coasts! I shall assuredly write rhymes; let the nine Muses prevent it if they can!" Martha Fricker had probably departed after her refusal of Burnett, for Samuel's timetable of domestic duties shows that they are to be shared only between himself, Burnett, and Sarah. The timetable remains an amusingly incongrous entry in his notebook, between literary allusions and data relating to the "first church in Britain"—"Six o'clock, Light the fires. Clean out the kitchen. Put on the tea-kettle. Clean the insides of the boiling pot. Shoes etc. C. & B. Eight o'clock, tea-things etc. put out and after clean up. Sara. One o'clock spit the meat. B & C. Two o'clock, vegetables etc. Sara. Three o'clock—Dinner. Half past three—10 minutes for clearing dishes." Whereupon the timetable disappointingly ceases.

By Coleridge it was doubtless more honored in the breach than in the observance. In the light of this timetable, the tale that Coleridge once came in tears to a friend to complain that he could not live with his wife if she was not brought to her senses appears less improbable. Was she, the friend asked, insane? No, said Coleridge, but a sane woman could hardly have required of a husband what she expected from him—that on the coldest mornings, even when the snow was on the ground and icicles hanging from the eaves of their cottage, she compelled him to get out of bed in his nightshirt and light the fire before she began to dress herself and the baby.

Certainly domestic duties did not prevent Coleridge from finishing "The Eolian Harp," begun in August. In this he appears as an idle dreamer, basking in the sunshine—a more characteristic attitude than cleaning the boiling pot. "Love," Coleridge once declared, "is the vital air of my genius." Now as he lay dreaming, love seemed to him to be the fundamental principle of the universe. But some vaguely pantheistic elements, which offended Sarah, apparently intruded:

But thy more serious eye a mild reproof
Darts, O beloved Woman! or such thoughts
Dim and unhallowed dost thou not reject
And biddest me walk humbly with my God.
Meek daughter in the family of Christ!
Well hast thou said and holily dispraised
These shapings of the unregenerate mind.

Charles Lamb, whose memories of Coleridge at The Salutation and Cat were still recent, when the poem appeared poked sly fun at Samuel's description of Sarah as his theological censor. "The conclusion of your *Religious Musings*," he told Coleridge, "I fear will entitle you to the reproof of your beloved woman, who wisely will not suffer your fancy to run riot, but bids you walk humbly with your God." He and his sister, Lamb said, had smiled at the "pleasing picture of Mrs. C. checking your wild wanderings, which we were so fond of hearing you indulge when among us. It has endeared us more than anything to your good lady; and your own self-reproof that follows delighted me."

Had Mary Evans heard of Coleridge's marriage when nine days later she married her man of "good fortune," Fryer Todd? Marriage was in the air then among Samuel's friends, and on November 14, also at St. Mary Redcliffe, Southey secretly married his beloved Edith Fricker, handed her over to Cottle's sisters for care and protection, and left at once for Lisbon to see his uncle there and determine his future career.

Aware of Southey's impending departure for Portugal but in ignorance of his marriage, Coleridge wrote him a letter the day before—a letter that as published covers eleven large pages of print—in which all Samuel's real or imaginary grievances against Southey find bitter and exaggerative expression. It was a strange letter for one happily married only five weeks before to write. The "pensive Sara" of "The Eolian Harp" would have looked more pensive had she seen her husband's bitter outburst to Southey in which sad memories

of the lost Mary Evans mingle with accusations of the betrayal of pantisocracy:

> Previously to my departure from Jesus College, and during my melancholy
> detention in London what convulsive struggles of feeling I underwent, and
> what sacrifices I made, you know....You remember what a fetter I burst,
> and that it snapped as if it had been a sinew of my heart. However I re-
> turned to Bristol, and my addresses to Sara, which I at first made from princi-
> ple, not feeling, from feeling and not principle I renewed; and I met a
> reward more than proportionate to the greatness of the effort. I love and I
> am beloved, and I am happy....And was not this your own plan? And the
> plan for the realizing of which you invited me to Bristol; the plan for which
> I abandoned my friends, and every prospect, and every certainty, and the
> woman whom I loved to an excess which you in your warmest dream of fan-
> cy could never shadow out?

The remainder of the letter was one long and ridiculously false diatribe
against Southey as a deserter, a traitor to pantisocracy, a selfish man who
would not share his legacy with his friends. "I neither have or could deign to
have a hundred a year," he cried, virtuously, little dreaming that within a few
months he would gladly accept a much larger annuity as well as another
substantial one—and without any offer or even thought of sharing it with his
friends! As for Burnett, Southey's cupidity, which Burnett accurately enough
"ascribed to an unparticipating propensity," had left Burnett brokenhearted
and useless, to be supported by Samuel: "Yet by my own exertions I will
struggle hard to maintain myself, and my wife and my wife's mother, and my
associate."

Coleridge had already begun to count the cost of marriage, and the result
had left him in no pleasant mood: "O! selfish, money-loving man! What principle have you not given up? Though Death had been the consequence, I would
have spit in that man's face and called him a liar, who should have spoken that
last sentence concerning *you*, nine months ago. For blindly did I esteem you.
O God! that *such a mind* should fall in love with that low, dirty, gutter-
grubbing Trull, *WORLDLY PRUDENCE*!!"

To blame Southey for all the mistakes, absurdities, and weaknesses in his
own life long remained a convenience for Coleridge in trouble, associated also,
quite falsely, with the loss of Mary Evans. "O!" he wrote to a friend, twelve
years later, "had I health and youth and were what I once was—but I played
the fool and cut the throat of my own happiness, of my genius, of my utility,
in compliment to the merest phantom of overstrained honour. O Southey!
Southey! an unthinking man were you—and are—and will be." But Southey,
now in Lisbon, probably ignored Coleridge's letter; certainly communication
between the former friends lapsed.

Despite Samuel's castigation of Southey as a traitor to pantisocracy, Cottle
soon remarked the same defection in Coleridge after marriage, and described
him as "consoling himself with the suspicion, not only that felicity might be
found on this side of the Atlantic, but that Clevedon concentrated the sum of

all the earth had to bestow....And this accompanied with the cheering assurance, that, by a merely pleasurable exertion he would be able to provide for his moderate expenses, and experience the tranquillizing joys of seclusion, while the whole country and Europe, were convulsed with war and changes.''

But upon Samuel this idyllic existence in the Clevedon cottage soon palled. He missed the Bristol Library and his Bristol friends, and Sarah was lachrymose when he left her to visit them. ''Not to adulterize my time by absenting myself from my wife,'' he resolved in April 1796. Nor did selling his poems to Cottle at a guinea and a half per hundred lines provide the easy subsistence he had anticipated. Nor did the poems themselves come easily. Cottle had hard work to extract from him ''copy'' for his forthcoming volume. Thus, although his generous friends—Poole, Wade, Cottle, and Estlin—replenished at need Samuel's ever empty pockets, he was soon faced with the necessity of finding permanent means of self-support. Two courses alone seemed to him possible: to turn Unitarian minister, or to edit a politico literary journal attacking the government.

Although Bristol's Unitarians readily welcomed so brilliant a youth to their ministry, his political lectures in Bristol prevented his preaching there; so instead he was cordially invited, through Estlin's influence, to give an ''inaugural discourse'' to the Unitarians of Bath. Anxious to preserve Samuel's dignity on such an occasion, Cottle and his friend Danvers, with high hopes, transported him thither in a ''Chaise.'' But the auspicious occasion proved a disappointment. Despite preliminary boosting of Coleridge as ''from Cambridge''—then considered a criterion of social and intellectual superiority—the congregation was ''the most meagre'' Cottle had ever seen. Cottle thought Coleridge's opening prayer ''formal, unimpressive and undevotional'': his sermon, merely his Corn Laws lecture. Perhaps worst of all was his proudly displayed blue coat and white waistcoat, which the shocked Unitarians had vainly attempted to make him veil in a preacher's black gown. Samuel's generous offer, amid little enthusiasm, to preach again that afternoon, attracted seventeen hearers of whom three soon walked out—perhaps because this sermon was his lecture on the Hair Powder Tax, with jokes omitted. ''We all,'' wrote poor Cottle, ''returned to Bristol with the feeling of disappointment. My regard for him,'' Cottle added, in a final devastating comment, ''was too genuine to entertain the wish of ever again seeing him in the pulpit.'' But it was not to be Samuel's last appearance there.

Coleridge now turned to his second plan—a newspaper, the *Watchman*. This, as its name implied, would supply honest and accurate information in place of a corrupt, government-controlled press. The scheme was impossibly ambitious, as ridiculous, indeed, especially for a one-man paper, as his pantisocracy had been. Despite his previous rejection—on the ground of ''monthly anxiety and quotidian bustle''—of a plan for a monthly magazine to be edited by Southey and himself, his *Watchman* was far more ambitious than that. To escape the stamp tax, it was to appear every eight days—a great disadvantage to subscribers and with each issue it offered: ''1.—A History of the domestic and foreign occurrences of the preceding days.—2.—The Speeches in both Houses of Parliament: and during the Recess, select Parliamentary speeches, from the commencement of the reign of Charles the First to the present era, with Notes historical and biographical.—3.—Original Essays and Poetry, chiefly or altogether political.'' There was more besides, including a promise to ''preserve Freedom and her friends from the attacks of Robbers and Assassins.'' The price for all this was four pence.

But before the time came to attempt the impossible task of fulfilling the promises of the *Watchman*'s prospectus, there was a delightful interval for Samuel of five weeks' adventures, of travel among strange men and manners, in strange regions. These were mostly among workmen and small tradesmen of the midland and northern manufacturing towns then developing whom Samuel must persudade to subscribe to his paper.

So, lightheartedly as ever when on some new adventure, he set out on January 9, 1796, on his crusade for ''Truth and Freedom,'' which was essentially—although later he forgot this—an attempt to gain subsistence for Sarah and himself:

> Ah! quiet Dell! dear Cot, and Mount sublime!
> I was constrain'd to quit you. Was it right,
> While my unnumber'd brethren toil'd and bled,
> That I should dream away the entrusted hours
> On rose leaf beds, pampering the coward heart
> With feelings all to delicate for use? . . .
> I therefore go, and join head, heart, and hand,
> Active and firm, to fight the bloodless fight
> Of science, Freedom, and the Truth in Christ.

''Reflections on entering into active life'' was his first title for the poem, later changed to ''Reflections on having left a place of retirement.'' One reason for quitting the cottage, which only Cottle mentions, was that their neighbors were ''a little too tattling and inquisitive.''

Samuel's new role as commercial traveler he combined with that of itinerant preacher. For, undeterred by the fiasco at Bath, he still hoped that if the *Watchman* failed, the Unitarian Church might shelter him. The enterprise was entirely congenial to his nature, and he entered with extraordinary zest into all the varied experiences of his journey. From flippancy to the amused, cynical realism that was a profound though little noticed element in his temperament, he surveyed with eyes of almost microscropic exactitude, city by city, the various personalities he encountered and endeavored to win for his cause.

His letters to his friends at this time read like pages from *Pickwick*, forty years before *Pickwick* appeared. At times, indeed, during his tour, he plays the role of Pickwick himself. It was the teacher and friends of Keats who called Coleridge ''a chameleon,'' and already he showed his instinct for assuming the various appearances that the cajolement of many and diverse individuals required. Entering the stagecoach in Bristol in holiday mood, he ''stumbled on a huge projection which might be called a belly with the same propriety that you might name Mount Atlas a molehill. Citizen Squelch-gut. Heavens! that a man should be unconscionable enough to enter a stage-coach, who would want elbow room if he were walking on Salisbury Plain!!!''

At his first call, Worcester, although he "marched in finery and cleanliness"—the blue coat and white waistcoat—down High Street, "Aristocrats and Clergy" were too influential to give the *Watchman* a chance. So Samuel hastened to Birmingham, where, as the "figurante of the circle," as he said, he was very happy. Twice on Sunday he preached sermons, "great part extempore, *preciously peppered with politics.*" But as at Bath, there was trouble about his "finery"; for Birmingham, made of sterner stuff, forced the black gown on him for preaching—to his great disgust. Some days later, still regretfully cogitating the matter, he decided: "I want firmness. I perceive I do. I have that within me which makes it difficult to say 'No!' repeatedly to a number of persons who seem uneasy and anxious."

His experiences in Birmingham included a "Calvinist tallow-chandler," whom he likened to "someone looking at me through a used gridiron, all soot, grease and iron." On another occasion, at a reception given in his honor, after drinking ale and smoking tobacco mixed with salt, he lay swooning and sick on a sofa as admiring visitors arrived to meet him. Restored to semiconsciousness and asked if he had seen the local newspapers, he replied, to the great merriment of the company, that Christians should not read newspapers. It is not surprising that after this, despite his social success, he was urged by his Birmingham friends to leave his canvassing for the *Watchman* to others. They assured him "in the most friendly and yet most flattering expressions, that neither was the employment fit for me, nor I fit for the employment."

On his way to Nottingham, he stopped at Derby to argue about religion with the atheistical and then famous Dr. Darwin, grandfather of the more famous naturalist. Either Sarah or his intention to become a minister or both had apparently dissipated many of his unorthodox opinions, of which in the past he had even been somewhat proud.

Nottingham, however, proved the highlight of the tour. There he at once became a social celebrity, which, like many egalitarians in politics, he particularly appreciated. "Coleridge, by God!" shouted an old college acquaintance as he was ushered in to a grand political dinner, and introduced to the richest people. Other festivities included a distinguished private dinner party given in his honor, entailing "the intolerable slavery of three courses," a grand public ball, where he found "the most numerous collection of handsome men and women" he had ever seen in one place. And *pour combien de bonheur*, on Sunday they let him preach in his "finery"—his "coloured clothes!" No wonder he joyously exclaimed: "I have got among all the first families in Nottingham, and am marvellously caressed!"

Sheffield proved a dismal contrast to Nottingham. Even the *Watchman* could not be offered there, for to do so would be to create a treacherous rival to the local democratic paper whose editor was in prison for his views. Nor were the persons there who most impressed him exactly pleasing: "a tobacco-toothed Parson with a majestic periphery of guts," and "a tall old Hag, whose soul-gelding ugliness would chill to external chastity, a cantharized Satyr.'' Nevertheless, there were compensations; the parson's wife proved to be ''an engaging little girl,'' and the ''old Hag'' ''an Angel of light.''

At Sheffield, too, the first news that his wife was ill reached him, making him ''distressed and sorely agitated.'' Stealing away for a quiet hour, he wrote a poem: ''On observing a blossom on the first of February, 1796,'' in which he touched upon his wife's illness and his own distress:

> I've stolen one hour
> From black anxiety that gnaws my heart;
> For her who droops far off on a sick bed.

Nevertheless, he did not at once abandon his intention to visit Manchester, Liverpool, and London before returning home.

At Manchester, however, more disturbing news of Sarah arrived, and via Litchfield, he returned to Bristol in low spirits, a prey to ''fears, doubts and difficulties.'' His past life now appeared but ''a feverish dream; all one huddle of strange actions and dim-discovered motives! Friendships lost by indolence, and happiness murdered by mis-managed sensibility.'' It was seldom throughout the remainder of his life that he saw himself so clearly and objectively, but already his haunting self-pity appears:

> Oh Nature! cruel step-mother, and hard,
> To thy poor, naked, fenceless child the Bard.

The cry of ''poor orphan'' was not easily drowned by later voices.

Directed to the generous Wade, Coleridge's outburst probably achieved its eleemosynary aim. A similar cry went out to the Birmingham minister, Edwards: ''Alas! the faces of strangers are but moving portraits—and far from my comfortable little cottage, I feel as if I were in the long, damp gallery of some Nobleman's House, amused with the beauty or variety of the paintings, but shivering with cold, and melancholy from loneliness.''

In mid-February Coleridge reached Bristol and found Sarah ill and pregnant, again living with her mother there. Then or before, the ''pretty cot'' at Clevedon was permanently abandoned.

Whatever the flying visits to the Midlands and the North achieved, it is certain that Coleridge's claim to have returned with the names of a thousand subscribers is a great exaggeration of the truth.

The months that followed Coleridge's return to Bristol were a time of exceptional anxiety and distress for both himself and Sarah. With a sick, pregnant wife, and himself unemployed save for unremunerative work on the *Watchman*, and penniless save for what he extracted from friends, he faced a bleak prospect. Nor can ''that Mrs. Fricker'' have rejoiced to welcome so impecunious a son-in-law to her house.

Certainly his lamentations were now unusually bitter. For his misery he this time blames everything and everybody but himself, even pantisocracy: "a scheme of virtue impracticable and romantic." Of course, Southey was now "a specious rascal who deserted me in the hour of my distress." For help he applied as usual to his Bristol friends, his letters often employing identical phraseology: his "quickset hedge of embarrassment" and the "groans of pain" from poor Sarah, for whom he shows in these woeful letters a sympathy and tenderness, later usually conspicuous by their absence. Piteously, too, he described himself, facing "poverty perhaps and the thin faces of them that want bread looking up to me."

Nor did he fail to make his helpers aware of the sad contrast between his present sordid occupation of editing the *Watchman*, forced upon him by poverty, and the great achievements of his genius, thus prevented. "O wayward and desultory Spirit of Genius! Ill canst thou brook a taskmaster! The tenderest touch from the hand of *Obligation* wounds thee like a scourge of scorpions!" His hatred of his editorial duties, he declared, was undermining his belief in God's providence. He regretted that he had once been prevented from becoming a shoemaker, so preferable was it to being "an Author by Trade." By mid-March he was "tottering on the edge of madness," and "obliged to take laudanum almost every night." Seldom indeed does Coleridge refer to his wife in his letters, and when he does it is nearly always to add pathos to his own misery. That Sarah was any happier than he is unlikely, and one is not surprised at his refusing Cottle's invitation on one occasion because "Mrs. Coleridge's spirits would not permit me." In mid-March he casually and mistakenly informed friends that Sarah had miscarried; a mistake he repeated shortly before his second child was born.

Nevertheless, Coleridge pondered abstractly, theologically, and philosophically his wife's nonexistent miscarriage, giving her in these aspects more attention than any he had devoted to her actual condition. By a miscarriage, he ruminated, "the thing which might have been a Newton or a Hartley has wasted and melted away." "The subject of Pregnancy" he thought "the most obscure of all God's dispensations," and "coercive against immaterialism." Indeed, "it starts uneasy doubts respecting immortality, and the pangs which the woman suffers seem inexplicable in the system of Optimism"—with which last opinion Sarah would doubtless have agreed. Pursuing such thoughts he came uneasily near atheism—despite his recent victory over Dr. Darwin—but was saved by the convenient and very Coleridgian solution: "*Incomprehensibility* is as necessary an attribute of the First Cause, as Love or Power, or Intelligence." For already Coleridge was showing his special talent as philosopher and metaphysician.

At any rate, while these subjects were being pondered, Samuel's less abstract epistles must have roused his nonphilosophical friends to practical efforts on his behalf, for late in March he and Sarah moved from Mrs. Fricker's to a new Bristol home, a house on Oxford Street, whence he could tell Poole: "*The Watchman* succeeds so as to yield a bread-and-cheesish profit." Yet even while inviting Poole and Edwards to be his guests, he emphasized his poverty: "My wife, my wife's mother, and little brother, and George Burnett; five mouths opening and shutting as I pull the string."

However, in mid-April he was cheered by the publication of his *Poems*. Samuel's signed receipt for Cottle's payment of thirty guineas for copyright still exists, to refute Coleridge's later assertion that he received only half the sum. Indeed, from Cottle by this time he must have received far more than thirty pounds. The original intention to publish Southey's poems with Coleridge's had perished in their quarrel, and each poet went it alone.

Coleridge's *Poems* consisted chiefly of the verses he had written in Cambridge, London, and Bristol, together with the long last poem, *Religious Musings*, of which he was inordinately proud. In Poole's presentation copy he wrote that however little Poole might admire his poems, he knew he would read them "with affection," and recalled the arbor in Poole's garden in which he had read many of them to his friend: "Dear Arbour! an Elysium to which I have so often passed by your Cerberus and Tartarean tan-pits!" Samuel's inscription in Cottle's copy was, like his letters to Cottle, more distant and slightly patronizing for an egalitarian: "On the blank leaf of my *Poems*, I can most appropriately write my acknowledgements to you for your too disinterested conduct in the purchase of them. Indeed, if ever they should acquire a name and character, it might be truly said, the world owed them to you. Had it not been for you, none perhaps of them would have been published and some not written."

Coleridge's opinion of the volume at this time he expressed to the radical poet John Thelwall, whose acquaintance he now made by sending him a copy. "You will find much to blame in them," he wrote, "much effeminacy of sentiment, much faulty glitter of expression. I build all my poetic pretensions on the *Religious Musings*." To Collier, the Shakespearean critic, Coleridge remarked fifteen years later:

> I freely own that I have no title to the name of a poet, according to my own definition of poetry. [He did not state his definition.] Many years ago, a small volume of verses came out with my name; it was not my doing, but Cottle offered me £20 [*sic*] when I much wanted it, for some short pieces I had written at Cambridge, and I sold the manuscript to him, but I declare that I had no notion, at the time, that they were meant for publication; my poverty, and not my will, consented. Cottle paid my poverty, and I was dubbed poet, almost before I knew whether I was in Bristol or in London. I met people in the streets who congratulated me upon being a poet, and that was the first notice I had of my new rank and dignity. I was to have had £20 for what Cottle bought, but I never received more than £15, and for this paltry sum I was styled poet by the reviewers, who fell foul of me for what they termed my bombast and buckram.

In his first public lecture, in the year 1811, Coleridge told his audience: "I was called a poet almost before I knew I could write poetry."

Coleridge's delighted description to Estlin of the reception given to his poems by the monthly reviewers was as unlike his account to Collier as the rest of it was from the actual facts. "The reviews," he wrote, "have been wonderful. *The Monthly* has cataracted panegyric, *The Critical* has cascaded it, and *The Analytical* has dribbled it with tolerable civility. *The Monthly* has at least done justice to my *Religious Musings*. They place it 'on the very top of the scale of Sublimity.' " And, on the same day, Samuel sent the same account to Poole.

Since his return to Bristol in mid-February, Coleridge had ceaselessly toiled, with endless lamentations, at his editorial duties, assisted only by the faithful Burnett, whose chief use appears to have been that of whipping boy. Advertised in London "by long bills in letters larger than had ever been seen before," announcing the first number for the impossibly early date of February 5, the *Watchman* did not appear until the first days of March.

The position in which Coleridge thus placed himself naturally gave him great cause for distress. With characteristic, reckless optimism, he had embarked upon an impossibly ambitious project, without considering what its actual achievement demanded. He was now understandably dismayed—particularly since he was never a ready writer. Yet he was now confronted by the necessity of filling, within an endless succession of eight-day periods, "thirty-two pages, large octave, closely printed," with articles on such a wide variety of subjects, including poems, as his syllabus had announced.

That in these circumstances the *Watchman* existed for ten weeks is surely matter for admiration rather than blame. Without journalistic experience, Coleridge at once found himself involved in various tasks to which he was a stranger. Besides writing copy for the paper, he was overwhelmed by correspondence about costs, organization, carriage, profits, contributions in verse and prose, requests to friends for contributions, delays, deliveries, nondeliveries, failures of distribution, and replies to private and public critical correspondents.

Nor did Coleridge possess the required editorial discretion. He shocked his serious, provincial, unsophisticated clientele, as well as his Unitarian, clerical friends, by publishing in the very first number, his flippant article "Fasts," with an epigraph from Isaiah: "Wherefore my bowels shall sound like an harp." The undergraduate "cleverness" that would have won the laughter and admiration of his Cambridge friends was poison for the *Watchman*. But at first, failing to realize this, Samuel was merely amused at the general dismay. A week later, however, when his mistake was brought home to him, he told some of his friends he was "ashamed. It was conceived in the spirit, and clothed in the harsh scoffing of an infidel."

Anonymous letters came to him, of course, and often amused him by their inept vituperation. "The digito-monstratus of Cambridge," wrote one: "political newsmonger, newspaper-paragraph thief, re-retailer of retailed scurrility, keeper of an asylum for old, poor and decayed jokes." Wrote another, "Sir, I detest your principles, your prose I think very so-so. But your poetry is so exquisitely beautiful, so gorgeously sublime, that I take in your *Watchman* solely on account of it. In justice therefore to me and some others of my stamp, I entreat you to give us more verse and less democratic scurrility. Your admirer, not esteemer."

The only effect such abuse had upon Coleridge, he said, was through his fear of financial loss. "I am perfectly callous," he told a friend, "except where disapprobation tends to diminish profit; there indeed, I am all one tremble of sensibility, marriage having taught me the wonderful use of that vulgar article, yclept *BREAD*." And he wrote to others in almost identical terms. His statement in the *Biographia Literaria* was, like other assertions in it, completely false. "I was most sincere, most disinterested," he there asserted, "my opinions were indeed in many and most important points erroneous: but my heart was single. Wealth, rank, life itself then seemed cheap to me, compared with the will of my Maker." He had been "persuaded by sundry philanthropists," he declared, "and anti-polemists to set on foot a periodical work."

Week by week throughout March and April Samuel's hopes for the *Watchman* rose and fell according to the reception given to each issue. But as letters from readers multiplied, urging mutually contradictory desires and advice, his heart sank: "The perplexities of my undertaking increase daily." London and Bristol, where general and political news appeared daily, wanted only "original matter" in the *Watchman*; but the Midlands and the North wanted no essays or poems but *news*. "To tell you the truth," poor Coleridge lamented to Poole, on April 11, "I do not think the *Watchman* will succeed. Hitherto I have scarcely sold enough to pay the expenses!" He was right: the decline continued to the not distant end. Soon he saw recent numbers, he said, "exposed in sundry old-iron shops for a penny a piece."

Hoping to delay the end until the twelfth number, he cried to Poole on May 5: "It is not pleasant, Thomas Poole! to have worked fourteen weeks for nothing—*for nothing*—nay, to have given the public in addition to that toil, five and forty pounds!" Such and other cries in Coleridge's letters at that time hardly prepare one for his urbane comment twenty years later in the *Biographia Literaria* on the *Watchman*'s demise: "In truth I cared too little for anything that concerned my worldly interests to be at all mortified by it." Eight days after his outburst to Poole, the next number, the tenth, appeared with a brief statement that it was the last. "The reason," it concluded with ironic concision, "is short and satisfactory—the work does not pay its expenses." To Poole the week before he had sent his swan song: "Mrs. Coleridge asks about baby-linen and anticipates the funeral expenses of her poor mother. O Watchman! thou hast watched in vain, said the prophet Ezekiel, when I suppose, he was taking a prophetic glimpse of my sorrow-sallowed cheeks."

From this fiasco Coleridge, in the *Biographia Literaria*, made a characteristically blameless, almost indeed triumphant, exit. As later on a similar occasion, he blamed the real or pretended dishonesty of others for his failure: he had been robbed by his London publisher, refused aid by others, and, but for the help of one faithful friend who paid eighty or ninety pounds, he would have been thrown into jail by his Bristol printer. But of all this there is no hint in his many intimate surviving letters at the time. In the *Biographia* his essentially altruistic motives are continuously stressed. "Completely hagridden by the fear of being influenced by selfish motives," he declared, he continued the work, even after "prudence dictated the abandonment of the scheme." Such was the strange work of time upon Coleridge's usually excellent memory.

That the *Watchman* lasted so long is, in fact, more surprising than its speedy demise. From first to last it contained within itself the germs of dissolution. A late start was followed throughout by belated political news previously published elsewhere, while the attempt to be impartial, above political parties, alienated the many who wanted their paper to reflect their own political views and prejudices. Coleridge's attack on Godwin and his rationalistic friends annoyed some while others objected to his castigation of Burke as a repressive reactionary.

Besides, Coleridge's dictatorial tone and his early exclusion of interesting, original material had quickly enveloped the paper in a dreary mantle of dullness. Indeed, one of Samuel's Cambridge friends, on hearing of the forthcoming *Watchman*, and mindful of Coleridge's indolence, had prophetically declared that after the first few numbers there would be little or nothing in the paper but parliamentary debates, with an editorial footnote, saying: "I should think myself deficient in my duty to the public, if I did not give these *interesting* debates at *full* length."

Nevertheless, it was on a final note of that "natural gladness" that won all hearts that Samuel's reminiscences in the *Biographia* closed, with an incident that may actually have occurred, and that he records as having happened a few months after the failure of the *Watchman*. "Of the unsaleable nature of my writings, I had an amusing memento one morning from our servant girl. For happening to rise at an earlier hour than usual, I observed her putting an extravagant quantity of paper into the grate in order to light the fire, and mildly checked her for her wastefulness; 'La, Sir!' (replied poor Nanny) 'why it is only Watchman!' "

7 "Dancing Demon" (1796-97)

"Would to God the dancing demon may conduct you at last in peace and comfort to the 'Life and labours of a cottager.' "
—*Charles Lamb to Coleridge, October 17, 1796*

Tom Poole, the moneyed tanner, whose life and influence were so intimately associated with Coleridge during his most critical and formative years, deserves more attention than he has hitherto received from Coleridge's biographers. How mutually antagonistic were elements of Poole's character and temperament the various descriptions of him left by his friends unconsciously reveal. "Rather rustic in appearance and provincial in his dialect," wrote one, "his clownish exterior, and rough imperious manner, with his disagreeable voice, spoilt by snuff, made a strange contrast with his great mental cultivation and excessive sensibility and tenderness of heart."

Poole's instinctive generosity of spirit was as evident in his plans for doing general good in Stowey as in his personal help to those in need. Yet his equally instinctive tendency to manage matters without being merciful to the feelings of the less capable, and his hasty temper, prevented many from appreciating him as he deserved. "There were many people in Stowey," said a friend, "who thought there was nobody like him, and who would say so with tears in their eyes; but there were always some who considered him a rather overbearing person, and remembered his revolutionary opinions with perpetual disapproval."

Poole's eccentricities and absentmindedness, "which often raised a smile at his expense," his incessant snuff-taking, which led one hostess after his visits to have her carpets immediately swept—all these were doubtless the unconscious expression of tensions created by Poole's nervous, complex temperament and social isolation. For Poole, like Coleridge, was in fact a déclassé. Highly intelligent, intellectually ambitious, yet almost entirely self-educated, he lived among peasants in a country village with no kindred soul to share his deepest interests. Alienated from the upper class by his radical and republican sympathies, Poole enthusiastically welcomed the friendship of Coleridge, glamorized for him as a brilliant Cambridge scholar, yet eminently friendly, human, and politically sympathetic.

A disappointment in love had permanently influenced Poole's deeply affectionate nature. Since rejection by his cousin, Penelope Poole, Tom had continued to live with his beloved mother and sister in his house near the tannery. His father was dead. His failure in love had doubtless influenced his belief "that woman is inferior to man"—an opinion not uncommon among masculine humanity. Nevertheless, he sustained a Platonic friendship, by letters, with his one feminine friend, Henriette Warwick. By the time Coleridge appeared, Poole's psychological orientation was predominantly masculine. How strong were his affections toward his men friends is revealed by the discovery, after his death, "in his bureau, carefully laid away among the sacred mementoes of those whom he loved best, a small packet labelled: 'The hair of my poor shepherd, who served me faithfully for twenty-three years.' "

Surely all this evidence of friends dovetails into a single psychological pattern, that of the (in Poole's case, unconscious) homosexual tendency. But the most significant evidence of this is quite unconsciously provided by Poole himself, when visiting Paris in 1802. There, amid the many and varied allurements at the Louvre, what most deeply moved him was the Apollo Belvedere. The experience so surprised him that naïvely and innocently he described it in a letter to Coleridge dated July 20:

"The first view of this statue astonishes you; it awes you; you can hardly look at it. A further contemplation has really a sublime moral effect. The stone makes you eloquent and perspicuous, it elevates your mind, and you feel that you are in the company of a 'superior being.' You leave it with regret, and you anticipate your return to it with a pure pleasure; it is not the feeling of returning to see a sight, but it is the feeling of being made wiser and better, of having your whole being dilated by its presence. I have said, and I repeat, that I can easily imagine that this statue could chain a man at Paris in the same way that the passion of love might." (Mrs. Henry Sandford, *Thomas Poole and His Friends* [London, 1888], p. 84).

Such an outburst from one so reserved and self-controlled as Poole surely confirms the masculine orientation suggested by the preceding evidence, and points to an innocent and unconscious but definite homosexual tendency—the unrecognized source of his affection for Coleridge, who himself in some slight degree appears to have had a similar tendency, equally unconscious. Today such innocence, even ignorance, of perversions, may seem strange, but was then common. As a recent writer says: "The Victorians' conception of love between those of the same sex cannot be fairly understood by an age steeped in Freud. Where they saw only beautiful friendship, the modern reader suspects perversion."

To Poole, upon the failure of the *Watchman*, Coleridge announced two new plans for existence—"the first impracticable, the second not likely to succeed." The first was to persuade some publisher to finance Coleridge and his wife at a German university, upon a promise that Coleridge would translate Schiller for him when he had learned enough German. Then the publisher would open a school for eight fortunate young men who would each pay a hundred guineas to study under Samuel's guidance, "Man as Animal, as an Intellectual and as a Religious Being," and so become "better Senators" than anyone in either House of Parliament. The second plan was "to become a Dissenting parson and abjure politics and carnal literature." This might force him to preach things that he did not believe, he said, but (employing the very argument that had so shocked and disgusted him when used by Southey), "Though not right in itself, it may become right by the greater wrongness of the only alternative—the remaining in neediness and uncertainty."

"Tom Poole," Southey once sardonically remarked, "is not content to be your friend; he must be your saviour." Samuel, always as ready to be "saved" as Poole was to save him, had also approvingly observed this trait in Poole. The truth of Southey's remark was now strikingly exemplified, for even before receiving Coleridge's two plans, Poole had persuaded a few admirers of Coleridge's verse to promise five guineas a year each for the next six years for Coleridge's sustenance, and so prevent the tragedy of his becoming schoolmaster or parson and depriving the world, as Poole wrote, of "the extraordinary marks of his sublime genius." These, together with his "honest heart" and fine principles, had aroused the contributors' "gratitude and admiration" and "irresistibly impelled" them to this action, in full confidence that a benevolent Providence would enable them with unabated cheerfulness to fulfill their engagement. Samuel, with unabated cheerfulness, accepted both their homage and their money, with a characteristically generous and condescending urbanity. "I feel myself rich in being poor," he wrote, "and because I have nothing to bestow, I know how much I have bestowed. . . .Concerning the scheme itself I am undetermined—not that I am ashamed to receive, God forbid!" But, he added in similar grandiloquent language that in fact, if he were hard-up again, "I can receive as I would bestow." Then in a sudden descent from his sublimities to the ridiculous Samuel continued: "God be ever praised for all things! Mrs. Coleridge loves you—and says she would fall on your neck and kiss you."

One of the donors' good wishes for Samuel was "that he may in peace enjoy the most perfect domestic felicity," for "he had united himself to her he loves, regardless of every other consideration." That, at least, was Poole's belief after receiving Samuel's letter on his marriage, describing himself as "united to the woman whom I love best of all created beings." The letter had probably inspired Poole to organize the annuity. Enthusiastically, Poole had seized the hand Samuel extended, and had overflowed in hackneyed rhetoric wishing them "a meridian bright and cloudless" on to "the soft close of a tranquil evening." But rising to a higher flight he had declared: "Providence has been pleased, if I may so express myself, to drop you on this globe as a meteor from the clouds, the track of which is undetermined. But you have now, by marrying, in some sense fixed yourself."

The inevitable visit to Poole soon followed, when Poole, obeying the ex-dragoon's order, sent "a horse of tolerable meekness" to meet him at Bridgwater. "Who should arrive but the famous Mr. Coleridge!" ironically exclaimed the critical Charlotte in her diary on that occasion: "I cannot form an opinion of him in so short a time, but could have discovered if I had not before heard it, that he is clever, and a very short acquaintance will unfold that he is extremely vain of it."

The saying "It never rains but it pours" was certainly justified at this time by the largesse now poured upon Samuel. On his return from Poole's, another diplomatically evoked donation awaited him from George Dyer, a kindly and poetical eccentric. "Deeply affected and almost agitated with that Gratitude, which if Philosophy discourage, Nature will more wisely compel," was Samuel's grateful reply. Next, John Fellows of Nottingham who had previously sent him and Sarah a parcel of stockings—the local product—now induced the literary ladies of that town to help Samuel, whose recent letter had touched Fellows's heart. So, each would subscribe a guinea toward his *Poems*, "for his disappointment in the *Watchman*." In reply, Samuel sent "my sincerest acknowledgements" to "the ladies who have honoured me by so delicate an act of liberality."

Ten days later came another gift, this time from no less august a source than the Royal Literary Fund, which sent him ten guineas on hearing that he was "a man of genius and learning, in extreme difficulties, proceeding from a sick family"—which included a prègnant wife and dying mother-in-law—who lived many years longer. Samuel's courteous acceptance of so small a sum was deservedly brief and slightly ambiguous: "You will, I trust, believe that I feel what I ought to feel for this relief so liberally and delicately afforded me, and that in happier circumstances I shall be proud to remember the obligation."

Despite these comparatively sordid material necessities of existence, Samuel's higher life of moral and intellectual preoccupation was meanwhile sustained by a lengthy philosophical, metaphysical, and religious debate with Thelwall, the poetic, democratic rationalist. This he did in a correspondence that followed Samuel's introductory letter and gift of *Poems* to him some weeks before. It was the kind of debate in which Samuel's still undergraduate and ever half-academic soul delighted: discursive, general, vague in argument, yet full of very definite though often questionable assertions, beginning and ending nowhere. Perhaps under Sarah's admonitions, Coleridge's Godwinian and pantisocratic principles, which had so recently led him to fear that in America the women would teach the children Christianity, had changed. Atheism, and Godwin as its evil exemplar, was now his main theme. Godwin's impossibly idealistic attitude to marriage Samuel now only saw as "free love" in its worst sense: "criminal." He would not "entrust his wife or sister or country" to anyone with such principles. Nevertheless, Samuel, being "a Necessarian," emphasized that he could not accuse Godwin of "guilt." His (never written) attack on Godwinism, *Critique on the New Philosophy*, he would soon publish. "*Marriage is indissoluble*," he emphasized: but not through any priestly magic. "Great indeed are the moral uses of Marriage. It is *Variety that cantharidizes us*. Marriage, that confines the appetites to one object, gradually causes them to be swallowed up in *affection*." Already after seven months, "the first fine careless rapture" of his marriage—as Browning would have said—was fading. Only a month before he had privately resolved "not to adulterize my time by absenting myself from my wife." It was the first rift within the lute. Already, too, he found in "property," "the Origin of all Evil."

But with the arrival of July Samuel's peace was threatened by an offer of work on the London *Morning Chronicle*, sufficient to support himself and his family. Thus menaced, he instinctively sought *advice* from his helpful Bristol friends: Estlin, treasurer of the new fund, Wade, and Danvers; but all were away. His letters to Estlin and to Poole breathed an unspoken prayer for salvation. "My heart is very heavy," he told Estlin, "for I love Bristol and I do not love London." This, too, he also told Poole, although but a month before he had told Fellows of Nottingham: "Indeed the Bristolians rank very low in the order of intellect; and form, I suspect, that subtle link, which (in the great chain of things) connects Man with the Brute Creation." "If I go," he now cried to Poole, "Farewell Philosophy! Farewell the Muse! Farewell my Literary Fame!"

But before the fatal day of decision arrived, exciting news came from Fellows. It was an alternative means of livelihood, for which Samuel had already promised "to sing 'lo Triumphe.' " A rich widow, Elizabeth Evans of Darley Hall near Derby, wanted him as tutor to her two sons. The possibilities thus presented to the poetic, romantic imagination were tremendous, and Samuel, taking his wife with him, "immediately set off" for Darley Hall. The meeting gave mutual satisfaction. For Coleridge the tutorship became "the object of my highest wishes," and despite the opposition of her relatives from father-in-law to grandfather, Mrs. Evans closed the deal at £150 a year.

Forgetting his moral objections to property and delighted with the roseate prospect, Samuel then made a serious tactical error. Leaving Mrs. Coleridge at The Hall, he hastened to Ottery to announce the good news and be reconciled with his family. His mother received him "with transport," George "with joy and tenderness," and the rest "with affectionate civility."

Cheered by this welcome and with delightful anticipations of life in Darley Hall, he reached Bristol on the return journey in high spirits. These were completely dashed by "a most impassioned" letter from Mrs. Evans, telling him all was over. If she appointed him tutor the wicked grandfather would disinherit her sons. "Farewell, pure and benevolent spirit," she concluded, "Brother in the Family of Soul. May a happier fate await you."

When he again met Mrs. Evans his tone was nobly tragic. "I cannot be said to have lost that which I never had," he said, "and I have gained what I should not otherwise have possessed—your esteem and veneration." This might well have left an ordinary lady speechless: but Mrs. Evans was not to be beaten—she could, indeed exquisitely, correct him: "Say rather my veneration and love!" Mrs. Coleridge, not daring to send the bad news to Samuel direct, had sent Mrs. Evans's note to him via Wade, with the cry, "Poor Coleridge, I cannot bear to think of his disappointment."

However, to sweeten the bitter draught, Mrs. Evans adroitly sent her two guests off in her carriage with her companion Miss Willet for a five-day visit to Matlock. The place was too full of painful memories of her late husband for Mrs. Evans to accompany them. Although Samuel found no compensation in Miss Willet, "an amiable old maid of about two and forty," for the absence of Mrs. Evans, he enjoyed Matlock, "monodized by Bowles." His time "was completely filled up with seeing the country, eating, concerts, etc. I was the first fiddle, not in the concerts, but everywhere else, and the company would not spare me twenty minutes together."

Next came a particularly delightful experience, a day's excursion to local beauty spots with Mrs. Evans and the ubiquitous Miss Willet. It included a country mansion full of Raphaels and Titians, a "thrice lovely valley," "without exception the most lovely place I ever visited," and Dovedale, "beyond expression tremendously sublime. . .the most tremendous of sublimities." There they "dined on cold meat in a cavern" before returning "quite exhausted with the rapid succession of delightful emotions." The final departure from Darley Hall was assuaged by a gift of 95 pounds in bank notes for Samuel, and for Sarah, all Mrs. Evans's baby-clothes, which, Coleridge unsentimentally remarked: "from the largeness of the quantity and the richness of their lace etc. . ., are very valuable." Tumultuous emotions swept through all as the last farewells were said. Mrs. Evans wept, again calling Samuel her "brother," and Samuel shortly afterward, called her "a woman of great mind and very great heart! She treated me," he said, "with esteem and affection and unbounded generosity."

In Derby a project, supported and probably instigated by Mrs. Evans, for a school to be run by Coleridge led him to claim a house then being built there, to order the chimneys to be altered to prevent smoke, and to agree on a rent of 12 pounds per annum; the landlord paying all taxes but the poor rate. Coleridge left the district the same day and apparently never troubled about the matter again.

The bad news of Darley Hall merely confirmed Poole's opinion of women. Samuel had left his defense in a woman's hands, and, of course, she had betrayed him! Poole was now "convinced that woman is inferior to man." Mrs. Evans had "vacillated" as no man would have done. Suddenly infected with Darley Hall rhetoric, Poole cried: "Woman, thou wast destined to be governed. Let us then bow to destiny." But innocent bachelor Poole, ignorant of woman's wiles, was wrong. Even Samuel seems to have been but a pawn in her game. For a year after his visit Mrs. Evans married one of his chief enemies, her late husband's half-brother. When told, Samuel said he was "not surprised," having "seen it even from the first week he was at Darley." O God! I wish. . .but what is the use of wishing!" he exclaimed; and he would say no more. No doubt his unuttered wish was that he had not left Mrs. Evans and gone to Ottery.

Samuel did not sink under the blow from Darley Hall but, as he said, "after the first moment, was perfectly composed, and continued calm and light-hearted." Poole, who had "sacrificed every selfish feeling" to encourage Samuel, was delighted that they were not to be separated. "My dear, dear boy," his letter to Samuel concluded, "God almighty bless you and assist you. Adieu! Adieu! Write! Write!" Samuel in reply thanked Poole for "that friendly heart"—feeling himself rich in Poole's love and esteem. "You do not know how rich I feel myself. O ever found the same, and trusted and beloved!" He would visit Poole, "if Sara will let me."

While Sarah, despite her condition, left Darley Hall alone for Bristol, Samuel in a private chaise went to Brimingham to spend a week with a Unitarian minister there, and preached for him the Sunday sermon. "*My chef d'oeuvre*," he complacently told his friends, adding that it was to be published. Even more important than his sermon was a new disciple, Charles Lloyd, the neurotic son of a wealthy banker and Quaker of Birmingham. Charles, now twenty-one, had been fascinated by Coleridge during his previous visit for the *Watchman*. Now hearing of the projected school at Derby, the poetical, unstable, "lost" youth, who disliked both banking and Quakers and held republican sentiments, yearned to join the "school," live with the ineffable Coleridge, feel the stimulus of his intellect, and imbibe his wisdom.

To Samuel at such a moment the advent of this enchanted son of a rich father seemed another interposition of Providence on his behalf. He approved the plan as enthusiastically as Charles himself. Summoned from Bristol shortly afterward by Lloyd's parents, Coleridge returned to Birmingham and had an interview that terminated in the banker's "joyful concurrence," and "thanks to Heaven" for the privilege Samuel accorded his son. Best of all, Mr. Lloyd also informed Coleridge that Charles was of independent means. Charles Lloyd, too, naturally recognized the providential nature of his meeting with Coleridge, and as Samuel described it, proclaimed "his joy and gratitude to Heaven," intending to be "always with me."

At this inconvenient moment before the last financial arrangements with Lloyd were completed, Sarah unexpectedly gave birth to a son. "Mrs. Coleridge was taken ill suddenly," Coleridge told Poole on September 24, 1796, "and before the nurse or sugeon arrived, delivered herself—the nurse came just in time to take away the afterbirth." He continued, "I was quite annihilated with the suddenness of the information—and retired to my room to address myself to my Maker— but I could only offer up to him the silence of stupified feelings." He wrote a sonnet on this experience, concluding with a prayer that his infant "may be born again a child of God." Then, taking Charles Lloyd with him, Coleridge set off for Bristol in the stagecoach. Fearing that the baby he had not wanted was dead, he wrote another sonnet on this experience as the coach rolled along. His first sight of the newborn baby was depressing—as he "looked on it with a melancholy gaze, not feeling that thrill and overflowing of affection which I expected." He named it David Hartley, after the philosopher of his present devotion. When the nurse told Mrs. Coleridge that she thought the baby resembled his father, Coleridge was not amused and commented to Poole: "No great compliment to me—for in truth I have seen handsomer babies in my life time."

Coleridge's enthusiasm for Lloyd's now living with them in Bristol was great: "Charles Lloyd wins upon me hourly; his heart is uncommonly pure, his affections delicate, and his benevolence enlivened, but not sicklied by sensibility. He is assuredly a man of great genius." All these fine qualities had been frustrated among "uncongenial minds." "For them to survive, Lloyd must be tête-à-tête with one whom he loves and esteems." In short, with Samuel. Already Lloyd was feeling the benefit of the change, for in three days Samuel had converted him from infidelity—Deism or Skepticism, neither Charles nor Samuel was sure which—to Christianity. It was an achievement that Charles celebrated in a very bad sonnet.

When in mid-October Samuel informed Lloyd's father that instead of running a school at Derby he would run a farm at Stowey, Mr. Lloyd disapproved. He was unimpressed by Coleridge's reasons: health, rustic simplicity, the moral grandeur of such poverty (with biblical quotations), the danger in towns of corruption from "politicians and politics" and of the destruction of "Christian graces." The change of plan was particularly made, he emphasized, to benefit Charles. But Quakers were not what Samuel expected. Mr. Lloyd swept all aside, including biblical justification of bucolic idealism, with the caustic remark that his new plan appeared "monastic rather than Christian."

So for Mr. Lloyd's benefit Coleridge next sent him an absurd syllabus of his son's projected studies, explaining that if Charles should ever resume his abandoned medical career, these would save his soul; for "most doctors are shallow animals, having always employed their minds about Body and Gut." As for Coleridge's former republicanism, which Mr. Lloyd disliked: "I have snapped my squeaking baby trumpet of sedition, and hung up its fragments in the chamber of penitences." He so liked the phrase that he repeated it to others on occasion. Despite Samuel's low opinion of medical science, Dr. Beddoes at this very moment, responding to a frantic appeal from Samuel, was treating Charles for epileptic fits. The curative "tête-à-tête" with Samuel had proved too strong for Charles Lloyd.

In the first days of December 1796, poor Mr. Lloyd was informed by Samuel of a "severe process of simplification" by which the soul-saving studies were scrapped, owing to the anticipated demands of "practical husbandry and horticulture." "The Voice within" had put "firm and unwavering negative" to Samuel's turning Unitarian minister or politician, and a school would ruin his health. Nevertheless, Charles, said Colerige, "vehemently" refused to leave him, and expulsion would endanger his health. If he remained, "to occupy a room in my cottage," it must be merely "as a lodger and friend, paying half-a-guinea a week exclusive of washing and any potation beyond table beer." There would be no servant, and Charles must furnish his own bedroom to prevent Samuel's "running into debt, from which may Heaven preserve me." Samuel's peroration was in his best style: "I have written plainly and decisively, my dear Sir! I wish to avoid not only evil, but the *appearances* of evil. This is a world of calumnies! Yes there is an imposthume in the large tongue of this world ever ready to break, and it is well to prevent the contents from being sputtered into one's face." But Charles's epileptic fits and the change of plan outweighed Samuel's rhetoric, and Mr. Lloyd called Charles home. There he remained over Christmas, busy extracting from his father permission to return to Coleridge.

Lamb, meanwhile, was overwhelmed by a domestic tragedy. His beloved and lovable sister Mary, in a first fit of what proved to be recurrent insanity, killed her mother and injured her father in a knife attack. Lamb, shocked and shaken, had asked Samuel to write him "as religious a letter as possible" for consolation. Samuel, ever ready to preach, exhorted him to practice Christian resignation and fortitude and, to at least his own satisfaction, proved that nothing could have been better for Lamb's soul. Mary was now confined in a madhouse where Lamb himself, disappointed in love and temporarily unbalanced, had recently been an inmate. In his misery Lamb accepted Coleridge's exhortations with gratitude. But soon recovering his normal critical mentality, Lamb genially yet sardonically taxed Coleridge with unorthodoxy and "blasphemy."

Shortly afterward, hearing of Samuel's plan to farm at Nether Stowey, Lamb preached to him in his turn: "I grieve from my very soul to observe you, in your plans of life, veering about from this hope to the other, and settling nowhere. . . . You seem to be taking up splendid schemes of fortune only to lay them down again; and your fortunes are an *ignis fatuus* that has been conducting you in thought, from Lancaster Court, Strand, to somewhere in Matlock; then jumping across to Dr. Somebody's, whose son's tutor you were likely to be; and would to God the dancing demon *may* conduct you at last, in peace and comfort, to the 'life and labours of a cottager,' " evidently ironically quoting from some letter from Coleridge to Lamb himself.

Despite Samuel's anxieties over Lloyd and Stowey, his friendly debates by letter with the rationalistic Thelwall continued in an atmosphere of calm abstraction. Their philosophical discussions were generally by-products of their "religious" arguments, which in turn often arose from "sparring about poetry," on which their views also differed. Coleridge was kind to Thelwall's mediocre poems, which offered full scope for destructive criticism. But Thelwall dismissed Bowles's sentimental sonnets as "Della Cruscan"; this, Samuel replied, "cut the skin and surface of my heart." With unconscious irony, Samuel also advised Thelwall, just as Poole had vainly advised Samuel, to "engage in some great work." Yet at the same time he confessed to Thelwall, "I compose very little—and I absolutely hate composition. Such is my dislike that even a sense of duty is sometimes too weak to overpower it." He told Thelwall, discussing life, "You, I understand, have adopted the idea that it is the result of organized matter acted on by external stimuli. Now as to the Metaphysicians, Plato says it is Harmony—he might as well have said a fiddle-stick's end—but I love Plato, his dear, *gorgeous* Nonsense."

Whatever his opinion of the soul, Coleridge now volubly asserted his adherence to Christianity, declaring that Newton, Locke, and Hartley had all abandoned skepticism for faith. "Now the religion which Christ taught," he told Thelwall, "is simply (1) that there is an Omnipresent Father of infinite power, wisdom and goodness, in whom we all of us move and have our being, and (2) that when we appear to men to die, we do not utterly perish, but after this life shall continue to enjoy or suffer the consequences and natural effects of the habits we have formed here, whether good or evil. This is the Christian Religion, and all the Christian Religion." That it was God the "Father" to whom Coleridge already turned, was natural to the fatherless "orphan" whose search throughout life for father substitutes—George, Poole, Words-worth—was instinctive. Toward the end, when all his earthly substitutes seemed to Samuel to have failed him, it was still to this external Father that he looked for salvation.

How far Samuel was completely serious in these discussions is not easy to determine. Often his mischievous, half-cynical humor broke through, as when he told Thelwall: "If my system should prove true, we, I doubt not, shall both meet in the Kingdom of Heaven, and I with transport in my eye shall say: 'I told you so my dear fellow.' " Much of the inconsistency in Coleridge's thought he in fact unconsciously explained in saying: "My philosophical opinions are blended with or deduced from "my feelings!" And Coleridge's feelings were already at times influenced by opium. There was essential truth, however harshly expressed, when Hazlitt, recognizing Coleridge's basic, largely unconscious skepticism, declared: "He had not been inconsistent with himself at different times, but at all times. He lived in a round of contradictions and never came to a settled point."

Throughout the year of Southey's residence in Lisbon, there had been no communication between him and Samuel. But when in May 1796 Southey found himself living opposite the Coleridges in Bristol, he is said to have broken the deadlock by sending across the street a slip of paper with a quotation from Schiller: "Thou leavest a void in my bosom, which the human race, thrice told, will never fill up." The story sounds more like a romantic invention by Coleridge than a probable action by Southey. At any rate, it was long before any friendly association for the two occurred; and for Southey at least, it was, perhaps, to quote Browning, "never glad confident morning again." The principals in whatever rapprochement was made may well have been the two wives, who were sisters.

Southey, reluctantly following the advice of his financially helpful uncle, had now turned to the study of law, hoping, however, to be able in time to live by writing. Certainly throughout the remainder of the year there was little pretense of real friendship between Southey and Coleridge. Southey dropped Samuel's part of *Joan of Arc* in his new edition of his poems, and Coleridge, on receiving a presentation copy, merely replied: "I thank you Robert Southey! for your poems; and by way of return present you with a collection of (what appear to me) the faults." These, he told Thelwall on the last day of the year, were chiefly lack of imagination and thought. "I think," he added, "that an admirable poet might be made by *amalgamating him and me. I think* too much for a *Poet*, he too little for a *great* Poet. He continued, "Between ourselves the *Enthusiasm* of Friendship is not with Southey and me. We quarrelled, and the quarrel lasted for a twelvemonth. We are now reconciled; but the cause of the Difference was solemn—and 'the blasted oak puts not forth its buds anew.' We are *accquaintances*—and feel kindliness towards each other; but I do not *esteem* or *LOVE* Southey, as I must esteem and love the man whom I dared call by the holy name of *FRIEND*. And vice versa Southey of me. I say no more. It is a painful subject.''

Nor was Coleridge's friendship with Poole now quite as close as before. From the time of his return to Bristol from Darley Hall Coleridge was haunted by a fear that Poole's affection for him had declined, as he at once told him, adding apologetically: "Indeed my soul seems so mantled and wrapped round by your love and esteem, that even a dream of losing but the smallest fragment of it makes me shiver, as though some tender part of my nature were left uncovered and in nakedness.'' For, he explained, "Where the friendship of any person forms an essential part of a man's happiness, he will at times be pestered by the little jealousies and solicitudes of imbecile humanity. Since we last parted I have been gloomily dreaming that you did not leave me so affectionately as you were wont to do.''

Was the "little jealousy,'' one wonders, caused by the advent of Poole's new protégé, Thomas Ward, "the young man with the soul-beaming face'' whom Samuel had just met? Ward, in fact, was fascinated by Poole, as Lloyd had been by Coleridge; and Poole and Ward now stood in the same relation to each other. Ward had also dropped the study of medicine and must live with Poole, or life would be void otherwise. So he became apprenticed to tanning and lived with Poole as if an adopted son. They played their favorite game of chess so enthusiastically that when Poole's mother, anxious about Ward's health, called "bedtime,'' they continued their game across the corridor from their respective bedrooms. In time Ward, like the "good apprentice'' of children's tales, became Poole's partner, and in later years, when Poole was a magistrate with official and social duties, Ward relieved him of much responsibility in the tanning business.

Poole's perfervid reply should have reassured Samuel, who was, said Poole, "the friend held dearest to me. *I say it thinkingly.* . . .By you, Coleridge, I will always stand, in sickness and health, in prosperity and misfortune, in vice . . .[probably a reference to opium deleted here] if vice should ever taint thee—but *it cannot.*'' At Samuel's request, Poole invited both him and Lloyd to come to Stowey, and sent horses for them to Bridgwater. But the visit was less happy than usual; for Coleridge wished to consult Poole about the plan to move to Stowey, and he found Poole less enthusiastic than he had hoped.

From the beginning of November to the end of the year, Samuel lived in a growing fear that his plan would fail. The cause was twofold: first, doubts of Poole's approval; second, the difficulty of finding a house at Stowey. "Irrationally strong,'' he described his anxiety on November 1. Two days later he was suffering from his usual anxiety neuralgia: such agonizing pains in "left temple, eye, cheek, jaw, throat and shoulder,'' that, "nearly frantic,'' he "ran about the house naked." It was probably Beddoes who prescribed the twenty-five drops of laudanum Coleridge was taking every four hours, greatly reducing the pains. When a relapse occurred, Beddoes increased the dose from sixty to seventy drops and, as Samuel said, "*sopped* the Cerberus just as his mouth began to open." He had, he said, "suffered more bodily Pain" during the attack than he had ever dreamed possible, and he praised "the ease and *spirits* gained from laudanum." Shortly afterward he spoke of "the languor and exhaustion to which pain and the frequent doses of laudanum have reduced me."

But Poole wrote more encouragingly about Stowey, and Samuel's spirits rose so far as to ask him to find "a fit servant for us—simple of heart, physiognomically handsome, and scientific in vaccimulgence," whom he would teach to cook. When his last two letters were left unanswered, Coleridge wrote again in rising hysteria. Every day for a week he had waited at the post office, "anxiously expecting" Poole's letter. It was not strange that Lloyd, of epileptic tendencies, had so soon collapsed in Samuel's company. Lamb, too, later feared the effect of Samuel's nervosity upon his sister, Mary.

During the following weeks of ups and downs, Coleridge's fears became obsessive, as Poole's letters encouraged or depressed him. For neither moral nor physical health, nor agricultural experience, was Coleridge's main reason for wishing to live in Stowey. To be near Poole, to have his protection and affection, his admiration and encouragement, including the practical one of his purse at need, was Coleridge's main incentive.

By the end of November 1796 Poole had found nothing better at Stowey than a squalid cottage in a squalid street; but Samuel dismissed all Poole's and Sarah's doubts about it: "It is not a beauty, but its vicinity to you shall overbalance its defects." Poole must take it for him—which doubtless meant pay the rent. His fears quieted, Coleridge now begged his "beloved friend" to "pardon his childish impatience." He now counted upon quitting his house in Bristol and being in Stowey before his present lease expired on Christmas Day. With renascent optimism, he faced the future in the bravest spirit, meaning "to work *very hard* as Cook, Butler, Scullion, Shoecleaner, Occasional Nurse, Gardener, Hind, Pig-protector, Chaplain, Secretary, Poet, Reviewer, and omniumbotherum shilling-scavenger. In other words I shall keep no servant, and will cultivate my Land-acre, and my wise-acres, as well as I can."

When in mid-December Poole made a final attempt to dissuade him from so foolish a project, all the old anxieties returned in full force. "O my God!" he cried on receiving Poole's "hasty and heart-chilling letter." Samuel's reply, of enormous length, took two days and a sleepless night to write, arguing, protesting, explaining, wheedling, using every means of justification, including emotional rhetoric, reproach, affectionate entreaty—and as usual at such times, emphasizing consideration for Mrs. Coleridge and now also for little Hartley: "By God, I dare not look at them. . . .Mrs. Coleridge has observed the workings of my face. . .and is entreating to know what is the matter. . . .O Thomas Poole! Thomas Poole! If you did but know what a Father and Husband must feel, who toils with his brain for uncertain bread! I dare not think of it. The evil Face of Frenzy looks at me. . . .Indeed, indeed, I am very miserable.''

So Poole's reasons were thrown to the winds. Lose his Bristol Friends? He had no friends in Bristol. Wade was leaving, and only Estlin and Cottle remained. How could they help him? ''not money—for a temporary relief of my wants is nothing—removes no gnawing anxiety and debases the dignity of man. Not their interest, for I can accept no place in State, Church or Dissenting Meeting.'' As for other suggestions: ''I could not love the man who advised me to keep school or write for a newspaper. He must have a hard heart.'' No, only Poole could help him—''O! a great deal!''—with daily advice on farming and soon, merely ''to pass across my garden once or twice a day for five minutes and set me right, and cheer me with the sight of a friend's face.'' No wonder poor Poole tried hard to divert his friend from a descent upon Stowey.

So Poole yielded, and Samuel, at once regretting his ''improper impetuosity,'' told Poole of the ''distressful dreams of falling down precipices''—doubtless due to the laudanum he was taking. In his sonnet of 1794, ''Pantisocracy,'' Coleridge similarly had written of those

> who start
> From Precipices of distemper'd sleep.

Now he asked God's blessing on Poole and on his ''Grateful and affectionate self. But bear with my infirmities!''

Some time before, Flower, the editor at Cambridge, had asked Samuel for a poem for the last day of the year, which hitherto he had been too worried to compose. To this he now turned, beginning his ''Ode to the Departing Year'' on Christmas Eve 1796 and completing it on Boxing Day. Poole's capitulation had brought Coleridge peace and harmony, and his ode began, as he later described it, ''with an address to the Great Being of Divine Providence, who regulates into one vast harmony, all the Events of Time, however calamitous some of them appear to mortals.''

So, on the last day of 1796, while the ''Ode to the Departing Year'' appeared in the *Cambridge Intelligencer*, Coleridge, after an emotional farewell to Estlin, set out with Sarah and the baby for Stowey, in a ''small wagon filled with boxes of books, chests of drawers, kitchen furniture and chairs, our bed and bed-linen.'' The move cost Samuel £110, which probably Poole or Estlin, or perhaps Mrs. Evans's present, helped to pay.

Such was Coleridge's entry with his wife and son into a new life as a farmer in Stowey.

8 Nether Stowey (1797-98)

"The light shall stream to a far distance from the taper in my cottage window."
—*Coleridge to John Thelwall, December 17, 1796*

As lightheartedly as he had set out on the *Watchman* crusade Samuel entered Stowey—in high spirits. A day or two later the house had been "set to rights" and "maid, wife, bratling and self" were "remarkably well." Coleridge loved Poole and his mother and was beloved by them: "We are happy." Sarah, in fact, was not happy. She missed her mother and sisters in Bristol, found the house but "a miserable cottage," and was grateful to Poole for making it "an abode of comparative comfort." The bitter contrast between it and her pretty cottage at Clevedon was greatly intensified for Sarah by memories of Darley Hall and rich, kind Mrs. Evans. "She sits and thinks and thinks of her, and bursts into tears," wrote Samuel, "and when I turn to her, says; 'I was thinking, my dear, of Mrs. Evans.' " But Samuel rejoiced that Lloyd, restored to health in the less exciting atmosphere of his Quaker home, was about to return to them.

To Samuel in his present mood their house appeared almost a palace—at any rate "better than we expected," and he proudly described its glories: a "comfortable bedroom and sitting-room" for Lloyd, and the same for himself and Sarah, a maid's room, kitchen, and outhouse. That the kitchen was ovenless may have escaped him, but it would not Sarah. However, there was also "a clear brook of very soft water" flowing past his front door on Lime Street, "a nice well of fine spring water" in the backyard, and a "very pretty garden" that would provide "vegetables and employment" for him. Indeed, he said, he was already "an expert gardener," with calloused hands as "testimonials of their industry." There was also "a sweet orchard" with a very convenient gate into Tom Poole's garden, leading to Poole's "bookroom" or library—where Samuel was to spend far more time than in gardening. Later, when Samuel's roseate vision passed, the "clear brook" became a "Gutter" an "odoriferous Lime Grove," and the cottage, "the little hovel." But that was not yet. To Estlin he concluded his survey: "You see, I ought to be happy—and thank God I am so."

In the genial excitement of his arrival in Stowey Coleridge sent Poole a facetiously rhyming invitation to dine with him on pork and potatoes.

For the moment his bucolic enthusiasm equaled that so recently experienced for pantisocracy and the Susquehannah. Henceforth his life should be happily divided between healthful, ennobling, physical labor in the garden and distinguished intellectual effort. As at Clevedon he made a timetable for himself: from 7:00 to breakfast at 8:30 he would work in the garden; then read and compose until midday. Then until 2:00 he would "feed the pigs, poultry, etc." From dinner to tea "work again," and from tea to supper, do his reviewing. "So jogs the day, and I am happy." Already he was growing "potatoes and all manner of vegetables," would "raise corn with the spade, enough for my family," and had acquired "two pigs and ducks and geese." He did not think it worthwhile to keep a cow since Poole provided all the milk they needed. Such is Coleridge's first and last appearance as a farmer.

"What does your worship know about farming?" Lamb asked him, skeptically inquisitive. No answer to the question anywhere appears beyond the indication so unintentionally provided by Coleridge himself, in his naïve story of his victory over Thelwall. For when Thelwall opposed religious instruction for children before they could give rational consideration to the subject, Samuel in reply merely pointed to his garden overgrown with weeds, saying: "The weeds, you see, have taken the liberty to grow, and I thought it unfair to prejudice the soil towards roses and strawberries." Certainly Samuel never "prejudiced the soil" of his garden toward anything.

Despite his arduous labors Samuel found occasional respite in the lighter, more frivolous social activities of Stowey. He was, he said, no doubt correctly, an "immense favourite" with "a number of very pretty ladies" with whom "I pun, conundrumize, *listen*, and dance. The last is a recent acquirement." To Gillman, in later days, Coleridge declared that his chief aim in going to Stowey was not to be near Poole nor to learn farming but to find rest and peace after political turmoil so that he might devote himself to poetry, ethics, and psychology, examine the foundations of religion and morals, and allay his religious doubts. Above all, he was anxious to "reconcile personality with infinity." It does not appear that either at Stowey or elsewhere he succeeded.

That he did much reading the list of his borrowings from the Bristol Library during these years clearly shows. "A library cormorant," he described himself, who particularly enjoyed "Metaphysics and Poetry and 'Facts of Mind,' " and he seldom read "but to amuse myself. . .almost always reading." Although, as in the past, the problems of philosophy, metaphysics, and religion, the opposition of heart and head, or materialism and religious mysticism, still dominated his thought and reading, he also went at times far afield to history and the literature of travel. "It was better for Coleridge, as poet, to read books of travel and exploration than to read books of metaphysics and political economy," said T. S. Eliot, with truth. Yes, Coleridge claimed that a poet must also be a philosopher. Of course, Coleridge did not return his library books on time, and the librarian's repeated but ignored request for their return produced from Samuel but contemptuously ironical insinuations about the illiteracy of the library committee: "Our learned and ingenious Committee, may read through two thousand four hundred pages of closely printed Greek and Latin in three weeks: I pretend to no such intenseness of application or rapidity of genius. . . . Yours in Christian fellowship." As for the librarian, "a dog," he told Cottle. "He has altogether made me pay 5/- for postage."

With the spring Coleridge's happiness departed. He complained of overwhelming demands from many quarters: Cottle nagged for poems for a new edition, editors nagged for overdue reviews, and Sheridan at Drury Lane wanted a tragedy, although, moaned Samuel to Cottle, "I have no genius that way." Nevertheless, his dream of vast wealth through the theater spurred him on. Besides, Lloyd had again departed—driven out of his mind by Samuel's too exciting proximity and by the death of his much-loved grandmother to whose memory Lloyd published a volume of verses, to which Coleridge contributed a bad introductory sonnet. Nor was his grandmother's death Lloyd's only misery. He wished to marry a Birmingham heiress, Sophia Pemberton; but his parents objected. And with Lloyd's departure went not only Samuel's eighty pounds a year rent, but also his hopes of a wealthy resident, married or unmarried, for years to come.*

Wandering as ever under stress of anxiety, Coleridge went to Brtistol to see Cottle, failed to call on him, and back in Stowey cited "a depression too dreadful to be described" as his reason. His state now, he said, was "calm hopelessness; every mode of life which has promised me bread and cheese, has been, one after another, torn away from me—but God remains." Nor did he forget that Estlin and Wade also remained. Lloyd's father sent Coleridge ten pounds. Thus encouraged, he returned to his never-never volume against Godwin and to his tragedy, *Osorio*.

But immediately another fit of wandering took him to Bristol again and on to Huntspill, to visit his other weak-witted pantisocratic acolyte, Burnett, prostrate by jaundice. To cheer him Samuel drank Burnett's smuggled

---

*Lloyd was gone, but was not to be forgotten. Later, released as cured from a private asylum, he married Sophia after much excitement, despite parental opposition. Jealous of Coleridge's attachment to Wordsworth, he vilified Coleridge to Lamb and Southey and caused a two year estrangement between them and Coleridge. To spite Coleridge, Lloyd withdrew his own verses, which at Lloyd's request Samuel had published with his own and Lamb's, in the second edition of his *Poems*. Coleridge's reply—made like Lloyd's through Cottle—was crushing: "I have no objection to any disposal of C. Lloyd's poems, except that of their being published with mine." In April 1798 Lloyd published "Edmund Oliver," a dastardly attack on Coleridge, who was obviously the "hero" of this tale, in which all Coleridge's infirmities are fully displayed. Coleridge's reply to this, which appeared in September 1802 in the *Morning Post*, was entitled "To One who published in print what had been entrusted to him by my fireside."

  Two things hast thou made known to half the nation,
  My secrets and my want of penetration:
  For O! far more than all which thou hast penn'd
  It shames me to have call'd a wretch, like thee, my friend!

Lloyd died in 1839 in an asylum in France.

brandy—"a compound of Hellebore, Kitchen grease and Asafoetida," said Coleridge, which gave him "brandiphobia." That was an illness from which, unfortunately, Samuel quickly recovered.

Back once more in Stowey, he returned with renewed energy to *Osorio*, and for the new edition of his *Poems* wrote his beautiful dedicatory verses to his brother George, who, however, said that Samuel was "displeased, and thought his character endangered by them." Written in May 1797, the poem incidentally provides one of the most charming glimpses of the Coleridges' domestic life in Stowey, when

> On some delicious eve,
> We in our sweet sequestered orchard-plot
> Sit on the tree crook's earthward; whose old boughs,
> That hand above us in an arborous roof,
> Stirred by the faint gale of departing May,
> Send their loose blossoms slanting o'er our heads!

In the background of this idyll was Poole, again stimulating the charitable to another contribution to the Coleridge fund. "Do not apply but to those who love him," Poole warned Estlin the treasurer, "for it requires affection and purity of heart to offer assistance of this nature to such a man." As doubts about Samuel's industry had arisen, Poole added: "Coleridge is industrious, considering the exertion of mind necessary when he works. The race-horse cannot always be on the turf." Even as Poole, aglow with benevolence and respect, was making these efforts for Samuel, Coleridge was entering for the first time the home of a man who would soon rival Poole in his affection and ultimately displace him.

William Wordsworth, then an almost unknown poet nearly three years older than Coleridge, was at once accepted by him as his superior in every way. "I feel myself a *little man by his side*," Coleridge told Cottle. Both similarities and differences in the temperaments and experiences of the two poets were such as made for mutual understanding and friendship. Wordsworth, son of a country solicitor and orphaned at an early age by the deaths of both his parents, had attended a village school situated amid the natural beauties of the Northern Lakes, and he had boarded with the kindly and simple peasantry there. At Cambridge, Wordsworth had preceded Coleridge. Only recently had the two poets met.

Wordsworth at this time was emerging from the darkest period of his whole life—caught in the French Revolution during a visit to France, he had escaped to England leaving behind him Annette Vallon, pregnant with his child, and still awaiting the marriage that, through real or imaginary impediments of war, never occurred. Denounced by angry guardians for his sympathy with the

Revolution and his *folie de jeunesse*, Wordsworth had abandoned his intention to enter the church. He remained lost and dejected, and with but slender means. But Dorothy, Wordsworth's devoted sister, braving the displeasure of her guardian uncles, had gone to live with her brother William at Racedown, a mansion near Stowey, let to them, rent free, during the absence of its owner.

There William and Dorothy lived for almost two years in happy solitude—he writing his poems, she managing the house and supplementing their small income by acting as mother and teacher to a little motherless boy, Basil Montagu, son of Basil Montagu, Sr. (1770–1851), barrister and writer. Deeply attached to each other, the brother and sister found mutual delight in their reading, in wanderings about the park at Racedown, and the lovely countryside. They even enjoyed their respective household duties. Wordsworth with his peasant experience liked the rural labors that Coleridge had only theoretically enjoyed. After "hewing wood and rooting up hedges" for an hour and a half, Wordsworth thought it "no bad employment to feel the 'penalty of Adam.'" Dorothy, for her part, far from demanding, as Coleridge had been, a housemaid "simple of heart, physiognomically handsome" or even "scientific in vaccimulgence," merely stipulated, "she must be a strong girl and cook victuals tolerably well."

When on June 5, 1797, Samuel appeared at Racedown, it was not the poets' first meeting. A casual encounter or two in Bristol, a recent call by Wordsworth on Coleridge that had cheered Samuel during his recent despondency, and some correspondence about their poems had already occurred. But now, with Coleridge's return call for Wordsworth's visit, the intimate period of their friendship began. From the first moment their meeting was peculiarly spontaneous and happy. Both William and Dorothy long remembered how Samuel on seeing them "did not keep to the high road," but "leapt over a gate and bounded down the pathless field, by which he cut off an angle."

Upon Dorothy Samuel's charm was immediate. "A wonderful man," she told a friend, "whose conversation teems with soul, mind and spirit; so benevolent, so good-tempered and cheerful." For the first few minutes she thought him "very plain"; but she forgot all defects of his features when he spoke. His eye, expressing "every emotion of his animated mind," was, she thought, truly the "'poets' eye in a fine frenzy rolling.'" She also noticed his "fine dark eyebrows and overhanging forehead."

Nor was Coleridge less impressed with the physically unlovely Dorothy, a new kind of woman to enter his life—free, unconventional, yet a lady, intelligent, spontaneous, affectionate, and passionately devoted to her brother and his poetry: Wordsworth's "exquisite sister...a woman indeed!— in mind and heart." As for her appearance, "if you expected to see a pretty woman you would think her ordinary; if you expected to find an ordinary woman, you would think her pretty! But her manners are simple, ardent, impressive." And prose proving inadequate to such a subject, Samuel slightly and purposely misquoted from his own "Destiny of Nations":

> In every motion her most innocent soul
> Outbeams so brightly, that who saw would say,
> Guilt was a thing impossible in her.

"Her information various," he continued, "her eye watchful in minutest observation of nature, and her taste a perfect electrometer; it bends, protrudes, and draws in, at subtlest beauties and most recondite faults."

As for William, although Dorothy had soon ceased to notice his physical defects, she once admitted: "He is however certainly rather plain, though otherwise has an extremely thoughtful countenance; but when he speaks it is often lighted up by a smile which I think very pleasing, but enough, he is my brother; why should I describe him? I shall be lauching again into panegyric." As she now observed, William lacked both Samuel's conversational ability and facility for friendship: "You must be with him more than once, before he will be perfectly easy in conversation."

Whatever reserve the Wordsworths felt on first meeting Coleridge was at once swept away by his habitual geniality and enthusiasm. Literature—poetry—their own above all, was the order of the day, and without delay they set to work. First Wordsworth read his latest poem, "The Ruined Cottage," which Coleridge praised to the skies. Then after tea, Samuel followed with two and a half acts of *Osorio*, which Wordsworth admired to Samuel's delight. The next morning, unsatiated, they listened while Wordsworth read his feeble tragedy *The Borderers*, which Coleridge thought "absolutely wonderful," quite Shakespearean in its "profound touches of the human heart"; indeed superior to Shakespeare, as "in Wordsworth there are no inequalities."

In such matters of mutual interest and appreciation and in continual wanderings about the countryside, the enchanted days of Samuel's visit to Racedown passed all too quickly. Coleridge, intellectually stimulating, brought William in his solitude a new creative companionship beyond what even Dorothy, more intuitive than intellectual or imaginative, could give in this manner. Coleridge, too, no longer solitary, spontaneously shared with William and Dorothy their wonderful unity of mind and heart.

But even at Racedown black care pursued Samuel, who, "shillingless," was forced to write, on two successive days to Estlin, as fund "treasurer," for money. This would be "the last year," he hoped, when he could "conscientiously accept" such contributions, "which in my present lot and conscious of my present occupations, I feel no pain in doing." Coleridge's return to Stowey was very short. The call of Racedown drew him back immediately. On July 2 he reappeared at Stowey, proudly driving a cart in which were William, Dorothy, and little Basil—with their luggage. They had not only come to be his guests but also to live near him if possible, having left Racedown forever.

Nor was it only Samuel's fascination that brought the Wordsworths to Stowey. An unpleasant atmosphere had been created at Racedown by its owner, who had just returned and was annoyed to find that it had been let rent free during his absence. Poole at once became the Wordsworth's "saviour," and found for them a charming house—which they always called "Alfoxden"—at a low rent. Poole stood surety in their lease when they signed it on July 14, 1797.

Samuel, ever sociable, had invited all his best friends, including Lamb, to be his guests in his Stowey cottage. Already overcrowded with the additions of the Wordsworths and Basil, "the little hovel" must have been unusually displeasing to Mrs. Coleridge, who was occupied with her domestic duties and her baby, Hartley. Among her guests she must have felt a complete outsider, preferring household tasks to accompanying them on their endless perambulations about the countryside. Having no love of country walks, she probably appeared to them an inferior person, almost a menial, indeed. There is certainly excuse, then, for suspecting a Freudian accident, when on the second day of the Wordsworth's visit, she upset a pan of boiling milk over Samuel's foot, which prevented his joining his guests on their walks. It was thus that Lamb, when he arrived at the cottage, found Coleridge *hors de combat*.

One evening, when Lamb and the Wordsworths were out walking, Coleridge limped his way to Poole's arbor and wrote one of his best and best-known poems, "This Lime-Tree Bower My Prison," beginning:

Well, they are gone, and here must I remain,
Lamed by the scathe of fire, lonely and faint,
This lime-tree bower my prison.

In revision he wisely dropped the second, self-pitying line.

When after a week at Stowey Lamb returned home, "the names of Tom Poole, of Wordsworth and his good sister, with thine and Sara's are become 'familiar in my mouth as household words,'" he wrote to Samuel, adding with a sudden change of tone, "Are you and your dear Sara—to me also very dear, because very kind—agreed yet about the management of little Hartley?"

Coleridge was now busy with the final preparations for the new edition of *Poems*, which soon appeared. He dropped much of his juvenile verse and also most of the political, "to widen the sphere of my readers," as he told Cottle. For the volume was to include only "my choicest fish, picked, gutted and cleaned." The most important additions were the "Reflections on Having Left a Place of Retirement" and the poem to George. *Religious Musings* and the "Ode to the Departing Year" were much revised.

In mid-May Southey had arrived at Portsmouth on his return from Portugal. Immediately after Lamb's departure from Stowey, Coleridge, now with Sarah the Wordsworth's guest at Alfoxden, sent him a long, expansive, and friendly letter—the first of its kind since their quarrel. In it he detailed all the exciting experiences in Stowey, particularly the glories of Alfoxden and the Wordsworths. He added a pressing invitation from both himself and William to visit them, offering to drive Southey and his wife to Stowey "in a one-horse chaise" if they would come. Nor need they fear, for he was "always very cautious and now no inexpert whip." But the Southeys did not come.

When on the following evening Thelwall, expected for several days, arrived at the Stowey cottage, he found Sarah, who had left Alfoxden to attend to domestic matters, "alone at the wash-tub. I have spoiled the soapsuds, however," Thelwall wrote from Alfoxden the next day, to his wife: "I slept at Coleridge's cot, and this morning we rose betimes, and came here time enough to call Samuel and his friend Wordsworth up to breakfast."

Thelwall's slightly satirical description to his wife of the rarefied atmosphere of this romantic coterie at Alfoxden—almost the only one by an outsider that is extant—also illuminates the slight sense of discomfort present in Lamb's letter after his visit. Lamb's explanation to Coleridge was "my silence was not sullenness," and he apologized for "behaving like a sulky child, but company and converse are strange to me. It was kind in you all to endure me as you did."

Everything, Thelwall now told his wife, had been "banished from my mind"—except herself and his babies—by the "enchanting retreat" Alfoxden, "the Academus of Stowey, and by the delightful society" there. They had wandered, he said, through their

> plantations, and along a wild, romantic dell, through which a foaming, rushing, murmuring torrent of water winds its long artless course. There have we. . . .a literary and political triumvirate, passed sentence on the productions and characters of the ages, burst forth in poetical flights of enthusiasm, and philosophised our minds into a state of tranquility, which the leaders of nations might envy, and the residents of cities can never know. Faith, we are a most philosophical party. . . .without any servant, male or female. An old woman, who lives in an adjoining cottage, does what is requisite for our simple wants.

Coleridge, too, on this occasion took stock of Thelwall, whom he liked "uncommonly well" as "a very warm-hearted, honest man." Yet they disagreed on "almost every point of religion, morals, and philosophy," wrote Coleridge—"He believes and disbelieves with impassioned confidence. I wish to see him *doubting* and *doubting*. . . .He is a man for action. He is a great favourite with Sara."

Glimpses of Samuel's everyday life in Stowey with the Wordsworths and Poole appear in one or two short notes that passed between them and are not lost: Will Poole send "a fore-quarter of lamb over to the Foxes" [Alfoxden]; will Poole "come over if possible by eleven o'clock, that we may have Wordsworth's tragedy read under the trees." Will "dear Poole send by Nanny, the coat etc. which you mentioned to me, as I wish to have it made fit for me by next Sunday." And Sarah asked Samuel to remind Poole of "some stockings, half silk and half cotton, which *you* could not wear." Samuel joked off the humiliation of needing Poole's old clothes: "You shall be my Elijah, and I will not reverentially catch the mantle which you have cast off. Why should not a Bard go tight and have a few neat things on his back? Ey?—Eh, Eh, God bless you and S. T. Coleridge."

The coat so jocularly acquired with biblical sanction was for the adornment of Samuel in the pulpit. For now, Sunday after Sunday, Coleridge was preaching in various places, including Bath and Bridgwater. He was, he explained, "unhired"—but doubtless was given his "expenses." The main reason for his preachings (besides his love of preaching anywhere and everywhere, as Lamb once told him), he explained to the "atheist reprobate" Thelwall: "Alas, I have neither money or influence, and I suppose, that at last I must become a Unitarian minister as a less evil than starvation." With this unhappy possibility in sight, Samuel addressed his Unitarian friends when in correspondence with them in a sanctimonious manner. Thus, when Flower at Cambridge lost a child, Samuel prayed for him to make "a sanctified use of your affliction," and "rolled his dreary eye from earth to Heaven"—much more followed in the same key. The dreary eye rolled from earth to heaven proved useful on at least one other such occasion.

But now, after Lamb, the expansive good-natured Cottle came to Stowey to see them, and he was enchanted with their way of life. Ecstatically he described his experience there: from Samuel's warm welcome and the tour through cottage and garden, consummated by a convivial scene with Poole and Coleridge in Poole's arbor, a scene that only Cottle's eloquence can fitly describe:

> After the grand circuit had been accomplished by hospitable contrivance we approached the "Jasmine Harbour." When, to our gratifying surprise, we found the tripod table laden with delicious bread and cheese, surmounted by a brown mug of the true Taunton ale. We instinctively took our seats; and there must have been some downright witchery in the provision which passed all of its kind; nothing like it on the wide terrene. . . .while the dappled sunbeams played on our table, through the umbrageous canopy. The very birds seemed to participate in our felicities, and poured forth their selected anthems. As we sat in our sylvan hall of splendour, a company of the happiest of mortals, the bright blue heavens, the sporting insects, the balmy zephyrs, the feathered choristers, the sympathy of friends, all augmented the pleasurable to the highest point this side the celestial . . . .While thus elevated in the universal current of our feelings, Mrs. Coleridge approached, with her fine Hartley; we all smiled, but the father's eye beamed transcendental joy. "But all things have an end."

Another visitor, a stranger who called about this time with some idea of living with the Coleridges, was a Richard Reynell, who arrived before Coleridge had returned from visiting Mrs. Barbauld, a popular poetess. Burnett, however, was there, and he introduced Reynell to the Wordsworths at Alfoxden. Soon Coleridge also arrived. Reynell found life in Stowey enchanting in its simplicity: "happy without superfluities," "domestic life in all its beauty and simplicity, affection founded on a much stronger basis than wealth—on esteem'' Sarah he admired: "indeed a pretty woman, sensible, affable, and good-natured, thrifty and industrious, and always neat and prettily dressed.'' Like Cottle, Reynell noticed Coleridge's affection for Hartley, "talking to him, and fancying what he will be in later days.'' But to Coleridge's disappointment, Reynell departed and did not return.

Thelwall, who had been particularly happy among the Stowey circle, now wished to live near them and asked Coleridge to find him a house. Although Coleridge acted with unusual determination and energy, he failed. For though Thelwall's arrest and imprisonment in the Tower and in Newgate on a charge of high treason were well remembered, his acquittal was forgotten. Protesting in late August at the political animosity toward Thelwall, Coleridge added: "The aristocrats seemed determined to persecute *even Wordsworth*.''

Thelwall's visit had, in fact, added fuel to the flames of suspicion already flickering about Coleridge and the Wordsworths, although they knew little or nothing of it. Political feeling ran very high at this time, for a French invasion was expected and mutinies had just occurred in the fleet. "We are shocked,'' Poole's acid cousin, Charlotte, wrote in her diary on July 23, "to hear that Mr. Thelwall has spent some time at Stowey this week with Mr. Coleridge, and consequently with Tom Poole. Alfoxden House is taken by one of the fraternity. . . .To what are we coming?''

That was the question many besides Charlotte were asking: "To what are we coming,'' with Thelwall and his friends settling in the neighborhood—Poole's friends, thought the villagers, must be dangerous Jacobins and atheists. Besides, Wordsworth, the man who had taken the large secluded house, had come from France, spoke French, had a woman living with him; his sister—of course—she would be! And a child with them! Yes, they agreed, Wordsworth was the worst, silent and dark, a desperate French Jacobin. The most damning fact about him was that he never mentioned politics! And Coleridge—the man who had so bewailed the death of Robespierre when visiting Poole—the Jacobin! And how extraordinary their behavior—wandering about the countryside by day and night, carrying camp stools, and making notes and sketches in books they carried, and walking a great deal by the river! They were, in fact, making notes of the scenery, and also of the river, which was to be the subject of a never-written poem by Coleridge. But Wordsworth, said the more charitable, might be merely a harmless smuggler! Indeed, one person had distinctly smelled brandy when passing the house, and was sure he had a still in the cellar.

From village busybodies to more important ones, the rumors spread, until the home secretary, the Duke of Portland, was warned of the dark deeds maturing at Stowey—"a very suspicious business'' with the villagers' damning details, from that of "the woman who passes for his sister,'' to the camp stools and notebooks. So, from the home secretary, the incriminating documents sped down Whitehall corridors to the permanent under-secretary of state, Mr.

King, who immediately dispatched a Home-Office detective, Walsh, to Stowey to unravel the mystery.

On August 11, 1797, Walsh reported his discoveries. A former servant at Alfoxden, whose unattractive but almost connotative name was Mogg, not only repeated the common charges, but added the damning fact that at Alfoxden they washed and mended their clothes on Sundays. Then, too, Mogg's friend of equally happy nomenclature, Christopher Trickle, who kept "the dog pound" at Alfoxden, had been asked by "the French people" if the river was navigable to the sea. They also kept no servant, had a number of visitors, "and were frequently out upon the heights most part of the night."

By special messenger this report sped to London, and the next day Mr. King, aroused by this alarming news, acted with great speed and energy. Walsh must "immediately proceed to Alfoxden," avoiding all "cause of suspicion to the inhabitants of the Mansion House there, narrowly watch their proceedings," but without alarming them, so that "they may be found on the spot." If becoming suspicious they fled, he must "follow their track," and if violent, he must get help from the local sheriff or magistrate.

Thus, by August 15, Walsh, quartered at the Globe Inn, Stowey, the nearest possibility to Alfoxden, and secretly listening to the villagers' talk, heard one ask the landlord "if he had seen any of those rascals from Alfoxden." to which the landlord replied that he had seen two of them the day before. Asked if they were French, he said, "No, no, they are not French, but they are people who will do as much harm as all the French can do." And Walsh believed, "This will turn out no French affair, but a mischievous gang of disaffected English men." The name of the tenant of Alfoxden, he had discovered, was "Wordsworth."

So the imbecile plot thickened, with messages and reports between Walsh and Whitehall; but unfortunately, the remaining documents in the case are "lost." Since Coleridge and Wordsworth knew nothing at the time, they were evidently never called to clear themselves of the suspicions. Long afterward in the *Biographia*, Coleridge gave his account of the incident, which, like some other things in that volume, is more imaginative than correct. Walsh, he said, had once crept up behind Wordsworth and Coleridge when they were discussing Spinoza, and had reported that he heard Coleridge call Walsh himself a "spynosy." Despite the poet's ignorance of Walsh's presence and errand in the neighborhood, the real smugglers there are said to have known it, and to have suspended their operations until after his departure. Doubtless Walsh soon found that it was a mare's nest, and he departed as quietly and suddenly as he had come. (Cf. E. K. Chambers, *Samuel Taylor Coleridge* [Oxford, 1938], pp. 80—82.)

The completion of *Osorio* in mid-October 1797 left Coleridge in a mood of emptiness, weariness and depressing consciousness of the play's defects. He felt also toward it that disgust which De Quincey described as the inevitable effect of opium to the addict's latest work. And at this time the presence of opium in Coleridge's life and work is evident in many ways. The passing of such a focus as *Osorio* for Coleridge's hopes, thoughts, and imaginings left no obstacle to the crowding fears and anxieties as to his means of support for himself and his family—fears that concentration upon his play had helped to keep at bay. He had, he said, "no hope of its success, or even of its being acted"; he felt, indeed, "an indescribable disgust, a sickness of the very heart," on hearing it mentioned, and "would rather mend hedges and follow the plough" than write another drama. Evidently by this time his recent agricultural enthusiasm was very dead.

Even amid his depression in the spring, he had heard

that divine and nightly-whispering Voice
Which from my childhood to maturer years
Spake to me of predestinated wreaths,
Bright with no fading colours!

This without undue modesty he had proclaimed in his verses to George. But now in autumn, that divine voice of the spring was silent. He bitterly complained of "having got nothing by literature" and that his fate was to become a Unitarian minister.

Restless, dissatisfied, unwell, looking to opium for consolation, Coleridge set out on a solitary excursion to clear his mind of the vapors and brighten his mood. He once remarked that some of his poems were "written after the more violent emotions of sorrow, to give him pleasure, when perhaps nothing else could." And thus it proved on this occasion; for when a day or two later he returned to Stowey, it was with a new poem, "Kubla Khan," in his pocket.

"A vision in a dream" in a "lonely farm-house," after taking opium and reading of Kubla Khan, a thirteen-century Chinese emperor; such was the substance of Coleridge's several accounts of the poem's origin. On waking, the whole poem, which he had composed in sleep, he said, remained in memory, and he had written so much down without hesitation, when he was disturbed by a caller, and could not afterward remember any more. Hence the uncompleted poem as it stands. Southey, acquainted like De Quincey with Coleridge's factual inexactitudes and opium habits, sarcastically remarked that "Coleridge had dreamed he had written a poem in a dream"—which may have been nearer to the truth than Southey perhaps believed.

Both De Quincey and the French poet Baudelaire, speaking from experience, described narcotic dreams, trances, or reveries, which closely resemble Coleridge's account of the origin of "Kubla Khan." De Quincey described his opium eater as "naturally seeking solitude and silence as indispensable conditions of those trances or profoundest reveries, which are the crown and consummation of what opium can do for human nature." And

Baudelaire speaks of "ce bouillonnement d'imagination, cette Maturation du rêve, et cet enfantement poetique auquel est condamné un cerveau intoxiqué par le haschisch."

Again in the real world of uncertainty and anxiety outside his dreams, Coleridge relapsed into a depression in which something of the opiate dreamy mood of "Kubla Khan" remained. It found expression in his letters in an abstract desire for "vastness" and "infinity"—the feeling he had absorbed as a small child during those night walks with his father who had spoken to him of the vast stellar spaces, and from those early fairy tales, which, he said, "habituated my mind to the Vast." He felt oppressed by an overwhelming sense of the littleness of things: "All things appear little—all knowledge that can be acquired, child's-play—the Universe itself—what but an immense heap of *little* things." He could, he said, "contemplate nothing but parts, and parts are all little. My mind feels as if it ached to behold something *great*—something *one and indivisible*." Only in this faith did natural beauty give him a "sense of sublimity or majesty! But in this faith, *all things* counterfeit infinity."

De Quincey, describing the sense of peace and calm, the lethargy induced by opium at one stage, said: "It seemed to me as if then first I stood at a distance, aloof from the uproar of life. . . .some sabbath of repose. . . .for all anxieties a Halcyon calm; infinite repose." That Coleridge was gradually emerging from such an experience his letters at this time strongly suggest. Losing a sense of spiritual essence in the universe, "I adopt the Brahman Creed," he told Thelwall, "and say it is better to sleep than to wake, but Death is the best of all!" He wished, "like the Indian Vishnu to float about along an infinite ocean, cradled in the flower of the Lotus, and wake once in a million years for a few minutes—just to know that I was going to sleep a million years more."

These, and similar remarks scattered through his letters and his notebooks both just before and just after the writing of "Kubla Khan" are full of the atmosphere of the poem. A few weeks before writing it he had expressed in his notebook his longing for "some wilderness plot, green and fountainous and unviolated by Man." In March of the following year, 1798, a letter to George shows how long this mood, these images (many first absorbed from reading), remained. A bad tooth and a bad dentist had troubled him, but, he tells George, "laudanum gave me repose, not sleep: but you, I believe know how divine that repose is—what a spot of enchantment, a green spot of fountains, and flowers and trees, in the very heart of a vaste of sands!" All this, I think, takes the reader nearer to the secret of "Kubla Khan" and its creation than any form of external analysis.

Early in November 1797, a mere three weeks after the walk from which Coleridge had returned with "Kubla Khan" in his pocket, he took the same walk with the Wordsworths. This time they continued to the wild, romantic Valley of Rocks, where Coleridge, still in a creative mood, suggested that he and Wordsworth should write a prose poem, "The Wanderings of Cain." Wordsworth, however, found the task impossible, and it was abandoned when

Coleridge had written the second canto in prose—a dull, horrifically supernatural tale, told in an unattractive mixture of the language of the Old Testament and Fossian, a wearisome, overdramatized production. Yet, in the eighteen lines of verse, in which Coleridge attempted to give the theme poetic form, something of the magic of this wonderful year appears:

> It was a climate where, they say,
> The night is more beloved than day.
> But who that beauteous Boy beguiled,
> That beauteous Boy to linger there?
> Alone, by night a little child,
> In place so silent and so wild—
> Has he no friend, no loving mother near?

For the exquisite moonlit nights of that season, which Dorothy also happily reports in her diary, here combine with Coleridge's deep, ineradicable pity for the "poor orphan" who was himself.

A few days later, on November 13 at half-past four in the afternoon, in dark and cloudy weather, Dorothy, William, and Samuel set off on another such walk. The thought of poetic collaboration with Wordsworth was still in Coleridge's mind, as well as the problem of meeting the expenses of their expedition. Since Coleridge had recently published some sonnets in the *Monthly Magazine*, he now suggested a combined poem to be sold to the editor for five pounds. For the first eight miles to Watchet, and in the evening there, they discussed the theme and treatment of such a poem. Coleridge, recalling the dream of a Stowey neighbor who had seen a visionary skeleton ship and crew, suggested the main idea. To this Wordsworth, who had just read Shelvock's *Voyages*, contributed the conception of a man's bringing upon himself the vengeance of the tutelary spirits of the region by killing an albatross, and added another suggestion, the navigation of the ship by dead men. But as with "The Wanderings of Cain," Wordsworth's attempt at collaboration broke down, and Coleridge continued alone until the following March, when he completed the poem. Thus was born "The Rime of the Ancient Mariner," the poem that has most preserved Coleridge's memory among a vast public, even to the present day.

This year at Stowey, with the inspiring companionship of William and Dorothy, was for Coleridge a wonderful year of lyrical-narrative inspiration, which never returned. "Half his time was passed in dreams," said Wordsworth after Coleridge's death.

In the *Monthly Magazine* for November 1797, Coleridge published a number of sonnets parodying the poetic mannerisms of several of his friends, including—as he told Cottle—Lamb, Lloyd, and Coleridge himself. Southey, rightly or wrongly believing himself to be ridiculed in the sonnet "To Simplicity," was offended with Coleridge, who, although apologizing, denied the charge. At the same time—employing what was to become his favorite Christian forgiveness technique, turning the tables upon an opponent—he told Southey: "I am sorry that I wrote them; because I am sorry to perceive a disposition in you to believe evil of me, and a disposition to teach others to believe Evil!''

Lamb, too, although apparently unresentful—if aware—of the parody of himself, was indignant for Southey, and said so. As the year 1797 died, so, too, apparently did the quarrel. At the same time came another disappointment for Coleridge and also one for Wordsworth: *Osorio* was rejected by Drury Lane and *The Borderers* by Covent Garden.

Despite this reverse, 1797 was certainly a wonderful year for Coleridge, not only for his poetic inspiration, but also for the pecuniary generosity he inspired in so many persons. Only eighteen months had passed since Poole formed his circle of annual contributors, and Coleridge received their first donations. It was only six months since Poole had raised their second response. But the forty or fifty pounds thus obtained were merely the curtain raiser to greater things.

Now, however, another well-wisher appeared: James Mackintosh, a well-known philosopher, politician, and historian, seven years older than Coleridge and, as yet, personally unacquainted with him.* Now, as one ''long an admirer of your genius,'' he wrote to Coleridge with great tact, kindliness, and deference, informing him that to be able to give him any assistance would be ''one of the greatest honours of my life.'' Unfortunately, not ''possessed of opulence,'' the best he could do for Coleridge, he said, was to inform him that his brother-in-law, Daniel Stuart, proprietor and editor of the *Morning Post*, offered Coleridge a guinea a week for contributions, although ''ashamed of offering so small a pittance.'' But if all went well, he ''would very gladly increase the salary.'' He also offered to ''urge the irresolute good nature of Sheridan'' to produce *Osorio*, and concluded: ''Suffer me to add that if by any means within my narrow power either now or hereafter I can show you in any degree my esteem for your virtue and my admiration for your genius, you will do me the greatest pleasure and honour by pointing it out.'' Coleridge accepted the offer, and from that time until his departure to Germany in the autumn of 1798 he sent an occasional sonnet to the *Morning Post*—but too sporadically to please the editor, Stuart.

Next, on Christmas morning 1797, an offer of £100 arrived from the two Wedgwood brothers, Josiah and Thomas, rich potters. Thomas had met Coleridge at Alfoxden in September, had doubtless fallen under his spell, and had heard of the Unitarian ministry as Samuel's impending fate. To save him for poetry and philosophy and from the Unitarian ministry, they had sent him this Christmas present, which he accepted, appropriately, on Boxing Day.

---

*James Mackintosh probably assisted in drawing the attention of the Wedgwoods to Coleridge, as deserving an annuity. It is said, however, that when Coleridge, on his return from Shrewsbury to Stowey in January 1798 paid a flying visit to Tom Wedgwood at Cote House near Bristol, he met Mackintosh there, in unfortunate circumstances. For other guests, bored by Coleridge's long philosophical monologues, which enchanted Tom Wedgwood, persuaded Mackintosh, well-known as a skillful debater, to dispute whatever opinions Coleridge expressed. This Mackintosh did so successfully that the humiliated Coleridge quickly departed. Whether true or not, it is certain that henceforth Coleridge showed bitter dislike of Mackintosh, on many occasions.

Coleridge, accepting it, said that it has relieved him "from a state of hesitation and perplexity" and given him the tranquillity and leisure of independence for the next two years." He was "not deficient in the ordinary feelings of gratitude," he added, but "would not find them oppressive or painful" if he were "acquiring knowledge for himself or communicating it to others," thus "contributing my quota to the cause of truth and Honesty."

So far all was clear and simple, and, so far as it went, satisfactory. But when a day or two later, through Estlin's contrivance, a pressing invitation to the Unitarian pulpit at Shrewsbury arrived, Coleridge was in a dilemma. The Wedgwoods' gift of two years' independence was, it seemed, incompatible with acceptance of this invitation; yet it meant security for life, and, except on Sundays, freedom. In this *embarras du choix*, Samuel wrote to ask Estlin's advice. Although his "heart had yearned towards the ministry," he asserted, conscientious scruples about some Unitarian dogmas had formed "almost insurmountable obstacles." He also asserted that he had delayed acceptance of the gift because of the doubts and difficulties of his situation, almost until the arrival of the invitation to Shrewsbury.

Estlin advised him to return the gift and take Shrewsbury. Samuel, choosing Shrewsbury—worth £150 per annum—as the better course, did so; but so cleverly that he captured both—indeed more than both. The letter of renunciation that he sent to Josiah Wedgwood, on January 5, 1798, was a masterpiece of its kind. In essence, of course, it was a superfine moral analysis and dissertation of which only the merest crude outline can be given here. He wished not to live a life of selfish isolation: "to preserve our moral feelings without withdrawing ourselves from active life." Rather than compromise in any "union of Religion with the Government," he would "undergo poverty, dependence and even death." But coming to practical considerations, he pointed out that even if he accepted their £100, "anxiety for the future would remain and increase," and to turn then to (journalism) would destroy "any delicacy of moral feeling," while to turn Unitarian minister would "warp the intellectual faculty." He concluded with a detailed account of all the material advantages that Shrewsbury offered—house, good salary, leisure, security for his family if he died, and exemption from military service. Thus he revealed to the Wedgwoods the magnitude of the sacrifice he must make if he accepted their mere £100. Hence he was being driven to accept Shrewsbury, despite his dislike of being "an hired teacher in any sect." The letter would have surprised Estlin!

To prevent any misunderstanding, Samuel, in a final passage, stated his minimum requirements for morally and intellectually regenerating humanity: "whatever is conducive to a man's real comforts is in the same degree conducive to his utility—a permanent income, not inconsistent with my religious or political creeds, I find necessary to my quietness—without it I should be a prey to anxiety, and Anxiety with me always induces sickliness, and too often Sloth; as an overdose of stimulus proves a narcotic." The thought of opium now was never remote.

This done, and having borrowed ten pounds from Estlin and five from Wade, Coleridge set off in mid-January 1798 to meet the Shrewsbury Unitarians. Mr. Rowe, the retiring parson, anxiously scanning each coachload of travelers as they arrived throughout the day but not finding Coleridge, at last returned dejectedly home, worried by the nonarrival of Coleridge who was to preach his trial sermon the next day. Even the last coach disgorged no clerical figure, only "a round-faced man in a short black coat (like a shooting jacket) which hardly seemed to have been made for him [evidently Poole's] talking at a great rate to his fellow passengers." Hardly had Rowe returned home, when the round-faced man in black entered, and dissipated all doubts as to his identity by beginning to talk. "He did not cease while he stayed; nor has he since, that I know of." Such was the description of Coleridge's arrival in Shrewsbury, written in later years of disillusion by Hazlitt, who was his enchanted listener when Coleridge preached the following day.

To young Hazlitt, not yet twenty years old, the preacher's voice as he announced the text "rose like a steam of rich distilled perfumes." As he prayed, it seemed "as if that prayer might have floated in solemn silence through the universe." Then Coleridge "launched into his subject—peace and war, church and state—like an eagle dallying with the wind." William Hazlitt, who had risen before dawn and tramped "ten miles in the mud" to hear the famous preacher, tramped home again, fascinated: he "could not have been more delighted" if he "had heard the music of the spheres."

Two days later Coleridge called on Hazlitt's father, the Unitarian minister of a neighboring village, and spent the night there. He enchanted young Hazlitt by his conversation and delighted his father. At breakfast a letter awaited Coleridge from the Wedgwoods, via Poole. It offered him an annuity of £150 without any conditions, strongly urging him to accept without "scruple or hesitation," and not give them "the real mortification" of a refusal. Having considered all possible candidates for the award, they had found that Samuel's "virtuous conduct" so far excelled that of the rest as to leave no doubt as to his claim.

Samuel's had been a long shot, but it had brought down the bird! "Coleridge," Hazlitt observed, "seemed to make up his mind to close with this proposal, in the act of tying on one of his shoes. It threw an additional damp on his departure."

Still fascinated, Hazlitt walked six of the ten miles back with Coleridge, who continued talking all the way, to Hazlitt's delight. Hazlitt also noticed his habit of "continually crossing me on the way by shifting from one side of the footpath to the other," seeming "unable to keep on in a straight line." To Hazlitt's surprise and joy, Coleridge invited him to visit him soon at Stowey. "On my way back," wrote Hazlitt, many years later when his youth's idealized vision of Coleridge had faded: "I had a sound in my ears—it was the voice of Fancy; I had a light before me—it was the face of Poetry." Throughout that winter one thought dominated all others in Hazlitt's mind: "I was to visit Coleridge in the Spring."

Since Mr. Rowe left Shrewsbury at once to find a house in Bristol and assist Estlin there, Coleridge was forced to take two more Sunday services and did not leave Shrewsbury until the end of January. The congregation, though small, was "cowed into vast respectfulness—but one shrewd fellow remarked that he would rather hear me *talk* than *preach*." The townspeople, "hot-headed aristocrats," were "dressy and fond of expense and the women very handsome." Had he remained, he was sure that they "would have behaved kindly and respectfully," but he "would have been plunged in a very maelstrom of visiting, with all its pomps and vanities, the mania of the place." Indeed, he quickly found that the minister there would have no such leisure and isolation as he had imagined: two sermons to prepare each week, many letters to write, "invitations to dinner, tea and supper, in each day, and people calling in, and I forced to return morning calls, every morning"; he could do nothing for the *Morning Post*. So ran Coleridge's account of his short ministry in Shrewsbury.

Coleridge's acceptance of the annuity was as dignified as his previous acceptance of the £100. He did not say like Hazlitt that he accepted the annuity before he got his shoes on—far from it—"It came upon my mind with such suddenness, that for a while I sat and mused on it with scarce a reference to myself, and gave you a moral approbation almost wholly unmingled with those personal feelings which have since filled my eyes with tears. I accept your proposal. . . .in the same worthy spirit in which you made it," and in the "hope that at some future period I shall have given a proof that as your intentions were eminently virtuous, so the action itself was not unbeneficent."

To his intimate friends Samuel at once announced, in ways suited to each, his good fortune, and to Shrewsbury he returned the payment for his visit, telling them of his withdrawal from the candidacy there. But the worthy inhabitants returned the money with an appreciative letter of regret, after his decision, finding in his refusal of payment "a fresh proof of those elevated sentiments which must add to our regret for the disappointment." Estlin, who wished Samuel to drop the annuity and stick to the pulpit, was shocked and disappointed. Poole, who read and forwarded the annuity letter, had at once urged acceptance with many and long arguments, believing "such benevolence the only pledge of our perfectibility." On hearing of Samuel's acceptance, Poole dashed to a party in town, was so cheerful, agreeable, and witty and sang so well, he told Coleridge, that everyone congratulated him without knowing the cause, though "joy beemed from every feature and action." Wordsworth's comment on the annuity a month later to a friend was the most intelligent, though prophetically pessimistic: "No doubt you have heard of the munificence of the Wedgwoods towards Coleridge. I hope the fruit will be good as the seed is noble."

Such was the climax of Coleridge's "Wonderful Year" with its wonderful verse and wonderful annuity: truly an "*annus mirabilis*," as it has been called.

Coleridge, preaching at Shrewsbury during the first days of 1798, was much missed by the Wordsworths, especially by Dorothy, then twenty-six years of age. She had been fascinated by Coleridge on first meeting him at Racedown. Like William, she had gladly moved to Alfoxden the previous July to be near Samuel. On January 3, 1798, when William and Dorothy returned to Alfoxden after a short visit to London, Coleridge had not come back to Stowey. In London on first meeting Southey, Dorothy had thought that although his "talents were certainly very remarkable," they were "much inferior to those of Coleridge."

Despite the unfortunate disappearance of much of Dorothy's *Journal* at this time, what remains unconsciously reveals an unusual mood in her, of restlessness and discontent, as, alone or with William, she wanders through the woods around Alfoxden, or watches the crescent moon, or Jupiter and Venus in a clear sky. The camaraderie, the deep affection of brother and sister, was a perfect sharing, even to gathering sticks together in the wood.

As January waned and no Coleridge appeared, Dorothy's discontent evidently increased. On January 27 even a walk with William proved "upon the whole an uninteresting evening." Similarly "uninteresting" was a walk three days later "to the blacksmith's and the baker's," despite William's exciting discovery of a "singular appearance about the moon." Seldom did Dorothy's interest turn definitely botanical, but one cold day, warmly sheltering under "the hollies, capriciously bearing berries," she asked herself: "are the male and female flowers on separate trees?" February came, but still no Coleridge. The evening was blusterous, but a "full moon rose in uncommon majesty over the sea," and Dorothy "sat with the window open an hour in the moonlight."

Two days later Coleridge reappeared, and the weather and the mood of the diarist visibly brightened: "February 3rd. A mild morning, the windows open at breakfast, the redbreasts singing in the garden. Walked with Coleridge over the hills. . . . never saw such a union of earth, sky and sea. . . . Returned to dinner at five o'clock. The moonlight still and warm as a summer's night at nine o'clock." The next morning, to Dorothy walking with Coleridge, everything spoke of spring: "the young lasses in their summer holiday clothes—mothers with their children in arms, and the little ones tottering by their side, midges spinning in the sunshine, the songs of the lark and redbreast, daisies upon the turf, the hazels in blossom; honeysuckles budding."

When sometimes Coleridge failed to appear at Alfoxden, Dorothy's interest waned, as before his return. It was thus on February 24 when, although sitting with William on their favorite hilltop overlooking the sea, she found the landscape only "mildly interesting." When on the following day Coleridge did not appear, Dorothy "lay down in the morning. Though the whole day was very pleasant, and the evening fine, we did not walk." But the next day Coleridge came, and she walked with him "nearly to Stowey, after dinner. A very clear afternoon. We lay sidelong upon the turf, and gazed on the landscape till it melted into more than natural loveliness. . .Walked to the top of a high hill to see a fortification. Again sat down to feed upon the prospect. . . .On our return, Jupiter and Venus before us." Surely Venus was in the ascendant. When exactly, one wonders, did Coleridge note in his private record: "Such light as Lovers love—when the waxing Moon steals in behind a black cloud, emerging soon enough to make the Blush visible, which the long kiss had kindled."* The note of reality is evident, "Who," one may ask, "was its inspiration?" Certainly not Mrs. Coleridge, away in her Stowey cottage expecting the birth of baby Berkeley, while little Hartley played near her. Perhaps the lost pages of Dorothy's diary could answer this question. Whatever the answer, these were certainly halcyon days for Dorothy and Samuel—such as they were never to know again.

Already their happy days at Alfoxden were numbered. On March 5 they heard that the owner of Alfoxden, Mrs. St. Albyn, having learned of the government spy and the Wordsworths' terrible doings, refused to renew the lease, which expired on Midsummer Day 1798. The Wordsworths' political reputation prevented any hope of obtaining another house near Stowey, and an inevitable separation threatened the Wordsworths' companionship with Coleridge. "The hills and the woods and the streams and the sea, and the shores would break forth into reproaches against us if we did not strain every nerve to keep their poet among them," Coleridge told Cottle, adding: "Without joking and in serious sadness, Poole and I cannot endure to think of losing him." "And Dorothy," he might have added.

From March 9 to 18 the Coleridges stayed with the Wordsworths at Alfoxden, and Dorothy's entries in her journal were, as she said, "neglected." But her walks with Samuel continued. On March 23 Coleridge dined again at Alfoxden—a notable occasion, for as Dorothy recorded: "He brought his ballad ["The Ancient Mariner"] finished." Coleridge's companionship with the Wordsworths had assisted poetic composition, particularly Wordsworth's example. In February Coleridge had written two of his finest poems, yet they were widely divergent in subject: the exquisite reflective poems, "Frost at Midnight," and his great "Recantation," as he first named it—his ode, "France," in which upon the French invasion of Switzerland, he recanted his Francophilism and transferred the spirit of liberty to the beauty and power of nature.

Religion, generally linked with his political and philosophical ideas, was much in Coleridge's mind at this time. To his brother George, on March 10, he wrote a long and interesting letter of this kind, which was perhaps more particularly inspired by his wish to obtain an invitation to Ottery than by abstract veracity. At any rate, it expressed a surprisingly close kinship of opinions with those of the politically and theologically orthodox clerical, George. What his reception was, when early in April he visited Ottery, is not known. On April 18

*The editor of Coleridge's notebook dates the entry indefinitely as 1779-1802.

he was back at Alfoxden dining and walking with his friends again. During his absence Dorothy, probably hoping for news of Samuel, visited Mrs. Coleridge.

On May 16, two days after Berkeley's birth, the Wordsworths and Coleridge set off to walk to Cheddar, which they reached the next day, after spending the night at Bridgwater. The second night they spent at Cross, where Coleridge wrote a letter to Estlin, which Wordsworth, who went on to Bristol, carried with him the next day. Meanwhile Coleridge and Dorothy apparently returned to Stowey. But as all the remaining *Alfoxden Journal* is missing after "Slept at Cross," the rest of the journey and even the day of return are unknown.

Coleridge's letter to Estlin, delivered by Wordsworth, was as full of admiration and praise of the bearer as ever. "I have known him a year and some months," he wrote, "and my admiration, I might say my awe of his intellectual powers has increased even to this hour—and, (what is of more importance) he is a tried good man." Wordsworth's only fault in Samuel's eyes—at least when writing to Estlin—was his unorthodoxy: "He loves and venerates Christ and Christianity—I wish he did more." So on that subject they were, he said, "habitually silent."

Two or three days after Coleridge's return from Cheddar, Hazlitt arrived for his promised visit in the spring. Coleridge at once took him to Alfoxden, but William had not yet returned from Bristol, and only Dorothy was there. They stayed the night, and Hazlitt read some of the *Lyrical Ballads*, Wordsworth's and Coleridge's latest poetry, in manuscript. After breakfast the next morning they continued to read them as they sat on the trunk of an old tree in the park, and Hazlitt felt "the sense of a new style and a new spirit in poetry." As Coleridge and Hazlitt walked back to Stowey that night, Coleridge talked continuously of Providence and kindred subjects, which included Wordsworth's weaknesses in his poems on simple human beings. These Samuel thought too "corporeal and matter-of-fact" for verse. But, said Coleridge, Wordsworth's philosophical poetry "had a grand and comprehensive spirit in it."

The next day Wordsworth arrived from Bristol and called at Coleridge's before going on to Alfoxden. This also seems to have been the occasion of Cottle's second visit to Alfoxden, but if so, it is strange that Hazlitt does not mention him. Yet in any case, Cottle's visit, even if a little later, must have occurred before Hazlitt's departure on June 10. Whether then or some days later—which is improbable—Cottle, yielding to the repeated and pressing invitations of both Wordsworth and Coleridge, who wanted their *Lyrical Ballads* published, drove Wordsworth down from Bristol—according to Cottle's own dramatic account—in a gig that also carried a cheese and a bottle of brandy for the frugal dinner they were to have with Coleridge on arrival at Alfoxden. But on the way a tramp stole the cheese. When they unharnessed the horse, the bottle of brandy fell, was broken, and its contents lost. Nor could William or Samuel or Cottle get the horse's collar off. Coleridge suggested that the horse was ill and had a swollen neck. But the servant girl arrived, turned the collar round, and, to the amazement of the three spectators, quietly removed it.

Hazlitt has left an unforgettable account of his first sight of Wordsworth, the "gaunt Don Quixote-like" figure, "quaintly dressed in a brown fustian jacket and striped pantaloons," the rolling, lounging gait, the "severe, worn pressure of thought about his temples, the fire in his eye, the intense, high, narrow forehead and Roman nose, cheeks furrowed by strong purpose and feeling, the convulsive inclination to laughter about the mouth, the deep gutteral intonation" of the North. Sitting down in the Stowey cottage, Wordsworth "instantly began to make havoc of the half of a Cheshire cheese on the table," and said triumphantly that "his marriage with experience had not been so unproductive as Mr. Southey's in teaching him a knowledge of the good things of this life." The next day Hazlitt and Coleridge went to Alfoxden, and Wordsworth read "Peter Bell" to them in the open air. Hazlitt noticed in the reading by both poets "a chaunt which acts as a spell upon the hearer and disarms the judgement."

There was, of course, during the three weeks of Hazlitt's stay, much walking and talking between Alfoxden and Stowey. There were talks and drinks in Poole's jasmine arbor, which had so delighted Cottle the previous year, and Coleridge and Hazlitt, accompanied by a Stowey native, John Chester (also fascinated by Coleridge), took the favorite walk to Lynton and the Valley of Stones. Chester, the silent, stolid, bowlegged peasant, following Coleridge with doglike devotion although he could not understand his conversation, attracted Hazlitt's attention and even sympathy. Yet "of the three," Hazlitt wrote in later years, "had I to choose during that journey, I would be John Chester." As they loitered by the sea, a fisherman described the failure of their attempt to save a boy from drowning on the previous day. When Coleridge expressed surprise at the risk they had taken in the attempt, the man replied: "We have a nature to one another." This pleased Coleridge, and immediately inspired a dissertation upon "disinterestedness."

During Cottle's visit there was much discussion about the price for the copyright of their poems and plays. Finally, although refusing his offer of thirty guineas for each of their tragedies, Wordsworth and Coleridge agreed to thirty guineas for their joint volume of poems, to be called *Lyrical Ballads*. They insisted at the same time that it should be published anonymously. "Wordsworth's name is nothing;—to a large number of persons mine *stinks*," Samuel genially informed Cottle on May 28.

By this time the Wordsworths and Coleridge were planning to go to Germany when the lease of Alfoxden expired on Midsummer Day 1798. When the first news of this expulsion reached them in March, Coleridge proposed "a delightful scheme," as William called it, that they all, even including Sarah and the family, should go to Germany for two years to study the language and "natural sciences." To this end, money from Cottle was needed. To obtain it Cottle had been invited to Alfoxden and induced to buy *Lyrical Ballads*. Continually during these last months at Alfoxden the plan for Germany was discussed. Coleridge had long hoped to learn German at a German university by getting publishers to finance him on his promise to translate Schiller's works for them afterward. Now with the Wedgwoods' pension, the plan seemed possible. The Wordsworths, too, were enthusiastic—particularly Dorothy, who was delighted to learn that in this way Coleridge would not be separated from them when they left Alfoxden. Besides, life in Germany was cheaper than in England, Dorothy declared, somewhat prematurely, and translations "the most profitable of all works." In that, she said she could do almost as well as William.

As June advanced, the restlessness of approaching departure infected all. On Sunday, June 10 Hazlitt said farewell to Stowey. He left with Coleridge, who was to preach at Taunton that day and meet Hazlitt again that evening at Bridgwater. On the way Hazlitt asked him if he had prepared his sermon. To this Samuel replied that he had not even thought of the text, but would think of it as soon as they parted. The next morning they set off for Bristol. There they parted, Hazlitt returning home. Not until two years had passed did they meet again; nor was there ever again for Hazlitt the enchantment of these first two meetings with Coleridge.

Coleridge spent the following day with Estlin, who "opposed my German expedition furore perreligioso, amicissimo furore." The next day Samuel called on Poole's friend Samuel Purkis, also a tanner, at Brentford. He liked both him and his wife and was driven by Purkis part of the way to Stoke d'Abernon, where Josiah Wedgwood had "a noble house in a rich pleasant country." Josiah received him with "joy and affection." On the third day there, however, Josiah became so worried about his wife's health that he took her to Dr. Beddoes in Bristol, leaving Coleridge with his brother Tom. With Tom, Coleridge passed the time "metaphysicizing so long and closely" that even Samuel became "a caput mortuum, merelees and residium." On June 18 Coleridge left for London, and he was back in Stowey when the Wordsworths quitted Alfoxden on June 25. From Alfoxden William and Dorothy went directly to the Coleridges' to spend a week with them before leaving for Bristol on July 2.

The harsh noises in the Bristol streets intensified Dorothy's distress at the loss of "the sweet sounds of Alfoxden." "I have not often felt more regret than when we quitted Alfoxden," Dorothy told her aunt, "I should however have felt much more if we were not likely in so short a time to have again the pleasure of Coleridge's society, an advantage which I prize the more, the more I know him." After a week with Cottle, William and Dorothy made a few days' walking tour along the banks of the Wye, during which William wrote his famous "Lines Composed a Few Miles above Tintern Abbey."

By August 3, when Coleridge, too, had just arrived in Bristol, his intention to take Sarah and the children with them to Germany had been abandoned, as to do so he "must *borrow*—an important, perhaps an immoral thing." This, with sublime innocence, he told Poole. "I guess Mrs. Coleridge's wishes tend the same way," he added, but for himself, the German plan was obligatory:

"of high importance" to both his "intellectual utility and moral happiness." Instead of his wife and family, the devoted yokel Chester would accompany him. One evening Coleridge suddenly suggested to the Wordsworths another "dart to Wales," this time to visit Thelwall who had a farm at Liswyn-on-Wye. At six o'clock the next morning they set off. "A very pleasant tour," Wordsworth described it, and even forty years later recalled Thelwall's "pleasant abode on the banks of the Wye."

Coleridge then returned to Stowey, while Dorothy and William, after superintending the printing of *Lyrical Ballads* in Bristol, went to London via Blenheim and Oxford on August 27. In London, before September 10, Coleridge joined them and made some useful calls, again including Mrs. Barbauld. He also called on a bookseller and publisher, Joseph Johnson, whom he persuaded to print a pamphlet containing "Fears in Solitude," "France," and "Frost at Midnight." On his first call, said Coleridge, Johnson received him "civilly," on his second, "cordially," and on a third visit wept when saying farewell, and Samuel departed with an order for thirty pounds upon Johnson's Hamburg agent.

On September 14 the Wordsworths, Coleridge, and Chester took the London stagecoach to Yarmouth, which they reached the following day. Samuel had "some long conversations" with Burnett, who was now a Unitarian minister there. The next morning, September 16, 1798, they sailed for Hamburg.

9 Germany (1798-99)

"I look back on my first sojourn in Germany and at a German University, as on a spot of sunshine in my past life."
—*Coleridge to James Gillman, Jr., August 10, 1829*

Their vessel, bound for Cuxhaven, left Yarmouth that Sunday morning, September 16, 1798, at eleven o'clock; and as the English coast faded away, Coleridge's domestic emotions kindled. He would return, he wrote to Sarah, "with an intenser affection, a proud nationality made rational by my own experience of its superiority." He also saw his "dear, dear babies as distinctly as if they had at that moment died and were crossing me in their road to Heaven!" An unhappy omen, for Berkeley he never saw again.

Nevertheless, far from being depressed while the Wordsworths and Chester were confined by sickness to their cabins, Samuel, "neither sick nor giddy but gay as a lark," as he told Sarah, remained on deck. In his letters to her and to Poole he wrote with the detailed realism so characteristic of him on such occasions, avoiding none of the physically unpleasant aspects of the voyage, from the stench of the bilge water to the "green and yellow specimens of the inner man" in passengers' basins.

Despite his clerical appearance, "all in black with large shoes and black worsted stockings," a party of three drunken Danes seized upon him as he lay asleep on the deck and made him "sit down and drink with them," which Samuel was evidently ready to do. Mistaking him for a priest they called him "Doctor Tology," until he told them he was no priest but "un philosophe." His philosophy he at once demonstrated by "drinking some excellent wine, devouring grapes and part of a pineapple—

Good things I said, good things I eat,
I gave them wisdom for their meat—

and in short time became their idol."

Soon Coleridge was their leading spirit, yet occasionally he remembered his "poor friends below, who in all the agonies of sea-sickness heard us most

145

distinctly shouting, singing, laughing, fencing, dancing country dances—in a word, being Bacchanals.'' Thus, in joking, ''dancing all together a kind of wild dance on the deck,'' in eating and drinking, the two days at sea passed gaily enough for them. A Dane, who was a Deist, surprised and disappointed to find the ''philosophe'' a Christian, retired to his cabin in temporary disgust. Coleridge, wrapped in his new overcoat, of which he was very proud—''a weighty, long high-caped, respectable rug''—lay down in one of the boats, and in poetic mood watched the stars and the foam flakes ''full of stars of flame,'' until he fell fast asleep. Soon rain drove him into the stinking cabin—or, as he expressed it to Sarah, he ''descended into Hell and rose again.''

His eye for character was as keen as ever. Amid all their revelry he noted sardonically his companions' ridiculous qualities—their mispronunciations, bad grammar, too affectionate attitudes toward himself, and other absurdities. ''This day enriched me with character,'' he told Sarah, ''and I passed it merrily.'' He promised to describe each of them to her, and he did so without fear or restraint, even of his own riotous behavior. Indeed, the full and frank and affectionate letters he now sent Sarah not only suggest a real intimacy with her such as Reynell had observed at Stowey but also cast doubt upon the extreme conventionality and fear of impropriety of which Samuel was soon to accuse her. To so priggish, humorless, and straightlaced a wife as Coleridge later described her no intelligent husband would have sent letters of such Bohemian jollity as these. Rather, they remind one of the girl who by her association with the godless, Jacobinical, free-love pantisocrats, had braved the censure of the ''respectable'' at Bristol, Clevedon, and Stowey.

Certainly at this time nothing is more conspicuous than Samuel's affectionate expressions in his letters to her. ''Good night my dear, dear Sara!'' he wrote in his first letter. ''Every night when I go to bed and every morning when I rise, I will think of you with yearning love, and of my blessed babies. Once more, my dear Sara; good night.'' Again and again from Germany he sent her such, and stronger expressions of his affection. True, she was absent, and with Samuel absence ever made his heart grow fonder.

But they were not at any rate empty words. ''The sky and colours of the clouds,'' he told her later, writing at eleven at night on arrival in Hamburg, ''are quite English, just as if I were coming out of T. Poole's, homeward with you in my arm.''

On Tuesday morning they reached the mouth of the river Elbe. As they entered the river and left the open sea and its dangers behind, Coleridge again felt what seemed to him the appropriate emotions, as when he left England. He ''thanked God for my safe voyage, and thought most affectionately with many tears of my wife and babies, and of my friend [Poole]—and of my friend at Bristol.'' But his bacchanalian companions dragged him away from the letter to Sarah: ''The noisy passengers swear in all their languages with drunken hiccups [sic] that I shall write no more—and I must join them. Indeed they present a rich feast for the dramatist.''

''Wordsworth shockingly ill, his sister worst of all—vomiting and groaning unspeakably,'' he told Sarah. But at last the rolling of the ship ceased as they proceeded and the Wordsworths appeared on deck. Dorothy was surprised to find the banks of the Elbe invisible so that the river appeared to her "a still sea." "Oh! the gentle breezes and the gentle motion!" she thankfully exclaimed after the horrors of her illness and of the cabin. Thinking of her return to it that evening she shuddered and felt sick. In the early evening they reached Cuxhaven, anchored off the town, and, as Dorothy's journal recorded, her party "drank tea upon deck by the light of the moon."

Upon the emergence of the Wordsworths the bacchanalian revels appear to have subsided. That the Wordsworths had not been deaf to the general noise, indeed that Dorothy had been wearied by it, is shown by her appreciation of the contrast between her peaceful moonlight tea party and the noise of the passengers: "I enjoyed solitude and quietness, and many a recollected pleasure, hearing still the unintelligible jargon of many tongues that gabbled in the cabin. Went to bed between ten and eleven. The party played at cards, but they were silent and suffered us to go to sleep."

For ten guineas—which Coleridge happily remarked meant only half a guinea for himself—the ship's captain took them another sixty miles up the river to Hamburg, and shortly after four o'clock on Wednesday afternoon they anchored off the town.

Wordsworth had found a more respectable friend on board than Samuel's associates, a distinguished French émigré, M. de Lautre. With him Wordsworth set off to find a hotel. Meanwhile, Chester and de Lautre's servant guarded Dorothy and the luggage while Coleridge dashed off to present letters of introduction. These, he declared later, brought him "no real service" beyond "distant ostentatious civility": except for the brother of Klopstock the poet. Like Dorothy and William, Samuel found Hamburg first and last an unpleasant place: "an ugly city that stinks in every corner." Wordsworth, though quietly resigned, was yet more damning: "It is a *sad* place; I have no doubt this city contains a world of wood and honest people, if one had but the skill to find them." Coleridge, making his way through the "narrow and stinking" streets, found everything he saw in Hamburg interesting. The "ladies all in English dresses and in the newest fashions": the young men who looked like "dashing English Bucks." He stared through house windows at the people inside "drinking coffee or playing cards, and *all* the gentlemen *smoking* at the same time—something no English gentleman would do in the presence of ladies in those days.

Soon de Lautre's servant found him and led him to "Der Wilder Man," the best hotel they could find, but inferior. "Not of the genteelest class," thought Coleridge regretfully, for he had reluctantly declined to leave the Wordsworths and become the rich, drunken Dane's guest for board and lodging at the best hotel in Hamburg. Instead, although Dorothy had a room to herself, Samuel had to share one with Chester, and William had to find one at the "Sea-Man's Hotel." However, on reaching "Der Wilder Man," Coleridge found his friends sitting "drinking some excellent claret," and he joined them "with no small glee."

Coleridge and the Wordsworths met Klopstock the poet, who proved even more disappointing than Hamburg. Coleridge thought his forehead lacked "comprehension," his eyebrows lacked "weight," his eyes lacked "moral or intellectual peculiarity," and his "general countenance," lacked "massiveness." He also thought Klopstock's wig "ugly" and that his hair-powder made his face "look dirty." When he answered Coleridge's Latin in French—which only Wordsworth could understand—and said that he was not particularly interested in German poetry, and in English preferred Glover to Milton, their disillusion with him was complete. But seeing the old man's swollen legs and remembering that he was "the venerable Father of German Poetry, a good man and a Christian," Coleridge almost wept.

During their few days in Hamburg the friends passed the time in the usual way of free, unshepherded tourists in unfamiliar places. They wandered aimlessly about the streets, entered churches, ate in cheap restaurants. Undeterred by a bad and dear dinner in a French hotel, they went on to a French play—which was worse. To Sarah Samuel described his experiences in the usual detail, even to his surprise at finding no prostitutes in the streets, and his and Wordsworth's discovery a week later that a whole street was specially allocated to them. Nothing, indeed, escaped Samuel's eye. To Sarah he sent lists of prices, ranging from "a fat goose" to playing cards and sticking plaster—which suggest that Sarah was still thinking of coming with her babies to join them somewhere in Germany. The shops open on Sunday and the people working there "inclined" Coleridge to "a strict Sabbatism." Did he remember the Sunday clothes-washing at Alfoxden, which had so scandalized Stowey? He now reflected, with a return to his earlier pantisocratic attitude, "the rich *may* play and the poor must work." Of religion in Germany he was already highly critical, especially in Hamburg. Only the pastors and peasantry pretended to be infidels in other parts of Germany, he said, "but in Hamburg they are not irreligionists, only they have no religion." "What the Hamburg merchants may be," he told a friend eighteen months later in England, "I know not, but the tradesmen are knaves, scoundrels with yellow-white phizzes, that bring disgrace on the complexion of a bad tallow candle."

Quickly wearying of Hamburg and anxious to find a pleasanter and cheaper place of residence, his companions appointed Coleridge as their "missioner" to Ratzeburg, which Klopstock's brother recommended, with offers of introductions. So at five o'clock on Sunday afternoon, September 23, Coleridge set out on his "mission." For Dorothy his absence, as before at Alfoxden, was a dull, somewhat unhappy time. An hour before Coleridge's departure, William left by boat for Harburg in the vain hope of finding a cheap carriage for sale. He did not return until the next morning. Then the monotony was broken by a gargantuan dinner with Klopstock and his relatives at his brother's home. Dorothy disliked young Mrs. Klopstock's vanity and manners and was shocked by her *décolleté* dress—"N.B. much exposed," she recorded. William emerged from the party with an even lower opinion of poor Klopstock than before, and Dorothy had a bad headache that lasted until Coleridge returned on the 27th.

William seemed as out of sorts as Dorothy when Samuel, delighted with the success of his "mission," ran him to earth in an inn where William sat "out of spirits and disgusted with Hamburg and Hamburgers, and resolved to seek cheaper residence more to the south." So Coleridge described him. After dispatching Coleridge to Ratzeburg on his "mission," Wordsworth, without waiting for the result, had decided to go elsewhere. To this decision he adhered on the ground of economy, although Coleridge had already booked rooms at Ratzeburg for Chester and himself.

Poor Dorothy, whose expectation of being again with Coleridge had alone mitigated the pain of leaving Alfoxden, evidently tried to prevent the impending separation. When Coleridge went to Remnant, Johnson's agent in Hamburg, for more information and was reassured about expenses of travel, Dorothy, although with "still a bad headache," followed him to discuss the question. She was skeptical of any economy in William's choice of some place in Saxony; "God knows whether he will succeed," Samuel complained of William to Poole. But Poole, already growing jealous of Coleridge's admiration for Wordsworth, welcomed the news of their separation. They had both "done perfectly right," he said, "so there is an end to our tease about amalgamation, etc. etc."

Wordsworth's own reference to the separation in a letter to Poole written on the day he and Dorothy left Hamburg, after Coleridge's departure with Chester, was brief and indifferent: "Coleridge has most likely informed you that he and Chester have settled at Ratzeburg. Dorothy and I are going to speculate further up in the country."

Lamb, hearing of the parting, suspected disharmony and sardonically informed Southey: "I hear that the Two Noble Englishmen have parted, no sooner than they set foot on German earth, but I have not heard the reason—possibly to give novelists (moralists?) a handle to exclaim— 'Ah me! what things are perfect?'"

Although biographers—with less knowledge than we have today—have readily accepted Wordsworth's assertion of economy as the sole reason for this sudden and surprising disruption of the party and of the long-discussed plans for mutual companionship in Germany, it is difficult not to believe that other reasons also played their part. Travel is an acid test of friendship, especially in a foreign country. Then, too, Samuel's behavior on the ship must have opened his friends' eyes to hitherto unsuspected Bohemian proclivities in his temperament; nor was Wordsworth the kind of man to appreciate them, especially if fearing possible repetition of such antics elsewhere. Nor may he have been indifferent to Samuel's future borrowing propensities, already involving Chester.

More important perhaps was the close friendship of Dorothy with Coleridge—the married bachelor abroad. Perhaps even Wordsworth felt some jealousy, for his possessiveness toward his sister Dorothy was a probable even if unconscious element in the whole complex. Dorothy, as the only woman with the three men, was in those days in an anomalous situation, and

Coleridge himself later described the attitude of the Germans toward Wordsworth with Dorothy, as regarding "sister" as merely a cover for "mistress."
Perhaps above all Wordsworth wished for peace and quiet, including separation from the restless, temperamental Coleridge, so that he might compose the
exquisite "Lucy" poems, already fermenting in his creative imagination.

At any rate, on Sunday, September 29, the grand festival of St. Michael for
which Coleridge delayed his departure by one day, Dorothy "walked with
Coleridge and Chester on the promenade," while William booked his seat and
Dorothy's on the Brunswick coach. The next morning at seven o'clock she
heard Samuel cursing the postillion for overcharging as he and Chester set off
for Ratzeburg. Three days later William and Dorothy left in the Brunswick
coach to "speculate further up in the country."

During his previous visit to Ratzeburg Coleridge had as usual noted
everything of interest on the journey. Now he poetically summarized it:

We rode in wicker wagon with our goods
O'er damned bad roads through damned delightful woods.

On that first visit, too, he had made friends with the military governor at a
table d'hôte feast in honor of Nelson's victory at the Battle of the Nile. "The
colonel very attentive to me indeed—so were all," he complacently recorded in
his notebook, adding "I was half tipsy." Now, on this second journey, they
reached Ratzeburg before nightfall and settled in their lodgings, with which
Coleridge was well pleased. His window commanded an "enchanting prospect" of the town, woods, and lake. The "peaceful" house itself, the home of
a "worthy and learned pastor, a widower with five children, was in all respects
comfortable." After Hamburg he now felt as happy as "a little fish thrown
back into the water," or "a fly unimprisoned from a boy's hand."

Happily pursuing his German studies, he delightedly learned from the
children chattering around him as they laughingly corrected his mistakes.
Bürger was his preference among the German poets he read, and *Leonore* he
thought better in the original than in all English versions, which must have included the recent and popular one by Sir Walter Scott. "Bürger's wife," he
breezily told Sarah, "was unchaste, and he died of a broken heart. She is now
a demirep, and an actress at Hamburg! A Bitch."

Study never destroyed Samuel's strong social instincts, and at Ratzeburg
they found particular satisfaction. Amid the strong anti-French feeling of the
time, English visitors in Germany were most warmly welcomed, and
Klopstock's letter of introduction to the mayor of Ratzeburg established
Samuel, to his extreme delight, as persona grata to a crowd of local bigwigs.
"The Gentry and Nobility here," he told Sarah, "pay me almost adulatory attention." His vanity—his defense against the inferiority feeling for which he
blamed his school—now had full play. The courtesy he received as an
Englishman and fellow-countryman of Nelson he largely misattributed to his
ode "France": when another, grander victory banquet and victory concert occurred, still celebrating the Nile battle, Samuel basked in Nelson's reflected

glory. When the band played "Britannia Rules the Waves," as he entered the concert room he accepted it as an honor to himself. The military governor and mayor of Ratzeburg continued to pay him, he believed, "particular attention" at public gatherings, and with his innate dramatic instinct, responsive to every environment, grave or gay, whether amid drunken Danes afloat or haughty, provincial VIPs ashore, the ex-Jacobin now assumed an almost ambassadorial dignity, as a kind of self-appointed representative of England.

Naturally, in these circumstances Samuel's satisfaction with life in Ratzeburg was immense. No wonder he described it nostalgically long afterward as "a spot of sunshine in my life." To Sarah and Poole he proudly recounted his grand experiences—conversazioni, with "Counts and landrosten bowing and scraping" to him, and "countesses old and young" complimenting him on his German (which was weak) and on his nationality. "To be an Englishman in Germany is to be an Angel," he declared. But to be an angel was never Samuel's forte and he described these brilliant occasions as "stupid things enough." Temperamentally, he was happier in the less inhibited environment of the ship, which he had never found "stupid." But to Sarah and Poole his satisfaction at his new importance overflowed: "We are very well and very comfortable"—the "we," the sole very occasional reminder of Chester's existence.

Samuel captured the heart of a countess—"a very beautiful little woman," as he told Sarah—by writing a wonderful German sonnet that has, however, disappeared. The countess had also "what is very rare in Germany, perfectly white regular French teeth." She invited Samuel to her home to meet her husband and promised, "I will sing to you and play on the guitar and the pianoforte."

From the window of his room Coleridge could see the seven church towers of Lübeck, some twelve miles distant at the end of the lake. In October he took a boat down the lake to the "old fantastic town," and he found the churchs so attractive with their old pictures and wood carvings that he regretted being unable to "loiter" away a week among them. Before returning to Ratzeburg he pushed on to the little village of Travemünde on the Baltic.

After two months of fine weather, November brought "chill, misty rains." "The Lake looks turbid," he complained, "and the purple of the woods has degenerated to a shabby dirt colour." Soon, however, he found some compensation in learning to skate, and particularly delighted in the less personally active pleasure of being dragged across the lake in an "Ice-stool" by tow-skaters "faster than horses can gallop." He had, as ever, an eye for beauty; the frozen lake and snow-covered fields and woods seemed to him no less beautiful than in summer. "O my God! What sublime scenery!" he exclaimed; "one huge piece of thick transparent glass"; and when at sunset the lake looked to him like great pools of bright red blood floating in a yellow-green sea, he cried to the absent Sarah: "O my God! how I wished you to be with me."

With the coming of winter to Ratzeburg, balls and concerts became weekly events. As at Stowey he was "pressed by all the ladies to dance." Anxiously awaiting letters from home, he told Sarah: "If I could, I am in no dancing

mood.'' His Stowey lessons had apparently been a failure. ''I am very proud
to hear that you are forward in the language, and that you are so gay with the
ladies,'' Sarah genially replied ''You may give my respects to them, and say I
am not at all jealous, for I know my dear Samuel, in her affliction [Berkeley
had caught smallpox] will not forget entirely his most affectionate wife.''
Another obstacle to Samuel's dancing was his horror at ''a most infamous''
new dance, ''the Waltzen,'' in which ''partners embrace each other, arms
around waists and knees almost touching, and they whirl round and round to
luscious music.''

Amid such lascivious scenes Samuel contrasted the immoral Germans with
the moral English. ''There is no country on earth,'' he somewhat quaintly
wrote, ''where the married women are chaste like the English. Here the married men intrigue or whore—and the wives have their cicisbeos. I entreat you,''
he begged Sarah, ''suspect me not of any cicisbeo affair. I am no Puritan; but
yet it is not custom or manners that can extinguish in me the Sacredness of a
married woman, or quench the disgust I feel towards an adultress.''

Samuel's letters to Poole were as affectionate (though sometimes lachrymose)
as those to his wife. ''Tell my dear Sara that I am well, very well. Go to my
house and kiss my dear babies for me. My Friend, my best Friend, my Brother,
my Beloved. The tears run down my face. God love you.'' So ends his first letter to Poole. ''My spirit is more feminine than yours—I cannot write to you
without tears,'' he tells him a month later, and so on throughout his time in
Germany. Such being presumably Coleridge's emotions under normal conditions, any delay in the arrival of letters intensified his feelings, as before
Stowey, into pathological anxiety. Because of his excitability, both Sarah and
Poole agreed not to inform him when Berkeley caught smallpox until all
danger was over, and they were glad that Samuel was not home. Nevertheless,
when at last the news reached him he burst into hyperemotional ecstasies,
praising ''God the Infinite, my Babes are alive,'' weeping for a day as passionately as if they had been dead . . .''My dear Sara! my love! my Wife!
God bless you and preserve us. . . .I pant to be at home with you.'' On the last
day of 1798, Mrs. Coleridge, particularly conscious of her husband's absence
during this time of trial and anxiety for Berkeley, went with the two children to
stay with her own family in Bristol.

On February 6, 1799, Samuel and Chester left Ratzeburg. ''Calm and
studious, reading German as English,'' and in ''old German'' superior to most
at Ratzeburg, so he claimed, he had decided to combine economy and study at
the University of Göttingen. There, too, he would ''imperiously exclude'' every
interest except the writing of a life of Lessing—never to be written. This would
not only help to pay Samuel's debts but also cure ''the disease of my mind,
comprehensive in its conceptions, but wasting itself in the contemplation of
many things it might do. The journey to Germany had certainly *done me
good*—my habits are less irregular; and my mind more in my own power. But I

have much still to do." Surely so promising a report, coupled as it was with a harrowing statement of debts, would loosen Poole's purse strings.

Traveling on the two coldest nights of the century, as he believed—"My God! Now I know what the pain of cold is and what the danger!" On the third day they reached Hanover, where through letters of recommendation, a baron introduced Coleridge to the local VIP's, even offering him a prince. But Coleridge, apparently overwhelmed, "deferred the honour"—yet carefully preserved the baron's card to show to Poole. Samuel's hotel bill, as inflated as himself, brought him to earth, made him realize the penalty of greatness, and forced him for the rest of the journey to eat where the postillion did, on cold meat for fourpence, and on coffee and a biscuit for a penny less.

Their first acquaintance with Göttingen as they entered the city on February 12, 1799, was the sound of whips cracking as students noisily steered ladies over the snow in horse-drawn sledges. "Four very neat rooms" at 25/- per month," he told Sarah, were his new quarters there; "a damned dirty hole," he described them in his notebook. He now went into excruciating financial calculations, which ended in his suspecting that he owed Chester "five pounds, twelve shillings," with very little cash left.

After his grand friends at Ratzeburg and Hanover Samuel thought little of mere professors, and the internationally famous Professor Heyne seemed to him but "a little, hopping, over-civil sort of a thing" who talked fast and coughed incessantly. The next day Coleridge matriculated and met some English students who took him to a club of "first class students" including nobility and Englishmen. Women students, of course, did not then exist. But the club, he told Sarah, disgusted him: the "roaring, kissing, embracing, fighting, smashing bottles and glasses against the wall, singing." All were drunk but the two Englishmen and Samuel himself, who—surprising if true—"drank nothing." The scene was even worse, he said, than what he had seen at Cambridge! Above all he detested the men's kissings and embracings: "a most loathsome business," which the English were known to hate. Sarah, too, found their "jovial parties, their manners and their mirth excessively disgusting."

The deep depression that Coleridge experienced at Göttingen supports one student's assertion that he was taking opium there. His imagination, he told Sarah, "is tired, down, flat and powerless, and I languish after Home for hours together in vacancy; my feelings wholly unqualified by *Thoughts*. I have at times experienced such an extinction of *Light* in my mind, I have been so forsaken by all the *forms* and *colourings* of EXISTENCE, as if the *organs* of Life had been dried up: as if only simple BEING remained, blind and stagnant!" The reason was not solely homesickness; it was also surely opium and also his dyspathy toward the Germans. "Love is the vital air of my genius," he told Sarah, "and I have not seen one human being in Germany, whom I can conceive it *possible* for me to love—no not one. To my mind, they are an unlovely Race, these Germans!" It was then natural for him to make friends chiefly among the English students, who particularly noticed how affectionately he spoke of his wife, and also that he did not attend church.

Another of Samuel's disappointments was the continued silence of William and Dorothy since their separation. To his "great anxiety and inexpressible astonishment," as he told Sarah, "where they are, or why they are silent, I cannot even guess." Then came a letter from William (lost) and probably also from Dorothy. For six weeks they had been in Goslar, dull, dreary without society or other means of speaking German. They would soon leave the place.

Samuel in December sent them hexameter verses, to illustrate a discussion on prosody:

> William, my teacher, my friend! dear William and dear Dorothea!
> William my head and my heart! dear poet that feelest and thinkest!
> Dorothy, eager of soul, my most affectionate sister!
> Many a mile, O! many a wearisome mile are ye distant.
> Long, long, comfortless roads, with no one eye that doth know us. . .
> William my head and my heart! dear William and dear Dorothea!
> You have all in each other; but I am lonely and want you.

William's reception of the verses was not effusive: "I need not say how much the sentiment affected me." He could offer no opinion on the meter. Dorothy's letters to Samuel now are an unspoken echo of the last sentence of his verses—"I am lonely and want you."

Throughout that winter, while William, ill with nervous pains, immortalized Dorothy and memories of his early days amid the beauties of the English lakes, Dorothy's thoughts strayed to the contrast between her dull life in Goslar—"all petty trades people, a low and selfish race, intent upon gain." she told her brother Richard—and "Coleridge, in a very different world from what we stir in: all in high life among barons, counts and countesses." Her regrets at not going with Coleridge to Ratzeburg must have now intensified; so too, her desire for his "natural gladness." She also feared that the separation from Coleridge would continue after their return to England, knowing as she now did that William would return not to Stowey but to the region of his childhood, which he was now reliving in imagination—more real to him than Goslar. To lure Samuel to the beauties of the North, of which he knew nothing, Dorothy sent him the now famous passage from *The Prelude* just then written, describing William's love of skating on Windermere. To this she added the affectionately malicious comment: "You speak in raptures of the pleasure of skating. . . .In the North of England, amongst the mountains whither we wish to decoy you, you might enjoy it with every possible advantage. A race with William upon his native lakes would leave to the heart and the imagination something more dear and valuable than the gay sight of ladies and countesses whirling along the lake of Ratzeburg."

Still further to entice Samuel northward, Dorothy added the nutting scene from *The Prelude* and invited Samuel to come "wherever we finally settle," and with William "explore together every nook of that romantic country. . . .I would follow at your heels and hear your dear voices again." Before posting, Dorothy snatched a last line, unconsciously pathetic—"You will write by the first post. . .Farewell! God love you! God bless you dear Coleridge, our very dear friend.'' The depth, sincerity, and sadness of her feelings evade the concealment of her former reserve.

That during this winter of Wordsworth's nervous tension and poetic inspiration created by memories of early days and by his love for Dorothy there had come a crisis in their mutual affection seems probable. Dorothy's friendship with Coleridge had inevitably in some degree affected her love for William, and surely William's love for her; a rival in Dorothy's heart could hardly please the brother who wrote of her:

> Sister for whom I feel a love
> That warms a brother far above. . .
> Why does my heart so fondly lean,
> Why, but because to you is given
> All, all my soul could wish from heaven?
> . . . .
> My dear companion of my lonely walk,
> My hope, my joy, my sister and my friend,
> Or something dearer still, if reason knows
> A dearer thought, or in the heart of love
> There be a dearer name.

Why, one wonders, of Coleridge's two surviving letters to Wordsworth at this time, had all been deleted save twelve lines expressing his admiration and affection for Wordsworth? As with the Alfoxden journal, a cautious censorship appears to haunt Samuel's friendship with Dorothy.

On Saturday, February 23—''a most delightful morning,'' said Dorothy—she and William left Goslar on foot for Nordhausen where they opened Samuel's latest letters and answered them. Dorothy's ''joy'' at seeing his handwriting again was so great that she ''burst open the seals and could almost have kissed them in the presence of the postmaster; but we did not read a word until we got to the inn, where we devoured them separately for at least two hours. . . .God bless you dear, dear Coleridge.''

William's reply, a contrast to Dorothy's, was formal, at times even subacid. To Coleridge's wish that they would come to cheap Göttingen, he replied: ''We must pursue a different plan. We are every hour more convinced that we are not rich enough [a sneer at the annuity and at Coleridge's chronic debts] to be introduced into high or even literary German society'' [a sneer at Samuel's boasts of his Barons, etc.]. All he and Dorothy wanted, he said, was a few people to talk German with. But ''as this blessing seems to be destined for some more favoured sojourners'' [another stab!], they must make the best of their lot, and would, weather permitting, ''saunter about'' for two or three weeks, ''at the end of which time you may be prepared to us in Göttingen. I do not say have the pleasure of seeing and conversing with you. There we can arrange everything respecting our return.'' He also [another stab?] ''wished not to be in debt when I return.''

Strangely formal, even unfriendly at times, Wordsworth's letter, like the

deleted ones, prompts speculation, however futile. But previous and later letters from William do lead to a suspicion that jealousy of Coleridge's annuity
and of his increasing friendship with Dorothy were affecting his attitude
toward Coleridge. One must not forget De Quincey's description of Wordsworth: "Whilst foolish people supposed him a mere honeyed sentimentalist
. . .he was in fact a somewhat hard pursuer of what he thought fair advantage."
De Quincey also spoke of Wordsworth's "masculine and Roman harshness."

Nor were Coleridge's comments on William at this time as reverent as usual.
"William seems to have employed more time in writing English than in study-
ing German," he told Sarah "No wonder! for he might as well have been in
England as at Goslar, in the situation which he chose, and with his *unseeking*
manners. His taking his sister with him was a wrong step. . . .Sister is considered as only a name for mistress. Still, however, *male* acquaintance he
might have had, and had I been at Goslar, I *would* have had them. But
William, God love him! seems to have lost his spirits and almost his inclination
for it." Wordsworth's expenses, he added, were almost less than they would
have been if he had stayed in England—"mine have been very great."

A month later in England, Mrs. Coleridge was plunged in grief by the sudden death of baby Berkeley in convulsions. "I wish I had not seen it," she told
Poole, "for I am sure it will never leave my memory." As before when
Berkeley caught smallpox, she and Poole agreed to keep the news from Samuel
for the present. "I will pass over all subjects with the greatest care," she wrote:
"for I well know their violent effect on him—but I account myself most unfortunate in being at a distance from him at this time, wanting his consolation as I
do, and feeling my griefs almost too much to support with fortitude." She was
indeed in unhappy circumstances, forced to depend upon Southey to arrange
the baby's funeral, and for his hospitality afterward at Westbury where he and
Edith were then living. Awaiting a letter from Samuel, she told Poole with
Grecian directness and simplicity, "I long for it—for I am very miserable."

Not until a month later was Coleridge informed of his baby's death. Then
Poole wrote to him, inculcating also academic, stoical consolation by exhorting him to remember that he still had Hartley, had lost nothing, in fact, as
Berkeley had not yet attained the age of reason, and Coleridge could have
more children if he wished! And, Poole concluded, he himself had had disappointments during the last month, "worse than the death of ten infants."
Poole can hardly have thus consoled Sarah, whose reaction to such argument
would not have been appreciative. Poole admired Sarah's self-control and emphasized it to Samuel: "She did all a mother could do. *But she never forgot
herself.*" Nor did Samuel when Poole's letter reached him in April. "I read
your letter in calmness," he replied, "and walked out into the open fields, oppressed not by my feelings, but by the riddles which the Thought of Death so
easily proposes and solves—never."

Ten days after Poole wrote, Sarah wrote to Samuel in a very different vein with the same unconscious pathos of sincere feeling simply expressed, with a kindness toward her absent husband that belies much of his later denigration of her.

My dearest Love, I hope you will not attribute my long silence to want of affection. If you have received Mr. Poole's letter you will know the reason and acquit me. My darling infant left his wretched mother on the 10th February, and though the leisure that followed was intolerable to me, yet I could not employ myself in reading or writing, or in any way that prevented my thoughts from resting on him. This parting was the severest trial that I have ever undergone, and I pray to God that I may never live to behold the death of another child. For, O my dear Samuel, it is a suffering beyond your conception! You will feel and lament the death of your child, you will only recollect him a baby of fourteen weeks, but I am his mother, have carried him in my arms and have fed him at my bosom, and have watched over him by day and by night for nine months. I have seen him twice at the brink of the grave, but he has recovered and smiled upon me like an angel, and now I am lamenting that he is gone.

Sarah's moving letter could only have been written by one with sensitive taste, deep feeling, and imaginative and literary ability in expression. Nor did Sarah ever overcome the sense of loss left in her by Berkeley's death. When in her old age her daughter Sara was collecting material for a life of her father (never completed), Mrs. Coleridge wrote on the back of this letter: "No secrets herein. I will not burn it for the sake of my sweet Berkeley." It is regrettable that so few of Mrs. Coleridge's letters to her husband have been preserved. They must surely have been even more interesting than her excellent letters to Poole, which have been published. Except for these, nearly all we know of Mrs. Coleridge comes from Samuel's references to her in his own letters to others.

Samuel's reply to Sarah's letter was, like that to Poole, an egotistic self-dramatization—a complete contrast in both spirit and expression to his wife's. Beginning with a long and very dull rhetorical sermon on immortality, he proceeded to sermonize her: "The few, the slow, the quiet tears that are shed are the accompaniments of high and solemn thought, not the workings of pain or sorrow." Indeed, he hoped that good would come of the baby's death, for "when in moments of fretfulness and imbecility [meaning, or course, Sarah's] I am disposed to anger or reproach, it will I trust be always a restoring thought—'We have wept over the same little one—and with whom am I angry?—with her who so patiently and unweariedly sustained my poor and sickly infant through his long pains—with her—who, if I too should be called away, would stay in the deep anguish over my death-pillow! Who would never forget me.' "

Perhaps Sarah was less consoled than Coleridge expected on reading the pompous little "Epitaph" on the death of *another* baby, recently written at the request of "an Englishman" with which his letter concluded. Hardly convincing, too, were Coleridge's verses that soon followed in reply to Sarah's

repeated wishes for his return. In one of these, he regretted he was not a little
feathery bird with two little wings, so that he might fly to her:

If I had but two little wings
And were a little feathery bird,
To you I'd fly, my dear!
But thoughts like these are idle things,
And I stay here.

Sarah, twenty years later, in a letter to Poole, recalled "many, many tender
and *some* very bitter recollections connected with Berkeley's birth and death,
sweet child! But I do not wish him here."

Whatever disappointments marriage to Samuel had brought her in the past,
now during the German adventure, came a greater one. Alone, without means,
forced, much as she hated it, to apply several times to Poole for aid: "until
Samuel makes some provision. Perhaps he may think I have enough to last until he returns, not knowing my situation." Week by week she anxiously
awaited his return, read his complaints of bitter homesickness, of a return
often announced but ever delayed—for Sarah a continual process of declining
confidence and respect. Mrs. George Coleridge, pitying her situation, kindly
invited her to Ottery, and Sarah appreciated the "very kind invitation."
There, troubled by the curiosity of some about her husband's changing and
complicated politics, she asked Poole's help. "It is very unpleasant to me,"
she wrote, "to be often asked if Coleridge has changed his political sentiments,
for I know not properly how to reply—pray furnish me."*

Late in April 1799 William and Dorothy "passed thro' and only passed
thro' " Göttingen wrote the disappointed Samuel who spent a day with
them and accompanied them five miles on their homeward journey. He
doubted William's ostensible reason for choosing to live in the Lakes instead
of in Stowey—the use of a large private library near him there. For
Coleridge well knew that Wordsworth was no great reader and probably suspected the truth—Wordsworth's memories of his happy childhood there, so
revivified and inspired at Goslar. So they parted again, "melancholy and
hypped," and William, said Samuel, was "affected to tears."

His discussion with William about living together in England Samuel
reported to Poole, who at this time, when writing to Coleridge, combined the
experienced wisdom of a somewhat anxious father with the tenderness of a
protective mother toward an absent and erratic son. Poole insisted upon the
learning of German as the overriding aim—"no poetry—no original composition," no talking in English, but he must make a strict arrangement of his time

---

*Mrs. Coleridge's use of furnish has been interpreted (wrongly) as an indication of illiteracy. In
fact, the word was often used in a similar way, by both Coleridge and Wordsworth, and was in
regular use by educated persons at that time. Nor was Mrs. Coleridge by any means the only person to be uncertain about the particular development of Coleridge's political opinions at any one
moment, as indeed her own question to Poole clearly shows.

and tie himself down to it. For Poole well knew Samuel's weakness. Yet Samuel reassured him: "I am very busy, very busy indeed!"—attending the classes of "several professors and getting many kinds of knowledge; but I stick to my Lessing."

As for the recent discussion with Wordsworth, Samuel informed Poole that he refused to go to the North, citing, as ever when it suited him, Sarah as an excuse for his decision: "The impropriety of taking Mrs. Coleridge to a place where she would have no acquaintance."

This he did not consider a year later, when, against her wishes, he took her there to live. But now Sarah and the expense of the move were "two insurmountable objections. Finally I told him plainly, that *you* had been the man in whom *first* and in whom alone, I had felt an *anchor*! With all other connections I felt a dim sense of insecurity and uncertainty, terribly uncomfortable." And ironically he referred to Wordsworth's excuse—"a library absolutely *necessary* to his health, nay to his existence."

Any rejoicing by Poole at the disagreement of Wordsworth and Coleridge would have been premature, for Samuel continued: "It is painful to me too to think of not living near him; for he is a *good* and *kind* man, and the only one whom in *all* things I feel my Superior." But he added, as balm for Poole, "my Resolve is fixed, *not to leave you till you leave us."* Coleridge also believed that his own fascination would bring Wordsworth back to live near him again. A few weeks later William—"right glad," as he told Cottle, to be back in England, "for we have learnt to know its value"—merely remarked of his last meeting with Samuel: "We left Coleridge well at Göttingen a month ago"—nothing more.

Meanwhile, despite Sarah's increasingly insistent appeals and his own promises to return, Samuel set off on May 11 with four of his English friends and a new disciple, the son of Professor Blumenbach, for the famous Brocken. Climbing the mountain, he discoursed to his companions on the Sublime and Beautiful, capping their extorted attempts at a definition of Sublimity with his own: "A suspension of the power of comparison." On the crest of the Brocken he gazed over the beautiful landscape and with tears in his eyes looked toward England.

> O dear England! how my longing eye
> Turned westward, shaping in the steady clouds
> Thy sands and high white cliffs! Sweet, native Isle,
> This heart was proud, yea, mine eyes swam with tears
> To think of thee, and all the goodly view
> From sovran Brocken, woods and woody hills
> Floated away, like a departing dream,
> Feeble and dim.

So at least he described himself in the Inn album at Elbinge. Nor was England the sole inspiration of Coleridge's emotional moment on the Brocken. For then, as "a gentle maid, our first and early love," the ghost of Mary entered his verse.

Since Coleridge's last meeting with the Wordsworths some resurgence of poetic ambition had occurred in him. But it led only to the discovery that, as he told Poole, "my poor Muse is quite gone." So, too, thought his friends, as he recited his attempts during their journey. They were a happy party nevertheless. Coleridge, some six years older than the rest, led and discoursed on the way, impressing them by his knowledge and talk but at times boring them with monologues.

Coleridge's gaiety and fun disarmed all resentment or wish to ridicule his failings, which included his evident vanity and his looking almost instinctively at himself whenever there was a mirror in the room. When quizzed about his slovenly dress he replied "with a singularly cockscombical expression of countenance," as one described him, that when he spoke his dress would not be noticed. Sometimes abandoning such metaphysical subtleties as the Sublime and Beautiful, or "The Essential Nature of Happiness," they found happiness itself in frolicking and singing for joy. A night at Blankenburg was merrily spent in singing patriotic English songs. And Samuel found "something inexpressibly charming" in the shocking waltz when danced by unsophisticated peasants showing "confident affection" instead of the "voluptuousness" it created "in the highest circles." Another of Coleridge's party, however, described the peasants' waltzing more realistically as being "in the true style, the man continually putting his leg between those of the woman, and his arm around her neck," while he smoked his pipe in her face. On Saturday night, May 18, they reached Göttingen again after a walk of thirty miles that day. Nor did Samuel's devotion to Lessing prevent another excursion shortly afterward, this time to the Hübichen-Stein.

Increasing debts now apparently synchronized with increasing homesickness and with increasing reports to Poole of intense study. "I read and transcribe from morning to night." had never before worked so hard as now, and *"my whole Being* so yearns after you, that when I think of the moment of our meeting, I catch the fashion of Germany Joy, rush into your arms, and embrace you—Methinks my Hand would swell, if the whole force of my feeling were crowded there. Now the Spring comes, the vital sap of my affections rises, as in a tree." To Josiah Wedgwood, already becoming suspicious of Samuel's devotion to study at Göttingen, he now sent an imposing report—of both aims and remarkable achievements in learning in many fields, linguistic and scientific, including the reading of high and low German, "the oldest German, the Frankish and the Swabian," physiology, anatomy, and natural history. He had also collected and read materials for a history of belles lettres in Germany before Lessing, and had made "very large collections for a Life of Lessing." This last has been his chief work at Göttingen, he said, and was to meet his expenses. All this led to a request to "anticipate for 40 or 50 pound" his annuity and to an incomprehensible financial statement in which both Chester and Wordsworth are included as his helpers.

On June 23, Midsummer Eve 1799, Professor Blumenbach, a physiologist and founder of the science of anthropology, gave a family supper of farewell for Coleridge, to which his companions on the Brocken came. The conversation in German was particularly lively and amusing, as one guest recorded. Coleridge was in high spirits and delighted the ladies as he talked away interminably, drawing from his pocket a little German dictionary from time to time when his vocabulary failed. "There was," wrote the guest, "something inexpressibly comic in the manner in which he dashed on, with fluent diction, but with the worst German accent imaginable, through the thick and thin of his subject." After midnight, as the day of Coleridge and Chester's departure dawned, Blumenbach's fascinated son sent Coleridge a sentimental note in German, which read: "When, dear friend, you admire Nature in your own country as we both did in the Hartz Mountains, you will remember the Hartz, and then I may hope that you will not forget me either. Farewell and happy journeying. Ever your Blumenbach."

At midday Coleridge and Chester departed on their homeward journey, accompanied by two of their English friends as far as Brunswick. All climbed the Brocken again on their way. But even to the last minute a tour of Denmark, Norway, and Sweden, proposed by Samuel, was delayed until some of his friends got permission from home. When it came these dashed off in a coach for Brunswick where they overtook the rest. A map was bought and studied; but Samuel's enthusiasm had now cooled and probably means were lacking. Finally, he deferred the tour until next spring. When it did happen, Coleridge was absent, and the tour was not a success. At Brunswick on July 3 Coleridge and Chester parted from their friends and by July 18 were again at Cuxhaven. There Coleridge was much distressed at the nonarrival of the box containing his clothes and thirty pounds worth of metaphysical books, not yet read but chosen as material for a dream magnum opus to which he meant "to dedicate in silence, the prime of my life." However, the box followed him to England, and before the close of July 1799 Coleridge and Chester were in Stowey again.

Of the inspiring hopes and projects with which Coleridge had gone to Germany he returned with little indeed to show. He knew little or no German when he left for Germany, and what he learned there was chiefly by conversation at Ratzeburg, not by definite linguistic study. The contemporary account of Samuel's farewell supper indicates some conversational ability in German when assisted by a dictionary. Too impatient to learn genders and inflections, Coleridge resembled the Latin students that Dr. John satirized, and "got his German from meaning, rather than his meaning from the German;" or as one critic more politely phrases it, "His comprehension of even involved philosophical argument is due to his power of grasping intuitively the larger units of sense, rather than to any knowledge of syntactical relations." His translations were often "free," and his philology often fanciful. "Nor," says the critic, "was his mastery of Old High and Low German as good as he claimed. . . .dabbling in these older dialects." As for his "very large collections for a Life of Lessing," all that has been found among his papers is a brief summary of a German summary of the standard biography of Lessing.*

Before leaving Germany Coleridge had some acquaintance with Kant's philosophy, whether in the original or in translation. He had also a considerable knowledge of Schiller, from whom he took the phrase "emotion recollected in tranquillity." This was used by Wordsworth in his preface to the second edition of *Lyrical Ballads*. Coleridge had not yet read Schelling. One later contemporary of Coleridge at Göttingen, named Benecke, asserted that when there, "Coleridge was an idler, and did not learn the language thoroughly." that he learned a long ode of Klopstock by heart, and declaimed it without understanding it, so playfully mystifying the English with the apparent rapidity of his progress.

When De Quincey's *Opium Eater* appeared in 1821, Benecke thought that it was by Coleridge, for he knew Coleridge took opium at Göttingen.

Whatever the visit to Germany achieved for Coleridge, its results were largely disappointing. His knowledge of German remained inadequate and his verse translations of German poetry were indifferent, both as translations and as English verse. Nor were his few original English poems of that time much better.

Such were the slender earnings from Coleridge's professedly arduous labors in Germany. The loss of the original poetic inspiration Samuel had enjoyed during "the Wonderful Year" seems to have been the most important and lamentable result of his absence from England.

Yet, looking back seventeen years later through the golden haze of memory to his German adventure, Coleridge wrote in his *Biographia:* "I made the best use of my time and means; and there is therefore no period of my life on which I can look back with such unmingled satisfaction." Later still it became for him "a spot of sunshine in my life."

*Much in this short survey of Coleridge's work in Germany is based on "Coleridge's Knowledge of German as Seen in the Early Notebooks" by Dr. E. M. Wilkinson, in *Coleridge's Notebooks,* ed. Kathleen Coburn (Princeton, N.J., 1957), 1:451-54.

10   Uncertainty (1799-1800)

> *"God knows where we can go; for that situation*
> *which suits my wife does not suit me, and what suits*
> *me does not suit my wife."*
> —*Coleridge to Poole, January 1800*

The twelve months that passed between Coleridge's return to Stowey in July 1799 and his departure with Mrs. Coleridge in mid-June 1800 to settle in Greta Hall were far from happy. For this there were several reasons, particularly the increasing disparity between Coleridge and his wife. Absence does not always make the heart grow fonder, and Sarah in her husband's continued absence had doubtless looked back with little satisfaction upon her four years of married life—years of hand-to-mouth existence, of poverty, of futile and ever-changing plans, and of ever-changing domiciles—the *Watchman,* Darley Hall, the school, the private students, the Stowey "farm"—all futile! And at Stowey there was virtual exclusion from her husband's intellectual friends at Alfoxden, where he almost lived, while she, sometimes servantless, did the housework in "the little Hovel" and attended to Hartley.

Not until six months after Berkeley's death had Samuel come back to her, despite her longing letters and his affectionate messages of homesickness promising an early return. For almost a year she had been left to face all the difficulties of life alone with her two babies, and had been forced to apply to her best friends, Poole and Southey, for help when little Berkeley died. Now, instead of the promised reward for her own sacrifices and for his important and abstruse studies in Germany, he had brought far less than nothing—overdrafts on Wedgwood's annuity and debts to his friends in Germany as well as in England. As for his year's arduous study, all he had to show was thirty pounds worth of metaphysical books bought for his great work—never achieved—and his pleasant memories of social life and excursion in Germany, which she could hardly be expected to enjoy. Perhaps worst of all, Samuel's chief excuse for the German spree, the famous life of Lessing, which he had told her in April "will of course establish my character for industry and erudition," and leave them "more than cleared" of debt, was proving a mere will-o'-the-wisp, like all the rest! Even his wonderful friend's vaunted *Lyrical Ballads* with some of her husband's poems "was laughed at and disliked by all," she was told.

Daughter of a man who several times had failed in business and had fallen from a good position into poverty, Sarah well knew the misery of such a life and had no wish to repeat the experience. From her unhappy childhood Sarah had doubtless, as if often in such cases, acquired an almost psychopathic fear of the failures and debts that her more Bohemian husband accepted as easily as he did the charities of his friends. Her middle-class pride also resented these as a bitter humiliation. In her eyes her husband was a failure: a man who could not or would not place family responsibilities first, nor achieve the poetical and literary success that he had often prophesied. Shortly after Samuel's return, his wife's anger must have increased when an attack on her husband, reprinted from the *Anti-Jacobin,* publicly accused Coleridge of having "left his native country. . . .his poor children fatherless and his wife destitute." Nor did Coleridge fulfill his threat to prosecute the paper for libel.

Coleridge, for his part, found his practical, middle-class wife unimaginative, "a philistin," more interested in worldly success than in poetic dreams or literary ambitions. Coleridge, on the other hand, was temperamentally unadaptable to the demands of the real world about him. Thus, below all lay a conflict of temperaments that permitted no compromise. Similarly, however unconsciously, working toward this estrangement of husband and wife was the close intimacy of Coleridge with the Wordsworths, which, while making Mrs. Coleridge feel an outsider, can hardly have raised her in her husband's esteem. Nor can one forget that a true mutual love had never existed between them. For the present, however, only the seeds of these sorrows were planted; the sad harvest was yet to come. By this time, too, Mrs. Coleridge must have been aware of her husband's addiction to opium.

Stowey, too, had lost its chief attraction for Coleridge—the companionship there of Wordsworth and Dorothy. Nor was this all. Even the faithful Poole, bitterly disappointed at Coleridge's failure to return from Germany with the materials of success as promised, was naturally less cordial, especially after the sacrifices he had made to help both Samuel and Mrs. Coleridge. Indeed from this time, though very gradually, Poole's appreciation of Mrs. Coleridge increased with the passage of the years, as that for her husband declined, until in later life it was to her alone that his letters and assistance were directed.

In these circumstances Coleridge's thoughts turned inevitably to help from friends and escape from Stowey. He, therefore, effected a reconciliation with Southey. Pleading for at least "the outward expressions of daily kindnesses" if they met, he described himself as "in declining health" and with "domestic afflictions hard upon me." This overcame Southey's reluctance. So in August Southey and his wife stayed with them in Stowey.

At once the two friends were talking, laughing, and writing at the same table as in their earlier days, while, wrote Southey, "the hours slip away, and the ink dries upon the pen in my hand." Lightheartedly, they jointly composed some would-be humorous verse, "The Devil's Thoughts," casually, as Southey described:

There while one was shaving,
Would he the song begin
And the other when he heard it at breakfast,
In ready accord joined in.

Before the end of the month both families visited Ottery and in early September went on to Exeter. Coleridge much preferred his family's "roast fowls, mealy potatoes, pies and clouted cream" to their "Church and King" politics. Southey was amused at the continual admonitions of old Mrs. Coleridge to Samuel when arguing with his brothers: "Ah! If your poor father had been alive, he'd soon have convinced you!" A five-day ramble with Southey around Exeter seemed "tame" to Coleridge after "Quantock, Porlock, Culbone and Linton."

Groundless fears that Hartley had caught the itch and given it to his parents with Samuel "bearing up against the FRESH of my wife's hyper-superlative grief on the occasion," as he sneered to Southey, chilled the return of the Coleridges to Stowey on September 24. Six days later the picture of the domestic atmosphere he sent Southey was both metaphorically and literally unpleasant: their "little hovel almost afloat, poor Sara tired off her legs with servanting," Hartley a nuisance, and the place "stinking of sulphur," which the local apothecary had prescribed as a disinfectant. Samuel himself was racked by rheumatism through not having changed his rain-soaked clothes.

Nevertheless, "sunk in Spinoza, as undisturbed as a toad in a rock," Coleridge himself was unaffected by his unhappy environment. A week later the "little Hovel" had become "Apollo's Temple in the odoriferous Lime Grove." His enjoyment in being such a "toad in a rock" he again described in mid-October to Southey, though still "harassed with the rheumatism. . . .My enjoyments are so deep, of the fire, of the candle, of the thought I am thinking, of the old folio I am reading—and the silence of the silent house, is so most and very delightful—that upon my soul! the rheumatism is no such bad thing." That was an attraction that increasingly dominated Coleridge's life and greatly helped to change his direction from poetry, creative art, to academic studies. In time it was to be no less opiate than the drug that often accompanied it.

From Stowey on October 15, 1799, after a short visit to Josiah Wedgwood at Upcott where Coleridge had been unwell and unhappy, he remarked to Southey in the course of a long letter: "The wife of a man of genius, who sympathizes with her husband in his habits and feelings is a rara avis with me." Sarah was to accompany him to Bristol for a few days, but he went alone, leaving her for weeks ignorant of his whereabouts. Then instead of going to London as intended, he suddenly dashed north with Cottle on October 22 to see the Wordsworths.

The Wordsworths were now at Sockburn in Yorkshire, a farm kept by old family friends, Tom and George Hutchinson. There, upon their return from Germany, William and Dorothy had found a temporary home. When Samuel and Cottle arrived on October 26, they found not only the Wordsworths and the two Hutchinsons, but also their sisters Mary and Sara, who helped their brothers to keep house. Samuel at once appreciated the frank Yorkshire cordiality of their welcome and thought: "Few moments in life are so interesting as those of our affectionate reception from a stranger who is the dear friend of your dear friend!"

The next day Wordsworth, anxious to find a permanent home for Dorothy and himself and no doubt also hoping to attract Coleridge by the beauty of the scenery to settle near them, set off with him and Cottle on a walking tour of the Lake District, nearby. On the third morning Cottle departed for London, and his place was taken for a day or two by Wordsworth's sailor brother John who was then on holiday. On reaching Grasmere, its beauty so enchanted William that he decided to make their home there.

From Keswick Samuel wrote to Dorothy of his delight in the new, strange scenery: "the divine Sisters, Rydal and Grasmere," the ascent of Helvellyn "on a day when light and darkness coexisted in contiguous masses, and the earth and sky were but *one*, and Nature lived for us in all her grandest accidents. . .you can feel what I cannot express for myself, how deeply I am impressed by a world of scenery absolutely new to me. . . .Why were you not with us, Dorothy?"

At Keswick Coleridge also received and accepted an invitation from Stuart to come to London and work for a time for the *Morning Post*. For another week Coleridge continued his tour with William, leaving him on November 18 and returning to London via Sockburn, where he stayed a week.

Emerging from the London stagecoach at midnight on November 27, 1799, London seemed to Coleridge "a huge place of sepulchres, through which hosts of spirits were gliding." Stuart's invitation to write for the *Morning Post* had brought Samuel to London, and to Stuart he soon made his way. With Stuart, Coleridge's previous relations had been but perfunctory. The occasional verses he had promised Stuart at a salary of a guinea a week had come so slowly that Stuart had protested. And Coleridge had neither called on him when leaving for Germany nor sent him contributions when abroad, as requested. But since Samuel's return to England, he had sent Stuart an occasional poem.

Nor on this present occasion was Coleridge's servitude—as he soon regarded it—to the *Morning Post* of long duration. It was, in fact, a mere four months, from December 1799 to the end of March 1800. Throughout these months Stuart often called on Samuel to discuss the next day's article—or "paragraphs" as they were called. Coleridge made "brilliant" comments, said Stuart, but "could not write daily on the occurrences of the day." Indeed, Samuel's principle for the *Morning Post*—"first make your thoughts scholastically accurate, then popularize"—was too impractical for daily political journalism. Yet, despite his dislike of such writings, the experience was to some extent beneficial; for "obliged to write without much elaboration," he achieved his wish to "improve in naturalness and facility of style."

Coleridge's continuous, plaintive protests at the slavery of his journalism surprisingly contrast with the force and vitality of such articles as his attacks on Pitt and on the continuation of the war and his rejection of Napoleon's attempts at peace. Throughout, Coleridge claims that his attitude is based on principles of general humanity, and above a narrow nationalism, in whatever camp. Closely analyzed and argued, they at times supplement abstract argument with vivid imagery.

Such direct and incisive writing was, in fact, largely due to the journalistic conditions in which it was produced and forms a striking contrast to the long, labored, involved periods of Coleridge's later leisurely prose. As Stuart said: "When Coleridge wrote in his study without being pressed, he wandered and lost himself. He should always have had the printer's devil at his elbow, with: 'Sir, the printers want copy.' "

That Coleridge himself clearly realized this is shown by his notebook entry of October 1800: "He knew not what to do—something, he felt, must be done. He rose, drew his writing desk suddenly before him. Sat down; took the pen—and found that he knew not what to do."

Despite Coleridge's contempt for mere money-grubbing journalism, the publicity it brought him appealed to his vanity, as he frankly admitted to Josiah Wedgwood: "It is not unflattering to a man's vanity to reflect that what he writes at night, will before twelve hours are over, have perhaps 500 or 600 readers!" It also pleased him to believe that he heard people in conversation and in parliamentary speeches employing some "happy phrase, good image or new argument" taken from himself; then, "quietly, in the silent complacence of your own heart, you chuckle over the plagiarism."

Lamb was now, like Southey, reconciled with Coleridge, and followed his journalistic activities with an interest genially satirical. In this mood he thanked Samuel for castigating the secretary for war for his bad syntax in "the luminous paper" in which in a "very novel and exquisite manner confined political with grammatical science." It must, he was convinced, have dealt a "death-blow" to that Ministry, and he expected Pitt and Granville to resign.

Nevertheless, Samuel's attendance at the great parliamentary debates brought him little satisfaction. Twice, when debates were postponed, he left the "hideously crowded House" in disgust, and when at last he heard Pitt speak he was disappointed; Pitt merely "argued" instead of "reasoning," and despite "the elegance and high finish of his periods," said nothing "rememberable." On hearing Pitt again he dismissed him as "a stupid, insipid Charlatan." His own report of Pitt's speech was made, he said, from "notes so scanty that Mr. Pitt is much obliged to me, for by Heaven, he never talked half so eloquently in his lifetime." Characteristically, he believed that his report "made a great noise in London," and he invented the tale—which Stuart denied—that George Canning had called on Stuart to discover the identity of the brilliant reporter. Charles James Fox Samuel thought "a great orator," but the rest of the speakers, "mere creatures;" he and Southey he said could have made a better speech than any of them.

Despite the excitement and publicity attending his parliamentary reporting, Coleridge quickly wearied of the speeches and of the personal inconvenience to himself occasioned by visits to Parliament. His assertion that he did not report there *ex officio* but went there merely for curiosity conflicts with his gloomy remark to Poole on one occasion: "Tonight I must go with Stuart to the House of Commons." At one time he complained of being kept in Parliament from eight one morning until three the next day with an additional five hours of writing and correcting—"a good twenty-four hours of unpleasant activity."

Perhaps a remark of Lamb's is the best explanation of Coleridge's exaggerated and fictional claims to preeminence among the personnel of the *Morning Post*. Coleridge, said Lamb at this time, was, throughout the years he had known him, "in the daily and hourly habit of quizzing the world by lies, most unaccountable and most disinterested fictions." Thus it was, with Coleridge and the *Morning Post*. In personal letters and in his *Biographia Literaria*, Coleridge made wide and various claims that fell little short of "the *Morning Post,* c'est moi!"—claims that Stuart categorically denied.

According to Samuel, Stuart had begged him to come and save his paper from shipwreck, and Coleridge had stipulated that the paper's politics be changed and that he be given the management of the literary and political departments. He also declared that, since his employment, the circulation of the expiring journal had increased enormously, and that Stuart had been so impressed as to offer him half share in the paper, worth £2,000 a year. But this he had refused, preferring "the country and the lazy reading of old folios, to two thousands times two thousand pounds." "Beyond £250 a year, he considered money as a real evil," he said he told Stuart. This, he sneeringly added, Stuart could not understand, "for such ideas are not animals indigenous to the longitude and latitude of the Scotchman's soul." Such was Samuel's report to Poole. That was one of the most reprehensible of Samuel's many unworthy sneers at his friends and benefactors; for his own letters often admit the extraordinary generosity with which Stuart treated him. Indeed, in one letter to Stuart, he declared that Stuart had "behaved with the most abundant honour and generosity" to him.

Stuart, while readily admitting Coleridge's journalistic ability within limits—his "good sense, extensive knowledge, deep thought and well-grounded foresight—so brilliantly ornamented, so classically delightful; the writings of a scholar, a gentleman and a statesman without personal sarcasm or illiberality of any kind"—was not blind to Samuel's shortcomings. He was aware of Coleridge's impracticability, continual short illnesses, and absences. Nor did Stuart consider Coleridge's contributions to the *Morning Post* so significant or important as Samuel described them.

Throughout his four months of journalism Samuel almost continuously wailed to his various friends that his numerous great (dream) works were being ruthlessly sacrificed to mercenary writing for the *Morning Post*. He had "newspapered it merely as a means of subsistence while doing other things," he moaned, and seventeen years later he declared in his *Biographia* that he had "wasted the prime and manhood of his intellect in labours which added nothing to his fortune or reputation." His sole consolation was the "gratification derived" from having raised the standard of dignity and morality in political journalism. Yet, in fact, as Stuart said, without the journalist's stimulus of immediate publication, Coleridge's literary plans and ambitions seldom matured.

As the new year 1800 advanced, Coleridge became increasingly weary and depressed. His chief anxieties were journalism, London, and the need of a settled home in the country where his great dream works could be written. By April, he soon calculated, he would be able to pay all his debts and escape. "In a few weeks," he told Josiah Wedgwood at the beginning of February, "I shall have accomplished my purpose—and then adieu to London forever." "I shall give up this newspaper business, it is too, too fatiguing," he told Southey a week later, and after two more days he cried to Poole: "My very soul is squeezed out." On March 1, after one of his suspicious and increasingly frequent absences, Coleridge definitely threatened to abandon regular work for Stuart. A few more "essays as soon as possible, in common honesty," he promised, "as I have received from you much more than I have earned. *After* these. . . .I will do what I can—only not for any regular *Stipend*. That harasses me."

Thus at the end of March, or perhaps early in April, Coleridge's present association with the *Morning Post* came to an end.

On December 1, 1799, Samuel, who had lost touch with his wife since leaving her for Bristol and London in mid-October, asked Cottle to find her and tell her that he wanted her and Hartley to join him in London. Mrs. Coleridge, meanwhile, knowing nothing of her husband's changed plans and sudden journey north, had returned to Stowey after visiting clerical friends in the country. Not finding Samuel at Poole's as she had expected, she had waited a month in her servantless home for news of him. The admirable Cottle now discovered her, and Samuel, having borrowed twenty-five pounds from Poole's friend Purkis, sent her money for the journey. Soon all were together again at Samuel's lodgings, 21 Buckingham Street, Strand. On March 2, Mrs. Coleridge left London to stay with another clerical family, that of the rector of Kempsford in Gloucestershire, who had been the curate at Stowey. That same evening Samuel celebrated her departure by getting "tipsy" at Godwin's, after moving to Lamb's the same day.

For Coleridge in London, life with Mrs. Coleridge proved as disappointing as it had been recently in Stowey. To Southey, even before Mrs. Coleridge's departure, he unburdened himself—in Latin—of the miseries her presence created for himself. While admitting her many worthy qualities, he complained of her entire devotion to her maternal cares and her indifference to his own pursuits. Even in the early days of his marriage, he said, he had often been very miserable, but now he stoically added the reflection that one cannot be fortunate in all things, and as time alleviates all sorrows, he was not merely resigned to his lot but even cheerful. "London does not suit either of us," he wrote.

As the weeks in London passed, Coleridge's letters increasingly reveal two contradictory tendencies of his nature affecting his way of life—the desire for repose, for solitude, dreams, thought, and natural beauty, on the one hand, and on the other, the stimulus of a strong social instinct. Thus it was that Coleridge, although intending a return to "retirement and rustication" in the country, now decided in London, "it is good for me to have a run of society."

So two evenings with Godwin, the atheistic abomination of a year or two before, were now "Noctes Atticae." But he privately thought Godwin "no great things in intellect," and when he heard that little Hartley had given him a painful "rap on the shins with a ninepin," Samuel regretted that he was not there to see it. Through Godwin he met others including the notorious radical Horne Took, then sixty-three. "A clear-headed old man," Coleridge thought him, but he disliked "a sort of charlatanry in his manner." Godwin also introduced Samuel to the anti-Pittite Sir Francis Burdett, whom he liked. But he was later so shocked by the loose conversation of Burdett and his friends that he escaped in a passing chaise.

As with Southey, Coleridge's magic worked with Lamb, and on the very day of Mrs. Coleridge's departure Coleridge went to live with him at 36 Chapel Street, Pentonville. Old quarrels were at once forgotten, and their friendship soon became as close as before. Coleridge had introduced Lamb to Godwin, and Lamb had "expected the roof to fall and crush the Atheist." Indeed, he expected that Godwin himself would have "horns and claws." In both expectations Lamb was disappointed, finding Godwin "quite a tame creature." Nevertheless, Lamb, who had recently, as he said, "determined to lead a merry life in the midst of sinners," had celebrated his meeting with "the Atheist" by being "drunk two nights running at Coleridge's." Coleridge praised Lamb to Godwin as "worth a hundred men of *mere* Talents." Lamb was grateful to Samuel for also introducing him to Stuart, although the introduction bore little fruit since Stuart thought Lamb unfitted for daily journalism—as no doubt he was. "He tends me," Lamb said of Coleridge, "amidst all his own worrying and heart-oppressing occupations as a gardener tends his young tulip."

"More winning and captivating manners than those of Mr. Coleridge when called forth, were never possessed by mortal," wrote the expansive Cottle. The London blue-stockings would have agreed with him. Such was their infatuation that, after Samuel's departure, Lamb complained of "a tribe of authoresses that come after you here daily, and, in defect of you, hive and cluster upon us." With a Falstaffian reference Lamb continued: "I forgive you: 'The rogue has given me potions to make me love him.' " The "tribe" included "that mopsey," John Wesley's niece, as well as the romantic Miss Hays, "a thing ugly and petticoated," said Samuel brutally. Even the kindly Lamb wrote:

God forbid I should
Pass my days
With Miss Hays.

Was it Mrs. Coleridge's impending departure that made Coleridge on March 1 write to Estlin a letter that might have come untouched from the hand of Dicken's Stiggins? After playing high jinks with Godwin and Lamb, Samuel now became exquisitely hypersensitive to moral issues. He had attended a party in London given by a Unitarian minister, Dr. Disney, which (unlike Godwin's) had deeply shocked him. It had also, one feels, failed to recognize Coleridge's importance. Dr. Disney had been wicked enough to send one son to Oxford and the other to Cambridge, "established and idolatrous" places—where they would learn only "gentlemanliness," infidelity, and "a deep *contempt* for Dissenters," of whom he was "proud" to be one. But the universities' cult of "the gentleman" was "a thing more blasting to real Virtue, real Utility, real Standing forth for the Truth in Christ, than all the Whoredoms and impurities which this gentlemanliness does most generally bring with it."

The contrast between purity of Estlin's high-toned provincial gatherings and the wickedness of Dr. Disney's was so poignant that Samuel's emotions overflowed: "My dear Friend!—In the crowded, heartless party at Dr. Disney's, O! how I did think of your Sunday Suppers, their light uncombrous Simplicity, the *heartiness* of manner, the literary Christianness of Conversation! Dr. Disney himself I *respect,* highly respect; in the pulpit he is an Apostle; *but there—there it stops!*" It was all very sad. Since the walrus and the carpenter wept together there had been nothing like it. And how shocked Estlin would have been, had he seen Samuel's genially blasphemous reference to Charles and Mary Lamb as "The Agnus Dei and the Virgin Mary" two days later in a letter to the atheistic Godwin! Nor must one forget that Estlin, like Stuart and others, sometimes assisted Coleridge in need.

Despite Coleridge's complaints of being "galley slave" to Stuart, "employed from I rise to I set, from 9 in the morning to 12 at night," he also contemplated, to relieve his chronic impecuniosity, the writing of many volumes—all dreams. A hotchpotch of skimmed histories, made "without any toil of brains" but with "some goodly title" might bring £100 in twelve weeks—even fifty pounds long before, in advance payment, if the publisher were cleverly managed. A schoolbook for Phillips, a publisher, was to bring him £150 in no time; but all it brought was a solicitor's demand for the repayment of the twenty-five pounds advanced, for no work appeared. Whereupon, "the fellow's name is so infamous," that Coleridge could not dream of becoming his "hack." When Godwin's novel, *St. Leon,* brought its author £400, Samuel contemplated "tossing up a novel" at the rate of a volume a week. Pondering Godwin's good fortune, he exclaimed to Southey in the words of Falstaff—whom Samuel in some ways resembled—"And Godwin got £400 for it—think of that, Master Brooks! [*sic*] Still needing money, he agreed in March to write for Longman, for £100, an account of his recent tour in the North—another dream volume!

Similarly stillborn were a number of ambitious articles for the *Morning Post,* including others on Pitt and on Napoleon (promised continually for the next ten years). Also unrealized was a series of articles on drama for which Coleridge haunted the London theaters, which he complacently remarked, "costs me nothing." Nor was this enough. Subordinating his pecuniary aims to a higher, moral purpose, he was, he said, "dedicating two mornings and one whole day" each week, despite his slavery to Stuart, to an *Essay on the Possible Progressiveness of Man,* which never progressed. The *Life of Lessing,* Coleridge's reason for his German adventure, never appeared, giving way to another dream production, *Essay on Poetry,* which, he declared, "would be a disguised system of morals and politics."

The only literary result of the German adventure was Coleridge's translation of Schiller's *Wallenstein.* This he did for the publisher Longman under the pressure of financial necessity and, as Stuart would have said, with Longman's "printer's devil at his elbow." Samuel's opinion of the play varied according to the occasion and his mood. In July 1800, shortly after publication, he described it as "a dull, heavy play, prolix and dragging." Later he spoke of it as "a specimen of my happiest attempt, during the prime manhood of my intellect, before I had been buffeted by adversity and crossed by fatality." Yet, the author of *Wallenstein,* Schiller, was far less enthusiastic. "The translator," he told a friend in 1801, "was a man of genius, but had made some ridiculous mistakes."

Coleridge, of course, did not achieve this translation without many groans and regrets: "O this translation is indeed a *Bore—never, never,* never will I be so taken in again. Newspaper writing is comparatively ecstasy!" "Working from morning to night and half the night too," yet still "too slow for the printer." "These plays play the devil with me." As for Schiller, when in 1801 Stuart tried to lure Coleridge from the North to meet Schiller in London, Samuel replied that he "would not stir twenty yards to know him."

Wallenstein brought Coleridge only another disappointment. The fifty pounds he received from Longman for it he dismissed with the scathing comment: "The whole work went for waste paper." "The same toil, time and effort," he said, for the *Morning Post* would have brought him ten times as much.

"These plays play the devil with me," Samuel had moaned in the depression brought by *Wallenstein,* and the devil had soon appeared as opium. To Godwin, while his translation was in progress, he complained that the work "wasted and depressed my spirits," leaving him "unfit for anything but sleeping or immediate society." In a letter to his friend Tom Wedgwood, also a drug addict, Samuel had written in January 1800: "Life were so flat a thing without enthusiasm—that if for a moment it leave me, I have a sort of stomach-sensation attached to all my Thoughts, like those which succeed to the pleasurable operation of a dose of opium." Thus, for at least once, Coleridge, who so often denied it, admitted that there were "pleasurable" sensations created by opium.

After Mrs. Coleridge's departure from London the haunting question for Coleridge of where to live—near Poole at Stowey again, or near Wordsworth and Dorothy in the North—insistently demanded decision, for his time for leaving London approached, and his wife's pregnancy advanced. Now that Coleridge had been made "independent" by the Wedgwoods, his relatives urged him to settle near them in Ottery. But "that," he told Southey, "I must *decline,* in the names of public Liberty and individual Free-agency. Elder Brothers, not senior in intellect, and not sympathizing in main opinions, are subjects of occasional visits, not temptations to Co-township."

From the beginning of the year 1800 until his departure from London, Coleridge continually debated with Poole the question of a new home, asking his friend to find another house for him in Stowey since he refused to return to the "old hovel" there. This, with increasing anxiety, Poole tried to do, as time passed and Coleridge's drift toward Wordsworth and Dorothy in the North became more evident. At the same time, however, Samuel's provisos to Poole became increasingly severe. He refused to share a kitchen in one house, and by mid-February 1800 he insisted on a garden—"not that I mean to work in it—that is out of the question."

The difficulty of finding a home was increased by a difference between himself and Sarah on the matter. For, as he told Poole, "Sarah being Sarah, and I being I, we must live in a town or else close to one so that she may have neighbours and acquaintances. For my friends form not that society which is of itself sufficient to a woman. I know nowhere else but Stowey, (for to Bristol my objections are unsurmountable). . . .God knows where we can go; for that situation which suits my wife does not suit me. A truth which always remains equally clear, but not always equally pleasant." Doubtless Mrs. Coleridge wished to live near her mother in Bristol, but Samuel cared as little for Bristol as for Ottery.

The rival attractions of Poole and of the Wordsworths were further complicated for Samuel by a sudden passion for the companionship of Southey. Ill from overwork, Southey was meditating emigrating to a warmer climate. To be near him would be a "mutual comfort" in literary work, and Sarah would be happy near her sister. For a moment, Poole and Wordsworth temporarily displaced, Coleridge even dreamed of living with Southey at Alfoxden. Something of the old pantisocratic dream revived as the time of Southey's departure approached, and he saw himself, with Southey and Wordsworth, "forming a pleasant little colony for a few years in Italy or the South of France! But no! Precious stuff for dreams and God knows I have no time for them."

Amid the complications of his existence, Coleridge at this time already felt that he was not made for the world, nor the world for him. He suspected that his ambitions exceeded all possibility of realization: "that the dedication of much hope and fear to subjects which are perhaps disprorportionate to our faculties and powers is a disease.'' ''But,'' he added, ''I have had this disease so long, and my early education was so undomestic, that I know not how to get rid of it.'' He was also unhappily conscious that his chief interests were in abstractions, predominating over those ''private and personal connections and interests'' which should have precedence.

Another cause of Coleridge's mental unrest was the increasing rivalry between his affection for Poole and that for Wordsworth—as the father figure Coleridge needed. The earliest, his brother George, had been gradually displaced by Poole, and now Poole was giving way to Wordsworth. Wordsworth probably knew little and cared less about this; but Poole knew and cared deeply. To Samuel he now wrote almost like a jealous lover, accusing him of ''treating me with unmerited silence'' and of ''prostration'' before Wordsworth. Samuel's reply, a brusque dismissal of ''such an absurd idea,'' was as little reassuring to Poole as the superlative praise of Wordsworth, whom Coleridge considered the equal of Milton. Then, the most powerful influence of all perhaps, came a long letter from Wordsworth written on Christmas Eve 1799, in which he spoke of the pain of parting from Samuel, and described his and Dorothy's horseride to Dove Cottage, their new Grasmere home, where they had lived for four days. He described their crossing of the Tees by moonlight and all the romantic scenery of their journey—waterfalls, streams, snow, mountains—everything to excite lovers of the fashionable ''picturesque.'' And to all this, Dorothy added a short postscript, no less compelling—''write soon, I pray you. God bless you. My love to Mrs. Coleridge, and a kiss for Hartley.''

April 1800 came, and with April, as long intended, Samuel set off again for the North, this time alone. ''Colridge had left us,'' Lamb somewhat peevishly told Manning on April 5, ''to go into the North on a visit to his god Wordsworth.'' The next day Samuel arrived at Dove Cottage and stayed there a month. A day or two after his arrival he sent Southey, about to sail to Lisbon, a letter of affectionate and sentimental retrospect. ''We cannot, if we would, cease to love each other,'' he wrote, and declared that if Southey were abroad a year hence, ''I and mine will join you;'' if in England, ''You must join us; though where we shall be, God knows! but in some interesting country it will be, in Heaven or Earth.'' A fortnight later Southey and Edith sailed for Lisbon.

On May 4, 1800, Coleridge left Grasmere for Bristol to meet his wife and to give the Bristol printers some of Wordsworth's poems for the new edition of *Lyrical Ballads*. Soon he was at Stowey as Poole's guest, and there on June 7 he informed Humphrey Davy: ''I have now finally determined on the North.'' A year previously, when Samuel had no wish to leave Stowey, he had stressed to Poole the ''insurmountable objection, the impropriety of taking Mrs. Coleridge to a place where she would have no acquaintance.'' Nor indeed did Mrs. Coleridge at any time wish to leave the Pooles and her other friends and helpers in Stowey. Nevertheless, Samuel now again used consideration for his wife as an excuse for going North. She ''had scarcely any society'' in Stowey, he now told Wedgwood, "and the nearness of Bristol connected me too intimately with all the affairs of her family."

Everything urged flight from town to town to the peace of the country. A week after he had informed Davy of his decision, Coleridge left Bristol with his wife and son for Dove Cottage and his new home, Greta Hall, which Dorothy had found for him near Keswick—"a house," as he had already told Godwin, "of such prospect I shall have a tendency to become a God!"

11   Greta Hall (1800-1801)

"A house of such prospect, that if . . . impressions and ideas constitute our Being, I shall have a tendency to become a God."
—Coleridge to William Godwin, May 21, 1800

When the Coleridges arrived at Dove Cottage on June 29, 1800, after spending a week in Liverpool with Dr. Crompton and among the local literati, Dorothy Wordsworth, who had keenly missed Samuel's companionship since their parting in Germany, had been eagerly expecting him for ten days. "Most delightfully situated," she described Greta Hall, "and contains all possible advantages, both for his wife and himself; *she* likes to be near a town, *he* in the country."

Samuel was not well—ominous of his future in the North, he had caught a bad cold at Liverpool. Yet since the day was very warm, all sailed on the lake. The next day he was down with rheumatic fever, which kept him and his family at Dove Cottage for a month. Ominous, too, of the opium that increasingly accompanied his frequent illnesses was his remark to Davy a little later, wishing he "could wrap up the view from my house in a pill of opium, and send it to you!"

Their last evening with the Wordsworths was very happy. All had tea on an island in the lake, while Samuel lay supremely content, dreamily watching "the woods and mountains and lake all trembling, and as it were *idealized* through the subtle smoke which rose up from the clear red embers of the fir-apples," as he told a friend. After tea they made "a glorious bonfire and danced around it."

On July 24, 1800, the Coleridges entered Greta Hall, intending to make it their permanent home. But Coleridge, who soon wearied of family life, remained there only fifteen months, returning to London in November 1801.

At first his delight in the beauty of the scenery around him overflowed in letters to friends, in which Samuel expatiated upon the sublimities of his environment: "Far beyond my expectations . . . six distinct landscapes . . . two lakes, vale, river and mountains, mists, clouds and sunshine making endless com-

176

binations, as if Heaven and Earth were talking to each other." The scenic beauty around Coleridge was an ever-present temptation to him to leave work and wander for days about the countryside. He delighted in the landscapes spread before him, ever changing as he walked and climbed. Often caught in showers during these excursions, Coleridge suffered much from consequent bouts of rheumatism, which kept him bedridden over long periods.

Coleridge found his bachelor landlord, William Jackson, and his house-keeper, Mrs. Wilson, agreeable neighbors. They lived in one of the two houses that, being under one roof, composed Greta Hall. With intellectual interests and a good library, Jackson, a retired carrier—the "Master" of Words-worth's *"Waggoner"*—was almost a humbler Poole. Jackson's pleasant housekeeper, Mrs. Wilson, soon became very fond of Hartley and was very helpful to Mrs. Coleridge during her pregnancy. Jackson, indeed, was so impressed by his distinguished tenant that he refused to charge any rent; but this Coleridge, with a magnificent and surely unique gesture, refused as unthinkable. Nonetheless, Jackson was soon involved in the complicated financial transactions created by Coleridge's debts and financial innocence. Coleridge's dependence upon the Wordsworths was now almost entire. Their mutual interests and affections remained, as well as the Wordsworths' old way of life, which so suited Coleridge. When Dorothy's friend Jane Marshall asked her how they passed their time at Dove Cottage, Dorothy replied: "I cannot tell you how we pass it, because though our employments are not very various, yet they are irregular. We walk every day and at all times of the day, we row upon the water, and in the summer sit a great part of our time under the apple trees of the orchard or in a wood close by the lake-side. William writes verses, John goes fishing, and we read the books we have and such as we can procure. We often have our friends calling in upon us." But Dorothy's life was less purely idyllic than her description, for her journal reveals many domestic duties—cooking, knitting, washing, and mending, with the help of a peasant woman who lived nearby.

Every day or two Samuel would appear at Dove Cottage when his health permitted and remain for several days. When he was ill William, often accompanied by Dorothy, would come on a similar short visit to Greta Hall. Now with Coleridge their way of life continued as Dorothy had described it (except when illness interfered)—walking, talking, reading, and writing poetry, and when boating, so occupied with their interests as to let the boat take its course unguided. But Mrs. Coleridge was still the outsider, as at Stowey: she was still "Mrs. Coleridge" for them, when the rest, except Coleridge, were called by their Christian names. But the intrusion—as Mrs. Coleridge must have seen it—of the Wordsworths into her home was now a much more frequent occurrence than in the Stowey days.

Nor were their hours conventional. To such walkers, the thirteen miles between Greta Hall and Dove Cottage meant little more than the three between "the little hovel" and Alfoxden, especially since sometimes they traveled on horseback or by chaise. The arrival of one or the other poet at his friend's home was equally welcome by day or night. It was thus, on the last day of August 1800, for example, when at eleven, Dorothy, "walking in the still clear moonshine, in the garden," was suddenly joined by Samuel, who had "come over Helvellyn" and was excited about his attempts to continue "Christabel." William, who was in bed, came down in his dressing gown. Samuel read part of "Christabel" to them, described the mountain beauties of his walk, and they "sat and chatted till half-past three the next morning." The next day all walked in the wood by the lake, William read his poems, and they bathed. After dinner Samuel discovered a rock seat in the orchard, and cleared it of overgrowth. But, tired, he went to bed after tea, and Dorothy "broiled him a mutton chop which he ate in bed." William continually unwell with nervous pains during poetic composition, also went to bed, while Dorothy and John Wordsworth sat chatting with Coleridge until near midnight. The next day there was more walking, and in the evening Dorothy again "lingered with Coleridge in the garden" when "John and William were gone to bed and all the lights out." The following day Samuel returned home, over Helvellyn as he had come.

Close as the association with the Wordsworths now was, it was less intimate than in the old Alfoxden days. Then Samuel was a southerner in the South; now the Wordsworths were northerners in the North—which made a difference. As Samuel had foreseen, familiar manners as well as familiar scenery were part of the nostalgia that took Wordsworth to the North. "He will never quit the North of England," Coleridge had told Poole in March. "His habits are more assimilated with the inhabitants there. There he and his sister are exceedingly beloved, enthusiastically. Such differences do small sympathies make—such as voice, pronunciation, etc." In Dove Cottage the Wordsworths were no longer isolated as at Alfoxden. Friendly visits to and from neighbors, and simple teas and dinners given and reciprocated were, in fact, frequent, now that the Wordsworths were back among the scenes and people of their early days. Local isolation was rather the case for Coleridge, a southerner in the North without previous associations with those about him.

Inevitably, the result for Coleridge was at times a feeling of greater loneliness and more solitary wandering amid the peace and beauty of nature. Nor was solitude then unwelcome. "Man," he had written, a year before, "is not meant to be able to communicate *all*; the greater part of his being must be solitary." At times, too, he delighted—like Dorothy—in the life of the small natural things about him that filled many pages of his notebooks: insects, birds, the worm that "in motion flattens its tail so as to make it an exact resemblance to the Head of the venomous serpent," "the aromatic smell of the poplar," "the dazzling silver of the Lake," "the beauty of ferns," the rustle of a leaf in the wind, which he first mistook for the noise of a grasshopper.

Nor did human qualities, grave, gay, and humorous, among the peasants escape Coleridge's eye and record: the butcher who would rather kill an ox than a chicken, "two drunken men arm-in-arm, the one imagining himself sober, the other acknowledging himself drunk," and (a contrast) "a child scolding a flower in the words in which he had himself been scolded and whipt." That, he continued, moralizing the experience, "is poetry; past passion with pleasure." Such are some of the private records of Coleridge, so widely varied, so sensitive, so intimate, that, far beyond his letters or his published prose, they reveal the Coleridge who won the hearts of so many who knew him.

In mid-November 1800 these wanderings, often latterly in driving rain, cold, and wind, brought him to bed again with rheumatic fever—and its cure, opium. Letters from Samuel, "very ill," came to Dove Cottage, and William, as soon as the "terrible rain" stopped, set off for Greta Hall, accompanied part of the way, "in starlight," by the anxious Dorothy: "very sad, unwilling not to go on." The next day came a letter from Samuel, now better, summoning Dorothy. So the next day, "a fine, clear frosty morning with a sharp wind," Dorothy left home, and after a solitary tramp of four and one-half hours, reached Greta Hall at 2:30, to find all well. Such was the devotion of the Wordsworths—sometimes accompanied by Sara Hutchinson—during Coleridge's illnesses at Greta Hall, at this time.

Opium no longer inspired such dreams as "Kubla Khan." Bright visions had given place to horror dreams, such as one he had on November 28, "a most frightful dream of a woman whose features were blended with darkness, catching hold of my right eye and attempting to put it out. I caught hold of her arm fast—a horrid feel. Wordsworth cried out aloud to me, hearing my scream. I heard his cry, and thought it cruel he did not come, but did not wake till his cry was repeated a third time." Three years later many similar experiences inspired Coleridge's despairing verses, "The Pains of Sleep."

Increasing Coleridge's self-disgust was the sight of Wordsworth's steady progress with his poem to Samuel, *The Prelude*—as he later name it—"His Great Work," as Coleridge, enraptured, called it. The contrast between Wordsworth and himself brought despair. "As to Poetry," he told Thelwall in mid-December, "I have altogether abandoned it, being convinced that I never had the essentials of poetic genius, and that I mistook a strong desire for poetic power." Two days later he told another friend: "Wordsworth is a great, a true Poet. I am only a kind of Metaphysician." Shortly before he had told Godwin: "Here you will meet with Wordsworth, 'the latchet of whose shoe I am unworthy to unlose.' " And again in March 1801 Coleridge told Godwin: "I have *forgotten* how to make a rhyme . . . the poet is dead in me. My imagination (or rather the somewhat that has been imaginative) lies like a cold snuff on the circular rim of a brass candlestick, without even a stink of tallow to remind you that it was once clothed and mitred with flame."

It was in this mood of despair, amid sickness and disillusion, that Coleridge, who only five months before had entered Greta Hall with such high hopes and intense delight, gloomily watched the year 1800 draw to its wearisome close. The contrast for Coleridge between himself, poetically sterile, and Wordsworth, now composing poem after poem, sometimes a new poem a day, doubly embittered Samuel's dismay, raised Wordsworth even higher in his conscious estimation, and encouraged a spirit of jealousy below the conscious level. "I abandon poetry altogether," he wrote: "I leave the higher and deeper kinds to Wordsworth, the delightful, popular and simply dignified to Southey; and reserve for myself the honourable attempt to make others feel and understand their writings, as they deserve to be felt and understood."

This last allusion to his future as a literary critic was largely inspired by Coleridge's present interest in the new long "Preface" to the forthcoming edition of *Lyrical Ballads* in two volumes, which appeared in January 1801 (dated 1800). The Preface, which Coleridge had originally inspired, he had almost forced upon the reluctant Wordsworth who preferred poems to criticism. That this now famous "Preface" expressed Coleridge's opinions at that time, as well as Wordsworth's, Coleridge then declared. "The Preface," he told Stuart in September 1800, "contains our joint opinions on poetry." Two years later he was to tell Southey, "although Wordsworth's *Preface* is half a child of my own brain. . . . I rather suspect that somewhere or other there is a radical difference in our theoretical opinions concerning poetry." That "difference" he was to elaborate in his *Biographia Literaria*.

When this edition of *Lyrical Ballads* appeared with its second volume consisting almost entirely of Wordsworth's poems, Coleridge immediately praised the new "Preface" as "invaluable," and gave superlative praise to Wordsworth and his poems, new and old. Wordsworth, he told Godwin, "by showing him what true poetry was, made him know that he himself was no poet."

Early in August Lamb, a little hurt by Samuel's departure for the North, told his friend Manning: "Coleridge is settled with his wife (with a child in her guts), and the young philosopher (Hartley) at Keswick with the Wordsworths. They have contrived to spawn a new volume of *Lyrical Ballads*, which is to see the light in about a month, and causes no little excitement in the *literary world*."

The presentation copy of the *Lyrical Ballads* sent to Charles Lamb got the poor man into trouble with the two poets, for it seemed to them that Lamb's appreciation was inadequate, and Lamb was firmly and solemnly rebuked. The actual letters have unfortunately disappeared but in Lamb's delightful account of the affair to Manning, on February 15, 1801, there is a clear reflection of it, as he warns him to beware of mentioning the work: "All the North of England are in a turmoil. Cumberland and Westmorland have already declared a state of war." "Four sweating pages," Lamb described Wordsworth's letter regretting that the book had not given Lamb more pleasure, and wishing his "range of sensibility were more extended," thus allowing him "large influxes of happiness and happy thoughts," with a "deal of stuff," said Lamb, "about a certain 'Union of Tenderness and Imagination.' " To Wordsworth's solemn protest, Coleridge also added his weight. "Starts up from his bed of sickness to reprove me for my hardy presumption," wrote Lamb, "four long pages, equally sweaty and more tedious assuring me that, when the words of a man of genius such as Wordsworth undoubtedly was, do not please me at first sight, I should suspect the fault to lie in me and not in them, etc. etc., etc., etc., What am I to do with such people? I certainly shall write them a very merry letter. My back tingles from the Northern castigation." Shortly afterward Lamb wrote: "Between you and me, the *Lyrical Ballads* are but drowsy performances." Unfortunately, Lamb's "merry letter" is lost.

On September 14, 1800, Coleridge's son Derwent was born, and two days later Samuel, who had previously got Poole as godfather, also offered the honor to Godwin and borrowed ten pounds from him on the strength of it—a debt he soon got Stuart to repay. A day or two after Derwent's birth Coleridge set off again, wandering: he stood entranced by the beauty of a "rainbow on Skiddaw," and, when the rains began, he noted the preceeding days as "an interval, during which I travelled much."

Within a week little Derwent fell ill, and Coleridge, despite his theoretical objections to baptism, agreed that the baby should be baptized. To the sympathetic Godwin, however, he detailed his real feelings: "At times I dwell on Man with such reverence, resolve all his follies and superstitions into such grand primary laws of intellect, and in such wise so contemplate them as ever-varying incarnations of the eternal Life, that the Llama's dung-pellet, or the cow-tail which the dying Brahman clutches convulsively, become sanctified and sublime by the feelings which cluster round them. In that mood I exclaim, 'My boys shall be christened!'" Coleridge then continued in a different mood: "Shall I suffer the Toad of Priesthood to spurt out his foul juice in this babe's face? Shall I suffer him to see a grave countenance and hear grave accents, while his face is sprinkled, and while the fat paw of a parson crosses his forehead?" Nevertheless, Derwent was now baptized. ("This christening of Derwent was doubtless a private rite. In Nov. 1803, all three children were publicly baptised" [J. Dykes Campbell, *Samuel Taylor Coleridge: A Narrative of the Events in His Life* (London, 1894), p. 115].

Not until the middle of 1801 did Coleridge's almost continuous illness improve. "Nine dreary months," he complained in July 1801, racked in bad weather by aches and pains "almost incredible," "reviving like a parlour fly" when the sun shone. And, as before, the Wordsworths and Sara Hutchinson constantly attended him.

Dorothy's enthusiasm for Samuel made her a severe critic of Mrs. Coleridge at this time. "A bad nurse for him," she thought her; while, in fact, Coleridge was thanking Stuart for sending him *Morning Posts*, "a great amusement to Mrs. Coleridge, during her long attendance at my sick bed." Dorothy admitted that "Mrs. Coleridge" had "several great merits"—not further identified—but was "a sad fiddle-faddler, would have made a good wife to many another man, but for Coleridge!! Her radical fault is want of sensibility, and what can such a woman be to Coleridge? She is much, very much to be pitied for when one party is ill-matched, the other necessarily must be so too."

Dorothy now often, calmly and unconsciously, displaced Mrs. Coleridge as Samuel's chief nurse. "We are never comfortable at Greta Hall, after the first two or three days," she complained. "This of course we do not mind while we are of any essential service to him."

Amid physical pain and mental anxiety, Coleridge was glad that, despite all, his mind remained clear and active and had "compelled into hours of delight many a sleepless, painful hour of darkness by chasing down metaphysical game." These months of illness, he said, he would look back upon "as a storehouse of wild dreams for poems." Samuel also hoped that "philosophy and poetry will not neutralize each other." But that hope, as he had already foreseen, was to be disappointed. Ever a prolific letterwriter, Coleridge, despite illness, now relieved his solitude in Greta Hall by informing his friends in at least eighty-two frequently long letters of his interests, his studies, and his general way of life, sometimes including his debts and need of money.

Coleridge's intellectual ambitions, as he described them to friends, were boundless. They included "completely extricating the notions of time and space" and "overthrowing Hartley's associative theory" and "the doctrine of necessity," thus destroying "all the irreligious metaphysics of modern infidels." A few days later, "about to solve the process of life and consciousness," he "found himself unaware at the root of Pure Mathematics: and up that tall smooth Tree, whose few poor branches are all at its very summit, and I climbing, by pure adhesive strength of arms and thighs—still slipping down, still renewing my ascent." Yet this was not enough. He also engaged, he said, in exacting "literary pursuits," which included "the Northern Languages, the Slavonic, Gothic and Celtic, in their most ancient forms, as an amusing study," and also, "as a serious object, a metaphysical investigation of the laws by which our feelings form affinities with each other, with ideas, and with words."

Despite these formidable projects and the hundred or so dream volumes awaiting his attention, Coleridge, encouraged by his intensive reading of the medieval scholastics into a sublime contempt for the modern, unmetaphysical "empiricists," yet also influenced by the increasing reputation of his friend Humphry Davy, turned his attention to contemporary science. "Facts," said Samuel scornfully, "are not truths, not conclusions, not even premises"—and so could hold no interest for him. These blind scientists asked only "How?" All he wanted to know was "Why?"

In this mood Dr. Beddoes, pursuing his medical researches, seemed to Samuel merely a man "hunting a pig with a buttered tail." This, however, did not deter Coleridge from urgently requesting Beddoes's attentions when ill. Nor was Coleridge's only recorded scientific experiment a stimulus to enthusiasm—rubbing a cat's back in the dark to get sparks, but getting only badly scratched hands.

The abstract scientific spirit—less remote, in fact, than Samuel's metaphysical one—seemed to him too remote from simple human emotion for moral sensibility to survive: "a young poet may do without being in love with a woman—it is enough if he loves—but to a young chemist it would be salvation to be downright romantically in love," which was unfair to the many young chemists who have found such "salvation" without difficulty, and even to Davy, who married a rich widow. Science, Dr. Erasmus Darwin, Godwin, atheism, all, he had long since declared, made us "the outcasts of a blind idiot called Nature," dooming each person to become "a clod of the valley," instead of being "the children of an all-wise and infinitely good God," and preparing him "for the enjoyment of immortal happiness"—which was Samuel's "Why."

The spirit of science he believed destructive of poetry. "I look at the mountains only for the curves of their outlines; the stars as I behold them, form themselves into triangles. . . . The Poet is dead in me." Newton was "a mere materialist": and he added the meaningless and foolish remark that "the souls of 500 Sir Isaac Newtons" would not equal a Shakespeare or a Milton. Three years afterward, with more caution or wisdom, he asked Poole to destroy the letter—but it still exists. Nevertheless, many years later, Coleridge stood reverentially before the statue of Newton in Cambridge.

Coleridge's attitude toward science at this time was in some degree apparently affected by its association with Coleridge's Bristol friend Humphry Davy, the scientist. At first Coleridge, in correspondence with Davy, made fun of science by asking Davy silly questions, such as why did his foot feel cold in hot water, and why did peppermints maké his breath cold? If Davy did not reply he threatened to send his question to the *Lady's Diary*, "where you may find fifty questions of the same depth and kidney . . . God bless you my dear Davy! Take my nonsense like a pinch of snuff—sneeze it off, it clears the head—and to sense and yourself again. With most affectionate esteem."

But science soon made Davy a famous and socially important person. In 1801 he was appointed director of the Chemical Laboratory at the Royal Institution in London. Upon this appointment, Coleridge's references to science in his letter to Davy became more serious. Thus, when Godwin regretted that Davy "should degrade his vast talents to chemistry," Samuel defended him, crying: "How, Godwin! can you talk of a science of which neither you nor I understand an iota?"—which was, in fact, what Samuel himself had done. But now, as he told Davy, he "defended chemistry as knowingly at least as Godwin attacked it," with the impressive metaphysical argument that chemistry "immaterialized the mind without destroying the definiteness of the ideas." So now Coleridge intended "to attack chemistry like a shark"—i.e., to study chemistry intensively.

When Coleridge found that Davy's galvanic electricity was attracting admiration, his own previous attitude requesting Davy's "metaphysical opinions" changed to "Are your galvanic discoveries important? What do they lead to? Would to heaven I had as much knowledge as I have sympathy." Three months later, when Davy was a professor at the Royal Institution, Samuel wished: "Success, my dear Davy! to Galvanism and every other ism and schism that you are about."

In his sudden passion for science, Coleridge got Wordsworth to order two copies of a popular botanical book and two microscopes for himself and Samuel. Wordsworth, in "Stanzas Written in a Copy of Thomson's Castle of Indolence," described their doings in verse:

Glasses they had, that little things display,
The beetle panoplied in gems and gold:

A mailèd angel on a battle-day;
The mysteries that cups of flowers enfold,
And all the gorgeous sights which fairies do behold.

Such, apparently, was the final limit of their botanical studies. But when a neighbor in the Lakes District thought of making a scientific laboratory in his house, Coleridge at once asked Davy for information on books, apparatus, cost, and "how to begin." Reassuringly, he added that they already had "an electrical machine and a number of little nick-nacks connected with it." The "little laboratory," "electrical machine," and its "little nick-nacks" apparently never reappear in Coleridge's published correspondence.

"You know how long, how ardently I have wished to initiate myself in chemical science—both for its own sake, and in no small degree likewise, my beloved friend!—he told Davy on February 3, 1801—"that I may be able to sympathize with *all* that you do and think. Sympathize blindly with it all, I do even *now*, God knows! from the very middle of my heart's heart; but I would fain sympathize with you in the Light of Knowledge." In May, hearing that Davy was lecturing in London, Coleridge assured him: "as far as *words* go, I have become a formidable chemist—having got by heart a prodigious quantity of terms etc. to which I attach some ideas—very scanty in number, I assure you, and right meagre in their individual persons." Yet, his innate metaphysical dissatisfaction remained. These scientists found "all *power* and vital attributes depend on modes of *arrangement*," which chemistry did not explain. Their "reasoning" too, he found "unsatisfactory," believing other "agents hitherto undiscovered" must be present. "This cannot be *reasoning;* for in all conclusive reasoning, you must have a deep conviction that all the *terms* have been exhausted." Still he reassured Davy as to science: "I grow however exceedingly interested in the subject." But how little his interest was in "the subject" he revealed a fortnight later, in confessional mood, to Davy: "I am sometimes apprehensive that my passion for science is scarcely true and genuine—it is but Davyism! That is, I fear that I am more delighted at *your* having discovered a fact, than at the fact's having been discovered."

Nevertheless, Davy, like Wordsworth, unconsciously aroused in Coleridge that undercurrent of jealousy which the success of friends always created in Samuel. "Dear Davy," he told Southey on October 21, 1801, "if I have not overrated his intellectual powers, I have little fear for his moral character. Metaphysicians! Do, Southey, keep to your own most excellent word, *Metapothecaries*." Yet, ten days later Coleridge assured Davy: "I do not know by what fatality it has happened; but so it is that I have thought more often of you, and I may say, *yearned* after your society more for the last 3 months than I ever before did—and yet I have not written to you. But you know that I honour you, and that I love whom I honour."

A month later, amid the excitements of London, Coleridge described to Godwin, in a mood of facetious irony such as Davy had evoked, his recent association with the Wordsworths. London, he said, was "A great change from the society of W. and his sister—for tho' we were three persons, it was but one God—whereas here I have the amazed feelings of a new Polytheist, meeting Lords many, and Gods many.''

On January 20, 1802, Coleridge went with Poole to London, where both intended to hear Davy's popular scientific lectures at the Royal Institution.

Although Coleridge meant to attend the whole course of Davy's lectures, he did not do so. Nor is this strange, for his main purpose at the lectures was to increase his stock of metaphors, he said. The notes he made at Davy's lectures were merely descriptions of the demonstrations, almost without mathematical formulas, but amusingly punctuated by occasional exclamations of aesthetic pleasure. "Ether burns bright in the atmosphere," he wrote, "but O! how brightly, whitely, vividly beautiful in Oxygen gas!. . . . The Cannon with Hydrogen and common air. Held the Cannon over the bottle containing Hydrogen gas—applied a Leyden phial to it—*bang*!. . . . if all aristocrats here, how easily Davy might poison them all.'' The lectures produced no radical effect upon Coleridge's basic attitude toward science, and Davy a year later, despite Samuel's wooing, justly remarked of him: "as yet he has not laid the foundation for the new world of intellectual forms.'' In mid-June 1804, in a letter to Sharp, Coleridge—evidently unconverted—accused Davy of "prostituting and profaning the name of philosopher, great philosopher, eminent philosopher, etc. etc. etc. to every fellow who has made a lucky experiment, tho' the man should be frenchified to the heart, and tho' the whole Seine with its filth and poison flows in his veins and arteries.''

The months of intermittent illness in 1800-1801 and the year following were a crucial period in Coleridge's life. They intensified by frustration his natural tendency to indolence and indecision, while the illness itself was devitalizing, and made more so by the addition of brandy and opium. It isolated him from action, both literary and physical, and it led him to solitary reading and abstract thought. It hindered public expression by written or spoken word. It provided both reason and excuse for increased dependence upon others, particularly for the money he continually needed. It also provided an excuse for endless postponements of his intended works. Below all was Samuel's increasing fear that his poetic inspiration was dead and that his academic studies were but inadequate compensation for such a loss. "Into a *discoverer* I have sunk from an inventor,'' he bitterly noted in June 1801. From this time Coleridge was the man T. S. Eliot has thus described: "For a few years he had been visited by the Muses, and thence forth was a haunted man'' (*The Use of Poetry and the Use of Criticism*: *Studies in the Relation of Criticism to Poetry in England* [New York, 1970], p. 68). In his dilemma Samuel tried to crush his literary ambitions. "If I know my own heart, or rather if I be not profoundly ignorant of it, I have not a spark of *ambition*,'' he told Stuart in October 1800, "and though my *vanity* is flattered, more than it ought to be, by what Dr. Johnson calls 'colloquial prowess,' yet it leaves me in my study. . . my taste in judging is far, far more perfect than my power to execute and I do nothing but almost instantly its defects and sillinesses come upon my mind.''

Restless, Coleridge wandered aimlessly about the country around, wishing so "to wander and wander for ever and ever,'' as he wrote in his notebook just before coming, on June 18, 1801, upon "a hollow place in the rock, like a coffin, . . . exactly my own length—there I lay and slept.'' That was not the last occasion on which the sleep of death seemed to offer him an escape from the frustrations of his existence. Yet in natural beauty he found consolation. Five days later he told Godwin, after detailing his various illnesses, "What uninterrupted rural retirement can have had to do in the production of these outward and visible evils, I cannot guess. What share it has had in consoling me under them, I know with a tranquil mind, and feel with a grateful heart.'' The fear that he would fail to realize the promise of his youth, already felt by Coleridge's friends—now haunted him, "till I am completely disgusted with my performance and wish myself a tanner or a printer, or anything but an author.'' Samuel wrote that in October 1800. Yet, in the following April Wordsworth could still tell Poole: "He is a great man, and if God grant him life, will do great things.''

So, too, in optimistic mood Samuel raised his own spirits and sometimes, deceptively, those of publishers by announcing another library of phantom works for which he occasionally obtained advance payment. Samuel's dream volumes at this time included: "Concerning Poetry and the Nature of the Pleasures Derived from It,'' a drama and a farce, and a work on Germany, now "suspended'' because of his metaphysical studies that were so important that to quit them "seemed to me a suicide of my very soul.'' Another was a work—never achieved—on Locke, Hobbes, and Hume, which was to be "a pioneer to my greater work''—the *Logosophia*, also unrealized. And, of course, leading this assemblage was the never finished but never forgotten "Christabel.''

What Samuel's dreams of travel to his land of heart's desire were his letter to Poole at this time clearly reveal, as well as his disgust with England, a land in which writers could not make a living—especially, one might add, if they did not write! "O for a lodge in a land where human life was an end, to which labour was only a means, instead of being, as it is, a means of carrying on labour,'' he cried. And again some ghost of his pantisocratic dream returned for a moment, as he imagined himself with Wordsworth and two or three local farmers, happy in America. When someone doubted his happiness there, telling him of "the society so bad, the manners so vulgar, the servants so insolent,'' Samuel dismissed all as "arrant ingratitude to a land where there is no poverty.'' Yet, the next day he cried: "My country is my country; and I will never leave it till I am starved out.'' But the dream of foreign adventure remained, and anxious, almost motherly Dorothy was now convinced that Coleridge "will never be well till he has tried a warm climate.''

During the fifteen months of Coleridge's residence at Greta Hall the friendship between himself and Poole gradually waned. Although he wrote to Poole on the very day of his entry into the house, his letter, strangely impersonal in tone, was evidently a reply to some letter from Poole reproaching Samuel for not having written to him since leaving for the North. The blame for this omission Coleridge now laid upon his recent illness at Dove Cottage. Only at the close of the letter did any hint of Samuel's affection for Poole appear. It was, however, merely in the formal ending: "God for ever bless you, my dear Poole—and your most affectionate friend, S. T. Coleridge." Poole in his reply evidently doubted the sincerity of Samuel's last words. For Coleridge's next answer to Poole continued, after the final conventional blessing, "For God's sake never doubt that I am attached to you beyond all other men." And in the same letter he invited Poole to be godfather to his expected child (Derwent) and to visit them at Greta Hall.

Coleridge may have forgotten, but Poole certainly had not, the promise Samuel had sent him from Germany: "My resolve is fixed not to leave you till you leave me!" That promise had been broken, Poole sadly perceived, because Samuel preferred the companionship of Wordsworth to his own. But Poole's affection for Samuel remained, creating at the same time in Poole a jealousy of Wordsworth.

Samuel's replies in October and December 1800 were evidently intended to allay, as tactfully as possible, the jealousy of Wordsworth he apparently detected in Poole. Thus to Poole's anxious letters Coleridge replied reassuringly in December: "Believe me to be what I have been ever and am, attached to you *one* degree more at least than to any other living man." Perhaps Poole was by no means reassured. The preceeding October Samuel, in a similar attempt to calm Poole, had falsely assured him, speaking of Wordsworth: "I see him upon an average about once a month, or perhaps three weeks." It would, in fact, seem that the substitution of "week" for "month" in this passage would have been nearer the truth.

Poole's replies to Coleridge's complaints during his illness at this time showed all the tender solicitude of an anxius mother to a sick and fretful child. Samuel must not "tumble about, on precipices," not go out in bad weather, not "remain with wet feet and wet clothes." He must take "appropriate exercise and appropriate clothing during that exercise." And Poole reminded him that if he had not left Stowey, "which I bitterly regret," he would not have been ill. Poole was also beginning to fear that the early promise of "genius" in Samuel had been delusory. Samuel was not only "a husband and father," he reminded him, but also "a spirit of much power cast among us—power, I trust, to be productive of good. But remember it has not yet fulfilled its errand. You are I know, impressed with this truth."

Poole was not the only benefactor disappointed in Samuel. Josiah Wedgwood began to fear that his annuity was preventing rather than assisting the appearance of the great works expected of Coleridge's genius. Divining Josiah's doubts and fearing for his annuity, Samuel sent him in February 1801 an imposing series of letters attacking the "empiricists," and he requested Josiah's comments upon them. When no reply came Samuel, disappointed in turn, expressed his fears to Poole. Nor was Josiah's later comment to Poole, enthusiastic. He knew little about metaphysics, he said, he was too busy to read the letters, but "from a cursory view he seems to have plucked the principal feathers out of Locke's wings."

Josiah's annuity had been given to Samuel to benefit humanity. The abstractions of metaphysics did not seem to Josiah, apparently, to best answer that requirement. Samuel had not been satisfactory in the preceding November when Josiah urged him to adopt a "pursuit." "You say most truly, my dear Sir," was Samuel's tart retort, "that a pursuit is necessary—*Pursuit*, I say—for even praise-worthy employment merely for good, or general good, is not sufficient for happiness, is not fit for men. . . . " To this Samuel added a simple, unmetaphysical postscript that even Josiah too well understood: "I cannot at present make out how I stand in a pecuniary way—but I believe that I have anticipated on the next year to the amount of £30 or £40—probably more."

From this time, too, not only did Samuel's debts increase, but his attitude toward them and toward his many and patient benefactors assumed a complacency, even at times when disappointed, an insolence, as of one demanding the payment of personal dues. Nor was he unaware of the benefits he bestowed upon his donors by thus enabling them to develop their generous impulses. "The art in a *great* man," he privately noted, "and of evidently superior faculties, to be often *obliged* to people, often his inferiors—in this way the enthusiasm of affection may be exerted."

To Poole he explained the causes of his poverty—a high moral standard, and his hatred of writing "merely for the bookseller, without any sense of the moral utility of what I was writing." Although poverty "stared him in the face," he was unafraid: he "dared behold his image miniatured in the pupil of her hollow eye." Of course Poole sent largesse. Amid the discomfort of penury, "dunning letters—all the Hell of an author," Samuel relapsed into the mood of his earlier radicalism, though he now abjured both Jacobins and aristocrats as without principles. Now the moral advantages of poverty particularly impressed him. Pondering the condition of the poor, Coleridge propounded a scheme for feeding them on bread and beer made from otherwise wasted acorns, but not apparently, intended for his consumption. So thinking, he imagined "little red apple-cheeked children" watering the oaks round their cottage doors in dry seasons—"Merciful God! what a contrast to the employment of these dear Beings by a wheel or a machine in a hellish cotton factory!" For Coleridge well foresaw the horrors of the machine age dawning about him.

Throughout the spring and summer of 1801 Coleridge continued to encourage in his friends the moral excellence of generosity until Poole, a particular target for such moral improvement, began to show signs of weariness and impatience. "You say, if you were an independent man . . . ," he replied to Samuel's complaint, "In God's name, why do you not think yourself independent?"—thus reminding him of the Wedgwoods' annuity—"besides what your own labours may produce." And if Coleridge died, as he so often feared, wrote Poole sarcastically, he would adopt one son and was sure someone would do the same for the other. They must "live within their income, be it what it will.'' He had seen larger families living happily upon less than Coleridge had, said Poole. In the same unusual mood of impatience with Samuel, Poole dismissed his unreal grumblings about the poor—''What have you to do with the poverty and misery and sufferings around you? Have you caused the havoc?'' For Poole, famous for his practicality and generosity toward the poor about him, was unimpressed. Even Samuel's illness was not ''really bodily,'' he suspected, but ''the consequence of an irritated mind.''

Coleridge's continued touting for the means of foreign travel—the Azores for the moment—for cheap living, and to save his life particularly irritated Poole. Instead of financing such an expedition, he merely offered to try to find a companion for Samuel, one who would meet all expenses. ''Set your house in order in the best way you can,'' Poole told him, and, he advised the dropping of metaphysics and poetry, and their replacement with remunerative writing. It was Poole's sharpest rebuke to Samuel, but it must have been accompanied by a substantial present, for despite Coleridge's annoyance, which later found expression, Coleridge's reply to Poole was very appreciative. But Poole's letter marked the end of his former prostration to Coleridge's ''genius.''

Whatever had been the mutual disillusion of Southey and Coleridge, it was now far exceeded by the increasing dissension between Coleridge and Poole. On August 25, 1801, after a short absence, Samuel found a letter from Poole awaiting him. It was the result of an application by Wordsworth on Samuel's behalf, and almost certainly due to Samuel's suggestion for a loan of £50 to help him to travel, if Poole could afford to lose it. Wordsworth had kindly hoped by this to help both friends, but it became merely an excuse for Samuel's anger with Poole, who now reminded Coleridge that his debt to him was not £37 as Coleridge had said but £52, and he offered a mere £20 instead of the £100 Samuel wanted. Poole also spoke of ''many claims'' on himself and suggested that Coleridge's brothers might help him. He also informed Coleridge that he had suggested that Coleridge should accompany Tom Wedgwood on a projected visit to Italy, but he had received no reply. Annoyed by this refusal of his demands, Coleridge allowed a fortnight to pass before replying. The delay, he said, was not due to lack of affection, but to his despair of saving his life, for to go abroad was now impossible. Not that his life was of any importance, ''but for a sense of duty'' he would ''resign it as quietly and blessedly'' as a babe falling asleep on its mother's breast. Toward Wordsworth's intervention he felt ''great repugnance''; and as for accompanying Tom Wedgwood—''O God! the very last thing I could have submitted to,'' save ''as a duty.''

Yet, less than a year had passed since Samuel—hoping to accompany Tom to Italy—had told Josiah Wedgwood: ''If, (disciplining myself into *silent* cheerfulness) I could be of any comfort to him by being his companion and attendant for two or three months, on the supposition that he should wish to travel and was at a loss for a companion more fit, I would go with him with a willing affection.'' Finally, taking a high, dignified pose, he now adjured Poole: ''Let us for the future abstain from all pecuniary matters.'' ''If I live,'' he continued, "I shall soon pay all I at present owe—and if I die, the thought of being in *your* debt will never disquiet me on my sick bed." As for his health, "I am going, as suspect"; and as usual with all his friends he detailed his latest symptoms. Nevertheless, evidently assisted by opium, Coleridge added, "My spirits are good—I am generally *cheerful*, and when I am not, it is only because I have exchanged it for a deeper and more pleasurable tranquillity." Upon a note of stoicism the letter closed. Comparing himself to the soldier who "rushes on the bayonet," he cried to Poole, "his trade has been to follow a blind feeling—and thereby to *act*—mine has been to contemplate—and thereby to *endure*." Twelve days later, hearing from Davy of the death of Poole's mother, Samuel sent him a sermonic letter of general pious moralizing and preaching for Poole's improvement. It concluded: "Come to me, Poole!—No—No—No—You have none that love you so well as I. I write with tears that prevent my seeing what I am writing."

Hurt by both letters, Poole replied in a sad and solemn tone; but instead of cash he sent advice not to leave England, ignoring Coleridge's impending demise. Coleridge's answer to this was the most offensive of all: a long satirical parody of Poole's frequent advice to him; an exhortation to Poole to "exert your faculties, devote yourself to some great work, as a solemn duty," despite his inevitable "intellectual disadvantages" as an inheritor of wealth. From this Samuel indicated and analyzed Poole's defects as they seemed to him, ending with an insulting description of an evidently analogical and im-aginary gabbling idiot, which caused a friend of Samuel's to ask him what it said: "To give advice, I replied; I know not what else an idiot can do, and any idiot can do that." After this Coleridge continued to express his "aversion to the Rich, Love for the Poor or the Unwealthy, and belief in the excessive evils arising from Poverty." "God love you, my dear Poole!" he almost contemp-tuously concluded, "and restore you to that degree of cheerfulness which is necessary for virtue and energetic well-doing."

Poole in his reply rightly described the letter as "outrageous." Upon this Coleridge demanded in a surly tone: "Was my society then useless to you dur-ing my abode in Stowey?" And he promised to visit Poole when he could raise £25, and "any *part* of this money that you can spare for the space of four *months*, I shall be glad to receive from you." The rest he would borrow from some other person. Ten days later came £25 from Poole, which Samuel im-mediately accepted in an ungrateful, thankless letter. Next Saturday, he said, he would go to London for ten days "to settle all my literary concerns with ad-vice for my future health, etc." Then he would go to Poole and others until the end of March. "Less than two months I shall assuredly not stay with *you*," he condescendingly informed him, presuming more than ever upon Poole's gen-uine affection for himself. Nevertheless, Samuel's delicate feelings never quite recovered from the wound, for which even eight years later he characteristically and falsely blamed Wordsworth; "a healed indeed but yet scarred wound between me and Poole," he told Stuart.

12 "Dear Asra" (1799-1801)

Dear Asra, woman beyond utterance dear!
—*Coleridge, "Dear Asra" (1801)*

Worst of all Coleridge's anxieties throughout these months at Greta Hall was a new love. In November 1799 he—as related above—paid a second visit to Sockburn, which lasted a week. Then he continued on his way to London. This visit was fateful for Samuel who found in Sarah Hutchinson, then twenty-four years of age, his love ideal. Coleridge's almost certainly platonic romance with Sarah Hutchinson ran its somewhat dreary course for several years, until years later it faded away in absence. It began on Sunday, November 24, 1799, when all were gathered around the hearth at Sockburn enjoying conundrums, puns, stories, and laughter, while Samuel furtively held Sarah's hand for a long time behind her back, and "for the first time was wounded by Love's dainty but deadly poisoned dart." Such, but in Latin, was Coleridge's version of the incident when in 1803, transferring various material from his notebooks of 1799, he added it to them. And now in 1799 during this visit to Sockburn Coleridge entered in his notebook, without comment or addition, the single line:

The long entrancement of a True-Love's kiss.

In later years Coleridge's daughter described Sarah Hutchinson as having "fine, long, light brown hair, her only beauty except a fair skin, for her features were plain and contracted, her figure dumpy, and devoid of grace and dignity. She was a plump woman of little more than five feet." Sara Coleridge might be suspected of prejudice against her own mother's rival, but Coleridge's friend of later years, Crabb Robinson, first meeting Sarah Hutchinson in 1815 (when she was forty years of age), was even less complimentary: "a plain woman—rather repulsive at first—but she improves on acquaintance greatly—a lively and sensible little woman." Coleridge's son Hartley, who never much liked her, was struck by her "shrewdness"—which, in fact, her letters clearly prove.

Sarah Hutchinson did indeed possess admirable qualities. She was a typical woman of the northern well-to-do farmer class of her period, with much common sense and self-command. But Love's "deadly poisoned dart" was shot before Samuel could discover Sarah's virtues. Whatever happened or did not happen at Sockburn, it inspired Coleridge to write a romantic, pseudomedieval ballad, "Introduction to the Tale of the Dark Ladie," which appeared a month later in the *Morning Post*. It was "a silly tale of old-fashioned love"—with, in fact, recognizable decor from Sockburn. A few of its good stanzas are now famous as a separate poem entitled "Love." They stand out in happy contrast to the general mediocrity of theme and expression in the rest of the poem. How much or how little of reality is embedded in this presentation of Sarah as the blushing, weeping maid who forgives her lover for gazing "too fondly on her face"—and so presumably for also holding her hand—it is useless, and so foolish to explore. For Sarah as Genevieve and Samuel as a medieval minstrel, have been reborn in the never-never land of sham romantic dream. It was in that land of Romance that Coleridge's "love" for Sarah Hutchinson was born and died, "His love for her," wrote a finally disillusioned Dorothy ten years laters, "is no more than a fanciful dream."

When Samuel returned to London at the close of 1799, the memory of Sarah Hutchinson at Sockburn was a new magnet drawing him back to the North. Against the combined attractions of Sarah Hutchinson and the Wordsworths, Poole in Stowey had little chance. Coleridge, now walking about London with "a little of Sara's hair" in his pocket—as he said—must evidently return to the North before long. For Sarah was now rechristened "Sara" by Coleridge as more poetic. And Sara had doubtless corresponded with Coleridge during his absence in London, reviving happy memories.

The arrival of Coleridge and his wife at Dove Cottage followed six month later, on June 29, 1800. Since Sara and her sister Mary often stayed with the Wordsworths, they must inevitably have appeared with William and Dorothy at times, when the Wordsworths visited Coleridge at Greta Hall. It was thus in November 1800 during Coleridge's illness that Sara arrived at Greta Hall to join the Wordsworths there in helping Samuel. When a week later, on November 22, the Wordsworths returned to Dove Cottage, Sara accompanied them.

From this time until the following April 1801, Sara Hutchinson was the guest of the Wordsworths, though also sometimes a visitor at Greta Hall. When she was at Dove Cottage Samuel's visits there, during intervals of health, were frequent. He was at Dove Cottage on December 5, 1800, when Dorothy and Sara "had a grand bread and cake baking," and were "all very merry" until midnight. Coleridge returned home the next day, but four days later the Dove Cottage party walked through snow to Greta Hall and stayed six days. Four days later still, December 18, 1800, Mrs. Coleridge came on a visit to Dove Cottage with Derwent, and after two days she was joined there by Samuel, "very ill, rheumatic, feverish"—as Dorothy noted.

Certainly Sara Hutchinson became a devoted assistant to Samuel at this time of need. Her hand as copyist appears at this time in Coleridge's notebook, including many pages of listed flowers transcribed from a popular book on botany. There is found Sara's insertion "forget-me-not," the name Coleridge gave to the flower then known as "mouse's ear." The forget-me-not appeared also in one of Coleridge's poems, "The Keepsake," inspired by memories or dreams of Sara in these days, recalling:

> That blue and bright-eyed floweret of the brook,
> Hope's gentle gem, the sweet Forget-me-not
> So will not fade the flowers which Emmeline
> With delicate fingers on the snow-white silk
> has worked (the flowers which most she knew I loved).

Doubtless Sara Hutchinson's reward for her devotion was the gift he now made her of corrected proof-sheets of the sonnets of the poetaster Anna Seward, "The Swan of Lichfield," as she was called. They contained an inscription from Samuel to Sara—"The Editor to Asahara, the Moorish Maid, Dec. 1800, Greta Hall, Keswick." By this time Samuel needed whatever consolation Sara could give. His passion for her—if such it can be called—was an addition to the many other causes of his increasing disquietude and indecision.

Sara Hutchinson's departure from Dove Cottage in April 1801 left Coleridge's mind divided between happy memories of her presence and the deeper gloom of her absence. The first found expression in rather weak amatory verses that Coleridge entitled "The Language of Birds"—

> "I love, and I Love," almost all the birds say,
> From sunrise to star-rise, so gladsome are they . . .
> 'Tis no wonder that he's full of joy to the brim,
> When He loves his Love and his Love loves Him.

In the opposite mood of misery, he told Poole, "I to the grave go down."

In mid-July 1801, declaring that he must go to Burham to borrow the works of Duns Scotus from the Cathedral Library there, Coleridge set off for Bishop Middleham, which was eight miles from the Cathedral City. Sara Hutchinson was now living at Bishop Middleham, keeping house for her brother George who had a farm there.

The week Coleridge spent with George and Sara was so happy that poetry returned and he wrote the ode "Tranquillity," a quality evidently embodied for him in Sara:

> The feeling Heart, the searching Soul,
> To HER I dedicate the whole.

So it was written at the time in Sara's little manuscript volume of poems, some transcribed at various times by Coleridge himself. His description to Southey of his visit to Bishop Middleham was in harmony with his poem: "A quiet, good family that love me dearly.'' George he thought ''a great humourist'' for making ''very droll verses in the Northern dialect and in the meter of Burns.'' All must have vivdly recalled the meeting at Sockburn nearly two years before, when he held Sara's hand behind her back and was wounded by the poisoned arrow of Cupid. Sara he admired as much as ever—''so very good a woman that I have seldom indeed seen the like of her,'' he told Southey. Certainly Sara, who a day or two later was copying pages of Thomas Aquinas's Latin for Samuel, fully deserved the praise he gave her. It was surprisingly unromantic after the ''Introduction to the Tale of the Dark Ladie.'' Seeing her thus, Coleridge gave way to violent feelings in his letter to Southey: ''Death! that everywhere there should be one or two good and excellent people like these, and they should not have the power given 'em . . . to whirl away the rest to Hell!''

At Bishop Middleham Coleridge spent a happy week with his friends until his departure for Durham on July 24 to borrow the neglected Duns Scotus, and as he said, ''set the poor gemman on his feet again.'' But Durham disappointed him. The town and his inn he disliked, and the cathedral library had only one work of Duns Scotus, the *De Sententide* that, along with Samuel's other needs—seventeenth-century editions of Aquinas, Suarez, and Aristotle—the ''stupid, haughty fool'' of a librarian was reluctant to send to the Middleham farm. ''A few books which nobody had read within the memory of man,'' said Samuel, disgusted with treatment so different from that he had received from the cathedral of Carlisle, which had been sending to Greta Hall, for the last four months, whatever books he desired.

After dining in Durham ''with a large parcel of priests, all belonging to the cathedral—thoroughly ingorant and hard-hearted,'' he sent his disgusts for Southey's sympathy. The miserable librarian, when asked for the works of Leibniz, had mistaken the German name for certain ''animalicula,'' and sent him to a local naturalist who sold microscopes. The tale too closely resembles Samuel's tale of Spinoza and ''Spynosy'' at Stowey for credence, and though in both cases he swore to their truth, his fatherhood of both speaks in their faces, and hovers in their characteristically unsubtle humor. However, the erring librarian repented, and after two disgusted days Samuel, still intent upon ''burning Locke, Hobbes and Hume under the nose of Duns Scotus,'' set out to walk back to his friends at Bishop Middleham and to set Sara to her copying.

The walk brought back Samuel's illness—pains and swellings, especially at night. The Durham doctor prescribed horse-riding and warm seabaths. So he and Sara rode away together to her brother Tom's farm, Gallow Hill, only six miles from Scarborough by the sea. Their first day's ride brought them to Stockton, where another brother, John Hutchinson, had a farm and a bank. Two more days riding brought them to Gallow Hill and Scarborough, on the last day of July.

Life at Gallow Hill during their ten days' visit was as pleasant for Samuel as Bishop Middleham had been. Every day or so, doubtless accompanied by Sara at times and perhaps also by Tom Hutchinson, Samuel rode to Scarborough and back to Gallow Hill. He was glad to find the open sea bathing effective, and he particularly delighted in defying his doctor, who while insisting upon *warm* sea baths had warned him against *"the open sea* as fatal to me." Instead of obeying, Samuel "came out all at once on the beach, and had faith in the ocean," as he told Southey, "bathed regularly, frolicked in the billows, and got a proper deal of good."

It was now "this spa *season*," as Sara two years before had described Scarborough to her cousin, John Monkhouse: "a very gay place, I assure you. The spas are thronging past daily, and we see coaches whirring by for ever. . . . " Exhilarated by his aquatic diversions, returned health, the fascination and devotion of Sara, and a victory over his doctor, as well doubtless as by the social gaiety of the spa, Samuel burst into joyous song, which he sent to Southey with the explanation: "On my first immersion—for alas! it is a long time since I have cropt a flowering week on the sweet Hill of Poesy."

God be with thee, gladsome Ocean!
How gladly greet I thee once more—
Ships and waves and endless motion
And Life rejoicing on thy shore.

Gravely said the sage physician,
To bathe me on thy shores were Death;
But my Soul fulfilled her mission,
And lo! I breathe untroubled breath.

It was all very exciting; but as the verses proceed, it becomes evident that Sara inspires more of the wonder and joy than the misguided doctor:

Me a thousand Loves and Pleasures,
A thousand Recollections bland,
Thoughts sublime and stately measures,
Revisit on the sounding strand—
Dreams, the soul herself forsaking,
Grief-like Transports, boyish Mirth,
Silent Adorations making
A blessed Shadow of this Earth!

O ye Hopes, that stir within me,
Health comes with you from above!
God is *with me, God is in* me—
I cannot die: for Life is Love!

Seven years later, "alone and hopeless," Coleridge recalled the last stanza: "seven years ago, but oh! in what happier times—I wrote thus!"

At Gallow Hill was Mary, Sara's sister, acting as housekeeper to her brother Tom. There was good food, which Samuel always particularly appreciated, whether at Ottery or Gallow Hill. And there were gatherings around the hearth in the evenings, just as there were before at Sockburn, which Tom had since vacated for Gallow Hill. Some ten years later Samuel recalled those evenings at Gallow Hill—the fire, Mary, Sara, and himself; Sara leaning with her head on her hand, her feet on the fender, the dog watching her face in the firelight, the last dinner at Gallow Hill with two fowls and delicious white sauce, the too salt cheese at Middleham, horses and riding to Scarborough, the volumes from the Durham Cathedral Library: such were his memories.

Nor was it ony in a prose version in his notebook that Coleridge recorded such memories of Gallow Hill. The following April 1802, in his verse "Letter to Asra" (as Sara now became), he incorporated a similar memory:

> that happy night,
> When Mary, thou [Sara] and I together were,
> The low decaying fire our only light,
> And listened to the stillness of the air!
> O that affectionate and blameless maid,
> Dear Mary! on her lap my head she laid—
> Her hand was on my brow
> Even as my own is now;
> And on my cheek I felt the eye-lash play.
> Such joy I had, that I may truly say,
> My spirit was awe-stricken with the excess
> And trance-like depth of its brief happiness.

In the revised and much improved version of "Letter to Asra," named "Dejection," these lines were among the omissions.

On August 9 Coleridge and Sara left Gallow Hill for Middleham where they arrived on the eleventh. For a week or more he remained there, took a sulphur bath at a neighboring health resort, and, when two young girls staying with the Hutchinsons at Middleham departed, he sent them off with flattering and flirtatious verses, excusing himself for being ineligible as a suitor, because

> *Nota bene, I'm married*;
> And coals to Newcastle must never be carried!!

On August 25 Coleridge reentered the gloom of Greta Hall.

On July 10, 1801, after a year in Portugal, Southey and his wife Edith returned to Bristol. There warm invitations from Coleridge awaited them, not only to visit Greta Hall, but even to settle there with the Coleridges, almost as one family. With unusual, almost Coleridgian emotion, Southey replied the following day: "Time and absence make strange work with our affections; but mine are ever returning to rest upon you. I have other and dear friends, but none with whom the whole of my being is intimate—with whom every thought and feeling can amalgamate. Oh! I have yet such dreams! Is it quite clear that you and I were not meant for some better star, and dropped, by mistake, into this world of pounds, shillings, and pence?" With the last sentiment Coleridge must certainly have agreed, but perhaps less so when Southey also declared: "I must spur you to something, to the assertion of your supremacy. . . ."

Coleridge received the letter during his first visit to Middleham and, delighted to learn of the Southeys' return and impending visit, replied no less affectionately: "Oh! how I have dreamt about you—Times that *have been*, and never can return, have been with me on my bed of pain, and how I yearned toward you in those moments." "But for God's sake, make haste and come to me," he wrote, "and let us talk of the lands of Arabia while we are floating in our lazy boat on Keswick Lake." In lighter vein he cried "O Edith! how happy Sarah will be."

Immediately after Samuel's return to Greta Hall the Southeys arrived. But after the southern charms of Portugal, the beauties of the English lakes District left Southey as cold as he found the English climate. Seeing Coniston and Windermere, he sighed for "the Mondego and the Tagus," and "Cintra my paradise." "I have lived abroad too long to be contented in England," he exclaimed, "I miss southern luxuries—the fruits, the wines; I miss the sun in heaven," and he longed to again "eat grapes and ride donkeys, and be very happy. This country is very beautiful but very cold," he said, "It disappoints expectation."

So after a fortnight at Greta Hall Southey, leaving Edith with her sister Mrs. Coleridge, set out to tour Wales with his friend Wynn. During the tour he received an offer of a secretaryship to the Chancellor of the Irish Exchequer, and being too poor to refuse it, reluctantly accepted. Before leaving for Dublin on October 7, he spent a few more days with Edith and the Coleridges at Greta Hall, where Edith remained after his departure. Coleridge, immediately informing Poole of Southey's appointment, dismissed his four hundred pounds a year as "nothing. But his society will be all the first and greatest people—and of course the *opening* is great. Men of Talents," he added, "are at present in great request by the Ministry; had I a spark of ambition I have opportunities enough—but I will be either far greater than all this can end in, even if it should end in my being Minister of State myself, or I will be nothing."

The meeting of Southey and Coleridge at Greta Hall had not entirely fulfilled the ecstatic anticipations of either. A sense of change usually haunts first meetings after long absence, especially after such absence abroad. The quarrels at Greta Hall now occurring between the two sisters, in addition to the usual ones between Coleridge and his wife, had not promoted Southey's happiness there. Indeed, Samuel later regretted to Southey, "that which, I fear, could not but have disturbed your comforts, when you were here last." Nor did Southey approve of Coleridge's treatment of his wife.

How remote Southey was from Samuel's adulation to the "great" he soon showed by his comments on his new associates in Dublin, whose "civilities excite more contempt than anger, but they make me think more despicably of the world than I could wish to do." Almost immediately after arriving in Ireland Southey followed his chief to London, calling again en route at Greta Hall to see Edith, and leaving for London on October 30. There Edith joined him early in November, and Greta Hall resumed its former way of life.

If Southey's visit to Greta Hall had failed to justify his expectations of an ecstatic reunion with a rare and kindred soul, Samuel was no less disappointed in Southey, as his notebook very clearly showed in a reference to his friend as *Australis*. That the main cause of difference with Southey was, for Coleridge, his inability to sympathize with him about his wife, Samuel clearly revealed when writing to Southey shortly after his departure for Ireland. "My mind is full of visions," he wrote, "and you had been so long connected with the fairest of all fair dreams, that I feel your absence more than I enjoy your society. That I do not enjoy your society so much as I anticipated that I should do, is wholly, or almost wholly, owing to the nature of my domestic feelings, and the fear, or the consciousness, that you did not and could not sympathize with them."

At this time Samuel turned for assistance from the unsatisfactory Poole to Stuart who responded by sending him thirty pounds. For this Coleridge expressed warm gratitude: "much affected by the wish you express that I had applied to you in my pecuniary Distresses." Five weeks had passed since Samuel warned Southey, "Do not work for Stuart—Hamilton [apparently an editor] is bad enough!" The rest evidently transcended words. But now from Greta Hall he told Stuart that what writing he had done for him was "not at all adequate to the money I have received," and at the same time, he informed him, "Southey, I am certain never thought otherwise than that you had behaved very handsomely with him!" and he begged Stuart to send the next quarter's *Morning Post*s to "a very dear friend" of himself and of Wordsworth, Miss Sara Hutchinson, who lived at Bishop Middleham and whose "pleasure of seeing the paper during the time I wrote in it, would be greater than you can easily imagine."

In generous mood Samuel made a new agreement to send more articles and poems to the paper, but a week later he told Stuart that he had had the "cholera morbus," he feared his widow must pay the sixteen guineas he owed Stuart, he was now in bed, and he found it "more than merely expedient to lie in perfect calmness"; and besides, "it can be, I suppose, of no great importance when I begin with you."

Upon Coleridge's return from Durham to Greta Hall at the close of August, Coleridge could not forget the memories of Sara Hutchinson as he had seen her during the few happy days at Bishop Middleham and Gallow Hill. A lost love idealized in absence fascinated his imagination and created more powerful emotions than a present reality. His attempt in his notebook now to express his experience in what would today be called eidetic imagery—imagery so externalized and realistic as to be almost a hallucination—reveals his clear consciousness of this: "images and realities in the eye of memory—fantastically, soul going into the heart of the survivor, and abiding there with its image." Throughout September he was thus haunted, and another entry in his notebook shows how real this imagery was to him: "Prest to my bosom and felt there—it was quite dark. I looked intensely toward her face—and sometimes I *saw* it—so vivid was the spectrum, that it had almost all its natural sense of distance and outness—except indeed that, feeling and all, I felt her as part of my being—'twas all spectral . . . the last image, how lovely to me now.''

Frustrated passion readily turns to compensatory imagery, and Coleridge's visions of Sara may well find their explanations in Coleridge's reference to her at this time in the following entry in his notebook: "Sara is uncommonly *cold* in her feelings of animal love." She is also "deficient in tangible ideas and sensations." And with characteristic mental subtlety Coleridge turned to consider the relation between the "tactual" and the imaginative.

Throughout that autumn of 1801 Coleridge confided to his notebook his secret unrest, which as before sent him wandering aimlessly about the country around Greta Hall. As he wanders the stream murmurs to him of Sara, "Why aren't you here?" So now love, it seems to him, demands that Sara be brought into his own private, metaphysical world: "Endeavouring to make the infinitely beloved Darling understand all my knowledge, I learn that art of making the abstrusest Truths intelligible and interesting to the unlearned."

Doubtless it was to this end that he had set Sara again copying for him, this time not the names of flowers but long extracts from minor writers on the seventeenth century: Henry More's nonsense about spooks and witches, Peter Heylyn on the Sabbath and persecutions, and Daniel Sennert's wearisome Latin and Greek lucubrations. Soon poor Mrs. Coleridge was busy copying, too, despite her domestic and maternal duties. She was doubtless inspired by the example of Sara to attempt rivalry with her for Samuel's affection. Samuel was also writing his verses "To Asra":

Dear Asra, woman beyond utterance dear!
This love which ever welling at my heart,
Now in its living fount doth heave and fall,
Now overflowing pours thro' every part,
Of all my frame, and fills and changes all,
Like vernal waters springing up through snow.

On October 21, 1801 (Coleridge's birthday, which as usual he thought was the twentieth), he sent Southey a long letter that began with his regrets that Southey's visit had been too short for him to appreciate the beauties of the Lakes District, and, continued into the arena of his domestic miseries: "Yesterday the snow fell—and today—O that you were here—" he began, "Lodore full—the mountains snow-crested—and the dazzling silver of the Lake—this cloudy, sunny, misty howling weather!—After your arrival I move southward in the hopes that warm rooms and deep tranquillity may build me up anew; and that I may be able to return in the spring without the necessity of going abroad." When Southey returned to Greta Hall Coleridge would go with him and Edith to London, and then either to Poole or Wedgwood "as circumstances direct." Although the cold weather agreed with him, he said that he was very ill and nervous. After this came the evident cause of his dejection: "Sarah—(*Mrs* Coleridge)—alas! we are not suited to each other. . . . I will go believing that it will end happily—if not, if our mutual unsuitableness continues, and (as it assuredly will do, if it continue) increases and strengthens, why then, it is better for her and my children, that I should live apart, than that she should be a widow and they Orphans.''

To Southey he now expressed his genuine concern for his family's future. He had thought much about marriage, he said, and was "convinced of its indissolubleness.'' If separation came he would provide for her and the children if possible, "that while I live she may enjoy the comforts of life; and that when I die, something may have been accumulated that may secure her from degrading Dependence. When I least love her, then most do I feel anxiety for her peace, comfort and welfare. Is she not the mother of my children? And am I the man not to know and feel this?''

In this mood as November approached, Coleridge planned once again to join the *Morning Post* and earn his bread by the sweat of his brow. But before his departure for London there was a ceremony on October 10 lasting from midday until 2:00 P.M. It was attended by Wordsworth and Dorothy and Coleridge—the completion of "Sara's Seat,'' of which she had laid the first stone in March. "William Wordsworth and his Sister,—with S. T. Coleridge built it, to wit, all the stonework; with the footstones—we being all there in hope and prayer, that Mary with Tom Hutchinson had then already set off, and were setting off, from Gallow Hill—on their road to Grasmere. God in heaven bless her and him too.'' Such was Samuel's account, scribbled on the flyleaf of one his volumes. Mary must have reached Grasmere safely, for on October 23 she arrived at Greta Hall. Only Sara was invisible.

Coleridge's last day in Greta Hall, November 9, promised to be sad and solitary as well as darkened by the knowledge of domestic failure. For Mrs. Coleridge had already gone with the children to Eusemere by Ullswater, the home of new friends, the Clarksons. Meanwhile, Coleridge in desolate Greta Hall unburdened his spirit to Southey as usual: "If my wife loved me, and I my wife, half as well as both love our children, I should be the happiest man alive—but this is not, will not be.'' But the day was not to end so. "Just before dark'' Dorothy Wordsworth and Mary Hutchinson arrived. "We enjoyed ourselves in the study,'' wrote Dorothy, "and''—with private jibe at the absent Mrs. Coleridge—"were *at home*.'' They all had supper at the Jacksons' next door, and then Dorothy wrote: "Mary and I sat in Coleridge's room a while.''

The following morning, when Coleridge departed for Eusemere and London, Dorothy's record was very sad: "Poor Coleridge left us, and we came home together.'' Nor was that all; Dorothy had burned her mouth with Coleridge's brandy, and Mary's feet were sore. But the thought of Coleridge haunted Dorothy: "Coleridge had a sweet day for his ride. Every sight and every sound reminded me of him—dear, dear fellow—of his many walks to us by day and by night, of all dear things. I was melancholy and could not talk; but at least I eased my heart by weeping—nervous blubbering says William. It is not so. O! how many, many reasons have I to be anxious for him!''

On Friday, November 13, 1801, Samuel left Eusemere at half-past six in the morning and took "the heavy coach" to Penrith, which he reached at nine o'clock after a somewhat exciting journey. First one of the horses fell down, and next "plunged, &c. &c. &c. and tore all the harness," while two women in the coach were "hurt and as horribly frightened." However, Sara Hutchinson awaited Coleridge at Penrith, and he spent the day there with her. Late on Sunday evening, November 15, he reached London.

Coleridge remained in London little more than three months. Southey was then in London, and Coleridge stayed with him for a week before moving to rooms in King Street, Covent Garden, which Stuart had found for him. Although physically and mentally unwell, he immediately set off to find friends who might be useful to him. With a new sense of freedom he told Godwin he felt "like a fish in air, dying from excess of oxygen—a great change from the society of Wordsworth and his sister—for tho' we were three persons, it was but one God." That was not very kind to Wordsworth.

Now he was "meeting Lords many and Gods many," he proudly informed Godwin, yet "more odd fish than rarae aves." However, he would breakfast with Godwin tomorrow since he thought he could afford the half-crown fare. But "miserably uncomfortable," he did not expect to stay long in town. Nor did he.

On Boxing Day, with twenty-five guineas borrowed from Stuart on the promise of more articles—never written—Coleridge left for Stowey, where Poole and Tom Wedgwood awaited him. On the way a night's hospitality given him by a Bath parson was repaid by a recitation of "Christabel," which delighted the ladies. The next day he joined Poole and Tom Wedgwood in Stowey.

On January 20, 1802, Coleridge and Poole returned to London to hear Davy's lectures—already described. In London Coleridge dined with James Mackintosh who had stayed two days at Greta Hall. But Coleridge could neither forgive nor forget Mackintosh's conversational victory over him at Cote House in 1798. Coleridge now found him "very entertaining and pleasant, but every inch the Being I had conceived him to be, from what I saw of him at Cote House." Nevertheless, the acquaintance with Mackintosh set Coleridge working hard—so he said—at another great literary phantom during these last weeks in London, "finishing the History of the opinions concerning Space and Time for Mackintosh," as he told Poole.

A fortnight before, Southey had written satirically about the project to a friend, saying: "A great metaphysical book is conceived and about to be born. Thomas Wedgwood the Jupiter whose brain is parturient—Mackintosh the man-midwife—a preface on the history of metaphysical opinons promised by Coleridge. This will perhaps prove an abortion . . . . It has, however, proceeded so far as to disturb the spiders, whose hereditary claim to Thomas Aquinas and Duns Scotus had not been disputed for many a year before. Time and Space are the main subjects of speculation."

Coleridge's friends in London followed his doings there with—sometimes not uncritical—interest. "Coleridge is in town," Southey told a friend. "You should commute your Star for the *Morning Post*, in which you will see good

things from him, and such occasional verses as I may happen to evacuate.''
Nor was Coleridge's regrettable habit of backbiting overlooked. Lamb heard
of it and passed on the gossip to Manning: ''Coleridge appears as much as ever
under the influence of a cold vanity, and does not spare absentem rodere
amicum . . . . Pity that such human frailties should perch upon the margin of
Ullswater lake. 'Pity,' say all the echoes in such a tone, so plaintive, I wish I
had my flute.''

On one of the last days of February 1802 Coleridge left London for Greta
Hall.

13 Travels with Tom Wedgwood (1802-3)

> *"I shall probably return to Crescelly—and then—God knows, where! . . . I don't see any likelihood of our going to the Moon, or to either of the Planets, or fixed Stars—and that is all, I can say."*
> —*Coleridge to Mrs. Coleridge, November 23, 1802*

The thought of seeing Sara Hutchinson again dominated Samuel's return journey to Greta Hall in February 1802. Instead of going via York on the way, to meet her there as intended, he went directly to Gallow Hill. He arrived at Gallow Hill on March 2 and remained eleven days. This visit was evidently less pleasant for Samuel than the last. All available illumination comes from more "straws in the wind;" but that the wind was stormy is clear. For Samuel, the absent idealistic lover dreaming of a kindred soul—which meant an obedient one—the reality was almost inevitably disappointing. That this was so his notebook entries and verses show. Coleridge's notes, far from complimentary, suggest a refusal by Sara to meet some wish of Samuel's—perhaps his wish to bring her to Dove Cottage or to Greta Hall. That his wish to do so had caused perplexity in Dove Cottage as well as anger in Greta Hall, Dorothy's journal suggests. On receiving a letter from Coleridge on February 26, she noted: "We were perplexed about Sara's coming," Dorothy at once wrote to Mary Hutchinson, while William wrote to Mrs. Coleridge. And Sara did not come.

Certainly Sara no longer enjoyed the tranquillity that had so impressed and inspired Coleridge before at Gallow Hill. "Sara in bad spirits about Coleridge," Dorothy had written on December 13, 1801. Indeed, Coleridge's notes at Gallow Hill now suggest discontent and sometimes strife: "Sara Hutchinson's new gospel—alias—Honesty." Nor was Samuel's plan for a poem on Asra romantic: "Can see nothing extraordinary in her—a poem noting all the virtues of the mild and retired kind." Perhaps it is as well that the poem was never written. Another unwritten poem on Sara, also noted at this time, was to be "on the length of our acquaintance—all the hours I have been thinking of her." One poetical plan—"on the endeavour to emancipate the soul from daydreams"—was partly achieved shortly afterward in "The Picture," or "The Lover's Resolution," in which he cries:

The Master-passion quelled,
I feel that I am free.

This poem was first published in the *Morning Post* on September 6, 1802.

In another entry Coleridge went to Nature for metaphors—surely of Sara and himself—"Waterfall—tiny—a leaf—still attracted still repelled." The final entry at Gallow Hill suggests a quarrel, followed by a sudden departure: "Friday, Marcy 12th, 'and wept aloud'—you made me feel uncomfortable. Saturday, March 13th, left Gallow Hill on the Mail in a violent storm of snow and wind."

On March 15, Coleridge arrived at Greta Hall, a week late. In London, happy amid social distractions, Coleridge, after describing them to his wife, had affectionately concluded his letter: "God bless you my dear Sara! I shall return in love and Cheerfulness." But now his reception at Greta Hall could hardly be beyond doubt. The visit to Gallow Hill had certainly broken the olive branches that Samuel had offered to his wife before leaving for the North.

Samuel's entry into Greta Hall proved on his arrival there to be merely an escape from the frying pan into the fire, for the shadow of Asra had evidently affected Mrs. Coleridge, and within four days Coleridge made another escape, this time to the warmth and sympathy of Dove Cottage. Coleridge arrived in weather so bad that Dorothy "did not wish or expect him . . . half-stupified, his eyes a little swollen from the wind." Such was Dorothy's description. For two days he remained at Dove Cottage, and there was much talk: doubtless of Gallow Hill and Sara, and of Greta Hall and Mrs. Coleridge. There was perhaps already some suggestion of a separation of Coleridge from his wife. Samuel went late to bed that night, and Dorothy, "much affected with the sight of him" and with her "spirits agitated very much," sat discussing matters with William until four o'clock the next morning. On March 28 William and Dorothy came to Greta Hall—"wet at skin" with the rain—and stayed until April 5. The day before leaving Dove Cottage for Greta Hall, Wiliam began one of his most beautiful and famous poems, the ode entitled "Intimations of Immortality."

In May Coleridge learned from a newspaper that a portrait of himself was being exhibited in London. "What it is, or whose, I do not know," he told Poole, "but I guess it must be the miniature which Hazlitt promised to Mrs. Coleridge; but did not give her, because I never finished my sittings. Mine is not a *picturesque* Face,—Southey's was made for a picture." Samuel was glad to hear that Poole had received another portrait of Coleridge—in pastel—painted in Germany by some unknown artist. (A reproduction of this portrait is found in *The Collected Letters of Samuel Taylor Coleridge*, ed. Earl L. Griggs, 6 vols. [New York: Oxford University Press, 1956–71], 1:470.)

Wordsworth, at this time, drew two verse portraits of Coleridge, no less interesting than any drawn by a painter's hand. In Wordsworth's "Stanzas," inserted in his copy of Thomson's *Castle of Indolence*, Coleridge appears as

A noticeable Man with large grey eyes,
And a pale face that seemed undoubtedly
As if a blooming face it ought to be;
Heavy his low-hung lip did oft appear,
Deprest by weight of musing Phantasyl
Profound his forehead was, though not severe;
Yet some did think that he had little business here;
Sweet heaven forefend; his was a lawful right;
Noisy he was, and gamesome as a boy;
His limbs would toss about him with delight,
Like branches when strong winds the trees annoy.
Nor lacked his calmer hours device or toy
To banish listlessness and irksome care;
He would have taught you how you might employ
Yourself; and many did to him repair—
And certes not in vain; he had inventions rare.

Wordsworth's second portrait of Coleridge at this time, a slightly critical one, appears in "The Leech Gatherer"—now better known as "Resolution and Independence":

My whole life I have lived in pleasant thought,
As if life's business were a summer mood;
As if all needful things would come unsought
To genial faith, still rich in genial good;
But how can he expect that others should
Build for him, sow for him, and at his call
Love him, who for himself will take no heed at all?

By this time, life in Dove Cottage was almost as uneasy as life in Greta Hall; but for a very different reason. William and Dorothy had reluctantly agreed that William must marry, and that Mary Hutchinson (Sara Hutchinson's sister), a friend of their childhood, should be his wife. Mary, it would seem, was chosen as an amiable, sensible, good, and stable woman, least likely to upset the happy companionship of the brother and sister in Dove Cottage. To this end they decided to first visit Annette Vallon and her and Wordsworth's little daughter Caroline in France. Thus it was that at the end of July Dove Cottage stood empty for a time, while Dorothy and William went on their French journey.

For Coleridge the loss of the Wordsworths' companionship, of the happy hours in Dove Cottage, was so bitter that he hardly dared to think of them. "I seem to be beating off all reference to them and their letters," he told Sara Hutchinson a month after the Wordsworths' departure. "I wish, I wish they were back. . . . Dear little Caroline! Will she be a ward of Annette? Was the subject too delicate for a letter? I suppose so." Coleridge would not visit Dove Cottage during the Wordsworths' absence: "Although I have no objection to sleeping in a lonely house I did not like to sleep in *their* lonely house." Nor did the Wordsworths forget Coleridge, who received many letters from them during their travels.

Some compensation for the Wordsworths' absence, however, now appeared in Coleridge's improved relations with his wife. "At home all is peace and love," he told Estlin on July 26, the day the Wordsworths left for Gallow Hill for France. Three days later he "rejoiced" to inform Southey "that now for a long time there has been more love and concord in my house than I have known for years before."

Unfortunately, even these brief assertions of domestic peace only led Coleridge to long, dolorous, and wearisome memories of his past sufferings, detailed with egotistic self-sympathy to Southey at the end of July and to Tom Wedgwood in October. The terrible threat of separation, he told Southey, was his method of reforming his wife: so "very awful a step" involving "such violent struggles of mind" that his "sleep became the Valley of the Shadows [sic] of Death," and his health "truly alarming." This threat "so alarmed Mrs. Coleridge, so wounded her pride," made her see her husband abroad, friendless, and "pining away," and herself a widow—"feelings wholly selfish," which, however, "made her *serious*. That was a great point gained—for Mrs. C's mind has very little that is *bad* in it—it is an innocent mind, but it is light, and *unimpressible*, warm in anger, cold in sympathy, and in all disputes uniformly *projects* itself *forth* to recriminate, instead of turning itself inward with a silent self-questioning."

The Wordsworths were not the only friends of Coleridge in France during this summer of 1802. In the spring Poole, also taking advantage of the Peace of Amiens, planned to tour France, Switzerland, and Italy. On May 2 he sent Coleridge a letter of reconciliation in which his inextinguishable love for Samuel struggled against his friend's apparent indifference. "Why is there so little communication between us?" Poole asked. He did not even know where Coleridge was, and at least so far as it lay with Samuel, he said: "Can you suppose me uninterested in your welfare, and in your happiness in every point?" And he went on to tell of his plans for a European tour, and requested information that might help him, and also suggestions for useful books. "This is a short letter to send you so far," he wrote. "but a *new* correspondence is always deficient in topics. Let me hear from you. I shall write to you again before I go."

Coleridge, annoyed at not being invited to accompany Poole replied in a tone of sulky friendship: "I were sunk low indeed, if I had neglected to write to you from any lack of affection," and he went on to complain, "I have neither been very well, nor very happy; but I have been far from idle." By the end of the year he said his metaphysical studies would be completed, a long poem would be begun, which, like a new volume of poems also announced as "about to be published," never appeared. As for France, he added, he had just refused an offer from an unnamed publisher to pay Coleridge's expenses in France for a tour there like Poole's, in return for descriptive letters on the tour, for publication. From Paris on July 20, 1802, Poole, fascinated by the Apollo Belvedere, recounted his extraordinary experience in detail, telling

Samuel: "This statue could chain a man at Paris to the same way that the passion of love might" (see chapter 7).

During these months of July and August 1802 Sara Hutchinson received at least six long letters from Coleridge, parts of which she transcribed. These transcripts consist of long passages factually descriptive of his mountain wanderings about Kewsick. Occasionally, even in these transcripts, an affectionate exclamation appears: "O dear Sara!—how dearly I love you! Dear Mary! Heaven bless you." Such are Coleridge's endings in two of thse transcripts. Once at least, more practical than poetic, Coleridge informed his friend: "*I have now no clothes but what are patched at the elbows, and knees, and in the seat*—and I am determined to wear them *out and out*—and to have none till after Christmas." Certainly Coleridge's need of money was not hidden! Elsewhere in these transcripts he actually repays "the darlings" (Sara and Mary Hutchinson) the five pounds he has borrowed from them.

Early in August Charles and Mary Lamb, having suddenly decided to visit Coleridge, surprised him at Greta Hall, where for the next three weeks they were his guests. To Manning, Lamb, in one of his most delightful letters, described this visit: "He received us with all the hospitality in the world, and gave up his time to show us all the wonders of the country," The Lambs arrived in glorious evening sunshine, which made Charles think "we had got into Fairy Land." "We entered Coleridge's comfortable study," wrote Lamb, "just in the dusk, when the mountains were all dark with clouds upon their heads. Such an impression I never received form objects of sight before, nor do I suppose I can ever again. Glorious creatures, fine old fellows, Skiddaw, etc. I never shall forget ye." Lamb continued, "Coleridge had got a blazing fire in his study; which is a large, antique, ill-shaped room, with an old-fashioned organ, never played upon, big enough for a church, shelves of scattered folios, an Aeolian harp, and an old sofa, half-bed, etc. And all looking out upon the last fading view of Skiddaw and his broad-breasted brethren."

With Coleridge as guide, the Lambs climbed mountains and enthused over the prospects until, as Lamb told Manning, "I have satisfied myself that there is such a thing as that which tourists call *romantic*." "I shall remember your mountains to the last day I live," Lamb told Coleridge on his return to London. "They haunt me perpetually. I am like a man who has been falling in Love unknown to himself, which he finds out when he leaves the Lady." The Wordsworths were absent on their French journey, but the Clarksons were in Dove Cottage, and Charles and Mary Lamb spent two days with them there before leaving the Lakes District.

Back in London Lamb confessed to Manning that mountain scenery had not destroyed his affection for the town: "After all, Fleet Street and the Strand are better places to live in for good and all than amond Skiddaw. Still, I turn back to those great places where I wandered about, participating in their greatness. After all, I could not live in Skiddaw. I could spend a year—two, three years—among them, but I must have a prospect of seeing Fleet Street at the end of that time, or I should mope and pine away, I know.''

If the Lambs' departure left Coleridge unhappy again in solitude, he must have been greatly cheered when the Wordsworths returned to Dove Cottage on October 6 after their long absence in France and London. But with them now—probably less pleasing to Coleridge as an omen of change—was Mary Hutchinson, whom William had married two days before at Gallow Hill. Dorothy, although too greatly affected by her brother's marriage to attend the ceremony, has left an interesting reference to it in the following passage from her journal:

> On Monday, 4th October 1802, my brother William was married to Mary Hutchinson. I slept a good deal of the night, and rose fresh and well in the morning. At a little after 8 o'clock I saw them go down the avenue towards the church. William had parted from me upstairs. When they were absent my dear little Sara prepared the breakfast. I kept myself as quiet as I could but when I saw the two men running up the walk, coming to tell us it was over, I could stand it no longer, and threw myself on the bed, where I lay in stillness, neither hearing or seeing anything till Sara came upstairs to me, and said, "They are coming." This forced me from the bed where I lay, and I moved, I knew not how, straight forward, faster than my strength could carry me, till I met my beloved William, and fell upon his bosom. He and John Hutchinson led me to the house, and there I stayed to welcome my dear Mary. As soon as we had breakfasted, we departed. It rained when we set off. Poor Mary was much agitated, when she parted from her brothers and sisters, and her home.

For Coleridge, as indeed also for Dorothy, Dove Cottage since William's marriage was not quite the same. Instead of rushing over to Dove Cottage upon the Wordsworths' arrival with his usual tales of woe, not until late on the fifth day after the Wordsworths' return did he reappear there. Now, too, for the first time, a note of disappointment with Coleridge enters Dorothy's diary: "We expected to have found Coleridge at home, but he did not come till after dinner. He was well, but did not look so." After two days at Dove Cottage Coleridge persuaded the three to return with him to Greta Hall. "We consented," wrote Dorothy, "Mrs. Coleridge not being at home."

By this time Coleridge had made a new and important friend, William Sotheby: whom he had met when Sotheby was touring the Lakes District with some idea of taking a house there. Of considerable social standing, this ex-dragoon, enthusiastic classicist and poet, some fifteen years older than Coleridge, seemed to Samuel worthy of cultivation. After Sotheby's departure Coleridge, still hoping to attract him to the Lakes, sent him a poem, inspired, he claimed, by the local scenery and entitled "Chamouny: The Hour Before Sunrise. A Hymn." The poem, he said, was inspired by the beauty of the neighboring mountains: "I involuntarily poured forth a Hymn in the manner of the *Psalms*, tho' afterwards I thought the Ideas &c. disproportionate to our humble mountains—and accidentally lighting on a short note in some Swiss Poems, concerning the Vale of Chamouny [Chamonix], and its mountain, I transferred myself thither, in the Spirit, and adapted my former feelings to these grander objects. You will soon see it in the *Morning Post*—and I should be glad to know whether and how far it pleased you." This pretense that local scenery had inspired Coleridge to write a "Hymn" and so to impress Sotheby was apparently incorrect, for it was principally a plagiarism from a German poem, Frederica Brun's "Ode to Chamouny." The following day, September 11, Coleridge's poem appeared in the *Morning Post*. Coleridge never admitted this plagiarism.

Throughout September and early October Coleridge continued in his correspondence with Sotheby the ingratiating attitude he had immediately adopted upon their first meeting. Sotheby he hailed as "a man of genius," along with many effusive expressions of affection for his family.

Literature, of course, was a principal subject in this correspondence with Sotheby. Of the "Preface" to Wordsworth's *Lyrical Ballads* he told Sotheby: "I must set you right, with regard to my perfect coincidence with his poetic creed. It is most certain, that that Preface arose from the heads of our mutual conversations &c. &c. the first passages were indeed partly taken from notes of mine, for it was at first intended that the Preface should be written by me."

Paying exaggerated homage to Sotheby as a critic, Coleridge promised him a translation of Gessner's "Der Erste Schiffer," which he said was ready for publication, although it was never finished. He even asked Sotheby to obtain publication of the poem for him, but when Sotheby asked for a copy, Coleridge explained inability to transcribe it because of pressure of work for the *Morning Post*. To Sotheby's daughter Coleridge sent part of his never completed poem "The Dark Ladie." This so pleased Miss Sotheby that Coleridge promised he would try to send her the remainder soon. Nor did Coleridge omit to tell Sotheby of his misfortunes with publishers.

On November 3, 1802, an invitation arrived from Tom Wedgwood inviting Samuel to meet him at Cote House near Bristol. Early the next morning Coleridge set off. After spending a night at Penrith in the home of the middle-aged Miss Monkhouse, who had helped to bring up the Hutchinsons when orphaned, and meeting Asra there, he joined Tom Wedgwood on November 12. But Tom was restless, and poor Coleridge, instead of being allowed to wallow in the comforts of Cote House as he had expected, was hurried off the next day with Tom and Tom's sister, Sarah, by post chaise through South Wales, including the Vale of Usk—"Nineteen miles of most delightful country," but "not comparable with the meanest part of our Lake Country," as Coleridge described it.

On November 15 they remained for a week at St. Clears, "a little hamlet nine miles from Carmarthen, three miles from the sea." There Sarah Wedgwood left them for Crescelly fifteen miles away, the country house of Mr. Allen, the father of Mrs. John Wedgwood and of Mrs. Josiah Wedgwood. At St. Clears Coleridge was happily lodged with his friend at the Blue Boar, "the most comfortable little public house I ever was in." There Tom so improved in health as to go "cock-shooting in high glee and spirits," said Coleridge, imputing the change to his own influence upon Tom. Nevertheless, for Coleridge Tom's recovery meant the end, he feared, of his hopes of accompanying Tom to Italy. Coleridge found Tom a delightful and instructive companion, with the *finest and sublest* mind and taste" Coleridge had ever met. Tom, however, was less than perfect. To attempt to touch him for money was hopeless. Far from lending money to Coleridge, he had even borrowed from him.

A sudden visit to Crescelly on Sunday, November 21, introduced Coleridge to old Mr. Allen and his family and friends; but the next day they returned to St. Clears. The night before at Crescelly, Samuel had sat up until midnight, much enjoying "sweetmeats and cream and fruit," and not able to sleep before two. Thus, returning to St. Clears, he was, he said, "in a very pleasurable state of feeling"—indeed "deliciously unwell." But no sooner did they reach St. Clears and the comfortable Blue Boar than Coleridge was whisked off to Narberth, twelve miles away. Coleridge's much tried patience now gave way. As for their next destination he exclaimed to his wife: "God knows where; . . . I don't see any likelihood of our going to the Moon, or to either of the Planets, or fixed Stars—and that is all, I can say."

Nor did the amenities of the White Hart at Narberth bring Coleridge any compensation for the loss of the comfortable Blue Boar. All day and all night he was exasperated by noises that, with characteristic realism, he described in detail—"Men and women, servants, drivers, waiters, master and mistress all talking at once, very loud." And when not quarreling and scolding, their loud laughter was as bad. The window of the sitting room was on the street level, admitting very clearly all the noises of the street: "women scolding the children, children trampling, laughing, screaming in play, yowling in earnest, bells ringing, dogs barking, all accurately imitated by a parrot: in its own natural scream." For the grand finale, as Coleridge was writing letters for Tom, a huge sheep dog burst through the glass window: "Crash! and down fell the dog into the room, just on my back." One night of this was enough for both Tom and Samuel, and the next morning they returned to Crescelly, where they remained almost a month.

The impression made upon Coleridge by his aged host, Mr. Allen, during his previous flying visit had not been entirely complimentary. He had made his first appearance at 4:30, just after dinner, and Coleridge had informed his wife: "Down came old Allen. O Christ! Old Nightmare. An ancient Incubus. Every face was saddened, every mouth pursed up! Most solemnly civil, like the Lord of a stately castle 500 years ago! Doleful and plaintive eke; for I believe that the Devil is twitching him home."

"Old Allen," it seems, had offended Samuel by talking him down during a Coleridgian monologue. This offense still rankled in Coleridge's mind when two months later he denounced in his notebook, "The Natural silence of old age" reversed through wealth, thus "making old age hateful—old Allen." So much for the first visit to Crescelly.

The second visit, longer, was to be an almost entirely happy experience for Samuel, settled for a time in the comfort he loved above all things. As usual in such circumstances, Coleridge charmed the company. "All kindness to me and in prodigious favour here," Tom Wedgwood described him; and Coleridge found Tom's sister, Sally, "a truly excellent woman; her whole soul is clear, pure and deep as an Italian sky." And since she was chiefly responsible for the comfort he enjoyed, "the most perfectly good woman I ever knew." She played "divinely" on the piano. There were also the three young Allens—Jessica, Emma, and Frances—"Sweet, cheerful, and most innocent girls," he told his wife, "I cannot help being idle among them. What sweeter and more tranquillizing pleasure is there, than to feel oneself completely innocent among completely innocent young women. Warm rooms, warm bedrooms, music, pleasant talking, and extreme temperance—all this agrees with me—and the best blesing, that results from all, is a *placid sleep.*—no difficulties in my dreams, no pains, no desires." Yet not everyone at Crescelly shared the general enthusiasm for Coleridge. Tom's other sister, Kate, for one, was no admirer. She disliked "his accent and exterior," and she thought that his "too great parade of superior feeling, and of excessive goodness and sensibility" suggested "conceit and a suspicion of acting." She thought that he would make an unsatisfactory husband and father.

Indeed, Coleridge's triumphal progress at Crescelly did not proceed without an occasional mishap. In some nameless discussion, Kate Wedgwood attacked him. On another occasion, when he began to shock the company with startling opinions on the Ten Commandments, his bête noire, "old Allen" tapped him on the arm and led him out of the room. Even worse was the irrepressible, convulsive laughter of the charming and intelligent Frances Allen, Samuel's favorite. When Coleridge read Wordsworth's "Leech Gatherer" and came to a passage—later expunged—describing the leech gatherer's skin as so old and dry that even the leeches could not stick to it, Coleridge, who was sitting beside Frances, felt her shaking with laughter and was very angry. Sternly closing his book, he begged her pardon for having read the poem to her, intimating that to a person with no genius it might well seem absurd. The whole company was shocked and embarrassed, Sally looked angry, and Frances feared her father would turn her out of the room. But Uncle Tom rose to the occasion, saying, "Well Coleridge, one must confess it is not quite a subject for a poem." For some days Coleridge contemptuously stopped his reading aloud if Frances entered the room. However, Frances was too pretty for Coleridge to remain angry long; soon he was very friendly to her again. One day he even gave her his personal history, including the comment at one point—which naturally surprised her—"and there I had the misfortune to meet with my wife."

Yet, as often when Coleridge and his wife were apart, his feelings toward her were unusually amiable. The comforts of Crescelly gave unwonted warmth to his affectionate messages to her, utterly remote from the spirit of his remark to Frances Allen. Throughout his visit to Wales he wrote to Mrs. Coleridge regularly once or twice a week, thus presenting perhaps the most extensive and intimate expression extant of one aspect of their relationship. Nevertheless, a hangover from the quarrel about Sara Hutchinson and Penrith had delayed the return of complete amity. There was little suggestion in what remains of his first letter to Mrs. Coleridge of the victorious husband and troubling wife converted to obedience by threats of separation, as described to Southey. Rather, the boot was on the other foot: "My dear Love—write as cheerfully as possible. I am tenderer, and more fluttery, and bowel-weak, than most. I cannot bear anything gloomy, unless it is quite necessary. Be assured, I will bring back (come home when I will) a pure, affectionate, and husbandly heart to [Passage cut]. Again and again for evermore God bless and preserve you, my Love! and me for your sake, and the sake of our dear Children—and try to *love* and be *kind* to those whom I love. I am, and will remain, Your faithful and affectionate husband, S. T. Coleridge."

Five days later he wrote to Mrs. Coleridge again, and, in the one page allowed to posterity, defended his own character: his independence, his indifferences to the opinions of himself held by persons whom he did not respect, "an independence of, and contempt for, all advantages of external fortune, that are not immediately connected with bodily comforts, or moral pleasures." "I *dislike* fine furniture," he continued, "handsome clothes, and all the ordinary symbols and appendages of artificial superiority—or what is called *Gentility*. In the same spirit, I dislike, at least I seldom like, gentlemen, gentlemenly manners, etc. I have no pride, as far as pride means a desire to be thought highly of by others. If I have any sort of Pride, it consists in an indolent . . . " [cut]. Next he contrasted his wife's character with his own, to show her inferiority, disliking what he considered her dependence upon the opinions of others.

Delighting in doctoring his family and friends, he now insisted upon dosing them with his latest nostrum, ginger tea, and when Mrs. Coleridge tried to persuade him to reduce his opium, he reported it as reduced to a mere twelve drops of laudanum a day—only one-eighth of his previous dose. Besides, laudanum, he told her, "was far less pernicious than tea." At any rate there was a thaw. "My dear Love" and "Your dear Husband" formed the beginning and the end of his epistle.

On hearing alarming news from Mrs. Coleridge, whose confinement was approaching, Coleridge immediately ordered her "INSTANTLY to get a nurse." Unfortunately, he suggested Sara Hutchinson as the best possible nurse for her. From this, he proceeded to reproach his wife for her resentment of his friendship with Sara, and to self-justification. In this, he showed toward her a Christlike spirit of forgiveness: "Heaven bear me witness, I often say in the words of Christ, Father forgive her! She knows not what she does. Be assured my dear Love! that I shall never write otherwide than *most* kindly to you, except after great *Aggressions* on your part." "I owe duties to my wife," he says, and equally solemn ones to himself, children, friends and society. "I can neither retain my Happiness nor my Faculties, unless I move, live, and love, in perfect Freedom, limited only by my own purity and self-respect. . . .My Love is made up 9/10ths of fervent wishes for the permanent *Peace* of mind of those whom I love, be it man or woman; and for their progression in purity, goodness, and true Knowledge. Such being the nature of my Love, no human Being can have a right to be jealous."

So—still in the spirit of pure Christian love—he dragged on his argument, assuring her, yet

"without offence to you, as Heaven knows it is without any feeling of Pride in myself, to say—that in sex, acquirements, and in the quantity and quality of natural endowments, whether of Feeling or of Intellect, you are the Inferior. . . .I have a *right* to expect and demand that you should to a certain degree love, and act kindly to those whom I deem worthy of my love.—If you read this letter with half the Tenderness with which it is written, it will do you and both of us, GOOD: and contribute its share to the turning of a mere Cat-hole into a Dove's nest. You know, Sally, Pally! I must have a joke—or it would not be me!

The need of nurses for Mrs. Coleridge also meant the need for money, as she well knew. After vainly waiting a fortnight for promised funds, she must have asked her husband again, for on December 4 he replied, regretting that she had not received the money, which he obviously had not sent her. There was "no reason," he explained, why he had not sent it. But "you know how hateful all money thoughts are to me!—and how idly and habitually I keep them at arm's length. The next day he sent her a draft for fifty pounds on their landlord Jackson—who perhaps did not accept it, for he was soon in financial difficulties.

Whatever the pecuniary conditions at Greta Hall, Mrs. Coleridge, if possible had to pay her debts to the local shopkeepers, but whatever else she did, so thoughtful for her was he, she must keep enough for her own needs: "Be sure not to leave yourself with less than £10, if possible . . . and therefore you had better not think of your mother; . . . If you are seriously ill," he wrote,

or unhappy at my absence, I will return at all hazards. God love you and have you in his keeping, my blessed Sara—and speedily restore me to you—I have faith, a heavenly Faith, that our future Days will be Days of Peace, and affectionate Happiness.—O, that I were with you! I feel it very, very hard to be from you at this trying Time—I dare not think a moment concerning you in this Relation, or I should be immediately ill. But I shall soon return—and bring you back a confident and affectionate Husband. Again, and again, my dearest dearest Sara! —my Wife and Love, and indeed my very Hope—May God preserve you! —And do you above all things take care of yourself.

A few days later, still hoping to bring his wife and Sara together, Coleridge continued to urge her: "I hope that Sara Hutchinson is well enough to have come in. It would be a great comfort that one or the other of the three women at Grasmere should be with you—and Sara rather than the other two because you will hardly have another opportunity of having her by yourself and to yourself, and of learning to know her, such as she really is. How much this lies at my heart with respect to the Wordsworths and Sara, and how much of our common love and happiness depends on your loving those whom I love,—why should I repeat?—I am confident, my dear love! that I have no occasion to repeat it." His letter ended on a note of affectionate hopefulnes: "without a single interruption I have continued for three weeks to think of you with love and tenderness, and this I regard as an omen for the Future." Samuel also sent his wife a list of masculine and feminine names—all queer ones—from which she must select, when the baby was born. "Sara," the name actually given to the child at birth, was not in the list, but perhaps it was not chosen by Mrs. Coleridge. On December 16 Coleridge and Tom Wedgwood set out on their return journey, which was to take them to Gramere and Greta Hall.

On Christmas Eve 1802 Dorothy, in Dove Cottage, was very happy:

William is now sitting by me at half past 10 o'clock. I have been beside him ever since tea, running [sic] the heel of a stocking, repeating some of his sonnets to him, listening to his own repeating, reading some of Milton's, and the *Allegro* and *Penseroso*. It is a quiet keen frost. Mary is in the parlour below attending to the baking of cakes, and Jenny Fletcher's pies. Sara is in bed in the toothache [sic]. . . . Coleridge came this morning with Wedgwood. We all turned out of William's bedroom one by one, to meet him. He looked well. We had to tell him of the birth of his little girl, born yesterday morning at 6 o'clock. William went with them to Wytheburn in the chaise.

Such was Dorothy's record.

On this Christmas Eve of 1802, Tom Wedgwood and Coleridge entered Greta Hall. However, Coleridge remained there only a week with Tom, and then left with him to visit Tom's friend at Glenridding.

On New Year's Day 1803 Coleridge, after only a day at Glenridding, walked the fifteen miles "over Kirkstone, an awful road over a sublime mountain by tarn and waterfall to Grasmere," to join Wordsworth, Mary, and Sara Hutchinson in Dove Cottage. Dorothy was at Great Hall helping Mrs. Coleridge with the new baby, but the next day she returned, with all the Dove Cottage inmates, who had gone more than halfway to meet her. On January 4 Samuel returned to Glenridding by the same route as before, and the following day he sent his "dear wife and dear love" a letter intended to be conciliatory—but little likely to achieve its aim. Fearing that she might think him "neglectful or unaffectionate" because he had neither called at Greta Hall nor written since his departure on December 30, he assured her that illness was the reason. "Heaven knows!" he continued, "I will build up my best hopes on my attempts to conciliate your Love, and to call it forth into hourly exercise and gentle compliances, by setting you the example of respectful and attentive manners. We cannot get rid of our faulty habits all at once; but I am fully sensible that I have been faulty in many things; tho' justice to myself compels me to add, not without provocation."

Inordinately long—despite the excisions of later vandals—the rest of the letter promised to try "to correct all little overflows of temper," while in return she must receive his admonitions "with love and a ready and docile mind." She must do everything to enable him to love her, and "bear with your little corrosions and apparent unimpressibilities." He allowed that she was "a good woman with a pleasing person, and a healthy understanding—superior certainly to nine women in ten, of our own rank or above us." But she must let him be "quite tranquil" and "above all have confidence in my honour and virtue—and suffer me to love and be loved without jealousy or pain"—"God send us Peace and Love. My dear Love!" he continued, "What a New Year's blessing it would be. O, and surely it shall be. My heart is full of Hope and Love." To secure these blessings he then informed his wife that on the morrow he would probably return to Greta Hall with Sara Hutchinson "on a double horse." At last, on January 7, 1803, Coleridge returned to Greta Hall accompanied by Sara Hutchinson, but not on a "double horse." There Sara remained only a few days.

One day after dinner, during a momentary recovery from illness, Samuel wrapped himself up warmly and walked with Sara to the Falls of Lodore and the Gorge of Borrodale. There, "on emerging from a grove," they saw the reddest star Coleridge had ever seen, as he told Tom Wedgwood two days later: "it *started* as it were, from the Heaven, like an eyeball of Fire." It was almost certainly of this visit of Sara to Greta Hall that Coleridge was thinking a year later, when in his notebook he wrote: "While I am talking of Government or War or Chemistry, there comes ever into my bodily eye some tree, beneath which we have rested, some rock where we have walked together, or on the perilous road edging, *high above* the Crummock Lake where we sat beneath the rock, and those dear lips pressed my forehead, or that Scale Force in its pride, as we saw it—when they laughed at us for lovers."

This short interlude with Sara Hutchinson at Greta Hall soon ended. As the time of parting approached, Coleridge's thoughts were of the bitterness of life without Sara. "Fear of parting gives a yearning so like Absence, as at moments to turn your presence into absence," he privately reflected. With the hope of foreign travel in mind, he dreamed of himself with Sara abroad: "A plain and simple English Maiden, Rome, Alps, and Apennines, Etna and Vesuvius—and now he, who loves her, whom her soul loves, is among them." Such was the note Samuel made five days after the walk to Lodore.

On January 20, 1803, Coleridge hurriedly left Greta Hall to meet Tom Wedgwood in Bristol and go with him to his brother John's place, Cote House, nearby. The mood in which he left Greta Hall, one of relief from the stress of frustration, found private expression in a favorite natural image: "Repose after agitation, pool under waterfall made by the waterfall." Privately, too, he noted a new sense of the tragic element in life: "A vision of this world, moral and physical, being pulled down, to build up a new one—and with such of the materials as are usable and good for anything—Heaven made of one sort, Hell of another." Beyond that he did not go. Evidently, the war with Mrs. Coleridge over Asra, which Coleridge had tried to end by loving and conciliatory letters from Wales, had broken out again, and Samuel after only a few days at home with his wife had once again sought safety in flight.

Five days later, January 25, 1803, they entered Cote House, but Samuel was disappointed. Mrs. John Wedgwood was ill, Tom "in very low spirits," John his brother "no favourite of mine," and Kitty, mindful of her dislike of him at Crescelly, had put him in the tower. So Coleridge almost at once returned to Bristol to stay with Southey. "Coleridge is with me at present," Southey told a friend on January 30; "he talks of going abroad, for poor fellow, he suffers terribly from his climate." Shortly before, Coleridge, in his uncertainty about being chosen by Tom as his companion abroad, had assumed indifference to travel when writing to Southey, and also pretended that his chief reason for going abroad would be the good of his wife and children rather than his own benefit in health. He "could be well content" to stay at Keswick and recover there, "for I love the place with perfect love."

Meanwhile Tom, perhaps resenting Samuel's hurried departure from Cote, revoked is intention to accompany Coleridge to Poole's, because of "spirits too low to move out." So Coleridge sent Poole a brusque note on February 2 complaining of cold, and he almost went to a hotel, ordering "a fire in a tolerably roomy bedroom." He would be at Bridgwater at noon on February 4, he added; "if you send in for me, well and good—if no, I must take a post-chaise." The old affectionate tone was now absent. But Poole could still make him comfortable, and a fortnight later, "pretty middling" in health, he was luxuriating in the comforts Poole provided. "I do not stir out of the house," he told Southey, "and as I have a delicious wood fire in my bedroom, I am very comfortable here. A little boy about nine years old, a sharp child, waits on me." He "dearly loved to be waited on by children," he said. "A penny and cheerful praise," gave them—and him—such pleasure. Two days later, one of his habitual complaints about his wife, to Southey again, was quaintly yet significantly associated with his present comfort at Stowey. "I am so weak," he wrote, "that warmth of manner in a female house-mate is as necessary to me, as warmth of internal attachment. This is weakness; but on the other hand I ought to say, in justice to myself, that I am happy and contented in solitude, or only with the common inhabitants of a bachelor's house:—an old woman and a sharp child."

Coleridge could still magisterially approve Tom Poole as "a very, very good man," despite incorrigible "little faults and deficiencies," but Tom Wedgwood increasingly disappointed him. Not merely did he postpone a decision about foreign travel, he had dragged Samuel after him in his wanderings about England and Wales, until Coleridge groaned to Purkis: "I am a comet tied to a comet's tail, and our combined path must needs be damnably eccentric."

But at the same time he sent Purkis a description of Tom Wedgwood very different from his recent depreciation of him to Poole during their quarrel. He now declared Tom: "a man of Genius, of exquisite and various taste, extensive information, subtle and inventive faculties, affectionate dispositions, of a prosperous family, and to crown all these things, with a large fortune, a fine person, a most benevolent heart, with a calm and comprehensive and acute understanding organizes into a genuine benevolence. And all these things are blasted by a thickening of the gut! O God! Such a tree in full blossom, the fruits all medicinal and foodful [*sic*]—and a grub, a grub at the root!''

But the comet remained as erratic as ever, to Samuel's increasing irritation and dismay. Instead of meeting the anxiously awaiting Samuel at Stowey, Tom merely instructed him after five days, to go with Poole to Gunville, where he would join them later. At the same time he refused Coleridge's companionship abroad on the previous plea of Samuel's poor health, which Coleridge had denied. Bitterly disappointed Samuel made light of the defeat as due to a temporary depression and stressed his affectionate fears for Tom if he went with a mere ''hireling;'' for Tom was ''too good and too valuable a man for such.''

So, ''crossly enough,'' Coleridge set off with Poole for Gunville on Friday, February 18, 1803, and quarrelled with him all the way, just as if Poole were Mrs. Coleridge. For Poole had insisted upon a ''one horse chair,'' when Samuel wanted a post-chaise. The result, as Samuel had ''most minutely foretold,'' was breakings-down, delays, wettings, and a much belated appearance at Gunville on Sunday afternoon—a day late.

Not until nine days at Gunville had passed and Poole had departed, did Tom arrive, worse in health and spirits than Coleridge had ever seen him. There Coleridge renewed his fight, but Tom was obstinate: needed someone who knew French and Italian and could ''take the whole business of the road off his hands.'' However the host, Josiah, now came to Samuel's aid so successfully, that the rosiest prospect opened for him. ''An accomplished, travelling servant, a covered gig'' and horses—''so to walk and ride and be carried, as one's feelings direct,'' Samuel told Poole. ''Tom Wedgwood fitted me out with clothes, etc.'' he added: ''I should like the plan extremely. But I am prepared for all and everything to bust like a bubble.'' And so it did. For just as Samuel and the Wedgwoods were about to leave for London and the Continent, rumours of renewed war with France arose, and everything remained in suspense. ''All being thus settled,'' the deeply disappointed Coleridge told Southey, ''*pounce*! comes this damned war business!'' But he maintained his pose that his sole interest in the matter was his ''affection for Tom Wedgwood. Otherwise I would rather have gone on my own bottom.''

Deeply chagrined at the turn of events, Samuel left Gunville with Tom and Josiah on March 14 for London. There Tom in some way eluded Samuel, and with surprising speed, left with a young artist for Paris on March 25. On May 16 however, they were forced back two days before England declared war. Mrs. Coleridge was troubled by bad dreams, and for once Coleridge found her interesting: ''Of what kind are the dreams? I mean are they accompanied with distinct bodily feelings—*whizzings-up* into the head, fear of strangulation, etc., or simply great fear from fearful forms and combinations—or both at once?'' So he recommended warm brandy and water when going to bed, in place of beer at supper.

In London Coleridge was again Lamb's guest, and found in social distractions some compensation for his recent disappointment. He met Davy, who he had often feared would be spoiled by success. Davy, probably unaware of Coleridge's generous fears for his moral integrity, observed him with a scientist's detachment, but not without a sensitive and kindly human feeling. Davy met Samuel "generally in the midst of large companies, where he is the image of power and activity. His eloquence is unimpaired; perhaps it is softer and stronger. His will is less than ever commensurate with his ability. Brilliant images of greatness float upon his mind, like images of the morning clouds on the waters. Their forms are changed by the motion of the waves, they are agitated by every breeze, and modified by every sunbeam. He talked in the course of an hour, of beginning three works; and he recited the poem of *Christabel* unfinished, and as I had before heard it. What talent does he not waste in forming visions sublime but unconnected with the real world! I have looked to his efforts, as to the efforts of a creating being; but as yet he has not laid the foundation for the new world of intellectual forms!"

Davy's opinion of Coleridge was essentially akin to Southey's. Another similar view of Coleridge came to Southey from a shrewd observer, John Rickman, Secretary to the Speaker in the House of Commons, who now made Coleridge's acquaintance. Though less kindly than Davy's, Rickman's description of Coleridge was no less true. For Rickman was a "little annoyed by a habit of *assentation* which I fancy I perceive in him; and cannot but think he likes to talk well, rather than to give or receive much information. I understand he is terribly pestered with invitations to go to parties, as a singer does, to amuse the guests by his talent: a hateful task, I should think. I would rather not talk finely than talk to such a purpose."

It was against this same habit of *assentation* that Southey prophetically warned Samuel a year later, when he told him: "it does vex me to see you so lavish of the outward and visible signs of friendship. . . . You have accustomed yourself to talk affectionately, and write affectionately, to your friends, till the expressions of affection flow by habit in your conversation, and in your letters, and pass for more than they are worth; the worst of all this is, that your letters will one day rise up in judgement against you. . . . and you will be convicted of a double dealing, which, though you do not design, you certainly do practice. . . . Your feelings go naked. I cover mine with a bearskin; I will not say that you harden yours by your mode, but I am sure that mine are the warmer for their clothing."

"If there should be war, I will immediately come to Keswick," Coleridge told his wife on March 24. Five days later poor Mary Lamb had one of her fits of intermittent insanity, and Coleridge took her to a private asylum. "She was quite calm," he told his wife, "and said it was the best to do so—but she wept bitterly two or three times, yet all in a calm way. Charles is cut to the heart." Although war with France was not declared until May 18, Samuel left by coach for Keswick on April 6. Almost his last act before leaving London was to insure his life for £1,000 for the sake of his wife. Coleridge's often expressed fears of almost immediate demise, form an amusing contrast to the request he now sent Godwin, to certify "that I have no distemper that tends to the shortening of life. . . ." Once insured, he urged Southey to do the same, as "the best *possible* way of saving money."

On Good Friday, April 8, 1803, Coleridge arrived again at Greta Hall suffering from influenza caught *en route*. Although cured with opium, it turned to rheumatic fever that kept him bedbound for a month, and uneasy throughout the early summer. When on May 20 he tells Poole that he is "now only somewhat better, and feels the infinite importance of the deepest tranquillity," one senses opium or ether in the air.

14 To Scotland with (and without) William and Dorothy Wordsworth (1803-4)

"I am enjoying myself, having Nature with solitude and liberty. . ."
—S.T. Coleridge to Mrs. Coleridge, September 2, 1803

Among the fashionable and distinguished visitors who flocked to the Lakes that summer of 1803, were Sir George and Lady Beaumont who soon became important friends of both Coleridge and Wordsworth. Sir George, seventh Baronet, educated at Eton and New College Oxford, and now fifty years of age, was a mediocre painter remembered for his "picturesque" principle that "a good picture should be brown like a good fiddle," and that every landscape painting should have a brown tree in it. Like his wife, Sir George practised the admirable spirit of Christian benevolence and courtesy, which was then a particular characteristic of "the English Gentleman" and the English "Lady."

At the lakes the Beaumonts were led by fate to lodge for a time in Jackson's part of Greta Hall. There Sir George soon discovered to his dismay that Coleridge was his next door neighbor. For during Samuel's recent visit to London he had met Coleridge at one of Sotheby's receptions, and had so disliked him that he now tried to avoid him. But when baronets were about it was impossible to evade Coleridge, and now a chance conversation with Samuel converted Sir George in no time into a firm and helpful friend: "A few years ago a violent democrat but now quite opposite," Beaumont described Coleridge to the diarist, Farington.

Coleridge, delighted to ingratiate himself with such socially distinguished and potentially useful persons as the Beaumonts, at once overwhelmed them with what Rickman would have called *assentations*, and with attentions, including an introduction to Wordsworth whose poems the Beaumonts much admired. "Half mad to see you," Coleridge told Wordsworth, when the idolizing Lady Beaumont had told him that if Wordsworth had entered the room "she believed she should have fallen at your feet." To Wordsworth Coleridge described his impression of kind, sentimental, religious, benevolent Lady Beaumont, as "a miniature of Madame Guion" [*sic*], the French mystic. He completed his picture of her with a quotation from his own *Osorio*:

A deep Enthusiast, sensitive,
Trembles and cannot keep the tears in her eye—
Such ones do love the marvellous too well
Not to believe it. You may wind her up
With *any* music!
but music it must be, of some sort or other.

Certainly Samuel lost no time in "winding her up" with his music, including long, poignant passages from "Dejection." When a fortnight later the Beaumonts had gone to stay with Lord Lowther, Samuel wrote to inform his "honoured friends" of his tears on their departure, and the "refreshment of heart" Cowper's Letters had brought him upon their recommendation. Even if he had "hunted through all the libraries of Oxford and Cambridge" he could have found nothing more pleasing, although he had begun to read them "merely as connected with you." When Sir George presented Wordsworth with a piece of land three miles from Greta Hall, so that the two poets might improve themselves and poetry by a closer association after Wordsworth had built himself a home on it, —which he never did—Samuel's expression of pleasure and gratitude to Sir George exceeded Wordsworth's.

William Hazlitt, now a young man of twenty-five, also came to the Lakes that summer and renewed his acquaintance with Coleridge and Wordsworth, whose portraits he painted. Wordsworth's was later destroyed as unlike him, and Coleridge's is lost. The Beaumonts rather depressingly thought Wordsworth's portrait suggested a "profound, strong/minded philosopher, not a poet." Another friend on seeing it exclaimed: "At the gallows—deeply affected by his deserved fate,—yet determined to die like a man." Coleridge disliked his own portrait but Hazlitt refused his request to change it, "because," said Samuel, "the likeness with him is a secondary consideration—he wants it to be a fine picture." A surprisingly "modern" outlook! But it depressed Coleridge nevertheless. "You and I, dear William," he wrote, "pass for an ugly pair with the lower order; which I foretell Dorothy will not admit." Yet a week later he praised both portraits to Southey as "masterly, . . .very much in the manner of Titian." But Southey, when he saw Hazlitt's portrait in an exhibition later, wrote the most devastating criticism of all.

"Monday morning, 20 minutes after 11, August 15, 1803, W. & D. Wordsworth, and S.T. Coleridge left Keswick, in the Jaunting Car, for Scotland, up the steep Hill to Threlkeld". . . .Thus, as in Samuel's notebook entry, the much discussed tour in Scotland began. Mrs. Wordsworth who had had no honeymoon remained in Dove Cottage to supervise domestic matters.

Although shortly before that date Coleridge had felt "in excellent trim for our journey," a relapse occurred, and he began the tour in very low spirits and very dissatisfied with himself. "Sloth, Carelessness, Resignation—in all things that have reference to mortal life is not merely *in* me; it is *me*." Thus he described himself to Southey the day before they started. Perhaps Samuel's dejection was partly due to his "anxiety" at having promised to find this "jaunting" car, which became an important element in their expedition. It was, as Coleridge described it to Southey: "An open vehicle," with "room in it for three on each side on hanging seats—a dicky box for the driver, and a space or hollow in the middle for luggage—or two or three bairns. It is like half a long coach, only those in the one seat sit with their *back* to those in the other, instead of face to face. Your feet are not above a foot—scarcely so much—from the ground, so that you may get off and on while the horse is moving, without the least danger. There are all sorts of conveniences in it." When the party had gone Mrs. Coleridge—left like Mary to manage her house—told Southey:

> Wordsworth is to drive all the way, for poor Samuel is too weak to undertake the fatigue of driving. He was very unwell when he went off, and was to return in the Mail if he grew worse. . . .I hope he will be able to go, for if the weather be tolerable, it will do him much good. . . .My husband is a good man—his prejudices—and his possessions sometimes give me pain, but we have all a somewhat to encounter in this life. I should be a very, very happy woman if it were not for a few things—and my husband's ill health stands at the head of these evils.

The day of their departure was hot, and for most of it they walked up hills and along rough roads beyond the power of Samuel's horse to pull them. Indeed they appear to have walked nearly all through the tour with an occasional short interval in the car.

On the second day they reached Carlisle during the assizes that sentenced Hatfield the bigamist and forger to death. Coleridge, according to his own account, "alarmed the whole court," by shouting "Dinner!" to Wordsworth who was on the other side of the hall. Dorothy stood at the door of the gaoler's house, while Wordsworth and Coleridge went in to see Hatfield. Samuel, who two years before had written two articles on him for the *Morning Post*, noted in his pocketbook that this interview with Hatfield was "Impelled by Miss Wordsworth," and that he found him "*vain*, a hypocrite. It is not by mere thought, I can understand this man," he noted.

Gretna Green the next day they found "dreary," and Coleridge the day after did not join his friends in their pious visit to Burns' grave at Dumfries, partly no doubt because of his well-known lack of interest in "historic monuments," and perhaps even more because of Wordsworth's having called on Coleridge's bête noire, Samuel Rogers the poet. From now onwards indeed, Coleridge began to withdraw both emotionally and in some degree physically, from his previous intimacy with the Wordsworths, who now often walked together in the evenings, while Coleridge on the plea of fatigue, remained at the Inn. When after leaving Dumfries they walked along the Valley of the Nith, which reminded Coleridge of Gallow Hill, his thoughts were, as often, with Sara.

A week after the beginning of the tour they entered Glasgow where Coleridge, with his usual detailed realism on similar occasions, noted what he considered to be all the defects and peculiarities of the town. Their wonderful "jaunting car" attracted the attention it deserved and understandably preferring to walk beside it, they had entered Glasgow.

The next day on leaving they were forced inside the car by the heavy rain, and amid the smiles and stares of the astonished adult populace, left the town in fine style accompanied by a bodyguard of delighted infants running alongside and attempting to enter it.

On the second day after leaving Glasgow, Loch Lomond reminded Dorothy of lines from Wordsworth's "Ruth, and her dreams of romantic love," which Dorothy no doubt recited as they walked along; for that same night Coleridge asked himself: "What? though the World praise me, I have no dear Heart that loves my Verses. I never hear them in snatches from a beloved Voice, fitted to some sweet occasion, of natural prospect, in Winds at Night." Coleridge's dark mood however, did not blind him to the beauties of the scenery through which they passed.

The happiest evening of the tour, at least for Dorothy and Samuel and presumably also for William, was that of August 27, spent in a ferryman's hut by Loch Katrine on their return from the Trossachs. There, together with another chance visitor—a drawing master from Edinburgh—they had, as Coleridge noted: "a merry meal in the hovel black and varnished and glistering with peat smoke, the fowls roosting in the chimney amid the cloud of smoke." Dorothy wrote:

> We caroused our cups of coffee, laughing like children at the strange atmosphere in which we were: the smoke came in gusts, and spread along the walls and above our heads, in the chimney where the hens were roosting like light clouds in the sky: we laughed and laughed again, in spite of the smarting our eyes, yet had a quieter pleasure in observing the beauty of the beams and rafters gleaming between the clouds of smoke. . . .When we had eaten our supper we sat about half an hour, and I think I had never felt so deeply the blessing of hospitable welcome and a warm fire." Nor was an external stimulus to hilarity lacking. The ferryman, she added, "did not refuse to let his wife bring out the whisky-bottle at our request: 'She keeps a dram,' as the phrase is." Dorothy was accommodated with a room and a bed, and the three men, in Coleridge's words, "slept in the barn among the hay." Samuel described the night to Mrs. Coleridge a few days later, as "the pleasantest evening I had spent, since my tour: for Wordsworth's hypochondriacal feelings kept him silent and self-centered.

That night's carousal proved two days later to have been valedictory; for Coleridge then decided to part from the Wordsworths who continued their tour, after Samuel had said farewell to them at Arrochar. "Poor Coleridge being very unwell," wrote Dorothy, "determined to send his clothes to Edinburgh, and make the best of his way thither, being afraid to face much wet weather in an open carriage. We portioned out the contents of our purses before our parting; and after we had lost sight of him drove heavily along." For Dorothy certainly, the loss of Coleridge darkened the day. "Perhaps had we been in a more cheerful mood of mind," she wrote, "we might have seen

everything with a different eye. Our thoughts were full of Coleridge. . . .I
shivered at the thought of his being sickly and alone, travelling from place to
place." Throughout the rest of their journey, the thought of Coleridge
haunted Dorothy's mind.

As often, poor Dorothy's sympathy was wasted, for Coleridge's immediate
reaction after their departure was far from sadness at the loss of friends nor
did he make for Edinburgh, but for the famous Glencoe that disappointed
him. Yet his walk there was happy although "barefoot," as he burnt his shoes
in drying them, and despite neuralgic pains in his head and face. "So happy
alone—such blessing is there in perfect liberty—he wrote to his wife on
September 2, and later in the same long letter: "I am enjoying myself, having
Nature with solitude and liberty; the liberty natural and solitary, the solitude
natural and free." And he contemplated a poem on the subject. His solitude
also allowed him to take opium without being observed by the Wordsworths—doubtless one reason for the parting.

As usual, Coleridge's feelings, whether happy or sad, mingled with his appreciation of the scenery through which he passed. The day after the parting
the raindrops on a lake spoke to him of "multitude & Joyance." On the same
day another sight evoked his feeling toward Wordsworth: "My words and actions imaged on his mind, distorted and snaky as the boatman's oar reflected
in the lake." Dyspathy toward Wordsworth, whatever the cause, certainly
played a large part in Coleridge's decision to separate during the Scottish tour.
"William proposed to me to leave them," he told Mrs. Coleridge; "I eagerly
caught at the proposal: for the sitting in an open carriage in the rain is death to
me, and somehow or other I had not been quite comfortable." This separation
of Coleridge and the Wordsworths recalls that in Germany five years before.

Certainly Wordsworth's account of the present parting as quoted in the
Memoirs, suggests the dyspathy between Coleridge and himself, which Coleridge at times openly asserted: "Coleridge was at that time in bad spirits, and
somewhat too much in love with his own dejection, and he departed from us as
is recorded in my sister's journal."

Coleridge's annoyance with Wordsworth extended to the partition of their
funds on separation—indeed, obliquely, poor Dorothy was also implicated.
"The worst thing was the money," Coleridge told his wife, "they took twenty-
nine guineas, and I six—all our remaining cash."

From Ballachulish on September 2, and from Fort William the next day,
Samuel complained to his wife of his miseries. He is penniless, needs £10, but
at worst "will *make* £5 do. You must borrow it of Mr. Jackson." He feared
one of his children had died—"an untried misery" he said, forgetting
Berkeley, whom Mrs. Coleridge could not forget! His health was but "middling," he took drugs only in fits of colic, had bad sleep and dreams, and since
his illness became asthmatic, "opiates produce none but unpleasant
effects. . . . I am hopeless." And after drinking "water by the roadside" he
had had an hysterical attack of weeping, pains, colic, and fatigue.

A similar state upon his entry into Fort William, apparently the same hysterical fit he mentioned to his wife, he described to the Beaumonts on September 22: "At Fort William on entering the public house I fell down in an hysterical fit with long and loud weeping to my own great metaphysical amusement, and the unutterable consternation and bebustlement of the landlord, his wife, children and servants who all gabbled Gaelic to each other, and sputtered out short-winded English to me in a strange style. . . ."

The next morning, Sunday September 4, on his way to Fort Augustus, cheered by the charge of only 5/10 for six meals and half a pint of whisky, he sat down on a convenient gravestone, took out his notebook, and solemnly inscribed: "Peace and blessing be with us all! With thee my Sara!" But which 'Sara,' who shall say? At Fort Augustus, while writing another letter to his wife, "the Governor and his wise Police Constable seized me and my letter, he told her. Later, "taken up for a spy and clapped into Fort Augustus," was his version to Southey. But his only private note on the matter is, surprisingly, merely: "Tuesday morning, Sept. 6. 11 o'clock. Left Fort Augustus, having breakfasted with the Governor." Was it literally or only ironically intended? Otherwise it is strange that Samuel, so proud of any social distinction, reserved this breakfast for his private record alone.

On September 11 he reached Perth after walking 263 miles in eight days—so he said. The next day he arrived by coach in Edinburgh. "A wonderful city! What alternations of height and depth!—A city looked at in the polished back of a Brobdignag Spoon," he thought, as they approached it. But in effect, there in Edinburgh, his tour of Scotland ended. Indeed he had gone there with the intention of returning to Greta Hall as speedily as possible. For at Perth letters from Southey informed him of the sudden death of Southey's baby daughter, Margaret, his first and long-desired child, and of the sudden dash of the parents to Greta Hall for sympathy. Upon this Coleridge had at once turned his steps homewards.

"An instructive though melancholy tour," he had described it to his wife, intending to retrace it on the map for her when he reached home. Melancholy in large part it certainly had been, and increasingly as the solitary days which at first pleased him, passed. Horrific dreams pursued him by night and day. "Frightful dreams with screaming" they were, that sometimes woke him and those about him. Sometimes on waking, he found his legs locked together and bruised in his agonized convulsions. "Relief and quiet sleep through camphor & ether," he once records. Hysterical weeping sometimes followed the dreams. "My spirits are dreadful," he told Southey, "owing entirely to the horrors of every night. I truly dread to sleep; it is no shadow with me, but substantial misery foot-thick, that makes me sit by my bedside of a morning and cry." In similar terms he described his state to his wife, and to his most intimate friends.

The effect upon him of Southey's sad letter was of course, intense. "I am stunned at present," he replied, "whatever comfort I can be to you, I will. I cannot stay a day in Edinburgh. I cannot chit chat with Scotchmen, while you are at Keswick, childless. I will knit myself far closer to you than I have hitherto done—and my children shall be yours till it please God to send you another.'' To Mrs. Coleridge his account was more emotional even than this. The letters he told her ''have stunned me, and I am afraid of hysterics, unless a fit of vomiting which I feel coming on, should as I hope it will, turn it off. I must write no more.''

To Southey he now sent verses—''The Pains of Sleep''—which gave expression to his misery. At Edinburgh the dreams still pursued him and there, at the Black Bull Inn, he composed an ''Epitaph'' for himself, which, he told Tom Wedgwood later, ''I composed in my sleep for myself, while dreaming that I was dying. To the best of my recollection I have not altered a word:

Here sleeps at length poor Col, and without screaming,
who died, as he had always lived, a-dreaming:
Shot dead, while sleeping, by the Gout within,
Alone, and all unknown, at E'nbro' in an Inn.

Since Coleridge's separation from the Wordsworths and his dyspathy towards William, his letters to his wife had been friendly and conciliatory. ''Misery is a misery-maker,'' he told her at Perth, alluding to his despondency, ''But do you try, and I will try: and Peace may come at last. . . .O Sara! dear Sara! try for all good things in the spirit of unsuspecting Love for miseries gather upon me.''

Now increasingly his thoughts of Asra appear in his private record. Alone in the landscape meditating an ode to Solitude, Nature and Liberty, the thought of Asra moves Coleridge: ''I feel here as if I were free to wander on the winds, a blessed Ghost, till my Beloved came to me. . . .'' He sees her, ''My Love,'' resting among ''the purple heath flowers: their shadows playing on her naked feet between the silken ligatures of her sandles.'' The unconscious significance of Coleridge's next image of himself as a ''mourning husband,'' may have escaped his observation despite his keen psychological insight: ''Such love as mourning husbands have. To her whose spirit hath been newly given, to be his Guardian Saint in Heaven.''

''Asra'' like Samuel, had her unhappy moods which also found expression in her letters. His fears, doubts, hesitancies when her letters reached him so disturbed him, that he now noted privately how on such occasions, uncertain whether she were ''affectionate or reproachful, mournful or happy,'' he would sometimes keep her letter half a day in his pocket, then peep into it at its end to find her mood, then leave it on his desk or again in his pocket, walk about the garden or his study for an hour or so in a ''flutter of feeling,'' then read or write until ''my spirits tamed,'' he could bear to read it.

Yet despite all these miseries, Coleridge filled many pages of his notebook with long detailed accounts and descriptions of the scenery and scenes through which he passed in his Scotch tour. Often also he observed factually, imaginatively, colorfully, humorously, or tenderly, according as the particular scene appealed to one or other of his various sensibilities. Often he combined the qualities of both painter and poet. This he realized, crying: ''It maddens me that I am not a painter, or that painters are not I.'' Some rocks appear to him ''like the tooth-sockets of some Mammoth among Mammoths.'' A milking scene delights him: ''What a joyous sight of cows and calves, a milking, lowing, browsing, multitude, with milking lasses chattering Erse. . . .'' Nor does his eye miss the antics of the wind: ''When nervously blown forwards, tumbling topsy turvey, in the strong wind.'' His eye for detail is no less active in the interiors of the inns he visits: noting pictures and all aspects that create their atmosphere.

How intimately he felt all the influences of the scenery, many a little vignette in his notebook shows: ''O that I had seen this in the evening a thumb's breadth from sunset; the solemn motion of the trees, is in such nights harmonious with the dimmer shape and deeper colours. As I write this, I turn my head, and close by me I see a Birch in full sunshine and the shadows of its leaves playing on its silver bark, an image that delighted my Boyhood, when I had no waterfalls to see. . . .'' His final verdict upon Scotland however, was soberly appreciative rather than enthusiastic. ''There are,'' he declared, ''about four things worth going into Scotland for, to one who has been in Cumberland and Westmorland. . .Loch Lomond, the Trossachs, the Falls of Foyers, and Edinburgh.''

After two days in Edinburgh, Coleridge left by coach for Carlisle and Penrith where he spent the night and must have met Sara, and reached Greta Hall at noon the next day, September 15, 1803.

15 Domestic Discord (1803-4)

"Mrs. Coleridge enjoys her old state of excellent health. We go on, as usual—except that tho' I do not love her a bit better, I quarrel with her much less."

—S.T. Coleridge to T. Poole, October 14, 1803

At Greta Hall Coleridge found with delight that one of his dearest wishes had been realized—Southey was already permanently installed there. This Coleridge had long planned and had attempted in various ways to achieve. To this end he had sent Southey several letters, not only of pressing invitation, but also of most practical details as to furniture, rooms, rent, and all other conceivable necessities. For Southey's companionship would be a great boon for Samuel, and, if the hopes of foreign travel Coleridge had cherished for many months were realized, Southey's care for Greta Hall and the Southeys and Coleridges there, would leave Samuel to wander about the world in happy freedom from family responsibilities. Indeed in his anxiety to obtain a domestic substitute, he had even attempted, when Southey hesitated, to inveigle Sotheby to Greta Hall instead.

Nevertheless, all was not *couleur de rose* now at Greta Hall. Southey had brought with him, not only his wife—Mrs. Coleridge's sister, but also Mrs. Lovell, another sister, a widow. But neither Coleridge nor his wife wished to live with Mrs. Lovell, whom Samuel thought too ill-tempered to recommend as governess to the Wedgwoods. Nor was Coleridge now enthusiastic about Mrs. Southey, the "dear sister" Edith of Coleridge's Pantisocratic days. Certainly after a month passed in the company of his wife's two sisters, Coleridge, wearied by the quarrels of the three whom he met at meals, found them "a very large bolus," and referred in most uncomplimentary terms upon the effect of the bolus upon his own digestion.

Fortunately the presence of Southey was great compensation for the "bolus" of the ladies accompanying him. And Southey was happy in renewing the old association with Coleridge. They were, said Southey, "the best of companions possible, in almost all moods of mind, for all kinds of wisdom and all kinds of nonsense." They now shared the rent of Greta Hall which was a little over twenty pounds a year for each. Economy as well as companionship had led Southey to join with the Coleridges. Six years later when it became clear that Samuel would never return there, Southey took the house himself on a lease of twenty-one years.

For Southey, despite his disappointment with Coleridge's failure to achieve his ambitions and his moral decline, still held him in high respect. "It provokes me," he had written to a friend in June, "when I hear a set of puppies yelping at him; upon whom he, a great good-natured mastiff, if he came up to them, would just lift up his leg and piss on. It vexes and grieves me to the heart, that when he is gone, as go he will, nobody will believe what a mind goes with him—how infinitely and ten thousand-fold the mightiest of his generation."

Nor was Coleridge's affection and admiration for Southey less enthusiastic than Southey's for Coleridge. To various friends Coleridge now lavished praises upon him: "the most industrious man I know or have ever known." "Southey" he hold Poole, "I like more and more. . . . Take him all in all, his regularity and domestic virtues, genius, talents, acquirements and knowledge—and he stands by himself."

As Southey rose in Samuel's esteem, Wordsworth at the same time fell. To Poole Coleridge explained his separation from the Wordsworths in Scotland on the ground of his feeling himself "a burden on them" and of William's hypochondria. Wordsworth made no such complaints of Coleridge merely telling Sir George Beaumont, with detachment, "when and why he left us. I am glad he did, as I am sure the solitary part of his tour did him much the most service. . . . Our carriage did not suit Mr. Coleridge, the noise of it being particularly unpleasant to him."

Nor was Coleridge's annoyance with Wordsworth only of the past. On September 25, ten days after Samuel's return from Scotland to Greta Hall, the Wordsworths returned from their tour to Dove Cottage in the late evening. They found "Mary in perfect health, her sister Joannah Hutchinson with her, and little John asleep in the clothes basket by the fire," as Dorothy described it.

Yet Coleridge paid no welcoming visit now to Dove Cottage. The first sight of him since the Wordsworth's return was when William visited Coleridge at Greta Hall on October 9. Dorothy, on the same day, was writing to Catherine Clarkson: "We have not seen Coleridge since our return. He is taking a violent medicine in the hope of bringing his disease to a fit of the Gout. . . . He performed miracles after we left him, in the way of walking, which proves an uncommon strength somewhere, but he is often dreadfully ill."

On the same day, Coleridge unburdened himself to Poole of grievances against Wordsworth. Samuel saw little of him as his health prevented visits to Dove Cottage "one third as often" as before, "and Wordsworth's indolence etc., keeps him at home. Indeed, were I an irritable man, and an unthinking one, I should probably have considered myself as having been very unkindly used by him in this respect." For he had seen Wordsworth "more and more benetted in hypochondriacal fancies, living wholly among *Devotees*—having every the minutest thing, almost his very eating and drinking, done for him by his sister or wife—and I trembled lest a film should rise, and thicken on his moral eye." Coleridge also perhaps, suspected a subtle change in Dorothy towards himself since the advent of Asra, and William's marriage. These circumstances, and Coleridge's own degeneration may well have changed the former fascination Dorothy had found in him into an almost maternal sympathy for "poor Coleridge." This he had felt during the Scotch tour, when at their parting he complained of feeling "uncomfortable." The feelings of the early days at Stowey between Coleridge and Dorothy could not escape the influences of the passing years and were not to be revived. As Mrs. Coleridge told Poole nine years later: "There will never more be *that* between them which was in days of yore."

Coleridge's disappointment was chiefly focused upon Wordsworth, whom he now saw as adulated not only by Dorothy but also by Mary. Even the admiring Robinson, on one later occasion when Sara Hutchinson had joined her sister Mary and Dorothy in the Wordsworth household, jested about: "Wordsworth and his three wives."

Coleridge also complained to Poole of Wordsworth's poetry, including regret that he written so many small poems lately as injurious to his poetic genius. Nevertheless, Coleridge heartily approved Wordsworth's continuing with *The Prelude*, his autobiographical poem, dedicated to Coleridge himself. Wordsworth, he said, should never have deserted this subject which suited his genius, for his other poems. "I have seen enough," he cried to Poole, "positively to give me feelings of hostility towards the plan of several of the poems in the *Lyrical Ballads*: and I really consider it as a misfortune that Wordsworth ever deserted his former mountain track to wander in lanes and alleys; tho' in the event it may prove to have been a great benefit to him. He will steer, I trust, the middle course. But he found himself to be, or rather to be called, the Head and Founder of a *Sect* in Poetry. . . ." For already Wordsworth's increasing reputation began to irk the ever jealous Samuel, who concluded by asking Poole to destroy this letter as well as one he had sent Poole depreciating Newton.

Poetry was not the only cause of Coleridge's complaints of Wordsworth; money was another. To be a friend of Coleridge was inevitably to be involved in his financial misfortunes; and now that Wordsworth had received the payment of the money so long owing to his father, Coleridge was almost immediately an interested party, just as he had been in his Pantisocratic days when Southey's windfall had occurred.

To meet his debts Coleridge now made some plans in which Wordsworth was called upon to give assistance. Coleridge's much mutilated letter of December 1803, to Sara Hutchinson, is obscure in detail but it includes a "sum to be repaid by Wordsworth at the end of the year, in case I should not be able to do it." This, he complained, "did not suit William." Dorothy had in fact, very politely told Coleridge on William's behalf: "Whatever best accommodates you, he should best like, only it would be more pleasant to us. . . . to have nothing to pay till the end of next summer—our affairs settled." However, on January 30, 1804, in a letter furtively sounding the Beaumonts for money, Coleridge, again in London, declared: "Wordsworth, after an obstinate refusal on my part for more than four months, has at length I may almost say—*forced* me to accept the loan of £100." The following March

Wordsworth certainly stood as security for the £100 Coleridge borrowed from Sotheby.

Hazlitt stayed in the Lake District until the late autumn sometimes taking country walks with Coleridge and Southey. Of one such walk through Borrodale on October 24, Coleridge privately decided: "Of course it was a mere walk." For like Hazlitt, Coleridge preferred to walk alone. "I must be alone," Coleridge pondered, "if either my imagination or heart are to be excited or enriched. Yet even so I worshipped with deep feeling the grand outline and perpetual forms, that are the guardians of Borrowdale. . . . The greater and perhaps nobler, certainly all the subtler parts of one's nature, must be solitary. Man exists herein to himself and to God alone. Yea in how much only to God—how much lies *below* his own consciousness." With such sentiments, no one would more readily have agreed than Hazlitt.

During these first weeks of his return to Greta Hall Coleridge spent much time sending long accounts to friends of his experiences in Scotland, particularly of his physical miseries, which still remained. In long assentatious letters to the Beaumonts he forged closer bonds of mutual friendship and sympathy. Even the most difficult hurdle, that of his early republicanism, he cleared with ease. For though due to "speculative principles wild as dreams," it was "perfectly harmless and Christian." Yet, as he told Sir George, he is "agitated," not only at writing to "you, added to the recollection of the unwise and un-Christian feelings" with which when young, "I contemplated all persons of *your* rank in Society."

Now, when a French invasion was expected, he felt many fears for Sir George's health "under the bustle of military preparation." "Are you much engaged in it?" he asked. His nights were filled with anxiety for the Beaumonts, "wishing they were farther inland" and he advised Sir George to go to his estate which was safer, and encourage his tenantry and colliers to join the army. As for himself: "If contrary to my deepest conviction, I find the Country in real Danger, I will stand or fall with it—and I trust, that I should not be found in my study if the French remained even ten days on British Ground." "At all events," he told Poole," *dulce & decorum est pro patria mori*—and I trust, I shall be found rather seeking than shunning it, if the French army should maintain its footing even for a fortnight."

With Lady Beaumont his task of "winding her up" was easier, as the music he played to her was akin to his own tastes and interests. Besides, it was she who now often took the initiative and played him *her* music; which included Pascal's *Lettres Provinciales*. Although, as he told her, "a wretched French scholar,"—confirmed by the misspelling of Pascal's name—he found a copy among Southey's books, and "seized it, O how eagerly! "It seemed to me as if I saw Lady Beaumont with my very eyes; and heard over again the very sounds of those words, in which she had expressed her enthusiastic admiration for him. "Indeed the book kept him out of bed, was in fact as marvellous in its effect on him as Cowper's Letters had been—"And the style a robe of pure Light."

Next, from her Ladyship came two volumes of Isaac Barrow's sermons with one passage marked as a favorite, which Coleridge found to be "an old friend and favourite of mine, beyond any other passage in any language" for creating admiration and surprise. "I pray," he added, noncommittally, "that I may read these excellent Sermons to such an effect, as will be considered by her Ladyship as the best possible Thanks." A month later, Coleridge commented in his notebook: "Barrow greatly inferior to all his great Predecessors, from Hooker to Taylor, in dignity of style. . . ." When Lady Beaumont sent him a "beautiful passage from her sister's letter," Samuel was "much affected." And in return for these kindnesses, he sent her his *Hymn Before Sun-rise, in the Vale of Chamouni*.

To Sir George at the same time, he promised verses—"My Translations from your drawings," that would make a volume if Sir George like them. He was himself "unusually pleased with what I have done," and "it seems as if I had more Love toward you than toward myself in my heart, while I am saying it." A little later his tone was somewhat less hopeful, as promised "specimens" of the "Translations" had apparently not appeared. Nevertheless, he hoped that the poems "will give evidence that the drawings acted upon my mind as Nature does, in its after workings. They have mingled with my thoughts and furnished forms to my feelings." But the "Translations" never appeared.

In early October, Samuel replied with exceptional warmth of affection to some enquiry about himself from his brother George. Although the day before, attempting to excuse his early republicanism to the Beaumonts as a reaction against his family, who "bigots from ignorance, remained wilfully ignorant from bigotry," he now told George of his "many tender yearnings" after them in Scotland, and George himself now became "dear friend of my childhood," "always loved and honoured." He also sent "a Brother's Love" to the whole Coleridge clan at Ottery by name. He had been "very deeply affected," he said, by George's remarks in his letter on Faith and Reason. So now he lovingly preached to George in return, not only on religion but on contemporary political evils. Instead of writing as he had done to Southey, "Pounce comes this damned war-business," he now spoke of it to George, in the unctuous tones he employed so often with Estlin: "Awful times. But God's will be done"—the invasion "a blessing"—so bad was England—and indeed Europe;—a lesson to them. Napoleon, he said, had heard that Coleridge was going to write and publish an article on him; was very anxious about it, and had sent the French Ambassador to Stuart to find out if it would be friendly. Probably like Coleridge's empty vaunts about his article on Pitt, this too was imaginary. What however was real—though not in fact realized—was Samuel's hope of passing Christmas and the spring at Ottery, "alone," if the necessary money could be found. As for his articles in the *Morning Post*, only "duty" had led him to make the "sacrifice" of quitting his "abstruce researches" for politics.

Sara Hutchinson, who had so occupied Coleridge's thoughts during his

Scottish tour, was not to be forgotten after his return to Greta Hall, as his notebook shows. The preceeding summer Coleridge's thought had turned from Sara for a moment to a horrified contemplation of the removal of Mrs. Coleridge, the chief obstacle of the consummation of his love for Asra: "There is one thing wholly out of my power, I cannot look forward even with the faintest pleasure of Hope, to the Death of any human Being, though it were, as it seems to be, the only condition of the greatest imaginable Happiness to me, and the emancipation of all my noblest faculties that must remain fettered during that Being's Life. I dare not for I can not: I cannot, for I dare not. The very effort to look onward to it with a steadfast wish would be a suicide, far beyond what the dagger or pistol could realize—absolute suicide, coelicide, not mere viticide. If I could secure you full Independence, if I could give too all my original Self, healed and renovated from all infirm habits, and if by all the forms in my power I could bind myself more effectively even in relation to Law, than the form out of my power would effect—then, *then* would you be the remover of my Loneliness, my perpetual Companion?" Certainly Coleridge would not dare to murder Mrs. Coleridge, but had she died, perhaps like Trollope's *Bishop of Barchester* on the death of his bullying wife, he would have prayed not to feel glad. Evidently too, *faute de mieux,* he could now contemplate, as in his pantisocratic youth, an irregular union with his beloved. Coleridge's wish to escape from his marriage now also found milder expression in another note: "A man who marries for love: a frog who leaps into a well. He has plenty of water, but he cannot get out again." Or was it a self-warning against Asra!

As Coleridge's mistaken "Birthday" October 20 approached, his emotions over Asra grew hysterical. Alone in his study the day before he cried, "O Sara! wherefore am I not happy!!! Why for years have I not enjoyed one pure and sincere pleasure!—One full joy!—." Thus his thoughts ran on until past midnight: "To-morrow my Birthday, 31 years of age!—O me! my very heart dies!—This *year* has been one painful dream. I have done nothing!—O for God's sake, let me whip and spur, so that Christmas may not pass without some thing having been done. . . ."

Day after day, memories and feelings inspired by Sara afflicted his body and mind. "The *aromatic smell* of the poplar" reminds him of Sockburn and his first meeting with Sara. In the moth beating against his lamp on the night of his actual birthday, October 21, he sees an image of himself. Even Sara's letters to him increased his anxieties. "If I have not heard from you very recently," he recorded, "and if the last letter had not happened to be full of explicit love and feeling, then I conjure up shadows into substances and am miserable." "Misery," he adds "conjures up other forms, and binds them into Tales and Events—the tale grows pleasanter—and at length you come to me; you are by my bedside, in some lonely inn, where I lie deserted—there you have found me—there you are weeping over me! Dear, dear Woman!" "When I am sad and sick," he brooded "I'd fain persuade my heart, I do not wish to see you; but when my nature feels a vernal breeze, a gleam of sunshine, and begins to open, O then I *long* for you, till longing turns to grief. . . ."

The essential egotism of Coleridge's "love" for Sara reveals itself in all these emotions and cogitations. She, however adored, is ever an attendant spirit upon himself, the lover. In his more realistic moods, Coleridge occasionally regarded his passion for Sara with his natural psychological insight. It is thus, when in one of these notebook entries, he describes with remarkable objectivity—even actually anticipating a term of modern psychology, "A lively picture of a man, disappointed in marriage, and endeavouring to make a compensation to himself by virtuous and tender and brotherly friendship with an amiable woman—the obstacles—the jealousies—the impossibility of it." And he determined to cure himself by "devotion to abstract sciences."

But below such causes of his misery as Mrs. Coleridge and Sara, lay another, deeper than all. This was a growing conviction that his early belief in his own genius had been mistaken, and that his friends were now also dubious as the years passed with little or no proof of high poetic power or intellectual excellence. This it was that impelled him to his agonized cry, on his "birthday": "I have done nothing!—O for God's sake, let me whip and spur, so that Christmas may not pass without some thing having been done. . . ."

These fears were not new to Coleridge. Throughout the preceeding spring and summer to allay them, in both himself and his friends, Coleridge had begun to create an enormous dream library of imaginary volumes. These he also announced to his friends as real or as impending realities. Occasionally,—presumably deceived by his imagination, affected by opium—he would announce to one or other that a volume of this library was ready for publication and request their assistance in finding a publisher. But when asked to supply the (nonexistent) manuscript, Coleridge would excuse its nonappearance on the ground of illness or pressure of work and study.

Even in July 1802 Coleridge had announced some of his dream volumes to Southey:—a work on the *Definitive Article in the Greek text of the New Testament* to be published "in a few weeks. . . .This is no mere dream," "like my hymns to the Elements; for I have written more than half the work." (But it was a dream). "I purpose afterwards," he continued, "to publish a book—*Concerning Tythes and Church Establishment*. For I conceit, that I can throw great light on the subject." He would also publish "very shortly," a book on contemporary poets and poetry, in two volumes.

Nevertheless Southey was unimpressed. "As to your Essays, &c. &c." Southey replied, "You spawn plans like a herring; I only wish as many of the seeds were to vivify in proportion. Your Essays on Contemporaries I am not much afraid of the imprudence of, because I have no expectation that they will ever be written. . . ." The following January 1803, Southey's disappointment with Coleridge's delays found expression to a friend:—"All other men whom I have ever known" he wrote, "are mere children to him, and yet all is palsied by a total want of moral strength. He will leave nothing behind him to justify the opinion of his friends to the world."

In the early spring of 1803 the phantom volumes poured forth—a volume of new poems, "a long comic poem of regular and epic construction, serious and pathetic in parts, and with the utmost beauty of imagery and poetic diction"; a tragedy and a farce, and a *History of Metaphysics in England,* in which "I have assuredly besprinkled Hume copiously from the fountains of Bitterness and Contempt". On their nonappearance, he prayed: "Have patience Lord and I will pay thee all!"

As the spring of 1803 gave place to summer with nothing done, Coleridge's sense of frustration increased and found frequent expression in his letters. "I am ashamed of talking about my intended works," he told Southey in May. "I am still in hopes that this summer will not pass away without something worthy of me." If God grant me only tolerable health this summer," he told Poole three days later, "I pledge myself to all who love me, that by next Christmas the last three years of my life shall no longer appear a blank." "During my illness," he told Godwin in June, "I was exceedingly affected by the thought that month had glided away after month, and year after year, and still had found and left me only *preparing* for the experiments which are to ascertain whether the hopes of those who have hoped proudly of me, have been auspicious omens or mere delusions—and the anxiety to realize something, and finish something has, no doubt, in some measure retarded my recovery." One of Coleridge's greatest anxieties at this time was his fear that Josiah Wedgwood, who was disappointed because Samuel had not yet produced some good book to improve the world, might withdraw the annuity he had given him. This indeed he did but not until nine years later.

Nevertheless, Coleridge now believed his prospects as a writer brighter than before. Above all was Samuel's great dream volume the *Organum vere Organum,* "the result of many years' meditation, and of various reading," which was to be "an instrument of practical reasoning in the business of real life." Surely a subject on which Coleridge could not be considered an authority! It was, he told Godwin, "a book by which the reader is to acquire not only knowledge but power." So much for the *Organum* which nevertheless occupied much of Coleridge's thought and time to the end of his life. So impressed indeed was poor Mrs. Coleridge by this portentous work that she proudly spoke of it to her neighbors.

The *Organum* was to be preceded by ten *Introductions* the first of which—never discovered beyond a few pages of a partly filled notebook—was, he said, now ready. Would Godwin find a publisher? But when Godwin immediately asked for the manuscript, essays for Stuart which never appeared and illness prevented his sending it. As for the promised volume of New Poems already "written or composed," they, said Samuel, "acted so perniciously on my disorder," that they could not be despatched. That they never appeared is not strange for Coleridge also complained bitterly that poetic inspiration was dead. "It seemed" he admitted, "a dream that I had ever *thought* on poetry—or had ever written it." Perhaps Coleridge now found some compensation in the appearance of a new edition of his old *Poems,* published with Lamb's assistance.

But the *Organum* was not enough for Coleridge. His dream library also contained an essay on the philosopher Hartley, a study of Chaucer, and contributions to the *Morning Post*. So far however, all were mere straws in the wind pointing toward his greatest plan, which was for Southey and himself to write a magnificent *Bibliotheca Britannica*. It was to be a history of British Literature, bibliographical, biological, and critical, with a catalogue of all extant books, in six or eight volumes. For this Samuel's plans were, for him, precise: "six months learning Welsh and Erse and writing a complete history of all Welsh, Saxon, and Erse books that are not translations." In October or November, this completed, he would proceed to Spain (if neutral) to throw light on Basque. Other subjects treated in the work would be metaphysics, theology, medicine, alchemy, law, ethics, philosophy of Catholicism, chemistry, surgery, navigation, travellers, and voyages, etc. throughout the centuries to the present day. It was all very stimulating, and besides, why not in this dream world live adventurously, like The Ancient Mariner and Christabel?

> Southey's reply to this was depressingly realistic: Your plan is too good, too gigantic, quite beyond my powers. If you had my tolerable state of health, and that love of steady and productive employment which is now grown into a necessary habit with me, if you were to execute and would execute it, it would be, beyond all doubt, the most valuable work of any age or any country; but I cannot fill up such an outline. No man can better feel where he fails than I do; and to rely upon you for whole quartos! Dear Coleridge, the smile that comes with that thought is a very melancholy one.

Southey was in fact repeating in politer language to Coleridge what he had previously written to a friend: "Coleridge and I have often talked of making a great work upon English Literature; but Coleridge only talks." And in talk the whole scheme passed.

Yet during these last months of 1803, Coleridge's physical existence was very different from that of his dreamworld of great achievement and fame. Behind this brave exterior Coleridge lived through a hell of bodily anguish, mental and emotional hysteria, anxiety, hope, and despair. From these, opium alone offered him a refuge. A week after his thirty-first birthday, Coleridge, late at night, dreaming and screaming, brought the whole household of Greta Hall to his room, "and," he noted later, "I continued screaming even after Mrs. Coleridge was sitting and speaking to me! O me! O me!"

Amidst these miseries Coleridge could always rely on Dorothy Wordsworth for comfort and consolation.

> We had a long letter from poor Coleridge, Dorothy informed Mrs. Clarkson on November 13, written in the languor of the first moments of ease after suffering the various tortures of tooth-ache, *teeth* drawing, rheumatism, sickness pains in the bowels, diarrhoea and worst of all a shortness of breath which has recently attacked him on the return of damp weather. His spirits and strength are yet wonderful: ill as he was on Friday I

should not wonder, if the weather were fine, should he walk over to Grasmere before Wednesday; he has intended coming for some time past but has been prevented by one ugly attack or another.

Poole, now estranged from Samuel, and less sympathetic than Dorothy, had recently and sarcastically replied to some of Samuel's many warnings of his own imminent death: "Be sure you leave strict orders if you die, to Mrs. Coleridge, or some one, to write to me immediately, that I may be certain while I do not hear from you that you have not been dead long." To Tom Wedgwood, Coleridge also complained: "Something there is in my stomach or guts that transubstantiates my bread and wine into the body and blood of the devil."

Meanwhile, Mrs. Coleridge, despite her unhappy life, was too busy with her domestic and maternal duties to seek a refuge in dreams and opium. A glimpse too we gain of her at this time with her two sisters and Southey in Greta Hall. "My wife," Coleridge told Sir George and Lady Beaumont, "is chin deep in occupation with the children and the meals, for we have but one servant, and can procure no other till November." Three weeks later, in mid-October, he told Poole: "Mrs. Coleridge enjoys her old state of excellent health. We go on as usual—except that though I do not love her a bit better, I quarrel with her much less. We cannot be said to live at all as husband and wife, but we are peaceable housemates."

At least one victory over her husband Mrs. Coleridge now achieved: a new baptism for all her children at the same time, on November 8, 1803. Yet while accepting his wife's wish in this matter, Coleridge was still dubious about the ceremony. Although he no longer saw in the christening, as three years before "the toad of priesthood. . . spurt out his foul juice. . . while the fat paw of a parson crosses his forehead," he still had reservations about such ecclesiastical ceremonies. So to his notebook he now confided:—"Baptism and Lord's Supper—and to see all the massacres attached to these"; and he wondered whether any church Sacraments "are of the *vital* or *true* parts of christianity."

Unfortunately both the Wordsworths,—Godfather and Godmother—were absent through illness. Nor was Sara Hutchinson present: "In bad spirits," said Dorothy, because her brother Tom had been forced by the landlord to leave their beloved Gallow Hill, and so far had found no refuge. Sara, who accused the landlord's wife of now wanting the farm for herself because Tom had so improved it, was much upset, "feeling," said Dorothy, "that they have no abiding place, and in short, that everything is unstable in this world." However, after a time of anxiety Tom Hutchinson, in March 1804, took a larger farm, Park House, near Penrith. Joannah took Sara's place there to help Tom, and Sara was free to help Mary again in Dove Cottage.

But Baptism and its theological validity could not banish from Coleridge's mind his overwhelming fears of failure to impress the world. What an impediment to success the wide range of his interests and ambitions had been, he now more clearly realized and on the day before the Christening, agonizing over the great variety of his dream works, he vowed "with a fervant prayer" for "enough of manly strength and perseverance to do one thing at a time."

So now he added a list of the works upon which he would concentrate his attention, including "Christabel," his dramas, *On Man, and the Probable Destiny of the Human Race—(My last and great work*—always had in mind.)" In addition to these, was his *Logic*, and "Revolutionary Minds" like Thomas Aquinas, Scotus, Luther, Baxter, and others.

On the second night after the Baptism the entry of Mrs. Coleridge awakened by his screams woke him from a horror dream of Boyer. The next day Coleridge was "frenzied with rheumatic tortures, now in the right jaws, teeth, face, eye and forehead, and now in the left; but wandering about, unable to sit, or lie—and miserable when in motion—from a stifling asthmatic flatulence."

But Coleridge's misfortunes in Greta Hall were not yet complete. From the external world he now received a shock that also of course, had strong emotional repercussions in him. On November 24 the new part of Greta Hall required by the Southey's residence was completed and changes in the Coleridge and Southey rooms were made. To his notebook, Samuel confided his distress: "Lo! on this day *we change houses*! All is in a bustle—and I do not greatly like *bustle*; but it is not that that depresses me, it is the *Change*—Change!—O Change doth trouble me with pangs untold!—but change, and change! change about!—But they shall not get me out—from Thee, Dear Study—I must write a poem on this.—But it is not the only thing—it is November 24, 1803. November 24, 1799, it was a Sunday, and I was at Sockburn!"—with its memories of Asra.

As the eventful day dawned, a restless Coleridge fearing for his study, had taken "a considerable quantity of laudanum." The fantastic results he minutely described and analyzed in his notebook. Next, at his bedroom window he surveyed and wondered at the simple grandeur of the view beautifully described by him in the same notebook entry:—"Darkness and only not utter black undistinguishableness—The grey-blue steely glimmer of the Greta, and the Lake—the black, yet form preserving Mountains—the sky, moon-whitened there, cloud-blackened here—and yet with all its gloominess and sullenness forming a contrast with the simplicity of the Landscape beneath. . . ." At such a moment we feel the tragedy of a man with sensibilities and mind too delicate and a will too weak for the roughness of daily human life. It is thus one sees Coleridge now, bewildered by frustrations, commonplace demands, and narcotic dreams, yet standing at his window in the darkness exquisitely responsive to the subtle beauty of the night. Thus for a moment, when not as so often, begging for sympathy, he appears a dignified tragic figure, unconsciously arousing our compassion.

How conscious Coleridge was of the truth of this, as also of his self-protective disguise in society, he revealed at this time to a friend, when he wrote: "I am far too contented with solitude. The same fullness of Mind, the same crowding of thoughts, and Constitutional Vivacity of Feeling, which makes me sometimes the First Fiddle and too often a watchman's Rattle, in Society, renders me likewise independent of it."

Two days after his nightwatch at the window, Coleridge wrote to Thelwall, who was touring the North, to bring him from "the best druggist in Kendal. . .an Ounce of crude opium, and 9 ounces of Laudanum, the latter put in a stout bottle and so packed up as that it may travel a few hundred miles with safety—The whole will cost, I believe, half a guinea. . . ." Thus Coleridge prepared for the journey to London and the foreign travel he was then contemplating. . . . To Thelwall, he explained his need of opiates as due to his physical ailments, adding, "I bear pain with a woman's Fortitude." More bad dreams followed in mid-December, dreams of Boyer again and Christ Hospital, and of fighting off a Cambridge "Harlot," with other horrific experiences. Such was Coleridge's state as the time for his departure from Greta Hall drew near.

On December 20, taking Derwent with him, Coleridge left Greta Hall for Dove Cottage, intending that Derwent should return home after a few days, while he would almost immediately continue his journey South. Unfortunately, a continuous sequence of illnesses and recoveries, due to the weather, kept him at Dove Cottage for a month. This present illness was a skin eruption which he diagnosed himself, and intended to cure by going to a hot climate which would cure the eruption, he thought, by increasing it. Nor would the physical effect of this cure, he believed, be all. By making him physically repulsive it would "kill all love not purely spiritual," as he confided to his notebook. Sara Hutchinson, then living with the Wordsworths in Dove Cottage, was inevitably associated in his mind with these cogitations about carnal and spiritual love.

So thinking of Sara he continued this:— "O! I should rejoice. My soul she would always love, the faithful Beloved!." Conscious of his asexual idealism, he noted: "Too much vital feeling and too little organic—what sort of Love is that." But in dreams by day and by night, the repressed impulse claimed compensation. Such was his dream of a man who "on the road to the Kingdom of Truth, falls into a criminal intercourse with a girl who is in love with him, whom he considers as the daughter of the King of the Land." Nor was Coleridge blind to its psychological significance. "O it was a wild dream," he cried, "yet a deal of true psychological feeling at the bottom of it." Sara also entered Coleridge's reading now, and in Donne and Daniel he finds her, inspiring in him the courage to sacrifice earthly bliss with her, so that he may find her again in Heaven, and is persuaded that grief for frustrated love is eternal.

Thus the month passed in Dove Cottage, until without returning to Greta Hall, Coleridge set out on Saturday, January 14, 1804, for London and "the South": For go South he must, where exactly, he did not yet know.

16   Escape (1804)

"I must go into a hot climate."
—S.T. Coleridge to Southey, January 11, 1804

From the King's Arms, Kendal, the next morning, January 15, 1804, Coleridge sent Richard Sharp a letter of thanks for a present of money. Congratulation, perhaps, rather than thanks, describes the letter, as in it Coleridge followed his usual technique on such occasions of praising himself to the donor for having encouraged in him the spirit of generosity. But on this occasion he does it obliquely through the description that he sends Sharp of his recent residence with the Wordsworths, whose chief reward for all the care they have lavished upon him during this last month was to feel the joy of helping him, and of finding in him an object on whom to bestow their love. Finally, he concluded with a delicate hint to Sharp: "my persuasion is strong as the life within me that a year's residence in Madeira would renovate me." And as soon as he reached London he would have the pleasure of thanking Sharp personally, "for I still hope to avail myself of your kind introductions." At the same time Coleridge wrote to Poole who was then in London, asking him if he could have a bed at Poole's lodgings, "or whether Mr. Rickman could let me have a bed for one or two nights," and as with Sharp, he impressed upon Poole his vital need of a voyage to Madeira. And if Madeira were impossible he would go to Ottery. But Poole must leave a letter for him at the Saracen's Head in London, where Coleridge would arrive on the twentieth of January.

So leaving Kendal on Sunday, January 15, by coach for Liverpool, he arrived there on Monday evening, and after spending several days with his Liverpool friend, Dr. Crompton, arrived on January 24, 1804, at The White Horse Cellar, Piccadilly, and was received by Poole "with wonted cordiality"—although four days ago Poole had vainly awaited him at The Saracen's Head until past midnight. So now Poole got him a bed in a neighboring coffeehouse where they breakfasted together at half-past-eight the next morning.

At nine Poole left for his "Parliamentary Office" (as Coleridge called it): "the WORSHIPFULL with his dozen clerks, and leaves me this nice parlour till 4 o'clock." Such was Samuel's report to his wife. For Poole had been invited by Rickman to make an abstract of returns relating to the condition of the poor, ordered by Parliament, and was now temporarily resident in London. However, Coleridge was able to enjoy his "nice parlour" alone for a time, as four days after Samuel's arrival, Poole left town for a week or more.

For Coleridge the days were by no means solitary. There were, of course, numerous letters to absent friends: grateful and affectionate ones to the Wordsworths, with thanks for their recent care of him during his illness; long, diplomatic and of course most affectionate and grateful ones to the Beaumonts; letters to Southey, Poole, Godwin and others, even two affectionate and hopeful ones to his wife:

> My dear Sara! believe me, hourly through the day, I am planning or praying for your comfort and peace: nor is it possible, that any name can be more affecting or sink into my heart, and my heart's heart, with a greater weight of duty, than that of the virtuous mother of my children. We will try hard, my dearest friend! that the severest judge shall be able to detect no other evil in us, than the—misfortune, I trust, rather than Evil—of being unsuited to each other."

Along with Coleridge's ever haunting sense of failure and with his increased drugging, drinking, and general moral decline, went an increasing bitterness, a jealousy of those friends and acquaintances who were outstripping him in the world's race for publicity, distinction, general, or official recognition. It is noticeable that his growing subtlety and realism in psychological self-analysis brought no corresponding realism, no moral improvement in his attitude toward the external world. From Kendal he had sent both Southey and Sharp letters containing depreciatory comments on Davy, and for years had sneered at Mackintosh to his friends. But both were now VIPs and they were honored with his earliest calls.

To Poole he reported his impressions immediately after these calls: Davy was growing worldly—"seems more and more determined to mould himself upon the Age in order to make the Age mould itself upon him. . . . O! it is a dangerous business this bowing of the head in the temple of Mammon, and such men I aptly christen *Theomammohists,* i.e. those who at one worship God and Mammon." For Davy was now not only a Professor at the Royal Institution and Director of its chemical laboratory, he had just been made also an F.R.S. But with Mackintosh it was worse; for he had just been made Recorder of Bombay, and also knighted: "I have called on Sir James Mackintosh who offered me his endeavors to procure me a place under him in India—of which endeavors he could not for a moment doubt the success—and assured me *on his honour - on his soul*!!! (N.B. HIS honour!!) (N.B. *his* soul!!) that he was sincere.—Lillibullero—whoo! whoo! whoo!—Good morning, Sir James." he told Poole.

At the same time, from the moment of Poole's departure on January 28, if not before, a continuous round of dinners and breakfasts and suppers with friends and acquaintances began. While dining with Stuart at a Strand restaurant, Coleridge had one of his attacks of diarrhoea, vomiting, sweating "like a tropical rain," immediately after the meal began. He was not fit to leave "till the watchman was crying 'past ten o'clock.' " The next day he prayed privately against the temptation to take opium out of the cupboard in his room. Nevertheless on that day he breakfasted with Greenhough, and for the second time dined with Davy. Reporting the occasion on the following day to Poole, Coleridge exclaimed in loyalty to Tom Wedgwood—"O! Davy *did* talk hard-heartedly about him yesterday."

On February 2, Coleridge dined with Godwin and made a scene. "Thundered and lightened with frenzied eloquence" said Godwin. For this Coleridge apologized the next day calling it "a tirade of drunken enthusiasm." It must be admitted, if Coleridge's account of the matter to Southey be correct, that Godwin had given him some provocation. Differences of opinion on religious and literary matters probably, as well as Samuel's recent protracted revision of a play by Godwin under pressure and supervision by its author,—to Samuel's disgust—played a part in the quarrel. Coleridge himself attributed his outburst to his own righteous indignation supplemented by "a plusquam sufficit of punch." Friendship was however restored at once as Coleridge immediately continued his intensive and detested revision of the detested play. Charles and Mary Lamb were among the guests, and were interested spectators of this dinner scene.

"Nothing," Coleridge told Wordsworth on February 8, "can exceed the bustle I have been in from the day of my arrival in Town." His hosts at many dinners and breakfasts with useful people of influence and generosity included Sharp, Rickman, whom he not only dined with, but determined to dine with "as much oftener as he will invite me, it being among my main wishes to be as much as possible with him." General Hastings not only invited him to dinner but brought along an escaped prisoner from France.

Amidst the "bustle" of his social life in London Coleridge did not forget the Beaumonts. On January 30, he sent them a long account of his physical miseries and stressed his need of a warm climate—either Madeira or Catania in Sicily—"if I can by any proper way arrange the means of so doing without injury or distress to Mrs. Coleridge: and of this I have now little doubt. Wordsworth, after an obstinate refusal on my part for more than four months has at length I may almost say—*forced* me to accept the loan of £100." Coleridge would also request another £100 from his brothers, who he said, could well afford it if he died and so could not repay the loan. But Sir George he most delicately indicated, must not be moved to sending him a contribution; that would prevent his ever writing frankly about his affairs to them again. Yet no request so crudely implied could come from Coleridge without a delicate vindication of it as a proof of his heartfelt affection for the Beaumonts: "I have prevailed on myself", he wrote—after a long effusive passage of warm attachment—"to write you what I am doing and how my affairs are situated now that all is settled, and I no longer risk that from your everflowing kindness, which would at once put a stop to my ever writing minutely of myself hereafter." Strange that such delicacy did not see the danger that all this might appear an oblique request for cash. At any rate it did seem so to the Beaumonts, for two days later came a promise of £100 from Sir George which Samuel refused with all gratitude and delicacy—just as he did the Wedgwoods' annuity. The result was still the same; Coleridge received from Sir George £100 a fortnight later.

Samuel in the same touchingly innocent way also invited himself to be the Beaumonts' guest at Stonehall, Dunmow, the Essex country home of Sir George's mother. The wonderful verses—"Translations" to be inspired by Sir George's mediocre drawings, had for some time fallen into that mysterious silence from which Coleridge's works seldom ultimately emerged. In this case as he told Sir George, he had lost notes of the drawings, "which from some over care of other I have mislaid, and by no industry of search can find." To see the originals was therefore necessary, and "I propose therefore, if it should be perfectly convenient to you, to pay you a visit for two or three days at Dunmow."

Thus it was that on February 7, at nine o'clock in the evening Samuel entered Stonehall, Dunmow, to be "welcomed with glowing affection." "I was welcomed" he told the Wordsworths, "almost as you welcomed me when first I visited you at Racedown." The attention given him by the Beaumonts and by "old Lady Beaumont now eighty-six, a sort of miracle for beauty, and clear understanding and cheerfulness," delighted him; while that of the servants, "in obedience to their master and mistress", would, he feared "effeminate" him if long continued. The Beaumonts' aristocratic courtesy he took as solely a tribute to his own personal qualities and declared them "good and pleasant people." Very happy in his environment, Coleridge of course found Sir George (as with others before) "a man of undoubted genius."

They discussed painting and painters and Samuel said no one had taught him so much in so short a time as Sir George had done. Painting and engraving Coleridge declared, "send us back with new eyes to Nature. . . . A man may employ his time far worse than in learning to look at a picture judiciously." Nor did Coleridge forget the ostensible purpose of his visit to Dunmow, Sir George's drawings. A dozen pages of his notebook are filled with explanatory notes and diagrams of the pictures, which, however, inspired no verses.

Nor was Coleridge's companionship with Sir George limited to intellectual and aesthetic subjects. On his third day at Stonehall he rode with him in Lord Maynard's Park, and as in his military adventure ten years before, fell off his horse. His private note of the incident was simple: "thrown off, etc, etc."; but to the Wordsworths he described himself a few days later as "dashed off my horse" which was so "galloping, kicking and plunging" that he thought it "mad". Yet when Sir George dismounted and caught it, and reinstalled Samuel on its back, it became "as mild as a lamb."

At the same time, beside his attentions to Sir George, Coleridge continued to capture the heart of Lady Beaumont by "winding her up with *any* music," as he had told Wordsworth, six months before. The "music" he now played to her, or let her play to him, was of the intimate, confidential, innocently sentimental kind, including religious thoughts and discussions of noble subjects; themes which Coleridge too could so eloquently expound. Thus it happened that on the Sunday following his fall Lady Beaumont confided to him some of the sweet simplicities of her infancy, particularly how before saying her prayers, she would try "to think of a mountain or great river, or something *great,* in order to raise up her soul and kindle it." And doubtless Coleridge interested her with similar edifying recollections of *his* infancy.

They had wonderful talks too about Coleridge's family and the Wordsworths: talks about Mrs. Coleridge and the children, he told his wife. The thought of Wordsworth's "domestic happiness, and his height and uniqueness of poetic genius," was so poignant said Coleridge, that tears rolled down Lady Beaumont's cheeks and even gathered in Sir George's eyes. Lady Beaumont's "quick enthusiastic feeling" reminded him of Dorothy Wordsworth but she lacked "Dorothy's powers." No wonder Samuel found the Beaumonts such "bewitching company" that he abandoned his eternal letter writing for a time.

Such was the visit to Dunmow as Samuel saw it—at least as he described it to his friends—all *couleur de rose* of the rosiest, including "such divine pictures and engravings." Only one thing failed to win his enthusiastic praise, the house itself, Stonehall: "An old house by a tan-yard with nothing remarkable but its awkward passages." But hardly less bewitching than his host and hostess were their wines—"rich and precious wines," whose names in some cases were new to him but all "agreed admirably" with his sensitive digestion. He was sure they would suit Wordsworth equally well and he got Wordsworth to send the Beaumonts copies of some poems that Coleridge had almost promised them.

At the beginning of Samuel's visit his health "greatly improved." This he largely attributed to the wines. When near the end of his visit his health deteriorated, the change he said, was due to a "heart-withering letter of absolute despair" from Tom Wedgwood—very ill—that arrived just as the weather turned wet. Thus Coleridge's last two or three nights at Dunmow were disturbed by bad dreams and his now frequent attacks of "asthma." This did not however, prevent his turning amateur physician to the Beaumonts. Soon after his departure from Dunmow he was getting from Davy "acid" for Sir George. To his distinguished patient Samuel sent long instructions and directions about it and other remedies: the acid to be drunk "thro' a glass tube."

Amid so many distractions and comforts the visit to Dunmow came all too soon to an end. Too soon, that is, for Samuel, for when Sir George called shortly afterwards on his friend Joseph Farington the landscape painter and diarist, he drily remarked that Coleridge "came for two days and stayed ten." Samuel told the Wordsworths on February 15, "I shall quit these good people with regret, for London." Two days later he departed. It was a triumphal departure. Samuel had tactfully—"mildly but firmly," as he said—refused on two occasions during his visit Sir George's offer of a hundred pounds. But now as Coleridge entered the London coach, the Beaumonts' servant handed him an envelope containing the twice rejected gift and a letter which for its delicacy, deliberate affection, and elevated good sense was " 'worth twice the sum'—to use a very vulgar phrase," as he told Southey. To Farington Beaumont expressed his opinion that "Coleridge had more learning, more reading than Wordsworth, but was not equal to him in poetic power," while Words-worth's poetry "had benefited him more, and more purified his mind than any sermons had done."

Immediately upon Coleridge's return to London the old round to breakfasts and dinners among the same circle of friends recommenced, so too did his hor-ror dreams and diarrhoeas, and the laudanum, opium and brandy as restoratives. During intervals of recovery he attended an occasional lecture by Davy who was giving another course of them at the British Institution.

His physical sufferings he described as usual in copious and often tedious detail in letters to friends—sometimes as part of a belated apology for absence from some party at which he had been expected. To Davy on one such occa-sion he protested against his own "very unjustly acquired character for break-ing engagements." And he emphasized the "extreme reluctance with which I go at all into company, and the unceasing depression which I am struggling up against, during the whole time I am in it which too often makes me drink more during dinner than I ought to do; and as often forces me into efforts of almost obtrusive conversation—acting the opposite of my real state of mind in order to arrive at a medium."

However true this may be, it is far from the impression many of Coleridge's letters give in describing his social experiences. At least one observer gained a very different opinion of Coleridge as a social being.* Amid his social suc-cesses he was still haunted by the consciousness of not having justified by achievements the literary expectations he had encouraged and obtained among his friends. "I have not been for some years," he told Rickman, "without great objects—and my indolence &c has almost altogether arisen from my hav-ing been too too constantly forced off from these objects—but enough!"

As with the Beaumonts these other social activities were not without per-sonal conveniences for Samuel of which he was shrewdly aware. Not only might well-to-do persons like Rickman and Sotheby fork out the needful when required, they might also provide useful introductions. So while Rickman could arrange free postage for Samuel's letters, Sotheby was asked to give him letters of introduction to the Governor of Malta, Sir Alexander Ball, and General Villettes, Commander of the troops there. At last Coleridge's waver-ing intentions had settled upon Malta, and as he informed Sotheby, he had "a wandering wish to get some small place in Malta or Sicily." He did not mind, he unselfishly remarked, if it occupied half his time: "for I have no wish to receive what I have not earned—a place of course, for the performance of the duties of which austere integrity and general information and sanity of mind" were the chief requisites.

In fact Coleridge's choice of Malta was chiefly due to his knowledge that his acquaintance, Stoddart, was now King's Advocate there and so might be useful to him. Some months before when Lamb first heard of Coleridge's wish

*Farington.

to travel, he warned him against "journeying to the green islands of the blest"; but now it was thus that Malta appeared to Samuel's romantic imagination as his plans matured. He had "little doubt" he told Wordsworth, "of a Vice-consulship." He was sure the climate would agree with him and life be "much cheaper. O what a dream of happiness could we not realize," he cried, when "my dear, dear friends," (the Wordsworths) joined him there.

This pleasant dream contrasted with the stern reality of borrowings from his brothers, to reach Malta. "For getting back I shall trust to chance," he told Wordsworth. To leave as little as possible to chance Samuel now continued to help his friends by making himself a target for their generosity—as he would have said. The generosity thus stimulated covered a wide field—topographical, financial, nautical, and itinerant.

On March 16, the Beaumonts returned to their London home, at the corner of South Audley Street and Grosvenor Square. The next morning Coleridge breakfasted with them and two days later returned as their guest remaining until his departure for Portsmouth on March 27. The night before his return he had been very ill again with "cholera morbus." He had, he now told Southey, been "conveyed by my own crawling limbs to Sir George Beaumont's where I have been ever since, tended most affectionately. . . . Your presence at Keswick is beyond all compare my greatest comfort."

The courteous attentions he received from the Beaumonts gave him an almost naïve pleasure and were much advertised in letters to his friends. "No parents, no brother or sister could have behaved with more anxious kindness to me," he wrote, and to the secrecy of his notebook confided: "My spirit watched as constantly and as slyly the numberless attentions of Sir George and Lady Beaumont, as an innocent young woman, pleased and uneasy, the intelligible all of a lover's behaviour."

Within the week of his arrival at the Beaumonts Coleridge recovered: was "in clear sunshine, out of the shadow of the wings of the destroying Angel," he told Tom Wedgwood; "Would to Heaven you were going with me" he added in a last vain attempt to lure Tom to accompany him abroad. On the same day, March 24, he booked his seat on the Portsmouth Mail for Tuesday evening, March 27. The day after the booking Coleridge sat for the painter James Northcote for his portrait commissioned by Sir George. Coleridge had to leave abruptly being again too ill to continue the sitting. Nevertheless Northcote completed the portrait without Coleridge the next day. Three days later Coleridge told Stuart: "I being exceedingly desirous that my friends in the North should possess a likeness of me, in case of my death, have authorised him to have it copied, if it continues to be admired as much as it has been." A good copy he had been assured, would cost only four or five guineas. Therefore, as he hoped to want no more money from Stuart beyond what Stuart had already given him, he ordered a copy of the portrait to be made and the bill went to Stuart to be settled:—"the last liberty of this kind I shall ever take." But this copy must be a good one so as to compensate if ever required for the loss of the original. That this copy has never been found either Fate, or perhaps Stuart, could explain. But Sir George Beaumont had two prints made of the portrait, one for Wordsworth, the other for Southey. Northcote's original portrait of Coleridge is now in Jesus College, Cambridge. Evidently the University has pardoned his irregular undergraduate life and uncomplimentary undergraduate verses.

Although on the day Coleridge sat for Northcote he described to Davy the illness that had interrupted the painting as a threat of "distempered sleep," he was well enough to dine that same afternoon with his host and hostess, (the Beaumonts) and their friends. "Distempered sleep," which had long since appeared in Coleridge's early sonnet *Pantisocracy* and more recently in *The Pains of Sleep,* was caused by opium. This he now plainly stated on the same day in his notebook, when evidently pondering the reason for his illness during the sitting that morning: "N.B. opium always in the day time increases the puffing asthma, eye closing, and startlings."

Coleridge's fellow guests at the Beaumonts' dinner party on that day were Farington and George Dance, an architect. The latter made a sketch of Coleridge. Although Samuel described himself to Davy as "with all my faculties beclouded" that afternoon, none of the diners noticed anything strange in him. Even the critically minded Farington, no great admirer of Coleridge, far from detecting "beclouded faculties" in him, found him particularly lively. To Farington's account of that evening we owe one of the most intelligent and objective descriptions of Coleridge in society that we have. "Throughout the Evening," Farington recorded, "Coleridge dominated the conversation," which was "very metaphysical," with Coleridge "analysing [*sic*] every subject." Samuel of course agreed with Sir George that painting required "more powers" than sculpture. He also said that "Nature" must be the basis of all poetry. Apparently forgetting his wish four years before "to toss up a novel" with Southey, he now denounced all novels, even the best, because "they afforded amusement to the mind, without requiring exertion." When Lady Beaumont asked his opinion about a ghost of which she had been told, Coleridge dismissed it as "an ocular spectrum" due to disordered imagination and nerves. Dr. Darwin the contemporary popular poet, he denounced as "a great plagiarist: "He was like a pigeon picking up peas, and afterwards voiding them with excrementitious additions."

Certainly Farington's impression of Coleridge was less than enthusiastic: "The evening was passed not in conversation but in listening to a succession of opinions and explanations delivered by Coleridge. It was all metaphysical, frequently perplexed and certainly at times without understanding his subject. Occasionally there was some brilliance, but I particularly noticed that his illustrations generally disappointed me and rather weakened than enforced what he had before said." When Coleridge read to them Wordsworth's verses *To a Highland Girl* and the sonnet composed upon *Westminster Bridge,* Farington noticed that "his dialect, particularly when reading, is what I should call broad Devonshire, for a gentleman. His manner was good-natured and civil, and he went on like one that was accustomed to take the lead in the company he goes into. . . . In coming away I expressed to Dance how much I was fatigued by that sort of confinement we had been under. He sympathized in it.''

The following day when Farington dined with Northcote and others Coleridge was discussed. When Sir George first praised him to Northcote the portrait painter had expressed surprise as Coleridge was "a *great democrat*.'' But Sir George replied that Coleridge's opinions were now altered. Opie, the painter, said Godwin had a high opinion of Coleridge's powers and of "*the riches* of his mind.'' Prince Hoare, artist and author, thought some of Coleridge's sonnets were very good, but Fuseli, who had met Coleridge at Johnson's the bookseller's, "thought little of him.'' Coleridge had mentioned to Northcote the "high family" of Sir George Beaumont on which Northcote had expressed his surprise that Coleridge, who had held all such distinctions so cheap, should give consideration to such a matter. Northcote had also been reminded of "the drone of a Presbyterian parson" when Coleridge read some of his poetry to him, but Lady Beaumont "appeared delighted.''

But whatever reservations some of Coleridge's critics might have, the Beaumonts had fallen under his spell, like so many others; and when a day or two later Sir George and Lady Beaumont called on Farington, Sir George spoke of his own "good fortune in having met with such a genius as Coleridge and a man of such a disposition that he would go to the end of the world to serve another. That Wordsworth, not himself was his theme, his friendship being above all self-love.'' Dr. Burney said "What he had seen of Coleridge's poems was of no value. . . . Here and there were a few touches of brilliance, but nothing solid.''

Northcote showed Farington his drawing of Coleridge, finished the day after it was begun but without further sitting than the first unfortunate one, and Farington thought it "very like.'' When Sir George's print reached William and Dorothy they were very critical, finding only parts of the face like Coleridge's, and Hazlitt's "so far as mere likeness goes, better; but the expression in Hazlitt's,'' Wordsworth added, "is quite dolorous and funereal.'' In this respect Wordsworth found Northcote's portrait "much more pleasing, though certainly far below what one would wish to see infused into a picture of Coleridge.'' But it was Southey who most completely damned the whole of the various portraits after seeing them several months later at an exhibition in London. "I went into the Exhibition," he wrote to Coleridge, then in Malta, "to see your picture which perfectly provoked me. Hazlitt's does look as if you were on your trial, and certainly had stolen the horse; but then you did it cleverly,—it had been a deep, well-laid scheme, and it was no fault of yours that you had been detected. But this portrait by Northcote looks like a grinning idiot; and the worst is, that it is just like enough to pass for a good likeness, with those who only know your features imperfectly. Dance's drawing has that merit at least, that nobody would ever suspect you of having been the original.''

During these last days in London before leaving for Portsmouth Coleridge was very busy; very "agitated" not only by the thought of leaving England but also by the anxiety of finding a ship and arranging his passage. He had hoped that Rickman would obtain a free voyage for him as the captain's friend. But Rickman seemed to Coleridge to have been indifferent. Samuel's final attitude to the much courted Rickman was bitter—for Rickman refused both free passage and free postage.

It was Sharp who found a ship, the Speedwell, for Samuel and brought its captain to him to arrange the matter. Coleridge went on board with him, found the ship "very neat but so small as to be literally a box." The next day he told Greenough: "Yesterday morning, weary of suspense and hearing nothing of a King's ship, I engaged my passage on board the Speedwell brig, John Findlay, Commander—of only 130 tons burthen, 35 guineas passage money, exclusive of wine, spirits and bedding!—Jesus Christ." After paying a deposit of £20, he heard to his annoyance that a King's ship "had been appointed, heaven knows how long. However all things are for the best, I hope, though if taken prisoner by an Algerian or a French man, I might be a little puzzled to develop the optimism on this side of the grave." When the next day he wrote to Rickman about coming with the Lambs to see him—his blasphemous mood was still active:— "The Virgin Mary and the uncrucified Lamb will come with me."

But the valedictory mood of some of Coleridge's last letters created a dignified even pious rhetoric, such as hitherto only Mrs. Evans on their parting at Darley Hall, had heard. Thus to the disappointed official of his insurance company he bade farewell with ecclesiastical solemnity: "I will offer up a solemn prayer for you with a fervent heart, among the names of my children and wife and friends, even as I mount the ship that may carry me perhaps to a burial in a foreign land. But if we have made God our Father, the whole universe must be our home! May the spirit of God aid us both so to do."

To others Samuel's farewells were almost brusquely practical. Thus, while too weak to bid a personal farewell to Greenough and wishing to avoid emotion, he concluded with unadorned practicability—"If you think it worth while, the brandy might be sent by one of the heavy coaches to-morrow morning. . . ." On the same day he wrote to the generous Sharp: "If gratitude consists in repaying love for love, merited esteem by merited esteem, and good services by earnest dispositions akin to them, I am and shall ever be, your grateful friend. P.S. If I draw at all, I shall draw on Mr. Stuart according to your letter."

Coleridge described himself on the day before he left London for Portsmouth as "miserably ill," "crawling" to the Strand—"I must be *carried* back." To those who for some or no reason had fallen into disfavour his farewells were nicely graduated, coolness and Christian piety being exquisitely blended into a vague aggrieved, and in extreme cases faintly insolent or even insulting tones.

So now to Sotheby who had vexed him in some way he sent a cool but pious farewell. Sotheby had given Coleridge a few days before £100, but had wanted security which Coleridge had induced Wordsworth, somewhat reluctantly to accept. But Coleridge had not been pleased and his last words to Sotheby in his last letter—or rather short note—were: "If I return, we shall be friends; if I die, as I believe I shall, you will remember me. Such remembrances do us all good. I pray fervently for you and Yours'. . . ."

But far worse than Sotheby were two other friends, Poole and Tobin, whose misdeeds he described to Southey. Coleridge it appeared, while staying recently with Poole, had quarrelled with him and gone to stay with Tobin, with whom he had quarrelled in turn. "Poole," he told Southey had since dared to send him an affectionate farewell letter— "good God! to believe and to profess that I have been so and so to him, and yet to have behaved as he had done—denied me once the loan of £50 when I was on a sick bed!" And a completely false version followed of his quarrel with Poole three years before about money. Even worse, Poole had not paid for Samuel's board and lodgings in London this time although he had had the benefit "of my *conversation* and the instruction he derived from it." Naturally therefore the errant Poole received a valedictory letter of a mere six lines saying Samuel was too weak "to take leave of you in person," and adjuring him: "May the Almighty guide you onward wherever and whenever the road leads to Happiness and that sole virtue which is in faith not in the outward works. S.T. Coleridge." Despite his promise in the note to write again to Poole before his departure he did not do so, and not until three years later did he write to him. Nor was the old relationship ever completely restored. When thirty-one years later after Coleridge's death, Poole reading Coleridge's letters in tears, came upon this farewell note, he "almost broke down" as Poole's biographer wrote.

The next sinner for castigation was of course Tobin whom shortly before, taking refuge with him from Poole, Coleridge had described to Poole as "an exceeding mischief-maker." Tobin, Samuel told Southey, had slept out after Coleridge's arrival at his rooms. He had left him "alone. . . no wine or spirit of any kind, and no human being within call." Nor was this all! Tobin had disobeyed Coleridge's command to call on Davy to explain Samuel's failure to keep an appointment with him. But Tobin had done worse than these things. He had tried to moderate Samuel's doping and drinking. Even at the last moment, when Coleridge was about to mount the Portsmouth coach, in the presence of Stuart and Lamb, Tobin appeared and reminded him of the paltry £10 Samuel owed him! No wonder then that some weeks later after leaving England, Coleridge sent Tobin a sarcastic letter beginning: "Men who habitually enjoy robust health have too generally the trick, and a very cruel one it is, of imagining that they discover the secret of all their acquaintances' ill-health in some malpractice or other." Two things that Tobin had done particularly angered Coleridge. The first was giving him advice, also one of Samuel's charges against Poole—the other, as Coleridge at least believed—was discussing his character and opium addiction with others. This was evidently a matter of common gossip among Coleridge's friends in London.

So now Coleridge's lengthy letter to Tobin warned him against people who not only imagined they discovered secrets but talked about them to friends.

"Those who are most fond of advising," he continued, "are the least able to bear advice from others. . . .I should often have been on the point of advising you against the twofold rage of advising, and of discussing characters. . . . Our friend's reputation should be a religion to us." After more preaching to the same effect Coleridge closed with an expression of high esteem for Tobin. Tobin in his reply the following August, wrote: "A letter of your fraught with advice against advising and other censorious matters was duly recieved by me."

Coleridge must also answer Davy who had sent him a parting letter tactfully mingling compliments to Coleridge's "genius" with gratitude for his beneficial influence upon Davy himself. It also included a very delicate hint of disappointed expectation: "You must not live much longer without giving to *All men* the *proof of power,* which those who know you feel in admiration. . . ." This time Coleridge far from being angry, answered Davy in a rare spirit of chastened truthfulness and friendly esteem. For Davy's hint was not forgotten although now for the present, Samuel had evidently forgotten his various recent aspersions against him. The letter he said had made him for the moment "able to hope for myself as you have dared hope of and for me." But "alas! such moments are neither many, nor of quick recurrence. There *is* a something, an essential something wanting in me. I feel it, I *know* it—though what it is I can but guess." He went on to identify it as he did elsewhere with "power" without "strength." His long letter closed with a perfervid assurance of "esteem and affection."

Inevitably it was the Beaumonts who received Coleridge's most fervent words of Farewell. Indeed his gratitude and affection required three letters for adequate expression—one to Lady Beaumont the day before he left for Portsmouth, one to Sir George and Lady Beaumont the following day, and the last to Sir George alone just before he sailed. The first to Lady Beaumont expressed his fear of being misunderstood in sending her Davy's eulogy of Coleridge's "genius." He explained that his real intention in sending it was to show them how greatly his friends overestimated him. His second letter written on his last morning at the Beaumonts was highly emotional. The night before alone in his bedroom, he said, sitting beside his fire and deeply moved by memories of the past, he had knelt and prayed for his hostess and host. But above all his grateful affection for his friends overflowed: "If I did not in my heart's heart cherish you, and (abstracting the hue of respect to the difference of your rank, which is with me a business not a force or of habit but of deliberate moral election) feel toward you, Dear Sir George and dear Lady Beaumont, even as tho'

We had been rear'd upon the self-same Hills,
Fed the same flocks by Fountains, Shades, and Rills. . . ."

He would remember their thoughts of him wherever he went, whether in this world or in the next. In his final letter addressed to Sir George, he continued the tone of its predecessor along with melancholy references to his physical and moral feelings, his "alienations from the spirit of Hope" caused by bodily suffering.

By this time his gratitude to the Beaumonts included not only the £100 Sir George had so delicately pressed upon him at Dunmow, but also the very earthly comforts he had provided at Coleridge's departure. "It would have affected you deeply," he told Southey, "to have seen the manner in which Sir George parted from me. His valet packed up everything, and did not leave me till I entered the mail. They stocked me with wine in stout bottles and lock-up cases, with medicine, portable soup, an elegant thing to lock up my letters, papers, &c. &c." Thus on March 27, 1804, amid farewell good wishes from Lamb and Stuart, Coleridge set off for Portsmouth.

Between 7 and 8 o'clock the next morning, Coleridge arrived at Portsmouth and took a room at the Crown Inn—"noisy, dirty inn"—"dirty, doleful inn"— to await the arrival of the Speedwell expected during the day, but which did not arrive till early in April.

"A dashing bookseller, a booted buckskin breeched jockey" named Mottley to whom Stuart had given him an introduction, proved also to be "a man of wealth and influence and a knowing fellow." He was also an agent for Sir Alexander Ball, the Governor of Malta. Mottley was most attentive to Coleridge, taking him through the dockyards where he "was lucky enough" to see the welding of an anchor. "Truly sublime" he found it—"the enormous blaze, the regular yet complex intertwisted strokes of between twenty and thirty men with their huge flailhammers. . . the shower of sparks, the iron dripping like a millwheel. . . . Verily it was an unforgettable scene." As in his early revolutionary days Coleridge pitied the workers—"Pitiable slaves working from 4 in the morning till 9 at night, and yet paid less than any other in the yard. They all become old men in the prime of manhood." He saw the rope makers and a machine "lately introduced after a rebellion amongst the men"—two thirds of the work should be done by machines thus easing labour" which now eats up the Ropemen like a giant in a fairy tale."

Coleridge's acquaintance with Mottley quickly developed into friendship. Mottley invited him to dine and Coleridge took advantage of the occasion to complain of the expense of living at the Crown Inn: "Mottley *congratulated* me that I got off so cheap. . . ." Immediately afterwards, Coleridge could tell his wife: "I am only at the expense of a lodging, at 1/2 a guinea a week, for I have all my meals at Mr. Mottley's."

Debts at Greta Hall were not forgotten by Samuel before his departure. Jackson, the admiring landlord at Greta Hall, although now like so many of Coleridge's helpers at one time or another, in financial difficulties, also assisted him in providing the means for his travels. Nor was Southey forgotten. Sending Mrs. Coleridge money to meet "little bills," Samuel also promised "in a few weeks I will leave you debtless at Keswick, debts great and small, save that which we both owe to Southey for his Vice-fathership." For Southey, remaining with his wife and family at Greta Hall now found himself accepting the responsibilities for Mrs. Coleridge and her children, which

Samuel had almost forced upon him by leaving England.

Nevertheless Southey sent Coleridge a very friendly farewell letter. He was, he said, surprised to learn that Samuel was really going abroad at last. "I shall often, Coleridge, *quanto minus est cum reliquis versari quam tui meminisse!* God grant you a speedy passage, a speedy recovery, and a speedy return! . . . I will write regularly and often. . . ."

On his last day in London Samuel sent a short note almost entirely practical to his wife, assuring her: "Do not be uneasy about money. If you want more, you shall have more." A month before, moved by receiving an account of the children from Mrs. Coleridge, Samuel's parental feelings had overflowed into an affectionate message, not only to them but also to herself. Weeping over her letter he wrote: "My eyes are still red with crying over it, for joy and tenderness and sorrow of absence—O my sweet Hartley! my darling—My own, very own Hartley!—and my Stump, my pretty affectionate Derwent'. . . . My very heart is still trembling,—and my very heart thanks and loves you, my dear! for your letter—be as minute about the children as you can—never let anything escape." A similar agonizing picture of himself Coleridge again drew for his wife's benefit in his last letter to her before sailing. "My dear Sara," he wrote, "the Mother, that attentive and excellent mother of my children must needs be always more than the word friend can express when applied to a woman—I pray you, use no word that you use with reluctance. Yet what we have been to each other, our understandings will not permit our hearts to forget! God knows, I weep tears of blood, that so it is! for I greatly esteem and honour you—Heaven knows, if I can leave you really comfortable in your circumstances, I shall meet death with a face, which I feel at the moment I say it, it would rather shock than comfort you to hear."

The Wordsworths of course would not allow Coleridge to leave England without a last affectionate farewell. "Our hearts are full of you" wrote Dorothy on April 3. "May God preserve you, and restore you to us, in health of body and peace of mind!"; and she continued with family news, visits from Sara, others from Mrs. Coleridge and the children and Dorothy's fears for Coleridge in stormy weather. William sent news of his poetry, of his additions to the poem dedicated to Coleridge, *The Prelude,* some of which Coleridge was already taking away with him. William's fears and affectionate message for Coleridge even exceeded Dorothy's: "Heaven bless you for ever and ever," he concluded, "no words can express what I feel at this moment, Farewell, Farewell, Farewell." Sara Hutchinson too must have sent Coleridge an affectionate farewell letter, not now forthcoming; nor are his letters to her or to the Wordsworths.

The state in which Coleridge left England in search of health was admirably described a few days before his departure by Southey to Rickman.

He is worse in body than you seem to believe Southey wrote, but the main cause lies in his own management of himself, or rather want of management. His mind is in a perpetual St. Vitus's dance—eternal activity without action. At times he feels mortified that he should have done so little; but his feeling never produces any exertion. I will begin to-morrow, he says, and thus he has been all his life long letting to-day slip. He has had no heavy calamities in his life, and so contrives to be miserable about trifles. Poor fellow! There is no one thing which gives me so much pain as the witnessing such a waste of unequalled power.

Four days later Southey told his friend Miss Barker:

Coleridge is gone to Malta, and his departure affects me more than I let be seen. . . . It is now almost ten years since he and I first met, in my rooms at Oxford, which meeting decided the destiny of both; and now, when after so many ups and downs, I am, for a time, settled under his roof, he is driven abroad in search of health. Ill he is, certainly and sorely ill; yet I believe if his mind was as well regulated as mine, the body would be quite as manageable. I am perpetually pained and mortified by thinking what he ought to be, for mine is an eye of microscopic discernment to the faults of my friends; but the tidings of his death would come upon me more like a stroke of lightning than any evil I have ever yet endured. . . .

17 "The Forlorn Wanderer"—In Malta (1804-5)

"Your kind reception of the forlorn wanderer gave me the greatest pleasure. . . "
—Mary Lamb to Sara Stoddart, June 1804

"Monday, April 9, 1804: to Gibraltar, and whithersoever else God will or suffer me to go." Such was Coleridge's first thought as the Speedwell set out on its "most prosperous voyage of eleven days," convoyed by the Leviathan, which Coleridge thought a "majestic and beautiful creature." Hoping to spend the time on board profitably, he had "written out with much pomp of promise," as he said, a plan to write letters, "fag Italian," and "finish my Christabel." "Spite of the toss and tumble of cruel rocking," he wrote letters to Lamb, Southey, and censoriously, to the errant Tobin; but little if any more of his plan was realized. Illness caused by the rocking ship (and by opium) soon laid him low, but he was not, he emphatically declared "sea-sick." It provided of course the usual gruesomely detailed material for letters. But for the last three or four days of the voyage to Gibraltar he rejoiced in feeling "uncommonly well," and was able to make the most of this five day's stay when they landed.

Throughout his wanderings abroad Coleridge showed the usual extraordinary breadth and variety of interests and attitudes; the most detailed and lively observation of the external world and its creatures,—particularly the humans—as well as his private world of religious-philosophic-metaphysical thought. His realistic appreciation of his two fellow passengers on the Speedwell was exactly what it had been during the *Watchman* crusade, sometimes even to the very words, as when he now described the fat woman voyager as one "who would have wanted elbow room on Salisbury Plain." The woman's table habits annoyed him as he watched her with a critical eye, and he was particularly revolted by her frequent selection of some specially alluring potato and her appreciative comments on it. For the other passenger he had even less sympathy—"a half-pay lieutenant turned small merchant," whose "bright eye over a yellow-purple face betrays to me that half his liver is gone or going."

From such uncharitable observations of human infelicity Samuel would turn to the beauties of nature about him: "All day during the sunshine, watched

255

with delight the two colours of the ocean; I have seen nothing like it hitherto, nothing so green, no green so bright and rich—and of violet purple, equal in light and richness. . . ." He traced familiar mountains in the clouds, rejoiced to see "the crescent moon with the old moon in her lap"—as in *Dejection*—and found pleasure in the idea of the ship itself, each part contributing to the efficiency of the whole. This it was, he said, that made the ship "picturesque," for "nothing more administers to the Picturesque than this phantom of complete visual wholeness in an object, which visually does not form a whole, by the influence *ab extra* of the sense of its perfect intellectual beauty or wholeness."

It was the memory of the idea of Sara Hutchinson more than the image that restlessly pursued Coleridge on the voyage, pursued him in thought by day and in dreams by night from which he often awoke weeping and screaming. The dreams inspired an attempt at poetic expression that petered out after eight lines giving place to an abstract analysis of the experience. "This in rhyme," he added, "and either greatly compressed or highly touched up. And now for the metaphysics"—This led to a psychological examination resulting in the opinion that its essence was self-pity "and pity had always pleasure as one of its component parts."

Yet his emotions continued in apparent detachment from his intellectual abstractions. "Why aren't you here?" he continually whispered, feeling a "yearning that at times passes into sickness of heart." His growing jealousy of Wordsworth's influence over Sara Hutchinson made him imagine Mrs. Wordsworth dead and Wordsworth married to Sara, with himself indicated as a mathematical minus quantity. Throughout his "love" is essentially self-love, as in his analysis he clearly saw: but in thought even as such, it spun a fine web:—"Long years of seriousness, of deep passion, awful incidents, seas traversed and the famous things of the world seen, and all connected with one abiding hope, one thought, one love,—this will surely give a delicacy, an awe, a fear of saying or doing light or coarse things in her presence, and lengthen out the passion, by still combining it with a manly feeling."

It was in a similar mood of metaphysical abstraction that Coleridge, sitting on a duck coop, "the ducks quacking at my legs," recorded his thoughts and feelings on the morning of April 19, as the Speedwell, driven by a brisk breeze at a speed which he was glad to note must prevent any sudden raid upon them by "privateers and corsairs," approached Gibraltar. "This is Spain!" he told himself. "That Africa! now then, I have seen Africa!" and he felt "a quickening of the movements in the blood." So now, as with Asra, the experience must be analyzed—to reveal after an immensely long and detailed dissection that his emotion was not due to any mere historical associations with the names *Africa* and *Europe*, because, as he reflected, he had less "pleasure in things contingent and transitory" than any person he knew, even than Wordsworth.

As the Rock came into view Coleridge traced "rude resemblances indeed, but yet resemblances to Keswick and Skiddaw" in the clouds. Thus "between 4 and 5, Thursday afternoon, April 19,—arrived at Gibraltar."

There he first discarded the clothing he had worn on leaving England: four flannel waistcoats, two pairs of flannel drawers, "under cloth pantaloons, and a thick pair of yarn stockings." He "passed nearly the whole of each day," he said, " in scrambling about on the back of the Rock among the monkeys. I am a match for them in climbing, but in hops and flying leaps they beat me." It was a healthy change from his besetting abstractions. So too was his interest in the town and in the various types of humanity he saw there: "Spaniards, Jews, Moors—a sweet English Lady—how straggled that angel face hither?" Just the place for a "character-painter" he thought, and longed for "a dozen plates by Hogarth" from it. The trees, flowers, gardens, even the weeds growing on the rock, he noted with delighted and observant eyes worthy of Dorothy herself.

Coleridge had stepped ashore with his "brain active," his "heart very full of love, tender recollections, and if possible, yet more tender hopes and dreams of the future"—so he described himself. But "a noisy dinner of 17 sea captains, indifferent food and burning wines," followed by his dragging "my now very tipsy captain" back to the Speedwell, where he left him "still drinking in his own cabin" with three other captains, Coleridge found less pleasing than the monkeys. He was delighted to find a cave that was "the very model" of his cave in *Osorio,* and he made friends with a Major Adye who invited him to dinner and sent a corporal to conduct him through the batteries. Later Adye, who had been a pupil of Coleridge's brother George, took a long walk with him which included another, even more delightful visit to the "cavern."

Gibraltar could not drive away Asra. He wanted the language of music he noted, to express the sad music in his heart—"like a faint pain, a spot which it seems I could lay my finger on." Whatever he was doing, he wrote, whether talking "loud or eager," reading, "meditating the abstrusest researches," or "laughing and telling tales of mirth," ever before him by day and in dreams by night, was the image of Asra. "Darling," he wrote in his notebook on his last day at the Rock, "my heart wishes and yearns, and stirs and bustles wishing." Yet how much of his love for her was in reality self-love emerges from his thoughts a few days later, when he similarly expressed "my utter want of sympathy with all ordinary love-poems, complaining of the cruelty of my mistress, of her attachment to another and—in short all that supposes that I could love with no knowledge of being loved in turn—or even with the knowledge of the contrary."

At half-past ten on Wednesday morning April 25, the Speedwell set out on the last lap of her voyage to Malta. For Coleridge this final stage of the journey was particularly unpleasant. "A miserable voyage indeed," with the exception of the last four or five days, he later described it—"for two days I was so ill that I expected to die." "A tedious series of calms and light winds and storms," drove them out of their course, and seasickness and indigestion aggravated, if not indeed caused by opium, played the devil with him. Storm and sickness brought him to his "bed" on May 5, and when the next day the mainyard of the ship was blown away, he lay calmly analysing the probable experience of being drowned in a cabin while seasick, and finally decided that he "could scarcely imagine a less desirable mode of death."

But even worse than sickness and drowning was the crisis of indigestion which followed the sickness and gripped him through "days of horror." Finally the surgeon on the "Maidstone"—which had replaced the "Leviathan"—had to be summoned with his instruments to relieve him of obstruction. Coleridge's characteristically and nauseatingly detailed accounts in his notebooks leave no doubt as to the agony he suffered. "A warning," he wrote at the end, no doubt a reference to the increasing doses of opium. In misery and self-abasement he cried: "have mercy on me, have mercy on me, Father & God!"

But when illness and thoughts of Asra did not distract him, he still regarded the world about him with unusually perceptive eyes. Seldom, surely, were the extrovert and introvert elements in a man so equally mingled. Nothing could be more mistaken than to picture Coleridge as an entirely introvert philosopher, a visionary, buried in abstract thought and self isolated from the world. To whatever in the outer world attracted or repelled him, he was ever most perceptive—though afterwards it might become the subject of a "metaphysical" analysis.

Thus it was when they now caught turtles and Coleridge transferred to his notebook exquisite verbal photographs of the scenes. But several days afterwards he cogitated: "the apparent *divisibility* of *Life* in the turtle—"*metaphysically,* what does it import?" A hundred aspects of the voyage that drew his attention produced in him similar reactions: the hawk that rested on the bowsprit and was shot at by sailors—"Poor hawk! O strange lust of murder in man!" Even the repulsive details of his chronic stasis did not prevent shortly afterwards a detailed analysis of sublimity, or speculation upon the melancholy influence of a waning moon, or upon the superstitious temper of sailors. It is not surprising that when "The Ancient Mariner" was republished in 1817 it contained additional touches influenced by this voyage.

Sometimes in lighter, more hopeful mood, Coleridge planned new literary works, plays with scenes based on Gibraltar and Malta, a *Spectator,* produced by himself, Southey, Wordsworth, Lamb, and a few others, unnamed. He even wrote a few jovially doggerel verses on the Captain; and at times, when able, he returned to his study of Italian. But deeper than all other moods was his bitter sense of failure, of frustration as a creative artist, the failure to prove to the world the possession of that "genius" of which he had been so sure.

The early stage of life with its hopes and expectations, he contrasted with age and its disappointments: "When young, come dancing in on the stage, and O then we sing so pretty—The World for a Lass: which we exchange in age for that doleful ditty, Alas for the World!" He would make a song of it, entitle it "Transpositions! Wonders of Transpositions." An additional element in his melancholy was the thought of Sara with William, Mary, and Dorothy in Dove Cottage, and his jealousy returned: "jealousies the chills of fever."

In the Speedwell itself he found imagery for the expression of his thoughts and feelings. On May Day when the ship, frustrated by contrary winds, was back where it had been some days before, Coleridge asked himself: "Alas! alas! what have I been doing on the great voyage of Life since my return from Germany, but fretting upon the front of the wind? Well for me if I have indeed kept my ground even!" Nine days later he again questioned himself: "Whither have my animal spirits departed? My hopes—O me! that they which once I had to check should now be an effort—Royals and Studding sails and the whole canvas stretched to catch the feeble breeze!" Conscious of his vast mass of material—thoughts, images, ideas—he pondered: "scarcely a day passes but something new in fact or in illustration rises up in me, like herbs and flowers in a garden in early spring; but the combining power, the power to do, the manly effective *will*, that is dead or slumbers most diseasedly." And he went on to consider poetry as a dream.

Thus time passed, until on May 18, 1804, about four o'clock in the afternoon, the Speedwell entered Valetta harbour and shortly afterwards Coleridge, now "in more than usual health," stepped ashore and proceeded to Stoddart's villa.

Coleridge had of course adopted Stoddart (who he said had invited him to Malta) as his guiding star there. Perhaps "the very kind invitation" he relied upon was the kind of invitation he had first extracted from the Beaumonts; for when Coleridge landed at Valetta and made straight for Dr. Stoddart's the welcome he experienced fell far below his expectations. When he arrived there only Stoddart's unmarried sister, Sara, was at home. Mary Lamb, Miss Stoddart's friend, had begged her and Mrs. Stoddart, "to be kind affectionate nurses" to Coleridge on his arrival—"to behave to him as you would to me or Charles, if we came sick and unhappy to you." But in the event, as Coleridge privately recorded, Sarah Stoddart, "not knowing it to be me, did not come down." And when she came down an hour later refused to "let the servant after two hours and a half, go to the next street to inform Stoddart of my arrival. 'No! there was no occasion!!' About nine o'clock Doctor Stoddart came in and received me with an explosion of welcome—that *as it should be*. An explosion of surprise and welcome, more *fun* and *affection* in his manner, but just as I wished it," Samuel told Mrs. Coleridge.*

---

*A minor official has asserted that when Coleridge arrived at the house, Stoddart was at a ball at the Governor's, when he was told that a gentleman from England wished to see him. 'My God!' said Stoddart, 'what has brought you here?' 'To see you.' 'Well, as you *are* here, one must be glad to see you. Come and have some supper.' Perhaps Coleridge was unduly sensitive, for Mary Lamb, on receiving Miss Stoddart's account of his arrival, replied: "your kind reception of the forlorn wanderer gave me the greatest pleasure." Cf. C.W. Dicke, *Papers of a Critic*, p. 17n.

Such a welcome, however, did not prevent Coleridge's remaining as the Stod-darts' "guest" for the next seven weeks, until a new and more magnificent asylum opened its doors to him.

Fortunately Coleridge found Mrs. Stoddart pleasanter than her husband: "I was much pleased with Mrs. Stoddart's manners and countenance." The next morning Coleridge, feeling "light as a blessed ghost brought my things from the boat." After dinner he walked with Dr. and Mrs. Stoddart about the town, which Coleridge noted in great detail and found "very wonderful," with its "massy endless walls and defiles." He romanticized grimly: "You can walk nowhere having whispers of suicide, toys of desperation, explosive cries of the Maltese vendors—shot up, broad and bulky noises, sudden and violent." He noted the people, "very dark, some almost black, but straight, clean limbed, lively, active—cannot speak in praise of their cleanliness." The Maltese women with their hoods he found "picturesque enough, but shockingly in-sipid—*all* and always." To Mrs. Coleridge he sent a similar account.

If Stoddart feared Coleridge's genius for crises he was soon justified; for a day or two later after dining out, Coleridge crawled to the house in a fever fit, and unseen, went to bed. There Stoddart found him and at his request gave him thirty drops of laudanum in warm lemonade, which soon cured him. "These accidents I think nothing of," he told his wife. Shortly afterwards came another crisis, when the Stoddarts' baby, born a week after Coleridge's arrival, died on June 5. On the night of her birth, Coleridge had a vision of his own lit-tle daughter Sara which "brought on a sort of hysterical fit" in which he was haunted by fears of her death. He dared not read letters from England if they came, yet also longed for them—"so terribly has Fear got the upper hand in my habitual feelings from my long destitution of Hope and Joy." And he wept and prayed for his children: "With tears and clasped hands I bless you." Thus he wrote to his wife, telling her also that he was "haunted by the thought that I have lost a box of books." "Again and again God bless you, my dear Sara!" he ended "Let me know everything of your health, &c., &c."

Coleridge had of course lost no time in making contact with the Governor* Sir Alexander Ball, and the Commander General Villettes, one of Nelson's Captains. On his first Sunday in Malta he had called on Ball and presented Sotheby's introductory letter shortly after attending church. "A very polite man" he found Ball, "but no hopes of any situation there." At the same time he also presented his letter to General Villettes—and noted the splendor of the Palace room. The next day Ball returned the call and introduced a Mr. Laing, chaplain to the governor and tutor to his son. Ball invited Coleridge to dine

---

*The Concise Dictionary of National Biography describes Ball as "commissioner of navy at Gibraltar; made baronet and Governor of Malta; rear admiral 1805." Campbell calls him "Civil Commissioner" p. 145. Chambers, High Commissioner, p. 180. The Concise D.N.B. calls General Villettes, Governor of Malta, 1801-7. From this variety I adhere, for convenience to Coleridge's word "Governor" for Ball, and likewise regard Villettes as Commander of the Forces in Malta. Coleridge miscalls him Valette and I quote the correct name—Villettes.

with him on the Thursday and offered him a horse to ride with Laing on the Tuesday to his country house, to St. Antonio. Thus social relations were established with the governor and also with the commander, quickly fostered with all Coleridge's now practised skill. But Malta itself, an island "about 20 miles by 12—a mere rock of freestone," greatly disappointed him: "a drearier place eye never saw—the dreariest of all dreary islands—nothing green meets your eye." But the climate was "delightful for 8 months of the year." The warmth suited Coleridge, and he believed himself the only Englishman on the island not troubled by the heat.

Three weeks after Coleridge's arrival the Stoddarts went on a holiday to Saint Julian's leaving Coleridge, as he said, alone in their "huge house." The change did not depress Coleridge who now happily declared, "I breakfast, dine and take coffee at the Governor's." Coleridge's talent for attracting favors was as active in Malta as in England, and soon he was settled in "A suite of delightfully cool and commanding rooms" in the Governor's Palace, "which Sir Alex was so kind as not merely to offer me, but to make me feel that he wished me to accept them." Stoddart had *"behaved well enough* said Coleridge, but he "would be much happier at the Palace."

Meanwhile the governor was thinking that Coleridge might be useful to him, while Coleridge was still thinking the same thought about the Governor, and was already, so he said, "writing for him to the last moment." Ball's chaplain-tutor and private secretary, Laing, was going with the governor's son to England. The under secretary was abroad. The public secretary (who died the next January) was very old and already useless. Although Coleridge's new rooms with a marvellous view of the harbour and sea—"a glorious sight"—delighted him, he soon complained of being "kept hard at work at the Palace" and considered himself "already as a sort of diplomatic understrapper." But he lost no time in entitling himself "private secretary" to the governor. His accounts of arduous duties were probably no more justified than his similar complaints about his publishers and the *Morning Post*; but his salary of £25 a month disappointed him—particularly no doubt, when he remembered Stoddart's £1,500 a year.

Probably De Quincey's assertion that Coleridge did not make a good secretary is true enough so far as the dull routine of such was concerned. But once installed semiofficially as an official mouthpiece of Malta, he characteristically decided to boost the island's importance (including his own) to a British Government that had not sufficiently realized the fact. To this end he produced a number of reports upon the place and persuaded Ball to send them to the Ministry in London. He also sent them to Stuart for publication in the *Courier,* "only," he warned, "not in the same words"—an action which Sir E.K. Chambers, who certainly would have known, described as "rather shocking to the official mind."

Coleridge told Sotheby that his letters of introduction "produced every effect that letters possibly could do," and although the acquaintance with General Villettes never advanced beyond his being "very attentive and polite, that with Ball proceeded to Samuel's great satisfaction. From the first Coleridge found him not only "markedly attentive," but even "friendly and confidential." A month later, when living in the palace, Coleridge praised him as "a very extraordinary man—indeed a great man; really the abstract idea of a wise and good Governor". Here for Samuel was almost a repetition of his comfortable life with the Beaumonts: but in a climate that suited him much better. "Sir Alexander Ball," he told Stuart, "is indeed in every respect as kind and attentive to me as possible, so that on the whole I am perfectly satisfied with the wisdom of the plan of coming to Malta."

In June when the hot weather came, Coleridge contemplated a visit to Sicily as "cooler and less dreary than Malta." As July opened his plan extended beyond Sicily to Naples, but he still intended to return to Malta. Perhaps he hoped by the change to escape the image of Asra which particularly haunted him this July, as his notebook showed. "My whole body and heart panting and shivering like an ague fit of Love," he wrote. Breakfasting with Ball and others on July 4, he saw a guest who so resembled Asra that he nearly fainted. It also made him feel that if the beloved died he could transfer his love to one "strikingly like, as truly one soul in two resembling bodies."

That evening in poetic mood, his longing found expression in a prose passage that was now his nearest approach to poetry; "The sun had set, a short half hour of tender, balmy darkness—and the moon rose, round and large, and scarcely confessed its waning.

> Stay Love! when the sun had set, I said. Under the tender darkness we sat, under the tree. The nightingale sings. The evening star is so large and beautiful, and the moon will soon rise.—O Evening—when Loneliness is Dreariness.—O Love—inspirer. Love—demander, the lonely Heart aches—even when it loves not, because it loves not—but Hope makes Dream. But him who loves and is not beloved.—But O to him who loves and is beloved, and never must attain.

A week later having been given a room at the Governor's country mansion St. Antonio, Coleridge moved there to escape the heat of the town. But there too was Asra—even while he was admiring a lizard in the garden—"O Sara! Yes, I could be happy here with *you*! Let me write to her to-day. . . ." And he turned again to the lizard. He thought once of writing a poem inspired by his eternal self-question of her: "Why are you not here? O no! O no! I dare not wish you here."

His external world stood in strange contrast to his inner misery. "As comfortable here as a man can be: and as happy as *I* can be, absent from England, and from all that makes England so dear to me," he told the Beaumonts on August 1. Three days later he described his good fortune to Southey in similar terms, concluding in a burst of enthusiasm: "and if living in lofty and splendid rooms be a pleasure. I have it."

Immediately afterwards he crossed to Syracuse, intending to tour Sicily at least. Free and with a new country before him, he was as active as always in such circumstances when in good health. Twice he climbed Etna he said, delighting in the spreading views as he climbed to the monastery where he passed the night before proceeding: "a wearisome road indeed, but I took it leisurely, and came into the monastery cool," though the ground had scorched his feet, he said. He had a primitive theological discussion with his guide, which finished with the guide crying: "Oh those damned priests! What liars they are. But we can't go to Heaven without them."

In Sicily as elsewhere, Coleridge's anti-Catholicism was an ever present influence; but later with wider experience, he much preferred what he believed to be Italian Catholicism to what he believed to be the Catholicism of Spain—a country he did not know. Italian Catholicism, he wrote long afterwards, is "pure Paganism, undisturbed by any anxiety about orthodoxy or animosity against heretics. Much more good-natured and pleasing to a traveller's feelings, and certainly not a whit less like the true religion of our dear Lord, than the gloomy idolatry of the Spaniards."

At Syracuse Coleridge met the British Consul Mr. Leckie, who must have sent a favorable account of him to Ball. On August 24, Ball replied that he thought the description "admirable" and added Coleridge's "Company will be a delightful feast to your mind." Ball also wanted Coleridge to make a financial survey of Sicily, and to help in the attempt to save the island from the French by persuading the King of Sicily to hand it over to Britain and receive in compensation, from Britain, an annual pension equal to the revenues he now enjoyed.

The only official affair in which Coleridge was implicated came just before his return to Malta and was described by him in letters to Ball. It began for Coleridge when a British merchant ship captured by French privateers—"ill-conditioned Ruffians," wrote Samuel—was brought into the harbor of Syracuse. Coleridge tried to discover how far the capture was legal, but failed. He then heard the ship had been ransomed. Later, when fighting had broken out between English and French sailors, the Governor of Sicily summoned Leckie and Coleridge accompanied him. When they stepped out of the carriage they saw by torchlight some 300 soldiers drawn up to prevent more trouble between the French and English. Leckie now argued with the Governor against the legality of the capture, while the French Commander threatened reprisals on the Governor if he handed them over to the British. Amid much confusion and debate as to illegality, Coleridge, according to his own account to Ball, threw in his weight and transcribed important documents. He had intended leaving for Messina, but not left instead for Malta to bring the Governor the latest news. Thus it was that about an hour before midnight on November 6, Coleridge left Syracuse and sailed for Valetta to inform Ball that the privateer had been released.

The two letters to Ball and a short business note to Stuart are all the correspondence written by Coleridge in Sicily that we have. Fortunately his notebook rather generously illuminates his life on the island. Little escaped his eye—the peasants, even the movements of the lizards and the frogs. Despite

his belief that "childish minds alone, can attach themselves to (so called) antiquities," he delightedly explored Timoleon's villa and the ruins of the great
fifth century fortress build by Dionysius the Elder at Euryalus, and rejoiced
there at "a glorious view indeed."

He became a regular attender at the opera, and one midnight only "the
voice of Conscience" prevented his visiting the Prima Donna of the Company,
Cecilia Bertozzi. He found pleasure in hearing the ragged boys and girls in the
street beautifully singing the songs from the operas that they had heard when
listening outside the theatre.

Unfortunately, he was also in the midst of fields of opium poppies; noticed
in detail the sowing of the seeds and collected some for himself. Immediately
after noting this, another entry like an earlier one made after taking opium,
describes his sensations as he lies in bed at six o'clock in the afternoon, watching the changing streaks in his bed curtains. During this period of Coleridge's life in Malta, the opium habit, as his daughter and De Quincey
later asserted, took a firmer hold upon him.

Coleridge's final opinion of the population of Syracuse immediately before
his departure, was less than complimentary—"12,000 inhabitants, of whom at
least 10,000 had better be out of existence. . . . I found no one native with
whom I could talk of anything but the weather and the opera; ignorant beyond
belief. The churches take up the third part of the whole city, and the priests are
numerous as an Egyptian Plague."

Coleridge's activities and observations in his outer world did not affect his
habitual inner life—thoughts of Asra and self-analysis. He jotted down some
tentative lines for "The Soother in Absence," and again noted "the aromatic
smell of the poplars," which always reminded him of his first meeting with
Asra at Sockburn.

As for himself, Coleridge apparently learned new manners from conversations with others at this time, presumably including Mr. Leckie—perhaps the
only person in Sicily to whom he could talk. "In company, indeed with all except a very chosen few, never dissent from anyone as to the *merits* of
another," he warned himself, "but content yourself by praising in your turn
the really good. . . .Coleridge! Coleridge! Will you never learn to appropriate
your conversation to your company? Is it not desecration, indelicacy, a proof
of great weakness and even vanity to talk &c, &c. ., as if you talked with
Wordsworth and Sir George Beaumont."

Similarly, from his consciousness of superiority, he warned himself against
arguing with others:

O young man, who hast seen, felt and known the Truth, to whom reality is a
phantom, and virtue and mind the sole actual and permanent Being, do not
degrade the Truth in thee by disputing—avoid it!   Until the Voice from
within tells him to speak out, he will remain silent, attempt no conversion of
others to the Truth. Till then, I am right willing to bear the character of a
mystic, a visionary, a self-important Juggler who nods his head and says, *I
could, if I would*; but I cannot, I *may* not hear the reproach of profaning

the Truth, which is *my Life*. . . . I might lose my Tranquillity, and in acquiring the *passion* of proselytism lose the *sense* of conviction. I might become *positive*! Now I am *certain*! I might have the Heat of Fermentation; now I have the warmth of Life.

He was also conscious that his virtues might be in alloy with some faults: "Do not be too much discouraged if any virtue should be mixed in your consciousness with affectation and imperfect sincerity, and some vanity. *Disapprove* of this—and continue the practice, and the good feeling even thus mixed. *It will gradually purify itself.* . . ." Such were Coleridge's cogitations on Sunday evening, October 14, 1804, in Syracuse.

A week later on his real birthday his mood was the usual one on those occasions, of gloomy soul-searching and shame for another unfruitful year with its broken vows. Why, he asked himself, had he "shunned and fled like a cowed dog" from the thought of his birthday and the realization that he was now thirty-two years old? "So help me Heaven! as I looked back and till I looked back, I had imagined I was only *31*—so completely has a whole year passed with scarcely the fruits of a *month*. O sorrow & shame! I am not worthy to live. Two and thirty years—and this last year above all others! I have done nothing!" It was in this mood of despondency that on the night of November 6 Coleridge returned to Malta.

On December 12, 1804, Coleridge sent his wife a letter in which the intention to impress her with a realization of his official importance is evident. Misleadingly pretending to have been "abruptly recalled" from Sicily, he explained in some detail why he had been "strenuous in awakening our Government" to the danger of allowing Sicily to fall into the hands of France. "I am constantly and even laboriously employed," he wrote, "and the confidence placed in me by Sir A. Ball is unlimited." He went on to speak of himself as to be leader in a corn commission to the Black Sea, whereas he was to be only a "substitute" for the leader if the leader, a Captain Leake, were called away. "If I could get off with honour, I would," he added, and in fact he didn't go. This final verdict on Sicily he now sent to his wife: "all is exaggerated grossly, except the abominableness of the Government, and the vice and abject wretchedness of the People."

He was disappointed too on his return to Malta to find that his fine room at the palace had been given to another official, and himself moved to a "garret at the Treasury," which boasted only a painted ceiling of Zephyrs: "Lord!—curly-pated heads spewing white smoke" and with four windows, "commanding a most magnificent view of open sea and lake-like harbours." He would only remain there he told Mrs. Coleridge, "till a suite of rooms can be fitted up for me at the Palace." But he seems to have remained in his "garret" to the end. On Christmas Day sitting there he described it again, somewhat sarcastically as his "sky-chamber," with only "six square yards" of available space, "with the four winds on the ceiling and the blast from each mouth of the curly-wigged Nobodies." Nor was Coleridge's financial position since his return to Malta better than before. "What I am to receive, I scarcely know," he told his wife. He had had only £50, and had been obliged to draw upon Stuart for another £50—which, of course, he "hoped to replace." For although "I dine at the Palace as confidential Secretary to the Government every day," he needed money for a few necessities "and the expense of my servant." Out of the £100 he had spent, he had repaid Stuart a debt of £25, and expected immediately to receive £100 as four months salary. Evidently Mrs. Coleridge needed such information as she probably had little or no money. So Coleridge promised to send her "£50 to pay my Life-assurance, and your Mother."

To such a nature as Coleridge's state officialism, although momentarily attractive to his vanity and self-importance, could not long appeal. His private comments in his notebooks after his return from Sicily, soon reveal a growing dislike of much about him. The mere expediency openly proclaimed that he found in political life shocked him. "No moral feeling" he noted. "The Cabinet would laugh aloud at such an idea. We are none of us in these things actuated by any notion of right or justice, and we know it!" Relegation to the "sky-chamber" had surely rankled, and the complaisance with which he now regarded his role in high matters of State made him sensitive to real or imagined slights, or to imagined subtle plans to make use of him. His sufferings took the form of impersonal statements in his record, as when he writes: "To enter a room, be loudly familiar with the Master and haughtily distant to a Stranger—a certain mark of a low mind." On the day after Coleridge's relegation to the "garret" he noted: "One of the heart-depraving habits and temptations of men in power, as Governors, &c. &c. is to make *instruments* of their fellow creatures. And the moment they find a man of honour and talents, instead of loving and esteeming him, they wish to *use him*—hence that self-betraying, side and down look of cunning &c.—and they justify and inveterate the habit by believing that every individual who approaches has selfish designs upon them." He also noted his dislike of "English Hauteur—want of smiles—all seem to wither in the aspect of their Pride/Scorn, and true alienation-alienum."

Lady Ball too annoyed him by defending Catholicism as better than no religion—which drew Samuel's private comment, "as poison to no sugar." Had our noble ancestors thought thus" he pondered, "we should now be slaves"—like the Sicilians. When one day as Coleridge was anxiously expecting letters, Lady Ball asked him "if I was not excessively impatient—I surprised her by saying—Not at all." But fearing "that in telling the truth I was conveying falsehood," he later "endeavoured to explain with propriety," that he was not impatient because he was anxious; "had much fear and little hope." Which it is to be also hoped Lady Ball understood.

By this time the novelty of his official position had quite worn off, and he was as weary of his duties as he had been at the *Morning Post*. Only "a fit of despair when life was a burthen" had made him agree to join the corn commission which he had later renounced.

England, being absent, became imaginatively alluring. "O God! O God!" he cried to his wife, "if that, Sara, which we both know too well, were not unalterably my lot, how gladly would I prefer the mere necessaries of life in England, to those obtained by daily effort." But his first duty he told her, was to make her as happy as he could, "compatible with the existence of that health and tranquillity (Joyless indeed both) on which the very power of doing anything for you must depend." And he agonized over the children "O my children! my children"—and blessed them all as usual. He concluded his letter to his wife: "I remain faithful to you and to my own honour in all things; and am most anxiously and affectionately, Your Friend and more than Friend, S.T. Coleridge."

As the year 1804 neared its end, Samuel's mood became increasingly despondent: his recourse to his favourite stimulants more evident at times. Doubtless his isolation in the "sky-chamber" intensified the temptation, not only by solitude, but also through the disappointment he had felt at his ejection from his former more impressive rooms, so pleasing to his vanity. On December 22 he made in a very large shaky hand, a private incoherent note, ending: "written in *involuntary* intoxication. God bless all!" The next day he recorded that he did not understand the note, which, he said, was written after colic pains cured by three glasses of whisky and water, "taken in despair." Self-abasement followed, including that for a "stupid drunken letter to Southey" written in the sprawling characters of drunkenness." If he should die before destroying his notebooks—"the history of my own mind for my own improvement—O friend! Truth! Truth! but yet Charity! Charity!" After this, save for one mild entry of self-examination, his notes remained entirely and abstractly metaphysical to the close of the year.

In this mood, Coleridge's thoughts again turned towards England. Indeed he told his wife in mid-December, if it were not for his dislike of living with her, he would come back to England at once. So instead, he commended her and the children to God.

On January 18, 1805 old Mr. Macaulay, the public secretary, died—"like a sleeping baby—during a tremendous storm of thunder and lightning." Coleridge was immediately appointed Acting Public Secretary in his stead, until Mr. Chapman the under-secretary who was to succeed Macaulay, returned from abroad. Coleridge, now given half the official salary of the post, thus received £50 monthly instead of the £25 he had so far received. To friends he complained that he had been promised the whole salary—which was most improbable. Sometimes he declared that he was being given less than half—which was incorrect. One of Coleridge's biographers, Campbell, found it "vastly amusing" to think of Coleridge with his political ideas acting as the public servant of the detested Castlereagh.

Immediately, despite his appreciation of his new dignified title which he sent to all his friends, and despite the pleasure Ball's friendship gave him, he again complained of the work entailed—of overwork and of absence from England. He would leave for England in March certainly, he told the Wordsworths the day after his appointment. A few days later he moaned to Southey that he was "employed from morn to eve in writing public letters, some as long as memorials."

His early resolution upon arrival in Malta to prevent brooding over his private miseries by filling his time with active interests and seeking company, had by this time, as his notebooks conspicuously showed, failed. The domestic problem, Sara Hutchinson, and the surrender to opium, ever increasing now, were chief agents in his mental unrest. Surely his unhappy inner life must have been in some degree visible, as well as the physical effects of the drug, to his friends.

In a long gloomy private note he made on January 11, 1805, he recalled how throughout his whole life from his earliest days, he had "always been preyed upon by some dread," and realized that his early love for Mary Evans, like that now for Sara, was "uncombinable with Hope." "It is most unfortunate that I so fearfully despondent should have concentrated my soul thus on one almost as feeble in hope as myself." Then came news that Jackson, now in financial difficulties, was selling Greta Hall, and that the Coleridges and Southeys were looking for a new home. Coleridge was much upset, fell ill and wanted to return to England, until he heard that the sale was revoked and life there would continue as before. As to what he would do or where he would go on returning to England, he had, as he said, "no idea."

His nervous dread was intensified by the uncertainty of his correspondence with his friends in England and of theirs with him. Some of his letters were burnt at Malta because of the plague which killed Major Adye who brought them. Others were thrown overboard from ships that were in danger of capture by the French. Doubtless these dangers were also used at times by Coleridge as an excuse when in fact he had not written. Dominated by this nervous dread he would as in the past, keep letters for hours, or even days, fearing to open them and learn some bad news; perhaps that one of the children or even his wife had died. "For so help me God!" he told Southey, "most ill-starred as our marriage has been, there is perhaps nothing that would so frightfully affect me as any change affecting her health or life." For the children, she was most necessary. He was, he told Southey, "ashamed to own to what a diseased excess my sensibility has worsened into."

In opposite moods of self-importance,* he proudly informed Mrs. Cole-

---

*In October 1834, Charles W. Dilke, Editor of the Athenaeum sent a messenger to Paris on behalf of the Magazine, to discuss a proposed Life of Coleridge in Malta. The Agent reported in part as follows: "Underwood and Mackenzie** say that there was more humbug in Coleridge than in any man that was ever heard of. Underwood was one day transcribing something for Coleridge when a visitor appeared. After the commonplaces, Coleridge took up a little book lying upon the table and said, 'By the bye, I casually took up this book this morning, and was quite enchanted with a little sonnet I found there.' He then read off a blank verse translation, and entered into a long

ridge and others of his full, majestic title—with the qualification "Acting" dropped—"Segretario Publico dell' Isole di Malta, Gozo, e delle loro dipendenze." Fifty times a day he had to sign his name with this title, he complained. For such work he quickly decided his half-salary was inadequate. Despite his free meals at the Palace with the Governor and his free quarters in his despised "sky-chamber," he told Southey "my profits will be much less than if I had employed my time and efforts in my own literary pursuits." Nevertheless he hoped to be able to pay all his debts, particularly that to Wordsworth, on his return. "I have scraped up by hard and slavish labour," he told Stuart on May 1, "about a hundred and fifty pounds, Maltese Currency, or a hundred and thirty English; but would to Heaven! I had never accepted my office as Public Secretary, or the former of Private Secretary. Even in a pecuniary point of view I might have gained twice as much, and improved my reputation. But regrets are idle!"

In this mood he told Southey in February "when I see *this* Booby with his ten pound a day as Mr. Commissary X, and *that* thorough-Rogue two doors off him, with his £15 a day, as Mr General Pay Master YZ, it stirs up a little bile from the liver, and gives my poor stomach a pinch, and when I hear you talk of having to look forward for an 100 or £150. But cheerily! what do we complain of? Would *we* be either of those men?"

Nevertheless he told Stuart in May, "Sir A.B. behaves to me with really personal fondness, and with almost fatherly attention. I am one of his Family, whenever my health permits me to leave my own house." That last qualification, like his remark that he spends nine days out of ten at the country house, Saint Antonio, suggests doubts as to his accuracy in many complaints of unending daily duties. He had "no head for politics" he told Southey, or he would explain to him how he had been working on memorials concerning Egypt, Sicily, and the Coast of Africa. He had also made a speech for some mysterious reason "in wig and gown" in the Admiralty Court. Many years later he told a Jewish friend that in Malta he had personally prevented an anti-Jewish pogrom. "A true Jack of all Trades" he described himself. In mid-March he despaired: "Mr. Chapman not yet arrived! and I am to stay another two months at least! O God, guide me aright!"

On April 1 Lady Ball, who was entertaining guests, heard of the wreck of Captain John Wordsworth's ship off Portland, with the loss of 300 men including the Captain. Remembering Coleridge had mentioned a friend Wordsworth, she sent for him and when he entered the drawing-room asked him if he knew Captain Wordsworth. "A little" he replied and was told of his death. Coleridge, overcome, left the room followed by Ball, "upon business," while

---

critique upon its merits. The same story, the same translation, and the same critique were repeated five times in that day to different visitors, without one word being altered. Mr. Underwood says that every one of his evening conversations was got up." Dilke, *Papers of a Critic*, 2 vols. (London 1875) 1:32-33

**Underwood and Mackenzie were Government Clerks in Malta.

another person invited him to dinner: "I was nearly strangled,—and at last just got out: I have just heard of the death of a dear friend, Sir! excuse me—and got home led by the Sergeant and followed to the door by Sir Alexander Ball." Such was Coleridge's account, written on the same day in his notebook.

Coleridge at any rate had no emotional reserve—at least in his written accounts of the news of John's death. To Mrs. Coleridge on July 21 when his imagination had been at work for nearly four months, he sent a far more dramatic version than the obviously more accurate one made at the time in his notebook. "On being told abruptly by Lady Ball of John Wordsworth's fate," he wrote, "I attempted to stagger out of the room, (the great saloon of the Palace with fifty people present), and before I could reach the door, fell down on the ground in a convulsive, hysteric fit. I was confined to my room for a fortnight after." His notebook disproves any confinement to his room at all. Describing the same event to Stuart on April 30, he had merely said he "heard abruptly, and in the very painfullest way possible in a public company."

Throughout April, although his actual references to John Wordsworth in his notebook are very rare, Coleridge was in very low spirits thinking of the unhappiness of the circle at Dove Cottage, including "deep-hearted and wide-hearted Dorothy, my Sister! my Sister! so like to myself in the forms of our hearts—Indeed, I am very, very, hopeless and heartless." On the same day, April 7, he pondered: "I am very mournful. Lord Nelson is pursuing the French Fleet and the Convoy is to be deferred. I feel glad—how can I endure that it should depart without me? Yet, if I go, whither am I to go? Merciful Providence! what a cloud is spread before me—a cloud is my only guide by day, and by night I have no pillar of Fire, nothing definite to alternate with the indefinite. . . ."

Letters lost, letters not arriving, work and delay in returning to England, brought him to his bed. No doubt opium was also involved. He determined to leave at the end of May, 1805 "even at the forfeiture of Sir A. Ball's goodwill."

Rickman heard years later that Coleridge and Ball "parted on the worst terms, on a mutual notorious hatred of each other." But of this there is little confirmation. Ball died in 1809. In 1810 Coleridge began his elaborate account of Ball as affectionately as ever, for *The Friend*. But the essay was never finished, as *The Friend* suddenly expired. Coleridge's posthumous eulogy of Ball does not necessarily confute Rickman. Certainly Coleridge's account to George of his detention by Ball in Malta was far from amiable. "Sir A. Ball" he wrote, "*intreated* me not to leave him until his absent Secretary returned. I could not say *no*! I did not *say, yes*! but I sullenly complied with him, and from that month lost all the little Spirits and Activity of mind which I had hitherto retained. . . ."

In late August Coleridge was still vainly longing to escape. "I have been flattering myself every week for the last six months" he told his wife, "that I should have permission and opportunity to go, but Sir Alexander has still contrived, in one way or another, to prevent it. Now however he has given me his solemn promise that as soon as I have written six public letters, and examined into the law-forms of the Island (which cannot take me more than a week altogether) he will forward me immediately to Naples, to send me home with despatches—which of course, would *frank me home*." As he was not sure of this he added he must retain £120 for possible expenses. "But, whatever money I am obliged to spend in travelling overland, will be amply repaid to me by the booksellers. It has injured by health very considerably, this continued disappointment."

There was the usual muddle with Coleridge's finances. As before, he had underestimated his debts to Stuart which were £61.11.5. and not £34 as Coleridge had imagined. He thereupon abandoned his intention to request another £50 from Stuart for himself and substituted one for £50 for Mrs. Coleridge, explaining that illness prevented his sending her £90 he had in hand. For as Coleridge told Stuart, he was "exceedingly anxious not to appear to make free with you in pecuniary matters."

At four o'clock in the morning of July 3, Coleridge noted "two shocks of an earthquake, very strong for Malta, shook my bed like a strong arm." To Mrs. Coleridge he reported it seven weeks later, as "a smart earthquake, which shook my bed and me in it as with a Giant's arm, but did no mischief. Ships sixty leagues distant from land felt it: and it appeared as if they had suddenly struck on a rough shore and were *raking* the stones." Shortly afterwards he saw a lunar eclipse but at first did not understand what he saw. As the moon reappeared he thought: "What a picture this of a man commencing life with a character utterly tarnished and gradually scouring itself and revealing by little and little till it became a Shakespeare or—"!! [*sic*]

"At last," on September 6, 1805, Mr. Chapman arrived and Coleridge was free. Despite Ball's efforts to keep him, he at once began to prepare for departure.

Coleridge's underlying mood since his return from Sicily despite his external cheerfulness was sad; the thought of Sara became yet more obsessive, suggesting in some ways the sustained excitement of unconsummated passion: "Oh Sara! I am never happy, never deeply gladdened," had forgotten the joy which used to fill his heart "as of a deep and quiet fountain." In private verse, as well as in prose, his longing for Asra found expression:

O! Asra, Asra! couldst thou see
into the bottom of my heart,
There's such a mine of Love for thee,
As almost might supply desert!

Of many similar verses Sara Hutchinson was also the inspiration.

With the sense of loss there mingled that of increasing but helpless self-disgust as he yielded to the craving for opium and alcohol. In moods of humility he thought how, with Sara's companionship, he would "be so very much a better man." But he was "not worthy" of her nor good enough to preserve hope. He must "perish." So influenced he neither gambled nor "connected himself with women even by thought." But illness and fear for his life drove him he moaned, "to stimulants that cannot but finally destroy me." In other moods Sara became an abstract ideal, and he felt "the grandeur of loving the Supreme in her—the real and symbolical united." In this mood he "loved her all the more as being capable of being glorified by me, and as the means and instrument of my glorification." Thus exalted, he attempted the next day to express his sublime emotions in verse; but like all such attempts now in his notebooks, it petered out after nine and a half mediocre lines. At another time he saw himself and Sara as "two birds of passage" helping each other "to support the long flight, the awful journey"—presumably of life.

The thought of his increasing surrender to narcotics and alcohol often tortured him; and he now recalled the names of poets who had become "Sots!—awful Thought!—O it is horrid!—Die my Soul, die!—Suicide—rather than this, the worst state of Degradation!" His disgust with this surrender, often associated with thoughts of Sara, appears again and again at this time in his notebooks. Frustration and suppression are the evident causes of his many dreams by night and day. Nor are these all. His cogitations now included self-discussion on religious questions, the Trinity, the Redemption, the assumption of Humanity by the "Godhead"—all marking the change now beginning in Coleridge from his earlier Necessitarianism and Unitarianism to Trinitarianism. But to Science he was still antagonistic: "a true Philosopher is something very different from a mere man of Science."

Shortly before the Secretary's return to Malta on September 6, 1805, Coleridge told his wife: "Sir Alexander Ball's kindness and confidence in me is unlimited. He told a gentleman a few days ago, that were he a man of fortune, he would gladly give me £500 a year to dine with him twice a week for the mere advantage which he received from my conversation, and for a long time past he has been offering me different places to induce me to return. He would give me a handsome house, garden, country house, and a place of £600 a year certain. I thank him cordially—but neither accept or refuse." Coleridge had also been offered "a fine opening in America," but "Wordsworth's aversion to America" stood in my way."

At 2 A.M. on the morning of the day following Chapman's return, Coleridge made the following entry: "Yes, a shocking recollection, that *years* have passed to a man in the prime of manhood, on every night of which he has dreaded to go to bed or fall asleep, and by that dread seduced to again and again and again poison himself." It was in this mood that sixteen days later, Coleridge finally "quitted Malta" at noon for Sicily and Italy. The next morning, September 24, 1805, he reached Syracuse with the world before him.

18   "The Forlorn Wanderer"—In Sicily and Italy (1805-6)

"Why is he wandering on the sea?
Coleridge should now with Wordsworth be."
—Mary Lamb to Dorothy Wordsworth, May 7, 1805

At Syracuse, Coleridge as before stayed with the Leckies. While there a providential apparition of Asra prevented his yielding to the renewed fascination of the Siren of Syracuse, the opera singer Cecilia Bertozzi. After six days with the Leckies, Coleridge set off to tour Sicily.

The country presented him with one enchanting scene after another. Valverde not only enchanted him by its beauty, but also presented the pleasing spectacle of "two very beautiful young ladies in chintz trousers, astride on very handsome ponies." Next Taormina's prospects "surpass, perhaps, all I have ever seen," he recorded. On October 3, 1805, when he reached Messina, even Taormina was surpassed.

His tour was both solitary and often melancholy, and the occasional irregular writing in his notebook suggests some form of intoxication—opium or brandy or both. This year as usual he mistook October 20 for his birthday, and also as usual on that day, was in melancholy mood—even more so than in previous years: "My Birthday! O Thought of Agony! O Thought of Despair! Drive me not to utter Madness!" Thus he privately recorded his misery at the thought of being thirty-three and with little done to prove his genius to the world. In deep misery he took a solitary walk "assuredly amongst the very loveliest prospects I have seen." So charmed was he that he wrote on the same day his private account of the scenes through which he passed; but only to end with an echo of his earlier misery: "O even but three years ago, how I should have *hoped* and schemed amid all this, but now I *hope* no more. O this *is* a sore affliction to be so utterly estranged from Hope. O miserable on my birthday too!"

Some three years later in another private note, Coleridge explained the main reason for the unusually melancholy mood that had mastered him at this time in Malta and afterwards, as he turned homeward—uncertain—lonely—lost—feeling above all that he had now crossed the dividing line between early life and age: "the melancholy, dreadful feeling of finding myself to be *man*, by a distinct division from boyhood, youth and young man!

Dreadful was the feeling—till then life had flown so that I had always been a boy, as it were; and this sensation had blended in all my conduct, my willing acknowledgement of superiority, and, in truth, my meeting every person as a superior at the first moment. Yet if men survive this period, they commonly become cheerful again. That is a comfort for mankind, *not for me*! There too lies part of the secret of Coleridge's contemplation of suicide on several occasions while in Malta. Now too his thought turned with morbid affection to Wordsworth: "O that my spirit, purged by death of its weaknesses, which are alas! my *identity,* might flow into *thine,* and live and act in thee and be Thou."

Coleridge also planned a cross country tour southward from Messina to Syracuse. Whether he carried out his plan or when he left Sicily we do not know.

When he again emerges from the obscurity that encompasses too much of Coleridge's life at this time, it is November 20 and he is in Naples. There the British Minister Hugh Elliot, bitterly disappointed Coleridge's expectations. For Ball, Samuel had told his wife a month before his departure from Malta, "would use his best interest with Mr. Elliot our Ambassador at Naples, to send me home with despatches."

But in fact, Ball's polite, almost impersonal note of introduction to Elliot, made no reference to Coleridge's official position or assistance, but presented him as a traveler, a private person of "literary fame," a "great genius," whose conversation would give Elliot "pleasure." Coleridge, who had so recently made a private note on the meaningless politeness of much official correspondence, had probably learned by this time that such introductions or testimonials are sometimes more significant in their silences than in their speech. Dated "23 October" the note was sent a month after Coleridge's departure from Malta, and was probably inspired by some reminder from Coleridge in Italy.

In these circumstances Elliot was unjustly vituperated by Coleridge, evidently in ignorance, for not giving him despatches and "franking him home." No mere facts ever prevented Coleridge when annoyed, from vilifying the offender; so now Elliot he declared, had by "inducements, at length persuaded" him to go to Naples, and when there had received him with "villainous treatment." A year later Coleridge informed his brother George that the French invasion of Italy was "the natural and necessary consequence of the mad and profligate, if not traitorous plans" of the wicked Elliot. Elliot indeed had proved "to be—everything that Sir Alexander Ball was not, and nothing that he was." Samuel's dislike even spread to the "sour looks" of Elliot's nine-year-old daughter.

For some unknown reason or none, Coleridge left Naples on November 30 and journeyed overland southwards to a place on the Gulf of Taranto, returning to Naples by December 14. He was evidently in a disgruntled peevish mood, for the next day he made a private note in mediocre Latin verse, protesting against some real or imagined "tyranny" over him by Wordsworth—one of his now periodic revolts against his own prostration before his friend.

Shortly afterwards he penned another morally indignant entry: "To notice with indignation the fortnightly lotteries at Naples." His moral revulsion appears to have been stimulated not only by his bad luck at a lottery in youth, but also by a similar attempt while in Malta of which only mysterious mathematical calculations remain. Upon his return to Naples Coleridge first heard of the death of Nelson at Trafalgar on October 21.

On Christmas Day 1805 Coleridge left Naples and set out for Rome. The following day entering the vale of Fondi, he noted its beauties: "Trees in their richest autumnal hues—the Appenines round hill, rising into sugar-loaf points, beautiful orange orchards. . . ." Peace and beauty were all about him! On the last day of the year he was in Rome exploring the Chiesa della Trinità de' Monti.

Hearing on New Year's Day 1806 that the French were expected in Rome on January 5, Coleridge pondered: "To stay or not to stay." That he did stay is clear from the next entry in his notebook: "5 Jan. 1806—Santa Maria Maggiore—glorious. . . ." That entry and the fact that Coleridge did not finally quit Rome until May 18, the absence of any reference in his notebook to such hairbreadth, dramatic escapes as he later described: Napoleon's frantic attempts to capture him—the Pope's assistance in escaping (not then resented as Catholic), all indicate that these yarns belong to "Fancy, or Imagination" rather than to fact.

What Coleridge actually did, however, was to become the guest of a new close friend, Washington Allston, an American painter of "the sublime," who was fascinated by Coleridge's conversation. Allston's house was in the beautiful country at Olevano, where the primroses springing up round Coleridge on March 9, made him ask himself "Am I at Keswick?"

But before moving to Allston's place, Coleridge had as ever found almost miraculously, a saviour and protector in Rome. This was a young art student Thomas Russell, whose father, a banker and proprietor of a transport firm at Exeter, knew the Ottery family. Thomas, according to Farington's account in his Diary, after visiting Gibraltar, Malta and Naples, reached Rome in January and remained there until he left with Coleridge in May. His description of finding Coleridge in Rome "in a destitute condition, his money being expended" agrees with Coleridge's own statement to his brother George months later: "my finances were exhausted; and my letters of credit I had left at Naples." A brief entry of Coleridge's made that Spring speaks for itself: "Received from Mr. Russell on credit 4 Doppios and four sequins—" This sum which Coleridge received—of course as ever, "on credit"—was worth in all about four pounds.

Russell, Farington adds, "became his friend and protector and relieved him from his difficulties, which had reduced his mind to such a state, as to cause him to pass much of his time in bed in a kind of despairing (and doubtless drugged) state." There is nothing in this unlike the Coleridge of recent years and of the year that immediately followed his return to England.

At Olevano Allston, some twenty-six years of age and Coleridge, mutually fascinated and complimentary became close friends. Coleridge honoured

Allston by revealing to him Mrs. Coleridge's inadequacies as he did with all his familiar friends. Coleridge believed he learned much good art practice and criticism from Allston. Allston's landscape with classical figures, *Diana and her Nymphs in the Chase* —an imitation of a Claude—so delighted Coleridge that he made a long prose description of it in his notebook and even contemplated a poem about it. Allston, a romantic of his period, almost dreamed in later life that his walks and talks with Coleridge "under the pines of the Villa Borghese" had been in fact with "Plato in the groves of the Academy." These walks and talks with Allston must have provided Coleridge with a rare opportunity of instilling into him his own aesthetic theory of the artist as Divine Creator. Certainly the talks were useful to Allston: for the lectures he gave when back in America, are said to have been "full of echoes of Coleridge." Allston also now began a never finished portrait of Coleridge and later in England painted another, now in the National Gallery.

Despite his perfervid anti-Catholicism, or perhaps to increase it, Coleridge was back in Rome on May 4, attending a beatification ceremony at Saint Peters. He made a note of the fact without other comment in his private record. In Rome Coleridge also made the acquaintance of another painter, George Augustus Wallis, an Englishman whose ten-year old son Trajan, used to accompany Coleridge on his walks about Rome. Hazlitt in his essay *On Patronage and Puffing,* describes how Coleridge after his return to England, bored an incredulous party of which Hazlitt was a member, with "a laboured eulogy" of young Trajan Wallis.

At Rome Coleridge's thoughts now turned towards England. So on May 18 1806, two years to the day since he landed at Valetta, he left Rome accompanied and assisted with unfailing patience and generosity by Russell, who in doing so sacrificed a visit to Switzerland. In Florence on June 17, Coleridge described himself in a letter to Allston, as having been "dangerously ill for the last fortnight"—smitten he believed by "a manifest stroke of Palsy" with violent vomiting and screaming. Not for the first time he dreamed of suicide from which the thought of his children conveniently saved him. But more convenient was Russell. "Nothing," he told Allston "can surpass Mr. Russell's kindness and tender-heartedness to me." To Allston as so often before to others, Coleridge's love and gratitude overflowed: "had I not known the Wordsworths, I should have loved and esteemed you *first* and *most,* and as it is, next to them I love and honour you. . . ." But Florence for Coleridge was not to be love and kindness alone. There was a haughty professor—ironically named by the Fates, Benvenuti—who, bored by letters of introduction, received Coleridge with "almost insulting coldness." Nor when the erring professor paid him a courtesy call would Coleridge be mollified.

Five days later at Pisa Coleridge had another attack of hysteria similar to that in Florence. The immediate aftermath of emotions kindled by both experiences was four lines of verse:

Come, come, thou bleak December Wind,
And blow the dry Leaves from the Tree!
Flash, like a Love-thought, thro' me, Death,
And take a Life that wearies me.

Hysterical emotion indeed haunted him during this last journey through Italy to Leghorn. His record of his emotional outbursts at this time occupies the greater part of the few entries he then made in his notebook, the rest consisting of some eloquent passages describing scenery which particularly appealed to him and some trivial memoranda. Other references to opium and "sotting" in the notebook may suggest that Coleridge's association with artists in Rome had encouraged Bohemian relaxation and intensified his fits of hysteria.

Coleridge's hysterical emotional crises reveal in his present record of them the same psychological mechanism as that of similar outbursts in his later years—the same emotions, fears, remorse, and despair; the same thoughts and imagery—fears of a child's death—fears to open a letter—death wishes for himself by suicide—and during a storm at Pisa, by lightning. He was also conscious, as these notes show, of guilt and failure in real life, of the evils opium, brandy, and ether were creating for him. Deep in his emotional disturbance lay his passion for Sara. For her he now indulged in vain dreams of impossible sacrifice: "O Dear John Wordsworth! Ah that I could but have died for you and you have gone home, married S. Hutchinson, and protected my poor little ones. O how very, very gladly would I have accepted the conditions. But thou art gone, who mightest have been so happy, and I live—to be increasingly (. . . .), body and soul—*live*—to die minutely." In these notes Coleridge often reveals his consciousness of his moral weakness as frankly as he details his physical ills to his friends. In one entry Coleridge briefly but clearly indicated the various phases of these emotional crises:

1. Uncomfortab(le)
2. O(pium) + B(randy)
3. Increased N(ervous) E(nergy)
4. Positive body pain
5. Remorse + despondency.

The next day, June 23, Coleridge and Russell left Leghorn for England on an American ship captained by an American named Derkheim, whom Coleridge soon eulogized as an angel and an exemplar of all American virtues. Later—as so often with Coleridge's helpers—he anathematized Derkheim as an emissary of the devil.

When Coleridge embarked he was still in "very low spirits." Throughout the voyage, according to his accounts of it after reaching England, he must have remained so; for he suffered a repetition of his illness on the outward voyage. He lay prostrated by obstructed digestion with the captain and Russell, "seriously alarmed for my life," nursing him with almost incredible devotion and emotion. Indeed "had not the captain loved me, as he often said, better than a brother, and performed all the offices of a nurse, I could not have survived.''

Although Coleridge had begun his voyage to Malta with an intention to improve his Italian he seems to have had little opportunity in Italy or elsewhere to do so. He apparently returned to England as he had returned from Germany before, with his linguistic ambitions largely unrealized. He read some Italian poetry of which he knew little or nothing before leaving England, but was no better in acquiring spoken Italian than German. "He never reconciled himself," says one critic," to the sound of Italian as spoken by the Italians, although he considered it delightful on English tongues.'' His visits to Sicily he had expected would give him better opportunities of learning to speak the language correctly. But he was disappointed. For, says the same critic, "he had apparently not anticipated the difference between the Italian spoken there and the Italian he had learned from his grammars.'' He was also disconcerted by the speed of Italian conversation in Sicily. In fact Coleridge's assertion to Stuart in a letter of July 6, 1804—"I shall soon be able both to speak and write French and Italian,'' was far too optimistic. Worst of all for the Coleridge who had left England with high hopes of finding health and a profitable sinecure was the thought of his return as a mere wanderer, "ill, penniless, and worse than homeless''—a failure in all things.

The absent Coleridge was not forgotten by his friends in England. They anxiously expected letters from him and when they did not arrive became still more uneasy. When Dorothy heard indirectly in May 1804, that Samuel had reached Gibraltar, she told the equally anxious Lady Beaumont: "It is a great comfort to us to know that he has got so far on his voyage." The following month Southey was relieved when in London, to have news of Coleridge through Lamb and others, and was glad to find a letter from Coleridge awaiting him at Greta Hall. Indeed Coleridge when absent, became an extraordinarily unitive influence upon his friends, including the Lambs and the Beaumonts. It brought the inmates of Dove Cottage and Greta Hall into far closer personal and friendly contacts than ever before. Lady Beaumont had been specially fascinated by the religious element in Coleridge who on parting had promised at her request to pray for her. Sara Stoddart in Malta, whose letters to her friend Mary Lamb seem providentially to have escaped the mishaps befalling Coleridge's many "lost" letters—sent the anxious Mary the long awaited news of Coleridge's arrival which was so long in coming directly from Coleridge himself. Mary Lamb who liked Mrs. Coleridge, sent her the latest news from time to time. This Mrs. Coleridge passed on to Dove Cottage whence it continued on its way to the Beaumonts. Nor were the Southeys less interested or less informed. Of course whoever in the circle received a letter from Coleridge himself must send its contents the same round. In this way, Mrs. Coleridge, hitherto the "outsider," was brought into closer friendly association with the Wordsworths than ever before. Invitations now came to her from Dove Cottage and were reciprocated from Greta Hall.

The picture that Dorothy Wordsworth sends Lady Beaumont of their life in

June 1804, reveals a surprising change in the relationships between Dove Cottage and Greta Hall. Dorothy, William, Mary, and Baby John had gone in their "little carriage"—the old "jaunting car" of the Scotch Tour—to Greta Hall where they "arrived at six o'clock in the evening, to the great joy of all the family for they had been long burning with desire to see the child." William had gone ahead "to warn them of our coming." Derwent ran about shouting "Mary's coming, Dorothy's coming." Mrs. Coleridge ran to meet them with little Sara in her arms, "Mrs. Lovell and Mrs. Southey followed, and all shouted with surprise at the sight of John." "Mrs. Coleridge is fat and looks well," Dorothy continued, "she seemed to be in pretty good spirits. As soon as possible. . .she intends bringing all her children over to spend a fortnight or three weeks with us." And Dorothy's frustrated affection for Coleridge in absence found satisfaction in his children. Nor was Wordsworth himself less anxious and interested.

When Coleridge's first letter to Mrs. Coleridge arrived late in August and reached Dove Cottage, William transcribed a large part of it for Sir George Beaumont, "to remove anxiety on your part." Despite the increasing demands made by family responsibilities upon Dorothy, her thoughts and fears were continually for Coleridge in Malta. She dreamed of going with William to meet Samuel in Switzerland on his homeward way. On Christmas day 1804, Dorothy's apprehensions found expression in a letter to Lady Beaumont: "Alas! we have had no letter from Coleridge. We are perplexed and distressed about him, and continually thinking about him in spite of our attempts to turn from the thought. We find our comfort here, that he is certainly at Malta and that every caution will be used to keep the fever out of the island. . . . We hear often from Mrs. Coleridge. She is in very good health, but does not know what to think about the non-arrival of letters and is very anxious. She and Derwent have been staying with Miss Sara Hutchinson at Park House!"

Regret for the lost companionship of Coleridge haunted the country walks of William and Dorothy at this time, and they found consolation almost from the moment of his departure, in planning to live near him wherever he might choose to settle upon his return. William was convinced that the climate of the North was injurious to Coleridge. "When Coleridge has found out a residence better suited to his state of health," he told Scott, in January 1805, "we shall remove and settle near him." Nor was Dorothy less enthusiastic about living near Coleridge. "We have entirely made up our minds upon quitting Grasmere, as soon as ever Coleridge has fixed upon and procured a proper residence for himself," she told Lady Beaumont in April (1805).

Mary Lamb, poetically inspired by the thought that Coleridge's return would console the Wordsworths for the death of their brother John, now asks Dorothy in a letter:

> Why is he wandering on the sea?
> Coleridge should now with Wordsworth be.
> By slow degrees he'd steal away

> Their woe, and gently bring a ray
> (So happily he'd time relief)
> Of comfort from their very grief. . .

Nothing more obviously suggests the spell Coleridge cast over his intimate friends. It was composed of some of his best extrovert qualities: his geniality—even bohemian sympathies—his spontaneous kindliness to those about him, his wit, his joyousness when in that mood, his endless play of imagination and fancy, his interesting conversation and pleasant humour, all contrasting with the darker, internal, introspective introvertive qualities they concealed. Wordsworth with rare penetration perceived all these contradictory elements in Coleridge and summarized them in his poem "A Character," which concluded with a vivid portrayal of Coleridge's spell over Wordsworth himself:

> I marvel, how Nature could ever find space
> For so many strange contrasts in one human face:
>
> . . . .
>
> This picture from nature may seem to depart,
> Yet the Man would at once run away with your heart;
> And I for five centuries right gladly would be
> Such an odd, such a kind happy creature as he.

Southey's description of Coleridge's appearance, as well as of his attractive personality, closely resembled that of Wordsworth. "You would have found him the most wonderful man living in conversation," Southey told Matilda Betham the miniaturist in 1808, "but the most impracticable one for a painter, and had you begun the picture it is ten thousand to one that you must have finished it from memory. His countenance is the most variable that I have ever seen; sometimes it is kindled with the brightest expression, and sometimes all its light goes out, and is utterly extinguished. Nothing can convey stronger indications of power than his eye, eyebrow and forehead. Nothing can be more imbecile than all the rest of his face; look at them separately, you would hardly think it possible that they could belong to one head; look at them together, you would wonder how they came so, and are puzzled what to expect from a character whose outward and visible signs are so contradictory."

Unfortunately, Coleridge's genial qualities find very little expression in his published correspondence.

Coleridge's own opinion of his face when Miss Betham invited him at this time to sit for his portrait, was even less flattering than Southey's. "My poor face is a miserable subject for a painter" he wrote in accepting the invitation, "for in honest truth I am what the world calls, and with more truth than usual, an ugly fellow." But the portrait was not painted until three years later. For Coleridge's attempts to reach Miss Betham's studio on this occasion always failed; sometimes he lost his way, sometimes he forgot the address—so at least he asserted.

As the year 1805 moved towards its close, expectations of Coleridge's reappearance intensified. They turned to impatience as he delayed and when winter arrived became gloomy fears and forebodings of evil: of shipwreck and disaster such as had destroyed Captain John Wordsworth. On Christmas Day 1805, Mary Lamb, replying to enquiries from the anxious Catherine Clarkson, wrote; "We have heard no more of Coleridge. I will certainly write the instant I hear from him. I have not the most distant idea where it is probable he will land." And she went on to dream of a "happy meeting" of Coleridge with the Clarksons and the Wordsworths early in the new year. But it was Dorothy, writing on that same Christmas Day to Lady Beaumont, who gave full rein to her emotions, her memories, and her fears:

> Poor Coleridge was with us two years ago at this time. . . . We hear no further tidings of him, and I cannot help being very uneasy and anxious: though without evil, many causes might delay him; yet it is a long time since he left Malta. The weather is dreadful for a sea voyage. Oh my dear friend, what a fearful thing a windy night is now at your house! I am too often haunted with dreadful images of shipwrecks and the sea when I am in bed and hear a stormy wind, and now that we are thinking so much about Coleridge it is worse than ever.

Until far into the new year Dorothy's fears continued, and were augmented by thoughts of Coleridge's dangers from the French, after hearing in March that Coleridge was in Italy. Mrs. Wordsworth and Sara Hutchinson, she said, were similarly distressed. "When I was alone in bed at night," she told Catherine Clarkson, "I could not banish the most dreadful images, and Mary and Sara have suffered in the same way." But all they could glean were generally odd scraps of news from various sources, seldom indeed from Coleridge himself.

Upon hearing that Coleridge was still on earth, as he was in Italy, Dorothy was greatly relieved. "A heavy burden is removed from our minds," she wrote. "We were wearied out with conjectures, and expectations worn out; for though every postday we trembled when the news was coming upstairs, 'no letters' yet we had scarcely anything like expectation left." But now they hoped Coleridge was "on his way home." In this manner, amid hopes and fears and disappointments, amid a silence broken at long intervals by vague rumors and reports, and a growing feeling of neglect—despite Dorothy's stout defence of her friend—the early summer of 1806 passed. "If you write to Mrs. Coleridge," Dorothy exhorted Catherine Clarkson on the last day of June, "do continue if possible to report something of the fine things said of him by the fine folks, for she would fain persuade us he is a perfect clown, at least in his appearance."

By August 1 William Wordsworth's anxiety for Coleridge, which was very real, had turned to irritation at his silence. "I do not know," he then told Sir George Beaumont, "whether my sister has written since we had another account of Coleridge; I am sorry I cannot say *from* him. He was at Leghorn with a friend on their way to England: so that we still continue to look for him daily. He has lost *all* his papers, *how* we are not told. This grieves and vexes me much." Southey too was both angry and sceptical. "I have no doubt," he wrote, "that the reason why we receive no letters is that he writes none; when he comes he will probably tell a different story, and it will be proper to admit his excuse without believing it." In this Southey was a true prophet. Coleridge's excuses, real or imaginary, were many and various. Many letters he had written to his friends in England he explained, had perished en route: some were burnt at Gibraltar because of the plague there; some had perished in the turmoil of war; and even on his return voyage to England when a "Spanish Privateer ruffian boarded us," Coleridge's important political papers were thrown overboard by Captain Derkheim for safety. "Probably," remarked Rickman, sceptical as Southey "these were papers he had intended to write."

Then suddenly, in mid-August, a fortnight after Wordsworth's irritated letter, there came glad news to poor Dorothy. Immediately she told Catherine Clarkson: "I have only just time to save the post, but I cannot wait another day for I have the blessed news to tell you that Coleridge is arrived. . . ."

PART II

1806–1816: 33–42 Years.

England again—New hopes and disappointments—Escape to opium and to Highgate

1   The Wanderer's Return (1806-7)

".. I found myself again in my native Country—ill, penniless, and worse than homeless."
                    —S.T. Coleridge to Josiah Wedgwood, June 25, 1807

On August 17, 1806, after a week in quarantine off Portland, Coleridge "leaped on land" at Halstow in Kent and went straight to "a curious little chapel" there, where he "offered as deep a prayer as ever without words or thoughts was sent up by a human being." He certainly needed aid, both divine and human, and having sought the former turned at once to its human counterpart. Taken by Russell to the Bell Inn, Cheapside, where the office of Russell Père was situated, Coleridge settled down for the night while Russell's clerk collected his lost luggage.

From the Bell Inn the next morning Coleridge wrote to the most like of human helpers, Stuart, who was at Margate on holiday, and told him of his plight: "I am too much agitated to write the detail, but will call on you as soon as my two or three remaining guineas shall have put a decent hat upon my head, and shoes on my feet. I am literally afraid even to cowardice to ask for any person or of any person." The next day, to Southey he described himself as "shirtless and almost penniless." He also wrote to Wordsworth, a letter, which like nearly all that Coleridge sent to him, has disappeared.

To enable Southey and also Mrs. Coleridge to feel something of Coleridge's gratitude to Captain Derkheim, Coleridge described in unnecessary and gruesome detail Derkheim's attentions to him during his illness on the return voyage. "Tho' as proud and jealous an American as ever even America produced," Derkheim "would come and even with tears in his eyes, beg and pray me to have an enema." Indeed, although "the strongest man on board," the demands of the enema had almost exceeded the Captain's strength. But a few weeks later when Derkheim failed to retrieve Coleridge's property from the Customs for him, the Captain fell from his higher state in Coleridge's opinion to the lowest depth. For Derkheim had refused to bribe the customs for Coleridge, owing, said Samuel "to a prejudice against smuggling almost peculiar to Americans and arising out of the happy state of a new country under a republican government." And not only had Coleridge's trunk been left in the Customs limbo, but also the forty volumes Derkheim had promised to bring by fours and fives each time, had not been touched. In fact the miserable man had got married and although Coleridge had given a string of pearls,

Derkheim had also taken some valuable Attar of Roses to give to his wife. To Coleridge's letters of reproach Derkheim had made no reply but merely sailed away. Nor was Mrs. Derkheim any more satisfactory than her husband. For when Coleridge went to her with his tale of woe all she said apparently was "Good God!" So poor Coleridge after returning from a fruitless errand to the Customs that brought him only wet shoes, "was obliged to keep my bed till yesterday evening." Finally Mrs. Coleridge's young brother, George Fricker, and Mrs. Clarkson went down to the Customs office and Coleridge's property was recovered.

In England however, Coleridge now found compensation for his personal misfortune. His native land so dispraised by Coleridge upon his departure for Malta now delighted him: "Immediately after my landing, health seemed to flow in upon me like the mountain waters upon the dry stones of a vale-stream after rains." Since leaving England he said he had "never enjoyed four *days* of such health."

After two days with Lamb in London Coleridge, postponing Stuart's invitation to join him in Margate, accepted the offer to stay in his empty house in Brompton. But already in two letters Coleridge had opened Stuart's purse even before his house. To Southey he sent a long and excruciatingly detailed account of his physical miseries during his recent voyage. To Stuart he also sent a long letter of discontents, disillusions, and hardships encountered during his wanderings. Immediately before leaving Italy Coleridge had received a letter from Stuart listing Coleridge's debts to him. This, Coleridge now told Stuart, had made him feel "very low," and "never for an hour ceased to prey on my mind." Duped and defrauded by the malignancy of men and fate he would have been "left starving in a foreign country" but for the generous care of a gentleman who befriended him. All this had prevented his sending £100 to Mrs. Coleridge. Such then was Coleridge's plight; the ruin of his hopes of helping his family by hard-won earnings through drudgery in Malta: "but enough!" he concluded. But it was not quite enough. Stuart's "loans" past, present, and future, must be gracefully acknowledged: "God bless you, my dear Sir! I have yet cheerful hopes that heaven will not suffer me to die degraded by any other debts, than those which it has ever been and ever will be, my joy and pride still to pay and still to owe—those of a truly grateful heart—and to you among the first of those to whom they are due." Thus with pious resignation was Stuart warned that he might have to look to heaven for the repayment of Coleridge's debts.

Soon Coleridge joined Stuart at Margate during several visits made from the close of August until Stuart's return to town on September 22. Stuart, having sold *The Morning Post*, had become proprietor and editor of *The Courier* with his old friend Street as joint editor. During the intervals of his visits to Margate, Coleridge transferred his residence to the office of *The Courier*, intending to make contributions to the paper. Like so many of Coleridge's writings, the articles he now promised Stuart on Fox and Pitt (both recently dead) were but a dream. Street however wrote one on Fox which Coleridge adversely criticized to Stuart; for Street was far less appreciative of Coleridge than Stuart was. At any rate, on September 27 *The Courier* published Coleridge's mediocre verses: *Farewell to Love*, suggested by a sonnet of Fulke Greville's.

News of Coleridge's arrival in quarantine off the South coast came to Greta Hall and Dove Cottage in the usual roundabout way. Russell had immediately informed his father at Exeter of their arrival in England, and he had informed Ottery that Coleridge was back and in distress. From Ottery the news came to Mrs. Coleridge, who in turn passed it on to Dorothy, who sent it to Catherine Clarkson and to Lady Beaumont. "Blessed news," said Dorothy, who charitably believed that Coleridge's silence was due to his fear "lest he should hear of some new sorrow." They had received she said "only one letter from him" since John Wordsworth's death. Excitement rose high at Dove Cottage and Greta Hall with the expectation of Coleridge's impending return to his family and friends. Dorothy, alone at Dove Cottage in joyous agitation, at once informed William, who with Mary and John was at Park House.

Meanwhile Mrs. Coleridge actively prepared for her husband's reception; preparations which little Derwent long remembered. "My mother," he said, "had taken my pillow for my father's bed, who required several. On her telling me this, I exclaimed, 'Oh! by all means. I would lie on straw for my father!,' greatly to my mother's delight and amusement. How well does this speak for my mother."

But disappointment soon followed as week after week passed with only broken promises of return to the North. Not less compelling was Coleridge's fear of appearing before his wife, the Wordsworths, and worst of all Sara Hutchinson, as a greater failure than he had seemed upon his return from Germany. For now he was "ill, penniless and worse than homeless," as he told Josiah Wedgwood ten months after his arrival in England. Nor was this all. The Coleridge who returned from Malta was all too obviously to his friends a changed man: lost, dejected and with the appearance of a victim of drugs and drink. Nor had he anything to show for his foreign adventure: not even the good health which was its much-proclaimed objective.

Mary Lamb after seeing him wrote at once to Dorothy, begging her to get William to consult with Southey to persuade Mrs. Coleridge to agree to a separation from her husband. Then William must come to town to see Coleridge. Mrs. Coleridge, pleased by the affectionate messages in her husband's letters, had no inkling of the bombshell of separation that was about to burst upon her and had written a happy note of expectation to Mary Lamb, which haunted Mary throughout the night following her letter to Dorothy. Thus it came that the next day Mary sent Dorothy a letter of repentance and renunciation saying: "Yesterday I wrote anxiously. . .and to-day I think of the letter I received from Mrs. Coleridge, telling me, as joyful news, that her husband is arrived, and I feel it very wrong in me even in the remotest degree to do anything to prevent her seeing her husband—she and her husband being the only people who ought to be concerned in the affair." The basic cause of her impetuous intervention, Mary added, was "the anxious care even to misery which I have felt since he has been here, that something could be done to make such an admirable creature happy."

Mary Lamb next decided that Coleridge must write to his wife and she would make him do it. "You must, positively must write to Mrs. Coleridge this day," she told him, "and you must write here, that I may know you write, or you must come and dictate a letter for me to write to her. I know all that you would say in defence of not writing, and I allow in full force everything that you can say or think, but yet a letter from me or you *shall go today*."

The result was Coleridge's first letter to his wife since his return. It was written on September 16, 1806. Five more letters to her followed at short intervals until the last on October 9, each with an unfulfilled promise of immediate return to Greta Hall; each with an excuse for not doing so.

Nor were these excuses entirely dishonest. For Coleridge was now busy in London seeking influential patrons in the hope of obtaining, on the strength of his official position in Malta, a sinecure or pension for himself. This he described in detail in letters to his wife. As for any active post, he would not consider such, having had enough of that in Malta. But Coleridge was unfortunate in these attempts. When he tried to see Lord Howick the Foreign Secretary, the porter, he told Josiah Wedgwood some months later, "repelled me from his door with gross insult. . . ." A similar attempt with Lord Holland had no better success.

"Fretted out of all patience," he described himself to his wife after these failures; but he was not surprised. I never expected anything from it," he told her. "As to sinecure places or pensions, they are out of the question for any but noblemen's sons, or the relations of men with great parliamentary interest. And as to active secretaryships, and all those situations which imply the continual subjection of one's own intellect to the views and purposes of another, I know them too well already; and £500 or even £1000 a year would be poor compensation.

Although he told his wife on September 29 "I visit nobody but Charles and Mary Lamb, and have not been to one public place," throughout September the intervals between his visits to Stuart at Margate were filled with similar frequent flying visits to the Clarksons, who were staying with a friend at Parndon some twenty miles from town. Despite more promises to Mrs. Coleridge of an immediate return to Greta Hall, he remained at Parndon until October 10, when he accompanied Mrs. Clarkson to her home at Bury St. Edmunds, as Mr. Clarkson was in London.

The atmosphere at Bury was evidently theological, for Coleridge recorded his high approval of the comment of the Clarksons' servant after she had heard a sermon by the famous Unitarian preacher and scientist, Dr. Price. "Neither the poor nor the Gospel appeared in it," she said. Coleridge, now anti-Unitarian and antiscientific, highly approved. "Excellent hit on the fine respectable attendants of Unitarian chapels, and the moonshine, heartless head-work of the sermons!'' he exclaimed. How shocked poor Estlin and the once admirable Unitarians of Shewsbury would have been!

But such cogitations were a mere childish playing with seashells on the seashore compared with the ocean of theological speculation, or rather Coleridge's clarification provoked by some questions put to him by the serious-minded Mr. Clarkson, theologian and antislavery propagandist. Mr. Clarkson's questions as repeated by the exhilarated Coleridge, included: ''What metaphysically the Spirit of God *is*? What the Soul? What the difference between the Reason and the Understanding?'' Thus stimulated Coleridge wrote to Clarkson on October 13 a long letter, almost a pamphlet. For Coleridge considered Clarkson's questions to be ''not more awful than difficult of solution,'' and this put him on his mettle. Only seven weeks had passed since Coleridge told Stuart of his vexation at ever having been ''a delver in the unwholesome quicksilver mines of abstruce metaphysics.'' He now returned to them and to the Kantian region of 'Reason versus Understanding,' which haunted Coleridge's thought to the end and in the process bored some of his hearers including Carlyle.

Perhaps Coleridge's return to metaphysics was largely a reaction against the different atmosphere of the races at Newmarket which he had visited the day before. Coleridge had appeared there in his usual semiclerical dress of a black coat, knee breeches, and silk stockings, and mounted on a scraggy horse with rusty and discolored harness. The amusement and ridicule Coleridge thus excited he met, according to his own account, with ready (though complicated and laborious) retorts, which he said shattered his tormentors. To the notebook he confided his condemnation of gambling. The impressions on the gaming tables left by the dice box spoke to him of ''the agony and spite with which many have been thrown.''

On October 14 Coleridge left Bury. Two days later he was in Cambridge which he had not revisited since his student days twelve years before. His private comments upon the visit were surprisingly free from the slightest touch of sentimentality as he walked about the town and the colleges: ''The young men seemed the very same young men I had left.'' The only changes were in those who had been his contemporaries: they were altered like himself he said. He visited the library of Trinity College and was introduced to Porson the famous professor of Greek. Porson, when Coleridge gained his one academic success, the medal for a Greek ode, had offered to show his colleagues ''134 examples of bad Greek'' in it. Probably Coleridge was unaware of this, but to Samuel's annoyance Porson had evidently forgotten who Coleridge was. ''He took no notice of me'' said Samuel, ''not even by an act of common civility. His pitiable state, quite *muddled*.'' For Porson now forty-seven was too fond of wine.

During the two months which had elapsed since Coleridge landed in England, the Wordsworths were increasingly disappointed by the lack of letters and by his delay in coming North to his home and friends. Also the news

Mary Lamb sent them of Coleridge's intention to separate from his wife increased their anxiety. Wordsworth, despite Coleridge's objection, threatened to come to London to see him unless he came home, and insisted that Mrs. Coleridge must be given reasons for his delay, or she and his friends at Dove Cottage be immediately informed that separation was imminent. To the Beaumonts, William and Dorothy sent the news that a separation was intended. "What a deplorable thing" wrote William to Sir George; and Dorothy discussed the question at great length with Lady Beaumont. "Mrs. Coleridge has many excellent properties," Dorothy told her, "as you observe; she is unremitting in her attentions as a nurse to her children, and, indeed, I believe she would have made an excellent wife to many persons. Coleridge is as little fitted for her as she for him, and I am truly sorry for her." Nevertheless, Dorothy still hoped separation might be avoided if only Coleridge could be persuaded to return home and find adequate compensation for the shortcomings of his wife in "the blessings of friendship. . .and devote himself to his studies and his children."

Thus in a state of continual expectancy all at Dove Cottage awaited Coleridge's arrival. But he did not come despite his promises to Mrs. Coleridge. At last in despair, near the end of October the Wordsworths left for Coleorton—a farmhouse in Leicestershire lent to them by Sir George Beaumont. Sara Hutchinson was to join them at Kendal and go with them to Coleorton. Meanwhile Coleridge, at last returning to Greta Hall, broke his journey at Penrith hoping to see Sara there, only to learn that she had just left for Kendal. So to Kendal he followed her and there the Wordsworth family found not only Sara as expected, but also the unexpected Coleridge. Coleridge shy of meeting the whole family, conscious as he was of the change in himself, sent word to Wordsworth to come to him at his inn; but the others came too. Dorothy vividly described the occasion later to Catherine Clarkson:

We all went thither to him and never never did I feel such a shock as at first sight of him. We all felt exactly in the same way—as if he were different from what we had expected to see; almost as much as a person of whom we have thought much and of whom we had informed an image in our minds, without having any personal knowledge of him. Alas! [she continued] what can I say? I know not what to hope for, or what to expect; my wishes are plain and fair, that he may have strength of mind to abide by his resolution of separating from Mrs. C. and hereafter may continue unshaken; but his misery has made him so weak, and he has been so dismally irresolute in all things since his return to England, that I have more fear than hope. He is utterly changed; and yet sometimes, when he was animated in conversation concerning things removed from him, I saw something of his former self. But never when we were alone with him. He then scarcely ever spoke of anything that concerned him or us, or our common friends nearly, except we forced him to it; and immediately he changed the conversation to Malta, Sir Alexander Ball, the corruption of government, anything but what we were yearning after. All we could gather from him was that he must part from her or die and leave his children destitute, and that to part he was resolved.

His fatness [wrote Dorothy] has quite changed him—it is more like the flesh
of a person in a dropsy than one in health; his eyes are lost in it—but why
talk of this? You must have seen and felt all. I often thought of Patty
Smith's remark. It showed true feeling of the divine expression of his
countenance. Alas! I never saw it as it used to be—a shadow, a gleam there
was at times, but how faint and transitory! I think however that, if he have
courage to go through the work before him, William's conversation and our
kind offices may soothe him and bring on tranquillity; and then, the only
hope that remains will be in his applying himself to some grand object connected with permanent effects.

From Sunday evening until Tuesday morning they all stayed with Coleridge
to cheer him. When the others left for Coleorton Sara and William remained
with him for another day before following the rest. Before leaving they obtained
a promise from Coleridge to join them at Coleorton after seeing his wife
again in Greta Hall. Dorothy found the journey to Coleorton with Mary, little
John and his two year-old sister Dora, wearisome. On October 30 the family
reached Coleorton as Coleridge entered Greta Hall. On the same day Sara and
William left Kendal for Coleorton by coach.

Southey was if possible even more shocked than Dorothy on first seeing
Coleridge. His countenance is more changed for the worse than I could have
believed possible. His eyes have lost all their life, partly from fat and still
more from the quantity of laudanum which he takes, and the quantity of
spirits. Nothing intoxicates him, and he is not sensible and will not be easily
convinced that he drinks enough to kill anybody—frequently when he was
at home nearly a bottle of rum in a day. "Do not talk about this for it is better kept to ourselves," he told a friend, "but he is in every way the worse for
his long absence, except for his understanding."

A week after Coleridge's return home Wordsworth wrote urging him to
drop his idea of giving lectures and come with Hartley to Coleorton and there
to write "Your Book of Travels which would be certain of a great sale." But
no reply came from Coleridge, fighting his battle for freedom at Greta Hall.
Dorothy described to Lady Beaumont on November 14 their life at Coleorton:
"My brother works hard at his poems preparing them for the press. Miss Hutchinson is the transcriber. She also orders dinner and attends to the kitchen; so
that the labour being so divided we have all plenty of leisure. . . .I have kept
back from speaking of Coleridge, for what can I say? We have had no letter
though we have written again. You shall hear of it when he writes to us."

"Finally resolved," wrote Coleridge in his notebook on November 12; and
amidst the domestic struggles broke his silence to the Wordsworths with four
letters in the next four days. Dorothy at Coleorton anxiously following the
course of events, was able to tell the no less anxious Lady Beaumont on
November 16, the latest news from the front. Mrs. Coleridge, she reported of
the separation, "has fully agreed to it." Coleridge would, as he wished, take
the two boys to see to their education and they would spend their holidays with
their mother. That this break-up of the family affected his wife—a devoted

mother—amazed Coleridge. "He tells us," Dorothy told Lady Beaumont, "that she breaks out into outrageous passions," fearing that "everybody will talk." Dorothy was much alarmed because Coleridge feared he had dropsy. Conscious of his duty to his boys, Coleridge expressed the best intentions—never fulfilled: the half of each day he would educate them himself and the other half they would spend in school. So Wordsworth told Coleridge to bring them both with him to Coleorton, and Dorothy glady expected them.

Without such encouragement from Coleorton and the offer of the place as an asylum, Coleridge might never have separated from his wife. Dorothy Wordsworth's dislike of Mrs. Coleridge had unconscious elements: her affection for Coleridge and love of his companionship which she doubtless expected to be as in the past, once the separation was made. Then too with her brother married and with Sara Hutchinson often helping and companioning William almost as Dorothy used to do, she must have felt comparatively lonely and no longer the only significant person in her brother's household.

What Lady Beaumont thought of all this we can only surmise. But Dorothy's replies strongly suggest that Lady Beaumont had spoken mercifully of Mrs. Coleridge, and nowhere in all the verbose explanation and condemnation of Mrs. Coleridge by Dorothy Wordsworth to Lady Beaumont, is there the slightest suggestion that Lady Beaumont joined in the attacks upon the ill-used victim of circumstance.

The miserably weak letter Coleridge sent to the Wordsworths on November 19 has been largely deleted but some of his charges against his wife remain and reveal his characteristic attitude of being the innocent sufferer. Gossip retailing remarks made by Mrs. Coleridge about himself—which can hardly have exceeded in bitterness his own remarks about her—made him cry: "Excess of my anguish." Her "mere selfish desire to have a rank in life" of which he complained, was in fact if true, merely a case of the kettle calling the saucepan black. Nor was this all; there were "her temper and selfishness, her manifest dislike of me (as far as her nature is capable of a *positive feeling*), and her self-encouraged admiration of Southey as a vindictive feeling in which she delights herself in satirizing me, etc, etc." Such were the childish moanings he poured into the too sympathetic ears of Dorothy and William. Probably, he concluded, he would come to "your mansion of sojourn" before any reply could reach him.

This puerile letter Dorothy received with such delight that she copied it for Catherine Clarkson on November 24 with the triumphant prelude:

I have at last the comfort of writing to you with a settled hope that poor Coleridge may be restored to himself and his friends. Lost he has been, oppressed even to the death of all his noble faculties (at least for any profitable work either in himself or for the good of others), but Heaven be praised, his weakness is conquered (I trust it is) and all will be well. Last night William and I walked to the post office (two miles off) tempted through the miry roads by the *possibility*, not the *hope* of a letter; but a letter we found, and I will give you his own words. . . .

Instead of appearing at Coleorton as promised Coleridge remained at Greta Hall, and four days after Dorothy's triumphant letter to Mrs. Clarkson he made an entry in his notebook which might have given Dorothy less pleasure than his declaration of a final break with his wife. For the sight of Sara Hutchinson at Kendal and the thought of her now with the Wordsworths brought on the old intense emotion, which he had declared dead when in Italy.

O Elpizomeme [the hoped for one], when shall I have to write a letter to you with no *other* sorrow to communicate than that absence from you, which writing itself implies? I know you love me! My reason knows it, my heart feels it—yet still let your eyes, your hands tell me—still say, O often and often say, My beloved! I love you—indeed I love you—for why should not my ears, and all my outward being share in the joy—the fuller my inner being is of the sense, the more my outward organs yearn and crave for it. O bring my whole nature into balance and harmony.

Two days later Coleridge replied to a letter of rebuke from his brother George who had received no letter from him since his departure for Malta. In his reply Coleridge told the full tale of his life in Malta as he now saw it, emphasizing his danger from the malevolence of Napoleon which he had by this time doubtless come to believe, and sympathizing with George in the departure of his brother Edward from George's school, which Edward had abandoned but which, said Coleridge, did not surprise him. Coleridge however did not mention separation from his wife.

On December 19 Dorothy Wordsworth informed Lady Beaumont: "We are in expectation every moment of poor Coleridge and his son Hartley." She had expected them "last night." Mrs. Coleridge was to move "southward in the spring" and to keep Derwent until she met Coleridge in London.

He writes calmly [wrote Dorothy] and in better spirits. Mrs. Coleridge had been outrageous; but for the last two or three days she had become more quiet, and appeared to be tolerably reconciled to his arrangements. I had a letter from her last week—a strange letter! She wrote just as if all things were going on as usual, and we knew nothing of the intentions of Coleridge. She gives but a very gloomy account of Coleridge's health, but this is her old way, without the least feeling or sense of his sufferings. [Dorothy hoped Coleridge would be better when with them.] As to drinking brandy, I hope he has already given over that practice; but *here,* I think, he will be tolerably safe, for we shall not have any to set before him, and we should be very loath to comply with his request if he were to ask for it. There may be some danger in the strong beer which he used formerly to like, but I think, if he is not inclined to manage himself, *we* can manage him, and he will take no harm, while he has not the temptations which variety of company leads him into, of taking stimulant to keep him in spirits while he is talking.

To this Dorothy added a postscript: "*Saturday morning*—No Coleridge last night, and it is now twelve o'clock and he is not arrived. . . ." Not until the following day, December 21, did Coleridge reach Coleorton with Hartley.

For Southey at any rate Coleridge's departure was no grief. Southey's son

Herbert was born on October 11, 1806, and his daughter, now two-and-one-half years old, had helped to heal the wound of little Margaret's death. Southey's biographer writes: "What with these children and the little Coleridges, Greta Hall soon became a gay and noisy place. It was an ideal house for a large family, and Southey's a proper spirit to preside over it. He treated his sisters-in-law—particularly Mrs. Coleridge who was his special butt—with continual banter and the children with a very reasonable indulgence." The two little Southeys and the little Coleridges delighted Southey as they played about the house, and a genial family spirit prevailed. He was also glad to receive his friends at Greta Hall. On the day Coleridge entered Coleorton Southey wrote to his brother who had recently left them: "What a difference has one week made in this house! Nurse gone—'Old love God and be cheerful,' as Coleridge calls her—Coleridge and Job (Hartley) gone, and now you also. . . ."

Coleridge's arrival at Coleorton delighted Dorothy as she almost immediately told Lady Beaumont:

> The pleasure of welcoming him to our house mingled with our joy, and I think I never was more happy in my life than when we had him an hour by the fireside: for his looks were much more like his own old self, and though we only talked of common things, and of our friends, we perceived that he was contented in his mind, and had settled things at home to his satisfaction. He has been tolerably well. . . . We shall drink a health to you on Christmas Day. You may remember that it is my birthday; but in my inner heart it is never a day of jollity.

On Christmas Day Coleridge wrote Mrs. Coleridge a fairly long and friendly letter. Absence was already working as usual on him, improving on a proximate reality. He had arrived safely though tortured on the way by boils that "bled, throbbed and *stabbed*. . . . At Coleorton, he said,

> we found them dining Sunday half past one o'clock—Today is Christmas Day. Of course we were welcomed with an uproar of sincere joy: and Hartley hung suspended between the ladies for a long minute. The children, too, jubilated at Hartley's arrival. . . . All here love him most dearly; and your namesake Sara Hutchinson takes upon her all the duties of his mother and darling friend, with all the mother's love and fondness. He is very fond of her. . . .

This must have delighted Mrs. Coleridge: "We all wish you a merry Christmas and many following ones." He will write again "at full the day after tomorrow. . . .this letter I mean merely as bearer of the tidings of our safe arrival. I am better than usual. . . .Believe me anxiously and for ever, your sincere friend, S.T. Coleridge." So ended the year 1806.

The new year at Coleorton began hopefully in a poetic atmosphere. On January 7 Wordsworth read aloud his additions to *The Prelude* composed during Coleridge's absence in Malta. These verses particularly interested Coleridge as they described the "wonderful year" of their first friendship at Stowey. Moved by these reminiscences and by the poetry, Coleridge now composed a poem *To William Wordsworth* praising him as an immortal poet and abasing himself in bitter acknowledgement of his own failure to achieve his early poetic ambitions. Invoking Wordsworth he cried:

> O great Bard!
> Ere yet that last strain dying awed the air
> With steadfast eye I viewed thee in the choir
> Of ever-enduring men. . .

Thus the poem begins with somewhat stilted and artificial rhetoric. Only when Coleridge proceeds to describe himself and his feelings, does the verse rise to the level of true poetry:

> Ah! as I listened with a heart forlorn,
> The pulses of my being beat anew
> And even as life returns upon the drowned,
> Life's joy rekindling roused a throng of pains—
> Keen pangs of Love, awakening as a babe
> Turbulent, with an outcry in the heart;
> And fears self-willed, that shunned the eye of Hope;
> And Hope that scarce would know itself from Fear;
> Sense of past Youth, and Manhood come in vain,
> And Genius given, and knowledge won in vain;
> And all which I had culled in wood-walk wild,
> And all which patient toil had reared, and all,
> Commune with thee had opened out—but flowers
> Strewed on my corse, and borne upon my bier,
> In the same coffin, for the self-same grave!

But even before the poem ended Coleridge's hope of poetic inspiration had risen again phoenix-like from its grave:

> Amid the howl of more than wintry storms,
> And Halcyon hears the voice of vernal hours
> Already on the wing.

Encouraged by the poetic atmosphere about him Coleridge now wrote to Southey in optimistic mood, believing that a new period of high poetic inspiration for him was beginning. Since he came to Coleorton he said, he had written "between 4 and 500 verses"—of which only those *To Wordsworth* are known. "I felt," he wrote, "as a man revisited by a familiar spirit, the first morning that I felt that sort of stirring warmth about the heart, which is with me the robe of incarnation of my genius, such as it is."

Unfortunately Dorothy's expectation of Coleridge's immediate improvement once he was free from the harmful proximity of his wife, was quickly disappointed. Instead of joyously absorbing the beneficial domestic influences at Coleorton, he was "neither in good health nor spirits" Wordsworth regretfully reported to Scott in late January: "How long he will stay I do not know," and he continued: "He talks of publishing, not *formal* travels, but certain remarks and reflections which suggested themselves to him during his residence abroad.''

Coleridge's long hesitation in finally separating from his wife irritated Dorothy, who almost as if she were Mrs. Coleridge, took command of the situation. ''Poor soul!'' she told Catherine Clarkson on January 20: ''he is sadly deficient in moral courage. . .he sayd he will write to-day to Mrs. Coleridge, his letter of final arrangements, but I shall depend upon him till I see the letter sealed up and directed.'' A week later Dorothy's hope for the destruction of Coleridge's taste for opium and brandy failed. ''Pretty well at present, though ailing at some time in every day,'' she told Lady Beaumont: ''He does not take such strong stimulants as he did, but I fear that he will never be able to leave them off entirely.'' When some weeks later Mrs. Coleridge replied to her husband's ''letter of final arrangements''—as Dorothy described it to Catherine—not without a touch of satisfaction—Dorothy added, the ''poor woman is almost frantic.'' But in believing that the moment of finality had now come, Dorothy was mistaken.

Nor was this all. For both Dorothy and Coleridge the approaching separation brought new problems. Coleridge and his two sons must live with the Wordsworths, all agreed. But as Dove Cottage was already too small for the Wordsworths' family alone, where were they to live when Coleridge and his sons joined them? ''But *where*?'' Dorothy asks Catherine Clarkson. Coleridge, who could always believe what he wished to believe and now wished to live with the Wordsworths in Greta Hall, also ''had an idea'' that Southey intended to quit the place with the rest. To this plan of Coleridge the Wordsworths reluctantly agreed. ''Though *very very* reluctantly,'' said Dorothy to Catherine. ''There would be something very unpleasant, not to say indelicate,'' she continued, ''in going so near to Mrs. Coleridge immediately after their separation. . . .Mary and I having many objections to Keswick, and a hundred more to taking Mrs. Coleridge's place in that house.'' Nevertheless for Coleridge's sake, the Wordsworths would if necessary sacrifice their own feelings. However to Dorothy's joy, Southey did not intend to quit the house. ''We are all right glad in our hearts to be released,'' she wrote. Although Coleridge was disappointed he denied any desire for Southey's removal or annoyance at his remaining in Greta Hall. His belief that Southey had expressed such an attention he told his friend, was due to his ''perplexed and absent state of mind.''

Southey in fact strongly disapproved of the separation. If he was able to live happily in the same house with Mrs. Coleridge, why could not Samuel do so? A little prejudiced perhaps against the Wordsworths, yet clear-sighted, Southey believed that their influence upon Coleridge's marriage had been unfortunate—a view which Coleridge himself afterwards expressed. To Rickman, Southey clearly described the situation as he saw it. Coleridge's intention to live with the Wordsworths he said, was due to ''his idolatry of that family. They have always humoured him in all his follies—listened to his complaints of his wife—and when he has complained of the itch, helped him to scratch, instead of covering him with brimstone ointment, and shutting him up by himself!'' Coleridge's habits, he continued, were "murderous of all domestic comfort.'' Rickman too had heard of Coleridge's calls for brandy in the mornings, "without respect of persons.''

For Coleridge this springtime at Coleorton in 1807, was darkened by jealousy of Wordsworth's friendship with Sara Hutchinson, who was now transcribing William's poems, as she had once transcribed those of Coleridge. Coleridge's jealousy was a reaction from the adulation of Wordsworth which Coleridge had just expressed in his poem. Coleridge's belief that Wordsworth was much superior to himself in all ways created a fear that Sara Hutchinson, now in constant association with Wordsworth, would prefer Wordsworth to himself. As Coleridge minutely contemplated the relations of Wordsworth and Sara his jealousy increased although it probably had no foundation in fact.

Only a week after Coleridge's arrival at Coleorton the first sign of his jealousy of Wordsworth at this time appeared. The three pages devoted to it in Coleridge's notebook have been destroyed and all that remains of this entry is: "THE EPOCH—Saturday 27 December 1806—Queen's Head, Stringston, 1/2 a mile from Coleorton Church, 50 minutes after 10. . . .'' The so deleted entry as it stands is baffling; but some little light is thrown, (perhaps rather on Coleridge's state of mind than on any real incident) by two later allusions to it in the notebooks.

Nine months later at Nether Stowey, Coleridge again cogitated the incident at Stringston which had so agitated him the year before. And he again records his agonies and self-questionings over Wordsworth and Sara:

O agony! O the vision of that Saturday morning—of the bed—O cruel! is he not beloved, adored by two—and two such beings—and must I not be beloved *near* him except as a satellite? But O mercy, mercy! is he not better, greater, more *manly*, and altogether more attractive to any (than) the purest woman? And yet, and yet, methinks, love so intense might demand love—otherwise, who could be secure? who could know, that his beloved might not meet his superior? Wordsworth is greater, better, manlier more dear, by nature, to woman, than I—I—miserable I!—but does he—O no! no! no! no! he does not—he does not pretend, he does not wish, to love you as I love you, Sara!—he does not love, he *would* not love, it is not the voice, not the duty of his nature, to love *any* being as I love you. No! he is not to be beloved—but yet, tho' you may feel that if he loved you, (tho' only) even *partly* as *I* love you, you should inevitably love him, love him to a degree in which you *cannot* love *me*—yet still he does not *so* love you—(no!) not in kind, much less degree—I alone love you so devotedly, and therefore, therefore, love me, Sara! Sara! love me! . . . Awakened from a dream of tears, and anguish of involuntary jealousy, ½ past 2—September 13, 1807.

How long Coleridge tortured himself with this real or imagined incident is revealed in another entry in his notebook made about a year later: "O that miserable Saturday morning! The thundercloud had long been gathering, and I had been now gazing and now averting my eyes, from it, with anxious fears of which I scarcely dared be conscious. But *then* was the first thunder-peal!

But a minute and half with ME—and all that time evidently *restless and going.*
An hour and more with Wordsworth in bed. O agony! and yet even. . . ." In
later life however, in a private memorandum Coleridge doubted the reality of
any grounds for his fears:

> That dreadful Saturday Morning at Coleorton, did I *believe* it? Did I not
> even *know* that it *was* not so, *could* not be so? Would it not have been the
> sin against the Holy Ghost, against my own spirit, that would have ab-
> solutely destroyed the good principle in my conscience, if I had dared to
> believe it conscientiously, and intellectually. Yes! Yes! I knew the horrid
> phantasm to be a mere phantasm: and yet what anguish, what gnawings of
> despair, what throbbings and lancinations of positive jealousy! Even to this
> day the undying worm of distempered sleep or morbid day-dreams.

From these outbursts of hysterical emotions the only solid but unexplained
fact that apparently emerges is that the three, whether alone or with others,
seem to have spent a night at an hotel near Coleorton—perhaps driven there by
bad weather during a walking tour in the district.

How long the jealous fits lasted is shown by a Latin verse—not very elegant
Latin verse—*Invocation to Wordsworth.* In this Samuel proclaims his impending demise because of Wordsworth's domination of Asra, who now ignores
Coleridge, all faith and loyalty destroyed. The date of the verses is unfortunately vague, some time between 1807 and 1810, and probably of the later
period when Sara's withdrawal from Coleridge was complete.

So these few weeks in the beauties and peace of Coleorton, which Dorothy
had fondly imagined would bring Coleridge tranquillity and productivity,
merely left him wallowing in a sea of frustrations. His anxieties were many: love
for Sara and Wordsworth, physical ills, surrender to opium and brandy and
the separation from Mrs. Coleridge. Too weak to complete the separation,
Coleridge still hesitated, intending to visit her from time to time despite having
separated from her.

At this very time, February 1807, Coleridge most clearly and proudly expressed to himself his psychological dissociations:

> Could I fear for a moment the supremacy of Love suspended in my nature,
> by accidents of temporary desire; were I conscious for a moment of an in-
> terregnum in my heart, were the rebel to sit on the *throne* of my being, even
> tho' it were only that the rightful lord of my bosom were sleeping, soon to
> awake and expel the usurper, I should feel myself as much fallen and as un-
> worthy of her love in any such tumult of body indulged toward her, as if I
> had roamed, like a hog in the rankest lanes of a city, battening on the loath-
> some offals of harlotry.

With much more to the same effect. Quite apart from the temperamental and
intellectual differences between Coleridge and his wife this basic attitude was
in itself sufficient, and indeed in reality a dominating element in the separation.

Such was Coleridge's state in February at Coleorton, where he also now continually contemplated departure. "Coleridge talks of leaving us in a fort-night" Wordsworth told Scott on March 2, "but as he is of a procrastinating habit" he might all the same, remain. Wordsworth's increasing alienation from Coleridge, was probably an intuitive recognition of Coleridge's jealousy. It now inspired Wordsworth's poem, *A Complaint*, written at Coleorton before Coleridge's departure:

There is a change—and I am poor;
Your love hath been, nor long ago,
A fountain at my fond heart's door,
Whose only business was to flow;
And flow it did; not taking heed
Of its own bounty, or my need.

What happy moments did I count!
Blest was I then all bliss above!
Now, for that consecrated fount
Of murmuring, sparkling, living love,
What have I? Shall I dare to tell?
A comfortless and hidden well.

A well of love—it may be deep—
I trust it is,—and never dry:
What matter? if the waters sleep
In silence and obscurity.
—Such change, and at the very door
Of my fond heart, hath made me poor.

Such as Wordsworth's reply to Coleridge's defection.

Early in April 1807, Coleride left Coleorton with the Wordsworths, Sara, and Hartley for London, to stay with Basil Montagu. "Very unhappy at Cole-orton from causes I cannot mention," Coleridge told his Bristol friend Wade the following August.

2 Separation (1807)

"A man who marries for Love is like a frog who leaps into a well—he has plenty of water, but he cannot get out again."

— *Notebook, Entry 1390—April-June 1803*

In London Coleridge soon turned to the payment of his debts in his usual manner by borrowing more money from his friends and then not paying his debts with it. From Wordsworth he had borrowed fifty pounds before leaving Coleorton, and his evident application to Stuart was disappointing. For Stuart now informed him that four years ago for the Scottish tour Coleridge had borrowed from Stuart on Wordsworth's behalf eighty pounds, but had paid Wordsworth only sixty pounds. "A strange absence of mind," Coleridge replied: "By what mistake (for I cannot, cannot degrade myself so far as to talk of motive) I could have commingled a debt of my own with Wordsworth's unknown to him or to you, is an absolute puzzle to me." An unsatisfactory result indeed after Coleridge's preliminary letter declaring that in comparison with Stuart's assistance to himself, his own contributions to the *Morning Post* and *Courier* were of little value. This Samuel said, he had always proclaimed to the world and always would do. As for those debts, "God in Heaven knows," he added "I would never repay if; if I *could* suspect of myself, that the repayment would in the least degree lessen my sense of obligation to you." However from Sotheby Coleridge extracted fifty pounds.

It was at this time that Coleridge began to create his reputation as a talker of genius who thus dominated social circles in London and attained a celebrity status which increased to the end of his life. Experience, an official position in Malta, as well as his travels in Italy, had given Coleridge a new social pose, even a certain pretentiousness. This enabled him calmly yet inexorably to hypnotize dinner parties by his "conversations." He brooked no rival and seldom permitted or needed an interrupting questioner or disputant.

Thomas Dibdin, a well-known bibliographer of the time, now first meeting Coleridge, found his conversation "as an intellectual exhibition altogether matchless." "The orator," he wrote, "rolled himself up, as it were, in his chair, and gave the most unrestrained indulgence to his speech." Much of his talk was of the relationship between Nelson and Lady Hamilton, and all knew Coleridge had been "Secretary to Sir Alexander Ball, Governor of Malta." "A copious field was here afforded for the exercise of his colloquial eloquence," wrote Dibdin, "For nearly two hours he spoke with unhesitating and uninterrupted fluency."

Coleridge's magnetic eloquence haunted Dibdin throughout the night: "It drove away slumber: or if I lapsed into sleep, there was Coleridge, his snuff box and his 'kerchief before my eyes—his mildly beaming looks—his occasional deep tone of voice—the excited features of his physiognomy—the secret conviction that the auditors seemed to be entranced with his powers of discourse." Nevertheless Dibdin disapproved of his conversion of the conversation into an uninterrupted monologue maintained by an "*emphatic* rather than *dogmatic* manner."

Writing of all this long after the first meeting with Coleridge, though surely not without earlier notes of it, Dibdin also summarized his various experiences of Coleridge as a talker: He was, he must admit, "a *mannerist*. It was always the same tone—in the same style of expression—not quick and bounding enough to diffuse instant and general vivacity; and the *chair* would sometimes assume the solemn gravity of the *pulpit*. In consequence, when heard repeatedly, this would have, and *did* have the effect of tiring." His conversation was always "delicate, reverend and courteous. The chastest ear could drink in no startling sound; the most serious believer never had his bosom ruffled by one sceptical or reckless assertion. Thinking and speaking were his delight; and he would sometimes seem, during the more fervid moments of discourse to be abstracted from all and everything around and about him, and to be basking in the sunny warmth of his own radiant imagination." It is recorded by one observer on another occasion that Coleridge sometimes took brandy as a stimulant before he talked.

Hazlitt about this time also heard Coleridge talking at one of Lamb's evening parties: "Riding the high German horse, and demonstrating the categories of the transcendental philosophy." During his visit to London, Coleridge first met Walter Scott, already a well-known poet who had been wanting to meet "that eccentric but admirable poet Coleridge," as Scott had described him five years before.

Early in May Coleridge arrived in Bristol with Hartley. There Mrs. Coleridge with Sara and Derwent had awaited him for two months in her sister's home. Their intention was for the whole family to leave Bristol in a few days to stay with Poole at Stowey. On June 4, a month after Coleridge's arrival, Mrs. Coleridge sent Poole a bitterly apologetic letter of endless delays due to her husband, and also informed him of their impending arrival at Stowey the next day. Yet even that, she warned Poole, was doubtful:

It is his and my present intention to leave Bristol to-morrow i.e. Friday morning but as it is utterly impossible for me to guess what that morning may produce (*near* although it is) that I write to request you, dear Sir, to pardon this want of punctuality, which believe me is not to be reckoned among my numerous faults. I have had all our clothes packed since Tuesday, and am waiting with great seeming patience to set off, yet it is my private opinion that we may not get off even to-morrow. I am well aware that this letter will not reach you until you have been 4 days in expectation of us, and I wish I had written on Tuesday after my first disappointment, to have saved you at least one day of expectation which I have so often smarted under.

Mrs. Coleridge was to "smart" again for not until the day after the morrow did they leave Bristol for Stowey.

Although Poole had to leave home on business on the day of their arrival, he was there to welcome them. Mrs. Coleridge long remembered "the radiant cordiality of welcome" with which they were received.

Time had worked its changes on both friends. Poole, no longer the mere tanner, had made Ward his partner, and had himself withdrawn from all practical aspects of his business. He was now a County Magistrate and recognized as an important person and leader in all beneficial and charitable enterprises in the district. At the same time he had quitted the old house, tanyard, and garden. Now, with mingled arrogance and democratic fervour he would exclaim to those about him during social occasions, in a voice harsh through incessant snuff-taking, "I am a plebeian. I am a tanner, you know, *I* am a tanner." And local wits called him "Lord Chancellor Hyde."

Since Poole's refusal to obey Coleridge's demands for cash and Coleridge's consequent neglect of Poole, the old spontaneous mutual sympathy no longer remained. Poole must have seen that convenience rather than friendship was the main reason for Samuel's visit. Disillusion not only with Coleridge as a friend, but also as an oft proclaimed "genius," similarly affected the present relationship of the two. For Poole's admiration had naturally yielded to doubt as Coleridge's unproductive years unrolled. Yet, as Poole later revealed, his affection for Coleridge still survived.

In Stowey Samuel anticipated a fortnight's ease and pleasure before proceeding with his wife and children to the Coleridges' home at Ottery. Mrs. Coleridge first demanded this visit in order to prove to her husband's relatives her own innocence and objection to the separation. After some reluctance Coleridge agreed to go there, believing that after the separation he might remain in Ottery with his two sons and teach in his brother George's school. This appeared the more feasible as Samuel's brother Edward, who had been Assistant Master there, had just vacated his post. This too would solve for Samuel the immediate problem of a subsistence for himself and his family.

To this end, immediately before leaving Coleorton, Samuel had written to George announcing his immediate arrival in Ottery with his family, the impending separation from Mrs. Coleridge, and his wish to settle there with his two sons and teach in the school. Then tactfully, he explained to George the necessity of this separation:

In short, with many excellent qualities, of strict modesty, attention to her children, and economy Mrs. Coleridge has a temper and general tone of feeling, which after a long—and for six years at least—a patient trial I have found wholly incompatible with even an endurable life, and such as to preclude my ever developing the talents which my Maker has entrusted to me—or of applying the acquirements which I have been making one after the other, because I could not be doing nothing, and was too sick at heart to exert myself in drawing from the sources of my own mind to any perseverence in any regular plan. The few friends, who have been witnesses of my domestic life, have long advised separation, as the necessary condition of everything desirable for me—nor does Mrs. Coleridge herself state or pretend to any objection on the score of attachment to me—that it will not look *respectable* for her, is the sum into which all her objections resolve themselves. At length however, it is settled (indeed the state of my health joined with that of my circumstances, and the duty of providing what I can, for my three children, would of themselves dictate the measure, tho' we were only indifferent to each other) but Mrs. Coleridge wishes—and very naturally—to accompany me into Devonshire, that our separation may appear free from all show of suspicion of any other cause than that of unfitness and unconquerable difference of temper. O that those who have been witnesses of the truth, could but add for me that commentary on my last words, which my very respect for Mrs. Coleridge's many estimable qualities would make it little less than torture to me to attempt.—However we part as friends. The boys of course will be with me. What more need be said, I shall have an opportunity of saying when we are together.

Before leaving Bristol Samuel received George's reply but as on many other occasions nervous fears prevented his opening it at the time. Not until he was in Stowey did he dare to read it and then was bitterly disappointed. George in fact was greatly upset by the news. He strongly disapproved of the separation. He could not receive Samuel and his family because of general illness and the distress Samuel's letter had given him. As for the school, George was now retiring he said, from his headmastership; "To come to Ottery," he added, "for such a purpose would be to create a fresh expense for yourself and to load my feelings with what they could not bear without endangering my life. I pray you therefore do not so. . . ." But generous as ever George continued:

> Whatever I can spare you in the pecuniary way for putting out your children or making you more comfortable shall be at your service, but peace of mind, if it is to be found here below, I must have. Resolve therefore wisely—your situation is no way desperate if your mind does not make it so. I shall be happy to hear from you and will exert myself to the utmost, when I have got rid of my present trouble, to serve you, but it cannot be by your coming here with your family at present. I know not scarcely what I have written, my mind is so agitated from within and from without. . . .For God's sake strive to put on some fortitude and do nothing rashly.

Such was the reply that Coleridge found when one day in Stowey, he first opened and read it—with rising indignation and amazement. So it seemed to Samuel his goodness, help, and generosity toward his brother were being flung back in his face as not wanted. Besides he had announced to others, including Sotheby and Wedgwood, his immediate departure for Ottery. The worthless George he refused to answer.

Coleridge never suppressed the open expression of his emotions and now to Wade in Bristol and to Davy in London—doubtless also to others—he denounced George as having invited them to Ottery and promising to pay all expenses of the journey. This appears to be the opposite of the truth—as also his pretence that he offered to go there against his personal wishes in order to be "an aid and comfort to him" in the school. He had, he said, disclosed the intention to separate from his wife because of "Wordsworth's advice that unless I disclosed my resolves of parting from Mrs. Coleridge to my relations and our common friends, she would never give up the hope of making me retract, as I had so often done before from pure weakness. . . ." It is surely not strange that Mrs. Coleridge soon left Nether Stowey and returned with the children to her sister in Bristol.

Now alone with Poole as the summer of 1807 waned, Coleridge wandered about Alfoxden and the Quantocks with happy memories of the past about him. It was not memories of Dorothy that now haunted him but of Sara Hutchinson—a natural consequence surely of his concentration upon the separation from his wife. So now the emotions created by Sara inspired a poem *Recollections of Love:*

How warm this woodland wild recess!
  Love surely hath been breathing here;
  And this sweet bed of heath, my dear!
Wells up, then sinks with faint caress,
  As if to have you yet more near.

Eight springs have flown, since last I lay
  On sea-ward Quantock's heavy hills,
  Where quiet sounds from hidden rills
Float here and there, like things astray,
  And high o'er head the sky-lark shrills.

No voice as yet had made the air
  Be music with your name; yet why
  That asking look? that yearning sigh?
That sense of promise everywhere?
  Beloved! flew your spirit by?. . . .

Despite the loss of the correspondence between Coleridge and Sara Hutchinson there is no doubt as to Coleridge's frequent letters to her at this time. Before leaving London, Coleridge had escorted Sara on her shopping expeditions there, and had seen her into the coach for Bury when she left him to visit the Clarksons. Although all that remains of a letter he sent her a day or two later is the final sentence, it shows his anxiety about her well-being. "I pray you" he wrote, "write immediately 2 or 3 lines to me, at Mr. Wade's Bridge Street, Bristol—just to let me know how you were, and how you are." Now too Coleridge showed unwonted energy in obtaining the release of Sara's sailor brother, Henry, from the press gang which had removed him from his ship into the navy. Requesting Sir George Beaumont's aid, Coleridge told him Henry "is the brother of the two beings, whom of all on earth I most highly honour, most fervently love." These he explained, were Mrs. Wordsworth (Mary Hutchinson) and her sister Sara. Sara's appeal for his aid, he told Beaumont, had brought him from his bed, "in consequence of a letter, which has deeply affected me, and of a name, which would be a spell to recall me for the time even from the verge of death.''

This in turn led Coleridge to another wail at the contrast between Sara Hutchinson's perfections and his own miserable partner. How could real life with Mrs. Coleridge compare with an idealised dream life with Sara Hutchinson! A month later he sent Stuart a kind of test paper for choosing a wife, evidently influenced by Sara Hutchinson's virtues and his wife's failings. Choosing a wife was, he wrote, ''a subject so full of anxious hope for you, so full of regretful anguish to me.'' How completely Sara Hutchinson dominated Coleridge's private thoughts and emotions since leaving Coleorton, his notebook clearly reveals. ''I yearn to make her love of me delightful to her own mind. . .'' he wrote in September 1807, ''She is all my vanity and all my virtue. . . .Self in me derives its sense of Being from having this one absolute Object.'' Without her love, he would be nothing but ''a haunting of the demon suicide. O! what mad nonsense all this would sound to all but myself—perhaps even she would despise me for it. . . .'' Thereupon his thoughts turn to Wordsworth and his own jealousy.

Among the many miseries that absorbed Coleridge's thoughts amid the ease and peace of Stowey was that of his sufferings through opium, ''a reprobate Despair, that snatches at the known poison, that suspends—alas! to aggravate the evil. . .and I know it—and the knowledge, and the fear and the remorse, and the wilful turning away of the eye to dreams imperfect, that float like broken foam on the sense of reality, and only distract not hide it, these are the wretched and sole comforts. . . O who shall deliver me from the body of his death. Meanwhile the habit of inward brooding daily makes it harder to confess the thing I am, to any one—least of all to those whom I most love and who most love me—and thereby introduces and fosters a habit of negative falsehood, and multiplies and fosters a habit, the temptations to positive insincerity. O God! let me bare my heart to Dr. Beddoes or some other medical philosopher. If I could know that there was no *relief*, I might then *resolve* on something. (Suicide?)—But the one ineradicable Idea, and unquenchable Yearning! - and the fear that death itself will but increase it! for it seems to have an affinity with Despair! O Asra! Asra!'' Yet almost immediately afterwards he wrote down in his notebook a long recipe for a concoction of laudanum.

Coleridge's unhappy domestic memories while in Stowey were now cheered by his first meeting with a new and important admirer, Thomas De Quincey. De Quincey, hypnotized by the *Lyrical Ballads* and especially by ''The Ancient Mariner,'' had vainly sought Coleridge during his absence in Malta, and now hearing that he was at Stowey arrived in hot pursuit of him at Poole's, only to learn that Coleridge was visiting friends at Bridgwater. There at last De Quincey discovered Coleridge standing ''in deep rêverie'' under a gateway, a stout person some five feet eight in height with fair complexion but black hair, and large, soft, dreamy eyes.

So abstracted from the external world was Coleridge that when accosted by

De Quincey he started, looked lost and confused "repeated rapidly a number of words which had no relation to either of us." But quickly restored to "daylight realities," Coleridge received the new admirer kindly, graciously led him to a drawing room of the house where he was staying as guest, "rang the bell for refreshments" and invited him to "a very large dinner-party on that day" at the house. In the meantime Coleridge treated De Quincey to a three hours "continuous strain of eloquent dissertation" on the great Hartley's philosophic errors, disowned now by Coleridge along with his Unitarian sympathies of previous years. He also told De Quincey that he now believed in prayer.

"In the midst of our conversation," wrote De Quincey, "if that can be called conversation which I so seldom sought to interrupt and which did not often leave openings for contribution, the door opened, and a lady entered. She was in person full and rather below the common height; whilst her face showed to my eye some prettiness of rather a commonplace order. Coleridge paused upon her entrance; his features, however, announced no particular complacency, and did not relax into a smile. In a frigid tone he said, whilst turning to me, 'Mrs. Coleridge'; in some slight way he then presented me to her: I bowed; and the lady almost immediately retired. From this short but ungenial scene, I gathered, what I afterwards learned redundantly that Coleridge's marriage had not been a very happy one." Despite his admiration for Coleridge De Quincey made his sympathy and esteem for Mrs. Coleridge very evident.

A more genial scene, at least for Coleridge soon followed when he took De Quincey to walk with him about Bridgwater in the early evening:

All the people of station and weight in the place, and apparently all the ladies, were abroad to enjoy the lovely summer evening; and not a party passed without some mark of smiling recognition, and the majority stopping to make personal enquiries about his health, and to express their anxiety that he should make a lengthened stay among them. . .Especially I remarked that the young men of the place manifested the most liberal interest in all that concerned him.

Such was their walk. "Rarely," wrote De Quincey, "perhaps never, have I seen a person so much interrupted in one hour's space as Coleridge, on this occasion, by the courteous attentions of young and old."

Even at the first meeting Coleridge confessed to De Quincey his opium habit, when perhaps with that intention, De Quincey told him that he took opium for toothache. Upon this Coleridge warned De Quincey against opium with such a "peculiar emphasis of horror" that De Quincey felt Coleridge "never hoped to liberate himself from the bondage," and in De Quincey's opinion he never did. "The gloom and the weight of dejection which sat upon Coleridge's countenance and deportment at this time" said De Quincey, deeply impressed him. "Never," he continued, "had I beheld so profound an expression of cheerless despondency. And the restless activity of Coleridge's mind, in chasing abstract truths, and burying himself in the dark places of human speculation, seemed to me, in a great measure, an attempt to escape out of his own personal wretchedness.'' This De Quincey says Coleridge later admitted.

Yet despite Coleridge's warning, De Quincey's own experiences with opium inspired his volume *The Opium Eater,* which appeared fourteen years later and made De Quincey famous.

Throughout the evening De Quincey's close observation of Coleridge continued: ''At dinner, when a very numerous party had assembled, he knew that he was expected to talk, and exerted himself to meet the expectation. But he was evidently struggling with gloomy thoughts that prompted him to silence, and perhaps to solitude: he talked with effort, and passively resigned himself to the repeated misrepresentations amongst his hearers. . . .'' Excited and delighted with the day's experiences, De Quincey could not sleep, so leaving Coleridge at ten o'clock he set off for Bristol, walking ''through the coolness of the night.''

Nor had Coleridge failed to impress his new admirer with his undeserved poverty. ''Was it possible that this ruin had been caused or hurried forward by the dismal degradation of pecuniary difficulties?'' De Quincey asked himself as he proceeded towards Bristol and thought of the signs of misery and decay in Coleridge. The result was that in Bristol he asked his friend Cottle to send Coleridge £500, as from an anonymous admirer. Cottle wisely persuaded De Quincey to reduce it to £300 and the following October offered it to Coleridge who, knowing pretty well whence it came, graciously accepted it. However upon acceptance, Coleridge with exquisite delicacy as on all such occasions, laid down stringent conditions—which proved in fact mere verbiage! Cottle must assure him that ''My unknown Benefactor is in such circumstances, that in doing what he offers to do, he transgresses no duty of morals or of moral prudence.'' Indeed, De Quincey's gift he could accept only ''as an unconditional loan—which I trust I shall be able to restore at the close of two years.'' However when some years later De Quincey in need requested its return, Coleridge was too impecunious to meet the request.

In his present circumstances Coleridge found that to remain indefinitely at Stowey as Poole's guest was the best and most pleasant course. He took horse exercise, stopped drinking brandy—so he said—and his health improved. This he said, was due to his ''being alone with Poole, and the renewal of old times by wandering about among my dear old walks, of Quantock and Alfoxden.'' He also visited friends in the neighborhood, including the Chubbs at Bridgwater, where De Quincey had found him. He called on his old acquaintances the Cruikshanks, the family of the agent to Lord Egmont. To Egmont Coleridge had referred ten years before in his republican enthusiasm as ''Lord Thing-a-my-bob—I forget the animal's name.''

Now, however, he was anxious to remove all suspicions of having favoured egalitarianism and was disturbed when Mary Cruikshank, the agent's sister, borrowed from a friend the first edition of Coleridge's early *Poems*—often politically inspired. ''With the kindest intentions,'' he told her, ''I fear you have done me some little disservice in borrowing the first edition of my *Poems* from Miss Brice. I never held any principles indeed, of which considering my age, I have reason to be ashamed. The whole of my public life may be comprised in eight or nine months of my 22nd year; and the whole of my political sins during that time, consisted in forming a plan of taking a large farm, in common, in America, with 10 or 12 other young men of my own age. A wild notion indeed but very harmless.''

He also found time while at Stowey to write to Mary Cruikshank on other subjects, giving her an account of a pleasant dinner with one of her friends which left him somewhat uncertain of his homeward way, after drinking a bottle of port and two glasses of mead. Coleridge did not forget Mary Cruikshank's social utility and Mary soon received from him a second (harmless) edition of his *Poems* with a request that she read some of it to Lord Egmont's daughter, Lady Elizabeth Perceval. This request he explained, was due to his sincere regard for Lady Perceval "of whose esteem, so far at least as not to be confounded with the herd of vulgar mob flatterers, I am not ashamed to confess myself solicitous.'' Yet with characteristic versatility he turned shortly afterwards to a deep theological discussion with Mary on his faith in miracles as essential to Christianity.

Upon Lord Egmont Coleridge had made, if we may believe De Quincey, a most striking impression. Even while De Quincey was at Poole's, Lord Egmont called with a present for Coleridge, "a canister of peculiarly fine snuff, which Coleridge now took profusely,'' and at the same time spoke of Coleridge "in the terms of excessive admiration,'' urging Poole to set him to "some great monumental work, that might furnish a sufficient arena for the display of his various and rare accomplishments; for his multiform erudition on the one hand, for his splendid power of theorizing and combining large and remote notices of facts on the other.'' Indeed Egmont suggested for Coleridge the writing of "a history of Christianity'' in its progress into various churches and sects and "the relations subsisting between Christianity and the current philosophy. . . .But at any rate, let him do something, for at present he talks very much like an angel, and does nothing at all.'' Lord Egmont, who had lent his carriage to convey Coleridge to Bridgwater on the quickly broken understanding that he would remain there only one night before returning to Poole's, now realized Coleridge's procrastination. He laughed at his own simplicity in believing Coleridge.

At last, in mid-September Coleridge left Stowey for Bristol, where Mrs. Coleridge and the children were awaiting him to take them back to Greta Hall. Since their rejection by Ottery, the separation seems to have been shelved for a time. But instead of going North, Coleridge resumed associations with old Bristol friends. With Cottle, whom he had not seen since his departure for Malta, he discussed religious questions, and Cottle, still ignorant of his opium addiction, was delighted to learn of Coleridge's abandonment of Unitarianism. Cottle was well aware of what Rickman called "Coleridge's habit of Assentation'' but on this occasion was convinced of Coleridge's sincerity: "I knew that Mr. Coleridge was somewhat in the habit of accommodating his discourse to the sentiments of the persons with whom he was conversing; but his language was now so pious and orthodox, that the contrast between his past and present sentiments was most noticeable. He appeared quite an improved character, and was about, I thought, to realize the best hopes of his friends. I found him full of future activity, projecting new works, and particularly a *New Review,* of which he himself was to be the editor!. . .and I thought the prospect never appeared so cheering." When shortly afterwards, Coleridge left Bristol for London, he did not see Cottle again for seven years. Coleridge's old Bristol friend, Estlin, the Unitarian Minister, was far from delighted with Samuel's new religious opinions. "A mere superstitious Calvinist," he wailed; and declared that Coleridge's intellect and genius were lost. Samuel in his new theological passion, next discussed with a local Baptist Minister such thorny problems as Redemption, Salvation, and the Trinity.

In Bristol, as in Stowey, personal failures dominated Coleridge's thoughts. In a "moulting peacock with only two of his long tail feathers remaining, and those sadly in tatters, yet proudly as ever spreading out his ruined fan in the sun and breeze" he found an apt symbol of himself. Despite the much vaunted purity of his love for Sara as an abstraction, he complained to his notebook now, that she did not grant him the "words, looks, chaste caresses, that innocent and loving brothers may to a twin sister."

Towards the end of October 1807, De Quincey in place of Samuel obligingly conducted Mrs. Coleridge and the children back to Greta Hall, where they arrived early in November. Coleridge meanwhile spoke of going to London to prepare a course of lectures for the Royal Institution where Davy was all powerful. While at Stowey Coleridge had thankfully accepted Davy's suggestions to give such a course. "I have now seriously set about composition" he replied on September 9, 1807, "with a view to ascertain whether I can conscientiously undertake what I so very much wish—a series of lectures at the Royal Institution. I trust I need not assure you how much I feel your kindness—and let me add that I consider the application as an act of great and unmerited condescension on the part of such managers as may have consented to it."

Probably Coleridge's anxiety about the lectures and a consequent recourse to opium explain the weeks of illness which immediately followed. On November 3, he told Cottle: "I have not been once out of house, since I saw you, and though somewhat better, am still confined." Three weeks later Coleridge left Bristol for London.

3 The Morgans (1807-8)

—Me did you soothe, when solace hoped I none!
And as on unthaw'd ice the winter sun,
Though stern the frost, though brief the genial day,
You bless my heart with many a cheerful ray.

—*S.T. Coleridge*
To Two Sisters *(Mary Morgan and Charlotte Brent)*
A Wanderer's Farewell. 1807

During his recent illness Coleridge had been affectionately tended by old Bristol friends—the Morgans. Henceforth for the next eight years they became his chief friends and protectors. The Morgan family consisted of John Morgan, a young retired solicitor and man of means, his wife Mary and her unmarried sister Charlotte Brent. The devotion of the two women to Coleridge in his illness evoked in him sincere gratitude, admiration, and praise. "Had I been a child or favourite brother," Coleridge told Dorothy Wordsworth on November 24, "I could not have received more affectionate attentions and indulgences. I never knew two pairs of human beings so alike as Mrs. Morgan and her sister Charlotte Brent and Mary and Sara (Hutchinson). I was reminded afresh of the resemblance every hour—and at times felt a self-reproach that I could not love two such amiable, pure and affectionate beings for their own sakes. But there is a time in life when the heart stops growing." Nevertheless Coleridge entered the dates of his friends birthdays in his notebook: "November 5, 1807—Miss Charlotte Brent's birthday—24; 14th June, Mrs. Morgan's (Mary Brent)—25;. . . 17 months difference."

On November 23, 1807, Coleridge arrived in London full of "grateful affection and most affectionate esteem" for the Morgans. He always particularly included Charlotte Brent, as he immediately informed them. But merely private expressions of his admiration for the two sisters was not sufficient; and *The Courier* published on December 10, Coleridge's verses entitled *To Two Sisters,* in which he paid public homage to Mary and Charlotte. Over the opening stanzas there surely broods also the spirit of Sara Hutchinson. Indeed the poem includes homage to her and to her sister Mary Wordsworth, as friends whose kindness to himself like that of Mary Morgan and Charlotte Brent, had earned his heart's devotion:

To know, to esteem, to love, and then to part
Makes up Life's tale to many a feeling heart;
Alas for some abiding-place of love,
O'er which my spirit, like the mother dove,
Might brood with warming wings! . . .

Coleridge's prevailing mood of sadness nevertheless dominates these verses. As ever in his writings of this kind, there is more about himself and his sorrows, than about those to whom he is paying homage. So he continues:

O fair! O kind!
Sisters in blood, yet each with each intwined
More close by sisterhood of heart and mind!
Me disinherited in form and face
By nature, and mishap of outward grace;
Who, soul and body, through one guiltless fault
Waste daily with the poison of sad thought,
Me did you soothe, when solace hoped I none!
And as on unthaw'd ice the winter sun,
Though stern the frost, though brief the genial day,
You bless my heart with many a cheerful ray;
For gratitude suspends the heart's despair,
Reflecting bright though cold your image there.
Nay more! its music by some sweeter strain
Makes us live o'er our happiest hours again,
Hope re-appearing dim in memory's guise—
Even thus did you call up before mine eyes
Two dear, dear Sisters, prized all price above,
Sisters, like you, with more than sisters' love;
So like you *they*, and so in *you* were seen
Their relative statures, tempers, looks and mien,
That oft, dear Ladies! you have been to me
At once a vision and reality
Sight seem'd a sort of memory, and amaze
Mingled a trouble with affection's gaze.

After this the poem drags on laboriously in merely conventional complimentary verse.

When Mrs. Coleridge and Southey saw these verses in the *Courier,* with their full title, *"To Two Sisters (Mary Morgan and Charlotte Brent) A Wanderer's Farewell,* they were not amused. Nevertheless "It is a beautiful poem" Mrs. Coleridge told Poole, "but it was, in my opinion, a most ungenerous action, the publishing of it, it abounds with gratitude to these young ladies, and bitter complaints and woeful murmurings at his own unhappy fate! Southey was sorry that he should do such an unmanly thing as publish such a poem, and I think his well-wishers must all condemn it."

The Grasmere circle were now increasingly disillusioned and disappointed as the weeks passed and the only letters with news of Coleridge were from his wife. "Coleridge has never written to us," Dorothy told Mrs. Clarkson on the 4th of November "and we have given over writing to him, for what is the use of it? We believe he has not opened one of our letters. Poor Soul! He is sadly to be pitied. I fear all resolution and strength of mind have utterly deserted him."

Stuart, always a friend to Coleridge, now allowed him to live at the office of the Courier, 348 Strand, "where there is a nice suite of rooms for me, and a quiet bedroom without expense" as he told the Morgans. De Quincey, who had come South again and followed Coleridge to London, has described Coleridge at this time in his rooms at the *Courier*. He found no such "nice suite of rooms" as Coleridge had described to the Morgans:

> In such a situation, annoyed by the sound of feet passing his chamber-door continually to the printing-rooms of this great establishment, and with no gentle ministrations of female hands to sustain his cheerfulness, naturally enough his spirits flagged; and he took more than ordinary doses of opium. I called upon him daily and pitied his forlorn condition. There was no bell in the room; which for many months answered the double purpose of bedroom and sitting-room. Consequently I often saw him, picturesquely enveloped in nightcaps, surmounted by handkerchiefs indorsed upon handkerchiefs, shouting from the attics of the *Courier* office, down three or four flights of stairs, to a certain Mrs. Brainbridge, his sole attendant, whose dwelling was in the subterranean regions of the house. There did I often see the philosopher with the most lugubrious of faces, invoking with all his might this uncouth name of Brainbridge, each syllable of which he intonated with long-drawn emphasis, in order to overpower the hostile hubbub coming downwards from the creaking press, and the roar from the Strand, which entered at all the front windows. "Mistress Brainbridge! I say, Mistress Brainbridge!" was the perpetual cry.

"My old woman," "the unlovable old woman" Coleridge called her.

In mid-December Coleridge decided to postpone his lectures until mid-January 1808 giving the illness of Davy as his reason or excuse. Near the end of the month, he left London for Bristol again to stay with the Morgans over Christmas and the New Year. On January 13, 1808, the day before his first lecture, he returned to town.

The unhappy contrast between his solitary and comfortless existence at the *Courier* office with only his old attendant Mrs. Brainbridge, intensified Coleridge's appreciation of the comfort and kindness he had enjoyed with the Morgans. In this mood, on January 22, 1808, Coleridge wrote to Mrs. Morgan a most affectionate letter. She had haunted his dreams as a "compassionate comforter therein, appearing, in short as your own dear self, most innocent and full of love." But the letter he said was not for Mary alone and he concluded with an effusion of blessings for the whole family, ending in a mournful sigh for himself: "Ah, who is there to bless S.T. Coleridge?" A week later, still longing for the companionship of the Morgans, he told John Morgan: "O would to Heaven you, and dearest Mary and Charlotte were within a few streets of me!''

As no reply had reached Samuel by February 10, Coleridge's fears of having offended the Morgans dictated another letter to them in which his uneasiness finds full expression:

> How can I have given offence? Did I write with too presuming a familiarity? I remember indeed, that once, and I fear more than once, I made myself an object of a little under-ridicule to Miss Brent from the earnest affection of my looks and manners towards her; but that was when she did not know what was at the bottom of my feelings—and that the highest and most holy remembrances of my heart and head were flashed upon the eye of the mind.

How much the companionship of the Morgans had unfitted Coleridge for his solitary existence in London when his usual ''illness'' again confined him to his room, he clearly revealed, crying: ''I have indeed no one to speak to—no gentle voice to listen to—no kind face to look at—and the heart aches to utter forth its sorrows somewhere.'' Then suddenly self-conscious he asked Mary to burn the letter. But with his emotions still inspiring him he continued at considerable length in the same strain; describing how time had weighed upon him without the Morgans' company and concluding ''O I pray you, love me! I ask no more.''

However, just as Samuel was sealing his letter, his fears lest the Morgans would not reply to him were laid to rest by the arrival of Mrs. Brainbridge with a parcel of gowns which he had asked Mary and Charlotte to make for him—evidently to be paid for—and to be presented to Sara Hutchinson and Mrs. Wordsworth from himself. Coleridge had forgotten the matter but the arrival of the parcel delighted him. ''O bless you!'' he wrote ''I am so fluttered that I cannot open it. But it will give me spirits to get up and I hope to sit up for the whole evening. . .''

On the same day, still moved by the arrival of the parcel and presumably by some letter from the Morgan sisters enclosed in the parcel, he wrote to them again calling them ''My lovely Mantuamakers.'' One of them he declared was ''a beautiful lady with a fine form, a sweet chin and mouth and bright black eyes. . .and another sweet young lady with dark meek eyes, as sweet a chin and mouth, and a general *darlingness* of tones, manners, and person.'' And he apologized for his loss of self-restraint in describing himself and his feelings in his last letter. But Samuel's wish to have the Morgans near him still remained and he now suggested to John Morgan the removal of the family to London where he would join them in some suitable lodging. Such a change from his loneliness he said would enable him to work. But behind his words and his present misery in solitude one also senses his fear that alone in *The Courier* office his opium habit must gain complete control.

Such was the physical, mental, and emotional background to Coleridge's forthcoming lectures: excitement with the Morgans, illness, opium and brandy, environment at the *Courier* office where he experienced loneliness without even peace and quiet. But worse, with all these influences there mingled a more profound emotional disturbance: extreme anger toward Mrs. Coleridge. Certainly, the angry emotions which Coleridge had discovered in himself near the close of 1807 were finding free vent throughout these earlier months of 1808 in his correspondence with his wife in Greta Hall and in his accounts of it to the Morgans.

Evidently the contrast between the comfort and attentions provided by the Morgans and what he considered the unpleasantness of his wife, was the basic cause of the quarrel he now engaged in against her. He felt outraged by what he thought was her indifference to his sufferings. Whatever letters she sent him whether sad or merry, all were bitterly and vehemently disapproved by Samuel who of course transmitted his misery to the Morgans for consolation.

That Mrs. Coleridge was not without complaint of her husband is evident in the letter she sent to Poole on December 28, 1807. Courteously implied rather than openly proclaimed, Samuel's shortcomings were not concealed. Very obviously expecting that her husband had not written after leaving Poole to thank him for his hospitality, she told Poole:

> I cannot endure to pre-suppose you never having heard anything of us, since Coleridge left your most hospitable dwelling: yet, what is more likely? However, when he at length joined us at Bristol, in such excellent health, and improved looks, I thought of days 'lang sine' and hoped, and prayed it might continue. Alas, in 3 or 4 days it was all over! He said he must go to Town *immediately* about the lectures, yet he stayed 3 weeks without another word about removing, and I durst not speak lest it should *disarrange* him.

Evidently Coleridge's improvement on arrival in Bristol had been due to Poole's control over him at Stowey and the change later was caused by opium again. Mrs. Coleridge then described how she had waited at Bristol for Coleridge's intended departure for London and the lectures, "had packed up every thing; Coleridge's things (as I thought for London) and our own," and then departed with De Quincey and the children for Greta Hall.

Coleridge's hatred of lecturing naturally affected his relations with his wife. When in Bristol before Mrs. Coleridge's departure for the North and her husband's for London, the domestic atmosphere had evidently been far from cordial. After her return to Greta Hall Coleridge's feelings towards her had not exemplified the adage that "Absence makes the heart grow fonder." Nor can Samuel's quarrel with brother George about the separation have lessened his animosity towards her. The message Coleridge had sent her in a letter to Southey in December 1807, was hardly cheering. For the next three weeks, he told her, he could send her no money beyond the Wedgwoods' annuity of £150, which he said, "is, and for the future will remain, sacred to her. . . .It has been a baddish year; but I am not disquieted."

When Mrs. Coleridge wrote in low spirits of lack of money, Coleridge bitterly complained of her to various friends. When he told her of his illness, he came to suspect that she thought him "hypochondriacal," and was much annoyed. But when as so often before, he told her he was dying—and "fearful suspicions entertained of the stone"—he told the Morgans her reply was: "from beginning to end, . . . in a strain of *dancing, frisking, high spirits* jokes—quite the letter of a gay woman writing to some female acquaintance in a house of mirth." Indeed, he cried, morally indignant and exasperated, all she had said after reading of his sufferings and impending death was in these words—neither more nor less—"Lord! how often you are ill! You must be more careful about colds."

He would keep both letters he said "and when I die, bequeath them with some other curiosities to some married man who has an amiable wife (at least a woman with a woman's Heart) to make him bless himself! Not a word respecting my tender and tearful advice to her about the children. . .not one simple expression that she was sorry that I was obliged to work and lecture while I was so ill—not one word of thanks for my earnest prayer that I might recover enough of my healthy looks, as to be able this spring to assure her an additional £1.000—O shocking! it is too clear, that she is glad that her children are about to be fatherless." Let us hope that the Morgans applied sufficient balm to Samuel's deeply wounded feelings.

The next *casus belli* was Derwent. His eyes needed attention for some slight trouble which soon passed. At Keswick he was being treated by a local doctor or chemist with Mrs. Coleridge's approval. Coleridge on hearing of this and ever anxious to play the physician, became most excited; the drops being given to Derwent at Keswick were most dangerous, "poison" he said, and if not given with the greatest care "would make his eyeballs start and shrink up in their socket." So Mrs. Coleridge must immediately send Derwent to the Morgans at Bristol, to consult a Dr. King there. Dr. King feared for Derwent's eyesight under the present treatment. But Mrs. Coleridge refused to part with Derwent, and Coleridge's anger against her greatly increased. "As to his being at Mr. Morgan's," she replied, "they are estimable people no doubt—but it is quite out of the question." This outrageous answer Coleridge repeated verbatim to the Morgans, exclaiming:

These are her very words. And this is her child!. . . Are they then not *my* children too? I have indeed no other proof, and can have none than their faces and their hearts; but I have to maintain them, to brood over them, to hope and fear and pray and weep for them. Whether or no they be my children, I am quite certain that I am *their* father. Did this woman bring me a fortune? or give me rank? or procure me introductions and interest? or am I now maintained in idleness by her money? O that I had the heart to do what Justice and Wisdom would dictate—and bring her to her senses! Henceforward I will trouble you no more with this hateful subject. But only think just enough of it, not to remain too much surprised that my spirit was so weighed down by her unfeelingness, her seeming pleasure at the anticipation of my being speedily got quit of—me, who in the worst of times had ever felt and expressed as much joy in her health, as my wife, and mother of my children, as if I had been married to you, or Charlotte, or Mrs. Wordsworth or Sara Hutchinson—I say, wonder not that I was overset—that I seemed to look round a wilderness, to hear in the distance the yell and roar of fierce animals, and to see no one that would give me even the help of comfort! Neither wonder nor be wounded, if in this transient infirmity of soul I gave way in my agony, and *causelessly* and almost *unknowing what I did,* cried out from on my *Cross,* Eli, Eli lama sabachthani! My Friends! my Sisters! why have you forsaken me! For tho' I should be stung to death, yet such is my nature, that let me die when I will, love will be uppermost—and if there be grief or disquietude, it will be the grief and disquietude of love.

Nevertheless, despite his promise to the Morgans not to complain to them of his wife again, his bitterness found yet stronger expression, significantly contrasted with his admiration for Charlotte. She however must have shown some resentment at his complaints for he now wrote apologetically to the Morgans:

I entreat dear Miss Brent to think of what I wrote as the mere *lightheadedness* of a diseased body and a heart sore stricken. . . .I love her most dearly! O had I health and youth, and were what I once was—but I played the fool, and cut the throat of my Happiness, of my genius, of my utility, in compliment to the mere phantom of overstrained Honour! O Southey! Southey! an unthinking man were you—and are—and will be.

Although a consolatory letter came from Morgan, when Coleridge replied on February 10 his letter contained another outburst against his wife. "My sleep was oversome" he wrote, "my nature had received a sting—my children and their mother haunted me in a hundred horrid forms—and the whole day I remained in a high fever." He was too unwell he said: "I must I fear, again put off a lecture." He must go into the country he declared, "in order to recompose my shocked, and shattered spirits. O friend!" he continued to Morgan, "*you* cannot comprehend how the poison works—to know, that an ungrateful woman has infused dislike of me into the mind of my own child, the first-born and darling of my hopes."

A fortnight later writing to his wife, Coleridge made an amende honorable. He had never known he said "any woman for whom I had an equal personal fondness—that till the very latest period, when my health and spirits rendered me dead to everything, I had a pride in you, and I never saw you at the top of our Hill, when I returned from a walk, without a sort of pleasurable feeling of sight, which woe be the wretch! who confounds with vulgar feelings, and which is some little akin to the delight in a beautiful flower joined with the consciousness! And it is in *my* garden. . . ."

Amidst these miseries Coleridge's surrender to opium played a large part. Realizing his failure to cure himself he now decided to return to Bristol and place himself under the care of Dr. Beddoes.* In this mood he wrote to the

---

*Coleridge was not the only patient of Dr. Thomas Beddoes, for they included the following opium addicts: Thomas De Quincey, Charles Lloyd, and Tom Wedgwood. V. *Opium and the Romantic Imagination* by Alethea Hayter (London, 1968) p. 27.

Morgans on February 17 as follows: "It is my wish and the Dictate of my reason to come to you, and instantly to put myself under Dr. Beddoes, and to open to him the whole of my case—But yet—forgive me, dear dear Friends! but yet I cannot help again and again questioning myself, what *right* I have to make your house my Hospital—how I am justified in bringing Sickness and Sorrow, and all the disgusts and all the troublesomeness of Disease, into your quiet Dwelling. Ah! whither else can I go?—to Keswick? the *sight* of that woman would destroy me. To Grasmere?—They are still in their cottage, one of their rooms is proved untenantable from damp—and they have not room scarcely for a cat—"

4   The Lecturer (1808)

"I tremble at the Lecture day."
—*S.T. Coleridge to Mrs. Morgan, Feb. 10, 1808*

Almost immediately after Coleridge's arrival in England, Davy, to assist the homeless wanderer had arranged with the authorities of the Royal Institution for Coleridge to give a course of lectures. To this Coleridge had somewhat reluctantly agreed. In the first letter to his wife since his arrival he told her, on September 16, 1806, that he was invited to give these lectures: an invitation "which I am much disposed to accept, both for the money and reputation." At this time as he told Mrs. Coleridge, his subject was to be "The Principles common to all the Fine Arts."

The news quickly spread to Dove Cottage where Dorothy heard it with alarm lest it entail the waste if not the destruction of his "genius." Lecturing she had told Lady Beaumont in late September 1806, would tempt Coleridge "to lower himself to his hearers," and also prevent his producing "some great work in prose or verse." Such a work the anxious Dorothy believed, "would turn his thoughts away from his own unhappy lot."

Shortly afterwards, on October 3, 1806, Coleridge reported to his wife his plans for lecturing at the Royal Institution and also at the London Institution. Every year he would give lectures and would also produce a new book. . . .This would bring him he expected, a respectable annuity of perhaps £400 a year." His intention in October 1806 he had told Mrs. Coleridge, was to lecture on the Fine Arts for which he was to receive £120. But when the lectures were actually given in 1808, the subject had been changed to the "Principles of Poetry." He also hoped for a lectureship at the London Institution which would be more important than the lectures—but this did not happen.

On the day of Coleridge's arrival in London from Bristol, January 13, 1808, to begin his course of lectures at the Royal Institution the next day, he attended a lecture given there by his friend Thomas Dibdin. Thence, at the invitation of another friend, he proceeded to "A sort of Glee or Catch Club" as he described it. This "much delighted" him as all present not only "appeared marvellously delighted" with their guest but even conferred upon him the right of free entry into "all the musical entertainments of the town." Reporting these doings to the Morgans he concluded "My own lecture commences tomorrow, till that is over I can think of nothing else."

So on January 15 Coleridge gave his first lecture, probably on Shakespeare and Poetry. It "made an impression far beyond its worth or my expectation," he said. But immediately afterward he felt so unwell that he returned to his solitary room at *The Courier* and went straight to bed. There he remained bedridden until February 5, when he reappeared and gave his second lecture which he told Southey, "I could scarcely read through. The animated passages, few as they were, I was obliged to omit—and scarcely took my eyes off the paper. As I went thither from my bed so I returned thence to my bed—and have never quitted it except for an hour or two, sometimes a little longer, sometimes less, at night to have the bed made." And he told his friends—as often—that he knew he was dying.

Such was Samuel's state on February 9. The next day he sent a similar account of himself to the Morgans, adding that if he did not immediately recover, he "must give up the lectures, and go somewhere or other. Whither, God knows, the Shelterer of the shelterless!" And he went on to inform them that the cause was "a slight cold" due to the strings of his undershirt being worn out and to having lost three of his six undershirts—"O it is a sad thing to be at once ill and friendless. . .Now I tremble at the lecture day."

De Quincey, fascinated by Coleridge and attending his lectures, was at Dorothy's request to send her reports of them. De Quincey was Coleridge's only caller. In his daily visits to *The Courier* bedroom he saw in this cheerless environment and in opium the basic cause of Coleridge's illness and depression. "Thus unhappily situated," said De Quincey,

he sank more than ever under the dominion of opium; so that at two o'clock, when he should have been in attendance at the Royal Institution, he was too often unable to rise from bed. Then came dismissal of audience after audience, with pleas of illness; and on many of his lecture days I have seen all Albemarle Street closed by a "lock" of carriages, filled with women of distinction, until the servants of the Institution, or their own footmen, advanced to the carriage doors with the intelligence that Mr. Coleridge had been suddenly taken ill.

On February 26 Lamb reported to his friend Manning: "Coleridge had delivered two lectures at the Royal Institution; two more were attended but he did not come. It is thought he has gone sick upon them. He a'n't well, that's certain. Wordsworth is coming to see him. He sits up in a two pair of stairs room at *The Courier* office, and receives visitors on his close-stool." Like others, Lamb knew the part that opium was playing in these illnesses. So too did anxious Dorothy Wordsworth, now telling Mrs. Clarkson: "I have no doubt that he continues the practice of taking opiates as much as ever," and she feared "it will never be otherwise." Coleridge had ceased to write to the Wordsworths and whatever gleanings from other sources Dorothy could obtain she passed on to Coleridge's devotees, Lady Beaumont and Mrs. Clarkson.

Davy was now as concerned about Coleridge as Samuel's other friends were. "Coleridge," he wrote, after disappointing his audience twice from illness, is announced to lecture again this week. He has suffered greatly from excessive sensibility, the disease of genius. His mind is a wilderness, in which the cedar and the oak, which might aspire to the skies, are stunted in their growth by underwood, thorns, briars and parasitical plants. With the most exalted genius, enlarged views, sensitive heart, and enlightened mind, he will be the victim of want of order, precision and regularity. I cannot think of him without experiencing the mingled feelings of admiration, regard, and pity.

At the end of February Wordsworth, fearing Coleridge was dying—while Dorothy at Dove Cottage anxiously awaited news—set off for London to save him. "Wordsworth, the great poet, is coming to town," Lamb told Manning and with a satirical touch at Wordsworth's growing fame and self-importance: "he is to have apartments in the Mansion House. He says he does not see much difficulty in writing like Shakespeare, if he had a mind to try it. It is clear, then, nothing is wanting but the mind. Even Coleridge a little checked at this hardihood of assertion." During her brother's absence Dorothy found some consolation in remembering that poor Coleridge "has often appeared to be dying and has all at once recovered health and spirits."

Wordsworth on arrival in London found less need for his help than he had anticipated. He thought Coleridge's illnesses were only such as Coleridge himself could cure or prevent—doubtless another allusion to opium and brandy. Nor was Wordsworth pleased at being unable to gain access to his friend until 4 P.M. in the afternoons. He and Coleridge went one day to see the Angerstein collection of pictures (which became the nucleus of the National Gallery); and although Wordsworth had little confidence in his own pictorial knowledge and taste—and Coleridge seems to have been no better—a Michaelangelo and a Rembrandt specially pleased Wordsworth, who duly reported the occasion to Sir George Beaumont. At Longman's they "dined with some curious fishes," as Wordsworth described the occasion to Sir Walter Scott. It was "upon the whole but a dull business, saving that we had some good haranguing, talk I cannot call it, from Coleridge."

Wordsworth broke his stay in London by two short visits to friends: the Clarksons at Bury and Sir George Beaumont's mother at Dunmow. He also attended two of Coleridge's lectures; the first was apparently Coleridge's third given on March 30, and the next on April 1. They "seemed to give great satisfaction" Wordsworth told Sir George, speaking somewhat impersonally; but Coleridge was "not in spirits, and suffered much during the course of the week both in body and mind." When Wordsworth now heard that Sara Hutchinson had broken a blood vessel, he abandoned a projected visit to Oxford and returned at once to the North.

On hearing of Sara's illness, Coleridge was much upset. As in the case of Derwent, the physician in Coleridge became dominant; he consulted three doctors about Sara he told the Morgans, and as before found that his selection of remedies exactly coincided with medical opinion. That poor Sara's "accident" was serious, he never doubted; nor did he doubt "that without the utmost care joined to the most favourable circumstances, comprisable in four articles—repose of body—tranquillity of mind—regular and gentle daily horse-exercise—and the preclusion of febrile excitement by unceasing watchfulness to keep the body open—by prepared kalimagnesia vitrioluta—or aromatic powder—she would vanish away from us, like a blessed dream." Fortunately—whether due to Samuel's prescription or not—Sara Hutchinson soon recovered.

Southey too was then in London and met both Wordsworth and Coleridge. But London smoke as usual affected Southey's health and he was confined for a time by a cold. Coleridge particularly wanted to see Southey "as he offered to recite my lectures for me at the Royal Institution," he told Mrs. Clarkson on March 9. "A little wounded at your not contriving to pass an evening with me," Coleridge told Southey a fortnight later.

Although throughout April Coleridge's lectures continued with more regularity, the beginning of the month brought Samuel an emotional shock when Mary Evans, now Mrs. Todd, suddenly appeared among his audience, and came to speak to him. Coleridge's evident ill-health affected Mary who had been drawn to the lecture room, not by the subject to be discussed, but by the fact that Coleridge was advertised as the lecturer. This unexpected encounter confused Coleridge and Mary immediately seized the opportunity to send Samuel an apology combined with an invitation to visit her and her husband. "I felt so great a desire to once more behold an old and esteemed friend," she wrote, "that I could not resist the opportunity that presented itself." And she expressed her concern at Coleridge's changed appearance. To have approached Coleridge at such a time she said, "was the effect of a momentary impulse". . ."an error of judgement—but not intended to give pain. Your sincere friend," she concluded, "Mary Todd."

Mary's letter drew from Coleridge a somewhat formal and distant reply. "Dear Madam," he began: "undoubtedly the first moment of the meeting was an awful one to me. The *second* of time previous to my full recognition of you, the Mary Evans of 14 years ago, flashed across my eyes with a truth and vividness as great as its rapidity. But the confusion of mind occasioned by this sort of *double* presence was amply and more than balanced by the after-pleasure and satisfaction. Truly happy does it make me to have seen you once more and seen you well, prosperous and cheerful—all that your goodness gives you a title to. I shall, as soon as I am at liberty, call on you and Mr. Todd, and believe me to be with most sincere regard and never extinguished esteem, Your friend, S.T. Coleridge." During the fourteen years of Mary Evans' absence "Brother Coly" had evidently died. There was little enough in the note to please an ageing woman with the memory of an early lover.

Mary's marriage, as Samuel doubtless discovered when he called on her ten days later, had not been happy despite the affluence of Mr. Todd. "I saw yesterday" Samuel told Stuart on the morrow of his visit, "such a counterpart of the very worst parts of my own fate, in an aggravated form, in the fate of the being who was my first attachment, and who with her family gave me the first idea of a *home,* and inspired my best and most permanent feelings."*

Nor was the unhappiness of Mary Evans the sole cause of Coleridge's distress. On the very day of his visit to Mary he had received news of more illness at Dove Cottage and also that Mrs. Morgan was in weak health. Hence, as he now told Stuart, he had "lain awake weeping for the greater part of the night." When Coleridge adds "I had been forced all yesterday evening to exert false looks and false spirits toward one whom I perceived worthy of absolute abhorrence," we may safely assume that he refers to Mr. Todd.

So Mary again passed out of Coleridge's life. Three years later when Mr. Todd had lost his fortune, Mary's home was broken up and her son placed under the care of her maternal uncle.

Others besides De Quincey observed the large proportion of fashionable ladies at Coleridge's lectures—an element that Coleridge ever appreciated. One of them left a convincing account of his manner on one occasion when, as she wrote, "the poet had either forgotten to write, or left what he had written at home. His locks were trimmed, and a conscious importance gleamed in his eloquent eyes as he turned them towards the fair and noble heads which bent down to receive his apology. . .I began to think as Coleridge went on, that the lecture had been left at home purpose; he was *so* eloquent—there was such a combination of wit and poetry in his similes—such fancy, such a finish in his illustrations; yet, as we walked home after the lecture, I remember that we could not call to mind any real instruction, distinct impression, or new fact imparted to us by the great theorist. It was all fancy, flourish, sentiment, that we had heard."

For many Coleridge's lectures and conversations were fairy gold that disappeared if examined. Many who came were more interested in Coleridge the man than in his subject. These afternoon lectures indeed were more social than serious occasions. Few if any of his hearers were professional scholars learned in the matter of Coleridge's course.

Among Coleridge's scattered lectures-notes there is an ornate and involved apology to his audience for what he felt had been a feeble performance at his last lecture, which must have been that of February 5. He had felt he said "exceeding depression this morning previous to my appearance before you, accompanied with a painful sense of self-dissatisfaction bordering on self-reproach. I could not but be conscious," he continued, "to how severe a trial I had put your patience and candour in my last lecture; and though it was through severe and still lingering bodily indisposition that my faculties had

---

*Three years before this meeting with Mary, Coleridge in Malta, in January 1805 had committed poignant memories of Mary Evans to his notebook. Examining his permanent anxiety state—or as he put it, "the fact that I have always been preyed on by some dread," he instanced his love for Mary: "a state of struggling with madness from an incapability of hoping that I should be able to marry Mary Evans (and this strange passion of fervent though wholly imaginative and imaginary love uncombinable by my utmost efforts with any regular hope, possibly from deficence of bodily feeling, of tactual ideas connected with the image-) had all the effects of direct fear, and I have lain for hours together awake at night groaning and praying."

been too confused. . .and that the most interesting parts of what I had selected I found myself too weak to recite aloud. . .yet I could not drive away the despondence of self-condemnation; and when, during the time I have now been addressing you, my mind gradually regained its buoyancy, I felt an increasing impulse, which I have thus yielded to, to attempt to remove from your feelings the disappointment from the past by hopes of something less unworthy of your attention in my future lectures."*

Throughout April the course seems to have continued with more regularity and as May dawned Coleridge turned from Shakespeare to Milton. The few fragments of lecture notes that survive do not support his expressed intention of writing out at least half the course beforehand. Unfortunately Milton's *Tractate of Education,* which as one biographer justifiably declared "cannot be regarded as a valuable contribution to educational theory," led Coleridge to give on May 3 a gratuitous double lecture of two-and-a-quarter hours on Educational Methods. This was a veritable hornet's nest at the time as the followers of two rival educationalists, a Dr. Bell and a Mr. Lancaster were at daggers drawn on the subject.

Bell, a clergyman supported by the church, advocated mutual discussion among schoolboys as the best method. Lancaster, a Quaker who admitted some "useful hints" from Bell, strongly denied accusations of plagiarism made by Bell's enthusiasts. Coleridge was also a great admirer of Bell and determined to grind the wicked Lancaster's face in the dust. After reading a passage from Lancaster's book on education while lecturing, Coleridge denounced his schools, which he compared to prisons or convict stations, and flung the book to the ground with a theatrical gesture of disgust. But Lancaster had his enthusiasts who "not two hours before my lecture"—as the indignant Coleridge told Bell, appeared at Coleridge's door with Lancaster himself intent upon an introduction which Coleridge refused, thinking it "very improper that I should go to an extemporaneous lecture of two hours, perhaps fretted and agitated"—and he spoke of "threats" against himself, which probably meant only the threat of another Lancastrian educational pamphlet.

The great educational lecture of two-and-a-quarter hours was delivered on May 3 to an excited and expectant audience. In form it apparently resembled the others in wide and vague generalizations without concrete examples. He praised "love" as the greatest educational medium while at the same time—despite Samuel's still Boyer-haunted dreams—he exalted corporal punishment for the "Spartan fortitude it excited." Religious training was

---

*"That he did actually spend a considerable amount of time and energy in preparation is proved by the mass of fragments and notes now in print. It has been established that he wrote a number of complete original lectures, pieced others together from notes and marginalia, and sometimes offered long translations from German sources. At other times, however, he seems to have improvised from the sketchy jottings in his commonplace books, and frequently to have arrived at the hall empty-handed, with less idea of the subject than his audience, who had at least looked at the announcement."

given importance in education and the Church respected. It is doubtful how many clergymen would have approved his attitude as noted by one intelligent hearer: "The veneration for the Supreme Being, sense of mysteriou existence not to be profaned by the intrusion of clear notions."

Speculation indeed was now rife as to Coleridge's religious convictions. His former pantheism was said to have been replaced according to some who considered him "the philosopher of the High Church Party" by belief in dogmatic christianity. Among others, the rumor spread that Coleridge had turned Methodist. This so disgusted Lady Holland that she wrote in her journal of that year, 1808: "His nature is radically bad, he hates and envies all that are good and celebrated and to gratify that spleen he has given into Methodism. . . ." This was the Lady Holland whom Byron was to describe a few months later in *English Bards and Scotch Reviewers* as the prudish moral censor of her husband's writings.

The recorder of this and other of Coleridge's lectures was a friend of Mrs. Clarkson, Henry Crabb Robinson, who through her written introduction received a note and free tickets from Coleridge, though apparently they did not meet in person until a year or two later. Robinson, educated in Germany, and now foreign editor of the *Times,* became an admiring though not uncritical friend of Coleridge in future years. This educational lecture Robinson described in a letter to Mrs. Clarkson as "most excellent, delivered with great animation and *extorting* praise from those whose prejudices he was mercilessly attacking. And he kept his audience on the rack of pleasure and offence two whole hours and ten minutes, and few went away during the lecture." But Robinson privately objected to Coleridge's silly dismissal of Voltaire as a "paltry scribbler." Nor can Robinson have been impressed by Coleridge's repetition of the simile of the neglected garden of weeds as an answer to those who opposed early religious teaching—an argument he had used against Thelwall at Stowey. Robinson found Coleridge "not very methodical"—and the later part of the lecture that dealt with the education of the poor "very useful but very trite." "In conclusion," wrote Robinson, he eulogized Dr. Bell's plan of education and concluded with a severe attack upon Lancaster for having stolen from Dr. Bell all that is good in his plans." Indeed Bell whose attitude seems to have been that of a gentleman, mildly attempted to restrain the bellicose enthusiasm of Coleridge.

The general reaction in fact, was less favorable than Coleridge had anticipated. "His attack on Lancaster" Robinson reported, "has given great offence. This was to be expected." The next day May 4 when the normal lectures were resumed one auditor, Edward Jerningham, who had approved the education lecture, thought Coleridge "appeared much dejected; his voice assumed a more plaintive sound while he told us that his last had given great offence in speaking the truth. He could hardly at times refrain from tears; long pauses intervened—and he seemed as if he did not well know how to proceed." After the lecture Jerningham spoke to Coleridge who told him that some of the

Committee of the Royal Institution were vexed with him, and one had attacked him at some social gathering and was so abusive that Coleridge had been forced to leave the room. Indeed the Committee of the Royal Institution at their next annual meeting censured Coleridge for introducing personal abuse into a public lecture.

Two days later on May 6, Coleridge lectured on Milton and one observer there noticed his manner of opening the lecture: "When Coleridge came into the box there were several books lying. He opened two or three of them silently and shut them again after a short inspection. He then paused, and leaned his head on his hand, and at last said, he had been thinking for a word to express the distinct character of Milton as a poet, but not finding one that would express it, he should make one, *ideality*. He spoke extempore." Robinson who also attended this lecture was disappointed. "The least interesting lecture I have heard," was his verdict. "The word *poetry* was not used till the lecture was two-thirds over, nor Milton's name till ten minutes before the close."

Even now Coleridge sometimes failed to appear. In mid-May he "begged a week's holiday" wrote Robinson, in order to publish his lecture on Education—which never was published. Another time an expectant audience—thrilled by the row about Bell and Lancaster—arrived at the lecture room only to be told by an official that their lecturer had fallen and hurt his head when stepping out of a boat. According to Jerningham, three weeks passed after this accident before Coleridge reappeared. On another occasion, looking "sullen" he explained that on his way to the lecture his pocketbook of lecture notes had been stolen. This, said Jerningham, "was not indulgently received, and he went through his lecture heavily, and without advancing anything that was spirited and animated."

De Quincey too observed the growing impatience of the audience with Coleridge's continual absences and pleas of illness. These, he said,

> which at first had been received with expressions of concern, repeated too often, began to rouse disgust. Many in anger, and some in real uncertainty whether it would not be trouble thrown away, ceased to attend. And we that were more constant, [De Quincey continued,] too often found reason to be disappointed with the quality of his lecture. His appearance was generally that of a person struggling with pain and overmastering illness. His lips were baked with feverish heat, and often black in colour: and, in spite of the water, which he continued drinking through the whole course of his lecture, he often seemed to labour under an almost paralytic inability to raise the upper jaw from the lower. Inevitably, [said De Quincey,] his lectures, being extempore and so composed in this state, reflected his own feebleness and exhaustion.

In this depression he felt "continual disgust from looking back upon his own ill-success; for assuredly, he never once recovered that free and eloquent movement of thought which he could command at any time in a private company. Such self-disgust De Quincey once wrote, elsewhere and speaking solely of personal experience, was one result of addiction to opium.

De Quincey also found Coleridge's illustrative quotations "haphazard" and ineffective:

> as injudicious and as inappropriate as they were ill delivered; for among Coleridge's accomplishments, good reading was not one; he had neither voice (so at least *I* thought) nor management of voice. . . .However, this defect chiefly concerned the immediate impression; the most afflicting to a friend of Coleridge's was the entire absence of his own peculiar and majestic intellect; no heart, no soul, was in anything he said; no strength of feeling in recalling universal truths; no power of originality or compass of moral relations.

This is not the place nor is the material adequate for any independent detailed appraisal of the content and form of these lectures. But a few notes upon which Coleridge almost certainly drew and the comments and criticisms of Robinson, Jerningham, and De Quincey are something more than candles in the dusk.

These lectures, like *The Friend* later, fell between the two stools of academicism and casualness—the latter by no means always the inferior portion. "Coleridge's digressions," wrote Robinson, "are not the worst part of his lectures; or rather, he is always digressing." Lack of method, of direction, of lucidity and clarity, a tendency to wander, reveal the amateurishness of the course. "My opinion as to the Lecturer," wrote Jerningham after attending the lectures on Shakespeare and Milton, "is that he possesses a great reach of mind; that he is a wild Enthusiast respecting the objects of his Eulogium; that he is sometimes very eloquent, sometimes paradoxical, sometimes absurd. His voice has something in it particularly plaintive and interesting. His person is short, thick, his countenance not inspirited with any animation." Coleridge's solemn promise to write his lectures first was apparently seldom fulfilled. Jerningham indeed tells us "He spoke without any assistance from a manuscript, and therefore said several things suddenly, struck off from the anvil, some of which were entitled to high applause, and others incurred mental disapprobation. He too often wove himself into the texture of his lecture."

Although in writing of Pitt in the *Courier* Coleridge had condemned his use of "general phrases unenforced by one *single image,* one single fact. . . ." Coleridge himself in his lectures continually made enormous generalizations apparently unillumined by definite examples. Very frequently vague dramatic impressions appear. It is thus when after discussing Milton's definition of poetry as "simple, sensuous, and passionate," he cries: "How awful is the power of words! Fearful often in their consequences when merely felt, not understood, but most awful when both felt and understood."

From such intensely personal responses Coleridge at other times reacts into the most abstract, sometimes the most metaphysical, analysis. Thus his definitions occasionally become for his audience "ignotum per ignotius," as with the conclusion of three pages defining taste: "Taste then may be defined—a distinct perception of any arrangement conceived as external to us, co-existent with some degree of dislike or complacency conceived as resulting from that arrangement, and this immediately, without any prospect of consequences, though this is indeed implied in the word 'co-existent.' " It reminds us of Robinson's remark in a letter to Mrs. Clarkson on May 15—"I came in late one day and found him in the midst of a deduction of the origin of the Fine Arts from the necessities of our being, which a friend who accompanied me could make neither head nor tail of, because he had not studied German metaphysics. . . .These are metaphysics enow for the present. . . ."

De Quincey, although an enthusiastic disciple of Coleridge, summarily evaluated the lectures on their conclusion: "For this series (twelve or sixteen, I think) he received a sum of one hundred guineas. And considering the slightness of the pains which he bestowed upon them, he was well remunerated. I fear that they did not increase his reputation; for never did any man treat his audience with less respect, or his task with less careful attention."

Coleridge meanwhile became disgusted with the Royal Institution's methods of payment as well as with the amount itself. "My lectures will be profitable" he had told Dorothy on November 24, 1807, but now in the event his discontent found expression to both Stuart and Sotheby. In February 1808 Coleridge had requested a large advance payment for his lectures and had received only £40 sent him by a servant with a merely verbal message. It was indeed he told Stuart on April 18, "for the travelling expenses of myself and family." This advance payment he felt had been made without sufficient care for his dignity; and therefore he would (but did not) return all the fees from the Institution to show his disgust. Consequently he required an additional loan of £100 from Stuart. Nevertheless, Samuel was not unmindful of his debts to Stuart. "Few things oppress my conscience so much" he told him, "as my repeated nonperformance of what I had engaged, and God knows! both meant and expected to have done for you. . . ." However, Coleridge was not unduly disturbed, finding a happy compensation for his unwritten articles and debts in the thought that if Stuart were like himself, the happiness he must feel in such exercise of his own generosity and in Samuel's love for him were better for Stuart than any mere repayment.

Despite the delicacy of Coleridge's feelings in this matter he nevertheless felt that further explanation was necessary as this new borrowing from Stuart was due to Samuel's (imaginary) return of his fees to the Royal Institution.

Not immoral pride. . .he wrote, I have less pride than most men I have known; but I owe it to my sweet children and to my friends, not to suffer myself to be treated ignominiously; or to be regarded as an hireling. . . .But to be insulted by people, to whom I had been under no obligation, *for* whom you in reality (which is *I* to them) had been paying, and to be treated as a shoemaker—or even worse—namely, with the idea—"We must not pay him all beforehand, or he may give us the slip"—as if I were a Sharper, supposing my powers to continue—or a Being without friends interested in my honour, supposing sudden death or incapacitating sickness—all this is rather too bad.

The borrowed money Coleridge now said he required to pay the premium for the coming year's insurance which he wished to increase by £1000. Stuart gave Samuel the £100 and Coleridge promised to order the Committees of the Royal Institution when the time for further payments arrived to send them to Stuart as part settlement of his debts. A year later in mid-April 1809, Coleridge kept his promise and sent Stuart £60 from the Royal Institution—but it was for Stuart to spend in paying expenses of *The Friend* which Stuart, obedient as usual, dutifully did.

Besides Stuart there was Sotheby, also touchable at need. So on April 28 Coleridge wrote to him: "Dear Sir, I esteem you; and am therefore desirous of your esteem. Nor have I ever ceased to feel an interest in your true fame." Then followed compliments on Sotheby's poems and next: "I said I was anxious for your esteem; but my thoughts are like Surinam toads—as they crawl on, little toads vegetate out from back and side, grow quickly, and draw off the attention from the Mother toad." Then came Coleridge's complaint, as to Stuart, of the rudeness of the Institution's Committee to himself. But for Sotheby the £40 mentioned to Stuart, as prepaid to him by the Committe (and so recorded by the Royal Institution) had shrunk to "£20."

I had told Mr. Barnard (of the R.I.) that whatever they meant to give me (about £90 or £100 remains of what he promised), it would be highly convenient to me at the present time—& (O fool!) assigned my family motives—they *sent* a servant with £20—and a verbal *message*. What am I to deduce? That if PAYED beforehand, I should not do my duty afterwards with such *briskness*? Gracious Heaven! and if their hearts did not dictate the contrary as to my motives, yet as men of the world would not a 5 minutes' calculation have shown them, that taking in my travelling expenses, & my necessary expenses in town, wholly on account of these lectures, compared with my cost supposing me at home or at—that too dear, dear home—at Wordsworth's, I must necessarily be out of pocket, with the £130 or £40? But sickness or death might prevent me from giving the whole course. Am I then so friendless, he cried, so unhonoured in the world, that there is no one Being who would step forward, and repay what was to be repaid, and save my Honour?- Wordsworth, his Wife, his Sister, his Wife's Sister, yea, his very Children, would all consent to live on bread and water for a year rather than suffer my name to have such a stain on it. Besides I was to have had an equal sum the former year for half the number of lectures. . . .If my paper had permitted, I would have explained to you the justifying circumstances, which suddenly drew back the £50, which I borrowed from you, and was on the point of paying—it shall be sent before I quit town.

On May 21 Coleridge in a letter to Wordsworth describes his unhappy state in the heat and bustle of these disgusting lectures, for which I received whole hods of plaster of Paris—flatteries about as pleasant to me as rancid large Spanish olives—these on the one side—and permanent hatred, and the most cruel public insults on the other—and all this to cost me at least sixty £, exclusive of lodgings, for which I pay either by obligation or by past services or both." [Coleridge also says he is to give a lecture on Wordsworth's] "system and composition, which will be, God willing! on Friday *after* next—as my first lecture on Modern Poetry is to be on *next* Tuesday.

However, God was evidently not willing, for neither lecture was given.

At last in mid-June Coleridge's weariness of lecturing and his annoyance with the Royal Institution reached its climax in a note of resignation which the long-suffering Committee must have been relieved to receive.

Painful as it is to me almost to anguish, [he wrote,] yet I find my health in such a state as to make it almost death to me to give any further lectures, I beg that you would acquaint the managers that instead of expecting any remuneration, I shall, as soon as I can, repay the sum I have received. I am indeed more likely to repay it by my executors than myself. If I could quit my bedroom, I would have hazarded every thing rather than not have come, but I have such violent fits of sickness and diarrhoea that it is *literally* impossible. S.T. Coleridge

Coleridge of course did not repay the Royal Institution the £40. Nor did he ever again lecture there. Whether this was due to Coleridge or to the Committee is a nice point that cannot now be determined. But however it was, the separation must have been mutually satisfactory.

With the advent of May and the end of the lectures approaching Coleridge, expecting to meet his wife in the North that summer, continued to extend the olive branch he had offered her two months before. "I have," he wrote, "been making some hitherto baffled attempts to leave you a complete independence—for—strange as it may seem, inoffensive a being as I am—I have many enemies—from what cause, but envy, God only knows. "Of course" he added, "when I come into the country, I come to Keswick."

To show his tremendous exertions on her behalf Coleridge continued with a long list of his recent engagements which included a reply to a letter from the Duke of Sussex, much correspondence, interrupted by numerous admirers and a complimentary dinner given by another. The next day he dined with the Bishop of Durham; the day following, after lecturing on education for two-and-one-quarter hours, he dined with the *Whig Club,* which he mistook for the *Literary Fund,* which had invited him to dine with them. On Wednesday after his lecture he went "to dine with the famous Rout-giving over-rich Mr. and Mrs. Thompson in Portman Square." There another guest insulted him because of his lecture on education for which the Thompsons "in agonies" sent him a letter of regret. Nor was this all. He was now "preparing tomorrow's lecture" he told Mrs. Coleridge, and besides was writing to the man—a knight—who had insulted him at the dinner. There were also other letters to write including replies to dinner invitations from Sotheby, Sir George Beaumont, and from the daughter of the Dean of Winchester. So ended this sociable week with Coleridge busily "preparing for the Press the lecture on education, in order to withstand the bullies of Lancaster's faction." "They," he said, "insult me in the streets." Now, my dear!" he addressed his wife, "I leave you to judge whether I *can* do more than I do—having besides all this to prepare William's poem for the Press" [*The White Doe of Rylstone*]. "I shall put a full stop to all this in a few days."

Upon the conclusion of the lectures—which were never in fact concluded—Coleridge went to stay with his friends the Clarksons at Bury St. Edmunds. There it would seem the devoted Mrs. Clarkson helped to restrain his indulgence in opium. Lamb writing to George Dyer on July 5, could not of course forbear punning over the present address: "Coleridge is not so bad as your fears have represented him; it is true that he is Bury'd, altho' he is not dead: to understand this quibble, you must know that he is at Bury St. Edmunds, relaxing, after the fatigues of lecturing and Londonizing."

On September 1, 1808, Coleridge arrived at the Wordsworths' new home in Grasmere—Allan Bank—where he remained until February of the new year, 1809.

5 Allan Bank (1808-9)

We are a nice round family you may think and when Coleridge's boys are here on a Saturday and Sunday a pretty noisy one—Even now I hear Coleridge making racket enough for twenty with Sissy (Dora Wordsworth) below. He does tease her in such a way for she cannot be too naughty for his taste; he calls her "beautiful Cat of the Mountains" and she is more like a cat with him than anything else. The moment he appears she puts on her airs.
—Sara Hutchinson to Mary Monkhouse, November 30, 1808

Wordsworth had arrived in London in February 1808 to help Coleridge and bring him back to Dove Cottage. Certainly the time was well chosen. To De Quincey on February 2, Coleridge wrote: "I have neither written to or heard from Grasmere for a long time. Should you have occasion to write, you will remember me to them, and that I hope to write soon. I have had to begin such a volume of letters to them dolefully, that I myself feel an insupportable disgust by anticipative sympathy, that I shrink away like a cowed dog from the task of adding to the number—and having nothing of joy to communicate to them, I would rather that they should hear of the contrary from others than from myself. That there is such a man in the world, as Wordsworth, and that such a man enjoys such a family, makes both Death and my inefficient Life a less grievous thought to me."

Ten days later he told the Morgans, "My mind had yearned only for those at Grasmere, and the society of *your* affectionate fireside." On March 9, when Coleridge was in London he told Mrs. Clarkson: "He is a comforter. God bless him and *his*! His friendship and that of his sister Dorothy are the only eminent events or *passages* of my life, (among those wherein my *happiness* has been involved) in which I have not been cruelly deceived or deluded taking however a full share of the blame to myself."

Wordsworth as we have seen, on hearing of Sara Hutchinson's illness suddenly returned home on April 3. Even in Dove Cottage the loss of Coleridge's companionship haunted them. "How happy are we altogether again! If but poor Coleridge were in the right way, we should be content," Wordsworth told Sir George Beaumont. To Dorothy, William must have given a glowing account of Coleridge as a lecturer; for much delighted, she told Lady Beaumont on April 20, "He is a wonderful creature, pouring out such treasures of thought and knowledge, almost, we may say, without premeditation, and in language so eloquent.'' Two days later she exclaimed to Catherine Clarkson: "Poor Coleridge! He has indeed fought a good fight, and I hope he will not yield; but come to us having accomplished a perfect victory.'' Since Dorothy's salutary experience at Coleorton, absence and forgetfulness had made her heart grow fonder, and all her former hopes for Coleridge had revived.

In June 1808 the Wordsworths—with Sara Hutchinson now recovering from her illness—reluctantly left the beloved Dove Cottage for a new home nearby, named Allan Bank. The change was due partly to the Wordsworths' increasing family, and not less to their hope that after the separation, Coleridge and his two sons would come to live with them there.

But this hope evolved at Coleorton had not been without its fluctuations. "When we engaged this house," Dorothy told Mrs. Clarkson on December 28, 1807,

> it was under the idea that Coleridge with his two boys would come and live with us, a plan to which we consented, in the hope of being of service to Coleridge, though we were well aware of the odium which we should draw upon ourselves by having the children under our roof. We do not, however, now think that Coleridge will have the resolution to put his plan in practice; nor do we now even think it would be prudent for us to consent to it, Coleridge having been so very unsteady in all things since his return to England. Had he acted with firmness we should willingly have encountered blame, as the only means of preserving Coleridge in quiet, and promoting his schemes for the education of his sons; but we had long experienced at Coleorton that it was not in our power to make him happy; and his irresolute conduct since, has almost confirmed our fears that it will never be otherwise; therefore we should be more disposed to hesitation; and fear, of having our domestic quiet disturbed if he should now wish to come to us with the children. I do not say that we *should not consent* but it would be with little hope; and we shall never *advise* the measure.

The Wordsworths followed with interest Coleridge's career as a lecturer. On hearing of his illnesses, absences, and miseries, pity and affection overcame their reluctance to share their home with him. For they still hoped to see great works from his pen.

On June 5, 1808, Dorothy Wordsworth just installed in Allan Bank, expressed to Catherine Clarkson her delight in the lovely views from its windows. Nevertheless in a mood of sentimental nostalgia for Dove Cottage she rejoiced that she could still head her letters "Grasmere," instead of "Allan Bank." Lovely views however were inadequate compensations for the ubiquitous chimney smoke which haunted nearly every room. So now save for the smoke, everything was ready for the reception of Coleridge; but Coleridge neither came nor wrote.

After waiting for a month, Dorothy, bitterly disappointed, complained to Catherine Clarkson: ". . .day after day I waited in the hope of hearing from Coleridge himself; and truly at last I had not the heart to write, we having written so many times to him urgently entreating him to write, yet having received no answer. . . ." So Dorothy requested Catherine, who was still hostess to

Coleridge at Bury, to treat her letter as if to Coleridge himself and so inform him of her feelings.

Such was the unhappy prelude to the battle of *The White Doe of Rylstone* waged between Coleridge and the Wordsworths, upon their entry into the house to which they had expected to welcome their absent friend. Nor had Wordsworth' visit to Coleridge in London been entirely happy. Wordsworth had sorrowfully observed Coleridge's illnesses and increasing recourse to opium and had complained to Dorothy of being refused admittance to Coleridge's room until four o'clock in the afternoon. He had also been bitterly disappointed by Coleridge's refusal to return with him from London.

The particular occasion of the quarrel that now occurred was Coleridge's undertaking to help Wordsworth by correcting his latest poem—the dull *White Doe of Rylstone*—and arrange for its publication by Longman.

The reception of the poem in manuscript by Wordsworth's friends had been somewhat depressing. Coleridge and Lamb—not surprisingly—had been less than enthusiastic when Wordsworth read the poem to them. Lamb had been severely rebuked by Wordsworth for his attitude: "I am much more sorry on Lamb's account than on my own," Wordsworth wrote to Coleridge, "Let Lamb learn to be ashamed of himself in not taking some pleasure." Nevertheless Wordsworth was now reluctant to publish the poem.

It was Dorothy, now more practical than aesthetic, who urged publication upon William.

> We are exceedingly concerned, [she wrote on March 31,] that you, William, have given up all thoughts of publishing your poem. As to the outcry against you, I would defy it. What matter, if you get your hundred guineas into your pocket. . .without money what can we do? New house! new furniture! such a large family! two servants. . .we cannot go on so another half-year. . .dismiss one of the servants, and work the *flesh off our poor bones.* Do, dearest William! do pluck up your courage, and overcome your disgust for publishing. It is but a *little trouble,* and all will be over, and we shall be wealthy, and at our ease for one year, at least. [William's marriage and the consequent family life had not been without its unconscious effect upon the once romantic Dorothy.]

Three weeks later Dorothy triumphantly informed Lady Beaumont: "The poem is to be published. Longman has consented in spite of the odium under which my brother labours as a poet, to give him one hundred guineas per thousand copies. . .according to the demand."

Since the increase of financial responsibilities consequent upon Wordsworth's marriage, Dorothy's attitude to William somewhat resembled that of Mrs. Coleridge to Samuel. Indeed Dorothy's anxiety now led her to prod Coleridge about the dilatory corrections of Wordsworth's manuscript and his negotiations on Wordsworth's behalf with Longman for its publication.

Unlike Coleridge and Lamb, Southey at any rate found the *White Doe* "most masterly." The poem he told Walter Scott, "affected me more deeply that I wish to be affected. . . ." But Wordsworth's doubts still lingered; and when Coleridge had been sufficiently prodded by Dorothy to send the manuscript to Longman, Wordsworth, without Coleridge's knowledge, withdrew it. Wordsworth's withdrawal and Dorothy's urgings much annoyed Coleridge particularly in the nervous state to which his lectures and opium had reduced him. A breach between the two friends was the result.

Evidently provoked by some complaint from Coleridge, Wordsworth replied in the spring of 1808, in a letter chiefly devoted to a devastating but not inaccurate analysis of Coleridge's temperament.

> There is more than one sentence in your letter, [wrote Wordsworth] which I blushed to read. These, [he said] were due to Coleridge's habit, which I think a very pernicious one, of giving by voice and pen to your most lawless thoughts, and to your wildest fancies, an external existence; thus furnishing the bad Soul as well as the good with an ever ready companion and encourager; and finding by insensible reconcilement fair and attractive bosom-inmates in productions from which you ought to have recoiled as monsters. Hence there is more than one sentence in your last letter (I cannot sully this paper by transcribing them) which would abundantly have justified me in passing over all the accusations it contains as utterly unworthy of notice, coming as they needs must have done from a man in a lamentably insane state of mind.

Coleridge's infantile charges against Wordsworth, William curtly repudiated, exclaiming: "First let me sweep away some of the rubbish of which I hoped to have never heard more." But soon he turned to Coleridge's suspicions about the Wordsworths' relations with Sara Hutchinson:

> Passing by many most reprehensible and ungrateful accusations against those I best love, [he wrote] I now come to one sentence in which you speak of Sara's letters being written under Mary's eye and mine; These words I deem both unmanly and ungentlemanly, and were almost the only words in your letter which roused me. Sara's letters, either those she writes or receives do not any of them pass under my eye, and I am surprised you should so far forget yourself as to use such an expression. She is 34 years of age and what have I to do with overlooking her letters! (It is indeed my business to prevent poison entering into her mind and body from any quarter, but it would indeed be an extreme case in which I should solicit permission to explore her letters to know whether such poison were contained in them. . .).
>
> I come now to the keystone of our offences, [he continued] viz, our cruelty, a hope in infusing into Sara's mind the notion that your attachment to her has been the curse of all your happiness. So far from our having done this the very reverse is the truth. They did not pretend to deny (for my part I have meddled little with the affair) that your passion was a source to you of much misery; but they always told her that it was a gross error to appropriate this to herself; they laboured to convincing her of this; telling her that your mind must have had such a determination to some object or other, that she was not therefore the cause, but merely to use your own distinction, the innocent occasion of this unhappiness, that in fact as far as *you* were concerned she might congratulate herself; had this passion fixed upon a per-

son of a different kind what might you not have suffered? You precipitate yourself into friendships (amities if you think the words too strong). . .and trust to Providence for pulling you out of them. . . .

In conclusion Wordsworth finished his letter with a scathing comparison of Coleridge and himself in such matters as he now raised: "I am not fond of making myself hastily beloved and admired, you take more delight in it than a wise man ought. I am naturally slow to love and to cease loving, you promptitude. . . ."

Had Coleridge received that letter surely he would never have come to Allan Bank. Yet by the beginning of August 1808, he was definitely expected there and Dorothy anxiously told Mrs. Clarkson: "We have heard nothing of Coleridge, I hope he will reach Grasmere this week." But not until 11.30 P.M. on the night of September 1, 1808, did Coleridge arrive there.

At this time life in the Wordsworths' new home was rather disturbed. Mrs. Wordsworth had sprained her arm; she was also expecting the birth of her fourth child, Catherine, almost immediately. In these circumstances Wordsworth and Coleridge with little Sara Coleridge left Allan Bank for Greta Hall on September 5. There Southey coolly observed their arrival. "Coleridge has arrived at last, about half as big as the house," he told his brother—"He came with Wordsworth on Monday, and returned with him on Wednesday. His present scheme is to put the boys at school at Ambleside and reside at Grasmere himself."

Little of the admiration which Southey had once felt for Coleridge had survived his return from Malta. This is also revealed in the description of Coleridge that Southey now sent to the miniaturist Matilda Betham:

You would have found him [he wrote], the most wonderful man living in conversation, but the most impracticable one for a painter, and had you begun the picture it is ten thousand to one that you must have finished it from memory. His countenance is the most variable that I have ever seen; sometimes it is kindled with the brightest expression, and sometimes all its light goes out, and is utterly extinguished. Nothing can convey stronger indications of power than his eye, eyebrow, and forehead. Nothing can be more imbecile than all the rest of the face; look at them separately, you would hardly think it possible that they could belong to the one head; look at them together, you wonder how they came so, and are puzzled what to expect from a character whose outward and visible signs are so contradictory.

Coleridge's meeting with his wife at this time seems to have been amicable. For upon his return to Allan Bank he at once sent her an unusually cheerful and affectionate letter. After describing his delight in having little Sara with him and in seeing her playing with the young Wordsworths he concluded:

Be assured, my dear Sara! that your kind behaviour has made a deep impression on my mind. Would to God it had been always so on both sides. But the past is past,—and my business now is to recover the tone of my constitution if possible and to get money for you and our children. I trust I shall never wilfully do anything to give you the least pain. Heaven knows! nothing is more at my heart than to be conducive to your comfort of mind, body and estate—for you mistake greatly, if you imagine I do not entertain both affection and a very great esteem for you. May God bless us both.

Although his next letter to Mrs. Coleridge written within a week was an excuse for work "suspended" through ill-health, he again sent her his blessing accompanied by a request: "And now may God bless you, my dear Sara! and put it into your head to make a pair or two of drawers for the thighs and seat of your affectionate friend and husband, S.T. Coleridge." Evidently for Coleridge separation did not imply the relinquishment of such wifely duties. Nor did it in fact prevent Mrs. Coleridge's spending a week at Allan Bank that winter with the Wordsworths and their children. Another guest of the Wordsworths at this time was De Quincey.

Sara Hutchinson was now domesticated at Allan Bank. "She has made up her mind to live with us," Dorothy told Catherine Clarkson on April 22; "therefore you may be sure she will be tenderly watched and treated as an invalid till she is perfectly strong—and perhaps alas! that may not be for years."

Coleridge's amiability to his wife was a reflection of his happiness at finding himself once more with the Wordsworths and Sara Hutchinson. To a correspondent he wrote on September 16: "I dare acquit myself of all partiality, though I affirm, that there does not exist a family in the Island better worth your acquaintance if simplicity, delicacy, purity of mind, affectionateness and good sense are of any value in this money-making planet of ours."

Henceforth until Coleridge finally left the Lakes, mutual visits between the families at Greta Hall and those at Allan Bank were frequent. Coleridge's relations with little Sara were vividly described in later years by Sara Coleridge herself. Her impartiality is beyond doubt for not only had she a great affection for both parents but also an admiration for her father's "genius" that remained throughout her life. At this time Sara suffered from night terrors of imagination.

Even Mama [she wrote], scolded me for creeping out of bed after an hour's torture, and stealing down to her in the parlour, saying I could bear the loneliness and the night-fears no longer. But my father understood the case better. He insisted that a lighted candle should be left in my room, in the interval between my retiring to bed and Mama's joining me. From that time forth my sufferings ceased. [Sara was very conscious of her father's affection for herself]. My father's wish it was to have me for a month with him at Grasmere, where he was domesticated with the Wordsworths. He insisted upon it, that I became rosier and hardier during my absence from Mama. She did not much like to part with me, and I think my father's motive, at bottom, must have been a wish to fasten my affections on him. I slept with him, and he would tell me fairy stories when he came to bed at twelve and one o'clock. I remember his telling me a wild tale, too, in his study, and my trying to repeat it to the maids afterwards. Some of my recollections are tinged with pain. [Sara recorded]: I think my dear father was anxious that I should learn to love him and the Wordsworths and their children, and not cling so exclusively to my mother, and all around me at home. He was therefore much annoyed when, on my mother's coming to Allan Bank, I flew to her, and wished not to be separated from her any more. I remember his shewing displeasure to me, and accusing me of want of affection. I could not understand why. The young Wordsworths came and caressed him. I sat benumbed; for truly nothing does so freeze affection as the breath of jealousy. The sense that you have done very wrong, or at least given great offence, you know not how or why—that you are being dunned for some payment of love or feeling which you know not how to produce or to demonstrate on a sudden, chills the heart, and fills it with perplexity and bitterness. My father reproached me, and constrasted my coldness with the childish caresses of the little Wordsworths. I slunk away, and hid myself in the wood behind the house, and there my friend John, whom at that time I called my future husband, came to seek me.

A letter that Sara Hutchinson wrote in November 1808 to her cousin Mary Monkhouse presents a pleasanter picture of Coleridge at play with the children at Allan Bank—particularly with little Dora Wordsworth: "We are a nice round family you may think and when Coleridge's boys are here on a Saturday and Sunday a pretty noisy one—even now I hear Coleridge making racket enough for twenty with Sissy (Dora Wordsworth) below—he does tease her in such a way for she cannot be too naughty for his taste; he calls her 'beautiful cat of the mountains!' and she is more like a cat with him than anything else—the moment he appears she puts on her airs. . . ."

Nor did Sara Coleridge forget Sara Hutchinson in her recollections of these days: "My father used to talk to me with much admiration and affection of Sara Hutchinson, Mrs. Wordsworth's sister, who resided partly with the Wordsworths, partly with her own brothers. At this time she used to act as my father's amanuensis. She wrote out great part of the *'Friend'* to his dictation." And Sara continued with the word portrait of Sara Hutchinson previously quoted.

Even before the close of the lectures Coleridge had begun to make plans for a new periodical, *The Friend*, to be conducted by himself as *The Watchman* had been. The idea of it he had vaguely mentioned to Cottle a year before; but only now did it become a definite project. Such a periodical with Wordsworth as his partner he calculated would bring him not less than from twelve pounds to twenty pounds a week. On the strength of this he would support Wordsworth he promised, in May 1808—if the paper appeared. Thus he would prevent his friend from sacrificing poetry to mere money making, which he feared Dorothy Wordsworth—owing to their straitened means—wished William to do.

In September 1808 Coleridge unwarned by his experience with *The Watchman*, was busy at Allan Bank advertising among friends and acquaintances his new project—which became a weekly paper, *The Friend*. Like *The Watchman, The Friend* was to be an extraordinary periodical. It was "not for the multitude," he said "but for those who by rank or fortune or official situation or talents and habits of reflection are to *influence* the multitude." It was "to found true principles, to oppose false principles, in criticism, legislation, philosophy, morals and international law." At a price of a mere shilling weekly *The Friend* was surely a bargain.

Although on occasion Coleridge's literary friends might be welcome as contributors, Coleridge himself was to be the presiding genius. To this work he brought he said "the results of a life of intense study and unremitted meditation; of toil; and personal travels; and great unrepaid expense." In this way he would now show the world that he had so often disappointed, what his genius really could accomplish. "I consider *The Friend,*" he told Sir George Beaumont in mid-December 1808, "as the main pipe, from which I shall play off the whole accumulation and reservoir of my head and heart." And employing again a favorite metaphorical phrase, he continued, "Hitherto I have layed my eggs with ostrich carelessness and ostrich-like oblivion. The greater part have been crushed under foot: but some have crawled into light to furnish feathers for other mens' caps—and not a few to plume the shafts in the quivers of calumny."

During these last months of 1808 Coleridge was very busy making preparations for the publication of the first number of *The Friend*, too optimistically planned for January 1, 1809. Some prospectuses had been printed and were now sent by Coleridge for distribution to various friends and acquaintances. These were generally accompanied by a long covering letter. In this way he called for assistance from Stuart, Southey, Davy, Street, and the Beaumonts. Others were Poole and Estlin whose friendship Coleridge had allowed to lapse. He also wrote to comparative strangers including Jeffrey and James Montgomery, as well as his neighbors in the Lakes, William Taylor and Thomas Wilkinson.

On December 3 1808, Coleridge sent Estlin a conciliatory letter confessing his previous addiction to opium which he said was now cured:

> When I was last at Bristol, not only was my health in a far worse state than I had resolution to make known; but my mind was halting between despondency and despair. On my return to the North I summoned up courage and put my case fairly under the care and judgment of a physician—and I have now almost recovered my former nature. . .I look onward to my future exertions. . .[he continued], with humble confidence. By the work, of which you have here the prospectus, I have received strong encouragements to the belief, that I shall do good. As I am almost sure. that in the subjects admissible in such a work, our principles are the same, I have no immediate motive to detail to you the tenets, in which we differ.

In conclusion he emphasized the importance of *The Friend* and of its moral aims:

> As to *The Friend,* I make no request to you. You will do me all the good, you can, compatible with the approbation of your own mind. I have received promises of support from men of very high name in the literary world—and as to my own efforts, I consider the work as the main pipe of my intellectual reservoir. The first essay will be—On the nature and importance of *Principles.* The blindness to this I have long regarded as the disease

of this discussing, calculating, *prudential* age—and to prove this and to show its consequences in morality, taste, and even in the common goings-on of daily life is my paramount object for the whole work. . . .

It is Dorothy Wordsworth who gives us the most intimate view of life at Allan Bank as the year 1808 closed.

> We are all well, and in good spirits [she told Jane Marshall on December 4]; but (alas!) we have had, and still have grievous troubles to struggle with in a smoky house—wet cellars—and workmen by the half dozen, making attempts, hitherto unsuccessful, to remedy these evils. We are making one effort more, and if that ends as heretofore, we shall be reduced to the miserable necessity of quitting Grasmere; for this house is, at present, literally not habitable, and there is no other in the Vale. You can have no idea of the inconvenience we have suffered. There was one stormy day in which we could have no fire but in my brother's study and that chimney smoked so much that we were obliged to go to bed with the baby, in the middle of the day, to keep it warm, and I, with a candle in my hand, stumbled over a chair unable to see it. We cooked in the study, and even heated water there to wash dishes, for the boiler in the back-kitchen could not be heated, much less the kitchen fire endured; and in fact partly on account of smoke in windy weather, and partly because of the workmen we have been for more than a week together at times without a kitchen fire. The servants, you may be sure, have been miserable, and we have had far too much labour, and too little quiet; but, thank God! my health has stood it very well, and my sister has not looked so healthy for these two years or been so strong.
>
> At the time of the great storm, [Dorothy continued], Mrs. Coleridge and her little girl were here and Mr. Coleridge is with us constantly, so you will make out that we were a pretty large family to provide for in such a manner. Mr. Coleridge and his wife are separated, and I hope they will both be the happier for it. They are upon friendly terms, and occasionally see each other. In fact Mrs. Coleridge was more than a week at Grasmere under the same roof with him. Coleridge intends to spend the winter with us. On the other side of the paper you will find the prospectus of a work which he is going to undertake; and I have little doubt but that it will be well executed if his health does not fail him; but on that score (though he is well at present) I have many fears. . . .Miss Hutchinson is with us—she has been dangerously ill—confined to her bed—but is now recovered.

As ever when in a new venture, Coleridge was all excitement and enthusiasm for *The Friend*. "I am hard at work" he told Stuart "and feel a pleasure and eagerness in it, which I had not known for years—a consequence and reward of my courage in at length having overcome the fear of dying suddenly in my sleep, which and, Heaven knows! which alone had seduced me into the fatal habit of taking enormous quantities of laudanum, and latterly of spirits too. . . .I left it off *all at once*. . . ." This was a new reason for his drugging which hitherto had been for "rheumatism." This habit too he now cited as the cause of his "lungs slightly affected as by asthma, and my bowels dreadfully irritable; but I am far better than I could have dared expect." Nor in fact did he ever abandon his opium habit which he told others was reduced to one-sixth. To some he spoke more cautiously. Although he had consulted a physician since his return to the North, as he had told Estlin on December 3 1808, "it could not be abandoned without loss of life" and he felt revived in spirit now that he had "no secret to brood over." In similar terms he spoke of himself to others whose help with *The Friend* he required. When shortly afterwards Coleridge heard of the death on December 24, 1808, of Dr. Beddoes aged forty-eight, he was much upset, particularly as he had recently required Beddoes' assistance in reducing his dose of opium. "A very severe and very abrupt blow. . ." he described the news to Stuart the following January: "Few events have taken out so much hope from my life." Fortunately the demands of *The Friend* left Coleridge little time for grief as with Wordsworth's help he continued to send out prospectuses wherever possible.

Allan Bank as Dorothy described it was certainly no ideal environment for Coleridge at this time when facing his responsibilities as editor and almost sole contributor of *The Friend*. Nevertheless, Dorothy could describe Coleridge as "well and in good spirits, writing letters to all his friends and acquaintances, dispatching prospectuses, and fully prepared to begin his work." Yet Dorothy still doubtful, wrote:

> Nobody, surely, but himself would have ventured to send forth this prospectus with no one essay written, no beginning made! but yet I believe it was the only way for him. I believe he could not have made the beginnings unspurred by a necessity which is now created by the promises therein made. I cannot, however, be without hauntings of fear, seeing him so often obliged to lie in bed more than half the day—often so very poorly as to be utterly unable to do anything whatever. To-day [she told Catherine Clarkson], though he came down to dinner at three perfectly well, he did not rise till near two o'clock. I am afraid this account of him may give you some alarm. I assure you, however, that there is no need to be alarmed; his health is much, *very* much better, and his looks are almost what you would wish them to be; and however ill he may have been in the mornings he seldom fails to be cheerful and comfortable at night. [Even while she wrote, Dorothy added,] Sara (Hutchinson) and he are sitting together in his parlour!. . .

At the same time Wordsworth was in his study with Mary dictating his pamphlet: *The Convention of Cintra*. Dorothy too had her companion, De Quincey. He "is beside me, quietly turning over the leaves of a Greek book," she told Mrs. Clarkson, adding in evidently cheerful mood, "Mr. De Quincey will stay with us, we hope, at least till the spring. We feel often as if he were one of the family."

6 *The Friend* Appears and Disappears (1809-10)

Its Object is—by doing as much good as I can—to do some service to my wife and children. . .
> —S.T. Coleridge to John Colson, April 18, 1809

The last No. of The Friend *lies on his Desk, the sight of which fills my heart with grief, and my eyes with tears. . .*
> —Mrs. S.T. Coleridge to Thomas Poole. [August 3, 1810]

To Stuart above all others Coleridge now turned for assistance in starting *The Friend.* From Stuart Coleridge for a long time had obtained journalistic advice and also, of course, money. So close was Stuart's involvement in preparations for *The Friend,* that between the opening of the year 1809 and the following June Coleridge sent him some twenty letters about the running and financing of the paper. Coleridge's gratitude to this "dear and honoured friend" found full and free expression in January 6, 1809: "The tears are in my eyes as I write, so that I can scarce see my paper—I would I could convey to you as by intuition, how much I love and esteem you. . ." and proudly he announced: "I have about 20 swelling names of earls and countesses and Bishops. . . ."

From the very first Coleridge's most intimate friends were dubious about the prospects of *The Friend.* When Lamb received from Coleridge what he called "a flaming prospectus" of *The Friend,** on the same day as the promise

---

*The "flaming prospectus" as it appeared in the first number of *The Friend,* is certainly interesting, perhaps even a little frightening for modest readers of *The Friend.*

"The object of *The Friend,* briefly and generally expressed, is—to uphold those truths and those merits, which are founded in the nobler and more permanent parts of our nature, against the caprices of fashion and such pleasures as either depend on transitory and accidental causes, or are pursued from less worthy impulses. The chief objects of my own essays will be:

The true and sole ground of morality or virtue, as distinguished from prudence:

The origin and growth of moral impulses, as distinguished from external and immediate motives:

The necessary dependence of taste on moral impulses and habits and the nature of taste (relatively to judgment in general and to genius) defined, illustrated, and applied. Under this head I comprise the substance of the lectures given, and intended to have been given at the Royal Institution on the distinguished English poets, in illustration of the general principles of poetry; together with suggestions concerning the affinity of the fine arts to each other, and the principles common to them all; architecture; gardening; dress; music; painting; poetry.

of a Christmas turkey from an acquaintance, he felt, he said, "more sanguine" of seeing the turkey, than of seeing Coleridge's review on the advertised date, January 1, 1809. Nor was he mistaken. "A very cheerful letter," said Lamb, accompanied the prospectus: "He says they are well there, and in good spirits and that he has not been so well for a long time. . . .Those who remember *The Watchman* will not be very sanguine in expecting a regular fulfilment of this prophecy. But Coleridge writes in delightful spirits, and *if ever*, he may *now* do this thing. I suppose he will send you a prospectus. . . ."

Coleridge's letter had arrived at a fortunate moment; when in fact Mary Lamb was expressing to Catherine Clarkson her annoyance with Coleridge for not calling on them when in London. "Coleridge in a manner gave us up when in town," she wrote "and we have lost all traces of him. . . .We expect *too much,* and he gives *too little.* We ought many years ago to have understood each other better. Nor is it quite all over with us yet, for he will some day or other come in with the same old face, and receive (after a few spiteful words from me) the same warm welcome as ever. But we could not submit to sit as hearers at his lectures and not be permitted to see our old friend when *school hours* were over."

Southey on receiving his prospectus was as pessimistic as Lamb. "For *The Friend* itself" he told Rickman, "you may whistle these three months, and God knows how much longer." Then followed a severe but not unfair criticism of Coleridge's doings as editor of his weekly review. "Hitherto however" Southey continued, "there is no blame attachable to him than that he carried a prospectus wet from the pen to the printer, without consulting anybody, or giving himself time for consideration, and so a day was fixed for the appearance of the first number which was impossibly soon. Meantime, a hundred difficulties open upon him in the way of publication. . . .The prospectus looks too much like what it intends to be, talks confidently to the public about what the public cares not a curse for, and has about it a sort of unmanly *humblefication* which is not sincere, which the very object of the paper gives the lie to, which may provoke some people, and can conciliate nobody. Yet, such as it is, I shall augur best of those persons who expected most from it, such a habit of thinking, and such a train of thinking is manifested there."

The opening out of new objects of just admiration in our own language, and information as to the present state and past history of Swedish, Danish, German, and Italian literature,—to which, but as supplied by a friend, I may add the Spanish, Portuguese, and French—as far as the same has not been already given to English readers, or is not to be found in common French authors.

Characters met in real life; anecdotes and results of my own life and travels, as far as they are illustrative of general moral laws, and have no direct bearing on personal or immediate politics;

Education in its widest sense, private and national;

Sources of consolation to the afflicted in misfortune, or disease, or dejection of mind, from the exertion and right application of the reason, the imagination and the moral sense; and new sources of enjoyment opened out, or an attempt (as an illustrious friend once expressed the thought to me) to add sunshine to daylight by making the happy more happy. In the words 'dejection of mind' I refer particularly to doubt and disbelief of the moral government of the world, and the grounds and arguments for the religious hopes of human nature."

In Coleridge's search for subscribers to *The Friend* at this time, even un-forgiven brother George was not forgotten. To resume relations with George was now a delicate matter; for not until after a year's silence had Samuel replied to George's letter opposing his arrival with his family at Ottery. In a letter of May 11, 1808, Samuel had however broken the ice by abusing George and at the same time requesting a copy of his birth certificate, which he needed for some increase in his life insurance. In the same letter he had reproached George and his wife for preventing his coming to Ottery and putting him to useless expense. He accused them of defamation and of complaining that he had not repaid his debts to George. Samuel's long rambling letter at first prevaricating, often untruthful, next turned from angry reproaches to Christian forgiveness, pathos, and boasting. Were not his friends, Samuel asked, as "honourable and splendid" as George's? Then too his relatives had spread lies about him. George's wife had told Samuel's "that I had been a very bad young man—that my brothers had done wonders for me, but she hoped now that I was *reformed,* I should be able to repay the money." Although poor he continued, he might have been "perhaps the wealthiest of the family." Indeed had he not believed that George was as generously inclined as Samuel's own feelings he would have taken steps to repay his debts to George immediately. So now George must at once tell him the amount of his debt which "shall be ultimately paid to you if I live—broken out of years, even tho' I shorten my own and my children's simple means—and if I die shortly, it *is* still mentioned in my will." Indeed if a few of his friends knew of the matter they would have paid it at once.

George's refusal to invite him, a "deserted orphan" to whom "every kind-ness appeared great" had harmed his reputation among some who knew of it. Nor was this all. There were the "little pangs" he had suffered "from my sweet children asking me why they must not see their Grandmamma, their uncles, and cousins," and he had also "endeavoured to compensate for the disappointment of a fond mother, who had indulged the venial pride of show-ing off her children" to the family at Ottery. The letter was a wonderful crea-tion worthy of the author of "The Ancient Mariner," and it concluded on a note of finality: "I need no answer. . . ."

Although there had apparently been no communication between the brothers since this angry letter to George the needs of *The Friend* had led Samuel to write again to him at the close of the same year. "I cannot bring myself to believe that you can be indifferent to any virtuous effort on my part," he wrote, sending George a prospectus and at the same time informing him, "I have received promises of support from men of the highest present celebrity, and shall have at least three bishops among my patrons. I play off my whole mind in this work, as from the main pipe of the fountain. Indeed it is high time." And he continued using terms rather similar to those of his letter to Sir George Beaumont. "Hitherto I have layed my eggs with ostrich careless-ness and ostrich oblivion—most of them indeed have been crushed under—yet some have crawled into light to furnish feathers for the caps of others, and not a few to plume the shafts in the quivers of the slanderers. . . .''

To this George must have replied with characteristic amiability; for in two letters of April 12 and April 18, 1809, Samuel again wrote to him of *The Friend* delicately hinting at its financial difficulties, asking him to obtain subscribers, and detailing all the obstacles and delays which had caused postponement of the publication from May 1 to the 14. This date too ultimately gave place to June 1, 1809, which became the actual publication day.

In January 1809 Coleridge had sent Stuart an advertisement of *The Friend* to be sent to several newspapers:—

On Saturday—will be published *The Friend*, a weekly essay by S.T. Coleridge. The object of this work generally expresed, is—to uphold those truths and those merits, which are founded in the nobler and permanent parts of our nature against the caprices of fashion, and such pleasure as either depend on transitory and accidental causes, or are pursued from less worthy impulses. A more detailed account of its purpose and chief subjects will be found in the prospectus of *The Friend*, which may be procured gratis, from the booksellers undermentioned. The events of the day, and all personal and immediate politics will be excluded.

The faithful Sara Hutchinson, so often Coleridge's amanuensis, wrote this advertisement and throughout the following months copied nearly all Coleridge's material for *The Friend*. Immediately afterwards poor Sara fell ill, even before Coleridge had finished distributing his advertisement. "So far I had written," he told Stuart, "when Sara Hutchinson's illness stopped me both by the necessary attendance on her and by the weight on my spirits."

The next trouble for Coleridge was to find a printer; with Savage, printer to the Royal Institution, no agreement was reached—by Stuart's advice. Pennington, a printer at Kendal, declined an offer and in February Coleridge persuaded John Brown of Penrith to become both printer and nominal publisher. Soon however Brown discovered that he lacked sufficient type for the job and Coleridge had to buy more for him at a cost of thirty-eight pounds, as well as a hand press that cost Coleridge an additional twenty-two pounds.

Coleridge was now busy writing essays for the paper and found the task "quite delightful by comparison with the troubles of setting up shop." But his troubles were by no means over. The stamped paper that he wanted in order to save the cost of postage must come from the Stamp Office in London. Stuart as usual arranged the matter and paid a necessary sixty pounds. Sheets were dispatched to Coleridge in April but went astray en route and did not arrive until early in May—much too late for the intended publication which had originally been fixed for April 1—"which," wrote Chambers sardonically in his biography of Coleridge, "seems not altogether an inappropriate date."* April proving impossible, Coleridge who had next hoped to publish on May 1, was thus again disappointed. At last on June 1, 1809, the first number of *The Friend* appeared

---

*E.K. Chambers, *Samuel Taylor Coleridge* (Oxford, 1930), p. 220.

This was not achieved without much nervous anxiety for both Coleridge and Wordsworth. On February 12, Coleridge had left Allan Bank and walked to Penrith to see his printer, Brown. He remained in the neighborhood staying with various friends until his return to Allan Bank in mid-June. During this time his resort to opium created gossip in the neighborhood.

William and Dorothy heard of Coleridge's doings in absence with growing despair; and William on March 30, 1809, expressed to Poole his fears for the future of Coleridge and his family, as well as for *The Friend*. "I cannot say that Coleridge has been managing himself well," he wrote, "and therefore I would not have you disappointed if *The Friend* should not last long; but do not hint a word of this to any body, as any thing of that kind should it come to his ears would completely dash him. But I must say to you to prevent mortification on your part that I have not much hope." Wordsworth's mood was not improved by Coleridge's failure to write to them during these months of absence. Dorothy at this time expressed similar doubts to De Quincey. At first, annoyed like her brother by Coleridge's silence, she relented on hearing from Samuel and told De Quincey: "Poor soul! he writes in bad spirits, and I have no hope." Thus with fluctuating hopes and fears Dorothy noted Coleridge's delays on which she perciepiently commented to De Quincey: "I much fear that there is little done on Coleridge's part, and that he himself is not sorry that there should be an excuse in which he has no concern."

Meanwhile Wordsworth, increasingly provoked by Coleridge's relapse into opium at Penrith and consequent postponements, wrote to him in no amiable mood: ". . .It is *absolutely necessary* that you should always be *beforehand* with your work. On the general question of your health, one thing is obvious, that health of mind, that is, resolution, self-denial, and well-regulated conditions of feeling, are what you must depend upon; that doctors can do you little or no good, and that doctors' stuff has been one of your greatest curses; and of course, of ours through you. Do not look out of yourself for that stay which can only be found within."

William and Dorothy were now almost angrily discovering what Mrs. Coleridge could have told them long before, that the separation the Wordsworths had so long assisted with the best intentions, would not cure her husband's weaknesses. Three weeks later William's report to Stuart on Coleridge was no better. "Of Coleridge or *The Friend*" he wrote, "I can say nothing satisfactory; it is nearly 3 months since he left us, and I have not heard from him lately. He is now (I understand) at Penrith whither he went from Keswick for the purpose of publishing *The Friend,* against the second Saturday of May: that is all that I know of his late movements."

Penrith as the printing and publishing centre for *The Friend* inevitably increased Coleridge's difficulties. The little Cumberland town, as De Quincey pointed out, was twenty-eight miles from Allan Bank and with the almost inaccessible Kirkstone Pass on the route. Nor was there any direct postal service to Penrith. "Purchasing such intolerable difficulties at the highest price" was De Quincey's description of Coleridge's choice of Penrith as headquarters for *The Friend.*

But nothing came from Coleridge at Penrith except ugly rumors of continual relapses into opium bouts. On the last day of May or perhaps on the following day, which also happened to be that of the first appearance of *The Friend*, Wordsworth's anxiety for Coleridge led him to write a long and illuminating letter to Poole.

I am sorry to say [he wrote], that nothing appears to be more desirable than that his periodical essay should never commence. It is in fact *impossible*—utterly impossible—that he should carry it on; and, therefore, better never begin it; far better, and if begun, the sooner it stops, also the better—the less will be the loss, and no greater the disgrace. You will consider me as speaking to you now in the most sacred confidence, and as under a strong sense of duty, from a wish to save you from anxiety and disappointment; and from a further, and still stronger wish that, as one of Coleridge's nearest and dearest friends, you should take into most serious consideration his condition, above all with reference to his children. I give it to you as my deliberate opinion, formed upon proofs which have been strengthening for years, that he neither will nor can execute anything of important benefit either to himself his family or mankind. Neither his talents nor his genius, mighty as they are, nor his vast information will avail him anything; they are all frustrated by a derangement in his intellectual and moral constitution. In fact he has no voluntary power of mind whatsoever, nor is he capable of acting under any *constraint* of duty or moral obligation. Do not suppose that I mean to say from this that *The Friend* may not appear—it may—but it cannot go on for any length of time. I am *sure* it cannot.

Coleridge I understand has been three weeks at Penrith, whither he went to superintend the publication, and has since never been heard of (save once, on his first arrival) though frequently written to. I shall say no more at present, but I do earnestly wish that you would come down hither this summer, in order that something may be arranged respecting his children, in case of his death, and also during his life-time.

I must add, however, that it answers no purpose to advise her (Mrs. Coleridge) to remonstrate with him, or to represent to him the propriety of going on or desisting. The disease of his mind is that he perpetually looks out of himself for those obstacles to his utility which only exist in himself. I am sure that if any friend whom he values were, in consequence of such a conviction as I have expressed, to advise him to drop his work, he would immediately ascribe the failure to the damp thrown upon his spirits by this interference. Therefore in this way nothing can be done, nor by encouraging him to attempt anything else. He would catch eagerly perhaps at the advice, and would be involved in new plans, new procrastinations, and new expenses.

I am, dear Poole, most sincerely yours,
W. Wordsworth.

I must repeat how much I wish to see you here as I cannot write what I think and feel. Pray burn this letter when you have read it.

On the last day of May William wrote to Stuart of Coleridge and *The*

*Friend** in similar terms. When on the following day the first number of *The Friend* appeared, Wordsworth was no less pessimistic. On June 4 Coleridge in Penrith replied indignantly to some refusal by Stuart of his latest demand for money for *The Friend*. "And God knows!" he wrote, "how reluctantly and with lingering and often imprudent delays I made each separate request. . . .But yet, my dear Friend! in what one instance did I apply to you undriven by an absolute necessity?. . ." Thus at great length, Coleridge continued his protest.

Nine days later Coleridge impressed upon Stuart the sobriety, regularity, and industry of his present way of life. "All my habits are what they ought to be" he wrote; "I rise every morning at 5, and work 3 hours before breakfast, either in letter-writing or serious composition." He was also he said, "abstemious" in his diet, took only a pint of beer a day, "and tho' forbidden by my medical attendant from trying again the desperate experiment of abandoning all at once that accursed drug, . . .Yet I have, with a far greater endurance of severest sufferings than I could have dared give myself credit for, reduced to a comparative trifle, less than one 20th part of my old doses." He had printed he said, 620 copies of the first issue, 650 of the second, "and so many more are called for, that I shall be forced to reprint both." For this of course Coleridge complained more money was required. But his appeals to Stuart, Clarkson, and Montagu were now rejected.

Perhaps Samuel found some comfort in Lamb's rather formal reference to *The Friend* on June 7, after reading the first number. "I congratulate you on the appearance of *The Friend,*" he wrote. "Your first number promises well, and I have no doubt the succeeding numbers will fulfil the promise."

At Farington's dinner party on July 12 Northcote, Farington recorded, "had seen the first number of Coleridge's periodical work, in which two points were particularly clear, viz. his exhibiting *himself* and his *conceit*. Many passages cannot be understood. The whole strange and as it seemed contemptible."

Upon Coleridge's return to Allan Bank on June 13, Dorothy took stock of the situation and reported it to Catherine Clarkson.

At ten o'clock yesterday morning Coleridge arrived [she wrote]: He had slept at Luff's and came over the Hawes, and was not fatigued. This you will say is a proof of his bodily *strength,* but such proofs we do not need; for what human body but one of extraordinary strength could have stood out against the trials which he has put his to? You will have seen from his sec-

*The title ran thus: *"THE FRIEND*; a Literary, Moral, and Political Weekly Paper, excluding personal and party politics and events of the Day. Conducted by S.T. Coleridge of Grasmere, Westmoreland. Each number will contain a stamped sheet of large octavo, like the present; and will be delivered free of expense, by the post, through out the Kingdom, to Subscribers. The price each number One shilling. Penrith: Printed and published by J. Brown."

ond number that he intends to have one week's respite. His reason for this is that many orders have been sent in from booksellers, and he wants to have the *names,* that the papers may be sent addressed to the respective persons. Whether it was absolutely necessary or not, to wait a week I do not know. I am, however, convinced that it is a wise thing; for by this means—if he makes good use of his time—he may get beforehand, and I am assured that without that, it would be *impossible* that he should go on. He is in good spirits, and he tells us that he has left his third number with Brown, who is actually printing it. At all events, I am glad that he is here, for if he perseveres anywhere in well doing it will be at Grasmere; but there is one thing sadly in his way. The stamped paper must be paid for with ready money, and he has none.

Dorothy also vividly described Coleridge's manner of life as editor of *The Friend* and her own reactions to his periodical so far.

There are a few passages in the two papers published which have given us pain [she told Catherine]: and which, if he had been at Grasmere, would never have appeared. The one where he speaks of the *one* poet of his own time. This passage cannot but have wounded Southey, and I think that it was unjust to Southey; besides it is a sort of praise that can do William no good. . . .I think it was beneath Coleridge to justify himself against the calumnies of the Anti-Jacobin Review, foolish to bring to light a thing long forgotten, and still more foolish to talk of his homesickness as a *husband,* or of anything relating to his private and domestic concerns. There are beautiful passages in both the essays, and everywhere the power of thought and the originality of a great mind are visible, but there is wanting a happiness of manner; and the first number is certainly very obscure. In short it is plainly shewn under what circumstances of constraint and compulsion he wrote; and I cannot enough admire his resolution in having written at all, or enough pity his sufferings before he began, though no doubt almost wholly proceeding from weakness; an utter want of power to govern his mind, either its wishes or its efforts. He says he rises at 6 o'clock in the morning; that is, he has done so for more than a week, nay, I believe a fortnight; and this morning, when I rang the bell to call the maid to fetch Catherine (Wordsworth) away, he came all alive to my door to ask if he could do anything for me. A week's residence in Thomas Wilkinson's humble cottage brought about this change, and I believe that Thomas, even at the last, was the father of *The Friend.* Coleridge was happy in Thomas's quiet and simple way of life, drank no spirits and was comfortable all the time, and Thomas urged him to the work.

Writing on the same day William told Stuart that despite his previous fears of the failure of *The Friend,* he was now more hopeful: "I now think it right to say that such appear to be the present dispositions, resolutions, and employments of Coleridge. . .that I am encouraged to entertain more favourable hopes of his exerting himself steadily than I ever have had at any other period of this business."

A week later Coleridge thanking an admirer for his "present," expounded at great length his own exalted moral aims in founding *The Friend.* "Nothing," he wrote, "but a deep and habitual conviction of its truth absolutely, and of its particular importance in the present generation could have roused me from that dream of great internal activity, an outward inefficience, into which ill-health and a wounded spirit had gradually lulled me. . . ."

As July ended, literary labors on *The Friend* occupied Coleridge. "Coleridge," Dorothy told De Quincey on August 1, "has been very busy of late, and his health and spirits are better—he has sent off the 3rd and 4th numbers of *The Friend,* and is at work daily."

Near the close of August Dorothy could still tell Catherine Clarkson, "Coleridge is going on well at present. The 4th essay will come out next week, and I know that he has the 5th and more ready."* Nevertheless, Dorothy's doubts had returned: "As to its future regularity, I dare not speak; only this I know, that he has no right to tax his customers with the stamp, unless he goes on differently from what he has hitherto done. At present he is full of hope, and has, I believe, made excellent resolutions."

By mid-September Coleridge's troubles about paper for *The Friend* were nearing their climax. Stuart's, Montagu's, and Clarkson's refusal had left him moneyless, angry, and naturally despondent. There was little in Coleridge's letters of this time to justify the placidity of Mrs. Wordsworth's report to De Quincey on September 12: "Coleridge has been very busy lately. You have received the 4th number, and will be glad to hear that the 5th and 6th are in the printer's hand. He has, of course, been in more comfortable health. Heaven grant this may last!"

An argument with Stuart next arose, when in reply to a new reproach by Coleridge of refusing to assist *The Friend*, Stuart proved that he had in fact offered financial help as far as the twentieth number. Stuart must also have spoken of the dullness of the paper for Coleridge now promised: "I feel confident, that my essays will increase in interest." During the first two weeks of October the quarrel between Stuart and Coleridge continued, Coleridge arguing that Stuart had approved the plan for *The Friend*, and denying a charge of vanity, though he admitted, "I once was fond of feeling my power perhaps in conversation." Indeed Stuart was evidently led, as Wordsworth had been a year before, to some plain speaking to Coleridge about his faults as Stuart saw them. However Coleridge now offered to send Stuart "two columns twice a week for the next twelve weeks" if Stuart wished. But he emphasized that *The Courier's* political attitude now no longer harmonized with Coleridge's "principles as anti-Jacobin, anti-Buonaparte." At this point if we may judge from Coleridge's published letters, silence fell between the two friends for the next eighteen months.

---

*"The continuity of issue was frequently broken—thus there were eight blank weeks between II and III; three between III and IV; one between XI and XII; one between XX and XXI; and one between XXVI and XXVII and last" (Campbell, p. 173). Chambers (pp. 221–25) gives the publication dates as No. 1, June 1st; No. 2, June 8th; No. 3, Aug. 10th; and from September 7th, the regular weekly issues were resumed. It failed to appear on Nov. 2nd, but except for that it ran continuously from September 7th to the end of the year (1809). The last issue appeared on March 15th, 1810 (Chambers, p.233)."

Fortunately Poole had already complied with Coleridge's appeal for money combining it however with demands for better management of *The Friend* in various ways. He would pay one-third of the stamp money needed, but on condition that Coleridge arranged for its repayment to himself. To this Coleridge agreed. Poole also suggested, as so many others had done, that improvements might be made in Coleridge's style of writing in *The Friend*. "All the defects you have mentioned," Coleridge replied, "I am perfectly aware of and am anxiously endeavouring to avoid. There is too often an entortillage in the sentences and even the thoughts, which nothing can justify. . . ." And in addition Coleridge requested, evidently as a compliment, that Poole would send him some material for *The Friend*. Nor was Southey outside the circle of *The Friend*. "Southey who has been my corrector," he now told Poole, "has been strangely oscitant—or—which I believe is sometimes the case, has not understood the sentences, and thought, they might have a meaning for *me* tho' they had not for him."

Relying upon the interest George had evidently shown in *The Friend* after receiving Samuel's letters of April, Coleridge now wrote him a begging letter. Flamboyantly rejoicing in the success of *The Friend*, which he said would bring him a profit of £500 a year, he went on to describe the many dream volumes of works, poems, political memoirs, a Greek grammar, a history of logic, etc., all "ready for the press as soon as I can procure the paper." Unfortunately however at the moment, he needed "to have £120 advanced, between two or three friends."

His financial need Coleridge continued to impress upon brother George by appeals for sympathy. As before to others, to George he now repeated his pathetic presentation of wife and children suffering permanently through Samuel's temporary lack of means. He could immediately sell *The Friend* to Longman for £300 a year but that would deprive his family of it as their property. Then too he had been betrayed by his most intimate friends—one, a gentleman unnamed (evidently Stuart), the other by name, Poole. Stuart he thus described: - "I had received the warmest promises from a gentleman who owes—(and he used to acknowledge it to others as well as in his letters to myself) a very large fortune not indeed *exclusively* to my efforts but so far that without them he could have done nothing—and what I did for him was shown by the fact, that when I began to undertake the literary part of the concern, the sale was 1100, and barely paid itself—when I left it, it was net £8000 a year, and the sale exceeded what had ever been known in a similar concern." A week before modestly offering Stuart some essays for *The Courier* as part of an inducement for a loan, he had told him, "I suppose the great sale of *The Courier* raises it above the want of literary assistance." As for Poole he told George, "I have no one to apply to except Mr. T. Poole—and tho' I never received a pecuniary loan from him but once, and that duly repaid, yet I have no reliance that he will step forward—tho' he is a truly good and indeed excellent man; but in the *natural* man of the very best of us there is a speck!"

To this effusion George, who probably knew more about Stuart and Poole than Coleridge suspected and resented the repetition of such pathetic appeals for money, angrily refused assistance. At the same time he returned Samuel's previous abusive letter of May 11, 1808 to him. Upon receiving George's letter Samuel immediately replied employing his favorite Christian technique, saying he had prayed for George and so held no resentment against him for his unkind letter. Indeed he continued, he no longer needed the money as his friends had readily supplied it—Coleridge's usual reply in such cases. Then he went on to dissect his own character. In humility he concluded, "God be my witness! I never uttered a disrespectful word concerning you to another person. . . ." As for money, he had never been in debt he declared, although "for 14 years" he had been "never with a spare guinea in my house, and often sorely wanting it." Yet "If impulses base as those you have ascribed to me had been compatible with my nature" he told George, "I should have been a rich man long ago: for few men have had more opportunities."

Two days later Coleridge sent Purkis a begging letter in which he appeared as a high-minded sufferer under George's cruelty. Pressed by his need for more paper, he tried to touch other friends for money with varying success, while Sharp not only offered the help requested, but also to advance the whole of the money that Coleridge needed if the other friends found assistance inconvenient.

Despite such encouragement, Coleridge soon wrote in despair to Southey, "What really makes me despond, is the daily confirmation I receive of my original apprehension, that the plan and execution of *The Friend* is so utterly unsuitable to the public taste as to preclude all rational hopes of its success." Complaints of the dullness of *The Friend* were now reaching Coleridge. To one critical reader he replied, "I must submit to be esteemed dull by those who sought chiefly for amusement." He could not he said "be surprised, however much I may have been depressed, by the frequency with which you hear *The Friend* complained of for its abstruseness and obscurity."

From this point Coleridge turned to defend his literary style from similar criticism. "A man long accustomed to silent and solitary meditation, in proportion as he increases the power of thinking in long and connected trains is apt to lose or lessen the talent of communicating his thoughts with grace and perspicuity. Doubtless too, I have in some measure injured my style, in respect of its facility and popularity, from having almost confined my reading, of late years, to the works of the Ancients and those of the elder writers in the modern languages. We insensibly imitate what we habitually admire. . . ." To another enquirer a little later Coleridge replied, "mere amusement is not the main object" of *The Friend*. Coleridge was however cheered by an appreciative letter from Lamb who much admired an article in *The Friend* on Luther. "God forbid," he wrote, "that a man who has such things to say should be silenced for want of £100. . . .Oh, that you may find means to go on!. . .Your letter has saddened me."

Early in November Coleridge unaware of the fact that his mother was dead, told Southey that he had received news that she was dying and wished to see him before she died. The news he said had come from Brother George in a friendly letter "but tho' my brother knows I am penniless, not an offer of a bank note to enable me to set off. In truth, I know not what to do—for there is not a shilling in our whole house." A few days later Coleridge received from Stuart, who now severed his association with *The Friend,* the depressing news that Samuel in the final account owed him a hundred pounds.

On Christmas eve 1809 Coleridge was writing essays for *The Friend* on Sir Alexander Ball, his former friend in Malta, who had died on October 20. Rickman on learning that Coleridge's articles on Ball were appearing, was far from optimistic, expecting from Coleridge on such a subject little or nothing beyond fulsome praise: "As usual in his conversation, so in his writing, he does the Devil's dirty work—flattery—without hope of reward; and now we are to expect a grand batch of it in the promised eulogy of Sir Alexander Ball, a man with whom he parted on the worst terms—on a mutual notorious hatred of each other. To be sure Sir Alexander's family will be *astonished* at a panegyric from S.T.C. Yet there is room for panegyric, and if C. had begun by saying 'Such is the infirmity of human nature that personally I could not endure this man, yet will I try to do justice to his merit,' this had been well. The courtesy is not very much unlike falsehood, and partakes of the old failing—flattery without benefit to himself." But before Coleridge's last article on Ball appeared, *The Friend* had ceased publication.

On March 15, 1810, the last number of *The Friend* appeared. From the beginning of the year Coleridge's best friends increasingly anticipated disaster. For their fears there were many reasons. In addition to the fundamental instability of Coleridge's nature there were also the impossibly ambitious scope of the periodical—even as shown in the syllabus—Coleridge's impracticable arrangements for the printing publication and sale of his paper, and worst of all its dullness, obscurity, and consequent lack of appeal for the average reader. Frequent interruption in the continuity of publication were another source of misgivings for both readers and for Coleridge himself.

Although on January 1, 1810, Lamb described *The Friend* as "occasionally sublime," he ominously continued, "The worst is, he is always promising something which never comes. . .but I rejoice that it lives." Characteristically incisive was Hazlitt's description of the paper: "An enormous title-page. . .an endless preface to an imaginary work." Poole on financially supporting *The Friend* at Coleridge's request had insisted as a condition that Ward, a London bookseller must receive all subscriptions. Now however, Ward, weary of the task, resigned in despair and only resumed it upon Coleridge's agonized supplication, "What I am to do God knows—and He only I believe!. . .For God's sake feel for me."

Although Coleridge's hopes for *The Friend* were already waning he told Poole in mid-January, when lamenting his difficulties over the journal, "My purpose is not to give up *The Friend* until it gives up itself." Yet shortly afterward he admitted to Lady Beaumont "My own hopes concerning *The Friend* are at dead low water." This was chiefly owing to the loss of subscribers of whom Coleridge was beginning to learn what he might well have suspected before, that the public were less avid of moral exhortation than he had suspected. Even of those who still subscribed he wrote, "alike joined in giving out *The Friend* as an unreadable thing—dull, paradoxical, abstruse, dry, obscure and Heaven knows what else! I am myself completely at rest. I have done my best." Yet in this darkness there was a gleam of light: ". . .even in its infancy *The Friend* has done some good—and an unspeakable comfort it is to me to reflect that what good it does must be of a permanent kind."

From the increasing charges of obscurity that were to be the main cause of *The Friend's* decease, Dorothy Wordsworth valiantly attempted to defend Coleridge but was by no means blind to both his and *The Friend's* defects.

I guess that you join the general complaint of obscurity [she wrote to Jane Marshall on February 21st], I allow that it almost requires the whole power and attention of the mind to understand the author, and that probably that mode of publication is not the proper one for matters so abstract as are frequently treated of—for who can expect that people whose daily thoughts are employed on matters of business, and who read only for relaxation, should be prepared for, or even capable of, serious thought when they take up a periodical paper, perhaps to read over in haste?

Nevertheless Dorothy was still hopeful: "We expected the number of subscribers to be very much diminished at the 20th paper; but it has not proved so, and there have been some new ones."

A week later Dorothy writing to Lady Beaumont spoke of Coleridge's disappointment after the critical twentieth number appeared on January 4,

Coleridge's spirits have been irregular of late. He was damped after the 20th number by the slow arrival of payments, and half persuaded himself he ought not to go on. [Dorothy continued with an admirable account of Coleridge and of his editorial work at this time], We laboured against such a resolve, and he seems determined to fight onwards; and indeed I do not think he has ever much reason to be discouraged, or *would have been* discouraged, if his spirits had not been damped; for there have been many untoward circumstances and much mismanagement to hinder the regular remittance of the money, and many people have not yet paid, merely from thoughtlessness, who, no doubt, will pay ere long; and the work cannot but answer in a pecuniary point of view, if there is not in the end a very great failure in the payments. By the great quantity of labour that he had performed since the commencement of *The Friend,* you will judge that he has upon the whole been very industrious; and you will hardly believe me when I tell you that there have been weeks and weeks when he has not composed a line. The fact is that he either does a great deal or nothing at all; and that he composes with a rapidity truly astonishing, if one did not reflect upon the large stores of thought which he has laid up, and the quantity of knowledge which he is continually gaining from books. Add to this his habit of expressing his ideas in conversation in elegant language. He has written a whole *Friend* more than once in two days. They are never re-transcribed, and he generally has dictated to Miss Hutchinson, who takes the words down from his mouth. We truly rejoice in the satisfaction which *The Friend* has spread around your fireside, and there are many solitary individuals who have been proud to express their thankfulness to the author.

Yet whatever the cause or causes, the intermissions between the few issues of the short-lived *Friend* were numerous and sometimes extensive. On several occasions when material was lacking, Wordsworth filled the gap. Thus with several poems and prose essays Wordsworth greatly assisted Coleridge from November 23, 1809 to January 25, 1810. Coleridge—as seven years later with the *Biographia Literaria*—rehashed his letters from Germany, to help at need.

Coleridge's troubles Sara Hutchinson of course shared. "He has had a vast of plagues," she told Mary Monkhouse on March 27, 1809. The "obstacles" to the success of *The Friend* she considered very great and Coleridge "least of any man I know is calculated to overcome them." For another year Sara continued to help Coleridge with *The Friend*, taking down from his dictation all the material he supplied. But in mid-March 1810 when little or no hope of saving *The Friend* remained, Sara Hutchinson gave up the work and went to join her brother, John Hutchinson, at his farm in Wales.

A month later Dorothy Wordsworth, describing Sara Hutchinson after her departure, wrote to Catherine Clarkson, "very comfortable and happy that she has been taken this journey. She is comfortable, but poor thing! she evidently feels a great want. There is not that life by the fireside that we have—they are sleepy before supper-time, being little interested in anything else than their own domestic or farming concerns, and people must languish with no other thoughts from morning to night."

With Sara's departure the publication of *The Friend* immediately ceased.

I need not tell you how sadly we miss Sara, [Dorothy told Catherine Clarkson], but I must add the truth that we are all glad she is gone. True it is she was the cause of the continuance of *The Friend* so long; but I am far from believing that it would have gone on if she had stayed. He was tired, and she had at last no power to drive him on; and now I really believe that *he* also is glad that she is not here, because he has nobody to tease him. His spirits have certainly been more equable, and much better. *Our* gladness proceeds from a different cause. He harassed and agitated her mind continually and we saw that she was doing her health perpetual injury. . . .As to Coleridge, if I thought I should distress you, I would say nothing about him, but I hope that you are sufficiently prepared for the worst. We have no hope for him. None that he will ever do anything more than he has already done. If he were not under our roof, he would be just as much the slave of stimulants as ever; and his whole time and thoughts, (except when he is reading, and he reads a great deal), are employed in deceiving himself, and seeking to deceive others. He will tell me that he has been writing, that he *has* written, half a *Friend*; when I *know* that he has not written a single line. This habit pervades all his words and actions, and you feel perpetually new hollowness and emptiness. Burn this letter [Dorothy next commanded Catherine]; I am loath to say it, but it is the truth. He lies in bed, always till after 12 o'clock, sometimes much later; and never walks out. Even the finest spring day does not tempt him to seek the fresh air; and this beautiful valley seems a blank to him. He never leaves his own parlour except at dinner and tea, and sometimes supper, and then he always seems impatient to get back to his solitude. He goes the moment his food is swallowed. Sometimes he does not speak a word and when he does talk it is always very much upon subjects as far aloof from himself, or his friends, as possible.

Soon Dorothy turned to Coleridge's love for Sara Hutchinson,

Do not think that it is his love for Sara which has stopped him in his work. Do not believe it; his love for her is no more than a fanciful dream. Otherwise he would prove it by a desire to make her happy. No! he likes to have her about him as his own, as one devoted to him, but when she stood in the way of other gratifications [evidently opium and brandy] it was all over. I speak this very unwillingly, and again I beg you *burn* this letter. [And Dorothy added] He speaks of *The Friend* always as if it were going on, and would go on, therefore, of course, you will drop no hint of my opinion. I heartily wish I may be mistaken.

Not until mid-October 1811 did Sara Hutchinson return to Allan Bank. By that time Coleridge had left Greta Hall for London.

As soon as Sara Hutchinson left Allan Bank Coleridge's thoughts turned to departure, first to Greta Hall, and from there to London. Nor did the now critical Dorothy apparently wish to detain him. "Coleridge talks of going to Keswick for a short time," she told Catherine, in the same letter of April 12, 1810, "I hope he will choose the time of Mary's confinement for his journey, as though he does not require near so much waiting upon as formerly, he makes a great difference—there is his parlour to clean, fire to light—sometimes gruel—toast and water—eggs—his bed always made at unreasonable times, and many other little things which tell in a house."

What little we may gather from the few letters Coleridge wrote between the death of *The Friend* and his arrival at Greta Hall, corroborate Dorothy's account of him at this time. In mid-April asking his wife, "My dear Love," when he could be received at Greta Hall as other guests were there including De Quincey, he told her he was "desirous to be with you and Sara [Coleridge] for a while. . . .I am middling" he wrote, "but the state of my spirit of itself requires a change of scene." Then, partly no doubt to please her, he enthused over his boys, "Hartley looks and behaves all that the fondest parent could wish. He is really handsome—at least, as handsome as a face so original and intellectual can be. And Derwent is 'a nice little fellow,' and no lackwit either. . . ." The next day excusing himself to Lady Beaumont for his delay in replying to her letter, he declared, "Idle I have not been absolutely—but willing to exert energy in any thing, only not that which the duty of the day demanded."

In this state a fortnight later Coleridge entered Greta Hall; depressed by the failure of *The Friend*, haunted and shattered by the separation from Sara Hutchinson, and somewhat disturbed by the responsibility for the maintenance of his wife and children, he sought escape in study. The present incentive to Coleridge's departure from Allan Bank was—as on a previous occasion— the impending birth of another little Wordsworth, William, born on May 12. Coleridge's original intention was to stay at Greta Hall only a few days until the excitement of the birth had subsided. But once installed there, he remained for some five months.

On August 3 Mrs. Coleridge described to Poole the state of her husband during this visit.

> I am sorry [she wrote] to add that, in all that time he has not *appeared* to be employed in composition although he has repeatedly assured me he was. The last No. of *The Friend* lies on his desk, the sight of which fills my heart with grief, and my eyes with tears; but I am obliged to conceal my trouble as much as possible, as the slightest expression of regret never fails to excite resentment—Poor Man!—I have not the least doubt but he is the most unhappy of the two; and the reason is too obvious to need any explanation—It must, however, be confessed, he has been in almost uniform kind disposition towards us all during his residence here; and all Southey's friends who have been here this summer have thought his presence a great addition to the society here; and have all been uniformly great admirers of his conversation; His spirits too, are in general better than I have known them for years, and I cannot divine the reason of his passing his hours in so unprofitable a manner.

"Yet," continued Mrs. Coleridge, "I must not say that his abode here has been without some advantages to us." In fact it appeared Coleridge was teaching both his wife and his daughter Sara Italian. Mrs. Coleridge "was rejoiced" when this began, "but" she added, "was afraid he would not persevere, and I am convinced he would very often have put off the child, when he could not find an excuse to send *both* away when our tasks were ready." Coleridge was also interested in the studies of the two boys at the Ambleside School in Greek and Latin and bought for them a Greek lexicon.

Dorothy's description of Coleridge at Allan Bank in her letter of April 1810 to Catherine Clarkson, suggested less studious propensities to Coleridge's attitude to his children. "The boys come every week," she wrote, "and he talks to them, especially to Hartley, but he never examines them in their books." Hartley was now fourteen and Derwent ten. As things were, the children were both a source of pleasure and of anxiety to their poor mother: "These dear boys" she told Poole, "are the source of much pleasure to me at present—Heaven only knows how long it will last!" For despite these causes for consolation, she was unhappy. "Heaven knows" she told Poole, "I am so bewildered about our affairs that I do not know what to wish or what to *do*. These lads too, Hartley in particular is fast approaching towards manhood—what can he think is to become of them if he does not exert himself."

"This very day" Mrs. Coleridge informed Miss Betham on February 16, 1811, "Coleridge left us four months ago, he had been here five months in better health, spirits and humour than I had seen him for any great length of time for years before.* I fear he has been different since he left us." Yet she con-

---

*During these months at Greta Hall, Coleridge—probably under pressure from Southey—gave him a few contributions to his *Omniana*.

tinued, since Coleridge's departure from Greta Hall, he "had not *once* addressed any of his northern friends," It was only by chance she said, that she had heard that he was now domiciled with the Morgans and had been applying for advice to Dr. Abernathy. "I wish Coleridge would write!" she added, "both Southey and myself have written often to him.

Modern criticism of *The Friend* is by no means laudatory. Even in 1884, Traill impatient with the dullness of *The Friend*, remarked: "We have, of course, to bear in mind that the standard of the readable in our grandfathers' days was a more liberal and tolerant one than it is in our own."* And he went on to point out that even Coleridge was conscious of this defect. "With perfect frankness indeed does he admit in his prospectus that he must submit to be thought dull by those who seek amusement only." Traill's sufferings as a reader of *The Friend* are very evident, leading to the conclusion, "Coleridge's own theory of his duty as a public instructor was in itself fatal to any hope of his venture proving a commercial success."**

But Traill's sufferings sink almost into insignificance before the vehement verdict of another sufferer from *The Friend*—Elton: "As a book it is impossible, and as a periodical it was still more so; words would be wasted on its shapelessness and its profusion of digressive rigmarole."*** Perhaps the kindest verdict one may pronounce upon Coleridge's unfortunate periodical is the one with which Dickens used to cheer unhappy aspiring novelists who had submitted their first attempts for his opinion: "Well! For those who like that kind of thing—it is just the kind of thing they'll like."

*Coleridge; by H.D. Traill, ed. 1909, p.127.
**Ibid., p.129.
***Survey of English Literature, vol. 2, by Oliver Elton, ed. 1920, p.126.

7 The Great Quarrel with Wordsworth (1810-11)

"There are not those beings on earth, who can truly say that having professed affection for them, I ever either did or spoke unkindly or unjustly of them."

—S.T. Coleridge to John Morgan, October 12, 1811

As preceding chapters have shown the mutual feelings of Wordsworth and Coleridge had gradually changed since Coleridge's visit to Coleorton. Wordsworth's disappointment in his expectation of seeing Coleridge's genius find expression in poetry or in prose and the failure of *The Friend*, had destroyed his hopes for him. There was also Wordsworth's disgust with Coleridge's surrender to opium and spirits. Finally a bone of contention between Coleridge and Wordsworth was Sara Hutchinson. How far Wordsworth's feelings towards Coleridge had changed since the Alfoxden days, his letter to Coleridge (surely never sent) written just before Samuel came to Allan Bank, had clearly shown in its devastating but true analysis of Coleridge's temperament. In all this there was sufficient combustible material for a big fire. To it Wordsworth unconsciously and with the best intentions soon applied the ignition spark.

Coleridge's journey to London was not solitary; His companions were Basil Montagu,* Mrs. Montagu, and their little daughter. The Montagus had called at Greta Hall in October on their return from Scotland to London, and had offered Coleridge a seat in their chaise as well as hospitality in their home. Coleridge gladly accepted their offer, which he had probably invited, and on October 18, 1810, they set off—stopping at Allan Bank on their way.

One of Coleridge's reasons for visiting London was supposedly to place himself under a Dr. Carlisle for treatment as an opium addict. Dorothy informing her friend in November of Coleridge's departure for London tartly commented, "The consulting Carlisle is quite a farce, but the Montagus say he seems disposed to be regular. For my part I am hopeless of him, and I dismiss him as much as possible from my thoughts." Nor was Southey's comment upon Coleridge's resort to Carlisle more sympathetic than Dorothy's. "Cole-

---

*Basil Montagu (Senior) Montagu had remarried.

ridge is in London'' he told a friend, ''gone professedly to be cured of taking opium and drinking spirits, by Carlisle—*really* because he was tired of being here, and wanted to do both, more at his ease, elsewhere. I have a dismal letter about him from Carlisle. The case is utterly hopeless.''

During the leisurely week's journey to town the idealized Sara Hutchinson haunted Coleridge's mind and filled his notebook with the usual sentimental yearnings. Strange discordant elements inserted in his love longings were reproaches to Wordsworth in pedestrian Latin verses, for opposing Samuel's passion for Sara, and also for opposing opium and alcohol.

As the coach rolled on towards London Coleridge meditated love as an abstraction from several standpoints: intellectually, metaphysically, psychologically, and religiously. He cogitated the difference between love and lust. Love not lust he knew must be the feeling roused in him in his noblest purest hours—when moved by Nature, Art, Science of high Morality. ''Why'' he asked ''I say, why, when ever I am best, and most worthy, most incapable of guilt or folly, do I then feel the Yearning, this intense *Love*? '' And he continued: ''Were Sara here, even the adored here, enjoying it with me then, then, it would be Heaven possessed-'' In this strain of romantic sentiment he relieved his emotions in crying to Sara: ''To bid me not to love you were to bid me annihilate myself.'' With these and more such rhapsodies, Coleridge beguiled the tedium of the journey to town. Such was the prelude of the great quarrel between Coleridge and Wordsworth.

On October 26, the travelers arrived at the Montagus' London home, 55 Frith Street, Soho. Two days after their arrival Montagu, who had been annoyed during their journey by Coleridge's habits, exploded into angry denunciations of them to Coleridge himself. According to De Quincey the immediate occasion of the quarrel was the annoyance of Montagu who was a teetotaller, when Coleridge ordered wine for dinner. Other accounts differ; but the fact seems to have been that within two days Coleridge's behavior as a guest, had so irritated Montagu that he managed to get rid of him. It was evidently the culmination of Montagu's irritation with Coleridge during the journey; but when Montagu exploded he cited Wordsworth as one who had warned him against taking Coleridge into his house.

Before the Montagus and Coleridge left Allan Bank Wordsworth in fact, with the best intentions, to prevent this very rupture between his two friends, which he foresaw, had privately warned Montagu that Coleridge's habits would make him a very difficult guest in the home of so industrious a worker as Montagu himself. This situation—particularly if other incentives were present—contained all the materials for a first-class quarrel. The main cause was of course the question as to what words Montagu had imputed to Wordsworth; what words Coleridge imputed to Montagu; what words Montagu said *he* had said, and what words Wordsworth said *he* had actually said. So finally, the question was, ''What had Wordsworth in fact said to Montagu?'' Unfortunately all parties whether Wordsworthian or Coleridgian, instead of seeing its absurdity, regarded the question as extremely serious, although Coleridge despite the bitter importance he attached to Wordsworth's words, never attempted to deny the facts they described.

Grieved and of course heartbroken, Coleridge withdrew to Hudson's Hotel in Covent Garden. There for the next few days he nursed his misery to his heart's content, contrasting his loyalty to Wordsworth, even self-sacrifice as he believed, with his betrayal by the Wordsworths—for even Dorothy was included. In fact Coleridge's chief bitterness was his realization that his deplorable habits were alienating his best friends. Mrs. Montagu must have attempted to console Coleridge in his misery, for on November 1 he told Sara Hutchinson's cousin, John Monkhouse, "Mrs. Montagu is indeed a very rare instance of the union of a very superior intellect with winning kindheartedness, and easy, matronly, confidence-winning manners." Some two years later when Coleridge had learned that Mrs. Montagu supported her husband and Wordsworth, he declared her as a "horror of women. . . ."

Coleridge's anger with the Montagus did not soon pass. In September 1814 he described himself to Stuart as having been "duped by fool plus fiend, I.e. Basil + Mrs. M. to travel 300 miles solely to put myself under his [Dr. Carlisle's] care."

Soon however, on hearing of the quarrel, came John Morgan on November 3, 1810, posthaste to Hudson's Hotel, to rescue the brokenhearted Coleridge. Eighteen months later, he described it thus to Wordsworth: "A most intimate and dear friend of Mr. and Mrs. Montagu's had urged Mr. Morgan to call at the Montagus in order to be put on his guard against me. He came to me instantly, told me I had enemies at work against my character, and pressed me to leave the hotel and come home with him."

It was in this way that Coleridge resumed residence with the Morgans, now at 7 Portland Place, Hammersmith. There as before, pleasantly ensconced with them, he again too readily yielded to the call of opium and brandy. This in turn stimulated the good Morgans to urge restraint. By this time, according to Southey, Coleridge's dose of opium was a daily pint. He found the Morgans' efforts to save him intolerable and burst from their house, as he had burst from the Montagus' and would later burst from the Gillmans'. On December 21, 1810, he took refuge in Brown's Coffee House in Mitre Court, Fleet Street.

In a kindly letter informing them of his whereabouts he apologized to the Morgans for the trouble he had given them, hoped they were not offended, explained that his sudden departure was due to self-dissatisfaction and his decision not "to trifle on any longer" but place himself under Dr. Abernathy, who now replaced Carlisle. These he said, were his aims: "to settle something by which I can ensure a certain sum weekly, sufficient for lodging, maintenance, and physician's fees." For this last he said, he must "raise" £2 or £3, to enclose in an introductory letter to Dr. Abernathy. That he did not intend to return to the Morgans became evident when he requested them to send him "all my books and papers with such of my linen as may be clean." Samuel's letter ended in the old way with adoration for the ladies for their many virtues and in this case, even a final rhyming couplet -

And looking t'wards the Heaven, that bends above you,
Full oft I bless the lot, that made me love you!

In his renewed solitude Coleridge can hardly have welcomed a letter from Southey urging his return to Greta Hall and his domestic responsibilities—duties that the hard-working Southey was now being forced to assume. The letter, Southey told a friend, was written "in plain but proper terms, asking him if he did not himself feel how idle it was to go about looking for external aid. . .urging him to return here, this being the best place for him whether he adopts a wiser mode of life or persists in his present destructive one, and beseeching him to let me be his task-master for three months. . . .Something too I said about his children. He has given me no answer, which is easily accounted for, for I have no doubt that this letter, as well as two former ones which I have written him, is still unopened." Southey's appeal of course failed.

Despite Coleridge's obvious intention to leave the Morgans, at least for a time, he must have soon returned to them for early in February 1810 he again departed: this time to live at 34 Southampton Buildings, Strand, where as it happened, Hazlitt was his neighbor. Here too, his stay must have been brief. For on March 12 he told Miss Betham he must return to the Morgans in Hammersmith on that day, "as I am not fit to be in lodgings by myself."

For various reasons Coleridge at this time was in a particularly emotional state. In society he doubtless sought forgetfulness of his unhappiness. Not only was he oppressed by the quarrel with Wordsworth but also by his difficulties in obtaining money for his needs: and (perhaps above all) by memories of the absent Sara. Now too came sad news of the death of his early Pantisocratic friend, George Burnett. Erratic, an opium addict, Burnett had wandered about the world in various activities—as Dissenting Minister, tutor to the sons of Lord Stanhope and Secretary to a Polish count. He had then returned to England bankrupt. During these years Coleridge's feelings towards Burnett had varied as toward all Coleridge's friends. At one time Burnett had seemed to him "a coxcomb mad with vanity and stupid with opium." On another occasion after an unexpected meeting with him, Coleridge declared: "It made my heart feel almost as if it was going to ache, when I looked at his eyes—they seemed thoroughly those of an opium chewer. . . ." For his miserable state Burnett blamed his Pantisocratic friends Southey and Coleridge and Pantisocracy. With this Lamb agreed saying that they had done harm to Burnett's "flimsy skull." And now Burnett lay dead in Marylebone workhouse under suspicion of suicide. Mary Lamb, overcome by the shock, was again in the asylum.

The opium-drugged eyes of Burnett surely still haunted Coleridge's memory—as well as the quarrel with Wordsworth—when on March 12 1811, he cried to Robinson, "Troubles, God knows! have thronged upon me—Alas! alas! all my dearest friends I have of late either suffered *from,* or suffered *for.* Tis a cruel sort of world we live in! "A moral obligation," he continued, "is to me so very strong a stimulant, that in nine cases out of ten it acts as a narcotic. The blow that should rouse, *stuns* me." This Southey unconsciously corroborated when he told Sir George Beaumont a fortnight later: "The more necessary it becomes for Coleridge to exert himself in providing means for meeting the growing demands of his children, the more incapable, by some strange and fatal infirmity, does he become of exertion."

The day following his outburst to Robinson and after "a mournful conversation" with Lamb, Coleridge went on to keep a dinner engagement with Lady Jerningham. "My head throbbing with long weeping and the unnecessary haste I made in fear of being too late, and the having to act before the curtain, as it were, afterwards." Lady Jerningham sent a friend an interesting description of Coleridge on this occasion. "He came. . .and displayed a superabundance of words," she wrote: "and though certainly clever, I think his ideas lack behind, which makes him in the space of an hour give several contradictory opinions. He deems himself obliged to play first violin, and was much fatigued with the violent exertion he made. . . ."

By this time, Coleridge and Robinson were personal friends. Robinson had first met Coleridge on November 14, 1810, at Lambs' and had immediately fallen—though not uncritically—under the spell of his conversation. "Coleridge." Robinson declared, cannot *con*verse, he *ad*dresses himself *to* his hearers. At the same time he is a much better listener than I expected." At this first meeting Coleridge held Robinson spellbound from half past three in the afternoon till midnight by his talk of a thousand things, including politics, metaphysics, the Regency, poetry, Kant, and Shakespeare. Yet to his diary Robinson confided, "Tho' he practises all sorts of delightful tricks and shows admirable skill in riding his hobbies, yet he may be easily unsaddled. . . .Gross inconsistensies might easily be obtained from him." And finally Robinson decided: "An incomparable declaimer and speechmaker, he has neither the readiness nor the acuteness required by a colloquial disputant." But such criticism did not prevent his close friendship with Coleridge, whom Robinson occasionally assisted; as for example by advertising Coleridge's lectures in *The Times.*

By April 23, 1811, Coleridge was back in Southampton Buildings from which he had recently fled to the Morgans because of his inability when alone, to control his addiction to opium. Soon, once again, he returned to the Morgans.

In the spring of 1811 Coleridge was evidently at his wits' end for money. In this dilemma he first extracted a mere twenty pounds from Longman as an advance payment for an edition of his poems, never made. After this "Jew bargain" as the discontented Coleridge called it, he enthusiastically accepted Godwin's invitation to dine with himself and Henry Grattan, the Irish statesman, and borrowed two pounds from Godwin at the same time. Godwin's request for repayment a week later received only an encouraging promise for the future.

Next Coleridge turned to Stuart, as often before when in need, offering him in return for his aid, daily work at *The Courier* office. When his mind was "once at ease," and the unpaid subscriptions for *The Friend* collected, as he told Stuart, he would repay all his debts to him. From such "Cormorants on the Tree of Knowledge" as publishers he cried, referring to Longman, he would protect "S.T.C. and his three little ones." Evidently unable to resist this appeal Stuart made an agreement with Coleridge which actually resulted in the appearance of 45 or more articles by him in *The Courier* between May and September 1811.

These articles cover a wide variety of topics ranging from attacks on Napoleon, on Catholicism, and the scourging of women prisoners, to such subjects as *Christ Hospital* and *A Death-bed*. One article by Coleridge criticizing the appointment of the Prince of Wales as Regent was attacked in the House of Lords, and another objecting to the selection of the Duke of York to be Commander-in-Chief to the Army was suppressed by the Government—to Coleridge's great annoyance.

Coleridge's style in these articles varied according to the subject, from the direct and concise writing characteristic of his earlier years, to the laborious prolixity of his later writing. Of this Coleridge was very conscious. What vetting of Coleridge's articles may have occurred in the *Courier* office we cannot of course know.

Some readers, as with *The Friend*, objected to what they considered Coleridge's obscurity and diffuseness. Apologetically Coleridge replied to these objections, telling Stuart: "I hope in another week's time I shall have learnt to compress, or rather to select, my thoughts, so as to make them more frequently admissible. . . .I feel I have yet to learn how much larger a space my scraps occupy in the paper, than I am the least aware of while writing them. What I had imagined a snug little paragraph turns out to be a column."

Throughout the first half of the year 1811, despite the misery of his quarrel with Wordsworth, Coleridge not only found as in previous years relaxation in the social life of London, he also, though now thirty-eight, suddenly blossomed as a beau of the period, to Dorothy's disgust. Charles Lamb observing this development, described it to Dorothy Wordsworth in the affectionately ironical style he now so often adopted toward Samuel. "Coleridge has powdered his head and looks like Bacchus, Bacchus ever sleek and young. He is going to turn sober, but his clock has not struck yet; meantime he pours down goblet after goblet, the 2nd to see where the 1st is gone, the 3rd to see no harm happens to the second, a fourth to say there's another coming, and a 5th to say he's not sure he's the last." Lamb's remark of "goblet after goblet" was substantiated by Coleridge himself in April 1811 when, after a dinner party, he told Stuart: "I arrived safe at my lodgings, about ½ past 12; but I have suffered, as I deserved, most severely for my intemperance." In this state he said, "I vow to God, and I pray, God help me to keep the vow, that I never hereafter will drink a single glass of wine during dinner. . . ." But both vow and prayer were obviously forgotten without delay.

Toward the end of the same month, Coleridge went to Richmond for a day or two and called on John May, a wealthy wine merchant who was a friend of Southey. There he met two of his nephews, John Taylor Coleridge (twenty-one years old), and his brother Henry Nelson (thirteen), the sons of Samuel's brother, Colonel James Coleridge, who had married a rich wife. John Taylor, delighted at this meeting, at once sent to his brother James a vivid account of his impressions. Coleridge's talk fascinated him during the two days they were together, "Every subject he was master of, and discussed in the most splendid eloquence, without ever pausing for a word. Whether poetry, religion, language, politics or metaphysics were on the 'tapis,' he was equally at home and equally clear. It was curious to see the ladies loitering most attentively, and being really uncommonly entertained with a long discussion of two hours on the deepest metaphysics. . . .He made a conquest of all men and women at Richmond; gave us analysis of long works which are to come out, recited songs and odes of his own, told stories of his youth and travels, never sparing himself at all, and altogether made the most powerful impression on my mind of any man I ever saw. Yet I saw and heard *some* things which I did not quite like." Nevertheless still fascinated, the two youths walked back with Coleridge to his inn while he continued his eloquent discourse all the way.

The next morning they all went to church. "He seemed full of calm piety," Henry Taylor noted "and said he always felt the most delightful sensations in a Sunday churchyard. . . .After the service, he was vehement against the sermon, as common place, and invidious in its tone toward the poor. . . ." That afternoon back at May's after another metaphysical talk, this time with a French professor, a lady sang Italian songs to Coleridge's delight. "He was enraptured" wrote John Taylor Coleridge, "his frame quivered with emotion, and there was a titter of uncommon delight on his countenance. When it was over he praised the singer warmly and prayed she might finish those strains in heaven!"

Now at times when in Hammersmith with the Morgans, Coleridge still received friendly visits there from the Lambs. Charles Lamb's occasional notes to John Morgan radiate geniality toward the Morgans and Coleridge. It was thus in early October 1811, when Lamb in a short note to John Morgan remarked, "Our dinner at Hammersmith must cool for another day. Where is the lecturer, quasi lecturus? He has not been heard of at his own abode this fortnight. . . ." Throughout this month, Coleridge combined social life with preparations for advertising the course of lectures he was to give immediately afterward.

On October 8, after dining at Godwin's with the Irish politician, John P. Curran, and John Wolcot, the poetical satirist, well known as "Peter Pindar," Coleridge found a letter from John Morgan. Once again Coleridge had evidently fled from the Morgan household for four days later he replied to John,

My disappearance from you, will have afforded sign and seal to all the unfavourable judgements prompted by feelings. . .which, Heaven knows
how! I have excited for the last 6 months or more in your wife and sister, I
am well aware. I say, Heaven knows how!—because I cannot torture my
memory into a recollection of a single moment, in which I ever spake,
thought, wished, or felt anything that was not consistent with the most
fondly cherished esteem, and a personal and affectionate predilection for
them.

And he continued in the same strain. Conveniently forgetful of his many letters denigrating his friends when annoyed with them, Coleridge now declared
to Morgan,

There are not those beings on earth, who can truly say that having professed
affection for them, I ever either did or spoke unkindly or unjustly of
them. . . .[And he proceeded to impute his present difficulties to] having
imprudently hoped too highly of men, including wicked publishers [who
had robbed him] and particularly "a Maecenas worth £50,000," [evidently
Stuart]. [Nor was this all; other woes were "clamorous letters" from Mrs.
Coleridge,] the never closing, festering wound of Wordsworth and his family, and other aggravations. [Finally Coleridge bade him] Think of me as one
deceased who *had been* your sincere friend.

Three days later, October 15, 1811, Coleridge posted this letter to John
Morgan together with a recantation and apology.

I intreat (and beg you to intreat for me) [it began] Mrs. Morgan and
Charlotte's forgiveness for the gross disrespect, which my absence and
silence render me guilty of. I am truly and to my very heart sensible, that it
has been such behaviour, as they and you had little merited from me—and
that the rudeness is a trifle compared with the apparent ingratitude. [Then
followed self-justifying excuses:] I can only palliate it by saying what is the
Truth and the whole Truth, that my intentions have not been guilty—that
the agitation and distraction of my mind have been the causes—that it was
intolerable to me to bring back to your Home of Peace and Love a spirit so
disquieted—that I feared the probable effects of vexation on my bodily
health and had solemnly vowed that I would never be ill 24 hours together in
your House. . .

And in conclusion he asked John Morgan to burn both letters.

8   More Lectures and Farewell to Greta Hall (1811-12)

". . .It is a matter of great importance to me, as far as I am unfortunately a husband, Father, &—not thro' any fault of my own—a debtor. Otherwise, from any lesser dictate than that of Duty, I would not have humbled myself to solicit favors from Newspaper People while Luxuries, as cabbage stalks, lay rotting on Dunghills—No, nor then—for there are worse Deaths than Starving, even if much easier ones were out of our power."
                                    —S.T. Coleridge to William Godwin
                                             November 8, 1811
                                    (Re. advertising his Lectures)

Early in November 1811 Coleridge began preliminaries for the lectures which he reluctantly contemplated. On November 4 he invited Thomas J. Pettigrew, Surgeon, Antiquary, and Founder (in 1810) of the London Philosophical Society to come and have tea or dinner with him and the Morgans in Hammersmith. Coleridge's letter included a request for permission to add the name of the London Philosophical Society to the advertisement of his forthcoming lectures. The close of the letter was impressive: "When I return to my house in Keswick (a large mansion occupied in common by me and Mr. Southey, the husband of my wife's sister) should choice or chance lead you to the Lakes, you will find house-room and a glad welcome there. . . ." The consequence was that Coleridge's advertisement duly appeared under the aegis of the London Philosophical Society.

How distasteful Coleridge found the necessity of again lecturing he very clearly expressed to Godwin four days after inviting Pettigrew. Amid the nuisance of advertising he cried: "It is a matter of great importance to me, as far as I am unfortunately a husband, father, and—not thro' any fault of my own—a debtor. Otherwise, from any lesser dictate than that of duty, I would not have humbled myself to solicit favors from Newspaper People while such luxuries as cabbage stalks lay rotting on dunghills—No, nor then—for there are worse deaths than starving, even if much easier ones were out of our power."

There was also the trouble of finding a Lecture room. After rejecting "The Coachmakers' Hall" as "having no literary or philosophical redolence, or rather smelling somewhat unsavoury to the nares intellectuales of all my wealthy acquaintance. . .'' he accepted the lecture room of the London Philosophical Society in Crane Court, off Fetter Lane. The room he approved for being ''spacious and handsome. . . fitted up in a very grave authentic poetic-philosophic style, with the busts of Newton, Milton, Shakespeare, Pope, and Locke behind the lecturer's cathedra.'' But there were drawbacks. The entrance, he told Dr. Bell the educationist, was ''disagreeable even to foot-comers, and far more so to carriages from the narrowness and bending of the Lane.'' Besides the locality was vulgar, Fetter Lane itself he said, ''renowned exclusively for pork and sausages.'' Later, annoyed by the smallness of his audiences he blamed Fetter Lane, yet gained some consolation in finding his hearers ''highly respectable.''

As the time for the lectures approached Coleridge as usual on such occasions called upon his best friends for their assistance in advertising them in the Press. Requesting Godwin's help in this way including payment for the advertisements, which he promised to repay Godwin when able, he also described him on the same day to Robinson as ''Godwin whom yet I have little reason to rely on.''

In his advertisement of these lectures Coleridge informed the public:

MR. COLERIDGE

will commence

ON MONDAY, NOV. 18TH,

A COURSE OF LECTURES ON SMAKESPEARE (sic) AND MILTON,

in illustration of

THE PRINCIPLES OF POETRY,

and their

Application as grounds of criticism to the most popular works
of later English Poets, those of the Living included.

After an introductory lecture on false criticism (especially in poetry) and on its causes: two-thirds of the remaining course, will be assigned, let, to a philosophic analysis and explanation of all the principal *characters* of our great dramatist, as Othello, Falstaff, Richard 3rd, Iago, Hamlet, etc.; and 2nd, to a critical *comparison* of Shakespeare, in respect of diction, imagery, management of the passions, judgement in the construction of his dramas, in short, of all that belongs to him as a poet, and as a dramatic poet, with his contemporaries, or immediate successors, Jonson, Beaumont and Fletcher, Ford, Massinger, etc. in the endeavour to determine what of Shakespeare's merits and defects are common to him with other writers of the same age, and what remain peculiar to his own genius.

The course will extend to fifteen lectures, which will be given on Monday and Thursday evenings successively. The lectures to commence at half-past 7 o'clock.

Single tickets for the whole course, 2 guineas, or 3 guineas with the privilege of introducing a lady; may be procured at J. Hatchard's, 190, Piccadilly; J. Murray's, Fleet Street; J. and A. Arch's Booksellers and Stationers, Cornhill; Godwin's Juvenile Library, Skinner Street, W. Pople's, 67 Chancery Lane, or by letter (post paid) to Mr. S. T. Coleridge, J. J. Morgan's Esq., No. 7 Portland Place, Hammersmith.''*

To cover such a course in fifteen lectures or even in seventeen, to which Coleridge extended it—the addition being due to his digressions and repetitions as he explained—was no mean order even if closely adhered to. But this Coleridge was far from attempting.

The unusual punctuality of Coleridge's attendance must surely have been due to the Morgans. So from November 18, 1811, to January 27, 1812, on Mondays and Thursdays at half-past seven in the evening, Coleridge resumed his reluctant role of public lecturer. These lectures too were particularly well reported independently by three persons, i.e. Crabb Robinson, John Payne Collier, and a Mr. J. Tomalin.

Coleridge's first lecture began with a reference to the difficulties confronting him in lecturing on so wide a syllabus. "The field," he told them, "is almost boundless as the sea, yet full of beauty and variety as the land: I feel in some oppressed by abundance. . . ." So too were some of the audience; for in his next lecture Coleridge began by informing his hearers that some had already complained of his incomprehensibility.

Ever ready to admire what he thought good yet seldom uncritical, the indefatigable Robinson allowed nothing to escape him. Of the first lecture he wrote:

> I fear the general opinion is not very favourable. It wanted popularity. And the moral remarks he made were not shown to have an immediate bearing upon the subject. . . . [These remarks Robinson found particularly boring as he had often heard them before from Coleridge, and he complained that there was] too much apology, too much reference to what he had before written, too much promise of what was to come. . . . The observations he made were in the main just and striking. But the lecture hardly equalled his conversation.

These remarks of Robinson's on the first lecture are a fair example of his general attitude to the course as a whole though several lectures excited his pleasure and admiration.

---

*Coleridge gave these lectures of 1811-12 on the following dates: Lecture 1, Nov. 18th; 2, Nov. 21st; 3, Nov. 25th 4, Nov. 28th; 5, Dec. 2nd; 6, Dec. 5th; 7, Dec. 9th; 8, Dec. 12th; 9, Dec. 16th; 10, Dec. 19th; 11, Dec. 30th; 1811: in 1812, Lecture 12, Jan. 2nd; 13, Jan. 9th; 14, Jan. 13th; 15, Jan. 16th; 16, Jan. 20th; 17, Jan. 27th. The last two lectures were additional. The material of all these lectures was in fact almost identical with that of the 1808 course.

Robinson found the third and fourth lectures disappointing through "repetition." His comment upon the fourth lecture was:

"The habit of thus chewing the cud of his past lectures will be offensive. Hearers require to have the sense of getting on. And I begin to fear that Coleridge's laziness will lead him to be content with dreaming on, playing over certain favourite ideas which he delights in but which some of his hearers will be tired of."

Although Coleridge began his lectures under a sense of oppression at the wide extent of his syllabus he often wandered beyond it in digressions on additional subjects. Robinson, lamenting this tendency in the fifth and sixth lectures wrote:

"Reviewers, French philosophy, precocity, etc. in the education of children, but unluckily scarcely one observation on Shakespeare, Milton, or even on poetry."

Another objector to Coleridge's digressiveness was Miss Mary Russell Mitford, a young writer of twenty-four who eight years later became famous as the author of *Our Village*. She came to Coleridge's lectures and to hear Coleridge's opinions on "Milton and Shakespeare, and criticism and poetry, and poets and critics, and whipping little boys, and love and philosophy, and every other subject that ever entered the head of man."

But Miss Mitford also acknowledged in Coleridge "that electric power of genius" by which despite all drawbacks Coleridge held his audience.

One unfortunate consequence of Coleridge's digressions was his frequent inability to deal with his main subject in the lecture as advertised. To hear Coleridge speak on *Romeo and Juliet* Robinson vainly attended four lectures, only to find at last the substitution of *The Tempest*—though "treated beautifully"—instead of the long-sought play he desired. At last at the seventh lecture *Romeo and Juliet* arrived and inspired a dissertation on love.

Robinson thought it "incomparably his best lecture." An unfortunate continuation of the same subject, Love, in the next lecture which degenerated into a consideration of "incest" Robinson thought "his worst." So the lectures proceeded under Robinson's vigilant eye.

Although Coleridge declares aesthetic principles to be essential for literary criticism, in these and other lectures we find little or no such practice. Instead, as with Shakespeare's characters, the criticism depends upon sensitive observation and comparison, occasionally including self-knowledge, as in his discussion of Hamlet's nature. This Robinson acutely observed. So too, long afterward did T. S. Eliot when he wrote: "For what is Coleridge's *Hamlet*: is it an honest inquiry as far as the data permit, or is it an attempt to present Coleridge in an attractive costume?"*

---

*Coleridge in his own copy of Shakespeare wrote: "I have a smack of Hamlet in myself, if I may say so." *Coleridge, The Work and The Relevance* by William Walsh (London 1967) p.57. The quotation from T. S. Eliot is in his *Points of View* (London, 1941) p.16.

Eliot's criticism is in general very just, but in the case of Hamlet, Coleridge's excuse had he but known it, might have been an unconscious recognition of the hysterical temperament common to both Hamlet and Coleridge himself. Nevertheless Eliot's criticism closely resembles a remark of Coleridge to Sotheby in 1802 when he wrote: "It is easy to clothe imaginary beings with our own thoughts and feelings; but to send ourselves out of ourselves, to *think* ourselves in to the thoughts and feelings of beings in circumstances wholly and strangely different from our own—*hoc labor, noc opus*—and who has achieved it? Perhaps only Shakespeare."

The lectures on Milton that followed generally pleased Robinson. But Coleridge's attack on Dr. Johnson when he called Johnson "a fellow' caused the audience to hiss their disapproval, which produced from Coleridge a lame apology. Coleridge's final lecture was, said Robinson, "exceedingly well attended."

A little later in his Reminiscences Robinson declared as his final verdict on these lectures, that they were "less interesting than they would otherwise have been, because having been lately much in his company, the leading ideas were familiar to me. The difference was not great between his conversation, which was a sort of lecturing and soliloquizing, and his lectures, which were colloquial, and in which, as he was himself aware, it was impossible for him to be methodical. And those hearers who enjoyed him most, probably enjoyed most his digressions." Robinson also noted that the average attendance at the lectures was about 150.

Robinson's comments and criticisms, interesting and valuable though they are, do not lessen the importance of the acounts left by the other reporters, Tomalin and Collier. From these we gather information which most usefully supplements Robinson's *Diary* and gives us a clearer insight into the actual methods and material of Coleridge's lectures.

Perhaps the most obvious characteristics include Coleridge's definitions by poetic imagery, which is more likely to attract than to enlighten a popular audience. It is thus when he defines poetry: "her seat is the bosom of God, her voice the harmony of the world." So too again of poetry: "pleasurable excitement is its origin and object; pleasure is the magic circle out of which the poet must not dare to tread." Similarly picturesque rather than enlightening is Coleridge's illumination of the necessity of correct thought, by describing the trained hunter of chamois leaping precipices which the untrained cannot cross. At other times Coleridge's imagery descends to cheapness, perhaps intended to be humorous. Thus he classifies readers as: "sponges, who absorb all they read, and return it nearly in the same state, only a little dirtied; sand-glasses, who retain nothing, and are content to get through a book for the sake of getting through the time; strain-bags, who retain merely the dregs of what they read"; and "Mogul diamonds, equally rare and valuable, who profit by what they read, and enable others to profit by it also."

Very obvious too in Coleridge's lectures are his devious approaches to the various subjects he intends to discuss. This made the wearied Robinson a year later describe them as "the introduction to the introduction" instead of a discussion of the subject chosen. It was thus when Coleridge now came to Pope. Before we can decide that Pope is a poet we must first learn the meaning of the word "poetry" but before this can be done, we must learn how words are used. So when he turns to *Romeo and Juliet* "it will be necessary for me to say something of the language of our country."

Thus again and again in his lectures, even when Coleridge remembers the subject he has advertised and which the audience have come to hear, obstacles are as numerous on his road as the "Surinam toads" of one of his favorite images and the prime object becomes an ever-receding vision never reached. Such characteristic deviations Hazlitt detected when he described Coleridge's readers as resembling disappointed pilgrims to Mecca, which they never reached.

Coleridge's love of vague generalizations in his literary criticism was far from the opinion he had expressed eleven years before in the *Morning Post*. There he denounced William Pitt's use of generalizations without related details: "Abstractions defined by abstractions! generalities defined by generalities." Such criticism Coleridge's own lectures too often invited.

Although Robinson was ever critical of the lectures and declared of Coleridge "I doubt much his capacity to render them popular," he also told Mrs. Clarkson: "the lectures have been brilliant in passages." Sarah Hutchinson's interest in Coleridge's lectures found expression in a letter to Miss Monkhouse on December 3, 1811. "Coleridge's lectures have gone on to the 4th," she wrote: "more than this we have not had an opportunity to learn—and that they give great satisfaction and are very well attended—though I am afraid they will not prove very profitable." Collier tells us of the lectures: "The series was delivered extemporaneously, (without the assistance of notes)." As usual, Coleridge excused his refusal to write lecture notes, on the ground that his extempore talking was more appreciated by his audiences than formal lecturing. Consequently, he never hesitated to wander far away from his advertised subject.

During the course of these lectures the accusation against Coleridge of plagiarism from Schlegel and the other German critics arose. After the lectures on *Romeo and Juliet* (December 9 and 18) a German in the audience came to Coleridge and after some courteous remarks, said "Were it not almost impossible, I must have believed that you had either heard or read my countryman Schlegel's lecture on this play, given at Vienna: the principles, thought, and the very illustrations are so nearly the same—But the Lectures were but just published as I left Germany, scarcely more than a week since—and the only two copies of the work in England I have reason to think, that I myself have brought over. . . ." To this Coleridge replied: "I had not even heard of these lectures, nor had indeed seen any work of Schlegel's except a volume of translations from Spanish Poetry. . . ." Such was Coleridge's account of the whole incident to another person.

Despite his denials, sometimes accompanied by dubious assertions of fact,

Coleridge certainly in later lectures was influenced by Schlegel. The German would surely have been surprised to learn that a month before, on November 6, 1811, Coleridge had written to Robinson: "I am very anxious to see Schlegel's *Werke* before the lectures commence."

Schlegel's lectures on Shakespeare, Coleridge himself declared, were presented to him in December 1811 and Robinson, reading the same work in February 1812 confided to his diary: "Coleridge, I find, did not disdain to borrow observations from Schlegel, tho' the coincidences between the two lecturers are for the greater part coincidences merely and not the one caused by the other."

Coleridge's defense to his correspondent in 1811 was essentially that the influence of Kant upon both Schlegel and himself completely accounted for the resemblance that existed at times in words as well as in thought, between Schlegel's lectures and Coleridge's own. "Not in one lecture, but in all the lectures that related to Shakespeare" he wrote, "or to poetry in general, the grounds, train of reasoning, etc. were different in language only—and often not even in that. The thoughts too were so far peculiar, that to the best of my knowledge they did not exist in any prior work of criticism. Yet, I was far more flattered, or to speak more truly, I was more concerned, than surprised. For Schlegel and myself had both studied deeply and perseverantly the philosophy of Kant. . . . Suppose myself and Schlegel (my argument not my vanity leads to these seeming self-flatteries) nearly equal in natural powers, of similar pursuits and acquirements, and it is only necessary for both to have mastered the spirit of Kant's *Critique* of the Judgment to render it morally certain, that writing on the same subject we should draw the same conclusions. . . ."

Such was Coleridge's explanation of these resemblances in 1811. But in 1818 in his anxiety to disprove a repetition of the same charge of plagiarism from Schlegel in the lectures he was then giving, he misdated his lectures of 1808 as having been given in 1802 or 1803—far too early for such plagiarism to be possible. "16 or 17 years ago," he wrote "I delivered 18 lectures on Shakespeare at the Royal Institution" which had contained the same material now attributed by some to Schlegel. Hence presumably Schlegel had no influence upon these lectures of 1818. Yet in 1813, requesting Mrs. Morgan to send to him in Bristol for lectures there, the very volumes of Schlegel which he denied having used in 1818 he wrote: "You will remember that I used to take them to the Surrey Institution."

However accidental the resemblance to Schlegel in Coleridge's earlier lectures there is no doubt as to Coleridge's indebtness to Schlegel's writings in the later ones.*

---

*Coleridge's plagiarisms and literary borrowings in verse and prose, including the *Watchman, The Friend,* and *Biographia Literaria* are presented in great detail by Norman Fruman in *Coleridge The Damaged Archangel* (London, 1972).

Despite Coleridge's disappointment in his moderate hopes of attracting swells to his lectures in 1811, some distinguished persons who were unacquainted with Coleridge did find their way to Fetter Lane, including Byron. He attended the ninth lecture and also the last but one. Whatever Byron may have heard of Coleridge's lecturing he went to the ninth lecture on December 16 in no friendly spirit. "C. is lecturing," he told a friend on December 6 " 'Many an old fool,' said Hannibal to some such lecturer, 'but such as this, never.' " Nor was Byron's attitude improved when two days later the poet Rogers informed him that Coleridge had publicly attacked the poet Campbell, author of *"The Pleasures of Hope,"* in his lecture. "C. has been lecturing again at Campbell" Byron told a friend on December 8, "Rogers was present, and from him I derive the information. We are going to make a party to hear this Manichean of poesy." So moved was Byron that on the same day he repeated his complaint against Coleridge to another acquaintance, saying: "C. has attacked the *Pleasures of Hope,* and all other pleasure whatsoever. Mr. Rogers was present, and heard himself indirectly *rowed* by the lecturer. We are going in a party to hear the new art of poetry by this reformed schismatic: and were I one of these poetical luminaries, or of sufficient consequence to be noticed by the man of lectures, I should not hear him without an answer. . . ." "To-morrow I dine with Rogers, and I am to hear Coleridge, who is a kind of rage at present," Byron told a friend a week later. Robinson, describing Byron on this occasion, wrote: "He was wrapped up, but I recognized his club foot and his countenance and general appearance."

Miss Mitford, the keen and rather amused observer of Coleridge's faults and failings as a lecturer, told a friend in a letter of December 15, 1811: "His pronunciation is an odd mixture of all that is bad in the two worst dialects of England, the Somersetshire and the Westmoreland, with an addition, which I believe to be exclusively his own, namely given to the *a* long as in 'wave' and 'bane,' a sound exactly resembling that which children make in imitating the bleating of a sheep, 'BA-A-A-A.' " Nevertheless in the same letter, she could write: "You would certainly have been enchanted, for, though his lectures are desultory in the highest degree. . .he has so much of. . .that power which fixes the attention by rousing at once the fancy and the heart - that the ear has scarcely the wish to condemn that which so strongly delights the intellect."

On January 27, 1812 Coleridge gave his last lecture, his seventeenth of this first course.

On February 10, 1812 Coleridge left London for Greta Hall on what proved to be his last visit to the North. He found the journey most unpleasant. His coach, named "Lousy Liverpool," which he thought "the worst coach on the road," was mobbed at Oxford by street louts shouting its unattractive name. The "pot-house" at which it stopped for an hour he found so vulgar that he dared not invite his undergraduate nephews to meet him. Increasingly disgusted as the coach moved on, Coleridge quitted it at Birmingham after foiling an attempt by dirty fellow-travelers to pick his pocket and resumed the journey in the "Bang-up."After spending four days with Dr. Crompton at

Liverpool and meeting the local intelligentsia, Coleridge continued his journey to Greta Hall.

Coleridge's arrival at Greta Hall was excellently described by Mrs. Coleridge to Poole the following October, 1812: "Coleridge came to us last February, took up the boys at Ambleside, rode through Grasmere without stopping at Wordsworth's!" For the quarrel still rankling in Coleridge's mind, prevented any association with the Wordsworths, still living at the Vicarage. "Poor Hartley," Mrs. Coleridge wrote,

> sat in speechless astonishment as the chaise passed the turning to the Vicarage where Wordsworth lives, but he dared not hazard one remark and Derwent fixed his eyes, full of tears, upon his father, who turned his head away to conceal his own emotions—when they had an opportunity they both eagerly asked the meaning of this paradox, and Hartley turned as white as lime when I told him that Mr. Wordsworth had a little vexed his father by something he had said to Mr. Montagu, which, through mistake, had been misrepresented: These children in the habit of going weekly to Grasmere, could not comprehend how these things were—Numerous were the letters and messages I received from Miss Wordsworth [she told Poole] to urge Coleridge to write to her and not to leave the country without seeing them; but he would not go to *them* and *they* did not come to *him.*

Nevertheless Mrs. Coleridge could describe her husband during this visit as

> cheerful and good natured and full of fair promises—he talked of our settling finally in London, that is when he had gone on for a year or so giving me, and all his friends, satisfaction as to the possibility of making a livelihood by his writings so as to enable us to live in great credit there. I listened, I own, with incredulous ears, while he was building these "airy castles" and calmly told him that I thought it was much better that I and the children should remain in the country until the Boys had finished their school-education and then, if he found himself in the circumstances that would admit of it, and would engage not to leave us all alone in that wide city, I would cheerfully take leave of *dear Keswick,* and follow his amended fortunes; he agreed to this, and in the meantime, a regular correspondence *was* to be kept up between himself, and me, and the children; and *never more* was he to keep a letter of mine, or the Boys', or Southey's *un*opened.

Despite the children's dismay on being forced to bypass the Wordsworths, Coleridge found both his sons and daughter "all the fondest father could pray for: and little Sara," he said, "does honour to her mother's anxieties, reads French tolerably and Italian fluently." Her aptitude for English also delighted him and but for fear of inconveniencing the Morgans, he would have taken her with him to London. He found her "such a sweet-tempered, meek, blue-eyed fairy, and so affectionate, trustworthy and really serviceable!" In this last quality young Sara had evidently been—like Sara Hutchinson—helpful as an amanuensis to her father. And he asked Mrs. Morgan and Charlotte Brent "to make up a little bonnet," for "little Sariola" so that she may remember them with grateful affection.

Of his sons too Coleridge was no less proud. "Derwent is the selfsame fond small Samuel Taylor Coleridge as ever" he told John Morgan. When he summoned them from school to meet him, Derwent "came in dancing for joy, while Hartley turned pale and trembled all over" before discussing Greek with his father. Hartley who Coleridge thought had "inherited his poor father's tenderness of bowels and stomach and consequently capriciousness of animal spirits" complained that the schoolmaster favored Hartley as his favorite but was severe to Derwent himself. But Derwent admitted that Hartley "*is* a genius!" Coleridge certainly needed this cheerful society of his children, for immediately after his arrival at Greta Hall, "storm and rain" outside and dampness within brought on "a violent cold." This prevented his departure for London, as intended, at the end of February.

But below all other disappointments and anxieties for Coleridge lay the memories of his quarrel with Wordsworth, particularly stimulated by the Wordsworths' proximity since his return to the North. Not less than his sons had Coleridge felt the pang of bypassing the Wordsworth's home as they returned to Greta Hall, "I passed thro' Grasmere; but did not call on Wordsworth" he told John Morgan: "I hear from Mrs. Coleridge, that he treats the affair as a trifle and only wonders at my resenting it—and that Dorothy Wordsworth before my arrival expressed her confident hope that I should come to them at once!! I, who for years past had been an ABSOLUTE NUISANCE in the family! . . .It will not surprise you," he continued,

> that the statements respecting me, and Montagu and Wordsworth, have been grossly perverted: and yet [de]spite of all this there is not a friend of Wordsworth's, I understand, who does not severely blame him, tho' they execrate the Montagu's yet more heavily. But the tenth part of the Truth is not known. Would you believe it possible, that Wordsworth himself stated *my wearing Powder* as a proof positive that I never could have suffered any pain of mind from the affair—and that it was all pretence!! God Forgive him.

How bitterly Wordsworth felt about Coleridge's refusal to see him during his visit to Greta Hall, Crabb Robinson clearly states: "Wordsworth dwelt on this circumstance, with more warmth than any other, particularly on the injustice done to his sister, who had been Coleridge's best friend at all times." And so for the time being, Coleridge and Wordsworth remained apart.

A month later near the end of March 1812 Coleridge again unburdened himself to John Morgan on the same subject: "the Grasmere business has kept me in a fever of agitation—and will end in complete alienation—I have refused to go over, and Wordsworth has refused to apologize, and has thus made his choice between me and Basil Montagu, Esq[re]. . . .I have been in such a state of fever and irritation about the Wordsworths, my reason deciding one way, and my heart pulling me the contrary scarcely daring to set off without seeing them, especially Miss Hutchinson who has done nothing to offend me. . . .I have suffered so much that I wish I had not left London."

Coleridge's faith in Sara Hutchinson would have been sadly shattered could he have seen the letter she wrote to her cousin John Monkhouse on March 28, 1812 two days after Coleridge's departure for London. "He is offended with William" she wrote, "or fancies himself so—and expected William to make some advance to him, which as he did not, he was miserable the whole time he was in Keswick, and Mrs. Coleridge was right glad to get him off again, for she had no satisfaction in him—and would have given the world, I dare say, to have had him well again with William. We are all very sorry that his visit has ended so, being persuaded that he never would have come down at all but in the hope of a reconciliation."

That the adored Sara Hutchinson whose love-lock Coleridge had worn next his heart on his journey North, was in fact by this time of Wordsworth's party, Coleridge soon learned. This was indeed a bitter blow for him. He had intended to send her his account of the quarrel "but" as he told Lamb shortly afterward, "desisted in Consequence of understanding that she had already decided the matter against me."

Coleridge would have been even more distressed, jealous as he was, had he known of the poems Wordsworth was now writing in praise of Sara. These included a short poem and two sonnets in which Sara's virtues were symbolized by her spinning wheel:

Short-lived likings may be bred
By a glance from fickle eyes;
But true love is like the thread
which the kindly wool supplies,
When the flocks are all at rest
Sleeping on the mountain's breast.

Wordsworth entitled it *Song for the Spinning Wheel*. The two sonnets which followed—also suggested rather than inspired by the same spinning wheel—similarly expressed Wordsworth's appreciation of Sara Hutchinson's domestic virtues, in sincere but somewhat clumsy verse.

On March 26, 1812 Coleridge left Keswick for Penrith and there took the coach for London, never to return. Even at Penrith Coleridge's obsession with the quarrel still pursued him and before taking the London coach he continued to unburden himself to John Morgan.

I have received four Letters in 3 days, [he wrote] about my not having called on Wordsworth as I passed thro' Grasmere—and this morning a most impassioned one from Mrs. Clarkson—Good God! how could I? How can I? I have no resentment—and unless Grief and Anguish be resentment, I never had—but unless I meet him as of yore, what use is there in it? What but mere pain? I am not about to be his Enemy—I want no stimulus to serve him to the utmost whenever it should be in my power. And can any friend of mine wish me to go without apology received, and as to a man the best-beloved and honoured, who had declared me a nuisance, an absolute nuisance—and this to such a Creature as Montagu? And who since then has professed his determination to believe Montagu rather than me, as to my assertion to Southey that Montagu prefaced his Discourse with the words - "Nay, but Wordsworth *has commissioned* me to tell you, first, that he has no Hope of you," etc. etc.—A nuisance!—and then a deliberate Liar! O Christ! if I dared after this crouch to the Man, must I not plead guilty to these charges, and be a Liar against my own Soul? No more of this!

Nevertheless before the close of his letter Coleridge could not resist another outburst:

> Mrs. Southey and Mrs. Coleridge who have twice debated the matter with Wordsworth as well as with his Sister, are most vehement against Wordsworth—and Mrs. C. says, she never in her whole life saw her Sister so vehement, or so completely overcome her natural timidity as when she answered Wordsworth's excuses—She would not suffer him to wander from the true point—Never mind, Sir! Coleridge does not heed *what* was said—whatever is true, his friends all know, and he himself never made a secret of—but that *you,* should say all this—and to Montagu—and having never at any one time during a 15 years' friendship given him even a *hint* of the state of your opinions concerning him—it is *you*, Sir! *you*—not the things said, true or false! Southey never says anything but only—*"that miscreant, Montagu"*— whereas (I have nothing to complain of in Montagu) I think him in error.

After a most fatiguing journey and three sleepless nights Coleridge reached London at five o'clock in the morning of April 14, 1812 took a room at the Bull in Mouth Inn as no "Post Chaise" was available, and slept there for "8 or 10 hours continuously." The next day in a letter to Mrs. Coleridge he informed her "I did not see the Morgans till just now." But now another cause of misery momentarily superseded his quarrel with Wordsworth. From Penrith he had told Morgan "I will send you up a Draft for the £50 to make all secure and your mind at ease." Yet now he told Mrs. Coleridge "I heard that Morgan had never received the Draft for £50, which fearful of my being detained I begged you to send to him, and on which you must never have received my letter. What a thunderbolt to me!"

A week later back with the Morgans now in Berner's Street—he described himself to Mrs. Coleridge "I feel myself an altered man, and dare promise you that you shall never have to complain of, or to apprehend, my not opening and reading your Letters. Ever since I have been in town, I have never taken any Stimulus of *any* kind, till the moment of my getting into bed, except a glass of British White Wine after dinner—and from 3 to 4 glasses of Port, when I have dined out." Coleridge also anticipated a new course of Lectures with high hopes of their success.

9 From Lecture Room to Theater (1812-14)

"It has been a good thing for the Theatre. They will get 8 or 10,000 £—and I shall get more than all my literary labours put together, nay, thrice as much, subtracting my heavy losses in The Watchman *and* The Friend—*400 £; including the copy-right."*

—*S.T. Coleridge to Thomas Poole*
February 13, 1813

Meanwhile the lectures continued. Doubtless stimulated by the Morgans Coleridge now planned a new course of lectures in high spirits. They were to be delivered in Willis's Rooms in Hanover Square, and Coleridge pleasantly contemplated a more aristocratic audience than Fetter Lane had brought him. So, he now made great efforts to secure important sponsors for the course. These required pleasant social occasions, to which he was never averse. An invitation from Sir Thomas Bernard, Founder of the Royal Institution, to a dinner at which Dr. Bell was to be his fellow guest, much pleased him. Nor was this all. As he told his wife with evident pride: "the Venerable Bishop of Durham has sent me a very kind message—that though he cannot himself appear in a hired lecture room, yet he will not only be my subscriber, but use his best influence with his acquaintance."

Coleridge was in fact now attempting to form an influential Committee among socially distinguished persons to boost his lectures. Earnestly begging Sharp to join it, Coleridge wrote: "The plan of my lectures has been patronized in a way which I should never have dared hope for," and he appended the names of Sir Thomas Bernard, Sir George Beaumont, Mr. Sotheby, Sir Humphrey Davy, "and (I have some reason to flatter myself) Earl Darnley." "Everything, my dear! goes on as prosperously as you could yourself wish," Coleridge now told his wife. As a further inducement Coleridge sent Sharp more details: "The Committee will be merely nominal, and it's chief purpose to give a *first impulse* to the fashionable world, and a respectability to the Lectures.—The form of Annunciation is as follows:

Lectures on the Drama.

Mr. Coleridge proposes to give a series of lectures on the Drama of the Greek, French, Italian, English and Spanish Stage, chiefly with reference to the works of Shakespeare, at Willis's Rooms, King Street, St James's on the Tuesdays and Thursdays* in May and June at three o'clock precisely. Each course will contain six lectures, at one guinea the course, the tickets transferable, and no more subscribers admitted than the room will conveniently accommodate.

Four days before his intended first lecture, which was to be on May 12, 1812, Coleridge wrote to Stuart for assistance in a mood of disappointment, as his great expectations had not matured. "I send you 7 or 8 tickets," he wrote, "entreating you, if pre-engagement or your health does not preclude it, to bring a group with you, as many ladies as possible, but gentlemen if you cannot muster ladies: for else I shall not only have been left in the lurch as to actual receipts by my great patrons (the 500 half promised are likely to shrink below 50) but shall absolutely make a ridiculous appearance. . . ."

But misfortune ever dogged the footsteps of poor Coleridge when he really tried to meet the responsibilities of life. It ever favored him when he tried to avoid them—which was perhaps an even greater misfortune. So now on May 11, the day before that fixed for the first lecture, Coleridge's progress was impeded by nothing less than the assassination of the Prime Minister, the harmless Sir Spencer Perceval. Immediately on hearing the news Coleridge, shocked, but ever ready to defer a lecture rushed off to Sir Thomas Bernard, who agreed with him that the opening lecture should be deferred for a week, until May 19.

Informing Southey of the postponement of the Lectures because of "the aweful Events of Yester afternoon"—the murder of the Prime Minister Perceval—Coleridge went on to describe with his usual admirable realism on such occasions, the effects of the murder upon a London crowd as well as upon himself. "I was turned numb," he wrote, "and then sick, and then into a convulsive state of weeping on the first tidings just as if Perceval had been my near and personal friend—but Good God! the atrocious sentiments universal among the populace. . . ." We may suspect in this, as often in Coleridge's writings, a considerable infusion of poetic licence. Certainly Coleridge's very practical note to Sotheby immediately after the murder, cancelling his lecture showed no such excessive anguish, but only a normal if slightly exaggerated expression of personal feeling towards the end.

Coleridge had in fact, as he told Southey, gone immediately to *The Courier* with the unfulfilled intention to write an article, evidently impelled, not on this occasion by his need for money, but by an instinct for the public expression of his feelings, such as he now urged upon Southey. On leaving the *Courier* "faint from the heat and much walking," he had gone into the bar of a "large public house frequented about 1 o'clock by the lower orders." What he saw there roused his political emotions to fever heat. He even wished a similar

---

*The days were changed to Tuesdays and Fridays, and the course ended on June 5, 1812.

assassination for Jacobins and those who advocated parliamentary reform—views held and proclaimed by Sir Francis Burdett, a well-known member of parliament. Exasperated by the memory, Coleridge told Southey:

> It was really shocking—nothing but exultation—Burdett's health drunk with a clatter of pots—and a sentiment given to at least 50 men and women—May Burdett soon be the man to have sway over us!—these were the very words. "This is but the beginning"—"more of these damned scoundrels must go the same way—and then poor people may live"—"Every man might maintain his family decent and comfortable if the money were not picked out of our pockets by them damned placemen"—"God is above the devil, I say—and down to Hell with him and all his brood, the Minister men and Parliament fellows"—"They won't hear Burdett—No! he is a Christian man and speaks for the poor" - etc, etc - I do not think I have altered a word.

The last lecture of the series was delivered on June 5, 1812. Of these lectures we have little record by the usual notes by Robinson. The course as described in Coleridge's syllabus published in *The Courier* on May 11, was identical with the "annunciation" he had detailed to Sharp shortly before. This ambitious program seems to have resulted in fact in a comparison of Classic and Romantic drama in relation to Shakespeare largely based upon Coleridge's recent reading of Schlegel.

Robinson's comments upon this course of lectures were in general similar to those he had expressed during the lectures of 1811:—appreciation mingled with regrets at digressions, and irritation at sometimes finding little or no reference to the subjects announced. Thus when Coleridge instead of discussing Modern Drama as promised, treated of Greek Tragedy, Robinson, though disappointed, admitted it was "excellent and very German. . . ." "Very German" too Robinson found the next lecture which was on Greek comedy "and, of course, much too abstract for his audience, which was but thin. Scarcely any ladies there. . . ." Finally, considering Coleridge as a man and as a lecturer Robinson declared:

> With such powers of original thought and real genius, both philosophical and poetical, such as few men in any age have possessed, Coleridge wants certain low and minor qualities which render his great powers almost inefficient and useless, while most subordinate persons obtain all the fame he merits. . . . In the future lectures, money is to be taken at the door. . . . I doubt much whether the experiment will succeed. He announced his lectures ill, as if he felt degraded by allusion to money matters; I felt degraded at hearing a great man refer to such a subject. . . .

During the interval which followed the last of his recent lectures until the opening of the next series on November 3, 1812, Coleridge apparently suffered a bad attack of illness and wrote but few letters to his acquaintance. From the Morgans in Berners Street, Coleridge sent Rickman a dinner-invitation on July 17. On August 7 he sent Stuart a detailed description of the illness which now troubled him and at the same time offered some fragments for articles, while pleading for money to settle an unpaid bill. On the same day he made a similar offer of fragments from his Notebooks to Murray and also spoke of his illness.

Nevertheless, five days later Coleridge was already making plans for a new course of lectures to be given at the Surrey Institution in London.* On October 21 he discussed with a member of the Surrey In-

---

*"I have here sent you a chapter of Contents of my proposed Lectures," he wrote, "in the formation of which I have been desirous to introduce as much variety of matter, as is compatible with unity of Object. . .of course, I have drawn out this Sketch far more at large (for the satisfaction of the Committee) than it need appear in a printed Announce[ment]. . . .

The "Contents" enclosed by Coleridge is as follows:

Lecture 1. That to use each word in a sense peculiarly it's own, is an indispensable Condition of all just thinking, and at once the surest, easiest, and even most entertaining Discipline of the mind. On the words, Beautiful, Sublime, Majestic, Grand, Picturesque, Fancy, Imagination, Taste.
Lectures 2 & 3. The falsehood of the almost universal opinion, that in the progress of civilized Life the invention of Conveniences, and Utilities precedes the Arts of Ornament proved by Facts, and *a priori* (i.e. from the nature of the Human Being). The fine Arts in the natural order of their Origination—Dress, Orchésis, (including all the arts of bodily motion, as mimic Dances, gymnastic Sports etc.), Architecture, Eloquence, Music, Poetry, Statuary, Painting, Gardening.
Lecture 4. *On Poetry* in general, and as common to ancient Greece & to Christendom. On the Poetry of the Ancients, as contra-distinguished from that of the moderns, or the differences of the Classical from the Romantic Poetry, exemplified in the Athenian Dramatic Poets.
Lecture 5. On the Mythology of ancient Greece, its Causes and effects—and the worse than ignorance, infused by our School Pantheons, and the mistaken Zeal of religious Controversy. The connection between the Polytheism, Ethics, and Republicanism of Greece: and (as thence deduced) the impossibility and (were it possible) the usefulness of modelling our Poetry, Architecture, Music, etc. on the Remains of the ancients. The *Spirit* of Poetry common to all ages—and to *imitate* the ancients wisely, we should do as they did, that is, embody that Spirit in Forms adapted to all the Circumstances of Time, State of Society etc.
Lecture 6. The *human* Causes, which the goodness of Providence directed to the Diffusion of Christianity, and it's temporal Effects, abstracted from all higher and purely theological Views—the Deluge of Nations—the Establishment of Christendom—and the formation of mixt [sic] Languages, in which the decomposed Latin became amalgamated in different proportions with the Gothic, Celtic, or Moorish—these collectively were called the *Romance*, and in this sense of the *mixed* as opposed to the simple or homogenous, I use the word *Romantic*—and not *exclusively* with reference to what we now call *Romances*.
Lecture 7. The characteristics of the Romantic Poetry, and the true Origin of the Romantic Drama in Shakespear. On the false points of view, from which Shakespear has been regarded as wild, irregular, etc. etc.—and proofs that a profound Judgement in the *construction* of his Plays is equally his Characteristic, as Genius, and deep Insight into human Nature—or rather that they are the same Power variously applied.
Lecture 8. A philosophical Analysis of Romeo and Juliet, and of Hamlet.
Lecture 9. Macbeth and Othello.
Lecture 10. Hasty Review of the most important of the other Plays—and the character of Shakespear, as a Poet and as a Dramatic Poet.
Lectures 11 and 12. Milton's Paradise Lost
(from letter to Richard Saumarez Esq., Surrey Institution, Blackfriars Road, Wednesday, 12 August (1812) cf. Griggs, 3: 418-19.)

stitution: "the persons and number I wish to have admitted." Nor is there another letter from Coleridge in his published correspondence until December 1, 1812.

The lectures which Coleridge was now giving at the Surrey Institution had commenced on November 3, 1812, and ended on January 26, 1813. They were given on Tuesday evenings. The first half of the course covered, as usual, wide fields ranging from the relation of words to thought, civilization and the arts, the poetry of Ancients and Moderns, Providence, and Christianity. The second half of the course consisted of Coleridge's old familiar themes relating to Shakespeare, his plays and poems, and Milton's *Paradise Lost*.

Although Robinson attended most of the lectures, even from the beginning his spirits flagged. "A repetition of former Lectures, and dull," he described the first lecture. "Pious cant" was his comment on the second. At the third he fell asleep. The next, the fourth, showed Coleridge "in a good vein" on poetry. The next two lectures outwearied Robinson who described the first of them as "A declamation on atheism" in which "he wasted his time on the introduction to the introduction." For his remarks on this subject Coleridge apologized at his next lecture before discussing Christianity. The final lecture of the course on Shakespeare, Robinson found "very eloquent and popular" and he added: "he is recovering lost character among the Saints." This was evidently true, for Robinson continued: "He was received with three rounds of applause on entering the lecture room and very loudly applauded at the close. During the evening he gained great applause by some eloquent *moral* reflections: and he *this* evening, as well as on the three or four preceding nights, redeemed the reputation he lost at the commencement of the course." We know from Coleridge's own words that in these twelve lectures at the Surrey Institution, he used Schlegel's lectures on Shakespeare.

From this public approval of Coleridge, Robinson turned to cogitate upon the lecturer:

> That Coleridge should ever become a popular man would once have been thought a very idle speculation. It depends on himself, and if he would make a sacrifice of some peculiarities of taste (his enemies assert he has made many on essential points of religion and politics) he has talents enough to command success but he must also add the power of repressing the avowal of his own favourite peculiarities in opinion and feeling, which I doubt he will ever be able to obtain. His general notions on party-topics will suit a large proportion of the public, and, tho' he is not yet a favourite, there is a general opinion in favour of his genius.

Before the close of 1813, Coleridge, reappearing after another opium bout, was in Bristol, the guest of Josiah Wade, making plans to give a course of lectures there. His original intention had been to give only five lectures of which the subject was to be Shakespeare; but because of his diffuseness he added one additional lecture to this part of the course, and ultimately two more on education. The price for a single lecture was 5/-and one guinea for the whole course.

It ran from October 28, 1813 to November 23, and Coleridge kept to his dates. No prospectuses seem to have been printed but brief reports appeared in the Bristol *Gazette* and elsewhere including Stuart's *Morning Chronicle* and *Courier.*

To Mrs. Morgan and Charlotte Brent in a series of letters extending from late October 1813 to the end of the year, Coleridge described at times in detail, not only his personal miseries but also his experiences, anxieties, and successes as a lecturer. "The proposed scheme of lecturing has met with such support that I have resolved on it" he told Charlotte Brent on October 24 "and I shall give the first at the White Lion on Thursday evening at 7 o'clock." The next day he told Mrs. Morgan,

> The subscription promises to go on with a steady breeze—but you must be so good as immediately on the receipt of this, to hunt out for me the three volumes of *Schlegel's Vorlesungen.* . .and likewise my two *square* thick Memorandum Books. . .I am sure you will be able, in the title pages of the books that are not bound, to distinguish the words Vorlesungen, at the top, and *Schlegel* as the author's name, at the end (excepting the place and name of the publisher)—Besides you will remember that I used to take them to the Surrey Institution. . . .

Coleridge hoped that as a result of these lectures he would be able to assist the Morgans and Charlotte in their financial difficulties due to John Morgan's bankruptcy. With this intention he sent Mrs. Morgan frequent reports as the lecture course proceeded. "Tolerably attended" he described his first lecture, "and I doubt not, the scheme will be profitable." To encourage the Morgans and also himself, he emphasized his successes as a lecturer. Thus reporting his third lecture to Mrs. Morgan he wrote: "My lecture of yester evening seemed to give more than ordinary satisfaction—I began at 7 o'clock, and ended at half past nine—*Mercy* on the audience, you will say; but the audience did not seem to be tired, and cheered me to the last."

After his next lecture Coleridge was less elated: "I confess that I am vexed at heart at the inferiority of the lecture I delivered tonight—tho' all I spoke to, said it was a whim of my own. But I know these things by tact." The day before his next lecture Coleridge attended a dinner party from which he emerged "little less than drunk." "All next day," he continued, "I looked forward with terror to the evening's lecture, but got over it so as to redeem the preceeding, and with an éclat equal to the third."

Coleridge's lecture on Education, his seventh, also intended as his last lecture in Bristol, was so well received that he gave one more on November 23. His success he of course detailed to Mrs. Morgan and Charlotte Brent. "I have not prepared one single word or thought, till 10 minutes before the lecture commenced," he wrote, "It was therefore quite in my fire-side way, and pleased more than any." So encouraged was Coleridge that he considered the possibility of giving another series of lectures in Bristol.

While lecturing in Bristol Coleridge also gave another lecture course at the fashionable suburb of Clifton. The lecture course advertised in the *Gazette* on

November 4, 1813 was on "the construction, metre, and characteristic beauties of the *Paradise Lost,* with illustrative readings on Milton in general, as a man, and a poet; on the distinction between the poetry of Polytheism, as existing in the republics of ancient Greece, and the poetry of Christendom—the causes and their results; that a just taste may and must be grounded on fixed principles; and the rules deducible therefrom, by which a tenable judgment, both positive and comparative, may be formed concerning poetry and the works of different poets."

Coleridge began his Clifton lectures in a depressed mood. ". . .what is most unfortunate" he told Mrs. Morgan, "is that to-morrow at one o'clock I must be at Clifton, tho' with no probability of even more than enough to pay the Lecture Room & the Printing. I have had experience enough to expect nothing but meanness from the fashionable world, and therefore shall not be disappointed. . . ." The morrow was equally depressing: - ". . .one series of such impetuous *Storms* of Wind, and Rain, that there were not above 8 or 10 persons there—I therefore took a Chair, drew round the fire, and chatted for an hour & a half." Such was Coleridge's opening lecture at Clifton on November 10, 1813. Too disheartened to appear at his next two lectures, Coleridge summoned enough courage for the last Clifton lecture given in November—only to find twelve persons present. On November 24, 1813, the day after his last Bristol lecture, Coleridge returned to London, to Mrs. Morgan and her sister, in Fitzroy Square.

Nevertheless, *Felix Farley's Bristol Journal* announced on December 4, 1813, a proposal for a new course of six lectures by Coleridge to begin on December 7. The next advertisement appeared in the *Bristol Gazette* on December 30—"Mr. Coleridge having been surprised and confined by sudden and severe illness at his arrival at Bath, six days before the promised commencement of his second course, 7th December 1813, respectfully informs his friends that this second course will commence on Tuesday 4th January 1814, at the White Lion. . . ." But not until Coleridge's reemergence from the shades in April 1814 was he able to deliver the promised course. This course given at the White Lion in Bristol, consisted of six lectures chiefly on Milton, beginning on April 21. Apparently Coleridge attended all these lectures.

During this spring of 1814 Coleridge's dreams of still more lectures were threatened by another attack of erysipelas. Indeed, as he told Cottle, because of his illness he had hardly been able to finish his recent course. Nevertheless he would give three lectures on the French Revolution, only one of which apparently, materialized. Coleridge's present enthusiasm for lecturing had survived his discouragement by the financial failure of his recent Bristol Lectures. These, he now told Cottle, "had *almost* paid the expenses of the Room, advertisements etc.,—whether," he added, "this be to *my* discredit or that of the Good Citizens of Bristol, it is not for me to judge."

Nevertheless Coleridge advertised in *Felix Farley's Bristol Journal* on April 2, 1814 a new course of lectures: "Mr. Coleridge has been desired by, several highly respectable Ladies to carry into effect a plan of giving one or two lectures, in the morning, on the subject of FEMALE EDUCATION, of a nature altogether practical, and explaining the whole machinery of a school organized on rational principles from the earliest age to the completion of FEMALE EDUCATION, with a list of books recommended, etc. so as to evolve gradually into utility and domestic powers and qualities of Womanhood. Should a sufficient number of Ladies and Gentlemen express their desire to patronize this plan, Mr. Coleridge will hold himself ready to realise it, at such time as may be found most convenient to his auditors.'' Nor were these lectures to be offered unconditionally: for the French Revolution a minimum of ''50 names'' was demanded. For the educational lectures—which were never delivered—the minimum attendance was increased to ''60 names.'' So ended Coleridge's last Bristol lectures. Until early in September 1814 he remained in Bristol under medical treatment.

Throughout the period of these lectures, Coleridge's emotional background varied from the misery created by The Great Quarrel with Wordsworth to his temporary public triumph as the author of *Remorse,* and again to the unhappiness due to the loss of Wedgwood's legacy.

On October 10, 1812 Drury Lane Theatre, rebuilt after a fire that had destroyed it, was reopened. Two brothers, James and Horace Smith, seized the occasion to publish as the poems of contemporary poets including Coleridge, their own satirical verses on them. These pretended to be ''addresses'' sent by the poets to the Manager of Drury Lane to be read on the opening night of the theatre and rejected by him. They were therefore entitled *Rejected Addresses.* The poem pretending to be Coleridge's was entitled *Playhouse Musings.* It was in weak blank verse and contained little to suggest Coleridge's solicitude for a donkey expressed in his early poem *To a Young Ass.* This poem was evidently parodied in James Smith's opening lines:

> My pensive Public, wherefore look you sad?
> I had a Grandmother, she had a donkey
> To carry to the mart her crockery ware,
> And when that donkey look'd me in the face,
> His face was sad! and you are sad, my public. . . .

Hence, Coleridge is ridiculed as a weak sentimentalist towards animal life and the strife of Nature:

> Nought born on earth should die. On the hackney stands
> I reverence the coachman who cries ''Gee,''
> And spares the lash. When I behold a spider
> Prey on a fly, a magpie on a worm
> Or view a butcher with a horn-handled knife
> Slaughter a tender lamb as dead as mutton,
> Indeed, indeed, I am very, very sick.

Thus the part of Smith's *Rejected Addresses* ironically imputed to Coleridge, ends.

Playhouse Musings was not overlooked by the reviewers. "Mr. Coleridge," wrote Gifford in the *Quarterly Review,* "will not, we fear, be as much entertained as we were with his 'Playhouse Musings,' which begins with characteristic pathos and simplicity." The *Edinburgh Review,* more correctly critical, described it as "unquestionably Lakish, though we cannot say that we recognise in it any of the peculiar traits of that powerful and misdirected genius whose name it had borrowed."

Although Coleridge affected to be indifferent to the parody of himself in *Rejected Addresses,* his attitude to Gifford's article was far from being indifferent. "The paragraph in the Quarterly Review" he told Southey in February 1813 "respecting me as ridiculed in the Rejected Addresses, was surely unworthy of a man of sense like Gifford. What reason could *he* have had to suppose me as a man so childishly irritable as to be provoked by a trifle so contemptible?" For Gifford had also found fault with *Remorse*, accusing Coleridge of having written many "weak and slovenly lines in so fine a poem," as Coleridge complained to Southey.

How intimately personal *Remorse* was to Coleridge, he now revealed to Southey when he wrote: "By 'Remorse' I mean the anguish and disquietude arising from self-contradiction introduced into the soul by guilt—a feeling, which is good or bad as the will makes use of it." And he continued by admitting and excusing his borrowings from Schiller's *Wallenstein*: "as to my thefts from *Wallenstein*, they were on compulsion from the necessity of haste—and do not lie heavy on my conscience, being partly thefts from myself, and because I gave Schiller 20 for one I have taken.' "—referring of course also to his own translation of *Wallenstein* published thirteen years before. Nevertheless he added, "I shall, however, weed them out as soon as I can, and in the mean time, I hope they will lie snug."

Before the close of 1812 Coleridge's play *Osorio*, now rewritten and renamed *Remorse*, had been accepted by Drury Lane through Bryon's influence, and throughout December 1812 and January 1813, was in rehearsal. Despite the stress of his lectures Coleridge also supervised these rehearsals of which he complained to Stuart on December 22: "I find the alterations and alterations rather a tedious business, and I am sure, could compose a new act more easily and in shorter time than add a single speech of ten lines—The managers are more sanguine far than I am, and the actors and actresses with the exception of Miss Smith, are pleased and gratified with their parts. . . ." Coleridge understood Miss Smith's dissatisfactions, believing that her part was "not appropriate to her talents . . . and I am labouring with much vexation and little success to make it better. She was offered a part that would have suited her admirably, but (I know not from what motive) refused it." It was thus that Coleridge, harassed by the conflicting demands of playhouse and of lecture room, of dissatisfied actresses and of literary critics, entered the new year 1813.

Throughout January both playhouse and lecture room continued to exact their tribute from poor Coleridge. Thus the January days sped by until

January 23, when the opening night of *Remorse* arrived. Three days later Coleridge gave the last lecture of his course to the very appreciative audience Robinson described.

The next day, delighted with his double success as dramatist and lecturer, Coleridge wrote to his wife in a jubilant mood: "I concluded my lectures last night most triumphantly, with loud, long and enthusiastic applauses at my entrance, and ditto in yet fuller chorus as, and for some time after, I had retired. It was lucky that, (as I never once thought of the lecture till I had entered the lecture box) the last two were the most impressive and really the best."

From the memory of his dramatic exit from the lecture room Coleridge's thoughts turned back to his experience on the preceding Saturday when he attended the first night of *Remorse*: "I suppose that no dramatic author ever had so large a number of unsolicited, and unknown, yet *predetermined* plauditors in the theatre, as I had on Saturday Night." But of course poor unfortunate Coleridge was not to enjoy these successes without a fly in the ointment. "One of the malignant papers," he continued, "asserted that I had collected all the *Saints* from Mile-End Turnpike to Tyburn Bar. With so many warm friends it is impossible in the present state of human nature, that I should not have many unprovoked and unknown enemies."

Then from such shadows the memory of his dramatic success returned. "You will have heard," he continued to Mrs. Coleridge "that on my entering the box on Saturday night I was discovered by the pit—and that they all turned their faces towards our box, and gave a treble cheer of claps." But he still had doubts of the final success of the play because of what he considered the inadequacy of the actors. Nevertheless *Remorse* ran for twenty nights and brought Coleridge three hundred or four hundred pounds—his statements varied. The printed pamphlet of the play reached a third edition and Coleridge was to receive from Pople the publisher two-thirds of the profits "on terms advantageous to me as an Author and honourable to him as a Publisher." Because of this he now sent his wife instructions to draw £100 within a month or three weeks upon a City firm and promised at the same time the payment of another £100 with little delay. "I hope likewise before Midsummer if God grant me Life" he added "to repay you whatever you have expended for the children." From so brilliant a success of their protégé the Morgan family could of course not be absent, "Morgan and the women. . .are at the theatre," Coleridge told Rickman on the third day of the play but, he explained that he was too excited to accompany them.

Even before such excitements Coleridge's dramatic ambitions had soared and before the close of 1812 he told Robinson "It is my hope and purpose to devote a certain portion of my time for the next 12 months to theatrical attempts."

Coleridge's elation at the applause and social recognition *Remorse* was producing continued into February 1813 when he proudly complained to Southey of the "endless Rat a Tat Tat at our black and blue bruised Door—& my two Master-Fiends Letters and Proof Sheets, to which indeed I must add a third,

their Compeer-invitations to large Dinners, which I cannot refuse without giving offence, yet never accept without vexation and involuntary bad humour
the morning before, and stomach and bowel disturbance the day after. . . ."

Poole who had sent Coleridge a congratulatory note on his success must be
answered. Breaking through the coolness that had overlaid their friendship
Coleridge replied in February 1813: "Love so deep and so domesticated with
the whole Being, as mine was to you, can never cease to be." And he continued
with a long quotation from "Christabel," beginning:

Alas! they had been Friends in Youth!
But whis'pring Tongues can poison Truth!. . . .

But Coleridge in any quarrel must always be an ill-used person, and in this
spirit he now told Poole: "Stung as I have been with your unkindness to me in
my sore Adversity, yet the receipt of your two heart-engendered Lines was
sweeter than an unexpected Strain of sweetest Music—or in humbler phrase, it
was the only pleasurable sensation which the Success of the *Remorse* has given
me."

Assuming a pose of boredom about the congratulations which had come to
him, he continued, "No Grocer's Apprentice, after his first Month's permitted
Riot, was ever sicker of Figs and Raisins than I of hearing about the
Remorse. . . ." After this, he repeated his graphic "Rat a Tat Tat" phrase he
had used to Southey. He had never seen the play since the first night he said. It
"had succeeded in spite of bad scenes, execrable Acting & Newspaper Calumny."

Coleridge's chief satisfaction over *Remorse* was the financial result for
himself. "It has been a good thing for the Theatre," he told Poole: "They will
get 8 or 10,000 £—& I shall get more than all my literary labours put together,
nay, thrice as much, subtracting my heavy Losses in *The Watchman & The
Friend*—400 £: including the Copyright." Three days later, in mid February,
he described his profits to Rickman as 300 £. This he adds, speaking of himself
in the third person "had elevated his estate to 0-0 from 0-yx." He also
believed the second edition of *Remorse*, "corrected and augmented," would
appear the next day.

But just before the success of *Remorse* a severe blow struck Coleridge—the
loss of half of the Wedgwoods' annuity. On November 9, 1812 Coleridge
received a letter from Josiah Wedgwood withdrawing his own contribution.
The remaining half, £75, contributed by Tom Wedgwood could not be
touched because of Tom's death. Alleging with some justification, his own financial losses, Josiah, while withdrawing his part of the annuity, declared that unless
Coleridge said he was "bound in honour to do so" he would not continue.

The correspondence which followed showed that true as Josiah's excuse
may have been, his disappointment with Coleridge was not without its effect.
Since Coleridge's return from Malta Josiah had been increasingly disillusioned
by Samuel's mode of life and failure to write the edifying books in expectation
of which the annuity had been granted.

After an interval of three weeks Coleridge had succeeded in overcoming the shock of Wedgwood's letter and was now able to express a dignified acquiescence. Nevertheless his consciousness of Josiah's disapproval is evident in his reply: "I should deem myself indeed unworthy of you and your revered brother's past munificence" his letter began, "if I had had any other feeling than that of grief from your letter: or if I looked forward to any other or higher comfort than the confident hope that, (if God extend my life another year) I shall have a claim to an acknowledgment from you that I have not misemployed my past years, or wasted that leisure which I have owed to you, and for which I must cease to be before I can cease to feel most grateful." He went on to cite his financial misfortunes: *The Friend* and the lectures. If these had succeeded he told Wedgwood, "it was my intention to have resigned my claims on your bounty. . . ." If his forthcoming play (*Remorse*) brought him the expected competence he continued, he would then be able "to bring into shape the fruits of 20 years study and observation." Next, from a vague reference to having been "calumniated," he concluded: "I beseech you, interpret it as a burst of thankfulness and most unfeigned esteem, not of pride, when I declare that to have an annuity settled on me of three times or thrice three times the amount, would not afford me such pleasure as the restoration of your esteem and friendship for your deeply obliged S.T. Coleridge."

In a short suave reply of apparent friendliness the virtuous Wedgwood adroitly admitted he had heard upon enquiry, ill but reliable reports of Coleridge which had given him "pain." Equally adroitly but still in the most friendly manner Josiah withdrew his association with Coleridge: "I have never ceased to feel most kindly towards you, and I believe I shall always retain the impressions that have been   made in me by our former intimacy, of your genius and of your tender and deep feelings. We have however lived so long without meeting and our pursuits and characters are so dissimilar that I cannot form a hope that we can again feel towards each other as we have done."

Mrs. Coleridge announced the loss to Poole with her usual self control.

Ah my dear Sir [she cried] Mr. Wedgwood, I daresay, little guesses the increase of anxieties his withdrawing his half of the annuity has caused me—but it was not to be expected that he could be interested about those whom he had never seen—I think if (he) had ever seen these children, he would not have had the heart to have withdrawn it—at least until one of them was in a way of providing for himself—but I blame nobody—and these murmurs of an oppressed heart, are only for the ears of an indulgent friend—this much more—and I have done—if it were not for the protection that Southey's house affords me—I know not how we should (all have gone on) at this present writing—I remain however in much trouble yet thankful for the blessings remaining to me—(I need not name them) and in the hope of better prospects or Coleridge's return even, dear Mr. Poole yours very sincerely. S.C.

Coleridge's comments to Stuart on December 22, 1812 upon his wife's reception of the bad news was terse, even laconic—"Poor woman! she is sadly out of heart in consequence of Mr. Josiah Wedgwood having withdrawn his share of the annuity. . . ." Although Coleridge had long declared that he had transferred the Wedgwood annuity to his wife, it was not until four years later that any legal transfer was made, and at that date it was of necessity only Tom Wedgwood's remaining half that could be transferred. Josiah Wedgwood's letter to Mrs. Coleridge on January 15, 1817 unconsciously suggests his sympathy with her. "Dear Madam," he wrote, "You will be so good in future as to draw on Messrs Thos. Coutts and Co. London for £75 a year, per procuration of S.T. Coleridge, and I must beg you to desire Mr. Coleridge will write to me that you have hitherto drawn for the annuity payable to him under the will of my late brother Thomas by his authority, and that he authorizes you to continue to do so." On hearing of Wedgwood's wish Coleridge quickly complied and henceforth Mrs. Coleridge became the legal, sole possessor of Tom Wedgwood's £75 a year.

10   The End of the Great Quarrel with Wordsworth (1811-13)

". . .so deep and so rankling is the wound, which Wordsworth has wanton-ly and without the slightest provocation inflicted in return for a 15 years' most enthusiastic, self-despising and alas! self-injuring Friendship. . . ."

S. T. Coleridge to Daniel Stuart
April 28, 1811

A main cause of Coleridge's unrest throughout the restless months of 1811 was the quarrel with Wordsworth, ever at the back of his mind. Inevitably news of the quarrel spread among the friends and acquaintances of all concerned and partisans appeared on every side. Arguments as to what words Montagu had used and imputed to Wordsworth, and as to what Wordsworth had actually said, developed with exaggerations and misrepresentations everywhere among the disputants. In all this, Coleridge, airing his complaints and describing his own sufferings real or exaggerated, played no mean part.

Mary Lamb, particularly concerned for Coleridge's mental state, urged Wordsworth to come to town immediately. Dorothy replied with an account of what William had said to Montagu and assured her that William felt no coolness to Coleridge. . . .A letter from Wordsworth however, seemed to Lamb too indifferent to be shown to Coleridge who nevertheless learned of it, and later rebuked Wordsworth for having written it. For the next eighteen months there was total silence between Wordsworth and Coleridge.

There is no direct record of what Montagu had said to Coleridge but extant letters and Robinson's diary repeat some of the obviously false and most objectionable terms: "Wordsworth *has commissioned* me to tell you, first that he has no hope for you; for years past you had been an ABSOLUTE NUISANCE in the family," and that Coleridge was "in *the habit* of running into debt at little Pot Houses for gin." Wordsworth was also said to have described Coleridge as a *"rotten drunkard* who was rotting out his entrails by intemperence." Such were the evident perversions of Wordsworth's well-intentioned warning to Montagu, on behalf of both friends. No one acquainted with Wordsworth could believe that such words *were ever spoken* by him nor surely by Montagu. That Wordsworth would not condescend to defend himself against such absurd charges was but natural. In these circumstances and hearing from various sources that Coleridge was well and cheerful and going about in society with his head powdered, Wordsworth dismissed his complaints as insincere.

It was Dorothy in letters to Catherine Clarkson who most clearly and fairly described the quarrel, although Dorothy too was not an entirely detached witness. Beside her natural desire to defend her brother, Dorothy had experienced from Coleorton days to those at Allan Bank, not only a disillusion with Coleridge like William's, but also the bitterness of discovering her mistake in believing that she could reform him where Mrs. Coleridge had failed.

Against Coleridge's version, or rather versions, as rumor brought them to Dorothy's ears, she now turned to defend William. After the months of Coleridge's residence at Allan Bank the Wordsworths well understood Montagu's disillusion with his guest. But Dorothy naturally resented Wordsworth's name having been introduced into their quarrel. "We find that Coleridge is offended with William," Dorothy told Catherine Clarkson in May 1811,

> I do not like to begin with such stories nor should I have mentioned it at all, if I had not thought that perhaps Henry Robinson may have heard something of it; and a mutilated tale might so come to your ears. In few words, I will tell you, though I am sure you would not be inclined to blame my brother whatever you might hear from other quarters. You know that Coleridge went to London with the Montagus, and that their plan was to lodge him in their own house, and no doubt Montagu expected to have so much influence over him as to lead him into the way of following up his schemes with industry. Montagu himself is the most industrious creature in the world, rises early and works late, but his health is by no means good, and when he goes from his labours, rest of body and mind is absolutely necessary to him: and William perceived clearly that any interruption of his tranquillity would be a serious injury to him, and if to him consequently to his family. Further he was convinced that if Coleridge took up his abode in Montagu's house they would soon part with mutual dissatisfaction, Montagu being the last man in the world to tolerate in another person (and that person an inmate with him) habits utterly discordant with his own. Convinced of these truths William used many arguments to persuade Montagu that his purpose of keeping Coleridge comfortable could not be answered by their being in the same house together—but in vain. Montagu was resolved. "He would do all that could be done for him and would have him at his house." After this William spoke out and told Montagu the nature of Coleridge's habits (nothing in fact which everybody in whose house he had been for two days has not seen of themselves) and Montagu then perceived that it would be better for Coleridge to have lodgings near him. William intended giving Coleridge advice to the same effect; but he had no opportunity of talking with him when Coleridge passed through Grasmere on his way to London. Soon after they got to London, Montagu wrote to William that on their road he had seen so much of Coleridge's habits that he was convinced he should be miserable under the same roof with him, and that he had repeated to Coleridge what William had said to him and that Coleridge had been very angry. Now what could be so absurd as Montagu's bringing forward William's communications as his reason for not wishing to have Cole-

ridge in the house, when he had himself as he says "seen a confirmation of all that Wordsworth had said" in the very short time that they were together. So however, he did, and William contented himself with telling Montagu that he thought he had done unwisely—and he gave him his reasons for thinking so. We heard no more of this, or of Coleridge in any way except soon after his arrival in town, by Mrs. Montagu, that he was well in health, powdered, etc., and talked of being busy—from Lamb, that he was in good spirits and resolved to be orderly, and from other quarters to the like effect. But in a letter written by Mary Lamb she says she knows there is a coolness between my brother and Coleridge. In consequence of this I told her what had passed between Montagu and William and assured her of the truth that there was no coolness on William's part. . . .We heard no more of the matter till the other day when Mrs. Coleridge received a letter from Coleridge about his MSS. in which he says as an excuse for having written to no-one and having done nothing, that he had endured a series of injuries during the first month of his stay in London—but I will give you his own words as reported to us by Mrs. Coleridge. She says "he writes as one who had been cruelly injured"—He says "if you knew in detail of my most unprovoked suffering for the first month after I left Keswick and with what a thunder-clap that *part* came upon me which gave the whole power of the anguish to all the rest—you would pity me, you would less wonder at my conduct, or rather my suspension of all conduct—in short that a frenzy of the heart should produce some of the effects of a derangement of the brain etc. etc."—so I suppose there is a good deal more of this, but she says he mentions no names except Mr. and Mrs. Morgan's. He says "I leave it to Mrs. Morgan to inform you of my health and habits" adding that it is to her and her husband's kindness he owes it that he is now in his senses—in short that he is alive. I must own that at first when I read all this my soul burned with indignation that William should thus (by implication) be charged with having caused disarrangement in his friend's mind. A pretty story to be told. C. has been driven to madness by W's cruel or unjust conduct towards him. Would not anybody suppose that he had been guilty of the most atrocious treachery or cruelty? But what is the sum of all he did? He privately warned a common friend disposed to serve C with all his might that C had one or two habits which might disturb his tranquillity, he told him what those habits were, and a greater kindness could hardly have been done to C for it is not fit that he should go into houses where he is not already known. If he were to be told what was said at Penrith after he had been at Anthony Harrison's, then he might be thankful to William. I am sure we suffered enough on that account and were anxious enough to get him away. I say that at first I was strong with indignation but *that* soon subsided and I was lost in pity for his miserable weakness. It is certainly very fortunate for William that he should be the person on whom he has to charge his neglect of duty—but to C the difference is nothing, for if this had not happened there would have been somebody else on whom to cast the blame. William wrote to Mrs. C immediately and wished her to transcribe his letter, or parts of it for C and told her that he would not write to C himself as he had not communicated his displeasure to him. Mrs. C replies that she is afraid to do this as C did not desire her to inform us, and that it may prevent him from opening letters in future etc. etc. I ought to have told you that C had a violent quarrel with Carlisle who refused to attend him as a surgeon after C had slighted his prescriptions. My dear friend you cannot imagine what an irksome task it has been to me to write the above, I would wish it to rest for ever. Time will remove the cloud from his mind as far as the right view of our conduct is obscured, and having deserved no blame we are easy on that score. If he seek an explanation William will be ready to give it, but I think it is more likely that his fancies will die away of themselves. Poor creature! unhappy as he makes others how much more unhappy is he himself.

Samuel's letter to his wife to which Dorothy referred, was written early in May 1811 when he gave as an excuse for his silence the terrible effects of the "thunder-clap" upon himself. When Wordsworth at last heard from Southey the words Montagu was said to have quoted as Wordsworth's he refused to believe it and declared (probably with truth) that Coleridge "had invented them." Yet by this time Coleridge had doubtless come to believe them himself. Wordsworth in fact regarded Coleridge's attitude to himself as a mere pretext "to break with him and to furnish himself with a ready excuse for all his failures in duty to himself and others."

To Stuart on April 28, Coleridge had already complained of Wordsworth.

So deep and so rankling is the wound [he said], which W has wantonly and without the slightest provocation inflicted in return for a 15 years' most enthusiastic, self-despising and alas! self-injuring friendship, (for as to his wretched agents, the Montagus, Carlisles, Knapps, etc. I despise them too much to be seriously hurt by anything, they for themselves can say or do) that I cannot return to Grasmere or its vicinity—where I must often see and always be reminded of him. Every man must take the measure of his own strength, I may, I do, regret my want of fortitude; but so it is, that incurable depression of spirits, brooding, indolence, despondence, thence pains and nightly horrors, and thence the Devil and all his Imps to get rid of them or rather to keep them just at arm's length, would be infallibly the result. Even to have only thought of W., while writing these lines, has, I feel, fluttered and disordered my whole inside.

In June 1811 the Wordsworths, having abandoned smoky Allan Bank, were busy settling down in a new temporary home in Grasmere, The Vicarage, where "a very pretty room" was reserved for Sara Hutchinson. Coleridge's children it was decided should no longer come for two days a week, as at Allan Bank. Dorothy now told Mrs. Clarkson: "the noise and confusion of so many children for so long a time in the house would be intolerable; but in fine weather they may always walk over on Saturday or Sunday morning, and spend the day with us."

Since Coleridge's quarrel with her brother Dorothy's disappointment with Coleridge had deepened into bitter despair of him. She could even find satisfaction in believing she had now lost her sympathy towards Coleridge, and could regard him with indifference. With severity she even criticized to Catherine Clarkson his articles in *The Courier*:

Poor C's late writings in *The Courier* have in general evidenced the same sad weakness of moral constitution to which you alluded in your last letter, as tainting his intercourse with his private friends, and his casual acquaintances also. They are as much the work of a party spirit, as if he were writing for a place—servile adulations of the Wellesleys. I speak of the general character of his paragraphs and short essays. No doubt there are amongst them sentiments of a better kind. It has been misery enough, God knows, to me to see the truths which I now see. Long did we hope against experience and reason; but now I have no hope! if he continues as he is. Nothing but time producing a total change in him can ever make him a being of much use to mankind in general, or of the least comfort to his friends. I am sure I have no personal feelings of pain or irritation connected with him. An injury done to my brother, or me, or any of our family, or dear friends, would not now hurt me more than an injury done to an indifferent person. I only grieve at the waste and prostitution of his fine genius, at the sullying and perverting of what is lovely and tender in human sympathies, and noble and generous; and I do grieve whenever I think of him. His resentment to my brother hardly ever comes into my thoughts. I feel perfectly indifferent about it. How absurd, how uncalculating of the feelings and opinions of others, to talk to your father and sister of dying in a fortnight, when his dress and everything proved that his thoughts were of other matters. Such talks will never more alarm me. . . .Only I must add that I fear he slackens at *The Courier* office, as there has been nothing of his for some days, and he has not written to Mrs. C since the time I mentioned; nor has he acknowledged the receipt of his MSS. which he was in a great hurry to receive, that he might publish them. By the bye he desired Charles Lamb to write to me about them; therefore, no doubt, he includes me in his resentment. I know not for what cause.

Two months later Dorothy informed Catherine that the Southeys were at Bristol and Mrs. Southey told her that Coleridge "had promised to return to Keswick in a month." Upon this Dorothy commented prophetically and with her now usual acerbity toward Coleridge: "I do not expect him in a year if he can stay on with the Morgans. It is a pity he is not obliged to supply himself with the means of actual living. While there is a house open to him he will go on far away from his family—and do nothing except by fits; he has not written in *The Courier* this long time. As Mr. Sharpe expressed it to me last Sunday 'Nobody has seen him in London. . . .' "

By December 5, 1811 Catherine Clarkson's indignation with Coleridge on behalf of Wordsworth had died down and she could write to Robinson sympathetically of Coleridge: "Of all men, there seems most need to say 'God bless poor Coleridge!' One could almost believe that an enchanter's spell was upon him, forcing him to be what he is, and yet leaving him the power of showing what he might be." Nevertheless reverberations of the quarrel still continued and two days later Mrs. Clarkson told him: "I have many reasons for wishing that Coleridge would write to me. Tell him from me that whether he write little or much I should be glad to hear from him. Don't tell him that you mentioned what he said respecting Wordsworth—I would rather avoid that subject if I could. It is possible that there might be something stern in Wordsworth's manner, but he has done so much for Coleridge—borne so much from him, that Coleridge ought to forget it. . . ."

On December 27, 1811 during Coleridge's series of lectures, Dorothy

Wordsworth gave a sardonic approval to Coleridge's intention. "It is well he has lectured," she told Catherine Clarkson, "as he probably would have done nothing else, and, having completed one design, there is better ground to hope that he may hereafter complete others. He has promised to come down to Keswick immediately after the Lectures. I wish he may; but I do not think he can resolve to come, if he does not at the same time lay aside his displeasure against William. Surely this one act of his mind out-does all the rest. . . ."

Mrs. Coleridge's comment upon the quarrel when writing to Poole on October 30, 1812 would not have pleased Samuel:

It has taught Coleridge one useful lesson, that even his dearest and most indulgent friends, even those very persons who have been the great means of his self-indulgence, when he comes to live *wholly* with them, are *as* clear-sighted of his failings, and much *less* delicate in speaking of them, than his wife, who being the Mother of his children, even if she had not the slightest regard for himself would naturally feel a reluctance to the exposing of his faults.

Back in London Coleridge continued throughout the spring and summer of 1812 his complaints of Wordsworth to various friends. On April 24 Coleridge recapitulated to his friend Sharp with increasing bitterness the sufferings Wordsworth had so wantonly inflicted upon him:

The conviction was forced on me, say rather pierced through my very soul with the suddenness of a flash of lightening that he had become my bitterest calumniator whom, to that very moment, I had cherished in my heart's heart—The benumbing despondency relieved by no gleam of hope, and only alternating with fits of (truly may I call it) mental agony, I even now scarcely dare look back on. But in the last worst affliction the cure was involved. I gradually obtained the conquest over my own feelings—and now dare call myself a freeman, which I did not dare do till I had been at Keswick, and satisfied myself that no possibility remained of my having been deluded.

Yet on the very day of his letter to Sharp he requested Mrs. Coleridge to obtain from Wordsworth via Southey, Wordsworth's *Essays on Epitaphs* for a new edition of *The Friend*; but they did not appear.

By this time Wordsworth was in London bent upon a final understanding with Coleridge while an anxious Dorothy besought William: "We long to hear from you—your first letter cannot tell us anything of the affair with Coleridge. . .I hope it will be over." Coleridge's attitude however was clearly expressed to Godwin on April 30: "You know I suppose that Mr. Wordsworth is in town—and I need not hint that it would be painful to me, *and I trust* to himself, that we should meet." A chief incentive to Wordsworth's visit to London had been the knowledge that the great quarrel was now the subject of scandal-mongering and tittle-tattle among various coteries there.

By this time the quarrel had become an engrossing subject for many of Coleridge's and Wordsworth's acquaintance. Of these Mrs. Clarkson was prominent, ardently throwing herself into the fray with varying feelings, at one time condemnatory of Coleridge, at others in relenting mood. Mrs. Clarkson brought in Crabb Robinson; and Coleridge sought comfort from John Morgan. Their letters are too many, too long, too repetitive for detailed reproduction here. Nevertheless some passages of these letters are too intensely personal for entire omission.

Robinson, who was attempting to promote a reconciliation between Wordsworth and Coleridge had been disgusted by gossip at a dinner party at Longman's. He reported it to Mrs. Clarkson who in turn passed it on to Dorothy Wordsworth and Sara Hutchinson. Thereupon all three ladies indignantly denied the expression attributed to Wordsworth. Mrs. Clarkson in her indignation cried that Coleridge "had better. . . .put a pistol to his brains!" but "turned sick at the thought."

From this time the contention between Coleridge and Wordsworth concentrated upon the question "what had Montagu really said." Coleridge had told Morgan on March 27, 1812, that Montagu told him during the quarrel: "Wordsworth had commissioned me to tell you &c." Henceforth this word "commissioned" began a new contention between Wordsworthians and Coleridgians. Mrs. Clarkson informing Wordsworth of "commissioned," begged him to "force an interview" with Coleridge for clarification of the point. Consequently Wordsworth sought an interview with Coleridge who refused, Lamb being the only intermediary.

Wordsworth was particularly incensed on hearing that Coleridge had begun a statement of his case to Sara Hutchinson but had abandoned it on hearing that she was against him. Such a statement Wordsworth declared angrily to Mrs. Clarkson, should have been sent to himself in the first place: "Why draw out a paper at all whose object it was to win from the sister of my wife an opinion in his favour, and therefore to my prejudice. . . ?" On the preceding day Wordsworth had found a letter from Coleridge but refused to open it unless he heard through Lamb that Coleridge declared it to be "nothing but a naked statement of what he believes Montagu said to him." He would then forward it to Montagu for his opinion of it.

From this point the altercation between Wordsworth and Coleridge again concentrated upon the words Wordsworth had used—according to Montagu and according to Wordsworth. Coleridge refused Wordsworth's suggestion that he, Montagu, and Wordsworth should meet to argue the question before Josiah Wedgwood as arbitrator. Thereupon followed a long, wearisome and largely repetitive argument in letters between the disputants. For them Lamb and Robinson acted as intermediaries. Wordsworth declared he had never used the words "rotten drunkard" and "nuisance" of Coleridge. Coleridge, although accepting Wordsworth's account of the matter, now charged him with unfriendliness in not giving it before. Yet Robinson believed Coleridge preferred Montagu's account to Wordsworth's. So Coleridge sent Wordsworth Montagu's words, which Wordsworth denied, and the contention by letters (largely destroyed) went merrily ahead. Wordsworth had *not* said he had "no hope of Coleridge," nor that he would "run into debt at little Pot Houses for gin"; neither had he called Coleridge a "nuisance."

The result was a reply from Coleridge on May 11, 1812, written in the most conciliatory and religious spirit,

> I declare before God Almighty, [he wrote] that at no time even of my sorest affliction did even the possibility occur to me of ever doubting your word. I never ceased for a moment to have faith in you, to love and revere you. . . .The rest of the letter was unimpressive and digressive filled with what people had said or were said to have said, and it ended on the familiar note of love and honour for Wordsworth:- the only offence I ever committed against you in deed or word, or thought—that is not writing to you and trusting instead to our common friends. . . .

The next day in a letter to Southey Coleridge wrote about Wordsworth's statement which had convinced him of Wordsworth's innocence: "I then instantly informed him that were ten thousand Montagus to swear against it, I should take his word not ostensibly only but with inward faith! . . .The affair between Wordsworth and me seems settled."

On May 20 Robinson "rejoiced" at his success with "*two such men*. . .one I believe the greatest man now living in this country and the other a man of astonishing genius and talents tho' not harmoniously blended as in his happier friend to form a great and good man."

Although Wordsworth could tell Mrs. Clarkson on June 4 of Coleridge: "I have seen him several times, but not much alone; one morning we had, however, a pleasant walk to Hampstead together." The feelings aroused during the great quarrel were never quite extinguished by either Coleridge or Wordsworth. Nor did the two ladies who had played no mean part in the quarrel regard Coleridge with the affection and admiration of the past, though they naturally welcomed the apparent end to the quarrelling. "I knew before that Coleridge was worthless as a friend—but nothing would have made me believe that he, who knew Wordsworth so thoroughly, and who must know himself—could have acted as he has by Wordsworth". Such was Catherine Clarkson's opinion. Dorothy Wordsworth's pleasure at the end of the quarrel—as she believed—was not less than Mrs. Clarkson's, but toward Coleridge her feelings were kinder. "How happy I am," she wrote to William on May 17, 1812: "that your mind is going to be settled about Coleridge—You have, in every part of the arrangement, acted wisely and becomingly—and I hope that such intercourse will henceforth take place between you as will be salutary to both parties. When you see him give my love to him. I suppose he will now receive it, though he has indeed acted to us all (and Sara and I could not possibly have offended him), as if he intended to insult us. I am sure he does not know the depth of the affection I have had for him."

Unfortunately, new tensions soon developed. The innocent cause of the first was little Tom Wordsworth's death on December 1, 1812. How the news reached Coleridge we do not know but within a week he sent Wordsworth a long, very Coleridgian consolatory letter which included an account of an intuition he had had of Tom's death at the time of its occurrence. From dreams of the Wordsworths and Sara Hutchinson he had woke three times that night "and each time found my face and part of the pillow wet with tears."

"Write? My dearest Friend!" he cried "O that it were in my power to be with you myself instead of my letter. . . ." The lectures he was giving he "could give up" he said, but the rehearsal of his play *Remorse,* must keep him in town at present, as "upon this depends my best hopes of leaving Town after Christmas and living among you as long as I live. . . ."

> O dearest Friend [he continued,] what comfort can I afford you? What comfort ought I not to afford, who have given you so much pain. . . ? There is a sense of the word, Love, in which I never felt it but to you and one of your Household! I am distant from you some hundred miles, but glad I am, that I am no longer distant in spirit, and have faith, that as it has happened *but once,* so it can never happen again. An aweful truth it seems to me, and prophetic of our future, as well as declarative of our present *real* nature, that one mere Thought, one feeling of Suspicion or Jealousy or resentment can remove two human Beings farther from each other, than winds or seas can separate their Bodies.

Such were the more important parts of Coleridge's letter which after a transition to theology and the comfort of belief in human "survival," concluded by assuring "Dear Mary," "Dear Dorothy," "Dearest Sarah!" that he was unchanged in his feelings towards them, was now living at his highest level, and was aware "that few things could more console you than to see me healthy and worthy of myself!" And the letter ended with "Again and again, my Dearest Wordsworth!! I am affectionately and truly your S.T. Coleridge."

Upon the receipt of this letter Dorothy's anger with Coleridge immediately evaporated—at least for a time. To Mrs. Clarkson, on January 5, 1813, she wrote: "I am glad to think that you will see Coleridge. Poor soul!—I only think of him now with my wonted affection, and with tender feelings of compassion for his infirmities. We have had several letters from him. Our sorrow has sunk into him, and he loved the darling the best of all our little ones. He talks of coming down as soon as possible, if his play succeds. I hope it will, and I am confident he will come."

Poor Dorothy can hardly have seen a comment by Coleridge made at this time in *Anima Poetae,* which however was not published until after Coleridge's death: "O that perilous moment (for such there is) of a half-reconciliation, when the coldness and the resentment have been sustained too long. Each is drawing toward the other, but like glass in the mid-state between fusion and compaction a single sand will splinter it." The remark was however both significant and prophetic. Only a month after Dorothy's optimistic letter to Mrs. Clarkson Coleridge was indignantly recapitulating to Poole the sufferings caused by Wordsworth's action. In this letter he expressed in plain words his realization that whatever apparent reconciliation occurred, his feelings towards Wordsworth could never be the same: "A reconciliation has taken place—" he cried to Poole, "but the *feeling,* which I had previous to that moment, when the 3/4ths Calumny burst like a Thunder-storm from a blue sky on my Soul—after 15 years of such religious, almost superstitious, idolatry and Self-sacrifice—O no! no! that I fear, never can return. . . .''

Nor was the mood of the Wordsworths without lingering suspicions of Coleridge. In these circumstances the grain of sand which in Coleridge's apothegm, prevented the fusion of the glass, was not wanting: indeed there were several grains: Dorothy vainly expecting Coleridge's letters, while Coleridge heard nothing of Wordsworth except indirectly. Other grains of sand were Coleridge's gift to Southey of a copy of *Remorse*, but none to Wordsworth; and instead of coming North Coleridge had gone to the seaside with the Morgans.

Even during these last days of the dying friendship between the Wordsworths and Coleridge Dorothy and Mrs. Clarkson continued to write of him with recurrent outbursts of affection and despair. It was Dorothy who on April 8, 1813 in her reply to Catherine Clarkson struck the final valedictory note: ''as to Coleridge you have done all that can be done, and we are grieved that you have had so much uneasiness and taken so much trouble about him. He will not let himself be served by others. Oh! that the day may ever come when he will serve himself! Then will his eyes be opened and he will see clearly that we have loved him always, do still (love) him, and have ever loved—not measuring his deserts. . . .God bless him.''

By this time in fact the quarrelling was over; the parting of Coleridge and the Wordsworths practically permanent. After Coleridge's removal two years later to Highgate where he remained for the last eighteen years of his life his relations with the Wordsworths were little more than a very occasional meeting when William was in London.

11   "Pitiable Slavery" (1813-16)

"I have strong hopes that I should emancipate myself altogether from this most pitiable Slavery, the fetters of which do indeed eat into the Soul."
—*S.T. Coleridge to R.H. Brabant*
[Late December 1815 - undated]

On August 10, 1813 Dorothy Wordsworth wrote of Coleridge to Sara Hutchinson: "Coleridge and the Morgans are coming down immediately, in such a hurry that they cannot wait for Southey. The Morgans intend to settle at Keswick for cheapness. Mary says, 'I suppose you know that the Morgans have *smashed*.' Now this I did not know, but I had heard that they were poor, and had had losses I believe."

Although the Morgans and Coleridge did not come to Keswick, Dorothy's information about poor John Morgan was only too true. John Morgan had, as Dorothy said to Sara Hutchinson, "Smashed"; was bankrupt. On October 15 Robinson recorded: "Coleridge's kind friend Morgan was forced to leave the country by pecuniary difficulties." Morgan in fact had fled to Ireland where he remained, consoled by the kindness of an Irish family which, said Morgan, "behaved extremely well" to him until the storm blew over when he returned to his family in England.

During John Morgan's absence in Ireland Coleridge, although in Bristol, busied himself in attempting to settle Morgan's affairs. To this end he tried to obtain the assistance of several Bristol friends, and was particularly anxious to save a tobacconist's shop in Bishopsgate Street owned by Charlotte Brent. To achieve this Coleridge persuaded a local clergyman, a Mr. Porter, to act as surety for £100 on her behalf. Coleridge, pleased with this success thanked Mr. Porter for his "friendly offer" in mid-October and a few days later dined with him. This friendship however was short-lived, for when a little later Porter refused to increase his responsibility beyond the original £100, the disappointed Coleridge told Morgan in June 1814: "There is a coolness between me and Porter. . . all common friends highly approve of my feelings and conduct. There is, I hear and fear, some danger that Porter's head will be turned by the flatteries and evening Ladies Parties of his parish."

Throughout October Coleridge, despite his lectures, was very busy with the Morgans' affairs, and in his correspondence with the two ladies he explained his difficulties in giving them the help they needed. Lloyd, the banker who

401

represented Charlotte Brent's creditors, soon fared even worse than Mr.
Porter in Coleridge's opinion. "I am indignant to the last degree at his conduct," Coleridge told Mrs. Morgan on November 5: "Shame upon the wretch!
to impose on, and act the bully-Creditor, toward a young lady ignorant of
business." Lloyd, he said, was responsible by his mismanagement for the delay with the £100 cheque. "I will take care" Coleridge wrote, "that the next £100
shall be ready money, and Charlotte should ask him why he had not taken the
former with the discount added: tho' there is not a tradesman in London but
himself, that would have been guilty of such meanness." But Coleridge was
willing to be co-trustee if Lloyd would accept his own surety to repay £90 "by
monthly installments."

Already, as ever with Coleridge in financial matters, his assistance to the
Morgans had become extremely complicated. "Be assured," he told his
friends, "I will [neither] neglect nor delay anything—pray write me if you
want any money for yourself. I can send you from 20 to 30 £ for your immediate use, and will do so by Sunday's post—I have not had time to call at
the Post Office to-day". Two days later Coleridge wrote again: "My dear
Friends—I write to-day for fear you should feel disappointed—but I must
write again to-morrow, because I think it better that Charlotte should pay the
100£ to Lloyd, and take his receipt as 'C.Brent'—not Brent & Co.—and I cannot procure a cheque to-day, being Sunday, or even a 100£ note—tho' the latter would, besides, be risking too much."

Coleridge in another letter to the Morgans also written on November 5,
1813, suggested increasing tension between himself and his friends, "if you
have been disappointed in not hearing from me (as I from you), it has not been
my fault." Thus he began, and continued evidently explaining some delay: "I
left instructions at the Post Office, that all my letters should be put in Mr.
Wade's box. . . ." The next moment however, Mrs. Morgan's letter arrived
and provoked from Coleridge for the enlightenment of the evidently disappointed lady a summary explanation of Coleridge's difficulties. The debts or
losses it appeared, were by this time greater than Coleridge had anticipated or
had indicated to the sureties and he dared not, as Mrs. Morgan evidently
desired, request an increase in their commitments. He must also explain his
delay in sending her various cheques that she and Charlotte had expected. He
himself was unfortunately short of cash, yet believed he could "command"
another £80. But he continued: "I doubt not that I shall be able to supply you
regularly with whatever is necessary for your immediate expenses."

On November 9, 1813, again worried by Mrs. Morgan's silence, Coleridge
wrote to her:

> My dear Friends, I can not express the uneasiness I have suffered, from not
> hearing from you. It REALLY so deprest [sic] my spirits, and so haunted
> me, that the lecture of to-night, which I had expected to have been the best
> and to have produced the most lively effect, that on Othello, was the worst I
> ever delivered—and a humiliating contrast to the lecture before. I so con-
> fidently depended on a letter from you by this day's post, that since two

o'clock, when Mr. Wade assured me that no letter had arrived, I could do nothing else but torment myself with conjectures and fancies. The root of the evil is, that neither of you ever formed a just appreciation of my affection towards you. You never believed that I loved you and Morgan, as (God knows!) I have done.

If he does not hear from Mrs. Morgan he must enquire elsewhere

to know what is become of you.—You cannot conceive, how unhappy this has made me—I pray God fervently, that it may be accident or even your fault—and not illness or any new misfortune. Sure, there cannot have been any thing in my latter letters, that has affronted you?—Pray, pray write immediately—and let the letter be circumstantial, first and foremost, as to Mary's health; secondly, as to your private and household bills, what have remained unpayed; and lastly, as to your immediate plans, and what you think of my proposal as to settling in or near Bristol for the next 4 months. . . .

Five days later Coleridge wrote in repentant mood:

My very dear Friends, When I wrote my last peevish and querulous letter (for which I am sorry but hope, you attributed it to its true cause, the anxiety of affection) I did not foresee the severe attack of illness, which I have since suffered, and tho' something better, still labour under. I dined on Wednesday at Mr. T. Castle's—felt myself uncomfortable—and whether from that cause, I drank more wine, or that the wine acted more on me, I was little less than drunk. . . .As you have forbad it (I hope to God! . .not from false delicacy), I shall not enclose in *to-day's* letter the 30 £ bank note, which I had procured. Whatever you wish, as to my coming up to town, I will most assuredly do—but it would add very, very greatly to my happiness, and I may add, to my well-being, if I could induce you to let me immediately find out some respectable family either at Clifton or at Frenchay where we all three might lodge and board, and have two bedrooms, and one sitting-room private to ourselves. I can feel and understand your objections; but I am certain, that the getting *them* over would greatly smooth the way to Morgan's comfortable return and settlement.

But the ladies, who had left Berners Street for Fitzroy Square in October, were reluctant to leave London for Bristol. So on November 18, 1813 he wrote: "If your feelings are insurmountable, I will take leave of my Bristolian friends, and instantly go off with you to Keswick. . . .But I will not say another word about it; only withersoever you go, I will accompany you, till I re-deliver the goods to the rightful owner J.J. Morgan, Esquire." And with a genial rap at Charlotte Brent's prudishness, he wrote: "Good night! Tomorrow I shall hear *from* you and *of* Miss Brent. *From* miss B.? O La! no! Write to a man, tho' old enough to be my father—! my neck-and-breast-kerchief is downright scorched and iron-moulded with the intensity of my expansive blush!"

Two days later, regretting their refusal to come to Bristol, Coleridge promised to go to them in London within a few days. If they were in Bristol he said, he would make £600 a year by holding discussion classes and giving private lectures, to teach "all the knowledge that a gentlemen ought to have." He would also have liked to conduct the ladies from London to live at Nether Stowey near Poole and other acquaintances of Coleridge.

On November 23, 1813 Coleridge gave his last lecture in Bristol and—as he promised—dashed to London to join Mrs. Morgan and Miss Brent in Fitzroy Square. Two days later he told Wade that Mrs. Morgan was too unwell to live in London.

On November 29, Coleridge left London with the two ladies whom he escorted to Ashley in Somerset. Thence Coleridge continued alone to Bath with the intention of leaving immediately for Bristol. At Bath however, illness confined him for the next three weeks to his room at the inn. On December 8 from Bath, Coleridge briefly informed Wade of his recent activities. "I left London the Monday before last, in the Reading Stage," he said, "to accommodate those with me stayed Monday night and Tuesday there—left Reading in a post chaise on Wednesday morning—arrived at Chippenham on Wednesday night—and at Bath on Thursday. . . ."

The journey had not been entirely harmonious and Coleridge's immediate expression of his feelings to Wade has been deleted by a later friendly hand. "The passions and pride of women," he continued, "even of in most respects good and amiable women!—passions that thwart all I do to serve them—the two sisters I have lodged at Mrs. Smith's, Grocer, Ashley, near Box—about four miles from Bath, and half a mile from Box—I could not leave them till they seemed settled—namely on Sunday—when missing the stage, and very unwell with a violent cold, I was obliged to walk to Bath thro' *such* a road, slip or slop, mud or mire, the whole way—and since my arrival at the Grey Hound, Bath, I have been confined to my bedroom—almost to my bed. . . .Pray for my recovery—and request Mr. Roberts's prayers—but for my infirm wicked heart, that Christ may mediate to the Father to lead me to Christ, and give me a living instead of a reasoning faith!—and for my health as far only as it may be the condition of my improvement and final redemption."

At Bath Coleridge had one of his worst opium bouts. It led to the following letter to Mr. Roberts (a Baptist Minister of Bristol) written almost a fortnight after the letter to Wade. "You have no conception of what my sufferings have been," he told Roberts, "forced to struggle and struggle in order not to desire a death for which I am not prepared—I have scarcely known what sleep is, but like a leopard in its den have been drawn up and down the room by extreme pain. . . ." The same day, 19 December 1813, Coleridge described himself in similar terms to Mrs. Morgan, repeating the simile of the "leopard in a den," which evidently pleased him. "Amidst all my anguish you and Charlotte were present to me—and formed a part of it"—he continued. Of the doctor attending him in Bath he spoke highly, and then informed Mrs. Morgan:—"I shall put myself into a post chaise this afternoon, please God! and proceed to Bristol—from thence, I will write you immediately. Feeble, as I am, and so deprest [*sic*] in spirit, I dare not come over to you—lest I should not be able to get away. . . .I will send you word as soon as I have settled myself in

Bristol—i.e. within 3 or 4 days. . . ." In a postscript he wrote: "If possible, I will come over on the 24th and spend Christmas Eve and Christmas Day with you." After this, with the exception of one brief note to Miss Brent written shortly before Christmas expressing his pleasure on learning of Mrs. Morgan's convalescence, we have no other letter from Coleridge, until he writes to Estlin on April 5, 1814.

Amid Coleridge's silence, Mrs. Coleridge anxious for news of him, wrote to Poole in February 1814:

> Our intelligent neighbour Mr. De Quincey tells me, that you have been with Mr. Coleridge in London during the last year; you would naturally imagine that he would mention this circumstance to me in his letters—but unhappily for me and the dear children, and I may add, for himself, his aversion to writing of every kind seems to strengthen with every absence—We have not seen him for two years—and it will be 12 months in March since he wrote to Keswick—having only sent me one letter during 2 years. When my brother Southey returned from London, Coleridge promised to accompany him; we were all sadly disappointed when the chaise arrived with only *one* person in it. Southey however assured us, that he would be here shortly, having gone to Bristol to deliver a course of lectures, after which he would set off for Keswick to meet the boys at the Christmas holidays.

So wrote Mrs. Coleridge, oppressed by many disappointments including the loss of half of her annuity. She was also very conscious of her dependence upon Southey and upon this note her letter drew to its close:—"If it were not for the protection that Southey's house affords me—I know not how we should all have gone on. . . ."

The months which intervene between Coleridge's illness at Bath in December 1813 and arrival in Bristol, until his removal to Highgate in April 1816 formed the period of his worst addiction to opium. Consequently opium appears more frequently at this time in Coleridge's correspondence than before.

It was now that Cottle, anxious to prevent Coleridge from wasting his genius in mere teaching and lecturing, planned to raise an annuity for Coleridge among Bristol friends. In discussing the subject with Southey, Cottle discovered for the first time and with profound shock, that Coleridge was an opium addict. He immediately warned Coleridge of the danger he was in and begged him to abandon the drug. Characteristically, Coleridge replied in a mood of profound misery and repentance. "You have poured oil in the raw festering wound of an old friend's conscience, Cottle!" he began, "but it is oil of vitriol!" And he continued in this strain to the end of his letter, in which however, he finally described his need of financial assistance. Of his bodily and mental sufferings, he went on to give a graphic description. "For years the anguish of my spirit has been indescribable," he wrote "the sense of my danger staring, but the conscience of my GUILT worse, far far worse than all!—I have prayed with drops of agony on my brow, trembling not only before the justice of my Maker, but even before the mercy of my Redeemer."

He was, he said "seduced into the accursed habit ignorantly" by illness. Indeed the cause was "not (so Help me God) by any temptation of pleasure, or expectation or desire of exciting pleasurable sensations."

In this last assertion Coleridge in fact contradicted his admission on other occasions, that "pleasure" was one of the attractions of opium for him. Coleridge's hope of reformation as he now told Cottle, unfortunately require the expenditure of one or two hundred pounds, "half to send to Mrs. Coleridge, and half to place myself in a private madhouse." Unfortunately also, Coleridge added, he was not yet able to repay Cottle the £10 he owed him.

Upon Cottle, now aware of Coleridge's failings, the request for financial assistance had no effect. Rather he next concentrated his energy upon the religious element in Coleridge's letter. He was, he said, "afflicted to perceive that Satan is so busy with you, but God is greater than Satan. . . ." To this Coleridge, dangerous as ever when in religiously repentent mood, replied with ironical suavity: "I have too much to be forgiven to feel any difficulty in forgiving the cruellest enemy that ever trampled on me: and you I have only to thank. . . ." And he repeated his previous request for money to assist his reformation. That Coleridge's request was again ignored by Cottle doubtless accounts for the theological onslaught upon Cottle which followed. However, Samuel's Bristol friend Hood produced the required money and enabled Coleridge to place himself under the care of a local practitioner, Dr. Daniel. But so angry was Coleridge, that he now described Cottle to Wade as "a man who is unworthy even of a rebuke from you." Soon friendly relations were restored when Coleridge was ill and Cottle broke a blood vessel. Shortly afterward in a letter to Morgan, Coleridge could speak of Cottle with affectionate disgust crying: "God bless him! He is a well-meaning creature; but a great fool!"

On May 14, 1814 Coleridge sent John Morgan, (now apparently living with his family at Ashley) a long self-exculpatory letter about his opium habit which the Morgans had vainly attempted to control. "I have been crucified, dead, and buried, descended into *Hell,* and I am now, I humbly trust, rising again, tho' slowly and gradually," he wrote. He lamented his sense of "guilt," including "ingratitude to so many friends who have loved me, I know not why; of barbarous neglect of my family; excess of cruelty to Mary and Charlotte, I have in this one dirty business of laudanum an hundred times deceived, tricked, nay, actually and consciously LIED. And yet all these vices are so opposite to my nature. . . ."

Coleridge also wrote to John Morgan of the doctors who had helped him in his fight against the domination of opium. As for Dr. Daniel, "at his second call," Coleridge wrote, the doctor said "that while I was in my own power all would be in vain—I should inevitably cheat and trick him, just as I had Dr. Tuthill—that I must either be removed to a place of confinement, or in all events have a keeper." The result was, according to both Coleridge and Cottle, that Wade hired a man to guard him from taking opium. However Daniel had made him much reduce the dosage and he expected to be completely cured within a few days. To Daniel he was very grateful; thought him: "the wisest of physicians to me." For Daniel, he said, "already from 4 and 5 ounces has brought me down to four teaspoonfuls in the 24 hours." To Daniel himself Coleridge sent on May 19 a revised extract from his "Pains of Sleep" as a token of "my life-long affectionate gratitude for my emancipation from a slavery more dreadful than any man, who has not felt its iron fetters eating into his very soul, can possibly imagine." On the same day Coleridge requested a friend to inform Mrs. Clarkson "that I have been for many months *worse than nothing*; but that by the grace of God, who has answered by fervent and importunate prayers for mercy, and for increase of faith and fortitude, and (instrumentally) by the great prudence, skill and gentleness of my medical attendant I am almost miraculously restored, and (as it were) *emancipated*." Nevertheless Coleridge refused to see John Morgan until after the impending cure.

Coleridge's fear of having deeply offended Mary Morgan and Charlotte Brent was apparently not only due to his shame about opium, but also to the disagreement with them occasioned by John Morgan's bankruptcy and Coleridge's attempts to assist them. As ever, his love for the ladies was still, he assured John Morgan, profound: ". . .strange as it must appear to them, and perhaps incredible, it is still true, that I not only have loved ever, and still do love them; but that there never was a moment in which I would not have shed my very blood for their sakes. . .and must take the alienation of Mary's and Charlotte's esteem and affection among the due punishments of my crime." There was however, a brighter side to the picture: "I am as much pleased as it is possible I can be at present, in the present state of my body and mind, at the improving state of your affairs. Nothing would give me truer delight than being recovered, to be able by my exertions to aid you: And assuredly, either this will (be) the case, or my death." I dare not ask you to give my love to Mary—it is sufficient that she has it, Coleridge told John in concluding his letter.

The artist Charles Robert Leslie in his *Reminiscences* praises Coleridge for his devoted attention to Allston when ill at this time. But soon Coleridge was very angry with Allston for not answering one of Coleridge's letters—as Coleridge himself so often did to his own friends. When shortly afterwards Allston called on Coleridge the breach was healed.

Allston was now dispirited by lack of patrons and by hostile critics, two misfortunes which of course immediately aroused the sympathy of Coleridge as a fellow sufferer. "Allston has not yet learnt all he will learn on the excessive meanness of Patrons" he told Morgan on June 11, 1814, "of the malignant envy and brutality of the race of Painters! . ." Early in July Coleridge called to see Allston's present work, "*The Dead Man Revived by Touching the Bones of the Prophet Elisha,* and was "more than gratified by the wonderful improvement of the picture. . .a perfect work of art" he found it: "such richness with such variety of colours, all harmonizing, and, while they vivify yet deepen, not counteract, the total effect of a grand solemnity of tint, I never before contemplated."

Before the close of July Coleridge, to assist Allston, who was evidently in difficult circumstances at this time, decided to write and publish in the local newspaper some essays on aesthetics which, strange to say, did actually appear in *Felix Farley's Bristol Journal* in August and September 1814, entitled: *The Principles of Genial Criticism Concerning the Fine Arts.* In these, however, Allston's name scarcely appears. In the only important reference to the artist Coleridge drew attention to "the admirable pictures now exhibited by Allston" in Bristol.

The *Essays on Genial Criticism* in the Bristol Journal were immediately attacked in the public papers by several critics, much to the annoyance of Coleridge who on September 10 expressed his feelings to the Editor of *Felix Farley's Journal* about them. Coleridge's long, facetiously caustic letter probably demolished the poor provincial critics.

In Allston, now ill and bankrupt and the target of hostile art critics, Coleridge saw a young replica of himself. So with extreme indignation, he appealed to Stuart in mid-September to intervene by persuading another newspaper "not to continue that accursed system of detraction and calumny against Allston." Allston's gratitude to his stout defender found expression in the painting of Coleridge's portrait that year in Bristol—now in the National Portrait Gallery, London. On August 16, 1814 Coleridge described in detail to Morgan his feelings about the portrait. "Of my own portrait," he wrote, "I am no judge—Allston is highly gratified with it. . .my face is not a manly or representable face—whatever is impressive, is part fugitive, part *existent* only in the imaginations of persons impressed strongly by my conversation—the face *itself* is a FEEBLE, unmanly face. . . .The exceedng weakness, strengthlessness, in my face, was ever painful to me—not as my own face—but as a face."

Never, despite his weak condition, was Coleridge so busy as now. He turned in July to coaching local actors who were about to present *Remorse* to the Bristol public. ". . .I am enforced to give one of the actors (whose name I know not) a meeting at 1/2 past 8 this evening at Mr. Ambrose's, he having to enact some part in the *Remorse*": he told Morgan, "and to-morrow morning at 1/2 past 8, Mr. Bengough, the Ordonio, is to breakfast here and have the part read and commented on to him." The result of these preparations was an announcement in the *Bristol Gazette* of July 28, 1814 that *Remorse* was to be performed in the Bristol Theatre on 1 August. The success of *Remorse* in Bristol would seem to be dubious if judged by Coleridge's pessimistic remark on the last day of the same month to Murray the publisher: "The *Remorse,* tho' acted 20 times, rests quietly on the shelves in the second edition, with copies enough for 7 years' consumption, or 7 times 7."

Prevented by an attack of erysipelas from visiting the Morgans at Ashley, Coleridge maintained a close correspondence with them throughout June and July 1814, chiefly concerning his health. He was still under the care of Dr. Daniel, but Daniel's attempt to reduce Coleridge's doses of opium caused him much suffering. "In head and vigour of mind I am not amiss," he told John Morgan in mid-June:—"in disposition to activity much improved—but subject at times to strange relapses of disquietude, without apparent cause or occasion.'' Shortly afterward he was able to visit the Morgans for a few days, and then returned to Bristol. "On my return the improvement of my health and appearance was so manifest and striking that all my friends triumphed in me" was the message he sent to Morgan on June 29.

The next day, in two letters to Morgan, he spoke of his long standing ill health and revealed another aspect of it seldom, if ever, mentioned to any previous correspondent. "I am almost certain," he wrote, "that there is a source of disease of 25 years standing at least, much more serious and which, if curable at all would be of incomparably more tedious cure than even old Blacky, alias opium." Coleridge evidently suspected venereal disease and forbade the ladies to read this part of his letter. "I gave you a hint," he told John, "that I had latterly from increased knowledge, begun to suspect a source of disease in myself anterior to, and even more serious than, the opium; and which had been, from its constitutional effects, the *cause* of my resorting to that drug: tho' from never having had any *'complaint'* in my whole life, and having since my twenty second year never had any illicit connection, I did not till lately even *suspect* it—from the *mistaken* supposition that strictures in the urethra always originated in some vicious cause." But having now read some books which greatly increased his fears, he had spoken that very morning on the subject to Dr. Daniel who suggested a medical examination, which he was to have the next morning. In his present state of suspense his "dread of having the worst, I suspect, ascertained. I write now," he continued, "merely to give an outlet to my anxieties—merely to be *doing* something." He would, he said, if possible, inform Morgan of the result of the examination before closing his letter. For two days Coleridge delayed the posting of the letter for this purpose; but a further delay by Daniel led Coleridge merely to promise Morgan a personal account of the result as soon as the examination occurred. "Whatever be the result," wrote Coleridge, "I will see you in a few days, and explain whatever is mysterious . . . Since I have read on the subject, I myself have no doubt of the melancholy fact."

By this time Coleridge had withdrawn from the hospitality of Wade in unfortunate circumstances due to opium. This inspired a penitential letter to his former host. "Dear Sir," he wrote on June 26th "For I am unworthy to call any good man friend—much less you, whose hospitality and love I have abused; accept, however, my entreaties for your forgiveness, and for your prayers."

"Conceive a poor miserable wretch, who for many years has been attempting to beat off pain, by a constant recurrence to the vice that reproduces it. Conceive a spirit in hell, employed in tracing out for others the road to that heaven, from which his crimes exclude him! . . . After my death, I earnestly entreat, that a full and unqualified narration of my wretchedness, and of its guilty cause, may be made public, that at least some little good may be effected by the direful example!"

When peace with France was prematurely proclaimed on June 27, 1814, Bristol rejoiced. Coleridge was one of those who contributed to its jubilation by designing a "transparency"—"a vulture with the head of Napoleon chained to a rock, and Britannia bending down, with one hand stretching out the wing of the vulture, and with the other clipping it with shears, on the one blade of which was written Nelson, on the other Wellington."

> We've fought for peace, and conquer'd it at last.
> The ravening vulture's leg is fettr'd fast.
> Britons, rejoice! *and yet be wary too*!
> The chain may break, the clipt wing sprout anew.

Whatever we may think of Coleridge's lines they were certainly prophetic. His transparency, however, caused him far more anxiety than amusement because of his fear of its being set on fire "from the obstinacy and self-conceit of the lighter and frame-maker." Consequently, until Coleridge "persuaded Wade to put all the lights out, we were in continual alarm, with three of us constantly watching the abominable lamps."

Throughout July 1814 the attraction of the Morgans at Ashley increased its hold upon Coleridge. "Suppose I borrowed Hood's horse for a fortnight to ride over myself, in order to give you a little horse exercise?" he asked Morgan on July 7. And he went on to say: "I begin to hope confidently that I shall be able to work *profitably*, and somewhere or other to renew our former relations. I can at all events get six guineas a week: and that in a country cottage would be ample for us."

From Ashley on September 12 Coleridge, now in happy mood, informed Stuart at length and in detail of his recent sufferings. He concluded his letter: "I am now joint tenant with Mr. Morgan of a sweet little cottage at Ashley, half a mile from Box on the Bath road. I breakfast every morning before nine—work till one—and walk or read till 3—thence till tea-time, chat or read some lounge-book—or correct what I have written—from 6 to 8, work again from 8 to bedtime, play whist, or the little mock billiard called Bagatell, and then sup and go to bed."

Soon Coleridge was writing for the *Courier* with unusual energy and regularity six political letters,* the style of which varied from the excellent directness and brevity of his earliest journalism, to the rambling and laborious and involved manner of so many of his later letters.

On November 23, 1814, Coleridge wrote to Stuart suggesting more essays and ten pounds as a "further loan." At the same time he informed his friend: "Monday after next (Dec. 5th) I expect as far as so perplexed a being dare expect anything, to remove to Calne, Wilts—at Mr. Page's, Surgeon." After this letter Coleridge disappears until he writes to Cottle on March 7, 1815.

---

*The six letters, two of which were published in two separate parts, appeared in the *Courier* on September 20 and 29; October 21; November 2; and December 3, 6, 9, and 10, 1814.

Meanwhile, Coleridge's friends and relatives wondered about him. "Can you tell us anything of Coleridge?" Southey asked Cottle on October 17, 1814. As the year 1814 closed Lamb, on December 28, asked Wordsworth the question that Southey and all Coleridge's intimate friends were asking: "Where is Coleridge?"

Cottle's reply to the many queries, "Where is Coleridge?" throws little light upon his way of life at the opening of the year 1815. "We merely knew," he wrote, "that Mr. Coleridge was gone to reside with his friend Mr. John Morgan at Caine; a worthy man, an only son, who had unfortunately lost nearly all his patrimonial property, the result of his father's many years' industrious toil, and on the wreck of which he had now retired to a small house at Calne, in Wiltshire." Coleridge was, in fact, now entering upon the darkest and the last phase of his entire surrender to opium.

It is Mrs. Coleridge who, in a letter to Poole on March 28, 1815, throws much needed light upon Coleridge's activities at this time at Calne:

> We have just received a letter from Mr. Coleridge's friend Mr. Morgan of Calne in Wilts. He says he is not entirely without hope that Coleridge will do something now for his family, as he is now in good health and spirits and talks of beginning in good earnest a German translation which will be profitable and which Mr. Morgan kindly promises to take all the fag of, and only require the business of correction from Coleridge, which will leave him at liberty to get his poems ready for the press; he says he had been at Devizes, Corsham on visits, and Bath, and at each place got ill and here he says he is far too much in company, but nothing shall be wanting on his part to be of use, and keep him in health. I am afraid he has still his old habit of swallowing opium, and if he continues in it I fear no good will ever come from him.

Coleridge's emergence from the shades is revealed in a letter to Cottle of March 7, 1815. In this, after informing him, "In health I am not worse than when at Bristol," Coleridge requested a loan of twenty-five pounds to meet his debts. "My embarrassements," he explained, "have not been occasioned by the bad parts, or selfish indulgences of my nature." When no reply came from Cottle, Coleridge told him: "My distresses are impatient, rather than myself." He felt himself, he said, a trouble to the Morgans—"a burthen on those to whom I am under great obligations, who would gladly do all for me; but who *have* done all they *can*!" And he again suggested an annuity for himself. Cottle thereupon sent Coleridge five pounds. But before it reached Coleridge, Cottle received from him another letter "far more harrowing than the first. This, wrote Cottle, "was the *last* letter I ever received from Mr. Coleridge." However, Cottle recorded a last meeting with Coleridge when Cottle, being in London in 1821, called upon him at the Gillmans' in Highgate, "when he welcomed me in his former kind and cordial manner. The depressing thought filled my mind that this would be our final interview in this world, as it was. On my going away, Mr. Coleridge presented me with his *Statesman's Manual*, in the bill-page of which he wrote, 'Joseph Cottle, from his old and affectionate friend, S. T. Coleridge!' "

To Dr. Brabant on March 10, 1815, Coleridge described his public appearance at Calne as an opponent to the new Corn Laws forbidding the importation of wheat until it reached a certain price. At a public meeting at Calne Coleridge not only addressed the meeting, but also drew up the petition that was to be presented to Parliament.

> Mounted on the butcher's table made a butcherly sort of speech of an hour long to a very ragged, but not butcherly audience; for by their pale faces few of them seemed to have had more than a very occasional acquaintance with butcher's meat. Loud were the Huzzas!—and if it depended on the inhabitants at large, I believe they would send me up to Parliament. I was not sorry to have an opportunity of showing that I had not supported Government so strenuously from the Treaty of Amiens to the present year from any interested motive, but from conscience.

Such was Coleridge's description of this incident.

Recently Coleridge had formed a friendship with the poet William Bowles who lived in the neighborhood of Ashley. Using Bowles's name as an introduction, Coleridge now sent Byron a manuscript copy of his own unpublished poems, with a request that Byron would assist their publication. They appeared later in *Sibylline Leaves*. In a covering letter Coleridge combined flattery of Byron with a detailed description of his own poverty. Byron, he wrote, would get better terms from the publishers than Coleridge could if he offered these poems to them himself.

Lord Byron, despite his previous annoyance at Coleridge's lecture in 1811, immediately replied on March 31, 1815, in a courteous and friendly letter in which he said, "It will give me great pleasure to comply with your request." And he went on to praise Coleridge as a dramatist, saying: "We have had nothing to be mentioned in the same breath with *Remorse* for very many years: and I should think that the reception of that play was sufficient to encourage the highest hopes of author and audience."

That summer Hartley, who had just matriculated at Merton, spent part of his vacation with his father at Calne. There Samuel and Hartley attended a performance of *Remorse* presented by a traveling dramatic company. In a letter to Dr. Brabant introducing the main actor of the company, Coleridge wrote: "I am myself so well satisfied both with the professional talents of his company and their regularity and moral deportment, that I have not thought myself justified in denying him a few lines to you. . . . On my conscience," he added, "they appear to me to act just as well as those on the London stage; indeed, far beyond my expectations." Some weeks later Coleridge described the acting of the play in similar terms to Byron.

Certainly *Remorse* caused no little excitement among the inhabitants of Calne and its neighborhood. Mrs. Morgan described the scene in a letter to Mary Lamb, and Mary Lamb passed on the news to Sara Hutchinson, quoting Mrs. Morgan's words:

Hartley Coleridge has been with us for two months. Morgan invited him to pass the long vacation here in the hope that his father would be of great service to him in his studies; he seems to be extremely amiable. Your old friend Coleridge is very hard at work at the preface to a new edition which he is just going to publish in the same form as Mr. Wordsworth's—at first the preface was not to exceed five or six pages, it has however grown into a work of great importance. I believe Morgan has already written [copied] nearly two hundred pages. The title of it is *Autobiographia Literaria* to which are added *Sibylline Leaves*, a collection of poems by the same author. Calne has lately been much enlivened by an excellent company of players—last week they performed the *Remorse* to a very crowded and brilliant audience; two of the characters were admirably well supported; at the request of the actors Morgan was behind the scenes all the time and assisted in the music etc.

Mrs. Coleridge, kept closely in touch with events at Calne by frequent letters from Hartley, duly reported them to Poole. She heard of the forthcoming *Biographia Literaria* with but chastened optimism: "Heaven knows I have great reason to pray for its success, but it appears to me that Mr. Morgan is too sanguine when he hopes Coleridge will get some hundreds for its publication." Then, turning to Coleridge's socialities, she continued: "General and Mrs. Peachey dined with Coleridge at Mr. Bowles's near Calne, the marquis of Lansdown heard him speak for 3 quarters of an hour at the Bible Society at Calne, and they saw him and Hartley at the play-performance of the *Remorse*, well enacted." Mrs. Coleridge's love for her children, found in this letter, as often, was given convincing expression; and of daughter Sara she now told Poole: "She is thought an interesting little creature, and I assure you, very amiable; How can her father bear to absent himself so long from her; I am sure he loves her notwithstanding."

Life at Calne, particularly amid such social distractions, required money; and this Coleridge in his usual way attempted to extract from friends and acquaintances on the grounds of real or imaginary publications including the *Biographia Literaria*.

Coleridge's next attempt to procure money, and by the same bait to obtain assistance, was again to Byron. So in mid-October 1815 Coleridge replied to Byron's sympathetic letter of March with an offer to send him pre-publication copies of the *Biographia* and *Sibylline Leaves* when printing was complete. And he humbly thanked "your Lordship" for the encouragement in dramatic writing of his "advice and favourable opinion." To this Byron immediately replied in a most friendly and complimentary letter in which he informed Coleridge that Walter Scott had introduced him to "Christabel," which he thought a magnificent poem, even superior to "Love" and "The Ancient Mariner." "Christabel" was, Byron said, "the wildest and finest I ever heard in that kind of composition." "Scott," he said, "is a staunch and sturdy admirer of yours, and with a just appreciation of your capacity, deplored to me the want of inclination and exertion which prevents you from giving full scope to your mind."

To this letter the delighted Coleridge replied on October 22, 1815, in the hope of soon sending a copy of "Christabel" "for your Lordship's gracious acceptance." Coleridge wrote, "I was much gratified I confess by what your Lordship has said of this poem, the *Love* and the *Ancient Mariner*, but I was far more affected and received a far deeper and more abiding pleasure from the kindness with which in the following [paragraphs] you have conveyed to me the regrets of many concerning 'the want of inclination and exertion which prevented me from giving full scope to my mind.'" From this Coleridge proceeded to a self-justification which ended, of course, in the excuse of his poverty for his failure to write the poems and books which he would otherwise have written. "Why," he asked,

> has not some one work already been produced, some thing that may be referred to?—And it is this my Lord! which delicacy forbad me to answer in a public work—but in private and to my friends I would ask in return: Has there been during the whole of my life since my return from Germany in 1800, a single half year, nay, any three months, in which I possessed the *means* of devoting myself exclusively to any one of many works, that it would have been my delight and hourly pleasure to have executed? So help me God! never one! At all times I have been forced in bitterness of soul to turn off from the pursuits of my choice to earn the week's food by the week's labor for the Newspapers and the like.

Three days later Coleridge wrote again to Byron. Although but a fragment of this letter remains and that containing only references to Coleridge's never completed dramas, the letter evidently accompanied the promised copy of the unfinished "Christabel," as Byron's reply clearly shows. Some months later Byron sent Coleridge £100. A consolatory letter from Coleridge to Allston dated October 25, 1815, on the death of Mrs. Allston some months before, included queries about the possibility of publishing Coleridge's works in America. It finally resulted in an American edition of the *Biographia Literaria* published at the same time as the English one in 1817.

From Coleridge's correspondence at this time various indications emerge of another surrender to opium. Such was the brief note that Coleridge now sent John Morgan: "My dear Morgan, To-morrow morning I doubt not, I shall be of clear and collected spirits; but to-night I feel that I should do nothing to any purpose, but and excepting thinking, planning and resolving to resolve—and praying to be able to execute—S. T. Coleridge." Another note, this time evidently to some local chemist, similarly speaks for itself: "Be so good as to send off a man with the paper which will accompany this note from [Mr. Morgan] as I shall want it, as a thing of necessity, by Sunday evening."

At the close of the year 1815 Coleridge in two letters to Brabant spoke of the efforts he was making to overcome his addiction to opium: "By following your plan, as far as the nature of my circumstances permits," he said, "I am as well, if not somewhat better, than I have been for some years." For Dr. Brabant was one of several medical men who took Coleridge in hand at this time. "Should I have such success in my dramatic enterprises," he told Brabant, as to be able to say—"for six months to come I am not under the *necessity* of doing anything!" I have strong hopes that I should emancipate myself altogether from the most pitiable slavery, the fetters of which do indeed eat into the soul. [And he continued:] In my present circumstances, and under the disquieting uncertainty in which I am, concerning my place of residence for the ensuing year, all I can do is to be quite regular, and never to exceed the smallest dose of poison that will suffice to keep me tranquil and capable of literary labor. What I refer to in this last sentence I would rather say than write to you—therefore be so good as to take no notice to it. It will be a sore heart-wasting to me to part from Mr. Morgan: for never was there a man of stricter integrity or higher honour, nor have I a more faithful, zealous and disinterested friend.

Before the close of 1815 Peacock's *Headlong Hall* appeared (although dated 1816) and in its satirical presentation of Coleridge similarly testifies to Coleridge's reputation as a scholar of wide knowledge. In *Headlong Hall* Coleridge appears as Mr. Panscope, "the chemical, botanical, geological, astronomical, mathematical, metaphysical, meterological, anatomical, physiological, galvanistical, musical, pictorial, bibliographical, critical, philosopher, who had run through the whole circle of the sciences, and understood them all equally well."

Peacock's satirical mood towards Coleridge had also found expression a year before in a satirical ballad, "Sir Proteus," ridiculing the leading romantic poets Wordsworth, Southey, and Coleridge, whom he associated with Coleridge's poem "The Three Graves," of which Coleridge's is the second:

The second of three graves did sing,
And in such doggrel strains,
You might have deemed the Elfin King
Had charmed away his brains.

And Peacock, essentially of the eighteenth century in his sympathies and as anti-romantic as Mrs. Coleridge, continued his satirical attack on Coleridge in the following trenchant footnote:

Surely this cannot allude to . . . the profound transcendental metaphysician of *The Friend*, the consistent panegyrical politician of the *Courier*, the self-elected laureate of the asinine king, the compounder of the divinest narcotic under the shape of a tragedy that ever drugged the beaux of Drury Lane, the author of that irresistibly comic ballad, "The Ancient Mariner," and of a very exquisite piece of tragical mirth, also in the form of a ballad entitled "The Three Graves," which read—"if you can!"

It is regrettable that Coleridge's letters contain no reference to this young satirist of twenty-nine who was acquainted with Lamb, Shelley, and probably in some degree with Coleridge.

"Where is Coleridge?" Lamb had asked Wordsworth at the end of 1814, and now, in the following year, Lamb again asked the same question in one form or another of Coleridge's friends. "Of Coleridge I hear nothing," he told Southey on May 6, 1815, "nor of the Morgans. I hope to have him a re-appearing star, standing up before me some time when least expected in London." He told Sara Hutchinson on October 19, evidently in reply to her question, "I hear nothing from Coleridge." Finally on December 25, 1815, Lamb, writing to Manning who was in China, spoke of Coleridge in the usual affectionately cynical, but also for the moment macabre, mood of the following passage in which he pretended to give Manning the latest news of friends in England, most of whom he pretends are dead: "Coleridge is just dead, having lived just long enough to close the eyes of Wordsworth, who paid the debt to nature but a week or two before. Poor Coleridge, but two days before he died he wrote to a bookseller proposing an epic poem on the "Wanderings of Cain," in twenty-four books. It is said he has left behind him more than forty thousand treatises in criticism and metaphysics, but few of them in a state of completion. They are now destined, perhaps, to wrap up spices."

Mrs. Coleridge had told Poole in March, "I am afraid he has still his old habit of swallowing opium," and the last of Coleridge's published letters of this year, 1815, besides many intervening ones, completely justifies her fear. For in late December 1815 Coleridge wrote, as on recent occasions, to a chemist at Calne: "Mr. Coleridge presents his respectful compliments to Mr. Kirkland, or the gentleman, his assistant—requests that there may be sent by the bearer three ounces of laudanum—(in the accompanying bottle—or whatever quantity it may hold) half an ounce of crude opium (if there be none purified)—and two ounces of the tincture of cardanum. As soon as the weather relaxes Mr. Coleridge will call in on Mr. Kirkland and settle his general account."

When on April 10, 1816, Coleridge wrote to Byron, opium still appears, but the mood, as often with Coleridge, is one of repentance. So to Byron Coleridge described his "daily habit of taking enormous doses of laudanum which I believe necessary to my life, tho' I groaned under it as the worst and most degrading of slaveries."

On the preceding day, however, although Coleridge can hardly have been aware of it, one of his medical attendants, a Dr. Adams of Hatton Garden, London, had written to a worthy apothecary of Highgate, James Gillman, on Coleridge's behalf. Describing Coleridge's condition, Adams requested Gillman to accept Coleridge in his home for a period of treatment, so that he might be carefully watched and prevented from taking surreptitious doses of opium. "A very learned, but in one respect an unfortunate gentleman," Adams described Coleridge, willing "to submit himself to any regimen, however severe." Adams continued, "I should not have proposed it, but on account of the great importance of the character as a literary man. His communicative temper will make his society very interesting as well as useful."

Thus it was that a day or two later Coleridge called on Gillman at his home, Moreton House on Highgate Hill, explained that to continue much longer with the drug or to abandon it suddenly would be equally fatal, and drove home the pathos of his situation by "repeating some exquisite but desponding lines of his own"—as Gillman described the scene. As usual Samuel's magic worked; and when an hour later he departed, promising to return in a day or two as a resident, Gillman was already hypnotized: "spellbound," he said, "without the desire of release." Such was Coleridge's introduction to the new life at Highgate which continued until his death there 18 years later.

Part III

1816-1834: 42-61 years (death). Highgate—Opium controlled— years of writing, talking, and fame.

1 Highgate Refuge (1816)

> *"My medical friend and his excellent wife, who has been a most affectionate and sisterly nurse to me . . . "*
> *—Coleridge to Hugh James Rose, September 17, 1816*

When on April 15 Coleridge reappeared to begin his life with the Gillmans, it was in the wake of his characteristically explanatory letter about himself, in which, with impeccable propriety of form, he also defined the terms upon which he would, as it were, accept their invitation to share the domestic amenities of their home. "Terms," he wrote, "proportioned to my *present* ability, and least of all things to my sense of the service." Any pecuniary inadequacy on his part, he suggested tactfully, must be offset "by esteem and grateful affection," and by the fact that he and Gillman would be "reciprocally serviceable to each other."

Besides, he assured them, his "ever wakeful reason and keen moral feelings" must prevent any inconvenience to themselves. His habitual truthfulness, he added, made lying impossible for him, but his "specific madness with regard to this detested poison" might lead him to "act a lie, unless carefully watched." Nor could they object, he felt sure, to a daily visit from his "literary counsellor and amanuensis" Mr. Morgan, from half past eleven till half past three. "I have been for so many years accustomed to dictate while he writes, that I now cannot compose without him. . . . He has kindly left his family for a month at Calne in order to be with me during such hours, as I should be otherwise alone." A fortnight later Lamb told Wordsworth, "Morgan is with us every day, going betwixt Highgate and the Temple." Nor was Morgan's duty confined to writing what Coleridge dictated. He became, in fact, a kind of general agent for Coleridge, particularly now in dealing with publishers.

Coleridge's kindly if slightly condescending tone, even in this annunciatory letter to the evidently impressed Gillmans, swept aside all difficulties as he declared: "I have taken no notice of your kind apologies—if I could not be comfortable in your house and with your family, I should deserve to be miserable."

Nor did his unfailing instinct for protective comfort now desert him. His trial month at Moreton House continued for another three, and henceforth he remained with the Gillmans in Highgate to the end of his life. Samuel's appreciation of the Gillmans was almost as great as theirs of him. "A man of strong, fervid and agile intellect," he thought Gillman, "and his wife it will be impossible not to respect, if a balance and harmony of powers and qualities, unified and spiritualized by a native feminine fineness of character, render womanhood amiable and respectable."

Intuitively recognizing his new friends' respective predilections, Coleridge adopted widely different attitudes toward them. Gillman's "strong, fervid and agile intellect" he at once fascinated by taking a cowry shell on the mantelpiece as his inspiration for a fervent denunciation of Unitarianism, contrasting "the beauty of the shell's exterior with the hollow murmuring sound" inside it. Toward Gillman's wife Anne he at first adopted a characteristically cumbrous style of persiflage, which changed with the years into solemn meditation or pious exhortaton. For Mrs. Gillman, said her granddaughter, "was a woman of pious beliefs."

Mrs. Gillman, indeed, was soon to become of first importance in Coleridge's life at Highgate, an importance based upon mutual respect and affection. To this Coleridge's daughter Sara later testified in a marginal note written in Christopher Wordsworth's *Memoirs* of his poet-uncle. Coleridge, she wrote, "was fondly attached to Sarah Hutchinson, and was afterwards very fond of Mrs. Morgan and Miss Brent and still more perhaps of Mrs. Gillman." It is perhaps significant that in Sara's list neither Dorothy Wordsworth nor Mrs. Clarkson nor Mrs. Coleridge appears.

Mr. Gillman, then thirty-four years old, ten years Coleridge's junior, and his wife Anne, were, said their granddaughter, "A harmoniously united couple, and were one in their affectionate devotion to the poet." "We met indeed for the first time," wrote Gillman in his *Life of Coleridge*, "but as friends long since parted who now had the happiness to see each other again. . . his manner, his appearance, and above all his conversation were captivating; we listened with delight."

That in these circumstances Coleridge should immediately make himself at home with such a family in its pleasant house was inevitable. The several servants, one of whom was soon especially allocated to himself and his comfort, were no small additional attraction.

Nor was the Gillmans' delight with their new acquaintance limited to his individual charm. Into their quiet, dull suburban life Coleridge brought important persons and interests which emphasized his social prestige in their eyes, and added a new element to their intimacy. So within a month of his arrival Coleridge was sending out such invitations to his friends as this to Stuart: "Mr and Mrs Gillman will be most happy to see you to share in a family dinner and spend the evening with us; and if you will come early, I can show you some most delicious walks." Until the last months of his life he continued to send out similar invitations, in which the Gillmans appeared as host and hostess with himself. The "most delicious walks" were many a pleasant stroll about Highgate, where, owing to his clerical style of dress and appearance, he was often mistaken by strangers for some local clergyman.

Within the domestic circle at Moreton House Samuel's success was all-embracing. Even the servants were proud to serve him, and his kindness to the two young Gillmans, James and Henry—which touched their mother's heart—even extended to tutorial supervision of an occasional and general kind. This last, however, had its disadvantages, as young James found on one occasion which years later he still remembered and described to his own daughter, who recorded it thus:

> My father in his youth was sometimes sent up to the poet's room by his parents to ask for assistance on some difficult point in his school studies; this the poet often volunteered to give; but on one occasion his mentor gave him such a long discourse interspersed with so many illustrations, even going back to the days of Creation, that waiting in vain for the desired elucidation, he was obliged to walk backwards to the door; then gradually in the same position going down the stairs, the Poet stepping down after him, still enforcing his argument—he had to take advantage of a third person's appearance, and retreat with his exercise out of the garden door.

To his intimate friends Coleridge readily acknowledged his good fortune, rejoicing after three months in "the fortunate state of convalescence, and tranquil yet active impulses, which, under Providence," he now enjoyed. At last he had found what he had so long sought: comfort, tranquillity, and irresponsibility. Charles Lamb, with whom Coleridge had spent a fortnight just before moving to Highgate, followed his doings with friendly but amused and critical eyes. For Lamb Dr. Gillman became, of course, "Dr. Killman," at whose house Coleridge "plays at leaving off laudanum; his essentials not touched; he is very bad." But there were wonderful recoveries. When he recited his poems to Lamb his face had "its ancient glory," so that he seemed to Lamb "an Archangel, a little damaged." Lamb had also been uncomfortably aware of Coleridge's almost mesmeric influence on him during his recent visit: "'Tis enough to be within the whiff and wind of his genius, for us not to possess our souls in quiet."

Certainly the craving for opium was not to be stopped by Coleridge's arrival at the Gillmans'. "No sixty hours *have yet passed* without my having taken laudanum," he had told Gillman in his annunciatory letter, and the servants "must receive absolute commands from you on no account to fetch anything for me." Yet only eight days after his arrival he was smuggling opium in with books from Murray—the first of the many supplies from various secret sources obtained throughout the following years. How far Coleridge's condition was by this time a subject of general scandal among his friends and acquaintances and beyond, the following malicious passage from a letter of Miss Mitford the novelist to a friend clearly reveals:

He put himself under watch and ward; went to lodge at an apothecary's at Highgate, whom he cautioned to lock up his opiates; gave his money to a friend to keep; and desired his druggist not to trust him. For some days all went on well. Our poet was ready to hang himself; could not write, could not eat, could not—incredible as it may seem—could not talk. The stimulus was wanting, and the apothecary contented. Suddenly, however, he began to mend; he wrote, he read, he talked, he harangued; Coleridge was himself again! And the apothecary began to watch within doors and without. The next day the culprit was detected; for the next day came a second supply of laudanum from Murray's, well wrapped up in proof-sheets of the *Quarterly Review*.

The American artist Leslie was as pleased with the Gillmans when he called on Coleridge as was Coleridge himself. "A delightful family," he found them, and the Gillmans were so pleased with Leslie that they invited him "to visit them at all times and to spend weeks with them," as Leslie told a friend. Leslie thought Mrs Gillman "a very excellent and charming woman" with "a very fine face," and willing to sit for him for her portrait whenever he wished. At Coleridge's request Leslie sketched the poet's face and later made another sketch, which afterwards became the model for Thornycroft's bust of Coleridge which stands in Westminster Abbey.*

Lamb, however, was less pleased than Leslie with both Coleridge and the Gillmans. He complained to Wordsworth that Coleridge was now invisible: "An odd person," he said, who "when he first comes to town is quite hot upon visiting, and then absolutely never comes at all, but seems to forget that there are any such people in the world." Mary Lamb a few weeks later, replying to Sara Hutchinson, wrote: "You ask how Coleridge maintains himself. I know no more than you do. Strange to say, I have seen him but once since he has been at Highgate, and then I met him in the Street." Lamb had called on Coleridge in Highgate one morning, but unlike Leslie had found "something in him or in his apothecary so unattractively-repulsing from any temptation to call again, that I stay away as naturally as a lover visits. The rogue gives you love powders, and then a strong horse drench to bring 'em off your stomach that they mayn't hurt you," Lamb added, quoting Falstaff. Another visitor to Highgate was Crabb Robinson, who, calling on Coleridge in mid-July, thought he had "profited already by the abstinence from opium; had never

---

*Some years before, in December 1811, Coleridge's friendship with a well-known painter and engraver, George Dawe, had inspired the following letter to Sir George Beaumont: "I slept in town in order to have a mask taken, from which, or rather with which, Dawe means to model a bust of me." Later he continued: "Mr. Dawe, a Royal Associate, who plastered my face for me, says that he never saw so excellent a mask, and so unaffected by any expression of pain or uneasiness." Coleridge ordered the mask to be sent to Sir George. "With it you will find a chalk drawing of my face which I think far more like than any former attempt, excepting Allston's full length portrait of me." This last, painted in Rome, was now waiting, he said, at Leghorn—with other valuable works, and "with no chance of procuring them." This portrait—never finished—is now in the Fogg Art Museum in the United States.

seen him look so well." Three days later Coleridge told Morgan, "I have had no relapse for three weeks, though I have been otherwise unwell twice."

Before the close of August Coleridge's thoughts were turning seaward. On the last day of the month he told Boosey, his London bookseller:

> I have some intentions of trying the Sea-air for a month, in company with the excellent family, whose House mate I at present am, and am likely to continue—I have of late been injured by over anxiety occasioned by overwork: & this latter on the account of others, not my own.—By the Sea side I hope to finish my *Christabel*: and if this and Tranquillity with exercise and change of air should give me confidence in myself, I shall probably attempt to realize a Plan which I have long had in agitation—viz—a fornightly or monthly Letter to my literary Friends in London and elsewhere concerning the real state and value of the German Literature.

It was thus that on September 19 Coleridge set off for Muddiford in Hampshire, "with my medical friend and his excellent wife, who has been a most affectionate and sisterly nurse to me," as Coleridge told a correspondent. He had come, he said, "for change of air and above all in the hopes of a deep tranquillity."

Toward the close of September Coleridge told an acquaintance: "I have endeavoured to prevent Mr. Gillman from knowing the extent of my late illness. From his wife, I could not conceal it." Lamb, in his now habitual half-appreciative, half-sardonic manner towards Coleridge, informed Wordsworth of their friend's departure for Muddiford: "He is gone to the seaside with his favourite apothecary, having left for publication, as I hear, a prodigious mass of composition for a sermon to the middling ranks of people to persuade them they are not so distressed as they commonly suppose. Methinks he should recite it to a congregation of Bilston colliers—the fate of Cinna the poet would instantaneously be his." For Lamb knew of the recent protest march to London of the miners of Bilston in Staffordshire until stopped by the police, and he had not forgotten that Cinna was murdered by the mob.

At Muddiford Coleridge was delighted with everything he saw. At the first sight of the sea he burst out:

> God be with thee—gladsome ocean,

quoting the verse he had composed at Scarborough, during that happy time fifteen years before with Sara Hutchinson beside him. He noted with approval the "green garden plot abounding in sea-rushes," which stood before the glass door of their parlour "with some potatoes that make most virtuous efforts to lift their dwarf heads above the ground, and a fine old mulberry tree with a seat under it." In a neighboring "sea ditch," some two or three yards wide, Coleridge and Gillman rowed a little boat and also paddled—in real "Ancient Mariner" style.

Nor did Coleridge lack suitable society. "A number of fashionable families" accounted for the "bathing machines" on the beach. One of these fashionable families included William Stewart Rose, nearly Coleridge's age, poet and translator and now reading clerk to the House of Lords and clerk of private committees. It was he who five months before had caused Coleridge such distress by refusing to lend him a book that he had tried to borrow. However, they had become friendly and Coleridge was delighted on arrival at Muddiford to find Rose there, "no unpleasant accession, both for his society and for his library." Besides, in Coleridge's words, "Mr. Rose has the prettiest, oddest cottage ever seen, about a furlong from our house here and overlooking the beach. It is circular, has an Italian Garden with a fountain, a handsome library, and a most luxurious Turkish tent . . . etc, etc." Gillman, too, must have liked Rose (or perhaps his dog) for he presented Rose with his one literary achievement, a work on hydrophobia.* To a poem that Coleridge was now contemplating in honor of his friend he gave the name of Rose's cottage "Gundimore." The poem apparently got no farther than that, but Rose, in his poem of the same name, more satisfactory biographically than poetically, wrote:

> And these "ribbed sands" was Coleridge pleased to pace
> Whilst ebbing seas have hummed a rolling base
> To his rapt talk.

Coleridge's appreciation of William Stewart Rose extended even to his Methodist valet with whom he formed a personal though temporary friendship due to mutual religious opinions. Before leaving Muddiford Coleridge presented his Methodist friend with a "corrected" copy of the recently published "Christabel" with a long inscription. The book Coleridge asked him to accept "as a *small* testimonial of Regard, yet such a testimonial as I would not pay to one I did not esteem, tho' he were an Emperor." Coleridge also promised to send him all his other works past and future.

Mrs. Gillman's domestic arrangements were, of course, perfect. Two maids came with the family and another "to *help* them," said Coleridge sarcastically, "lest they overwork themselves. She is too good." It was Coleridge's nearest approach to a critical comment upon his admired hostess. And now he wrote to Gillman's assistant, Williams, a letter whose contents were remote from his usual fields of discourse, requesting two pairs of his own "worsted" stockings and another pair for Mrs. Gillman, also a third pair for himself, black ones—with the proviso: "if the black have not holes, send them too"; mere details but significant of Coleridge's gradual immersion in the Gillmans' domestic life. Indeed, Coleridge now made comparisons of the prices of meat and vegetables at Muddiford with those in London. And like some old nurse

---

*Gillman also began a never completed biography of Coleridge, the first and only volume of which appeared shortly after Coleridge's death.

he made up playful baby names for the Gillmans' little son: "Hen-Pen, alias learned Pundit, alias infant Conchologist, alias Child of the sun, Day-boy (though now he sleeps throughout the night sweet and sound with me) and Jack-a-Lanthorn Sun-spot, alias mischievous doggie, alias Fish of all Waters, alias kissable Vagabond, and Comfort of his Mother's Heart." Thus by childlike playfulness and intimacy, as well as by intellectual remoteness and social distinction, Coleridge found his way into Mrs. Gillman's heart.

When Dr. Gillman returned to Highgate to pursue his study of hydrophobia, Coleridge sent him a philosophical clarification of the subject. "You must seek the *reality* not in any imaginary (chemical) *elements*," he wrote. "I begin with directing your mind to the idea of EXISTENCE . . . but as *existence* simply, as that which is the same in all things, the A, the Ω, and (more truly still,) the copula of the two, that in which both are one, and in which each involves the other—is the one indispensable condition of philosophizing." From this Coleridge proceeded to point out to the unphilosophic Gillman that "by the eternal Identity of Allness and Oneness, the whole Universe becomes an infinity of Concentric Circles," and so on.

But poor Dr. Gillman remained unilluminated and must have found a suspicion of irrelevance between Coleridge's philosophy and hydrophobia. For Coleridge replied: "It is your anxiety only and your lively perception of the inappropriateness of what I have hitherto written, that make the thought appear *in nubibus* or beyond your comprehension." And in his anxiety to save his friend from the influence of "mere science," he promised to devote his evenings to the instruction of Gillman for the sake of the work on hydrophobia.

In mid-November Coleridge returned to Highgate, doubtless with Mrs. Gillman and the children. "The sea-air did me good," he told Brabant, "and the benefit would have been far greater if I could have added leisure."

Such visits to the seaside for reasons of health—which Coleridge found good for both body and mind—were made annually during most of the years of Coleridge's life with the Gillmans.

2   The *Lay Sermons* and *Biographia Literaria* (1816-17)

> *"My chief purposes were, 1, to defend myself (not indeed to my own Conscience;) but as far as others are concerned, from the often and public denunciation of having wasted my time in idleness—in short, of having done nothing—2, not merely to state my own principles of Taste, but to settle, if possible, and put to rest with all men of sense the controversy concerning the nature and claims of poetic Diction."*
> —*Coleridge to John Hookham Frere, July 2, 1816*
> *(on the* Biographia Literaria)

Need of money, the peace and ease of life with the Gillmans, and doubtless also their tactful encouragement quickly led Coleridge to turn to writing with (for him) unusual intensity and persistence. The result was, first, the publication of the two never-finished poems, "Christabel" and "Kubla Khan," together with "The Pains of Sleep," in a small volume published by Murray in May 1816. The next year he produced *Sibylline Leaves*—a collection of poems which included and for the first time acknowledged Coleridge's authorship of "The Ancient Mariner."

For Coleridge, however, poetry was now almost a thing of the past, and he turned to prose. In 1816 and 1817 respectively, Coleridge's two "Lay Sermons" were published. The first was entitled, "The Statesman's Manual; or the Bible the best guide to political skill and foresight. A lay sermon addressed to the higher classes of society." The second was entitled "Blessed are ye that sow beside all waters. A lay sermon addressed to the higher and middle classes on the existing discontents." In this same year, 1817, Coleridge's most ambitious work, *Biographia Literaria*, also appeared.

So far so good. But for Coleridge the consequences of this literary activity were most unpleasant: first, relations with his publishers and, next, the opinions of his critics. Throughout the following months Coleridge almost continuously opposed, valiantly yet often untruthfully, the demands and complaints of his printer and publishers for proofs promised but not forthcoming.

Gutch in Bristol was now printing for Coleridge proofs of the *Biographia Literaria*, including *Sibylline Leaves* which was originally intended for the second volume of the *Biographia* but which appeared as an independent work. Coleridge's reply to Gutch's complaints of delays was the accusation that careless posting by Gutch had caused Coleridge unnecessary expense as well as the increased cost due to printer's errors. When Gutch in turn sent his bill, Coleridge accused him of overestimating the amount of material required for the *Biographia*. Gutch, he said, had created a large gap which Coleridge must fill. Gutch had also, to Coleridge's great annoyance, asked Mr. Gillman to extract payment from his penniless guest. Upon this Coleridge transferred responsibility for the payment of Gutch's account to his publishers, Gale and Curtis. This merely extended the battlefield, for Gale and Curtis demanded the return of Gutch's proofs before they would settle Samuel's account. Gale and Curtis were not only publishing the "Stateman's Manual," but were also committed to publishing a new edition of *The Friend*—which appeared in three volumes in 1818.

The change to Gale and Curtis (soon Gale and Fenner) brought Coleridge no relief. No more than Gutch were they reconciled to Samuel's endless delays in sending their material, and they refused to regard his excuses as a drug victim with sympathy. Nevertheless, in May 1817 they paid Gutch's bill and agreed to publish the *Biographia Literaria*. At the same time they demanded Coleridge's play *Zapolya* as security for the cost of publishing his works.

But this led to further and worse trouble between publishers and author. Fenner and Curtis began to print *Zapolya* as a separate volume, but Coleridge sternly forbade them. On learning something of the truth Curtis called on Murray, and to his surprise he discovered that Murray possessed rights not only over *Zapolya* but also over the *Biographia* and the *Sibylline Leaves*, which Fenner and Curtis in complete ignorance had already undertaken to publish. Murray, it also appeared, had paid Coleridge £100 (£200 in fact) for his publication rights over these volumes.

On learning these facts the appalled Curtis remonstrated with Coleridge, crying in his indignation: "To hear of £100, when you had named but £50, and of any other individual being promised the publication of the *Life* after all that has occurred—Look at it dear Sir." Coleridge's conduct, he added, had "exposed" the firm to the danger of "offering the *Life* in a public sale room on which a brother tradesman claims a serious advance, and of which he may yet prevent the publications." Neverthless, Curtis published *Zapolya* before the close of 1817 as "A Christmas Tale," which the author described as a "dramatic poem, in humble imitation of the *Winter's Tale*."

Next, unwarned by recent experience, Coleridge and Curtis undertook a new and more ambitious project, nothing less than the *Encyclopaedia Metropolitana*, "a History of Human Knowledge" in twenty-five volumes. Coleridge's enthusiasm dominated the plan. He wrote the prospectus and the "Introductory Essay on Method," and arranged the *Encyclopaedia*'s entries, not on some commonplace alphabetical system but on "a correct philosophical method" of his own.

When poor Curtis pleaded for an alphabetical arrangement on the ground of convenience, Coleridge, disgusted by so unphilosophical an attitude, replied: "in *all* things, we *all* of us arrange in the same way—A and the opposite of A (say B) and that in which A and B co-exist." Thus, naturally, "*Agriculture* must of necessity follow the tract on *Political Economy*, and precede *Manufactures* and *Handicrafts*." But even Coleridge found "Law" rather a hard nut to crack, as it must be divided between "Morality," "Biography," and the last eight volumes of the whole *Encyclopaedia*. There was, he assured Curtis, no difficulty in his plan, but there might be in finding men with "the grand REQUISITES, Appropriateness of ability, harmony and RELIABILITY."

As before, Coleridge's delays provoked remonstrances from Curtis, to which he replied: "I became bewildered, wrote and wrote and destroyed and erased, until I scarcely knew whether I was on my head or my heels." And again as before, Coleridge's need of money entered the fray. This, he said, was the basic cause of his frustrations and delays. His debts, he told Curtis, were a mere £300, of which half was due to Gillman for "board, lodging, medical attendance, washing, letters, parcels, and such like et ceteras, for the last year." As security for the settlement of these debts, he told Curtis, he would offer his past, present, and future works. Yet at this time Coleridge was lamenting to various friends that his critics had made his works unsalable. He rejected the publishers' condition that he work only on the *Encyclopaedia* and live near Curtis's brother, their printer, in Camberwell, where he (Coleridge) would be closely watched.

From May to August 1817 the battle between Coleridge and his publishers continued, until on August 18 a final agreement was reached by which Coleridge handed them as security for the payment of his debts all his works that they were publishing. At the same time he was removed from any further association with the *Encyclopaedia* beyond the prospectus and the "Introductory Essay on Method," which he had already written. Coleridge's language about his publishers was now as unrestrained as his anger. The *Encyclopaedia* when published—under the direction of Coleridge's bête noire, Stoddart—he denounced as a "Humbug" "an infamous catch-penny or rather catch-guinea." As for Coleridge's "Introductory Essay on Method," it was, he declared, "so bedevilled, so interpolated" that he could not decide whether it was "more disreputable to me as a man of letters or dishonourable to me as an honest man." Nevertheless, Coleridge produced his own separate edition of "Method" before the close of 1818.

Meanwhile, as we have seen, Coleridge's other works were appearing. The two "Lay Sermons" were due to the social unrest in England which followed immediately upon the end of the war with France. Coleridge's recent sympathy with the poorer classes in their protests against the Corn Law had now given place to his basic conservatism.

In this mood he wrote his "Lay Sermons," telling "the higher classes" to read their Bibles and the populace to detest demagogues. The first "Lay Sermon," the "Statesman's Manual," was a slim volume with an appendix of essays on "Reason, Understanding and Religion," and "Present State and Prospects of Philosophy." The tract was, of course, characteristically discursive, impractical, and in general pessimistic as one must be about a generation that ignored the basic fact that "Unity—Omneity—Totality" were of primary importance in statecraft.

Into his tract Coleridge poured streams of consciousness which were in fact the essence of his now famous "Conversations:" reason *versus* understanding, the wicked scientific and philosophical empiricists (especially Hume), and the wickedness of France, the scientists' spiritual home. The governing classes, he argued, needed reeducating to "a more manly discipline of the intellect; in short, a thorough recasting of the moulds, in which the minds of our gentry, the characters of our future land-owners, magistrates and senators are to receive their shape and fashion." But "suffice it for the present to hint the master-thought," which was the Bible. Nor was the influence of the Bible to be limited to the upper classes: "Of the labouring class who in all countries form the great majority of the inhabitants, more than this is not demanded, more than this is not perhaps generally desirable." The Bible he saw as the best of all educators because it was inspired by divine knowledge, particularly evident in its exaltation of ideas and principles above mere facts of history and science. Leading ideas in the rest of the tract are chiefly moralistic analyses of what Coleridge regards as the basic but largely unrecognized causes of the present social and political evils.

In his second "Lay Sermon" Coleridge emphasized, evidently for the middle classes, the sermonic element in his tract. The tone of the preacher gently pleading with the "higher classes," which he had adopted hitherto, he now discarded for the hortatory dictatorial style of the stern moralist, urging more particularly on the middle classes their duties to society. But for individuals like himself—intellectuals, artists, and such—he introduced an escape clause which, nevertheless, included the duty of employing their talents in high achievement: "Not by genius or splendid talent: for these, as being gifts of nature, are objects of moral interest for those alone to whom they have been allotted. Nor yet by eminence in learning; for this supposes such a devotion of time and thought, as would in many cases be incompatible with the claims of active life. Erudition is, doubtless, an ornament that especially beseems a high station: but it is professional rank only that renders its attainment a duty."

The second "Sermon" is a curious mixture of Coleridge's characteristic moral and intellectual attitudes toward contemporary social and political trends, with some rathr amateurish economic analysis lit at times by characteristic flashes of Coleridge's native intuitions. Demagogues and "political empirics" are lashed with Biblical quotations as enemies of liberty and harmful to the people. He touches upon economic-political conditions: the temporary prosperity caused by the war and its sudden collapse with the peace. He defends, cursorily, pensions and sinecures and capitalism, but is evidently more interested in the wider themes and general principles presented by morals and manners and the underlying causes, as he sees them, of their decline and of the existing distress. These causes, he finds, are particularly the decline of respect among the lower classes for rank and ancestry, the eclipse of philosophy by empiric science, lack of ideas among statesmen, the decline of an intellectual attitude in religion. All these give Coleridge the scope he desired for preaching, denouncing, and exhorting—at much greater length than in the first "Sermon," if we except the appendices there.

Coleridge showed much concern about his second "Lay Sermon." He looked forward, he said, with "far greater pleasure" to presenting a friend with a copy than he had with the first. He particularly prided himself upon having adapted the style of the middle class public, and when a *Times* critic described the second "Sermon" as "in the same style and manner as the first" Coleridge was annoyed. "The first I never dreamt would be understood (except in fragments) by the general Reader," he exclaimed, "but of the second I can scarcely discover any part or passage which would compel any man of common education and information to read it a second time in order to understand it."

Nevertheless, Coleridge privately feared that his two "Sermons" might well be above the heads of the general public. Indeed, he begged Street to read them and mark any page that seemed to him beyond easy comprehension by such. Coleridge's political opinions were, in fact, too personal, too much a mixture of keen intelligence and personal prejudices, too remote from party programs and slogans, for frank expression where the approval of the general public was sought. Of this Coleridge was very conscious. Already he foresaw not "Truth but Expediency," preached by demagogues to an uncritical and acquisitive populace. In such a world he foresaw the decline and ultimate extinction of individual values and rights, and so he attacked the demagogues as the chief enemies of liberty. Toward these "vipers" he had "a feeling more like hatred than I ever bore to other flesh and blood. So clearly do I see and always have seen, that it must end in the suspension of freedom of all kinds. Hateful under all names these wretches are most hateful to me as Liberticides. . . . O! that conscience permitted me to tell the whole Truth! I would, methinks, venture to brave the fury of the great and little Vulgar as the advocate of an Aristocracy, for by a Fool-or-Knave-ocracy must man be governed."

Whatever elation Coleridge felt at the publication of his work was quickly damped when the opinions of the literary critics appeared. Even the small pamphlet of poems previously mentioned, published by Murray in 1816 upon Byron's recommendation, created a withering reply from Hazlitt.

Hazlitt's early idolatry for Coleridge the Jacobin had, by this time, changed with Coleridge's own political development or, as Hazlitt saw it, apostasy. He now attacked Coleridge with all the rage of the iconoclast in Leigh Hunt's *Examiner*, on June 2, 1816. He particularly distressed Coleridge by denouncing "Christabel" as "like moon-beams playing on a charnel house, or flowers strewn on a dead body." Yet Coleridge himself described "Christabel" the following year in his *Biographia Literaria* as "a work that pretended to be nothing more than a common faery tale," and he wondered at the "expressions of admiration" it had evoked in earlier years, long before publication: admiration he now considered "utterly disproportionate" to its value. He also bitterly complained in the *Biographia* of friends and acquaintances and others who had highly praised the poem before publication, but now "abused" it. The basic inspiration of the never-completed "Christabel" was the then popular "Tales of Terror," or "Gothic Novels," which Coleridge as a literary critic had publicly condemned, even when composing "Christabel" and the essentially similar "Kubla Khan" and "Ancient Mariner."

Poor Mrs. Coleridge, partly influenced no doubt by the literary critics and by Southey, heard of the publication with dismay. "Oh! when will he ever give his friends anything but pain?" she cried to Poole, speaking of her husband: "he has been so unwise as to publish his fragments of "Christabel" and "Koula-Khan" [*sic*]. . . . We were all sadly vexed when we read the advertisement of these things." At least Mrs. Coleridge was in good company, which even included Lamb. In 1803 Lamb had recognized "Christabel," which he called "that sweet maid," as essential poetry. But he now declared: "It should never have been published, that no one understood it, and Kubla Khan is nonsense." Just before the publication of these poems, Lamb had, in fact, expressed a similar opinion of "Kubla Khan": "Coleridge repeats so enchantingly that it irradiates and brings heaven and elysian bowers into my parlour while he sings or says it; but there is an observation: 'never tell thy dreams,' and I am almost afraid that *Kubla Kahn* is an owl that won't bear daylight. I fear lest it should be discovered by the lantern of typography and clear reducing to letters, no better than nonsense or no sense."

"Kubla Khan" also produced in Hazlitt, as in Lamb, an instinctive recognition of its musical quality in conflict with his critical reaction. That the poem almost attained the wordless significance of music he realized, saying that it "shows that Mr. Coleridge can write better *nonsense* verses than any man in England. It is not a poem but a musical composition." And after quoting from it, he added, "We could repeat these lines to ourselves not the less often for not knowing the meaning."

The "Statesman's Manual" gave Hazlitt more opportunities to criticize Coleridge. Of these he took full advantage. Before the actual appearance of Coleridge's tract, Hazlitt, in a pretended review of it, attacked Coleridge, remarking at the same time that as Coleridge's writing was always incomprehensible there was no need to read it before reviewing it. Nevertheless, upon the publication of the "Statesman's Manual," Hazlitt renewed his attack upon Coleridge.

In these reviews Hazlitt, with keen insight and sometimes with wicked exaggeration, wittily denounced Coleridge's defects. He accused Coleridge of "moving in an unaccountable diagonal between truth and falsehood, sense and nonsense, sophistry and commonplace. A matter of fact is abhorrent to his nature; the very *air* of truth repels him. Two things are indispensable to him—to set out from no premises, and to arrive at no conclusion."

Yet Hazlitt clearly recognized Coleridge's powers of thought and of imagination: "Without will or sense, his genius has angels' wings, but neither hands nor feet. He should live in a world of enchantment." Nor did Coleridge's already celebrated conversational powers escape a bitter-sweet comment: "Talking away among his gossips. . . . He is fit to take up the pauses of conversation between Cardinals and Angels. . . . Let him talk on for ever in this world and the next; and both worlds will be the better for it. But let him not write, or pretend to write nonsense. Nobody is the better for it." Hazlitt was bitter, but his bitterness was brilliant. Lamb's comment to Wordsworth on Hazlitt's article was subtle and discerning: "Have you read the review of Coleridge's character, physiognomy, etc? his features, even to his *nose*! O! horrible licence beyond the old Comedy . . . God bless him, but certain that rogue . . . has beset him in most unmannerly strains. Yet there is a kind of respect shines through the disrespect."

Coleridge, when aroused, had nothing to learn from Hazlitt in vilification, and the elements of truth in Hazlitt's diatribe exacerbated his distress. "A most brutal attack," he privately complained, "as unprovoked as it is even to extravagance false, on me both as a man and an author." He continued with a highly colored account of Hazlitt's escapade in the Lake District, and how he and Southey had saved Hazlitt "at our own hazard from infamy and transportation in return for his having done his best by the most loathsome conduct (known to all the neighbourhood of Keswick and Grasmere but ourselves and the Wordsworths) to bring disgrace on our names and families."

Hazlitt's attacks on Coleridge were psychological rather than literary or political. Coleridge's "thoughts and theories," said Hazlitt, came and went like "the sails of a windmill." His "reasonings trying in vain to chase his fancy" dissolved and changed as rapidly as clouds and dreams do. Indeed, Coleridge in his "weary quest of truth" reminded Hazlitt of "mendicant pilgrims trudging across the desert with their faces turned towards Mecca, but contriving never to reach it." And Coleridge's fear of the masses Hazlitt here described as "the palsy of death." This last phrase, like Hazlitt's earlier charge of "servility," struck deep into Coleridge's emotions.

At last, in July 1818, after all the vicissitudes of its career, the *Biographia Literaria, or biographical sketches of my literary life and opinions* was published in two volumes. Shortly afterwards, *Sibylline Leaves* also appeared. A year before the publication of the *Biographia* Coleridge informed Frere, when speaking of the work, "My chief purposes were, 1, to defend myself (not indeed to my own Conscience;) but as far as others are concerned, from the often and public denunciation of having wasted my time in idleness—in short, of having done nothing—2, not merely to state my own principles of Taste, but to settle, if possible, and put to rest with all men of sense the controversy concerning the nature and claims of poetic Diction.''

This final form of the *Biographia* was, in fact, not that originally intended. At one time it was, as we have seen, meant to be a ''Preface'' to an edition of Coleridge's poems; and later as a ''Preface'' to the never-completed *Logosophia*. Such a variety of intentions for the work was inimical to its unity; and when ''the blunder of my printer,'' as Coleridge complained, forced him to write ''from 150 to 200 pages additional'' to fill the gap in the two volumes, which Coleridge said was due to Gutch's overestimation of the space required for a single volume, all hope of unity was lost. Indeed, the *Biographia* became, as Coleridge rightly called it in his fourth chapter, an ''immethodical miscellany.''

Yet Coleridge, despite his grumbles about the extra work involved, merely filled the gap in volume two with almost any old material that came to hand: the letters from Germany, already used in the *Friend*; some articles from the *Courier*, including Coleridge's criticism of *Bertram*; and a continuation of the critique on Wordsworth begun in the first volume. The *Biographia* closed with a ''Conclusion'' that attempted to confound Coleridge's critics and improve his public image, thus fulfilling the intention that Coleridge had expressed to Frere. From such a hotchpotch orderly development and progression cannot be expected; not is it to be found. Coleridge described the *Biographia* as ''this exculpation,'' alluding to his critics' charges, and he immediately afterwards wrote: ''What my additonal purposes were, will be seen in the following pages. It will be found that the least of what I have written concerns myself personally.'' That last remark was extraordinary for an autobiographer to make, especially one who was to expound ''my principles in Politics, Religion, and Philosophy'' and also their relation ''to poetry and criticism.''

An implicit confession of the failure of the *Biographia* as a biography he made in the final chapter when he promised to write a new ''autobiography.'' He wrote, ''No private feeling that affected myself only, should prevent me from *publishing* the same (for *write* it I assuredly shall, should life and leisure be granted me).'' But this promise, like so many of Coleridge's, remained unfulfilled. Nor could Coleridge's son Hartley have been enthusiastic about the *Biographia*; for after his father's death, when reluctantly accepting a commission to write an ''Introduction'' to it, he replied: ''I confess I would rather it appeared in connection with the *Poems* or almost any other of the works—for admirable as much of the *Biographia* unquestionably is, it is more fragmentary and worse put together than any of them.'' Nor was Hartley's ''Introduction'' ever written.

Coleridge indeed, frightened by his hostile critics, was in too cautious a mood to present an interesting autobiography to the public. Such a work required not discretion but the frankness of his remark to Poole twenty years before: ''As to my Life, it has all the charms of variety: high Life, and low Life, Vices and Virtues, great Folly and some Wisdom.''

But after limiting the *Biographia Literaria* to his literary life, Coleridge discovered that he had little to write about. In this dilemma he adroitly turned to his literary associations with such distinguished contemporaries as Southey and Wordsworth. At the same time, by disassociating himself from their faults, he seemed to acquire much of their distinction without appearing to desire it. Thus, too, the printers' gap was partly filled. The attacks of Coleridge's critics also supplied him with material for two chapters of counterattack. These critics haunt the remaining pages of the book.

Coleridge's consciousness of digressions is revealed in the opening sentence of his fourth chapter, that on Wordsworth: "I have wandered far from the object in view." Such was his return to his literary theme—Wordsworth. Immediately afterwards come five chapters on philosophy, chiefly attacking his bête noire, once his hero, the philosopher David Hartley, and the "mechanists" of 17th and 18th century scientific thought. Two more chapters are largely devoted to warning would-be writers of the dangers and disappointments menacing them, including, of course, once more the critics.

Unfortunately, the great discussion of the imagination, which Coleridge in the *Biographia* announced was about to appear in a later chapter, never appeared. It was replaced there by another, written by a "friend"—who was Coleridge himself—explaining its non-appearance because of the incomprehension of the ordinary reader.

A leading subject in volume 1 of the *Biographia* was Coleridge's distinction between fancy and imagination, "the generic difference between the faculties of Fancy and Imagination," as he described it to his friend Brabant two years before the *Biographia* was published.*

Another subject still haunting Coleridge's mind was the charge of plagiarism from Schlegel and Schelling created by his lectures. This, too, found a place in the *Biographia*, and as before he both denied and half-admitted it. "An identity of thought or even similarity of phrase," he warned his readers, "will not be at all times a certain proof that the passage has been borrowed from Schelling." In "self-defence," he continued, first alluding to Schlegel, "many of the most striking resemblances, indeed all the main and fundamental ideas, were born and matured in my mind before I had ever seen a single page of the German Philosopher; and I might indeed affirm with truth, before the more important works of Schelling had been written, or at least made public."

Also haunting Coleridge's mind and recently discussed in the "Statesman's Manual" was the question of reason versus understanding. This, he said, had been his main reason for creating *The Friend*. This question he claimed to have discovered by himself, although he later found it, he said, implied or stated "by the authority of our genuine divines and philosophers, before the Revolu-

---

*This distinction between fancy and imagintion was not Coleridge's original idea, but had long been traditional among writers and literary critics of the age.

tion." Yet on this subject Coleridge is no more illuminating than on imagination, merely trailing off immediately into his journalistic experiences with the *Watchman* and *The Friend.*

It was probably dearth of material as well as personal interest that sent Coleridge in the second volume of the *Biographia* back to Wordsworth.

So when in the *Biographia* Coleridge again turned to Wordsworth he now examined in great length and in great detail Wordsworth's defects in theory and in practice—often laboriously. Indeed, he at times treated Wordsworth's generalizations with a wealth of references and particularity of interpretation, which largely presented them in a misleading light. As a recent critic, Graham Hough, well says of Coleridge's attack on Wordsworth's "Preface" to the *Lyrical Ballads,* "He (Wordsworth) is concerned with what happens, or should happen, in the poet's mind in the act of composition. Coleridge, in these passages at any rate, is concerned with the *fait accompli*; with what happens in the reader's mind in the act of appreciation or judgement. . . . In fact, they were hardly talking of the same things." (Graham Hough, *The Romantic Poets* [London, 1965], p. 68.)

Thus it was that Coleridge now devoted a chapter of the *Biographia* to a detailed exposition of what he believed Wordsworth really meant to say in his "Preface": Yet for this there was some excuse, for the "Preface" as a whole was not well written, and to a reader acquainted with all the details of its origin it presents an uncomfortable conglomeration of Wordsworth's own attitude as a creative poet with Coleridge's critical and philosophical conversatins.

In this way, Coleridge's concentrated destructive criticism of Wordsworth's "Preface" was mingled with occasional eulogy. But his criticisms were far from suggesting that the "Preface," in fact, largely incorporated Coleridge's own ideas. On September 30, 1800, Coleridge had told Stuart, "The Preface contains our joint opinions on Poetry." Nevertheless, within two years Coleridge had been conscious of some disagreement with the opinions expressed in Wordsworth's "Preface."

To Southey on July 29, 1802, he had declared, "Although Wordsworth's Preface is half a child of my own brain, and so arose out of conversations so frequent that, with a few exceptions, we could scarcely either of us, perhaps, positively say which first started any particular thought . . . yet I am far from going all lengths with Wordsworth . . . I rather suspect that somewhere or other there is a radical difference in our theoretical opinions respecting poetry."

Coleridge, who detested adverse criticism of his own works, and was well aware that Wordsworth's attitude in this respect resembled his own, can hardly have anticipated a cordial approval from his friend. Although Coleridge finally attacks Wordsworth's "detractors," it is with an energy evidently inspired more by his own sufferings than by Wordsworth's. Such hostile critics he describes as "rogues" who reduce writers and poets "to all the wretchedness of debt and embarrassment."

That Coleridge indeed anticipated Wordsworth's dislike of his treatment of the "Preface," he clearly showed on several occasions. "I have no doubt that Wordsworth will be displeased," he told Brabant on July 29, 1815, "but I have done my duty to myself and to the public." Shortly afterward to Stuart he sent the following apologia, saying that what he had written was "in the hope of settling the controversy on the nature of poetic diction. I fear, that my reasonings may not please Wordsworth; but I am convinced, that the detection of the faults in his Poetry is indispensable to a rational appreciation of his Merits." This apologia was probably more ingenious than sincere. Coleridge's anger with Wordsworth since the great quarrel had now combined with jealousy of Wordsworth's domination over Sara Hutchinson—who was now copying Wordsworth's poems as she had once copied Coleridge's. To these causes for jealousy must be added the general acknowledgment of Wordsworth as the leading poet of the time and Coleridge's bitter realization that his own poetic inspiration was dead. All, consciously or unconsciously, doubtless played a part in Coleridge's attack on Wordsworth's theory and practice of poetry.

In the *Biographia* itself, Coleridge, evidently feeling the need for some excuse for his attack on Wordsworth, wrote in reference to "the detractors from Wordsworth's merits":

> Much as I might wish for their fuller sympathy, I dare not flatter myself, that the freedom with which I have declared my opinions concerning both his theory and his defects, most of which are more or less connected with his theory, either as caue or effect, will be satisfactory or pleasing to *all* the poet's admirers and advocates. More indiscriminate than mine their admiration may be: deeper and more sincere it can not be. . . . His fame belongs to another age, and can neither be accelerated nor retarded. How small the proportion of the defects are to the beauties I have repeatedly declared; and that no one of them originates in deficiency of poetic genius.

Despite this placatory passage in the *Biographia*, the fears of Wordsworth's displeasure, which had assailed Coleridge before the work's publication, continued after its appearance. Eighteen months before its publication he told Sotheby, as he had often told others before in one form or another: "It will not please Wordsworth, or," he added optimistically, "Wordsworth's detractors." On sending the newly published volumes to his son Derwent he wrote in similar vein, at the same time trying to dispel any suspicion in Derwent's mind of illwill towards Wordsworth. He feared, he said, that Wordsworth might be "offended," adding: "Of one thing I am distinctly conscious that my main motive and continued impulse was to secure, as far as in me lay, an intelligent admiration of Mr. Wordsworth's poems."

Yet, however strange it might seem to Coleridge, Wordsworth *did* resent this extraordinary defense of his poetry. His comments upon it, although characteristically restrained, show by their long continuance how deeply he must have resented Coleridge's criticism of his "Preface." To one inquirer Wordsworth replied immediately after the appearance of the *Biographia*: "I have not read Mr. Coleridge's 'Biographia,' having contented myself with skimming parts of it.'' He added, ''Indeed, I am heartily sick of even the best criticism.''

Thirteen years later, refusing the request of a minor poet to criticize a poem, Wordsworth replied: ''I am not a Critic—and set little value upon the art. The preface which I wrote long ago to my own Poems I was put upon to write by the urgent entreaties of a friend (Coleridge), and heartily regret I ever had anything to do with it; though I do not reckon the principles then advanced erroneous.'' Eight years later, replying to some similar requests from another correspondent, Wordsworth employed almost the same terms, saying that he had been ''prevailed upon by Mr. Coleridge to write the first Preface to my Poems—which tempted, or rather forced, me to add a supplement to it.''

Lamb, who knew Wordsworth's real feelings, had no doubt of their depth and intensity and prophesied that Wordsworth ''will never speak to Coleridge again.'' Robinson was more explicit than Lamb as to Wordsworth's dislike of Coleridge's criticism: ''Coleridge's book has given Wordsworth no pleasure, and he finds just fault with Coleridge for professing to write about himself and writing merely about Southey and Wordsworth. With the criticism of the poetry too he is not satisfied. The praise is extravagant and the censure inconsiderate. I recollected hearing Hazlitt say that Wordsworth would not forgive a single censure mingled with 'however great a mass of eulogy.'''

Another friend and benefactor of Coleridge, Stuart, was deeply grieved by Coleridge's false and malicious reference to him in the *Biographia*. For there, describing his work for the *Morning Post* and *Courier*, Coleridge wrote: ''In these labours, I employed and, in the belief of partial friends wasted, the prime and manhood of my intellect. Most assuredly, they added nothing to my fortune or my reputation. The industry of the week supplied the necessities of the week.'' In justifiable anger, the generous Stuart went down to Gillman's and warmly reproached Coleridge for what he had written. Some four years after Coleridge's death Stuart justified himself against Coleridge's insinuations in the *Biographia Literaria* by publishing in the *Gentleman's Magazine* in May 1838 some of Coleridge's letters to Stuart expressing deep gratitude to him for various payments for Coleridge's debts.

It was unlikely that Hazlitt, with his chattering clarity of mind and diction, would ignore the many opportunities given him in the *Biographia* for resuming his attacks on Coleridge. So, in the *Edinburgh Review* of August 1817, he pointed out that the *Biographia* was not what it pretended to be, biographical: it was less an account of Coleridge's ''Life and Opinions'' than ''An apology for them.'' He added, ''There were some things readable in these volumes,'' and he did not doubt that if the author had only ''made them a little more conformable to their titles, they would have been the most popular of all his productions.'' But Hazlitt was by no means blind to the hotchpotch, the obvious bit of bookmaking, that the *Biographia* largely was, with its series of unfulfilled promises, of deferred statements and evasions.

Equally direct and incisive is Hazlitt's harsh criticism of Coleridge himself:

"Mr. Coleridge with great talents, has by an ambition to be everything, become nothing. His metaphysics have been a dead weight in the wings of his imagination—while his imagination has run away with his reason and common sense. He might, we seriously think, have been a very considerable poet—instead of which, he has chosen to be a bad philosopher and a worse politician." That was not very different from T. S. Eliot's comment on Coleridge over a century later: "It was better for Coleridge as poet, to read books of travel and exploration than to read books of metaphysics and political economy. . . . The author of *Biographia Literaria* was already a ruined man. Sometimes, however, to be a 'ruined man' is itself a vocation." (T. S. Eliot, *The Use of Poetry and the Use of Criticism*, p. 69.)

Upon Coleridge's discussion in the *Biographia* of poetic diction, Hazlitt says an admirable final word: "As we think the common or natural style is the truly dramatic style, that in which he (the poet) can best give the impassioned, unborrowed, unaffected thought of others . . . The beauty of poetic diction is, in short, borrowed and artificial. It is a glittering veil spread over the forms of things and the feelings of the heart; and is best laid aside when we wish to show either the one or the other in their naked beauty or deformity." Hazlitt's examination of the question leaves nothing more to be said. Where Coleridge had touched in his book on matters in which Hazlitt was implicated, Hazlitt openly refused to enter into debate as possibly a departure from impartiality.

One reason for Coleridge's wish to improve his public image by the writing of the *Biographia* was to counteract the accusation in the *Anti-Jacobin* of 1799 that he had "left his poor children fatherless and his wife destitute." But in foolishly reviving the matter in the *Biographia* he gave another critic, John Wilson ("Christopher North"), an additional opportunity for an attack. This Wilson quickly seized in the October 1817 number of *Blackwood's Magazine*, in a review of the *Biographia* in which he cruelly declared: "A man who abandons his wife and children is undoubtedly both a wicked and pernicious member of society; and Mr. Coleridge ought not to deal in general and vague terms of indignation, (as he had done in the *Biographia*) but boldly affirm if he dare, that the charge was false then, and would be false now if repeated against himself." This did not satisfy Wilson, who continued his attack on Coleridge with an analysis of his character made with bitter clarity like Hazlitt's, but with his own comparative vulgarity of tone. Yet, also like Hazlitt, he admitted Coleridge's genius.

The *Biographia*, Wilson said, "lays open not unfrequently, the character of the Man as well as of the Author." Indeed, he added, the book entails "sacrifice of personal dignity," and he believed that henceforth it is

impossible that Mr. Coleridge is but an obscure name in English literature. In London he is well known in literary society, and justly admired for his extraordinary loquacity; he has his own little circle of devoted worshippers, and he mistakes their foolish babbling for the voice of the world . . . except a few wild and fanciful ballads, he has produced nothing worthy of remembrance. Yet insignificant as he assuredly is, he cannot put pen to paper without feeling that millions of eyes are fixed upon him: and he scatters his Sibylline Leaves around him, with as majestical an air as if a crowd of enthusiastic admirers were rushing forward to grasp the divine promulgation.

Much general denigration of Coleridge followed in Wilson's critique. Southey and Wordsworth were, said Wilson, well known and appreciated: "But Mr. Coleridge stands on much lower ground, and will be known to future times only as a man who overrated and abused his talents." Various aspects of Coleridge's life were treated with contempt, including his management of the *Watchman*, his wit and associations, and his political evolution: "We have no room here to expose, as it deserves to be exposed, the multitudinous political inconsistencies of Mr. Coleridge. . . . We believe that all good men, of all parties, regard Mr. Coleridge with pity and contempt."

Nevertheless, Wilson admitted that being a poet Coleridge had occasionally illuminated, however awkwardly, the nature of poetry:

As Mr. Coleridge has not only studied the laws of poetical composition but is a poet of considerable powers, there are, in this part of his book, many acute, ingenious, and even sensible observations and remarks; but he never knows when to have done—explains what requires no explanation—often leaves untouched the very difficulty he starts,—and when he has poured before us a glimpse of light upon the shapeless form of some dark conception, he seems to take a wilful pleasure in its immediate extinction, and leads "us floundering on and quite astray" through the deepening shadows of interminable night.

Wilson went on to ridicule Coleridge's treatment of fancy and imagination, at the same time ridiculing, rather vulgarly, his lectures.

Coleridge's distinction between fancy and imagination Wilson satirically described as "unequalled in the annals of literary history," and he sarcastically symbolized Coleridge's chapter on this subject in the *Biographia* by a humorous imaginary picture of Coleridge the lecturer, announcing it to his audience:

The audience is assembled—the curtain is drawn up—and there in his gown, cap and wig, is sitting Professor Coleridge. In comes a servant with a letter; the Professor gets up, and, with a solemn voice, reads to the audience.—It is from an enlightened Friend: and its object is to shew in no very courteous terms either to the Professor or his Spectators, that he may lecture, but that nobody will understand him. He accordingly m akes his bow and the curtain falls; but the worst of the joke is, that the Professor pockets the admittance-money,—for what reason, his outwitted audience are left, the best way they can to "fancy or imagine."

That such a critic as Coleridge could mistake Wilson's article for the work of Hazlitt is surprising.

Wilson's sneer in *Blackwood's*, about Coleridge having deserted his wife and children, so rankled Coleridge that he consulted Robinson with the intention of suing Wilson for libel. When Robinson dissuaded him from such a course, Coleridge sent Robinson a long letter of self-justification in which he said:

> I can prove by positive evidence, by the written bargains made with my booksellers, etc., that I have refused every offer, however convenient to myself, that did not leave two thirds of the property sacred to Mrs. Coleridge—and that I have given up all I had in the world to her—have continued to pay yearly £30 to assure her that if I live to the year 1820 will be nearly £2000—that beyond my absolute necessities (in which I count those things that are indispensable to my being able to do anything) I have held myself accountable to her for every shilling—that Hartley is with me, with all his expenses paid, during his vacations—that I have been for the last six months and now am laboring hard to procure the means of having Derwent with me.

Coleridge's daughter Sara said that the insurance taken out in 1803 for Mrs. Coleridge realized about £2,560 on Coleridge's death.

Perhaps Wilson's conception of Coleridge's obscurity was influenced by the satirical portrait of Coleridge which had appeared the preceding February in Peacock's latest novel *Melincourt*. In this, Coleridge is "Moley Mystic, Esq., of Cimmerian Lodge." Mystic is an expositor of "the system of Kantian metaphysics, or grand transcendental science of the *Luminous obscure*." Nor is this all, for Mystic is also described as "the Poeticopolitical, rhapsodicoprosaical, deisidaemoniacoparadoxographical, pseudolatriological, transcendental meteorosophist, Moley Mystic, Esquire."

Cimmerian Lodge itself, is shrouded in fog: "The fog had penetrated into all the apartments: there was fog in the hall, fog in the parlour, fog on the staircases, fog in the bedrooms;

The fog was here, the fog was there,
The fog was all around.

For even "The Ancient Mariner" must be parodied. In Mystic's library the obscurity of the house "was condensed almost into solidity." There Mr. Moley took his "synthetical torch which shed around it the rays of transcendental illumination" and, thus equipped, conducted his guests through his fog-shrouded estate, "pointing out innumerable images of singularly nubilous beauty," where, in fact, his visitors "could see nothing but the fog."

Poor Coleridge's hopes of improving his public image by writing the *Biographia*, although unrealized among his immediate contemporaries, certainly succeeded with admiring strangers in later years. The book which had brought him such devastating personal analysis and ridicule from the professional critics also annoyed Byron and Scott. The reason for this was his attack on Maturin's play *Bertram*, which was accepted by Drury Lane, when *Zapolya* had been rejected. Coleridge's criticism of *Bertram* lacked nothing of Hazlitt's bitterness, which Coleridge so detested, and concluded in the same style with the remark that the play ends "as it began, to wit, in a superfetation of blasphemy upon nonsense.'' Doubtless *Bertram* deserved the castigation that Coleridge gave it, but it inevitably suggested, and perhaps partly was, the revenge of a defeated rival. Nor was this all; Drury Lane, which had rejected *Zapolya*, must be chastised, including its "mercenary manager," as Coleridge described him. The manager, indeed, was said to have complained of Coleridge's "damned metaphysics.'' Byron, who had kindly sponsored the two plays at Drury Lane, was disgusted by Coleridge's attack on *Bertram*, and perhaps even more by Coleridge's description of the theater manager. Even before seeing the *Biographia* Byron's mood was evidently unfriendly, despite the £100 he had sent Coleridge. For about the very time of the *Biographia's* appearance, asking the publisher Murray for literary news, Byron demanded with satirical jocularity:

> Have you had no new Babe of literature ... . .
> No city Wordsworth, more admired than read.
> No drunken Coleridge with a new "Lay Sermon."

But writing again to Murray three months later, after reading the *Biographia*, Byron's genial derision of Coleridge had changed into anger. After complaining of his attack on *Bertram*, and "this long tirade on Drury Lane," Byron cried: "He is a shabby fellow, and I wash my hands of and after him."

In *Don Juan* Byron repeated the charge of drunkenness against Coleridge which he had made in his letter to Murray:

> Thou shalt believe in Milton, Dryden, Pope;
> Thou shalt not set up Wordsworth, Coleridge, Southey;
> Because the first is crazed beyond all hope,
> the second drunk, the third so quaint and mouthy.

On reading these lines Coleridge was more moved by the charge of drunkenness than by all the other ridicule of himself in the poem. On September 4, 1819, Coleridge sent Byron the following letter:

> My Lord, That I should be selected by you to share such immorality as Time may confer upon your *Don Juan*, demands my acknowledgement, the quality of which is enlarged by the charge of inebriety you prefer against me. Had you adorned me with indolence and irresolution the commendation had been just, but the more elegant acquirement of intemperance it were flattery to attribute to me. This example of your Lordship's taste and knowledge would embolden me to esteem you as among the first of our great writers if you would condescend first to avoid a too servile flattery of your contemporaries, and next to obtain correct information on the habits of those you celebrate. The sobriety of this letter, is the unhappy proof of the extravagance of your praise. I am your Lordship's obedient sober servant, S. T. Coleridge.

How little Coleridge's protest affected Byron, Byron showed three months later in Venice, when he added to Canto 3 of the poem another satiric reference to Coleridge, whose:

. . . flighty pen
Let to the Morning Post its aristocracy;
When he and Southey, following the same path,
Espoused two partners, (Milliners of Bath.)

Scott, who had introduced *Bertram* to Byron, was no less annoyed by Coleridge's attack on the play but showed greater consideration than Byron toward Coleridge. Writing to Maturin, Scott said:

Let me entreat you to view Coleridge's violence as a thing to be contemned, not retaliated— . . . the opinion of a British public may surely be set in honest opposition to that of one disappointed and wayward man. You should also consider en [sic] bon Chretien, that Coleridge has had some room to be spited at the world, and you are, I trust, to continue to be a favourite with the public so that you should totally neglect and despise criticism, however virulent, which arises out of this bad fortune and your good. . . . Upon my own part I can only say that I have no habits of friendship, and scarce those of acquaintance with Coleridge—I have not even read his Autobiography—but I consider him as a man of genius, struggling with bad habits and difficult circumstances.

3   Last Lectures and Political and Religious Essays (1818-32)

"I am . . . deep in the anxieties of a course of Lectures. . . . My poverty and not my will consenting."
—*Coleridge to H. F. Cary, January 30, 1818*

In January 1818 Coleridge, stimulated by his need of money and also by the wish to assist Derwent's education, began another course of lectures. At this time he was in bitter conflict with his publishers, who complained of his delays in providing material for the projected *Encyclopaedia*. Hence he now described himself to his new friend Cary as "deep in the anxieties of a course of lectures, *a course* to which (My poverty and not my will consenting) I have been driven by the unspeakabilities of those worthy Arcadians, Messrs. Curtis and Fenner. There is," he continued, "a degree of baseness and profligate dishonesty which I never had had, and probably never shall have, courage to anticipate, however suspicious the circumstances; as long as God permits the men to *look* tolerably like human flesh and blood."

Nor were Coleridge's complaints about his lectures by any means confined to Cary. To almost all his correspondents at the time of these lectures he groaned or anathematized as his moods drove him. To newspaper editors he was particularly eloquent. "Woe is me!" he cried to Mudford, the new editor of the *Courier*, "that at 46 I am under the necessity of appearing as a Lecturer, and obliged to regard every hour that I give to the PERMANENT, whether as poet or philosopher. . . . Woe from without," he continued, "but well for me, however, from within that I have been more sinned against than sinning." In such strains he invoked the assistance of the London newspapers, who generously advertised and reported his lectures and received in return warm expressions of gratitude.

On hearing of Coleridge's intentions Lamb (and Wordsworth, who was in London) came to the rescue, each writing independently to J. P. Collier, to help make Coleridge's lectures a success. "He is in bad health and worse mind," wrote Lamb,

and unless something is done to lighten his mind, he will soon be reduced to his extremities; and even these are not in the best conditions. I am sure that

you will do for him what you can; but at present he seems in a mood to do
for himself. He projects a new course, not of physic or metaphysic, nor a
new course of life, but a new course of lectures on "Shakespeare and
Poetry." There is no man better qualified (always excepting No. 1); ... . To
be serious, Coleridge's state and affairs make me so; and there are particular reasons just now, and have been any time for the last 20 years why he
should succeed. He will do so with a little encouragement. I have not seen
him lately; and he does not know that I am writing. Yours (for Coleridge's
sake) in haste. C. Lamb.

About the same time Wordsworth, showing no animosity to Coleridge
despite their quarrel, wrote in similar vein to Collier, hoping for the success of
Coleridge,

to whom all but certain reviewers wish well . . . he gained some money and
reputation by his last effort of the kind, which ws, indeed, to him no effort,
since his thoughts as well as his words flow spontaneously. He talks as a
bird sings, as if he could not help it; it is his nature. He is now far from well
in body or spirit; the former is suffering from various causes and the latter
from depression. No man ever deserved to have fewer enemies, yet, as he
thinks and says, no man has more or more virulent . . . We are all anxious
on his account . . . . He means to call upon himself, or write from
Highgate, where he now is.

Coleridge's preparations for the lectures, which were to be given in the
Philosophical Society's "great Room"—"the old shop," as he called it, in
Fleur-de-Luce Court, Fleet Street—followed their usual course. There was the
canvassing of friends, and the publication of a prospectus and syllabus. The
former was intimidatingly pedagogic. The syllabus covered in fourteen lectures
a period that extended from the "Manners, Morals, Literature, Philosophy,
Religion, and the State of Society in general, in European Christendom, from
the eighth to the fifteenth Century." It was to end with the fourteenth lecture
which was "On the corruption of the English Language since the Reign of
Queen Anne, in our Style of Writing Prose," followed by "A few easy Rules
for the Attainment of a manly, unaffected, and pure Language in our genuine
Mother-tongue, whether for the purpose of Writing, Oratory, or Converse."
This was to be followed by a "Concluding Address."
    According to his own account—or rather one of his accounts—Coleridge
took particular care in the preparation of his material. "I shall have written
every lecture, just as if I had intended to read them," he told Robinson, "but
shall deliver them without book." After almost a year's interval he told
another correspondent, referring to these same lectures of 1818,

The fact is this. During a course of lectures, I faithfully employ *all* the intervening days in collecting and digesting the materials, whether I have or
have not lectured on the same subject before, making no difference. The
day of the lecture, till the hour of commencement, I devote to the consideration, what of the mass before me is best fitted to answer the purpose of a

lecture—i.e. to keep the audience awake and interested during the delivery and to leave a *sting* behind , i.e. a disposition to study the subject anew, under the light of a new principle.

However, he asserted, even when he had written out some of his lectures, "partly from the wish to possess copies that might afterwards be marketable among the publishers," he soon found that his extemporary passages were the most appreciated. On such occasions, he said, "I have been obliged to push the MSS away and give the subject a new turn. Nay, this was so notorious that many of my auditors used to threaten me when they saw any number of written papers on my desk, to steal them away, declaring they never felt so secure of a good lecture as when they perceived that I had not a single scrap of writing before me." This remarkable behavior of the audience was apparently not observed by Coleridge's various critics. "I take far, far more pains," he said, "than would go to the set composition of a lecture, both by varied reading and by meditation, but for the words, illustrations etc. I know almost as little as anyone of my audience . . . what they will be five minutes before the lecture begins. Such is *my way* for such is *my nature.*"

Coleridge's assertion that he never repeated the material of earlier lectures is not only disproved by the facts, but even in his syllabus he now declared that "in these lectures will be comprised the substance of Mr. Coleridge's former courses on the same subject." This was, however, qualified by the cautious addition: "enlarged and varied by subsequent study and reflection." During these lectures the old charges of plagiarism from the Germans were revived and incorrectly denied again by Coleridge. Coleridge was also annoyed by Wordsworth's remark in 1815, in a preface supplementary to his own poems, that a German critic (whom Coleridge identified with Schlegel) had been the first to appreciate Shakespeare. By contrast, Coleridge declared that his praise of Wordsworth had created the hostility of critics to himself.

Gillman, who attended these lectures, was, of course, most enthusiastic: "He was billiant, fluent and rapid; his words seem to flow, as from a person repeating with grace and energy some delightful poem." Gillman also described an extraordinary lecture that Coleridge gave by invitation at the London Philosophical Society, the subject of which was unknown to Coleridge until announced after his arrival. This subject was "The Growth of the Individual Mind"—which was, in fact, akin to Coleridge's "Essay on Method." "A pretty stiff subject they have chosen," he whispered to Gillman as he mounted the platform after asking Gillman to watch and observe the effect of the lecture on the assembly, and should he appear to fail, to clasp his ankle, but if the audience appeared interested, to let him continue. Gillman wrote, "He was brilliant, eloquent and logically consecutive. The time moved on so quickly that on looking at my watch, I found that an hour and a half had passed. Waiting therefore for a desirable moment, I prepared myself, to use his own playful words 'to punctuate' his oration and I pressed his ankle, when bowing graciously and with a benevolent and smiling countenance he presently descended."

Among those who attended Coleridge's course of lectures in 1818 were at least three persons who recorded their impressions: J. H. Green, H. C. Robinson, and another, a Mr. H. H. Carwardine of Colne Priory, in Essex. In his first lecture, after discussing Shem, Ham, and Japheth as founders of the human race, Coleridge turned to discuss classic and romantic art. His treatment Carwardine found inadequate, and he summarized his final impressions thus: "Mr Coleridge has a solemn and pompous mode of delivery, which he applies indiscriminately to the elevated and the familiar; and he read poetry, I think, as ill as any man I ever heard."

On January 27, 1818—the night of Coleridge's first lecture—Robinson first attended one by Hazlitt, who was then lecturing on the English poets at the Surrey Institution on Blackfriars Road. Robinson then proceeded to the Philosophical Society to hear Coleridge. "Hazlitt's lecture," he wrote, "delighted me much by the talent he displayed. "But Coleridge's lecture Robinson found "heavy." Coleridge himself wrote to Mudford, "My lectures are, though not very numerously yet very respectably attended—and as respectfully *attended to*." Later he regarded them, said Gillman, as "the most profitable of any he had given." Robinson, on this first evening, was pleased to find "a large and respectable audience, generally of superior-looking persons, in physiognomy, rather than dress. Coleridge treated of the origin of poetry and of Oriental works; but he had little animation, and an exceedingly bad cold rendered his voice scarcely audible."

Although Gillman considered that the lecture room was in "an unfavourable situation," another hearer, a Mr. Allsop, described the lectures as "constantly thronged by the most attentive and intelligent auditory I have ever seen." Gillman also tells us that the audience included distinguished persons. Lamb—who apparently received tickets late—seems to have attended, but not until after the tenth lecture. In mid-February Lamb told Mrs. Wordsworth:

> S. T. C. is lecturing with success. I have not heard either him or Hazlitt, but I dined with S. T. C. at Gillman's a Sunday or two since and he was well and in good spirits. I meant to hear some of the course, but lectures are not much to my taste, whatever the lecturer may be. If *read*, they are dismal flat, and you can't think why you are brought together to hear a man read his works which you could read so much better at leisure yourself; if delivered extempore, I am always in pain lest the gift of utterance should suddenly fail the orator in the middle, as it did me at the dinner given in honour of me at the London Tavern. "Gentlemen," I said, and then I stopped.

Robinson's comments on these lectures were, on the whole, unfavorable. But the second lecture, which was on Gothic literature and art, he found "much more brilliant than the first and seems to give general satisfaction." So Robinson's varied comments on each lecture continued, until before the close he was forced to leave and go on circuit as a barrister. He wrote, "More entertainment than instruction [on Shakespeare] . . . splendid irregularities throughout"—"rather less interesting . . . dwelt on mere accidents which served to bring out some of his favourite ideas, which after a certain number of repetitions became tiresome.''

At the sixth lecture Robinson found the room "fuller than I had ever seen it," and he was forced to take a back seat. There were important persons there, he noticed, including Coleridge's bête noire Sir James Mackintosh, in a party with "some genteel women." They were, wrote Robinson, "in a satirical mood and made sneering remarks as it seemed, throughout the whole lecture. Indeed, Coleridge was not in one of his happiest moods." His subject was Cervantes, but Robinson found that "he was more than usually prosing and his tone peculiarly drawling." After the ninth lecture—on "Wit and Humor"—Robinson wrote: "I fear that Coleridge will not on the whole add to his reputation by these lectures."

Sara Hutchinson, although not among Coleridge's audience, followed the lectures from a distance with a curiosity that was less than affectionate. So, too, did the once admiring Catherine Clarkson, whose guest Sara Hutchinson at this time was. "Have you been at Coleridge's lectures, which I see puffed and advertized in the *Morning Chronicle*?" Sara Hutchinson asked her favorite cousin, Tom Monkhouse, in January 1818. A week later, she again wrote to Tom:

> We see Coleridge both advertized and puffed in the *Morning Chronicle*. I am glad to find that he intends publishing the lectures and wish he may do it—because then he will have his own—else it is scattering his knowledge for the profit of others. It is wonderful that the first lecture was true to the prospectus, but indeed he has exhibited such wonders lately: Pray have you any conversation with him—and did he inquire after "my dear" or his other friends? I was afraid that he would have favoured Mrs. Clarkson or me with a letter, because he asked me the address, but I hope he has forgotten it. If he should ask you, try to evade the question, for we are neither of us ambitious of the favour, especially as an answer *would be required*.

Sara Hutchinson's hope of seeing the lectures published was never realized.

Whatever the deeper feelings of Sara Hutchinson toward Coleridge now, her interest in him was certainly far from dead. A fortnight later she wrote again to Tom: "I see Coleridge proceeds regularly. Tell me what sort of a figure he cuts and in what spirits he appears to be. *The Morning Chronicle* puffs him very much." In April she again asked Tom for news of Coleridge, satirically using an expression that Coleridge had evidently employed in addressing her during some recent conversation in London: "Have you ever seen Zapolya my dear? since the lectures, or do you hear how he is going on?."

Dorothy Wordsworth's awareness of Catherine Clarkson's changed feelings toward Coleridge since his quarrel with Wordsworth, and consequently now of his coolness toward Catherine, was revealed when Dorothy wrote to her in March 1818: "I guess Coleridge will not call upon you." Yet only nine months previously Coleridge, speaking of Mrs. Clarkson to Robinson, had said: "You can scarcely conceive how much I love that lady. O me!"

From a curious incident created by Coleridge at the close of his lectures, Mrs. Clarkson's attitude toward him found clear expression. After the first few lectures Coleridge, oppressed by the realization that he was failing to include much of the material promised, published in the *New Times* on February 4 a letter of public apology for his shortcomings, which concluded: "I solicited, and how solicit the attendance of all who had or shall have attended me to a supernumerary lecture, at the end of the course, given gratis, and composed wholly of poetic translations, in chronological order, and concluding with an original poem." Nor did Coleridge immediately forget his promise. On May 22 the *Times* announced that "Supernumerary Lectures, consisting chiefly of free translations from the poets of the Middle Ages woven into a poem descriptive of the same, will be given on Tuesday evening, May 26th." The evening came, and the audience—but no Coleridge!

Even six months later Mrs. Clarkson had not forgotten this incident. "You heard perhaps," she asked Robinson, "what an ungracious leave Coleridge took of his auditory last Spring—calling them together to hear the gratuitous lecture, causing them to be told that he was too ill to meet them, but as soon as he recovered they should be sure of the lecture—Either he never recovered, or he forgot his promise." Thus, with no "supernumerary lecture," the course ended in the middle of March.

Shortly before the end of 1818 Coleridge began a new course—or rather two concurrent courses—one on literature and the other on philosophy. These were now held at the Crown and Anchor Tavern in the Strand, where there was a large room often used for public lectures. As ever, Coleridge approached his task reluctantly, complaining of the necessity, "not my will consenting." The usual procedure followed: prospectuses and letters to friends, to Mudford, and to others of the press, while he lamented, as so often before, that the great *Logosophia* would never be finished.

On December 14, 1818, the first of the fourteen philosophical lectures was given. It was a week late owing to the death of Queen Charlotte. For the same reason the first literary lecture was delayed until December 17. Coleridge's material in these Shakespearean lectures, was, of course, much as before. Thelwall enthusiastically reported upon the first literary lecture in his paper the *Champion*, saying that Shakespeare's qualities "were demonstrated with a truth and beauty which he only can arrive at who writes profound philosophy with exquisite taste and depth of poetic feeling."

Over another literary lecture the *Champion* was no less enthusiastic, describing it as "a splendid and ingenious display of metaphysical criticism and poetic enthusiasm . . . many ideas as just as beautiful." Nevertheless, it regretted the time wasted in "the almost unintelligibly ambiguous apologies for belief in ghosts and goblins." So Coleridge pursued his way along the lines he had previously advertised in the syllabus, which states that each play was to be studied "scene by scene, for the purpose of illustrating the conduct of the plot, and the peculiar force, beauty, and propriety of the language, in the particular passages, as well as the intention of the great philosophic Poet in the prominent characters of each play, and the unity of interest in the whole and in the apparent contrast of the component parts.''

Coleridge's interest in the philosophical lectures that he proposed to give was from the first perhaps greater than he took in the literary ones; but at the same time his fears for their success were also great. To Collins the painter he spoke of the small attendance that he sadly anticipated, which, nevertheless, he believed would find the philosophical lectures ''far more generally interesting and even entertaining, than the title.'' This expectation was satisfied at his sixth lecture on January 25, 1819, which was on ''the character of Our Lord as a philosopher, as the Union of the Truths and the Supplement of the inherent imperfections of Philosophy.'' Very successful, he described it to Rose, ''as far as can be judged from the satisfaction of a not very numerous tho' highly respectable Audience.'' Nevertheless, the absence of several friends from this lecture was a disappointment for Coleridge. Most disappointed, too, was Mrs. Gillman, absent through illness, ''tho''' wrote Coleridge to Tulk, ''of the whole of the two Courses it was the Lecture on which she had most calculated.'' Coleridge himself considered these lectures ''the most *entertaining* course of any, I have yet given.''

Coleridge delivered the last of his philosophical lectures on March 29, 1819. Besides the original delay in starting caused by the Queen's death, there were two interruptions in the sequence of the course, one in December due to the Christmas season and another at the beginning of February, through illness. The philosophical lectures, like the literary, naturally followed Coleridge's characteristic method—large generalization of favorite ideas such as ''polarity'' and the condemnation of ideas which he disliked—e.g. materialism— instead of factual historic detail. Notices in the press and the reports of the shorthand writer commissioned by Coleridge's friend Frere not only described the above elements in the lectures, but also observed, as with the literary lectures, ''rich metaphor,'' novelty of treatment, and similar praiseworthy qualities. But all was not praise: ''a very curious intelligent discourse,'' wrote one critic, ambiguously, and described Coleridge's treatment of Homer more directly as what ''might have been more effective by being more correct.''

The twelfth lecture, advertised as on ''Dogmatical Materialism,'' was, of course, a repetition of Coleridge's frequent attacks upon modern science made throughout many years. Merely experimental mechanical science was now, he complained, being equated with philosophic truth and religion: ''the restoration of ancient geometry, aided by the modern invention of algebra, place the science of mechanics on the philosophic throne.'' Nevertheless, the increasing influence of science had probably unconsciously affected Coleridge's opinion of Bacon and Newton, formerly regarded by him as of the Scientific Devil's Party. But now by some metaphysical conjuring they were transformed into philosophical soul mates.

Before the close of the lectures the old charge of plagiarism was again brought against Coleridge in a letter published in the *Morning Chronicle*. This critic denied Coleridge's claim to have been the first to discover "that the judgement of Shakespeare was, in all his writings, equally, if not more conspicuous than his genius," and he threw doubt upon Coleridge's ignorance of Schlegel's earlier identical criticism of Shakespeare, pointing out that Coleridge had studied in Germany.

At the penultimate lecture of the course Coleridge informed his audience that the next, the final lecture, would be "a review of all the preceding course and the application of it." Coleridge's consciousness of his digressions was evidently much in his mind, when at the opening of this final lecture he declared: "We have passed through a long and wandering road, which has often appeared to turn back upon itself." Thus the lecture proceeded until a quotation from Coleridge's "Lay Sermon" brought it to an end. Lamb, who was no lover of lectures and was somewhat peeved at Coleridge's continued absence in Highgate, received his lecture ticket coolly, citing a promise to attend a farce at Covent Garden as an excuse for his absence, and complaining: "It never lies in your way to come to us. But dear Mahomet, we will come to you."

As on previous occasions the financial results of both the literary and philosophical lectures were disappointing. For his scanty audience Coleridge found various excuses: inadequate advertising, although the press had been generous in its notices and reports; the competition of many others lecturing on kindred subjects, of which there were several, including Thelwall, at the time; bad health; the Queen's funeral and the mourning season; Christmas parties; and the attractions of the theaters. But, he asserted, his failure was not due to any dissatisfaction felt by his audience.

Coleridge's habitual nervous fears on such occasions beset him throughout the courses and were inevitably accompanied by severe self-criticism—of a kind. In this mood he thought the tenth lecture of the philosophical series "a poor one, I hope I shall be able to say my worst." With the lecture on *Romeo and Juliet*, however, he was "pleased even beyond my anticipation." Nor was Coleridge unaware of some criticisms of his method in lecturing—obscurity, prolixity, personal asides, and the serpentine turns and phrasing, and deviations into personal annoyance—by critics and others, such as Hazlitt.

Coleridge's lectures did not entirely suit his audience, nor his audience his lectures; for along with some of the general public for whom his lectures were primarily intended there also came loyal friends—most of them highly educated, including the philosophic surgeon Green, the Dante scholar Cary, Leslie the painter, the now invaluable Allsop, and the indefatigable Gillman. To please these and at the same time the general public was almost an impossibility, and whatever style he adopted was open to criticism by one or another section of his audience. The description of the lectures by one recent editor, Kathleen Coburn, as "both superficial and difficult" is not surprising. Nor can critical readers quarrel with the same editor's comment when she says: "Reading the lectures, now, one has to endure dullness, repetition, digressions, generalisations without substantiation, over-emphasis, gaps, and infuriating circumlocutions. The lectures admittedly are often disappointing in the extreme."* Thus the lectures brought Coleridge little but dissatisfaction, both financial and critical. Indeed, his consciousness of these defects and his sense of failure poor Coleridge expressed in a dolorous letter to Mulford in mid-February 1819: "I imagine that my ill health and despondency, that barely enable me to give the lectures themselves respectably, but utterly unfit me for all awkward exertion and canvassing, that these, joined with my solitariness, and unconnection with parties of any kind, literary, religious, or political, are the main causes of my failure." What wonder that poor Coleridge wrote on his manuscript at the end of his last lecture, "Monday, 29th March, 1819 fourteenth of the Philosophical course and the last (O pray Heaven, that it may be the last) of All!" and so it was.

One of the illuminating general comments upon Coleridge's literary lectures is that of Elton, who wrote:

We are seldom sure that his lectures on Shakespeare and the poets are saved for us in his actual words, as they are mostly preserved by dutiful reporters. But they were evidently discursive in essence. Even a stronger will than Coleridge's would have had much to contend with, in the task of shaping the rich material given to him by his far ranging, accumulative, and illustrative intellect, which continually throws off new ideas, like the "vortex-rings" of smoke, that propagate yet others by a strange process till they are lost in vanishing film just as the beauty and structure of the pattern is eluding our sense.

Whatever the disappointments of these lectures, whether for lecturer or audience, they brought Coleridge a new and important friend. This was Thomas Allsop, a young stockbroker who was only twenty-three years old but with intellectual interests, who introduced himself to Coleridge in a note handed to him just before his first lecture. The following day Coleridge replied to it, disclaiming appreciation of flattery, but accepting the young man's admiration and his suggestions of some addition to the syllabus. "Believe me," Coleridge concluded, "with great respect, your obliged fellow-student of the true and the beseeming." The extreme graciousness of Coleridge's reply combines with Allsop's later generosity toward him to suggest that in some way Allsop's generous nature revealed itself in his introductory letter.

A close intimacy with Allsop, both epistolary and personal, quickly followed and continued for many years. Coleridge was often Allsop's guest and met prominent political or literary persons at his house. Often, too, Allsop was Coleridge's guest at Highgate. On one of the rare occasions when Coleridge quarreled with Gillman, it was with Allsop that he found a temporary refuge.

Whether Coleridge was aware of it or not, Peacock's satirical interest in him

---

*Kathleen Coburn, ed. *The Philosophical Lectures of S. T. Coleridge* (New York: Philosophical Library, 1949), p. 37.

had by no means ceased. In November 1818 Peacock's new novel *Nightmare Abbey*, presenting Coleridge as Mr. Elosky, "a very lachrymose and morbid gentleman, of some note in the literary world but in his own estimation of much more merit than name," added new touches to Peacock's satirical portrait.

Shortly before the close of these lectures Coleridge's occasional sympathy for the sufferings of the poor, which had led him recently to oppose the Corn Law, led him to support with similar enthusiasm the Cotton Factory Bill which attempted to prevent the employment of children in factories. Sir Robert Peel's Bill he now supported with unusual energy, denouncing the employment of children in factories as "soul-murder and infanticide," and the members of Parliament who opposed the bill as representing "Boroughs in hell . . . " As for the poor children, "whose condition is an abomination which has weighed on my feelings from earliest manhood, I having been indeed an eye-witness of the direful effects" of such employment.

Now momentarily remote from the political attitude of his "Lay Sermons," he rhetorically asked Green "whether some half score of rich capitalists are to be prevented from suborning suicide and perpetrating infanticide and soul-murder." This call for action even drew Coleridge from his Highgate retreat to the Spring Garden Coffee House in London, "for which," he said, "no inducement would have been sufficient, but the belief that it was my duty." In this belief he had gone to London to discover the *Courier*'s attitude in this crisis: What was Mudford's opinion, he asked, on "1) The poor Laws, and the state of the labourers, agricultural and manufacturing, at large; 2) the education of this class; 3) the necessity of a corresponding education of the higher and middle classes; 4) the state of the punitive laws; 5) the existing state of the Press, etc" In April 1818 Coleridge published two pamphlets* that he had written on the subject, mainly directed to points that he had discussed with Mudford and written in his early admirable, direct journalistic style, so different from his now usually involved, prolix, "serpentine" manner which in his notebooks he had associated with "genius." When on the last day of the month the bill was passed by the Commons, Coleridge told a friend with a touch of complacency: "I have reason to think that my efforts have not been without their effect." Nonetheless, Coleridge was by no means blind to his self-sacrifice in supporting the bill: "Heaven knows," he told Robinson while awaiting the fate of the bill in the Lords "I am seriously hurting myself in devoting my days daily in this my best harvest-tide as a lecture-monger, so that I am most disinterestedly interested in the fate of the measure, yet interested I am."

---

*Remarks on the objections which have been urged against the principle of Sir Robert Peel's Bill, 1818" and "The Grounds of Sir Robert Peel's Bill vindicated, 1818." No other edition of these pamphlets was published, except one privately printed in 1913. A year after the appearance of the pamphlets Peel's Bill was finally passed by Parliament as a whole.

On January 26, 1822, Coleridge wrote to Murray suggesting the publication of a new volume entitled *Aids to Reflection in the formation of manly character on the several grounds of Prudence, Morality, and Religion: Illustrated by select Passages from our elder Divines, especially from Archbishop Leighton*. Murray did not publish the work, which was shortly afterwards accepted by Taylor & Hessey and appeared in 1825.

To Taylor & Hessey on August 8, 1823, Coleridge described the volume thus: *"Aids to Reflection*: or Beauties and Characteristics of Archbishop Leighton extracted from his various wirtings and arranged on a principle of connection under the three heads of 1) Philosophical and miscellaneous. 2)Moral and Prudential. 3)Spiritual—with a life of Leighton and a critique of his writings and opinions—with Notes throughout by the Editor." The first edition appeared with a long list of corrections, and the presentation copies had as many more added in manuscript.

The *Aids to Reflection* became the most popular of Coleridge's prose works and was greatly appreciated by certain religious circles in England and in America. Various distinguished persons at the time expressed their deep appreciation of the book; Julius Hare considered Coleridge to be "the true sovereign of modern English thought," and, among others, Frederick Dennison Maurice and John Sterling felt that they "owed even their own selves" to the *Aids to Reflection*. Irving, too, was an admirer and so was the Bishop of London, William Howley, who delighted Coleridge by sending him a letter of commendation after reading the work. Although Coleridge asserted that his publisher Taylor was converted by the *Aids*, John Henry Newman, the most famous of contemporary theologians, was much shocked by it, calling it "a liberty of speculation which no Christian can tolerate—conclusions which were often heathen rather than Christian."

As usual with Coleridge's works the publication of the *Aids to Reflection* brought him little material satisfaction. He complained of a lack of financial success, and of neglect or abuse by the professional citics. "I have not had interest enough," he told a friend, "to procure by *Aids to Reflection* even a mention in any one of our numerous Reviews, Magazines, or Literary Gazettes—but on the other hand, numerous Detractors have been successfully industrious in exciting a prejudice in the minds of the London publishers against any work from my pen, as obscure, brain-wrenching and unsaleable."

Coleridge would have found little consolation in the comments of his biographer H. D. Traill in 1884 on the *Aids to Reflection*. "There seems to me to be less charm of thought," he wrote, "less beauty of style, less even of Coleridge's seldom-failing force of effective statement, in the *Aids to Reflection* than in almost any of his writings." He continued:

As a religious manual it is easy to understand how this volume of Coleridge's should have obtained many and earnest readers. What religious manual, which shows traces of spiritual insight, or even merely of pious yearnings after higher and holier than earthly things, has ever failed to win such readers among the weary and heavy-laden of the world? And that Coleridge, a writer of the most penetrating glance into divine mysteries, and writing always from a soul all tremulous, as it were, with religious sensibility, should have obtained such readers in abundance is not surprising. But to a critic and literary biographer I cannot think that his success in this respect has much to say.

Oliver Elton, thirty-six years after Traill, began a discussion of the *Aids to Reflection*, with as little enthusiasm as that of Traill. "Coleridge," he said, "hardly wrote anything in prose that can be called a book, though we can carve one out of the midst of *Biographia Literaria*. His *Friend*, *Aids to Reflection*, and the like are mostly aggregations of formless discourses, circling in each case round certain leading ideas, but scattering off into meteor-fragments." Elton's brief analysis of the work gives us, however, a clearer understanding of it than do most critics:

> What may be called the missionary prose of Coleridge is also well seen in his *Aids to Reflection*, which aims at sketching for the plain, convinced, and cultivated rather than scholarly Christian, a rational groundwork for his faith, in its connection with pure philosophy on the one shore and on the other with the truth given by spiritual experience; the bridge being laid, as we should expect, across the depths of moral psychology, in which Coleridge is so painfully at home. The Kantian distinction between the "reason" and the "understanding" he interprets as severing the faculty that gives us the higher truths immediately, from that which works in a lower and more limited way, in the empirical field and through logical categories.

Coleridge regarded the *Aids* as only part of his great philosophic design (never realized), the *Logosophia*. A second edition of the *Aids* appeared in 1831, and for the next twenty years the book was frequently republished in England and in America.

One last work from Coleridge's pen appeared five years after the *Aids to Reflection*; it was entitled *On the Constitution of the Church and State, according to the idea of each; with aids towards a right judgment on the late Catholic Bill*. This tractate even the critical Elton described as Coleridge's "one shapely and orderly work in prose," and "the most lucid and able product of his reasoned conservatism. It is a most skilful attempt to rest Church and State in their British guise on a high philosophic basis, by defining and connecting the essential idea of each!"

Coleridge analyzes the "State" into: the "Landowning Nobility" who create the House of Lords; the "Mercantile Classes"; and the "Labouring and the Professional Classes" who form the House of Commons. The king is the head of all, or rather the "beam of the balance" as to the "duties and privileges of each class." Coleridge includes in this work a vindication of the clergy, or to use his own word for them, the "Clerisy."

For Coleridge this "Church," together with the secular groups, forms the "State." For his "idea" or ideal Coleridge, in effect, goes back to the Middle Ages. The "Clerisy" are not only concerned with theology and worship, but also with men's brains as well as with their souls. Their task is to maintain the true historical feelings and the national and immortal life of the country. One result of Coleridge's book was the reputation of being a High-Churchman and Tory and of originating ideas which ultimately led to the Oxford Movement. Before the close of the year of its publication, 1830, a second edition of *Church and State* appeared.

Nevertheless, *Church and State* apparently found no more favor with the professional critics than the *Aids to Reflection* had. Hazlitt died in 1830, but John Wilson now ridiculed Coleridge in the September 1831 number of *Blackwood's Magazine*, in a style which again suggests a somewhat crude imitation of Hazlitt. Writing under the pseudonym of "Christopher North," he compared Coleridge with the sun that glorifies everything it shines upon, and with the "affable Archangel Raphael in the Garden of Eden." He continued, "Simpletons say he knows nothing of science; we have heard him on chemistry puzzle Sir Humphry Davy—and prove to our entire satisfaction that Leibnitz and Newton, though good men, were but indifferent astronomers. Besides, he thinks nothing of inventing a new science, with a complete nomenclature, in a twinkling . . . We only know that Coleridge is the alchemist that in his crucible melts down hours to moments—and lo! diamonds sprinkled on a plate of gold!"

Early in February 1832 Coleridge vainly attempted, through Henry Nelson Coleridge, to persuade Wilson as editor of *Blackwood's Magazine* to publish several of his essays. When by May 26, 1832, no reviews of Coleridge's writings to encourage the republication of *Church and State* had appeared, Coleridge wrote to Blackwood himself to further his aim. "I should accuse myself of cowardice and ingratitude," he wrote, "if I hesitated to avow and assert my conviction that in the long, never flagging Height and Sustainedness of irony, in the continuity, variety and strength of wing, and in the value, the worth, the deep importance of the moral and political truths which it has streamed forth with eloquent wisdom, '*Blackwood's Magazine*' is an unprecedented Phenomenon in the world of letters, and forms the golden—alas! the only—remaining link between the Periodical Press and the enduring literature of Great Britain."

Having thus paved the way for repeating the request for Blackwood's support of his work, Coleridge continued:

> Having now given the relief of an outlet to the "gathering of the waters," to the feelings and convictions that have so long been astir within me, do me the justice to believe that it is from far other impulses than those of authorial vanity and craving for praise that I give vent to my regret that no notice was taken of my "Essay on the Constitution of Church and State according to the Idea of each," a copy of both the first and second edition of which I expressly desired the Publisher to transmit to you.

4 Life with the Gillmans (1816-30)

"I feel more and more that I can be well off no where away from you and Gillman."
—*Coleridge to Mrs. Gillman, June 17, 1818*

"I never did know the Master and Mistress of a Household, and the Household in consequence so estimable and so amiable as the Gillmans! . . . *God bless them!"*
—*Coleridge to an unknown correspondent, October 20, 1829*

From the time of Coleridge's entry into their Highgate home, the progress and vicissitudes of his friendship with the Gillmans naturally became one of the chief interests in his life. Nevertheless, by the irony of fate opium—the cause of Coleridge's acquaintance with the Gillmans—was also an ever present danger to their friendship. Mr. Gillman, warned by Coleridge himself to prevent surreptitious additions to his allowance of the drug, had appointed Mrs. Gillman to watch over Coleridge and, if necessary, to protect him from himself.

Not until May 1818, two years after his first period of domicile with the Gillmans, did Coleridge leave their home for a short time. On this occasion the cause was political and humanitarian, a dash to London to help the cause of the factory children. The next occasion on which he temporarily deserted the Gillmans was a visit of a fortnight's duration to Green's parents in their pleasant home near Maldon in Essex. On June 17 he wrote to Mrs. Gillman, "My very dear Sister and Friend," describing his pleasant environment: "the gardens . . . a perfect blaze of roses, yet I feel I do not receive the fifth part of the delight which I derived from the flower pots at Highgate so tended and worshipped by me." He continued, "Indeed, I actually make up a flower pot every night in order to imitate my Highgate Pleasures." Mrs. Gillman also had to be assured that she had no rival in his present hostess. Mrs. Green, it appeared, "in 20 years would never be above or beyond *liking* . . . she wants a *soothingness*, a something I do not know what, that is tender."

Mrs. Gillman's natural impatience for Coleridge's return also had to be placated. To return immediately, he emphasized, was impossible "without great unkindness." Unfortunately, his philosophical studies with Green, he explained, would detain him for a few more days. Mrs. Gillman, moreover, had to be left in no doubt of his preference for Highgate:

> Do not take it as words of course when I say and solemnly assure you, that if I followed my own wishes, I should leave this place on Saturday morning: for I feel more and more that I can be well off no where away from you and Gillman—May God bless him! for a dear friend he is and has been to me. Again and again and again, God bless you my dear friends, for I am and ever trust to remain, more than can be expressed, my dear Anne! Your affectionate, obliged and grateful, S. T. Coleridge.

The following October, when the new edition of the *Friend* appeared, it carried the following dedication: "To Mr and Mrs Gillman, of Highgate, these volumes are dedicated, in testimony of high respect and grateful affection, by their friend, S. T. Coleridge."

From the first Coleridge was happy in Highgate. The environment, in fact, attracted him on the one hand by its scenic beauty and on the other by its facilities for distinguished social intercourse. The first appealed to his love of silent contemplation, the second to his equally strong social instinct. So situated, comfortably ensconced with the fascinated Gillmans, and within easy reach of the town, Coleridge naturally felt no inclination to quit Highgate and remained there until the end of his life. His appreciation of the natural beauty in Highgate found occasional expression in his letters and was also remarked on by some of his friends. Highgate in May Coleridge found especially attractive in this way, and in the same month three years later he rhapsodized to a Cambridge acquaintance on "the paradisiacal loveliness of the walks about here—above all, of Caen Wood. As to nightingales—they are almost as numerous with us and as incessant in song as the frogs with you!" Nightingales particularly appealed to Coleridge, and Leslie the painter, his neighbor, described how, when Coleridge heard them on one occasion as he and Leslie walked in a Highgate Lane, "he easily distinguished and pointed out to me their full rich notes among those of other birds."

Coleridge's love of Highgate and its beauty deepened with the passing years. This we see in Leigh Hunt's description of Coleridge in 1828 in *Lord Byron and Some of His Contemporaries*:

> Mr Coleridge is fat, and begins to lament, in very delightful verses, that he is getting infirm. There is no old age in his verses. I heard him the other day, under the grove at Highgate, repeat one of his melodious lamentations as he walked up and down , his voice undulating in a stream of music, and his regrets of youth sparkling with visions ever young . . . . It is no secret that Mr Coleridge lives in the Grove at Highgate with a friendly family, who have sense and kindness enough to know that they do themselves an honour by looking after the comforts of such a man. His room looks upon a delicious prospect of wood and meadow, with coloured gardens under the window, like an embroidery to the mantle. I thought, when I first saw it, that he had taken up his dwelling-place like an abbot. Here he cultivates his flowers and has a set of birds for his pensioners, who come to breakfast

with him. He may be seen taking his daily stroll up and down, with his black coat and white locks, and a book in his hand; and is a great acquaintance of the little children. His main occupation I believe, is reading. He loves to read old folios, and to make old voyages with Purchas and Marco Polo; the seas being in good visionary condition, and the vessel well-stocked with botargoes.

Coleridge's amusement at Leigh Hunt's portrait of him was doubtless due to his recognition of its essential truthfulness and kindliness.

Yet, however bright the prospect at the Gillmans, the opium cloud loomed ever on the horizon. Such was the case at Ramsgate in the autumn of 1822, after Gillman had returned to Highgate and Coleridge remained with Mrs. Gillman and her sister, Miss Harding. After Gillman's departure Coleridge, probably to indulge his craving for opium, took a room for himself in another house. His excuse was to be nearer a favorite bathing place. But he also complained to Gillman of feeling a dyspathy at meals when alone with Mrs. Gillman and Miss Harding. The "dyspathy" that appeared at Ramsgate was still in evidence after Coleridge and Mrs. Gillman returned to Highgate. After disagreeing with Mrs. Gillman's dismissal of a servant for flirting with a visitor, Coleridge left the house and wrote to Mrs. Gillman, reproaching her for "the manner in which you broke away from me."

Toward the close of 1823, while Coleridge and Mrs. Gillman were again at Ramsgate enjoying their usual autumn holiday, Mr. Gillman superintended the move from Moreton House to another Highgate house, No. 3 The Grove. Charles Lamb, paying his first visit with Mary to the new house, gloomily foreboded evil consequences for its inhabitants. Lamb's words—as Coleridge later remembered them—were, "that they had never known a valued family change their old dwelling for a grander house and finer chattels without leaving the better part of themselves and their happiness behind." Lamb's fears were quickly justified, for before the close of the month Mrs. Gillman, who was in a nervous state, slipped and fell on the unfamiliar stair.

On December 10, 1823, Coleridge, much moved by the accident, described it in dramatic detail to Allsop, remarking that he had recently warned Mrs. Gillman "with some acerbity" to be careful of such a mishap.

Mrs Gillman in stepping from my Attic slipt on the first step of a steep flight of nine high stairs, precipitated herself and fell head foremost on the fifth stair, turned head over heels, & when at the piercing scream I rushed out, I found her on her back on the Landing place, her head at the wall, her feet and legs on the two last stairs . . . the small bone of her right arm was broken & her wrist sprained—no fever supervened—and her nerves are nearly restored to their former tranquillity. Even now the Image and the terror of the Image blends with the recollection of the Past a strange expectancy, a fearful sense as of a something still to come.

Shortly afterward Coleridge sent other more exaggerated accounts of the accident to Mrs. Aders and to the publisher Hessey.

Late in March 1824 the harmony of the Gillman ménage was woefully disrupted when Coleridge's secret purchases of opium beyond the limit allowed by Gillman were discovered. The usually mild Mr. Gillman actually lost his temper and Coleridge fled to the Allsops. To make matters worse—and perhaps also his temper—Dr. Gillman was suffering badly from a fresh attack of blood poisoning in one arm due to an injury which dated from a postmortem examination nine years before. At the same time Mrs. Gillman, in an anxious state, had gone to London—obeying, she said, her husband's command.

Coleridge remained some ten days with the Allsops until Mr. Gillman discovered him there and, on April 7, triumphantly bore him back in a coach to Highgate. Alone with the sick Gillman who returned to bed, Coleridge, "almost hysterical," remained to tend him, and after two days, as Gillman refused all professional attendance, he begged Green to come and if possible to bring another doctor with him.

Meanwhile Mrs. Gillman, anxiously but vainly awaiting a letter from Coleridge or at least from Allsop, remained in Chelsea haunted by fears of a permanent separation from Coleridge. In this state and unaware that even as she wrote Coleridge was being brought back to The Grove, Mrs. Gillman sent him a heartfelt letter of self-reproach, fearing that "my cool behaviour" had caused Coleridge's flight to Allsop. "Yet," she wrote,

indeed I feel for you *as formerly*, and know not how to bear up against the fear of losing you. If you have been in despair take courage, a *little* time, patience and *prudence* will set all to rights, and we may once more all three be happy. Gillman thinks you want to leave us. Pray come to me here if you do not judge wrong. Mr. G would not disapprove it I am sure. Only convince him that you love him and will not be so inconsiderate again, and all will yet be well. I will learn a lesson and not suffer my own impatience at your faults, for so I call them, to put me so much out.

If Coleridge could not or would not write to her, then Allsop must, she added—Indeed, if he did not come to her, Allsop must do so, and her letter ended in a final impassioned appeal for a return to the *status quo ante*:

I scarcely know how to appear tranquil and wish like you I could abstract myself from my heartfelt pain even for a short time. I shall call on you as I return home. . . . I do reproach myself bitterly, but as yet have said little to Mr Gillman—for as far as he is concerned you have been sadly in fault, and it is best perhaps to let just anger pass by a little. He is likewise much hurt about your Book [*Aids to Reflection*] not being out, and this appears reasonable. But still I do believe that things may yet be settled— . . . My ignorance and suspense are very painful. Gillman loves you so much, I am sure if things are well arranged matters may be adjusted. And I feel confident that the happiness, perhaps well doing of all *three* is concerned, so do not let us two suffer pride or temper to interfere in such a serious affair where there exists so much love. I should not write this but that I am persuaded of your attachment being unaltered . . . I wish above all things to see you. Yours as ever,—A. G.

When Mrs. Gillman returned home ten days later she must have found Coleridge there also. So after this storm in a teacup, life at the Gillmans' soon returned to its former tranquillity. The day after Mrs. Gillman's return was, as Coleridge did not fail to remember, "the eighth Anniversary of my Domestication at Highgate!" A week later he told Allsop: "Mrs. Gillman is much better—and all goes on with much kindness and kind attentions, which in part I attribute, perhaps erroneously, to some conversation on the subject between you and her—I am content, well knowing that the genial glow of Friendship once deadened can never be rekindled."

It is not surprising in the circumstances that scandal connected Coleridge's name with Mrs. Gillman's. Charles Lamb first heard of it when dining that summer with a parson, who had been his and Coleridge's contemporary at Christ's Hospital. "After dinner," Lamb told Robinson in November,

> we talked of Coleridge, and F who is a mighty good fellow in the main, but hath his cassock prejudices, inveighed against him on the moral character of Coleridge. I endeavoured to enlighten him on the subject, till having driven him out of some of his holds, he stopt my mouth at once by appealing to me whether it was not very well known that Coleridge "at that very moment was living in a state of open adultery with Mrs. Gillman at Highgate?" Nothing I could say serious or bantering after that could remove the deep inrooted conviction of the whole company assembled that such was the case!

Before the close of the year 1824 Coleridge's old relations with the Gillmans had been restored. At Ramsgate with Mrs. Gillman, Coleridge was worried by sympathetic feelings for the absent Dr. Gillman, whose troubles at this time were complicated and exacting. To Gillman, still haunted by his hydrophobia thesis, Coleridge now offered the consolation of a new theory, no longer based on Coleridge's "philosophy" but on his "scientific" understanding of the problem; i.e., "that the nerves act on the brain or central power, but that the brain does not act on the nerves."

But worse than hydrophobia for Gillman was his recent defeat in an election, apparently for some medical distinction. This defeat he attributed to the machinations of an unscrupulous rival. Coleridge's involvement in the affair is obscure, but his many letters to Gillman of sympathy and self-vindication occupied a large portion of his time when he was at Ramsgate in 1824. Mrs. Gillman, too, was unhappy at Ramsgate, wishing to be near her husband in his misery. For Mr. Gillman was, almost in Coleridgian fashion, broken-hearted. Thus it was that Coleridge came to compare, for Gillman's benefit, Mrs. Gillman's virtues with his own. "Need I say," he told a friend, "that I have had the same feeling tho' there is this shade of difference between the characters of your friend and your wife, that she is more haunted by the Past and especially by regrets where she seems to herself to have been out of the way when there was a duty of Business or Feeling to be performed—while I am more prone to project my thoughts and anxieties into the Future."

Immediately there followed a new misery for poor Mr. Gillman due to the rivalry of parties wanting or opposing a new school chapel at Highgate. "Mrs. Gillman," he said, "is silent, but sorely cut at heart—tho' she says it is only her head." Whether Mrs. Gillman's unhappiness was for her husband or for Coleridge's continual desire to leave her at Ramsgate and join him is perhaps, "like the Song of the Sirens," as Sir Thomas Browne once wrote, "not beyond conjecture." Had she discovered that, despite the upheaval in the Gillman home a few months before caused by Coleridge's secret purchases of opium, he was still acting in the same way?

Almost immediately after receiving Mrs. Gillman's emotional letter in April, Coleridge used some of the hundred pounds he had received from the Royal Society of Literature, upon their election of himself as an Associate, to pay the local chemist, Dunn. To Dunn he owed £25 which, apologizing for long delay, he now promised to send him, explaining that an earlier settlement was impossible without "imprudent exposures." Finally he ordered Dunn: "Destroy this instantly." Whether Dunn's bill was paid now or not, Coleridge was again apologizing to Dunn five months later for further delays in payment, while at the same time he ordered additional supplies of opium, which Coleridge considered necessary for work even if not for life. The chemist's apprentice used to fill Coleridge's laudanum bottle, which held "a twelve ounce pint," every five days—for Coleridge's calls for such refills were far more regular than his payments.

Early in February Coleridge, writing to Allsop, whose letter he had just received, gives us one of the few intimate glimpses of his domestic life with the Gillmans: "It was eleven o'clock this morning when Mrs. Gillman brought up your letter—and as soon as I had shaved and shifted, which from a distressful night and increased pain in a wrong place, altho' in *recto* I could not accomplish till 12, I walked out to con over the letter."

A few days later Coleridge sent Allsop another, less pleasant glimpse of his domestic life. Mrs. Gillman by this time, after nine years' life with Coleridge, was (like Lloyd and others who at one time or another were closely associated with Coleridge) falling into a state of permanent anxiety. Coleridge was, he told Allsop, "almost incapacitated from thinking of and doing any thing as it ought to be done, by poor Mrs. Gillman's restless and *interrogatory* anxieties, which in the first instance put the whole working hive of my thoughts into a whirl and a buzz, and then, when I see her care-worn countenance and reflect on the state of her health, (and it is difficult to say which of the two, ill-health or habitual anxiety is more cause and more effect) a sharp fit of the heart-ache follows." Mrs. Gillman's disappointments with Coleridge were increasing as she lost faith in her ability to cure him of his weaknesses. The shock to her of the secret supplies of opium was still active. Was she aware, a week after Coleridge's present complaint, that another little note had gone to Dunn promising early repayment of the debt with interest, as "the last sheet of my work is now going to the press?" Mrs. Gillman, disheartened by Coleridge's endless delays and excuses for unfinished work, was, in her anxiety for his welfare—perhaps also for the repayment of his debts to her husband—so pressing him as to disturb his own temper. "There is no medium," Coleridge continued with evident exasperation to Allsop, "either the unworthy notice-exciting *Unnoticing* and feverish mock-indifference of a quarrel, or to be fidget-watched and 'are you going on?'—'what are you doing now?'—'is this for the book?' &c &c. Precisely as if I were Henry at his lesson." A month later he told Tulk, "Mrs. Gillman being inexpressibly dear and valuable in my eyes. . .has been evidently declining since that dreadful fall."

This late spring of 1825 brought Coleridge fears not only of the loss of friendship, but even of Mrs. Gillman's death. There was illness everywhere in the new house at the Grove. "We have had a continued succession of illnesses, in our family here," he told John Taylor Coleridge on April 8: "at one time six persons confined to their beds. I have been sadly afraid that we should lose Mrs. Gillman, who would be a loss indeed to the whole neighbourhood— young and old." A fortnight later he told Derwent: "Mrs. Gillman, I am sorry to say, is rather declining than advancing—Good God! what a loss she will be, should it please God to take her!" Fortunately, Coleridge's fears proved unfounded; for Mrs. Gillman outlived both Coleridge and her husband.

With summer came a new responsibility for Coleridge: that of the Gillmans' younger son Henry, who had spent a year in a local school and, as it seemed to his mother, had not merely wasted his time but lost all power of attention. Mrs. Gillman was in sad straits about him. "That dear and excellent woman," Coleridge told his nephew Edward, the Eton master, "Mrs. Gillman, has for the last two months or more eat, drank, woke, slept, thought, dreamed nothing but Henry Gillman and Eton College," the school to which Henry was now to be sent. "Poor lady! it makes my very heart ache to see her, worn as she is to a shadow—grieving and mourning" at poor Henry's present state. Little Henry was a nervous child, which is hardly surprising for one of his age living in the Gillmans' home. In these circumstances Coleridge came to his rescue and conducted him to Eton, where his nephew Edward was expected to be a tower of strength for the boy, the Gillmans, and Coleridge himself. On July 24, 1825, safe at Eton with Henry, Coleridge reported the results of his mission to the Gillmans: "All things equal to our wish and perhaps beyond our expectations." Henry was placed in the fourth form and would be elected into college the next day.

Nor did Coleridge fail to make an impression at Eton. "I raised the House last night by the long and loud screams and distressful noises in my sleep," he told the Gillmans; "I was quite unconscious of what had occurred in the morning—I doubt not this often happens; but at Highgate I am not so within hearing." Despite this incident Coleridge was well satisfied with his own reception at Eton. "*Nothing* can *surpass*," he wrote, "the flattering attention that has been shewn me by the Provost, Dr. Keates, Fellows &c, &c" and Henry was "so good a boy" that Coleridge allowed him to describe everything himself in a letter to his parents. However, Coleridge's report on him to his nephew Edward, when Henry was about to enter Eton, was less appreciative.

Illness, of course, had prevented Coleridge from concentrating upon Henry's education during this interval as fully as he had wished, but "if I had the strength and the conveniences of *flogging* him, instead of scolding or confining, more would have been done."

But soon there came bad news from Eton. Henry was unsatisfactory and must be sent home. So on October 20, which as usual he mistook for his birthday, Coleridge set off to bring the little sinner back, forbidding either Mr. or Mrs. Gillman to accompany him. Coleridge's mediation was so successful that Henry was allowed to remain at Eton. Henry, however, was incorrigible, and soon the Gillmans received another notice of his expulsion from the school. On this occasion Coleridge retired from the scene and Henry's elder brother James brought the boy to town and put him on the boat for Ramsgate, where Coleridge, Mrs. Gillman and her friends and relations were taking their usual holiday. Henry's downfall affected both Mr. and Mrs. Gillman with nervous fears for their son's future. Even worse was poor Henry's rejection after Eton by a local school near Ramsgate. Finally Henry found a refuge in Shrewsbury School.

Coleridge's position as one of the Gillman family was now well established. The affection that they felt toward him was as great as if he had been a child of their own. His gentle, pleasant manner, the aura of intellectual distinction which he exhaled, the important people he increasingly brought to Highgate, all blended to strengthen the ties which bound the Gillmans to him; these only a rare fit of petulance ever broke. In general, the domestic harmony in the Gillmans' home was evidently perfect. Such was the case at the beginning of May 1827, when Mrs. Gillman left in Coleridge's room a pot of myrtle. This quickly inspired a most flowery letter of thanks. The myrtle, he emphasized, would endure "in the rich innocence of its snow-white blossoms!" when the rose, eglantine, honeysuckle, and jasmin had all perished. So with Mrs. Gillman's myrtle, "Our own myrtle plant remains unchanged, its blossoms are remembered the more to endear the faithful bearer."

Nor were Coleridge's attentions to Mrs. Gillman entirely confined to sentimentalities. A few months later, in a more practical mood to assist Mrs. Gillman's return to health, he for the moment reversed their usual roles of protecting and protected and persuaded Mrs. Gillman to drink a little wine. In a letter to a friend Coleridge delightfully described the incident: "Tho' the Constantia, is a most exquisite Cordial—for Mrs. Gillman being rather weakly and dining by herself at an early hour, I insisted on opening a Bottle for her, in the belief that as she scarcely ever tastes wine, a small glass daily for four or five days would speed her convalescence,—and tasted it myself, so as to be able to confirm her judgement." Fortunately, the wine met with his approval and, as he said, he was "learned enough in the Heraldry of Wine."

Very practical, too, were the instructions and exhortations that Coleridge now sent young James Gillman upon his entry to St. Johns at Oxford, inculcating undeviating devotion to his studies both secular and religious. Coleridge's opinion of humanity, as expressed at this time to Mr. Aders,

strongly contrasted with his attitude toward young James. "The older I am,"
he wrote, "the more charitable I grow, and the worse I think of men in
general, an apparent paradox; but a truth which every man who both *thinks*
and feels, will sooner or later find the truth of."

The summer of 1828 was a time of Continental travel for both Dr. Gillman
and Coleridge, but not together. Dr. Gillman, as medical adviser to the Duke
and Duchess of St. Albans, accompanied them on a tour of the Continent. On
June 21 Coleridge, with Wordsworth and his daughter Dora, left for the
Continent and did not return until August 6. During these weeks they visited
Belgium, the Rhineland, and Holland.

The tour did not pass unrecorded by observers. In Brussels they met an
English writer and journalist, Thomas Colley Grattan, who accompanied the
party to the field of Waterloo and for three days along the Meuse. Grattan,
who described the experience, was much impressed by Coleridge's monologues. These included a denunciation of Newton's theory of light, which
neither Coleridge nor Grattan understood, and also a wide variety of Coleridge's favorite subjects—grammar, natural beauty, painting, etc. Grattan,
profoundly impressed, noted that "in everything that fell from Coleridge that
evening there was a dash of deep philosophy." Nevertheless, Grattan's ecstatic
appreciation of Coleridge's talk concluded on a surprisingly sober note:

> Coleridge's talk was not absolutely tiresome, only somewhat drowsy. I
> thought it would be pleasant to fall asleep to the gushing melody of his
> discourse, which was rich in information and suavity of thought. But
> there was something too dreamy, too vapoury to rouse one to the close
> examination of what he said. Logic there no doubt was, but it was
> enveloped in clouds. You were therefore delighted to take everything for
> granted, for everything seemed to convince—because it took a shape and
> colour so seductive.

Like Grattan, Coleridge's more critical listeners too often found Coleridge's
talk fairy gold which, beyond his mesmeric influence, and in the cold light of
reason, lost its glitter and charm.

By contrast with Coleridge, Wordsworth was unimpressive and disappointing: "at times fluent but always commonplace," said Grattan. Wordsworth,
he found, merely spoke of the aspects of the scenery through which they
passed and did not, like Coleridge, couple it with "moral beauty." Wordsworth, he said, "did not talk well. But in fact he had no encouragement. He
had few listeners; and what seemed rather repulsive in him was perhaps chiefly
from it's grating contrast to the wonderful attraction of Coleridge."

At Godesberg where the wealthy Aders had a castle, Mrs. Aders was hostess
to Coleridge and his party. Another guest already there, a young man from
Oxford—Julian Charles Young—Mrs. Aders mystified by pressing him to
remain until some distinguished guests, whom she expected but refused to
name, arrived the next day.

To Young's meeting with Coleridge and Wordsworth the next morning we owe an inimitable description of the two poets on their tour. "I had scarcely entered the room," wrote Young,

and was trying to improve a bad sketch I had made the day before, when an old gentleman entered with a large quarto volume beneath his arm, whom I at once concluded to be one of the anonymous gentry about whose personality there had been so much mystery. As he entered I rose and bowed. Whether he was conscious of my well-intentioned civility I cannot say, but at all events he did not return my salutation. He appeared preoccupied with his own cogitations. I began to conjecture what manner of man he was. His general appearance would have led me to suppose him a dissenting minister. His hair was long, white and neglected; his complexion was florid, his features were square, his eyes watery and hazy, his brow broad and massive, his build uncouth, his deportment grave and abstracted. He wore a white starchless neckcloth tied in a limp bow, and was dressed in a shabby suit of dusky black. His breeches were unbuttoned at the knee, his sturdy limbs were encased in stockings of lavender-coloured worsted, his feet were thrust into well-worn slippers, much trodden down at heel. In his ungainly attire he paced up and down, and down and up, and round and round a saloon, sixty feet square, with head bent forward, and shoulders stooping, absently musing and muttering to himself, and occasionally clutching to his side his ponderous tome, as if he feared it might be taken from him. I confess my young spirit chafed under the wearing quarter-deck monotony of his promenade and, stung by the cool manner in which he ignored my presence, I was about to leave him in undisputed possession of the field, when I was diverted from my purpose by the entrance of another gentleman whose kindly smile and courteous recognition of my bow, encouraged me to keep my ground, and promised me some compensation for the slight put upon me by his precursor. He was dressed in a brown holland blouse; he held in his left hand an alpenstock, (on the top of which he had placed the broad-brimmed "wide-awake" he had just taken off), and in his right a sprig of apple-blossom over-grown with lichen. His cheeks were glowing with the effects of recent exercise. So noiseless had been his entry that the peripatetic philosopher, whose back was turned to him at first, was unaware of his presence. But no sooner did he discover it than he shuffled up to him, grasped him by both hands, and backed him bodily into a neighbouring armchair. Having secured him safely there, he "made assurance doubly sure" by hanging over him so as to bar his escape, while he delivered his testimony on the fallacy of certain of Bishop Berkeley's propositions, in detecting which, he said he had opened a rich vein of original reflection. Not content with cursory criticism, he plunged profoundly into a metaphysical lecture which, but for the opportune intrusion of our fair hostess and her young lady friend, might have lasted until dinner time. It was then, for the first time, I learned who the party consisted of and I was introduced to Samuel Taylor Coleridge, William Wordsworth and his daughter Dora.

As news of the presence of the two poets spread, the neighboring intellectuals, including Niebuhr the historian and Schlegel, flocked to the Aders' castle to meet them. In Brussels Coleridge had pontificated upon the German language, "upon which subject," said Grattan, "he was quite at home." But at Godesberg Coleridge's German was so weak that Schlegel, the only English-speaking German among them, begged him to speak English: "Mein lieber Herr," said Schlegel to Coleridge, "would you speak English: I understand it; but your German I cannot follow." So as formerly with Tieck, they conversed in English. To soften the impasse, Coleridge and Schlegel indulged in mutual compliments on each others' translations. But soon, in discussing Byron and Scott, they differed. When Schlegel praised the two poets, Coleridge decried them—Scott for having "so few quotable passages"; while Byron, he declared, "is a meteor, Wordsworth is a fixed star."

While at Godesberg Wordsworth attended a banquet given by Mrs. Aders on July 6 although her husband was in London. The occasion was the anniversary of the Aders' wedding day. Coleridge, unfortunately, was too ill to be present. Comedy, however, was not lacking as Mrs. Aders described the scene to Robinson, including "the awe which the poets of the two nations had, one of the other, except Schlegel who 'entertained' Wordsworth in English by abusing England through thick and thin." When one of the ladies present asked Schlegel "to repeat some lines in honour of the day," Schlegel asked Wordsworth to do it. Wordsworth obeyed but "declared that he preferred good plain prose on such occasions and proposed a toast in a few words. Whereupon two other ladies "left the room and composed some satirical rhymes upon the want of gallantry and promptness of the Poets of our Day, which were read with great delight, and all the cakes and dishes were stript of their flowers to crown the young poetesses." Doubtless the wine was better than the ladies' verses.

During their two or three weeks together and particularly during a journey down the Rhine to Bingen, the observant Young accompanied them and recorded many interesting aspects of the two poets' mutual relationship. Like Grattan, Young remarked that Wordsworth let Coleridge do all the talking, but noted the beauties of the scenery himself as to one of equal mind, and showed the same attitude and pleasure in talking to children. But Coleridge talked as if to display his superior knowledge and intelligence and made Young feel awkwardly inferior as so much was unintelligible to him. Despite their vanity, said Young, the poets showed no mutual jealousy. Wordsworth's silence, he found, was due to consideration for Coleridge's "inordinate loquacity." Coleridge, he said, "always speechified or preached." But the two poets were not uncritical of each other when talking to Young alone. "Wordsworth," he said, "in speaking of Coleridge, would admit, though most regretfully, the moral flaws of his character, for instance, his addiction to opium, his ungrateful conduct to Southey, and his neglect of his parental and conjugal obligations. Coleridge, on the other hand, forward as he was in defending Wordsworth from literary assailants, had evidently pleasure in exposing his parsimony in the same breath in which he vaunted the purity and piety of his nature." Mrs. Aders' admiration of Coleridge was not to be affected by her acquaintance with his companion poet. She was, she said, "delighted" with Wordsworth but still claimed "our old affectionate friend

Coleridge as *my* Poet.'' The tour was completed by a visit to the chief Dutch cities and, via Antwerp, back to Ostend and England.

The poetical fruits of Coleridge's travels were two weak and would-be-humourous sets of verses on the "stinks" of Cologne. He had occasionally been unwell while abroad but now felt better for the tour and was in good spirits. But in England he must face the repayment of his debts to various friends who had helped to finance the tour. In his difficulties he wrote to Dora Wordsworth for enlightenment. It seemed to him, he told her—"if I understand it"—that he owed £20 to Aders and £11.15/4 to Wordsworth. "Does William want the money *immediately*?" he asked.

On October 20, 1828, Coleridge left with Mrs. Gillman for Ramsgate, despite his premonition that he would not live to visit it again. Unless he went, Mrs. Gillman would not go, though she much needed it for her health, he told Stuart, from whom he had obtained £20 for the expedition. Dr. Gillman evidently wished Mrs. Gillman to accompany Coleridge to Ramsgate, to protect him from opium; or, as Coleridge told Stuart: "Gillman has a nervous aversion, formed during the first year of my inmateship in his family, to my remaining here for any length of time, without his wife." For whether at Ramsgate or Highgate, Coleridge must not be left without her guardianship. "Merely a nervous caprice," Coleridge considered Dr. Gillman's care for him, "but somehow or other he attributes to Mrs. Gillman a sort of talisman in respect of my health and comforts—and is haunted with the thought, that some ill-luck would happen" if he were ever alone. Coleridge was far too intelligent not to divine the truth.

To Dr. Gillman he sent a detailed account of their life at Ramsgate. They traveled as usual by steamer, a slow journey, for they left in a fog and the tide was against them. Poor Mrs. Gillman "was not ill, but quite lifeless." Miss Harding joined them; "she lives next door—and is chatty, as usual," he wrote. Mrs. Gillman bathed and had pony rides as before, and Coleridge anticipated great benefit to her health. His birthday, which occurred immediately after his arrival, "was suffered to pass undrunk, and unblest," he told Dr. Gillman. On November 25 they returned by coach to Highgate.

The sense of parental responsibility toward his own family, which Coleridge had acquired in recent years and which extended to little Henry Gillman in his Eton adventure, now revealed itself in a protective attitude toward the elder brother, James Gillman. Coleridge, after guarding Susan Steele from the advances of a suitor on the ground that she was to be the fiancée of James, later cautioned him against engagement in the mood of "look before you leap." Thus it is difficult to decide whether his marriage to Miss Steele two and a half years later was or was not assisted by Coleridge's interference. Coleridge's influence upon James's visit to Germany during the intervening period is evident in his letters. Besides urging him to study German, Coleridge also touched upon the picturesque aspects of the country: "That rich golden gleam, which distinguishes the surface of the soil at evening twilight" and "the endless castles, too, like mice-excavated Stilton cheese."

Lamb, now in Enfield, asked Mr. Gillman on October 26, 1829, "How can I account for having not visited Highgate this long time? Change of place seemed to have change me. How grieved I was to hear in what indifferent health Coleridge has been, and I not to know of it! A little school divinity, well applied, may be healing," he added, sending at the same time a copy of Thomas Aquinas for Coleridge. "Well, do not break your lay brains," he told Gillman, "nor I neither, with these curious nothings. They are nuts to our dear friend, whom hoping to see at your first friendly hint that it will be convenient, I end with begging our very kindest loves to Mrs. Gillman." Six days before Lamb's letter to Gillman Coleridge sent an unnamed correspondent a particularly detailed eulogy of the Gillmans:

> Of our fellow men we are bound to judge comparatively—of ourselves only, by the *Ideal*. Now verily, judging comparatively, I never did know the Master and Mistress of a Household, and the Household in consequence so estimable and so amiable to the Gillmans! The general Hospitality, without the least self-indulgence, or self-respecting expenses, compared with their income; the respectability and even elegance of all the appearances; *the centrality*, to whatever is good and love-worthy in the whole neighbour-hood, old and young; the attachment and cheerfulness of the servants, and the innocence and high tone of principle which reign throughout, would really be a very unusual combination, even though Mrs. Gillman herself had been a less finely natured and lady-like Being than she is. Would to God that I had Health and Opportunity to add 5 or 6 hundred a year to remove all anxious thoughts,—and that I could but render it possible and advisable for dear Mr. Gillman to have a two months' tour whither he liked every year! God bless them!

In the *Keepsake* for 1829 Coleridge's gratitude to Mrs. Gillman found public expression in a few lines of his poem "The Garden of Boccaccio"; for although Mrs. Gillman is not named, she is the obvious subject, when he writes:

O Friend! long wont to notice yet conceal,
And soothe by silence what words cannot heal.

As the spring of 1830 dawned Coleridge was evidently meditating flight from the Gillmans, of which Lamb, at any rate, had knowledge. He was also aware of Coleridge's friendship with the notorious and fanatical preacher Edward Irving and ironically associated the two as seeking a refuge in St. Luke's Hospital for the insane. For, referring to Coleridge, Lamb asked a friend on March 8, 1830: "Does he talk of moving the quarter? You and I have too much sense to trouble ourselves with revelations. . . .Tell Coleridge that he has to come and see us some fine day. Let it be before he moves, for in his new quarters he will necessarily be confined in his conversation to his brother prophet."

Whatever had been Coleridge's momentary intention to leave the Gillmans in March, life with them was on the whole too pleasant for a permanent departure. In May his gratitude and devotion to Mrs. Gillman inspired the following letter, in which he, nevertheless delicately, indicated that her reward must come from Heaven alone:

Dear Mrs Gillman, Wife of the friend who has been more than a brother to me, and who have month after month, yea, hour after hour, for how many successive years, united in yourself the affections and offices of an anxious friend and tender sister to me-ward! May the Father of Mercies, the God of health and of all salvation, be your reward for your great and constant love and loving kindness to me, abiding with you, and within you, as the spirit of guidance, support and consolation! and may His Grace and gracious Providence bless James and Henry for your sake, and make them a blessing to you and their father! And though weighted down by heavy presentiment respecting my own sojourn here, I not only hope but have a steadfast faith that God will be your reward: because your love to me from first to last has begun in, and been caused by what appeared to you a translucence of the love of the good, the true, and the beautiful from within me—as a relic of glory gleaming through the turbid shrine of my mortal imperfections and infirmities—as a light of life seen within "the Body of this Death!" because in loving me you loved our Heavenly Father reflected in the gifts and influences of his Holy Spirit! S. T. Coleridge.

From the spring of 1830 until the close of the year Coleridge continually complained of illness. In mid-May he felt a "languid yearning after an extrication from 'the body of this death.' " In July he repeated to Poole his complaints about the "brink of the grave" and his wish for escape from "the Body of this Death."

Such complaints from Coleridge were far from new. The physical miseries, which he had apparently endured and had so often described in letters to his friends, continued to afflict him throughout his years of residence with the Gillmans. During those eighteen years he wrote over a hundred letters to various persons, detailing the many illnesses which continually attacked him. These included stomach troubles, chest pains, and disordered kidneys, depression, nightmares causing shrieks, coughs, boils, jaundice, erysipelas, and rheumatism. How far these were real and caused by opium, how far imaginary and due to the same cause, it is impossible to determine. Yet until near the close of Coleridge's life these illnesses appear to have had very little influence upon his physical and mental activities.

5 Social Occasions (1817-30)

"We have a party to-morrow at six o'clock. In addition to a neighbour, and ourselves, and Mrs. Gillman's most unmrsgillmanly sister (but N.B. this is a secret to all who are both blind and deaf) there will be the Mathews . . . and Charles and Mary Lamb, who will stay the night, and we can get your bed at the same place."
— *Coleridge to Thomas Allsop, May 1821*

Despite Coleridge's literary labors and battles with his publishers, he nevertheless found time for considerable social activity both in London and—increasingly as the years passed—among his distinguished neighbors in Highgate. Coleridge's behavior at these parties was not invariably the same. At the more conventional, serious-minded ones, he delighted some and bored others with his endless monologues. On more hilarious occasions his natural gaiety—described by both Gillman and Wordsworth—found full vent.

In June 1817 a dinner invitation came to Coleridge from Joseph Henry Green, who was hitherto unacquainted with Coleridge. The invitation had been suggested by Coleridge's friend Robinson: and the result was that Green became one of Coleridge's best friends. The occasion for the dinner was the arrival in London of a distinguished German scholar, Johann Ludwig von Tieck, who, of course, would be a fellow guest with Coleridge and Robinson at the dinner. To meet Tieck, who was to make researches in London on Shakespeare and his contemporaries, two other Germans were also invited. Coleridge, in fact, was not unacquainted with Tieck, having met him in Rome.

Robinson found the occasion "an afternoon and evening of very high pleasure indeed." But "Coleridge was not in his element. His German was not good, and his English was not free. He feared he should not be understood if he talked his best. His eloquence was therefore constrained," Robinson wrote. Nonetheless, Coleridge found it "a most DELIGHTFUL EVENING," as he told his bookseller the next day when ordering the immediate delivery of all Tieck's works.

Hopes for the establishment of a club in London to foster interest in German literature were then in the ascendant, and this, almost inevitably, was discussed during the dinner with Tieck. Coleridge much hoped that a first meeting of the society could be held before Tieck's departure so that he "might very probably mention it with honour in his writings. . .and this would give a respectability to such an Institution that would be of the greatest service. I have little doubt that with proper measures taken, we should have two or three of the Royal Family, and count no small number of high titles on our list of members.''

Coleridge's interest in Tieck did not end with the dinner party, and two days later he playfully threatened never to forgive Robinson unless he soon brought Tieck to dine at Highgate. For there, Tieck would see the beauty of Caen Wood (Kenwood) with its "delicious groves and alleys. . .a grand Cathedral aisle of giant lime trees.'' Indeed, it it were convenient for Tieck to remain and sleep at the Gillmans' he would be welcome, and "if then return he must,'' he could leave for London the next day. He also much wished to introduce Tieck to Frere,—"a genius"—and all at Highgate would be "most happy if Green could come too.'' Thus, the acquaintance with Green quickly developed for Coleridge into a life-long friendship. Five days later, not having heard from Robinson, Coleridge repeated his invitation in increasing excitement, fearing that Robinson had been offended by the familiarity of his letter and, as an additional allurement, he promised "a Fête Champètre in Caen Groves.''

One morning four days later Robinson, Tieck, and Green took the stagecoach to Kentish Town and walked on to Highgate. There a happy and expectant Coleridge awaited them. Gillman, who seems to have been always available, joined them; and Robinson recorded that the time until four o'clock passed "very agreably indeed" in general conversation. "Coleridge read some of his poems and he and Tieck philosophized. Coleridge talked most. Tieck is a good listener, and is an unobtrusive man,'' he wrote. Tieck, fascinated by Coleridge's conversation, remained overnight.

At the end of the month Robinson, after a private talk with Tieck, recorded Tieck's impressions: "He has no high opinion of Coleridge's critique, but he says he has learned a great deal from Coleridge, who has glorious conceptions about Shakespeare. Coleridge's conversation he very much admires, and thinks it superior to any of his writings.'' At the same time Coleridge was telling Frere, who had not been able to see Tieck, of his "Genius" and his knowledge of European languages and literatures, ancient and modern. Indeed, he had found him "astonishing"; he had felt like "a mere schoolboy" in his company. For when Coleridge had quoted some of the most obscure lines in Shakespeare, Tieck had always continued the quotation and could even "tell you the place and page in one or more editions,'' which must have made Frere thankful for his escape. Although Tieck spoke English "very pleasingly,'' each had conversed as "far the best" in his own language very happily, without conscious translation. And to Coleridge's delight the excellent Tieck knew all about animal magnetism, a subject that then greatly interested Coleridge.

On July 4 Tieck left for Oxford, and before his departure Coleridge showed unusual activity on his behalf, requesting from Frere introductions for him at Oxford and Cambridge. To Green, who had long wished to study philosophy in Germany, Tieck recommended a course at Berlin. There Green soon went.

He returned in November and resumed his acquaintance with Coleridge. Coleridge evidently thought of accompanying Green, for he now asked Tieck: "Pray, how much could a single man *live at* in Berlin, say for half a year, economically yet decently? I include Lodging and Board only. I have a strong wish to pass 5 or 6 months there." But this he never did.

To Tieck at Oxford Coleridge, though no mathematician, he sent a warning against the mathematical genius, Newton. Newton he condemned for "the assumption of the *Thing*, Light, where I can find nothing but *visibility*. . . Before my visit to Germany, I had adopted the idea that Sound was = Light under the prepotence of Gravitation, and Colour = Gravitation under the prepotence of Light; and I have never seen reason to change my faith in this respect." Newton's theory of light Coleridge had summarily dismissed to Tieck as "monstrous fictions!"

In August 1817 Southey, returning to Keswick from a visit to the Continent, remained for a short time in London. There he found a letter from Coleridge, whom he had evidently not visited before his departure from England. "For God's sake," Coleridge had written, "do let me know of your arrival in London; it is so very important that I should see you." And now in his unrest Coleridge wrote to Southey again: "I have been waiting for your return with painful anxiety." He had heard from Hartley of Southey's return, and but for the effects of calomel and colocynth, and various other unfortunate accidents, he would have called on him immediately.

Southey's reaction was not enthusiastic. "I shall go to Highgate to-morrow," Southey told his wife in mid-August.

I gather from his note which I received this morning that he looks towards Keswick as if he meant to live there. At present this cannot be for want of room. . . . If he meant to live with his family it must be upon a separate establishment. I shall neither speak harshly nor unkindly, but at my time of life, with my occupations the thing is impossible. This is a hateful visit and I wish it were over. He will begin as he did when last I saw him, about Animal Magnetism or some equally congruous subject, and go on from Dan to Beersheba in his endless loquacity.

Probably Coleridge's recent "defence" of "Wat Tyler" still rankled in Southey's mind. The "Wat Tyler" incident dated back to the preceding February, when Southey's dramatic poem, "Wat Tyler"—written in his early Jacobinical years but never printed—was used by his political enemies in a pirated edition, of which, until it appeared on the streets, Southey had no knowledge. Its sale of 60,000 copies delighted his opponents. In Parliament Southey, the distinguished poet laureate, was accused of political apostasy. Coleridge, against whom the same charge was leveled at other times, defended Southey in four articles in the *Courier*, which so adversely criticized the poem that they gave Southey far more annoyance than pleasure. Privately Coleridge described "Wat Tyler" as "a wretched mess of pig's meat." Now in the *Courier* he described it as "a silly yet poisonous book," lamented its harmful influence, and felt "compunction for thus advertising it." Dorothy Wordsworth remarked, "If I were in Southey's place I should be far more afraid of my injudicious defenders than of my open enemies. Coleridge, for instance, has taken up the cudgels; and of injudicious defenders he is surely the Master Leader. . . .He does nothing in simplicity—and his praise is to me quite disgusting." The excitement about "Wat Tyler" now gave Hazlitt another opportunity to attack Coleridge, too tempting to resist. In the *Examiner* he anonymously ridiculed Coleridge's "flabby defence" of Southey and his "methodistical casuistry." And not only Coleridge but also Southey and Wordsworth he labeled "apostates."

During the years which followed in Highgate Coleridge often visited his friends in London. These included the Lambs, who were then living in The Temple, which they left in the autumn of 1817 for lodgings on Great Russell Street, Covent Garden. Coleridge often attended Lamb's famous suppers in The Temple, and one of the distinguished guests, the well-known lawyer Thomas Noon Talfourd, has described the effect of Coleridge upon the company: "There, Coleridge sometimes, through rarely, took his seat and then the genial hubbub of voices was still, critics, philosophers and poets were contented to listen; and toil-worn lawyers, clerks from the India House, and members of the Stock Exchange, grew romantic while he spoke. Lamb used to say that he was inferior then to what he had been in his youth; but I can scarcely believe it." Sometimes at these meetings in The Temple Coleridge was induced—as elsewhere—to recite "Christabel" and "Kubla Khan."

When Lamb moved to lodgings on Russell Street he continued his famous suppers. One of the best descriptions of those convivial meetings was given by Lamb's friend George Daniel, whose chief interests were old books and drama. "After winding up a narrow pair of stairs," he wrote, "a visitor on entering a middle-size front room, would dimly discern through tobacco smoke that was making its way up the chimney, and through the keyholes, a noble head, worthy of Medusa, on which were scattered a few grey curls among crisp ones of dark brown and an expressive thoughtful set of features inclining to the Hebrew cast." Such was Daniel's description of Lamb.

From Daniel's account the following picture emerges in which Coleridge dilates upon Shakespeare until some bored person jokingly interrupts him, encouraged by the mischievious Talfourd while the "sad looking and sickly" Hood makes "pointed puns." Daniel continues, "A plentiful supper would follow after which the goblets were refilled, the pipes re-fumed and the talk resumed for another pleasant hour or two. The company then took their leave (Coleridge generally lingering lag-last) bidding each other 'good night,' while labour, returning to its daily toil was grumbling '*good morning*!' "

Despite Coleridge's depression, the year 1817 closed for him in a genial social atmosphere, as several of his acquaintances recorded. On December 27 Robinson dined at Tom Monkhouse's with Wordsworth, Mrs. Wordsworth, Sara Hutchinson, Coleridge, and Hartley. "I was for the first time in my life," Robinson recorded, "not pleased with Wordsworth, and Coleridge appeared to advantage in his presence. . . .The manner of Coleridge towards Wordsworth was most respectful, but Wordsworth's towards Coleridge was cold and scornful.''

Three days later Robinson again met Coleridge and Wordsworth at a party given by Lamb. Coleridge, said Robinson, "had the larger number of guests around him. . .while Wordsworth was for a great part of the time engaged tête-à-tête with Talfourd. I could catch scarcely anything of the conversation; but I heard at one time Coleridge quoting Wordsworth's verses, and Wordsworth quoting—not Coleridge's—but his own.''

Despite Coleridge's occasional attendance at Lamb's suppers, Lamb was keenly and unhappily conscious that Coleridge's move to Highgate was largely preventing their old companionship. In October 1818 Lamb wrote to Southey: "I do not see S.T.C. so often as I could wish. He never comes to me; and though his host and hostess are very friendly, it puts me out of my way to go to see one person at another person's house. It was the same when he resided at Morgan's. Not but they also were more than civil; but after all one feels so welcome at one's own house.''

The social possibilities of Highgate were, in their own way, as attractive to Coleridge as London's. At Highgate new friends and acquaintances gathered about him, and, when the quarry seemed worth the trouble, he did not hesitate to take the initiative. It was thus when the popular comic actor Charles Mathews came to live near him. In a letter of May 1819 to Mathews, Coleridge offered his services—"as now an old stager at Highgate, or as the author of *Remorse*." He continued with a genial play upon Mathews' well-known title for his entertainments—"*as a friend*, you will always find me AT HOME.''

The acquaintance with Mathews that followed soon developed into friendship. A few months later Coleridge, with the Gillmans and others, was dining at Mathews' and more or less enjoying a rehearsal of Mathews' *At Home* entertainments. As Mathews' comic imitations of Coleridge on the stage were then famous, and as another guest, James Smith, had satirized Coleridge in his popular *Rejected Addresses* eight years before, Coleridge must have felt himself very much "At Home." An invitation from Mathews shortly afterward to meet Walter Scott threw Coleridge into a perplexity of indecision. Surely Scott, he debated, should have called *on him*, living so near to Mathews, so an acceptance of Mathews' invitation might compromise his dignity. "Yet I dared not purchase the gratification at so high a price, as that of risking the respect which, I trust, has not hitherto been forfeited," he wrote, revealing his anxiety to Allsop. The crux of his dilemma, he next admitted, was: "I seem to feel that I *ought* to feel more desire to see an extraordinary man than I really do feel.''

Mathews' actress wife, Anne, an observant admirer of Coleridge, has given us realistic accounts of qualities in Coleridge seldom remarked on by his other friends. She emphasized the kindly element in his nature, and his love of her flower garden delighted her: "As he went he gathered them till his hands were full. . .he doted upon flowers, and discoursed so poetically upon them.''

Anne Mathews was no less impressed by Coleridge's kindness to her when she was ill. The memory of Coleridge "coming down the hill, one stormy and severe winter's night to cheer me with an entertaining book, . . .and sitting with me and a friend. . .in my dressing-room, reading, and commenting on what he read, until I forgot my indisposition" remained with her to the end of her life.

Anne's perception of the Pickwickian element in Coleridge gives us a rare insight into this aspect of his influence over others. It forms a striking contrast to the facile romantic glamor that too often magnifies the appreciations of those who knew Coleridge only as poet and philosopher. "The simplicity of Mr. Coleridge's character on familiar occasions," she wrote, "gave us infinite amusement, which on his perceiving it, he allowed, with a smile against himself, while some charming remark would increase our enjoyment, and he would leave with his benevolent features beaming with good humour and kindness." Nor did they less enjoy a frequent incident. For on leaving, Coleridge, intent upon his conversation, had to be saved by his hostess from walking through a mirror which he mistook for an open door. Evidently, the easy theatrical atmosphere of the Mathews home appealed to the Bohemian strain in Coleridge's temperament. He himself had an actor's sense of a situation and ever instinctively reacted to it, whether it called for a genial freedom or a highly dignified personality.

Of this latter quality in Coleridge Charles Lamb, who had little sympathy with dignified self-importance, was very conscious. Once Anne Mathews witnessed Lamb's reaction to Coleridge's exaltation of Lamb himself. It was the occasion of Coleridge's first introduction of Lamb to Mr. and Mrs. Mathews. This Anne admirably describes:

We found Mr. Coleridge anxiously waiting for Lamb's arrival. . . .AT LAST Mr. and Miss Lamb appeared, and Mr. Coleridge led his friend up to my husband with a look which seemed to say, "I pray you, like this fellow." Mr. Lamb's first approach was not prepossessing. Guessing that he had been extolled, he mischievously resolved to thwart his panegyrist, disappoint the strangers, and altogether to upset the suspected plan of showing off. The Lamb, in fact, would not consent to be made a lion of, and it followed that he became puerile and annoying all the day, to Mr. Coleridge's visible mortification. Before dinner he was suspicious and silent, as if he was taking measure of the man he came to meet, and about whom he seemed very curious. The first glass of wine set his spirit free, and he became quite impracticable. He made the most absurd puns and ridiculous jokes, and almost harassed Coleridge out of his self-complacency, though managed to maintain a tolerable degree of evenness with his tormentor, now and then only rebuking him mildly for what he termed "such unworthy trifling." This only served to exasperate the perverse humour of him it was intended to subdue; and once Mr. Coleridge exclaimed meekly, after some very bad joke, "Charles Lamb, I'm ashamed of you!"—a reproof which produced only an impatient "You be hanged!" from the reproved, and another jest, more potent than the former, was superadded to his punning enormities. Mr. Lamb's last fire, however, was at length expended, and Mr. Coleridge took advantage of a pause to introduce some topic that might divert the party from his friend's determined foolery. He chose a subject which he deemed unlikely, if not impossible, for Lamb to interrupt with a jest. Mr. Coleridge stated that he had originally been intended for the pulpit, and had taken orders—nay, had actually preached several times. At this moment, fancying he saw something in Lamb's face that denoted a lucid interval, and wishing to turn him back from the nonsense which had so "spoiled the pleasure of the time" with a desire also to conciliate the "pouting boy," as he seemed (who, to our observation, was only waiting for an opportunity to revenge himself upon his friend for all the grave checks he had given to his jocular vein during dinner), Coleridge turned benignly towards him, and observed—"Charles Lamb, I believe you never heard me preach?" As if concentrating his pent-up resentment into one focus, and with less of his wonted hesitation, Lamb replied, with great emphasis, "I never heard you do anything else!"

A note from Lamb to Coleridge toward the end of the year 1820 forms an unintentional but amusing comment upon Coleridge's occasional denials to friends that he borrowed books without permission and failed to return them. This scandalous report Coleridge had asserted was due to Lamb's intemperance. But Lamb now wrote in evident irritation with Coleridge: "Why will you make your visits, which should give pleasure, matter of regret to your friends? You never come but you take away some folio that is part of my existence."

Naturally more pleasing to Coleridge was another note that reached him in the last month of the year, an invitation from Pettigrew—who was now cataloguing the library of the Duke of Sussex—to dine with the duke. He would have been, he told Pettigrew in reply, "a far stranger animal" than he was, "if my wishes were not . . . excited, and my vanity gratified by the opportunity offered of meeting His Royal Highness, the Duke of Sussex, and sitting down with him at the same table." Once or twice before in 1820 fortune had smiled upon Coleridge in this way; through Frere's commendation "one or two public men" including Lord Liverpool had wished to meet Coleridge, but naturally the duke's invitation was a greater consolation to Coleridge in his misfortunes than the solace of lessor celebrities. Yet even now fate was unkind; for Coleridge, it appeared, was too poor to travel the six miles journey to the duke and too unwell to leave the care of the Gillmans.

In May 1821 Coleridge invited Allsop to a social evening: "We have a party *to-morrow* at six o'clock," he wrote. "In addition to a neighbour, and ourselves, and Mrs Gillman's most unmrsgillmanly sister (but N.B. this is a secret to all who are both blind and deaf) there will be the Mathews (Mr and Mrs '*At home*' Mathews I mean)—and Charles and Mary Lamb, who will stay the night, and we can get your bed at the same place."

In the spring of 1822 Coleridge sent Mr. and Mrs. Allsop two invitations to social occasions at the Gillmans. His relations with Allsop had been somewhat strained lately as Allsop, despite Coleridge's denials, believed that he had divulged to friends the secret of Allsop's recent marriage. Thus it was that Coleridge's first invitation, written on April 17, was particularly affectionate to

Allsop, in hope of a reconciliation. They were to meet Charles and Mary Lamb at dinner, and, to lure the somewhat aloof Mrs. Allsop, he would show her the beauties of Highgate and hoped that they might hear the nightingales sing.

Shortly afterward, on May 30, Coleridge's second invitation to the Allsops followed, but in a postscript to a letter which requested Allsop, who was already security for fifty pound of Coleridge's debts, to increase it by another £100. The security, he emphasized, was merely nominal, as it was certain that the debts would soon be paid. Mrs. Allsop's apparent detachment from these friends of her husband was probably a not unreasonable dislike of such claims upon him. The invitation which followed showed more interest in Allsop's society than in his wife's despite the nightingales: "Charles and Mary Lamb and Mr (not Mrs) Green dine with us on Sunday next: and are to see Mathews' Dramatic Picture Gallery. Can you and Mrs Allsop join the party? Or if Mrs. Allsop's health should make this hazardous or too great an exertion, can you come yourself?—I am sure, *she* will forgive me for putting the question." As Coleridge heard during the following month of the birth of Allsop's daughter, the secret of the marriage could not in any case have continued. Probably, too, Mrs Allsop's condition also accounts for her apparent aloofness.

At Mrs. Aders's Christmas party of 1822 Coleridge and Robinson were among the guests. "A large party," Robinson recorded.

> Splendid dinner prepared by a French cook and music in the evening. Coleridge was the star of the evening. He talked in his usual way, but as well and with more liberality and in seemingly better health than when I saw him last, some years ago. But he was somewhat less animated and brilliant and paradoxical. He had not seen Wordsworth's last works, and spoke less highly of his immediately preceding writings than he used and still does of his earlier works. He reproaches him with a vulgar attachment to orthodoxy in its literal sense. The latter end of the *Excursion*, he says, is distinguishable from the former, and he can ascertain from internal evidence the recent from the early compositions among his works. He reproaches Wordsworth with a disregard of the mechanism of his verse, and in general insinuates a decline of his faculties. Of Southey's politics he spoke also depreciatingly—he is intellectually a very dependent, but morally an independent man. In the judgment of Southey I concur altogether. Of Wordsworth I believe Coleridge judges under personal feelings of unkindness. The music was enjoyed by Coleridge, but I could have dispensed with it on account of Coleridge himself. "For as eloquence the soul, song charms the sense."

So amid music, eloquence, and French cooking, the Christmas of 1822 passed.

"We are about to have an inundation of poetry from the Lakes; Wordsworth and Southey are coming up strong from the North," Lamb told a friend on March 11, 1823, and soon the "inundation" had engulfed both Coleridge and Lamb. A dinner party at Monkhouse's on April 4, 1823, was the beginning for Coleridge of a springtime round of social festivities, which a happy recovery from the imprisoning illness of the last three months allowed him to undertake. Robinson, one the guests, confided his sober account of the occasion in his diary.

April 4th—Dined at Monkhouse's. Our party consisted of Wordsworth, Coleridge, Lamb, Moore and Rogers. Five poets of very unequal worth and most disproportionate popularity, whom the public probably would arrange in the very inverse order, except that it would place Moore above Rogers. During this afternoon, Coleridge alone displayed any of his peculiar talent. He talked much and well. I have not for years seen him in such excellent health and spirits. His subjects metaphysical criticism—Wordsworth he chiefly talked to. Rogers occasionally let fall a remark. Moore seemed conscious of his inferiority. He was very attentive to Coleridge, but seemed to relish Lamb whom he sat next. Lamb was in good frame—kept himself within bounds and was only cheerful at last . . . I was at the bottom of the table, where I very ill performed my part . . . I walked home late with Lamb.

Lamb's account of the same occasion written the next day "with an aching head—for we did not quaff Hippocrene last night"—was characteristically lively: "I dined in Parnassus, with Wordsworth, Coleridge, Rogers and Tom Moore—half the poetry of England constellated and clustered in Gloster Place! It was a delightful evening. Coleridge was in his finest vein to talk, had all the talk, and let 'em talk as evilly as they do of the envy of Poets, I am sure not one there but was content to be nothing but a listener. The Muses were dumb, while Apollo lectured on his and their fine Art."

Nor was the host, Monkhouse, less pleased with the party than his guests. "*Five of the Most distinguished Poets of the age*," he told his fiancée, Miss Horrocks; "the party went off in the most delightful way, being as Rogers pronounced it, *the most brilliant thing* this Season. It wanted nothing to make it complete but Sir George and Lady Beaumont who were quite distressed that they were so engaged that they could not come. Coleridge was most eloquent and C. Lamb most witty but perfectly *steady*. Lord Lowther was asked but was obliged to leave town yesterday." But there were others who could and did attend—Mrs. Wordsworth, Sara Hutchinson, Mary Lamb, and Mrs. Gillman.

The next day, April 5, 1823, Robinson attended a musical party—which he had arranged—at the Aders', to which Monkhouse, Flaxman the sculptor, Coleridge, Wordsworth, Rogers, the Gillmans, and others all came. Robinson noted the different reactions of the poets to the music: "Wordsworth declared himself perfectly delighted and satisfied, but he sat alone, silent, and with his face covered, and was generally supposed to be asleep. Flaxman, too, confessed that he could not endure fine music for *long*. But Coleridge's enjoyment was very lively, and openly expressed."

At the close of the month social engagements still occupied much of Coleridge's time and attention. Mrs. Coleridge and her daughter Sara had won the affections of all the Coleridges at Ottery and had in this way doubtless assisted the rapprochement of Coleridge with his brothers.

"Your Uncle and Aunt, Colonel and Mrs. James Coleridge with Fanny" (their daughter), he now told Derwent, were in London and—with evident satisfaction—he was to dine with them on May 1 at the invitation of their son, Henry Taylor Coleridge.

Nine years had passed since James, annoyed at being expected to contribute to Hartley's education, had called Samuel "mad" and had wished that opium might rid the world of him. Nor had Coleridge's comments upon his brothers for many years been more complimentary. Now, however, with Coleridge safely ensconced at Highgate with a growing reputation and James the husband of a rich wife, their mutual feelings had changed. Indeed, five years ago they had met in London and had liked each other. Thus it was that Coleridge accepted his nephew's invitation with an enthusiasm which strangely contrasted with his cool rejection of the previous one of two months before, when Coleridge's wife and daughter were John Taylor Coleridge's guests.

"God willing," he now answered his nephew on April 23, 1823, "I shall not fail to be in Hadlow St. at the time appointed—and congratulate you on the arrival of so dear and precious an Assortment—. Be pleased to make my affectionate respects to my Brother and Sister—and most cordially to Fanny whom I seem to love with a double love—direct and reflected from little Sara, to whom she has been so altogether a Sister—God bless you, and your dear Lady . . . S. T. Coleridge." Unfortunately, no Robinson was present to record the meeting of James and Samuel at the party on May 1, but the next day Robinson attended Green's party at Lincoln's Inn Field, of which he has left a charming vignette: "A very genteel dinner and an agreeable party, Coleridge was the only talker, and he did not talk his best: He repeated one of his own jokes, by which he offended a Methodist at the whist table, calling for her *last trump* and confessing that though he always thought her an angel he had not before known her to be an archangel." What Mrs. Gillman, who was present with her husband, thought of the incident, we unfortunately do not know.

When in the summer of 1823 Lamb and his sister moved to Colebrooke Cottage in Islington, there were inevitably dinner parties for Lamb's friends. At two of these Coleridge, Mrs. Gillman, and Tom Hood the poet were guests. Hood long remembered the scene: "the contrast to Lamb" made by "the full-bodied poet Coleridge with his waving white hair, and his face round, ruddy and unfurrowed as a holy friar." With himself as subject Coleridge seldom lacked inspiration, and he now amused the company by describing a portrait of himself that was being painted as an unintentional barometer of his popularity. When the critics praised him, the painter came to him to make progress with the portrait. When the critics frowned, the painter stayed away.

Hood's description of Coleridge on these occasions is one of the most percipient of the many left by Coleridge's auditors:

What a benign, smiling face it was! What a comfortable, respectable Figure! What a model, methought, as I watched and admired the "Old Man eloquent" for a Christian bishop! But he was, perhaps, scarcely orthodox enough to be trusted with the mitre . . . . Amongst other matters of discourse, he came to speak of the strange notions some literal-minded persons form of the joys of Heaven; joys they associated with mere temporal things, in which, for his own part, finding no delight in this world, he could find no bliss hereafter, without a change in his nature, tantamount to the loss of his personal identity. For instance, he said, there are persons who place the whole angelical beautitude in the possession of a pair of wings to flap about with, like "*a sort of celestial poultry.*" After dinner he got up, and began pacing to and fro, with his hand behind his back, talking and walking, as Lamb laughingly hinted, as if qualifying for an itinerant preacher.

Now in full sail, by his eloquence with its far-fetched images, he enthralled the enchanted Hood. "With his fine, flowing voice," Hood continued,

> it was glorious music, of the "never-ending, still-beginning" kind; and you did not wish it to end . . . . You knew not whither, nor did you care. Like his own bright-eyed mariner, he had a spell in his voice that would not let you go. To attempt to describe my own feeling afterwards, I had been carried, spiralling, up to heaven by a whirlwind intertwisted with sunbeams, giddy and dazzled, but not displeased, and had then been rained down again with a shower of mundane stocks and stone that battered out of me all recollection of what I had heard, and what I had seen!

Nor were the year's festivities ended. Shortly after his return to Highgate Coleridge dined at Lockhart's with Tom Moore and others. Moore, too far from Coleridge, could hear only "the continuous drawl of his preachment." But later, when the ladies had retired, he moved close to Coleridge, whose "subjects were chiefly Irving and religion." Coleridge told them he was now writing "on Daniel and the Revelations, and his notions on the subject." These, said Moore, "as far as they were at all intelligible, appeared to be a strange mixture of rationalism and mysticism." Thus he described "the gift of tongues to have been nothing more than scholarship or a knowledge of different languages," and, after quoting Erasmus and Plato in support, he described his unsuccessful efforts to convert Irving to his view. Coleridge also recited some of his own later poems, including his "Epitaph". Some music with Moore's songs inspired more flights of oratory, "the music, like the honeysuckle round the stem, twining round the meaning, and at last over-topping it." And Moore wrote, "Over-topping the meaning" not a little applicable to his own style of eloquence."

The popular oratorical preacher, Edward Irving, who the year before had been appointed to the chapel at Hatton Garden in London, was now drawing crowds to see and hear him as if to a theater. He was now "the present idol of the world of fashion, the Revd. Mr. Irving, the super-ciceronian, ultra Demosthenic Pulpiteer," as Coleridge described him after hearing him preach. Coleridge's attendances at any church were very few and far between, and his visit to Hatton Garden was less religious than social. For, as Coleridge explained, he was "obliged to meet Mr. Irving at the table of a friend." Dorothy Wordsworth, on reading in a newspaper Irving's "description of the joys of Heaven," thought it "*worse* than a Methodist rant."

On Christmas Eve 1823 Coleridge annoyed Mrs. Allsop, not surprisingly, but inviting her husband to dine with him and the Gillmans "on Christmas Day—or on New Year's Day—or on both!"—without mentioning her name except for a concluding "kindest regards." Mrs. Allsop now replied to

Coleridge's invitation. "This was a season of *Family* re-unions," she wrote tartly, but her husband was staying with his parents. To this Coleridge sent her a characteristically apologetic letter explaining that it was understood Mrs. Allsop was always included in the invitations to her husband. Mrs. Gillman, he added, had not expected Mrs. Allsop would wish to be away from home and the children at that time. But Mrs. Gillman was still shaken from a recent fall and he had not dared to show her Mrs. Allsop's letter. So under the shadow of separation from the beloved Allsop, the year 1823 reached its end. The Gillmans' move in 1823 to a larger house (described later) presented Coleridge with an even better environment for social distractions than he had had before. Of this Coleridge made full use, until, near the close of his life, increasing illness prevented almost all social activities.

In April 1824 Coleridge was able to describe himself as having been "for three or four days in the feverish excitement of some almost necessary visitings and dinner parties occasioned by Mr Wordsworth's and his family being in town." During the next few months Coleridge often dined with various friends, both at their houses and at the Gillman's. From Ramsgate the following October he wrote: "I am perplexed by solicitations to dine with the men of title—to meet the Duchess of Leinster and offers to have only a very *small* party etc.—Sir Charles Des Voese is a good natured Irish Baronet, of high connections and large estates in both countries, Sir Alexander Johnson you will probably become acquainted with and will like." Before leaving Ramsgate with Mrs. Gillman on November 30 Coleridge attended at least two pleasant "musical" parties, but, nevertheless, he was weary of "importunately repeated invitations to dinner parties."

After the return to Highgate Coleridge's social engagements continued, and soon he had made friends with two Italian political refugees: Gioacchino de Prati (1790-1863) and Gabriele Rossetti (1783-1854), the father of the poet and painter Dante Gabriel Rossetti.

On May 18, 1825, Coleridge lectured to the Royal Society. The next day he described this experience to his nephew John Taylor Coleridge thus: "I inflicted the whole essay (an hour and 25 minutes) on the ears of the R.S.L. with most remorseful sympathy with the audience, who could not possibly understand the 10th part—for let it's merits be what they may, it was not a thing to read to, but to *be read by*." The essay was printed with the following title: "*On the Prometheus of Aeschylus; An Essay, Preparatory to a series of Disquisitions respecting the Egyptian in connection with the Sacerdotal Theology, and in contrast with the Mysteries of ancient Greece.*" Two days later Coleridge dined at Sir George Beaumont's with a fellow guest, "The Bishop of London and his angel-faced wife," as he did not fail to inform his friends.

The following month Coleridge dined at Sir George Beaumont's with Southey, who was about to visit Holland, and a day or two later he "made an unusually copious dinner, and drank at least a bottle of wine" at Sotheby's. In December Coleridge was much occupied in making the acquaintance of Joseph Blanco White (1775—1841), an Irishman born in Spain. Formerly a Catholic priest, he had rejected Catholicism and moved to London, where in 1814 he entered the English Church. In this year 1825 Blanco White's *Evidence against Catholicism* appeared, and it doubtless was the main cause of Coleridge's interest in meeting and entertaining its author.

Certainly White unconsciously inspired perhaps the most ornate of Coleridge's many alluring invitations to his own friends and acquaintances. Coleridge's nephews, Edward and Henry Nelson, were visiting him in a day or two and they much wished to meet White, whom they both admired. Although his knowledge of White's weak health, he wrote on December 12, "make my hopes burn very dim, yet I cannot help *trying*—so far as to assure you in my own name, my nephews', and Mr and Mrs Gillman's, that you would confer an especial delight on us all, if you would join the party. We shall dine at an early hour—about 4: and a well-aired Bed and Bed Room with a Fire in it will be prepared for you."

But this was not sufficient for Coleridge, who must now tell White that if he could not accept this invitation another would be sent to him in due course: "Oblige me with a single line by the return of Post—and let it be, Yes! if *that* be possible with *safety*. But if you are convinced, that you could not come but at a hazard, I retract my request, and tho' the *wish* will survive, yet it shall be swallowed up in a larger, as Jonas in the Whale, to be cast on shore again, sub dio in a more genial season." And Coleridge signed his letter with "unmixed esteem and cordial regard." Evidently the chief cause of Coleridge's extreme courtesy in this letter was the visit which White had made the previous July. He had come "in a glass coach," as Coleridge had proudly informed his nephew Edward Coleridge, and during many hours of talk Coleridge found the interview "highly gratifying to me . . . that he had the 'Aids to Reflection' at his fingers' ends." Coleridge would have been less pleased could he have foreseen that a year after Coleridge's death White would turn again, this time to the Unitarians.

Throughout the following years, 1826 and 1827, Coleridge's round of parties at home and abroad continued with little intermission. They included a dinner at Sir George Beaumont's with J. H. Frere as a fellow guest, and Coleridge's generosity in inviting his friends to dine at the Gillman's was endless. It included a large party there with de Prati again as one of the guests. Another such party a little later included Frere, Green, and Tulk.

The year 1827 opened with an invitation to Poole on January 3 to dine and spend the day with him at Highgate. But in Coleridge's invitation the old affectionate note to Poole was now lacking: "I write now, *not* to say how glad I shall be to see you to-morrow: for that would be wasting ink and paper and postage, not to add pen, time and daylight, in mere superfluities—but to transmit to you Mr and Mrs Gillman's best respect." Such was the chilly opening of Coleridge's letter to Poole. It was a far cry from the ebullience of Coleridge's invitation to White.

Throughout the following months of this year, among the friends who came to Highgate were Basil Montagu, his wife, Irving, and the Aders.

In the autumn, again at Ramsgate, Coleridge proudly informed the absent Gillman that he had dined with Sir George Gray and met Sir William Curtis. On November 22 he and Mrs. Gillman returned to Highgate.

An attack in January 1828 of erysipelas—the disease which later killed him—did not prevent Coleridge the following month from enjoying a party at Green's home. The principal cause of enjoyment was Leigh Hunt's description of Coleridge in *Lord Byron and Some of His Contemporaries*, which had recently appeared. Hunt's description Green thought "whimsically contrary to the truth." But Colerige disagreed, thinking it half true as a portrait of himself and very amusing. "I have not laughed so loud and long for many a month as I did on reading Leigh Hunt's character of me!" he told his nephew Henry. And he continued with a subtle analysis of Dryden's assertion:

Great wit to Madness sure is near allied.

No description of Coleridge in these later years is more important than Leigh Hunt's for those who wish to know the real Coleridge of everyday life. "Mr Lamb's friend, Mr Coleridge, is as little fitted for action as he, but on a different account," Leigh Hunt began. He continued:

His person is of good height, but as sluggish and solid as the other's is light and fragile. He has perhaps suffered it to look old before its time, for want of exercise. His hair too is quite white, (though he cannot much exceed fifty); and as he generally dresses in black, and has a very tranquil demeanour, his appearance is gentlemanly, and begins to be reverend. Nevertheless, there is something invincibly young in the look of his face: it is round and fresh-coloured, with agreeable features and an open, indolent good-natured mouth. This boy-like expression is very becoming to one who dreams as he did when he was a child, and who passes his life apart from the rest of the world, with a book and his flowers. His forehead is prodigious,—a great piece of placid marble; and his fine eyes, in which all the activity of his mind seems to concentrate, move under it with a sprightly ease, as if it were a pastime to them to carry all that thought. And it is pastime.

Next, opposing Hazlitt's description of Coleridge's nature as ethereal, Leigh Hunt presents his own conception of Coleridge as "a good-natured wizard, very fond of earth, and conscious of reposing with weight enough in his easy chair, but able to conjure his etherialities about him in the twinkling of an eye. He can also change them by thousands, and dismiss them as easily when his dinner comes. It is a mighty intellect put upon a sensual body; and the reason why he does little more with it than talk and dream is that it is agreeable to such a body to do little else."

Turning aside for a moment to comment upon Coleridge's ability as a talker, Leigh Hunt asserted: "Mr Coleridge will persuade a Deist that he is a Christian, and an Atheist that he believes in God. . . . However, if the world is to remain always as it is, give me to all eternity new talk of Coleridge, and new essays of Charles Lamb. They will reconcile it beyond all others; and that is much.''

The following month Coleridge sent a remarkably enthusiastic letter to the minor Scottish poet Thomas Pringle (1789-1834), inviting him to one of his Thursday parties. Pringle, a friend of Scott, had spent a few years in South Africa which had inspired his best-known poem ''Afar in the Desert.'' He was now back in England, where he was appointed secretary to the Anti-Slavery Society.

Coleridge, accidentally lighting upon ''Afar in the Desert,'' told Pringle that he ''was taken so completely possession of that for some days I did little else but read and recite your poem, now to this group and now to that—and since that time have either written or caused to be written, at least half a dozen copies—With the omission of about four or at the utmost six lines I do not hesitate to declare it, among the two or three most perfect lyric poems in our language.'' The acquaintance with Pringle proved useful to Coleridge, for a year later Pringle became editor of the periodical *Friendships Offering*, to which Coleridge contributed poems.

Before Coleridge left for the Continent in June 1828 Frederic Mansel Reynolds, who became editor of the *Keepsake* the following year, called on Coleridge and offered him fifty pounds for contributions to this annual if he promised to contribute to no other annual in 1829 save Alaric Watt's *Literary Souvenir*. The selection of Coleridge's poems chosen by Reynolds was ''Alice du Clos; or, The Forked Tongue,'' ''The Garden of Boccaccio'' and some ''Epigrams.'' But not until Coleridge's return from the Continent did he make the copies which Reynolds required; a year later ''The Garden of Boccaccio'' appeared in Reynolds' annual.

After his return from the continental tour, Coleridge attended a party given by Reynolds on August 18, which was far more exciting than most of the parties that Coleridge attended. Theodore Hook, the wit, novelist, and practical joker, aroused the Bohemian element in Coleridge which produced the scene described by another guest, Lockhart, as follows:

much claret had been shed before the *Ancient Mariner* proclaimed that he could swallow no more of anything, unless it were punch. The materials were forthwith produced; the bowl was planted before the poet, and as he proceeded in his concoction, Hook, unbidden, took his place at the piano. He burst into a bacchanal of egregious luxury, every line of which had reference to the author of the *Lay Sermons* and the *Aids to Reflection*. The room was becoming excessively hot: the first specimen of the new compound was handed to Hook, who paused to quaff it, and then, exclaiming that he was stifled, flung his glass through the window. Coleridge rose with the aspect of a benignant patriach and demolished another pane—the example was followed generally—the window was a sieve in an instant—the kind host was furthest from the mark, and his goblet made havoc of the chandelier. The roar of laughter was drowned in Theodore's resumption of the song—and window and chandelier and the peculiar shot of each individual destroyer had apt, in many cases exquisitely witty, commemoration.

"Like a wild school-boy at play" was another guest's description of Coleridge; but in walking home with Lockhart Coleridge entertained him "with a most excellent lecture on the distinction between talent and genius, and declared that Hook was as true a genius as Dante—that was his example."

We need not wonder that Coleridge's reply a week later to another invitation from Reynolds to a party was as exuberant as this: "I cannot bring myself to resign the pleasure I have promised myself in being once more *hook'd* on the whirl-about car of the portly god Bacchus, with wit, laughter, jest and song on the wooden-horses, like the children at Bartholomew Fair—Gladly would I make one in the train, tho' in the character of old Silenus sitting on his ass . . . unless ill."

A month later Coleridge told a friend, "Tomorrow evening or Tuesday morning I am engaged to pay my long delayed first visit to my dear friends, Charles and Mary Lamb, at Enfield." On October 20, despite a bad bout of erysipelas, Coleridge left for Ramsgate with Mrs. Gillman and her sister, and he returned to Highgate after a month's stay there.

Amid declining health Coleridge's social activities henceforth also declined, until in July 1830 he told Poole, "Since we last met, I have been brought to the brink of the grave thro' a series of severe sufferings that would have removed all terror from the anticipation even if I had ever associated any painful thought with the extrication of my spirit from 'the body of this death' . . . this is one of my *badly* days . . . I am yet in the land of the living." Yet even in Coleridge's last years, as will be seen in a later chapter, social diversions were not entirely abandoned.

6 Parental Responsibilities (1817-30)

"It is afflictive enough, that we have not one family house, as the natural centre for all of you and your Home . . . . I have felt this want very poignantly and not without an after-relish of mortification."
—*Coleridge to his son Derwent, February 2, 1826*

Coleridge's quiet regular life at the Gillmans' now combined with the increasing complexities of his children's affairs to lead him to assume parental responsibilities hitherto neglected. On May 6, 1815, Hartley registered at Merton College, Oxford, as the possessor of a small grant known as a postmastership. William Coleridge, Hartley's uncle, a fellow of Christ Church, had secured it for him. Influential friends also contributed to Hartley's expenses. In this Southey and Wordsworth led the way. They were assisted by the Beaumonts, Poole, Cottle, Montagu, and the Coleridges of Ottery.

Now two years had passed. All Coleridge's children were growing up, and his own former mood of despair had yielded. to the gracious influences of the Gillmans. So he began to follow his children's careers like a model father. When in June 1817 Hartley spent the summer vacation with his father at the Gillmans', Coleridge was not disappointed in the youth, who would be twenty-one in September. "His manners rather eccentric," he described Hartley, "otherwise he is in head and heart all I ought to wish." Requesting Poole to invite Hartley to Stowey, as he wished to see his birthplace, Coleridge told Poole: "He is very much improved, and if I could see him more systematic in his studies and in the employment of his time, I should have little to complain of in him or to wish for." Coleridge wrote to his wife on August 2, informing her that Hartley (who had returned from Poole's) had left for Oxford two days before. "I have paid his bills at Highgate," he told her, "boots, pantaloons, etc., together with the money in his pocket somewhat about £18."

Nor was this all. He also promised his wife "£50 at six weeks," vowing at the same time to observe the strictest personal economy himself. In this Coleridge was doubtless encouraged by the fact that the Gillmans, moved by his complaints of cruel and avaricious publishers, had reduced their charges for his board and lodging. "You or the children," he added, "will have every shilling beyond my necessities." Coleridge, however, had to leave for "the seaside for six weeks." The expense would be twenty pounds, but his health required

488

the change; and he would finish "Christabel" there, which would more than repay the expenses of his holidays.

Coleridge did not forget his other children at this time. If Mrs. Coleridge could afford to send Derwent to him in November with "the proper fit-out that he may want," he would try to repay her for the expense within six months. Dorothy Wordsworth, now a pessimistic critic of Samuel, heard of Derwent's projected visit to his father with dismay. "I cannot see any good that can possibly arise from this," she told Catherine Clarkson, "unless it forces his father to exert himself to put the boy forward, or forces him to confess openly that he cannot do anything—which will at least compel him to perceive that he or his children had, and have friends, ill as he thinks he has been used in the world."

So much for Hartley and Derwent! But Sara was by no means forgotten in Samuel's letter to his wife. "Would to God! I could hit on a possibility of seeing my dear Sara," he cried. "I would work night and day to bring it about—but unfortunately, we have no bedroom and she could not sleep out." Derwent's intended visit to his father did not take place. Now seventeen years of age, he had accepted a temporary post as tutor in a private family. On hearing of this Coleridge grudgingly assented: "if it pleases your mother and Mr Southey as much as it seems to please the Wordsworths, let it please you for the present." Derwent, indeed, had been disappointed by the failure of influential friends to obtain for him a grant at Cambridge. Hartley, however, spent the winter vacation with his father in Highgate. The visit was evidently a success, for on January 10, 1818, Coleridge told his friend Wrangham: "Hartley Coleridge is with me, and both he and his brother Derwent and his sister are everything the fondest father could wish. He returns to Merton, Oxford, on the 17th."

Fifteen months later Coleridge heard the delightful news that Hartley, who had taken a second class in his examination, had received a fellowship at Oriel College. To friends Coleridge expressed his pride in his son's achievement in gaining the fellowship, and he emphasized Hartley's brilliance in defeating "candidates of powerful talents . . . as a classic, a logician and a theologian." Nor did he forget Derwent, "whose abilities, principles and industry are as great a blessing to me as his brother is." Hartley's success revived Coleridge's hopes of Derwent's entry into Cambridge despite the previous disappointment. Hence came new anxieties about the means and more complaints of Samuel's own poverty. "But God's Will be done!" he moaned. "I have retained a calm conscience—and my children will inherit my principles . . . And these are blessings for which even poverty and detraction are but light counterweights."

Mrs. Coleridge's response to the news of Hartley's success was characteristically direct and realistic: "The news most recent and consequently nearest to my heart," she told Poole in April 1819—"I can hardly believe it possible." The Wordsworths, too, rejoiced and so did Mr. Dawes, Hartley's old schoolmaster at Ambleside, who gave the boys a holiday to celebrate the event. "The boys all huzza'd and there was *such an uproar*," Mrs. Coleridge told Poole. Such was the tale little William Wordsworth brought from school.

The following September, when young Sara was nearly seventeen years of age, her mother sent Poole an interesting glimpse of the children's life together in Greta Hall: "Hartley always discouraged his sister's erudite propensities, and tells her that Latin and Celibacy go together; but she playfully answers, 'Not the less for this, cease I to wander where the Muses haunt.' Derwent encourages and instructs her; they read Tacitus, Livy, Virgil and Cicero together; and when tired of these, she turns to Ariosto, Tasso, Chiabura [Chiabrera] and Dante."

The years that had embittered the feelings of Dorothy Wordsworth and of Sara Hutchinson toward Coleridge appeared to have had the opposite effect on Mrs. Coleridge. For the feelings of her husband and his continued silence and absence, combined with the tales which came to her of his opium and brandy, finally persuaded her that the separation that she had once detested was now for the best. Reunion with him was evidently impossible. "There is no chance of seeing him here, and for myself I have long since ceased to wish it," she told Poole in August 1818. Nevertheless, Mrs. Coleridge enjoyed the distinguished social atmosphere created by those who came to see Southey, the poet laureate, in this summer of 1818. Indeed, the domestic scene lives on her page when she tells Poole: "At the hour of nine we all assemble at the breakfast table—S his wife and two eldest daughters, myself and Sara, all well, except the good lady of the house who is in a very complaining way at present, (Mrs Lovell always breakfasted *alone* in the school-room and Hartley *alone* in his study). A note is brought in—Sir G and Ly B's compliments hope to see the whole party to dinner including the young ladies. We promise to go—." That afternoon at the Beaumonts, Mrs. Coleridge and Sara met Mr. Collins, whom the Beaumonts had commissioned to paint Sara's portrait.

"He has made a likeness of Sara in an oil painting in the character of Wordsworth's 'Highland Girl,' " she told Poole. "Wordsworth," she added, "admires the picture but objects to Sara's style of person and character of countenance for the subject she, he thought, might do for a sylph." The painter and the Beaumonts all liked the painting, which was exhibited the following spring in London. Before that Coleridge had already seen the picture privately, and his elaborate explanation to Collins of its effect on him suggests that, owing to long absence from Greta Hall, he was unable to estimate its value as a likeness. But he found it "exquisite" as a picture, which "has quite haunted my eye ever since," and "taken as a mere fancy piece, it is long since I have met with a work of art that has so much delighted me." If, however, he "described it as the union of simplicity with refinement," that would still be inadequate, he considered. Pictures of the Lake District poets were much in the air just now. A year before, Wordsworth's portrait had been painted by Richard Carruthers, which Southey thought a good likeness. Now, in November 1818, Coleridge told Charlotte Brent: "Leslie contrived to take a head of me which appears to be the most striking likeness ever taken—perhaps because I did not sit for it.''

When good news of Samuel came to her Mrs. Coleridge was pleased: "Mrs George Coleridge tell me," she wrote "that his brother the Colonel was much please with his society in town, in the Spring, and a gentleman, a friend of Colonel Coleridge's thought he had never been so agreebly entertained in his life, and that S.T.C. was the most astonishingly eloquent man he had ever known." At times Mrs. Coleridge's attitude toward her absent husband takes the tone of a mother sympathizing with a sweet misguided child—which in some ways he was. In this mood she described a romantically poetic visitor as necessarily pleasing Derwent, who "is full as romantic as ever his poor father was at his age."

For her daughter Sara Mrs. Coleridge's care and affection were as great as for her two sons. She had herself taught Sara Italian, learning it for that purpose, and from Sara's earliest years she had encouraged her studies. With pride she approved Sara's reading of *Don Quixote* in Spanish and later announced with natural pleasure the publication of Sara's translation of Martin Dobrizhoffer's *Latin History of the Abipones*, which Sara had made to help pay Derwent's university expenses. Promising a copy of the book to Poole on November 7, 1821, Mrs. Coleridge wrote with characteristically restrained disappointment: "Of course the Translator's name is *not* mentioned." Coleridge's reaction to the publication was more emotional: "unsurpassed for pure mother English by anything I have read for a long time." Lamb's comment on Sara's achievement—or rather on Sara herself—was amusingly critical: "I have seen Miss Coleridge, and wish I had just such a daughter. God love her! To think that she should have had to toil through five octaves of that cursed . . . Abbeypony History, and then to abridge them to three, and all for £113. At her years, to be doing stupid Jesuits' Latin into English, when she should be reading or writing Romances. Heaven send her uncle [Southey, who had suggested the work] do not breed her up a Quarterly Reviewer."

Nor were Mrs. Coleridge's letters to Poole confined to speaking of her children. "A few letters from C lately who is in his *better* way," she reported in April 1819, fearing "his lectures were not very profitable to him as he has not made me any remittance in consequence. Lady Beaumont, however," Mrs. Coleridge continued, "wrote to say she had seen him in Grosvenor Square [the Beaumonts' London home], and he was in better spirits than she had hoped to find him." To some gloomy foreboding of Poole Mrs. Coleridge replied, "What you say about S.T.C. is likely enough to happen. Alas, I dare not look forward: It seems to me impossible we ever should live together under a roof of our own, for we have not the means. Our separation has on the whole been for the best. You will easily see why. I grieve on the Children's account, poor things." The contrast between her husband's career and the increasing success of Southey, poet-laureate and well-known writer, a "lion of the Lakes," as she called him, was bitter to Mrs. Coleridge. People, she told

Poole, came to the church to be shown his pew there, and those with introductions came to the house. Coleridge, too, was angrily aware of this same contrast, and of his wife's admiration in this respect for Southey—a feeling which she no doubt readily expressed at times in her letters to her husband—most of which have disappeared.

In the spring of 1820 Coleridge was particularly happy in the company of Hartley and Derwent, who stayed with him for some time at the Gillmans'. "Nothing can exceed their fondness for their father," Coleridge told Allsop on April 10. "Would to Heaven, their dear Sister were with us—the cup of paternal joy would be full to the brim!"

This happy prelude ill prepared Coleridge for the crushing blow which followed two months later when he heard that Hartley had been expelled from his fellowship at Oriel College, Oxford. The charges against him were intemperance, general inattention to discipline, and undesirable associates. When on June 30 the news of Hartley's disgrace reached Coleridge, "a very heavy affliction came upon me," he told Allsop the following day, "with all the aggravation of Surprise—sudden as a peal of thunder from a cloudless sky." Derwent, who was with his father at the time, never forgot how deeply moved he was. Long afterward he wrote: "I have never seen any human being, before or since, so deeply afflicted. Not, as he said, by the temporal consequences of his son's misfortune, heavy as these were, but for the moral offence which it involved." Derwent had immediately, on the arrival of this news, set off for Oxford, while his father remained to write to Allsop and anxiously awaited the news that Derwent was to bring him on his return. "The worst news that ever reached my ears," Mrs. Coleridge, sad but self-controlled, told Poole the following March, while Hartley, having found a refuge with the Montagus in Bedford Square, translated *Medea* and prepared a volume of his own poems for publication. "Sometime hence when he shall have given sufficient proofs of steadiness of conduct, he will prepare himself for holy orders," continued Mrs. Coleridge with admirable practicality—"his letters on this subject are very affecting." As for Derwent, she told Poole, "his poor brother's misfortunes are a great burden upon his spirits at times and his father's situation in *mind*, *body* and *estate* oppresses him much."

Meanwhile, Coleridge was informing his friend Allsop of all the details, so far as he knew them, of Hartley's disgrace. His own knowledge of the matter was merely second hand, transmitted to him by the Gillmans, who had received a letter from Hartley's cousin at Oxford, John Taylor Coleridge, giving but few details of Hartley's expulsion. Then, characteristically reverting to his own personal sufferings caused by Hartley's faults, Coleridge described Hartley's intemperance as due to constitutional spontaneity, which even in early days led him to snatch whatever food or wine was placed before him, and which only recently the Gillmans and Coleridge himself had vainly attempted to eradicate when they saw Hartley "pouring glass after glass, with a kind of St Vitus nervousness."

The shame Coleridge now felt for his favorite child, whose virtues and weaknesses he had long suspected to be a repetition of his own, brought the past with Coleridge's own schemes and weaknesses before him. In this his innate impulse to self-expression found an unhappy satisfaction in the relief of opening his heart unrestrainedly to a friend—as often before to others. So now he made a full and humble confession of his opium addiction to Allsop.

Mistakenly believing that Hartley had returned to his mother instead of coming to him, Coleridge's outraged paternal affection and egotism—"as though I were not his father," as he told Derwent—resented Hartley's absence as an insult both to himself and the Gillmans. So to Derwent Samuel relieved his feelings, describing his nightly hysteria. "Last night," he wrote, "I screamed out but once only in my sleep. O! surely if Hartley knew or believed that I love him and linger after him as I do and ever have done, he would have come to me!"

Hartley, in fact, had not gone to his mother, who indeed was as deeply disappointed as her husband at her son's failure. Immediately on hearing the news she had turned to Sara Hutchinson for consolation. "Poor Mrs. Coleridge wants sadly to see me to talk about her unfortunate son," Sara Hutchinson told Mrs. Wordsworth. "The Fellows have stretched their power to the utmost—nothing can be proved against him," she wrote: "but indiscretions . . . but they wanted to be rid of him." For Mrs. Coleridge she had much sympathy: "I am truly sorry for her—for what can the poor helpless creature do for himself! She is very anxious that the best of it should be made to the Beaumonts."

Samuel, his emotions at least temporarily exhausted, turned in September to the practical aim of restoring Hartley's lost fellowship. With this intention he obtained two letters from Hartley stating the facts of the case as he saw them, and then on October 13, accompanied by Allsop, he set off for Oxford to fulfill this intention. There he would see Dr. Copleston, provost of Oriel, the chief authority respecting the fellowship. He would discuss the whole matter with him, present Hartley's account of it, and plead for leniency.

The result of the interview was, however, for poor Coleridge, most unsatisfactory. Instead of considering Hartley's return, the college authorities gave his father shocking details of his son's behavior as a Fellow, which had so scandalized them. Hartley had returned late at night drunk, so endangering the college with the risk of fire from his candle; he was absent from morning chapel; and he "was fond of society very different from that of his own Common Room, and by no means respectable." Therefore, "upon mature consideration of the case we were all of opinion that he was not fit to be admitted an Actual Fellow,—and that had we known a tenth part of what his Probationary year had brought to light, he never would have been elected at all." Such was the ultimate conclusion of this formidable university committee. Although expressed by Copleston with Oxonian courtesy and consideration, the Fellows' decision could not be changed. Before the day ended Copleston sent Coleridge a letter of sympathy, regret, and consolatory recognition of Hartley's good qualities. Allsop, who returned immediately with Coleridge, described their journey to Highgate as "perhaps the most painful recollection (one excepted) connected with the memory of Coleridge." But that was written after Coleridge's death.

Still anxious, Coleridge persuaded Hartley in the autumn to send explanatory, exculpatory letters with all the papers relating to the matter to all who had financially assisted him at Oxford, including Lady Beaumont, Poole, and others. For these Coleridge made preliminary drafts. "I have been more than usually unwell, with great depression of spirits, loss of appetite, frequent sickness, and a harrassing pain in my left knee," he told Allsop on November 26. He continued: "and at the same time anxious to preclude as much as I can the ill effects of poor Hartley's unhappy procrastination— . . . and this I could only do by taking on myself as much of the document writing as was contrivable." In this mood Coleridge drafted an enormous Coleridgian letter of tactful humility in which Hartley is made to say: "I cannot too soon enter a *disclaimer*, by a distinct declaration, that I do not put my veracity against the veracity of the Provost and resident Fellows of Oriel; but my disavowals against the assertions of their *informers*, whose evidence I solemnly assert to be false."

In mid-October, after a stormy meeting of the Fellows, Hartley's expulsion was confirmed and a solatium of £300 was offered to him for his immediate needs. On October 20 Copleston met Coleridge in London to discuss the matter, including the solatium. This Coleridge haughtily rejected, saying: "If my son be innocent of heavier part of your charges, far be it from me to persuade him to compromise his honour; if, after all his denials to me, he is guilty—he may do as he pleases but I will not be the channel of conveying the money to him." Nevertheless, indecision remained. Hartley consulted friends, including Wordsworth, Frere, and the Gillmans, and all advised rejection of the solatium. More letters to everybody by everybody followed, resulting in an impasse due to the college's refusal to agree to Hartley's terms of acceptance, which would imply a refutation of their more serious charges. Finally, Hartley accepted the money as a mitigation of a too harsh sentence, but on the condition that this acceptance implied no dishonor. Perhaps Derwent's summary remark on his brother's fall is the fairest: "The sentence might be considered severe, it could not be said to be unjust." At any rate poor Hartley's future path in life was devious and intemperate.

Hartley's failure evidently aroused fears in Coleridge for the future of Derwent. Thus on May 16, 1821, to guard Derwent from mishaps, Coleridge sent him a very long letter of warnings and advice. From dubious hopes of giving Derwent financial assistance at Cambridge he cried: "and God forbid but that by hook or crook you shall be enabled to make both ends meet, without incurring any Cambridge debt—the very thought of which agitates me." From this, Coleridge's thoughts turned for a moment to his debts to the Gillmans and his dubious hopes "of re-imbursing my best friends, Mr & Mrs Gillman, whose very virtues do at times throw me into a gloomy mood. How can it be otherwise when day after day I see them so generous, so high-hearted, and yet so industrious, self-denying, and economic—I know that they are at this moment out of pocket by me to between 3 and 400£.''

Then Coleridge reverted to Derwent, who, he warned, must be careful, if offered any high academic position at Cambridge, of its possible effect on his health. Fortunately, Derwent's health was never thus endangered, as no such position was ever offered to him. As alternatives Coleridge indicated to his son satisfactory possibilities: ''You may be a Tutor in a wealthy or noble family—you may (& I fondly hope you will) be a Clergyman—a Man of Letters—a Secretary to a Public Man.'' That Coleridge who so complained throughout his life of being a ''man of Letters'' should thus advise his son may seem extraordinary.

Despite his gratitude to the Gillmans, Coleridge's tardy realization of parental responsibilities now made him regret his lack of a home for his family and their friends. ''Would to God, my dearest Boy,'' he cried to Derwent, ''that I had a home of my own for you and your friends . . . it makes my heart ache, to know that I have not: tho' I have all and more than all, I fear, that my affectionate and more than generous Host and Hostess can supply, consistently with the performance of their own duties.'' And both Hartley and Derwent stayed with their father at the Gillmans' in the summer of 1821.

With the opening of the new year 1822, disturbing news about Derwent reached Coleridge. Unlike Hartley who had gained only a second class in his examination at Oxford, Derwent had gained a first in both his exams, but he had in the latest result been placed a little below his previous position in the first class. So terrible a failure as this slight decline in position by Derwent called for stern correction and exhortations by his father, who had far less sympathy for the blameless Derwent than for the erring Hartley, in whom he saw a replica of hmself. So now in mid-January 1822 Coleridge's annoyance found vent. The failure must be due to the shocking life Derwent was leading at Cambridge:

> extra-academic society, concerts, balls—Dressing, and an hour and a half or two hours not seldom devoted to so respectable a purpose—O God!—even the disappointment as to your success in the University, mortifying as I feel it, arising from such causes and morally ominous, as it becomes in your particular case and with the claims, that *you* must recognize on your exertions, is not the worst. This accursed coxcombry . . . sends a ferment into the very life-blood of a young man's sense and genius—and ends in a schirrus of the heart.

To bring home the full force of Derwent's wicked doings, Coleridge gave a remarkable description of his own immaculate way of life ''in my first term'' at Cambridge—as memory recalled, or distorted it. ''I read hard and systematically'' he wrote.

> I had no acquaintance, much less suitable, (i.e.) studious, companion in my own college. Six nights out of seven, as soon as chapel was over, I went to

Pembroke, to Middleton's [the present bishop of Calcutta] rooms—opened the door without speaking, made and poured out the tea and placed his cup beside his book—went on with my Aeschylus or Thucydides, as he with his mathematics, in silence till ½ past 9—then closed our books at the same moment—the size and college ale came in—and till 12 we had true Noctes atticae which I cannot to this hour think of without a strong emotion—With what delight did I not resume my reading in my own rooms at Jesus each following morning. Think you a ball or a concert or a lady party, or a literary club, would have left me in the same state?

Near the end of this long and angry letter to Derwent Coleridge reveals its basic inspiration. He had heard that Derwent, resenting his dependence on his father's friends, had described himself to a lady as a "mere poor child of charity"—a "mere almsman." Coleridge indignantly demanded, "Should a son have placed his father in so degrading a point of view and this in a letter to a vulgar tattling woman?" Piqued by this incident, Coleridge informed his son with paternal dignity: "I can spare a certain sum which is at your service, and which I consider as your's." He concluded, "I am not angry, Derwent!—but it is calamitous that you do not know how anxiously and affectionately I am your *Father*."

On receiving Derwent's reassuring reply Coleridge, somewhat mollified, answered him on January 15: "Of course, I am glad to be able to correct my fears as far as public balls, concerts, and time-murder in Narcissism—glad, because your character will be less *noised* and publicly talked of, as a gay youth."

Poor Derwent would perhaps have been astounded to learn of Coleridge's enthusiastic support at Cambridge of the French Revolution, by writing, in a train of gunpowder, "Liberty and Equality" on the lawns of Trinity, and setting it alight with the help of a fellow student, afterward Lord Lyndhurst.

Coleridge's anger was by no means soothed at this time by a letter from his wife, who, lacking information about Hartley's fellowship and the £300 solatium, reproved him for his long silence and his indifference toward his children, besides warning him against undue severity toward them. In reply Samuel cited the Gillmans' admiration for the delicacy with which he treated his sons. Nor was this all. Another dispute about Hartley immediately arose, in which Coleridge's wishes were opposed by Mrs. Coleridge, Southey, and the Wordsworths. The innocent cause of this contention was a kindly offer by Mr. Dawes to take Hartley as a teacher in his school. Samuel's fears for his son amid the temptations of London led him gladly to accept the offer for Hartley. This was much to the indignation of the others, who accused him of burying Hartley in the country. Hartley, however, accepted the post. To Dawes Coleridge wrote in high praise of Hartley's virtues, but he added that he had one great defect: "a narrow proud egotism . . . and for this very reason he is too often as selfish as a Beast." This, Coleridge added with unconscious humour, was unlike himself!

The opposition of Southey and Wordsworth to Coleridge's plan to send Hartley schoolmastering at Ambleside still rankled in Coleridge's mind, particularly because of a letter Wordsworth had written to Gillman. "Mournful," he told Allsop on May 30, "as my experience of Messrs Southey and Wordsworth in my own immediate concerns had been, of the latter especially, I was not prepared for their late behaviour as the contents of Mr W's Letters to Mr G [Gillman] were calculated to produce."

Throughout the summer and early autumn of 1822 Derwent and Hartley continued to cast shadows over their father's life. "It is now between four and five weeks since Derwent left Cambridge, spent 6 or 9 days in London, and then came to me evidently ill," he told John Taylor Coleridge on July 15. The illness was a fever which kept Derwent in bed nearly a month, while his father anxiously watched over him. At the same time Coleridge lost all sight of Hartley during one of the long disappearances that became Hartley's lifelong habit. He asked Taylor Coleridge not to give him any of the money that he held for Hartley, if Hartley turned up and asked for it. However, by August 4 the shadows were lessening, for Derwent was now out of danger and Hartley was about to go to the North to help Mr. Dawes. Characteristically doubting his ability as a schoolmaster, Hartley had only very reluctantly assented to his father's wish after a violent argument between the two, in which Coleridge said that, as Hartley had failed to maintain himself by writing for the press, he should accept Dawes' offer. Coleridge's annoyance at these inconveniences created by his sons turned to anger against his wife for her opposition to Hartley's rustication at Ambleside which he told Allsop was "much against the wish of his selfish *worretting*, ever-complaining never-satisfied Mother. He might go to perdition body and soul, the trouble, embarrassment and anguish remaining on my shoulders, rather than be saved at the risk of any occasional annoyance to her, or Mr Wordsworth's disapprobation—but hang her! she is not worth vexing about [sic] . . . it is grounded in pure selfishness." However, Mrs. Coleridge's protests were ignored, and by mid-November Hartley was teaching in Dawes' school. "Hartley Coleridge is with Mr Dawes," Dorothy Wordsworth told a friend a few days later. "He has not been long enough to have proved his skill and patience as a teacher; but Mr Dawes says he is very steady. He is the oddest looking creature you ever say—not taller than Mr de Quincey—(who was very small) with a beard as black as a raven. He is exactly like a Portuguese Jew." Thus it was that poor Hartley turned to the North—and never saw his father again.

On January 3, 1823, Mrs. Coleridge and Sara arrived at Moreton House, Highgate, on a visit to Coleridge, as he had anticipated to Allsop. For the last two months Mrs. Coleridge and Sara, now a charming girl just turned twenty, had been making a leisurely journey down to Ottery and the Coleridge family, besides calling on several old friends on the way. Mrs. Evans of Darley Hall—the scene for Mrs. Coleridge of bitter-sweet memories of twenty-two years ago—had welcomed them in the kindest manner, and Sara, as Mrs. Coleridge proudly told Poole, had "entered into correspondence with one of the ladies." Thence they proceeded to the Clarksons' home, now at Playford near Ipswich. After Christmas they departed for Highgate. There with Samuel, who had not seen Sara for ten years and found her "a sweet and delightful girl," they remained until the end of January. Three days after their arrival, Coleridge's two nephews, Henry Nelson Coleridge and John Taylor Coleridge came to Highgate and met Mrs. Coleridge and Sara for the first time. Although the visit of Mrs. Coleridge and Sara was marred by Samuel's illness, the account that Mrs. Coleridge sent to Mrs. Wordsworth was "cheerful," as Mrs. Wordsworth described it to Lady Beaumont. For many years Sara had longed to see her father, but unfortunately what she now thought of him we do not know.

At the end of January mother and daughter left Highgate for London, to stay with John Taylor Coleridge and his wife. There Sara was much admired for her beauty and the literary talent shown in her translation of the Latin *History of the Abipones*.

But Sara was by no means far from romance by this time. When recently Tom Poole had teased Sara, suggesting that such a bookworm would never desire a husband, Mrs. Coleridge had prophetically replied, "On the contrary, I am sure she will change her condition as soon as she can get the man of her heart." And now at Highgate the prophecy was fulfilled: for almost from their first meeting, Sara and her cousin Henry Nelson Coleridge fell in love. Before Sara and her mother left London at the end of February 1823 Sara and her cousin were secretly engaged. Henry Nelson, a serious Cambridge graduate who was twenty-four years old, had, shortly before Mrs. Coleridge's visit to Highgate, begun to call regularly on Coleridge whom he much admired, in order to take down his conversations which ultimately appeared as *Table Talk* in 1835, the year after Coleridge's death. "Sara and myself, are solemnly engaged to each other," the young man noted in his diary on March 5, 1823.

Sara's engagement was to last six years before it terminated in marriage, and it was kept secret from Coleridge for some time. Was it an inkling of this, or merely the inconvenience caused by the irruption of his wife and daughter into his peaceful dictation of the *Logosophia* to his enthralled pupil, that made Coleridge write on February 9, 1823, so churlish a refusal of John Taylor Coleridge's invitation to dine with them all? Nor was he well enough to visit Mrs. Coleridge and Sara in London. So February came to an end, and Mrs. Coleridge and Sara departed for Ottery. A few days later Lamb, in a letter to a friend, wrote the swansong of their visit with a rare sympathy for all. "The she-Coleridges have taken flight, to my regret," he wrote, "with Sara's own-made acquisitions, her unaffectedness and no-pretentions are beautiful. You might pass an age with her without suspecting that she knew any thing but her mother's tongue. I don't mean any reflection on Mrs Coleridge here. I had better have said her vernacular idiom. Poor Coleridge, I wish he had a home to receive his daughter in. But he is but a stranger or a visitor, in this world."

A fortnight later Coleridge complained to Mrs. Aders of his illness. "During the whole of my dear girl's stay in town," he wrote, "it confined me to my chamber—Even while she and her mother were at Highgate, I never had the power of going to town with them—and during the 5 weeks' interval between their leaving Highgate and returning for *one* day to take their parting leave for Devon, I never saw them." Two days before Coleridge's letter Mrs. Coleridge, with Sara amid the Ottery Coleridges, sent Poole a characteristically incisive comment upon their recent visit to her husband: "you will be pleased to hear," she told him "that our visits at Highgate and Ottery have been productive of the greatest satisfaction to all parties." The complacent tone of her remark was natural to a mother, for evidently Mrs. Coleridge was thinking rather of the secret engagement of Sara than of her husband.

The year 1824 opened badly for both Coleridge and his wife, who were much upset by Derwent's refusal, on quitting Cambridge, to return there in the hope of a fellowship or even to become a parson. Poor Mrs. Coleridge described the situation to Poole in February:

> In the midst of my perplexities on Derwent's account on his quitting Cambridge. I had only then learnt that he objected to taking orders at present, should not stand for an honour, not choosing to take the chance of a second rate one, and had not chance of a fellowship! Thus you see, my dear Mr. Poole, there is little else but disappointment for poor Sara, and me, to say nothing of S.T.C. & Hartley, the poor father is very much wounded by all this, but I hope his next letter will be written in a calmer state of mind, for poor Derwent has *now* done his best in accepting the situation of third Master of Plymouth School, from whence I have just received a good account of his health and determination to perform all the duties of the situation with the utmost regularity.

Characteristically calm and practical, Mrs. Coleridge, with no futile lamentations, gave Poole more details of Derwent's situation as well as Hartley's:

> He will, however, find it a very different sort of employment to the studies of a College, though he tells me he shall have leisure for his own improvement which he shall make a point of, and that having been previously acquainted with the other masters he feels himself already quite at home. The salary is 150 per annum, and he has an Exhibition or two for a few years with about 20 per annum, the income of which he must resign to me and his brother as we must, out of our little, pay his debts at Cambridge, something between 150 and 170 pnd, rather more than we expected, owing to his *not* having drawn on *that young friend*, I mentioned to you, from motive of delicacy, and never having had rooms in College—beside, maintaining himself through several vacations, a thing not calculated upon in the general way. Hartley says his brother is a beautiful Classic, and might have got a Fellowship at Oxford.

Mrs. Coleridge had better news of Hartley:

> Of Hartley I can send you a more cheering account—he has persevered very contentedly in the School, the profits of which nearly paid his expenses last half year; he wrote some articles for the B.C. which help him, and he is now

writing the *Article on Poetry* for the Encyclopaedia Metropolitana, which, perhaps, I mentioned in my last; it has been long in hand; but he would have finished it by this time, if our neighbour at Greta bank, Mr Calvert, had not prayed him to take his son, a youth of 18, as an evening pupil—much against all our wishes, as literary studies suit him better in the evening, and it is proper that he should walk and pay visits in the evening.

Young Sara, of course, was not forgotten by her mother, who gave Poole the following intimate glimpse of her.

Sara is translating an old French Memoir entitled—Memoirs of *The Chevalier de Bayard*. . . . She thinks it more difficult than the Latin of *The Abipones* for the warriors terms are so numerous, etc.—She had done what *is* done in the absence of her uncle [Southey] and as he has not yet read her performance I know not whether she will succeed or not; but I daresay it will do, for she is never weary of turning to books of reference, dictionaries, (of which this library furnishes several in old French) &c. Many of the Chevalier's exploits were acted in Italy so that she has immense folios of Italian Histories to look into, all of which is an amusement and a thing for which she seems to have a passion. She is, however, obliged to do very little of this work at one time on account of the eyes. Murray is to publish it in the summer, *in one volume*.

In this letter of February 1824 to Poole Mrs. Coleridge unconsciously reveals herself as a good impartial mother to her children, keenly, yet quietly observant of their individual temperaments and doings, interested, yet uncritical of their feelings and always helpful.

Far otherwise was Coleridge when he heard of Derwent's evil doings: irreligious rationalism instead of a clerical vocation. For Derwent, so different from Coleridge, there could be no such sympathetic understanding as for Hartley, so like himself. The basic cause of Derwent's wickedness, he told a Cambridge don, was vanity: "Vanity was so manifestly at the bottom of the whole, but I was more mortified by the shallowness than frightened by the profligacy and wickedness of his creed." However, a week later Coleridge sent the don better new of his errant son. "I have received a comfortable letter from Derwent," he wrote, "so far at least that he is determined to lay aside all his imagined convictions and consider as tho' they never had been."

During the following months young Sara Coleridge continued her translation of *Le Chevalier de Bayard*. In the spring of that year 1824 Sara called on her publisher in London and doubtless again visited her father in Highgate. "Sara thinks, by what I have said, that you will imagine that her papa never writes to us," Mrs. Coleridge now reported to Poole. "He does write much oftener than before he saw his daughter, but he is long in answering our letters; when we wish an immediate return we address our inquiries to Mrs Gillman who never keeps us in suspense."

Hartley had quickly vanished from the scene so far as his father was concerned. His schoolmastering at Ambleside had been of short duration, and he had now opened a school of his own, attended by fourteen boys. Of this no more is heard. But if Hartley was beyond reach, Coleridge could now unburden his mind and feelings to Derwent. In this mood he wrote to Derwent on December 21, 1825, complaining of "petty embarrassments." He cried, "I find myself decaying before I ever felt myself ripe." The list of miseries and grievances which followed, concluded with a new one: "I go from month to month as if I had no sons in the world, never hearing of you or Hartley." The *causa causans* of this letter was Coleridge's failure to obtain the assistance of John Taylor Coleridge in getting for Derwent a chaplaincy to the bishop of Quebec.

Nevertheless, Coleridge had been glad to find a change in Derwent, who, having now abandoned his temporary atheistical opinions, had returned to Cambridge and no longer refused to enter the church. For a time, indeed, Coleridge had feared that Derwent would become a wandering stone like his brother Hartley. Such being the situation, Coleridge improved it by sending Derwent, on January 4, 1826, a warning as to the importance of "will" in religious faith, with a copy of his *Aids to Reflection.* Speaking as "the father and not the author," he begged Derwent to give the work his most earnest and "unprejudiced attention." He also invited Derwent to come to him at Highgate.

His son's visit, however, brought Samuel a terrible shock—the news that Derwent meditated marriage to a young lady named Mary Pridham. Clearly, this called for the sternest of warnings—founded, of course, on Coleridge's own unfortunate experiences of marriage, to which, however, he naturally made no specific reference, but which Derwent must have well understood. "Experto Crede!" he cried.

> That the most heartwithering Sorrow that can betide a high, honourable, morally sensitive and affectionate-natured Man, (a guilty conscience excepted) is: to have placed himself incautiously in such a relation to a Young Woman as neither to have it in his power to discontinue his attentions without dishonour and remorse, nor to continue them without inward repugnance, and a future *life* of Discomfort, of vain Heart-yearnings and remediless Heart-wastings distinctly before his eyes—as the alternative—Either misery of Remorse, or Misery of Regret!

In this strain he continued, finally crying, "For God's sake, think and think again before you give the least portion of your own free-agency out of your own power. You give away more than Life." And he concluded by emphasizing that he was giving only general principles on the subject, not intended for particular persons.

Later, having heard the pleasant news that Mary Pridham was the daughter of a wealthy family, Coleridge's fears for Derwent vanished, and he most affectionately welcomed Mary Pridham in October 1827 as "my unseen daughter elect." Indeed, Mary Pridham inspired a poem beginning "Dear tho' unseen!'' and ending, "A father's blessing on Thee, gentle Maid.''

On first hearing of her son's engagement, Mrs. Coleridge was as unhappy as her husband had been—and largely for the same reasons: "I hope no child of mine," she warned Derwent on January 30, 1826, "will marry without a good certainty of supporting a family. I have known so many difficulties myself that I have reason to warn my children!'' Three days later young Sara told Derwent: "Your hint about 'marrying as soon as may be' had plunged Mama into one of those bogs of doubt and discomfort.''

As on previous occasions, but now more strongly than before, Coleridge felt the inconvenience of separation from his family. In this mood he told Derwent of his regrets:

> that we have not one family House, as the natural centre for all of you and your Home, as often as your calls admitted. I have felt this want very poignantly and not without an after-relish of *mortification*, with regard to your Sister: tho' as it is the only instance, and stands in contrast with the Rest, I should be an *Unthank*, if I did not turn away my eye from it—the more so, as the Obstacles have not been mere Excuses.—As the matter is, my intended argument holds—we must make the best of it—& not by neglect or long intervals of silence aggravate the evil.

Indeed, he added, if only his health were better and Hartley reformed, "What a comfort and delight it would be to have him with me, as a Literary Partner!'' He also asked Derwent to write and tell his mother how ill his father had been, and, as she was worried about her insurance money, to tell her that Mr. Green would pay for the insurance as long as he lived and would allocate money for it in his will. For further reassurance to Mrs. Coleridge, he added that, whatever his debts to the Gillmans might be at his death, they would make no claim upon this insurance money. Coleridge's hopes for Derwent's future were now rising since his decision to enter the church. His father now finally decided that Derwent "has a very fertile but somewhat shallow Surface-soil-below. I hope and I believe, there is rock and springs of pure water.''

Coleridge was still vexed by his failure to get Derwent ordained and installed in a curacy. The bishop of London had refused even Lady Beaumont's attempt to persuade him to ordain the young man, and neither of the two Coleridge nephews, John Taylor nor William Hart, bishop of Barbados, would help Derwent to a curacy. The following year, however, Coleridge's fears for Derwent ended when, on July 15, 1827, the bishop of Exeter ordained him. Next came a curacy at Helston in Cornwall, under a cousin, the Reverand James Duke Coleridge. It was soon followed by his additional appointment as master of the grammar school there. "Derwent," Mrs. Coleridge told Poole in the summer of 1827, "I am glad to say, is *performing* very industriously at his curacy at Helston where I am told he gives satisfaction to his parishioners.'' And she added a realistic description of the advantages and disadvantages of Derwent's life at Helston. Before the close of the year, on December 6, 1827, Derwent Coleridge married Mary Pridham at Helston. In 1841 he was appointed principal of St Mark's College in Chelsea, and he later became rector of Hanwell.

When at last Samuel heard of Sara's engagement to her cousin, Henry Nelson Coleridge, he was displeased. He objected to the marriage of first cousins in general, and a penniless barrister was not the husband he would choose for his daughter. Coleridge was also offended with Henry Nelson for other reasons, despite the record that the nephew was still making of his uncle's sayings. Henry Nelson had accompanied his cousin, William Hart Coleridge, bishop of Barbados, to his distant see, and Coleridge, who had appealed to the bishop without success to assist Derwent to a curacy, suspected Henry Nelson had not helped him in the matter. But even worse, Henry, as a result of his visit to the bishop, had written a book on the West Indies, which Mrs. Coleridge thought "very lively," but which Coleridge, although then ignorant of Sara's engagement, disliked for what he suspected to be an undignified reference to her: "I love a cousin; she is such an exquisite relation, just standing between me and the stranger to my name, drawing upon so many sources of love and tying them all up with every cord of human affection—almost my sister ere my wife!" Coleridge so resented the offending passage that he secured the withdrawal of the volume, which was republished with omissions in 1826.

So now, awaiting Sara's arrival and hearing from Mrs. Gillman some hint of the engagement between Henry Nelson Coleridge and Sara, Coleridge wrote to his wife for further information. In reply both Mrs. Coleridge and Sara wrote to him and, he told Edward Coleridge, "left me nothing to be informed of." It was now too late, he said, for him to express what his thoughts would have been had he been sufficiently in their confidence to be told of the engagement when it first occurred. But even in reticence his anger was apparent. To marry Sara to such an impecunious barrister as Henry Nelson he regarded with dyspathy, but he did not feel able either to oppose or sanction it: "For the man and the father are too strong in my soul, for me not to shrink from the thought of my only daughter—and *such* a daughter—condemned to a miserable heart-wasting; or not to regard the alternative as a *lesser evil*. I have not the heart either to pass such a sentence, or in any way to be aidant thereto." Two years before he had dictated to Henry Nelson for *Table Talk* his opinions on just such a marriage as this, and his attitude now was consistent with the ideas he then expressed: "Up to twenty-one, I hold a father to have power over his children as to marriage, after that age, authority and influence only . . . I should incline to disapprove the marriage of first cousins; but the Church has decided otherwise."

At length, on September 17, 1827, Sara arrived at Highgate. Coleridge found her "all the most ambitious father could desire. I have no fortune to leave, no *trust* of this kind in the transfer of which I have any interest of duty and therefore it has ever been my fixed principle in respect of marriage that, after my children have reached the years of discretion—as a friend I was ready to give them my best advice if it were asked, while it could be of any service; but as a father I had only my prayers and my blessing to give," he told Mrs. Coleridge.

Since August 1827 Henry Nelson Coleridge's visits to Highgate to record his uncle's conversation had been suspended, owing to Coleridge's dislike of his courtship of his daughter; and they were not resumed until April 1830. But now in August 1829, amid preparations for the impending marriage, Henry Nelson called at Highgate and after meeting his uncle went on to Ottery, and thence continued his journey to Greta Hall where he arrived on September 1, two days before the wedding. Meanwhile, on August 28 Coleridge wrote to Derwent mentioning Henry's visit, but making no allusion to the approaching marriage. His nearest approach to the subject, which had evidently appeared in Derwent's letter, was a sardonic reference to the approaching honeymoon: "the Mel Lunaticum (Lunare is the purer Latin, I believe) Temporis and gentle privacy of recent bliss is to have the Public House—the little romantic inn, I should say, at Pattersdale for its locality." Next, suddenly changing the subject, Coleridge told Derwent—who was now a father—"I am in a degree very unusual for me fidgetty to see and kiss my little Derwent." He also informed his son that Lady Beaumont (who had died on July 14, 1829), had left him a legacy of fifty pounds which he was sending to Mrs. Coleridge for Hartley, adding "Would to God! it had been twice ten times the sum." To Derwent's wife Mary he sent his usual blessings and praises.

In mid-July 1829 Mrs. Coleridge anticipated Sara's marriage in a state of anxiety and depression. Nor was the latest news of Coleridge remedial. "Your account of S.T.C. was better than the one contained in a letter last morning from our excellent friend, Mrs Gillman," she told Poole. "You must have met him in a lucky hour—she says he has been a great sufferer of late, and has rallied at short intervals only; he has been obliged to keep much to his room, even at meals, and for the present has given up his Thursday evening parties—she says, be assured we will take all possible care of him, but every species of excitement must, for the present, be kept from him, for fear of increasing the tendency to erysipelas that Mr Gillman so much dreads. This account of her father," Mrs. Coleridge continued,

> has distressed Sara greatly, and added some weight to her present anxieties respecting the approaching change in her condition, separation from her dear, and most highly-valued friend R.S. (Robert Southey) her beloved cousins, poor Hartley, the Wordsworths,—her aunts, *All*; this most delightful land of her birth—and last, not least, I guess, the parting with her Mother, by whose side she has lived, (with the exception of a year and a half's absence in the South, and a few occasional months' absence beside) for more than 26 years, and being an only one, she has been to that mother, almost *more* than a daughter.

Mrs. Coleridge's anxiety for her daughter's future happiness now found detailed expression to Poole:

> In the month of September her cousin, H(enry) N(elson) C(oleridge), if nothing should happen to prevent, means to join us here; and they are to be united at out parish church of Crossthwaite, and then proceed to a lodging

in some one of the vales, perhaps Grasmere for 3 for 4 weeks—before going finally to town, where I am sorry to say, it seems her lot to dwell; which would be no matter of regret to either of us, if she were a strong woman, and had no such decided habits fitting her for a quiet life in the country. A barrister's wife sees but little of her husband, so that Sara will be transported from a *too* bustling family, to one of utter loneliness, except from occasional vistiors—she thinks she shall find plenty of employ, and amusements, for her leisure and I pray that she may find it so. The lawyer's vacation lasts 6, or 7 weeks in autumn, which, in many instances is spent in the country. If they have their health, and his business increases, all will I hope, be well—he is very rheumatic at present, or rather has been so this spring—and is just, only, convalescent. Perhaps you know that he has resigned the Secretaryship to King's College, London—it was calculated by the committee, that 2 secretaries could not be afforded, in which case Henry could not remain, as it would take up *more* than the whole of his time. This resignation has been a great grief to me, and occasioned great opposition to their immediate union, on the female part, but we gained nothing by resistance, and the thing is, it seems, to take place, relying on an increase of business, and on the being made reporter of the New court of Equity next year which would fully compensate for the loss of the Secretaryship to the new College.

On September 3, 1829, at Crossthwaite Church as Mrs. Coleridge had anticipated, the marriage of Henry Nelson Coleridge to his cousin, Sara Coleridge, took place with éclat. Mrs. Coleridge, in a much happier mood, described the event to Poole three weeks later:

Henry is quite enchanted with all here—and full of thankfulness for the manner in which everything was conducted to do them honour on the important day, which happened to be fair, *all through* for a wonder; Mr John Wordsworth performed the ceremony—Mr Southey gave the bride away—Mr Senhouse with his 4 young ladies (bridesmaids), General and Mrs Peachey with my sister, Martha, and all our girls, making 8 bridesmaids including Dora Wordsworth, Miss Trevenan etc. accompanied them to church in four carriages all private over which was a saving of expense to us; (Henry brought a carriage with him from Lancaster, which his brother-in-law, Mr Patteson has spared him for the time he stays). After church a very elegant breakfat was ready prepared, in part, on the evening before, under the superintendence of Edith and her sister, in Mr Southey's study, which went off well, and at one o'clock the separations began—the pair, for Pattersdale, the rest for Derwent-Water bay, the present residence of Mr Senhouse, where a dinner, ball and supper was given, and they separated at 4 the next morning.

Nevertheless, contemplating her impending departure from Greta Hall and her friends in the Lakes District, Mrs. Coleridge was far from elated. "Do not suppose that I went to this merry meeting," she continued to Poole. "I remained at home with my poor sister Lovell, and even, began some of my packing, such as books, which was better than sitting quite still, and thinking of the miseries of quitting a beloved residence of 29 years duration which, you will see, by this date I have just undergone." In a postscript she added: "Mrs Gillman writes us that S.T.C. is a good deal indisposed."

In her previous letter to Poole of July 15, Mrs. Coleridge had mournfully described her intended journey after the departure of her daughter and son-in-law: "As soon as I can get away, I am to go to Helston, for a *long* visit—where I shall finally settle I know not, yet: [Derwent] and his wife say my natural home is with them—time will show; at my age, perhaps, it ought not to be a matter of *very great moment* where the time is past [*sic*] between the present and the last home—but old age is full of doubts, fears, and cares, unknown to earlier years." Shortly after the wedding Mrs. Coleridge paid a visit to Rydal Mount, before going on to Helston in Cornwall to stay with Derwent and his wife and to see their new baby. One of Derwent's parishioners who had attended the wedding brought Mrs. Coleridge back with her to Cornwall in her carriage. On the way Mrs. Coleridge visited several friends. A little later she made a permanent home with Sara in London and returned only once (in 1831) to Greta Hall. Sara never returned.

Poor Hartley, although absent from the wedding festivities, was not unmindful of them and sent his mother a cheerful message which strangely contrasted with the gloomy forebodings of his mother and sister: "Happy, most happy and full of hope am I!"

Mrs. Coleridge's distress on leaving Keswick was not chiefly at leaving Greta Hall but principally at leaving the vicinity of poor Hartley, wandering like the winds about Lakeland, restless, drinking, deeply repenting in profound Christian humility, but utterly unable to repress the wandering instinct which he had inherited from his father. His mother always provided for Hartley's needs; unhappy but never unsympathetic, she never lost patience with her son.

To Mrs. Clarkson in April 1830 Dorothy Wordsworth described Hartley's way of life in interesting detail. "Worst of all," she wrote,

> is Hartley's hopeless state. We had provided good lodging for him, he had no one want, was liked by the people of the house, and for seven weeks was steady and industrious. Money came to repay him for his work, and what does he do? Instead of discharging just debts, he pays a score off at the public house, and with eight sovereigns in his pocket takes off—is now wandering somewhere, and will go on wandering till some charitable person leads the vagrant home. We have only heard of his lodging at first at different inns—this no doubt while the money lasted—and since of his having been seen on the roads, and having lodged in this Barn or that. It has been my sad office, to report to his poor mother of his doings, but my *late* reports have been of cheering kind. I now dread the task that is before me. I shall not, however, write till he is again housed with the charitable Matron who is willing again to receive him. You will perhaps say, my dear friend, "Why do you not rouse the country and send after him? or at least yourselves seek him out?" Alas, we have done this so often without good coming. We are determined not to stir—but it is impossible not to be very much distressed and uneasy in mind, and especially for his Mother's sake.

Derwent saw Hartley but twice in these later years, first in 1843 and again on his deathbed in 1849.

The marriage of Derwent and that of Sara inevitably brought new interests into Coleridge's life of a less abstract nature than metaphysics, philosophy, or theology. On April 2, 1830, Dorothy Wordsworth sent news of the Coleridges to Crabb Robinson. "S. T. Coleridge continues to live at Highgate as usual," she wrote, "—attacked by occasional fits of sharp illness; but always, to a certain point, recovering from them—and I believe, he is publishing some new work—upon the old abstruse subjects. His daughter is happily settled near him in London, but they cannot see much of each other. To walk is impossible—and to be otherwise conveyed is too expensive for a young lawyer's wife who has his [sic] fortune to make. . . . Miss Hutchinson is with the Southeys."

Five days later Dorothy Wordsworth sent Catherine Clarkson the latest news of the Coleridges:

> Poor Mrs Coleridge! We miss her very much out of the country, though we saw little of her. She regrets what she has lost bitterly, yet is well pleased with her daughter-in-law, and has great comfort in Derwent, but at her age it is a great change—to a boarding school with ten boys in the house—and a little baby to boot, and another expected ere very long—but in September (and this I think is no cause for joy) Sara is to be confined—and, of course her mother goes to nurse her and I almost fancy that after that time Sara will not be able to go on without her help.

From Derwent's home at Helston on June 25, 1830, Mrs. Coleridge informed Poole: "Sara wishes me to be with her at her expected confinement which will take place at Hempstead, (by the blessing of Providence) where her husband has taken a small furnished house." In mid-September 1830, Mrs. Coleridge described to Poole her arrival at her daughter's house in London,—which was to become for both mother and daughter a permanent home:

> I found myself at Downshire Hill before the young couple had risen, which Sara was a little annoyed at, not expecting me so early. I found Sara in much better condition than I had ever hoped, though not without all the minor annoyances of her situation, from the thraldom of which she expects to be relieved in the course of the next week . . . Mrs and Mr Gillman were here this morning, and have taken Henry away in their carriage to see his uncle, who is very poorly at this time; I have not yet seen him, but as soon as he is well enough, after his daughter is safe in bed he will come over."

On October 7, 1830, Sara's first child, a boy, was born. The next day Mrs. Coleridge informed Poole of the birth:

> Yesterday forenoon, about 11 o'clock Sara was safely brought to bed of a boy who, with his mother, is going on well. He is about middle size, a little more than 8 pounds in weight. All parties seem satisfied with his appearance, but his father thinks he is too much like himself to be pretty; he wished for a girl, but is too happy at the well-doing of his wife to care, very much, about the sex of the child for she is better than could have been ex-

pected. I wrote in her room and she has just requested her kindest, best regards to you. Poor father at Highgate, has been very nervous about her, he will be now, relieved.

"Mrs. Coleridge is the proudest and busiest of Grandmothers," wrote Dorothy Wordsworth to Mrs. Clarkson in November. "Sara an excellent nurse and her husband the most contented of men . . . Poor S.T.C. declining in Body, but they tell us is as vigorous as ever in mind."

In mid-August 1832 Coleridge went to Hampstead for the christening in church of his granddaughter Edith, Sara's second child. He spent the day with the family, including Mrs. Coleridge, who sent Poole an account of her husband's visit in a letter of general gossip. "What will perhaps greatly surprize you as it did all his friends," she wrote, "the grandfather came from Highgate to be present, and to pass the rest of the day here!" As young Gillman, now the "Revd. James," performed the ceremony and brought Coleridge and took him back at ten o'clock that night, undue exertion by Coleridge was not required. Mrs Coleridge was glad to say that when Henry called the next day, he found "grandfather none the worse for the exertion he had made." Indeed, Coleridge's chief exertion appears to have been talking, for as Mrs Coleridge described it: "His power of continuous talking seems unabated, for he talked incessantly for full five hours to the great entertainment" of the few friends assembled.

Mrs. Coleridge also asked Poole to send her son-in-law any poems that he had by Coleridge, as Henry was preparing a cheap edition: "Could you have the goodness to spare us what you have by you—it would be a great charity—we hope that something may be made for him, for, of course, he must 'sorely want it'"

The influence of Coleridge's experience at the baptismal service he soon revealed in his conversation with his son-in-law Henry Nelson Coleridge, which was later published in *Table Talk*. "I think the baptismal service almost perfect," he told his son-in-law, "None of the services of the Chruch affect me so much as this. I never could attend a christening without tears bursting forth, at the sight of the helpless innocent in a pious glergyman's arms." Coleridge's sonnet "My Baptismal Birthday" was entitled in Mrs. Gillman's MS. copy "Lines composed on a sick bed, under severe bodily suffering on my spiritual birthday, October 18 [1832]." The poem ends thus:

> The heir of Heaven—henceforth I fear not death,
> In Christ I live! in Christ I draw the breath
> Of the true life!—Let then earth, sea, and sky
> Make war against me! On my front I show
> Their mighty Master's seal. In vain they try
> To end my life, that can but end its woe.—
> Is that a death-bed where a Christian lies?—
> Yes! but not his, 'tis Death itself there dies.

7   The Talker (1823-30)

"In truth, he's no beauty! cry'd Moll, Poll, and Tab,
But they all of them own'd He'd the gift of the Gab."
—Coleridge (on himself) to Mrs. Charles Aders, November 1833

"He talks as a bird sings, as if he could not help it; it is
his nature."
—Wordsworth to J. Payne Collier [late 1817]

Before the close of November 1823, during Coleridge's absence with Mrs.
Gillman at Ramsgate, Dr. Gillman moved their home from Moreton House to
No. 3 The Grove, also in Highgate. This house now bears a plaque in com-
memoration of Coleridge's residence there.

Coleridge was delighted with his new home, not only for itself, but also for
the extensive views spread before the window of the back attic that—rejecting
a second floor room next to the Gillmans—he had chosen for himself. "A large
and handsome mansion," he described the house, "and the view from the window
of the attic, which I have chosen as my bed and bookroom, commands a view
over Southampton Farm, Kenwood and Hampstead, not surpassed within a
hundred miles of London." He told a friend, "Our new home is and looks
comely, and of an imposing respectability; the views from the garden-side are
substitutes for Cumberland especially from the attic in which I and my books
are now installed; Mr Gillman has shown much taste in smartening, smoothing
and re-creating the garden, a gloomy wilderness of shrubs."

A room on the floor below his attic was also allotted for his sole use, where
he could dictate to his literary helpers and meet his friends. Characteristically
punning, he spoke of his evenings dedicated to serious discourse with his admiring or merely curious visitors as "Attic Nights." A year or two later the
beneficent Gillmans delighted Coleridge by rebuilding the attic and leveling its
sloping ceiling.

It is Carlyle, in one of the finest passages of his prose, who give us the best
introduction—though slightly ironic—to this final period of Coleridge's
career:

Coleridge sat on the brow of Highgate Hill, in those years, looking down on London and its smoke-tumult, like a sage escaped from the inanity of life's battle; attracting towards him the thoughts of innumerable brave souls still engaged there. His express contributions to poetry, philosophy, or any specific province of human literature or enlightenment, has been small and sadly intermittent; but he had, especially among young inquiring men, a higher than literary, a kind of prophetic or magician character. He was thought to hold, he alone in England, the key of German and other Transcendentalisms; knew the sublime secret of believing by "the reason" what "the understanding" had been obliged to fling out as incredible; and could still, after Hume and Voltaire had done their best and worst with him, profess himself an orthodox Christian, and say and print to the Church of England, with its singular old rubrics and surplices at Allhallowtide, *Esto perpetua*. A sublime man; who, alone in those dark days, had saved his crown of spiritual manhood; escaping from the black materialisms, and revolutionary deluges, with "God, Freedom, Immortality" still his; a king of men. The practical intellects of the world did not much heed him, or carelessly reckoned him a metaphysical dreamer: but to the rising spirits of the young generation he had his dusky sublime character; and sat there as a kind of *Magus*, girt in mystery and enigma; his Dodona oak-grove [Mr. Gillman's house at Highgate] whispering strange things, uncertain whether oracles or jargon.*

In his new home, No. 3 The Grove, Coleridge was very happy amid surroundings which Carlyle thus describes:

He would stroll about the pleasant garden with you, sit in the pleasant rooms of the place,—perhaps take you to his own peculiar room, high up, with a rearward view, which was the chief view of all. A really charming outlook, in fine weather. Close at hand, wide sweep of flowery leafy gardens, their few houses mostly hidden, the very chimney-pots veiled under blossomy umbrage, flowed gloriously down hill; gloriously issuing in wide-tufted undulating plain-country, rich in all charms of field and town. Waving blooming country of the brightest green; dotted all over with handsome villas, handsome groves; crossed by roads and human traffic, here inaudible or heard only as a musical hum: and behind all, swam, under olive-tinted haze, the illimitable limitary ocean of London, with its domes and steeples definite in the sun, big Paul's and the many memories attached to it hanging high over all. Nowhere, of its kind, could you see a grander prospect on a bright summer day, with the set of the air going southward,—southward, and so draping with the city-smoke not *you* but the city.

Such was the view which lay before Coleridge's eyes. He loved to see the sunsets from his western window, and on evenings of unusual beauty he would call those at hand to see and share his rapture. His nephew, Henry Nelson Coleridge, never forgot a Midsummer Day of 1827, the sun setting in splendor

*Thomas Carlyle, *Life of John Sterling* (1851), chap. 8 (Coleridge).

over Caen Wood, the evening peace about them as Coleridge stood gazing silently at the scene for nearly ten minutes, "in an almost trance-like state; his eyes swam in tears, his head inclined a little forward, and there was a slight uplifting of the fingers, which seemed to tell me that he was in prayer."

At Grove House Coleridge passed the last ten years of his life with but a very occasional and short intermission to visit his friends, except for the continental tour with Wordsworth and his daughter Dora. At Grove House, on Thursday afternoons and evenings, Coleridge's famous "conversations" were held. To Stuart, in July 1825, Coleridge gave an interesting description of these Thursday meetings. "I hope," he wrote,

> you will remember our Highgate Thursday Conversation Evenings on your return to town: because if you come once, I flatter myself, you will afterwards be no unfrequent Visitor. At least, I have never been at any of the town Conversazioni, literary or artistical, in which the conversation has been more miscellaneous, without degenerating into *Pinches*, a pinch of this, and a pinch of that, without the least connection between the subjects, and with as little interest. . . . There is one thing too, that I can not help considering as a recommendation to our Evenings, that in addition to a few Ladies and pretty Lasses we have seldom more than 5 or 6 in company, and these generally of as many different professions or pursuits—a few weeks ago we had present, two Painters, two Poets, one Divine, an eminent Chemist and Naturalist, a Major, a Naval Captain and Voyager, a Physician, a Colonial Chief Justice, a Barrister and a Baronet—&c. This was the most numerous Meeting we ever had.

These meetings had soon developed from the frequent visits of many friends and unknown admirers, whose unexpected calls sometimes inconvenienced both Coleridge and the Gillmans. Henceforth, in addition to these Thursday conversations, encouraged and assisted by the Gillmans—who paid all expenses and were delighted to meet Coleridge's distinguished acquaintances—Coleridge generously increased his dinner parties and receptions, in which the Gillmans were co-host and co-hostess with himself.

Not only dinner guests but also ever larger numbers of serious-minded souls, including many Americans, came to see and hear the renowned talker, whose "Conversations"—which, as Madame de Staël had said, were in fact "monologues"—covered anything and everything, from the ordinary topics of the day to the rarest regions of metaphysics, religion and political idealism. Coleridge's own opinion of these monologues he once clearly expressed to Allsop, saying, "a *conver*-or, to mint a more appropriate term, *one*-versatione." These "conversations" would now be recognized as streams of subconscious thoughts and feelings, largely expressive of the leading ideas and opinions long cogitated, which throughout so much of Coleridge's life he had intended to present to the world in a hundred dream volumes. So now, as the sole occupant of his small stage at The Grove, he found satisfaction for his past disappointments, as well as for his simple vanity, in dissertating to his small but select audiences, which, merely by their presence, testified to his fame. Thus, heedless of his hearers and of time, he allowed his streams of the subconscious to flow without restraint. It is, therefore, not surprising that the responses of members of Coleridge's audiences varied at times from enthusiastic admiration to doubts and disappointment.

That such unrestrained talk might be sometimes due to hysteria Coleridge had once unconsciously recognized when, annoyed with Poole's good advice, he compared Poole to a half-witted fool talking nonsense mechanically, unable to stop. Basically, too, a later critic of Coleridge, Walter Bagehot—who was eight years old when Coleridge died—expressed a similar opinion in his description of these "Conversations"; for Bagehot knew much about Coleridge from reliable sources. Although trenchant, Bagehot showed a psychological insight rare in his time when he wrote,

> In fact, the habit of continuous speech is a symptom of mental deficiency. It proceeds from not knowing what is going on in other people's minds. Samuel Taylor Coleridge, it is well known, talked to everybody, and to everybody alike; like a Christian divine, he did not regard persons. "That is a fine opera Mr. Coleridge," said a young lady, some fifty years back. "Yes, Ma'am; and I remember Kant somewhere makes a very similar remark, for, as *we* know, the idea of philosophical infinity . . . " Now this sort of talk will answer with two sorts of people—with comfortable, stolid people who don't understand it at all—who don't feel that they ought to understand it—who feel they ought not—that *they* are to sell treacle and appreciate figs—but that there *is* this transcendental superlunary sphere, which is known to others—which is now revealed in the spiritual speaker, the unmitigated oracle, the evidently celestial sound. That the dreamy orator himself has no more notion what is passing in their minds than they have what is running through his, is of no consequence at all. If he did know it, he would be silent; he would be jarred to feel how utterly he was misunderstood; it would break the flow of his everlasting words. Much better that he should run on in a never pausing stream, and that the wondering rustics should admire for ever.

So much for the Devil's Advocate! But without exaggeration, certainly many of Coleridge's admiring hearers during this final period of his life resemble the rustics of Goldsmith's *Deserted Village*, when listening to the schoolmaster:

> While words of learned length and thundering sound,
> Amazed the gazing rustics ranged around,
> And still they gazed, and still the wonder grew,
> That one small head should carry all he knew.

Nor was Bagehot more merciful to Coleridge's mental weakness of indecision, as the following passage shows: "On what plan, Mr Coleridge, are you arranging your books? inquired a lady. Plan, Madam? I have no plan: at first I had a principle; but then I had another, and now I do not know."

Wordsworth, whose opinion of Coleridge's talk was probably less remote from Hazlitt than his occasional kindly references to it might suggest, had written in 1817: "He talks as a bird sings. As if he could not help it: it is his nature." Ten years after Coleridge's death Wordsworth likened his talk to "a majestic river, the sound or sight of whose course you caught at intervals, which was sometimes concealed by forests, sometimes lost in sand, then came flashing out broad and distinct, then again took a turn which your eye could not follow, yet you knew and felt that it was the same river; so," he said, "there was always a grain, a stream, in Coleridge's discourse, always a connection between its parts in his own mind, though one not always perceptible to the minds of others."

For Coleridge as well as for his audiences this final essentially conversational period of his life was particularly satisfactory. From the poetry of his early years he had passed to political journalism, and from journalism to written work and lecturing; but to none had he been entirely devoted. Journalism and lecturing he had always hated; the writing of books he had always found so difficult that hardly any of those he dreamed of were written, and what he did write disappointed him financially and tortured him through hostile criticism. In these weekly conversations he evaded hostile critics and satisfied his social feelings and somewhat naïve vanity.

Whatever his audiences felt about them, Coleridge himself greatly enjoyed his weekly performances. They were, he said, far superior to all such, "literary or artistical," that he had attended in London. Despite his studied, benevolent modesty, his pleasure in his growing fame was evident, and if his audience included any "man of rank," as he called such, his pleasure was greatly increased. For Coleridge was more interested in the social standing of his hearers than in their intellectual qualifications. Yet the list of some seventy persons who recorded their impressions of these meetings does not include many of high intellectual importance, even in their own day, and fewer still who are now remembered.

The fame of these orations was spread not only by individual enthusiasts, but also by such journalists as John Wilson (the famous "Christopher North"), then well known for his *Noctes Ambrosianae*, who, in 1827 with a touch of Carlyle's acidity, wrote of Coleridge in that work: "You don't know Samuel Taylor Coleridge—do you? He writes but indifferent books, begging his pardon; witness his *Friend*, his *Lay Sermons*, his *Aids to Reflection*; but he becomes inspired by the sound of his own silver voice, and pours out wisdom like a sea."

Coleridge was ever ready for conversation, or rather monologues, with his friends when they called upon him—at all times, not only on the Thursdays specially reserved for these semipublic orations. Among the most regular attenders at these were Leslie the Royal Academician, Judge Talfourd, Basil Montagu, The Right Honorable J. Hookham Frere, Professor J. H. Green, Archdeacon Julius Hare, John Sterling, Henry N. Coleridge the poet's nephew, and Lord Hatherly. Others who came included Mr. and Mrs. Aders, William Collins the painter, Thomas Chalmers (a distinguished preacher), and Stuart the newspaper editor.

Carlyle's description of the protagonist in these performances, Coleridge himself, is as percipient as his general account of Coleridge at Highgate, previously quoted:

The good man, he was now getting old, towards sixty perhaps; and gave you the idea of life that had been full of sufferings; a life heavy-laden, half-vanquished, still swimming painfully, painfully, in seas of manifold physical and other bewilderment. Brow and head were round and of massive weight, but the face was flabby and irresolute. The deep eyes, of a light hazel, were as full of sorrow as of inspiration; confused pain looked mildly from them as in a kind of mild astonishment. The whole figure and air, good and amiable otherwise, might be called flabby and irresolute; expressive of weakness under possibility of strength. He hung loosely on his limbs, with knees bent and stooping attitude; in walking he rather shuffled than decisively stept; and a lady once remarked, he never could fix which side of the garden walk would suit him best, but continually shifted, in cork-screw fashion, and kept trying both. A heavy-laden high-aspiring and surely much-suffering man. His voice, naturally soft and good, had contracted itself into a plaintive snuffle and singsong; he spoke as if preaching,—you would have said preaching earnestly and also hopelessly the weightiest things, I still recollect his "object" and "subject," terms of continual recurrence in the Kantean province; and how he sang and snuffled them into "Om-m-mject" and "sum-m-mject" with a kind of solemn shake or quaver, as he rolled along. No talk, in his century or in any other, could be more surprising.

In September John Wilson as "Christopher North," now more appreciative, praised Coleridge's conversations in His *Noctes Ambrosianae*, saying: "I have heard Coleridge. That man is entitled to speak until Doomsday—or rather the genius within him—for he is inspired. Wind him up, and away he goes, discoursing most excellent music—without a discord—full, ample, inexhaustibly serious and divine." In later years Bryan Waller Procter (Larry Cornwall) recalled Coleridge's conversations of this time: "He talked with everybody, about anything . . . but he seldom talked of himself or his affairs."

Despite Coleridge's many divergent interests throughout the year 1827 his regular "Conversations" continued. A frequent visitor among Coleridge's audience on these occasions was a young barrister twenty-six years of age, William Page Wood—"Learned and Pious"—who on being made Lord Chancellor in 1851 became Baron Hatherley. Hatherley's recollection of these visits is particularly interesting. "Every Thursday evening was spent by Mr and Mrs Montagu at Highgate, in the company of Coleridge," he wrote.

I had the privilege, through Mr Montagu's kindness, of frequently accompanying him on these pilgrimages, and I entertain most lively recollections of many an evening passed there of highest enjoyment and interest. It is well known that Coleridge poured out all the riches of his prodigious memory, and all the poetry of his brilliant imagination, to every listener. I was not so only addressed myself, but I heard the whole of the poet philosopher's favourite system of Polarities—the Prothesis, the Thesis, the Mesothesis, and the Antithesis—showered down on a young lady of seventeen, with as much unction as he afterwards expounded it to Edward Irving.

The record made by the then famous Edinburgh preacher and professor of philosophy Thomas Chalmers of his first visit to Coleridge's talks on May 10, 1827, gives us a particularly intersting glimpse of the occasion:

Irving and I went to Bedford-square. Mr and Mrs Montagu took us out in their carriage to Highgate, where we spent three hours with the great Coleridge. . . . His conversation, which flowed in a mighty unremitting stream, is most astonishing, but, I must confess, to me still unintelligible. I caught occasional glimpses of what he would be at, but mainly he was very far out of all sight and all sympathy. I hold it, however, a great acquisition to have become acquainted with him. You know that Irving sits at his feet, and drinks in the inspiration of every syllable that falls from him. There is a secret, and to me as yet unintelligible communion of spirit between them on the ground of a certain German mysticism and transcendental lake-poetry which I am not yet up to. Gordon [a clerical friend in Edinburgh] says it is all unintelligible nonsense, and I am sure a plain Fife man as uncle "Tammas," had he been alive, would have pronounced it the greatest *buff* he had ever heard in his life.

Coleridge's nephew and son-in-law, Henry Nelson Coleridge, whose admiration for his uncle's talk had led him (as previously stated) to copy during several years, in private audiences, the words of wisdom that fell from Coleridge's lips at the time and to publish them as *Table Talk* a year after Coleridge's death, felt, however, that he had failed in *Table Talk* to create an adequate appreciation of these conversations.

"When I look upon the scanty memorial, which I have alone preserved of this afternoon's converse," Henry Nelson Coleridge wrote on June 24, 1827, "I am tempted to burn these pages in despair. Mr Coleridge talked a volume of criticism that day, which printed *verbatim* as he spoke it, would have made the reputation of any other person but himself. He was, indeed, particularly brilliant and enchanting; and I left him at night so thoroughly *magnetized*, that I could not for two or three days afterwards reflect enough to put anything on paper."

On February 4, 1827, John Abraham Heraud, a minor poet and writer then twenty-eight years of age, first met Coleridge. During this private interview he was much impressed by Coleridge's eloquence:

The venerable sage received me with great urbanity—at once ingenuous and engaging. . . . He then spoke profusely on the subject of his philosophy, and of some late chemical experiments that had corroborated certain *a priori* reasonings. He contended that systems of philosophy, to be true, must be constructed on *a priori* grounds, and that experience could only confirm them. The process of right reasoning, he said, was cathartic; a cleansing-away of all matter derived through sensuous media, and a proceeding in the light of ideas without regarding phenomenal facts—in a word, upon premises altogether and purely ideal, arriving at the appropriate conclusion. Having arrived at which, we should hold our systems up, and ask, does Nature echo this? And Nature will echo it, if care has been taken that all the premises should be included in the deduction. If only half the truth be taken, the conclusion must be erroneous. This was the case with Spinoza. While Spinoza supposed that phenomena were objects only, and not subjects also, "not all the powers of heaven and earth," said the eloquent and venerable man, "could invalidate his argument." But some time before his death, Spinoza began to suspect that they were subjects as well, which half of the truth added to the other half, will lead to a correct result. The things of experience and sense are Subject-Objects. In these few words I have abridged a conversation of two hours. He then read to me some manuscript poems, and invited me to his Thursday evening colloquies.

So impressed was Heraud by Coleridge's talk, that he incorporated some of it in his best-known poem "The Descent into Hell." "Have you seen Heraud's *Descent into Hell*?" a friend asked Lamb when the poem had just appeared. "No, I only wish I had," was Lamb's reply.

Another person, Henry Holland, a distinguished physician, later medical attendant on Queen Victoria and Prince Albert and made a baronet, met Coleridge on various social occasions during these later years. Nearly forty years after Coleridge's death, Holland published his *Recollection of Past Life*. "I saw Coleridge more rarely," he wrote of this time,

and never took a place among the worshippers at his shrine. I recollect him only as an eloquent and intolerable talker; impatient of the speech and opinions of others; very inconsecutive, and putting forth with a plethora of words, misty dogmas in theology and metaphysics, partly of German origin, which he never seemed to me to clear up to his own understanding or to that of others. What has come out posthumously of his philosophy has not removed this imputation from it. I suspect his "Table Talk," as we have it in the very agreeable volume bearing this title, to have been sifted as well as abridged by the excellent judgment of the Editor.

The spring of the year 1828 brought the usual socialities for Coleridge, although in these later years they took place more often at the Gillmans' than elsewhere. On April 28 Coleridge replied to a request from Sotheby to bring the popular American novelist, James Fenimore Cooper, to visit him at Highgate, giving a cordial assent to a visit from both. Almost a week before Coleridge had met Cooper at Sotheby's, along with Walter Scott, at dinner on April 22. On entering the drawing room Cooper had found Coleridge there, "a picture of green old age; ruddy, solid and with a head as white as snow." Coleridge was just greeting him with a benevolent smile when Scott and Lockhart entered.

Throughout dinner Coleridge preserved an unusual silence, which ended when the ladies withdrew, and the conversation turned to Sotheby's translation of Homer, which inspired in Coleridge a characteristic "dissertation" that silenced the rest of the company and continued for more than an hour. When Sotheby once or twice attempted to intervene in opposition, "the reasoning," wrote Cooper, "was taken out of his mouth," and on reflection Cooper thought that "the exhibition was much more wonderful than convincing." He continued, "Scott sat as immovable as a statue . . . evidently considering the whole as an exhibition rather than as an argument; though then he occasionally muttered, "eloquent!", "wonderful!", "very extraordinary!" and Lockhart, Cooper added, "caught my eye once, and he gave a very hearty laugh, without making the slightest noise, as if he enjoyed my astonishment. When we rose, however, he expressed his admiration of the speaker's eloquence." Even when a knocking at the dining room door summoned Coleridge and the listeners to join the waiting crowd in the drawing room. Coleridge did not stop but continued for another half hour, until Mr. Southeby rose and the séance came to an end.

Scott's journal also contains an account of this evening, which shows that he followed Coleridge's argument on Homer:

> April 22nd 1828, Lockhart and I dined with Sotheby where we met a large dining party, the Orator of which was that extraordinary man Coleridge. After eating a hearty dinner, during which he spoke not a word, he began a most learned harangue on the Samothracian Mysteries, which he considered as affording the germ of all tales about fairies, past, present and to come. He then diverged to Homer, whose Iliad he considered as a collection of poems by different authors, at different times during a century. There was, he said, the individuality of an age, but not of a country. Morritt, a zealous worshipper of the old bard, was incensed at a system which would turn him into a polytheist, gave battle with keeness and was joined by Sotheby our host. Mr Coleridge behaved with the utmost complaisance and temper, but relaxed not from his exertions. Zounds! I was never so bethumped with words.

The part played by Coleridge when Sotheby and Cooper visited him some time later was, of course, another such monologue for the edification of the company, on various subjects. He went out to meet his guests when they arrived in a manner which Cooper described as "frank and friendly, the poet coming out to us in his morning undress, without affectation, and in a very prosaic manner." A picture by Allston, which the painter had presented to Coleridge, now inspired a repetition of one of Coleridge's favorite stories, the tale of how it had been mistaken by a picture dealer for a Titian, who, on discovering his mistake, was dumbfounded.

> We then adjourned to the Library. . . . The conversation had wandered to phrenology, and Mr Coleridge gave an account of the wonders that a professor had found in his own head, with a minuteness that caused his friend to fidget . . . I never knew a person of real genius who had any of the affectations of the smaller fry, on the subject of their feelings and sentiments. If

Coleridge was scholastic and redundant, it was because he could not help himself; to use a homely figure, it was a sort of boiling over of the pot on account of the intense heat beneath.

In May, dining at Lady Beaumont's, Coleridge delighted his hostess by convincing her "that metaphysics, so far from deadening the spirit of imagination, had added new wings from the power of contrast." Lady Beaumont wrote to him later, referring to one of Coleridge's poems that he had recited—"the last specimen you read is a proof of your not having deceived yourself." The letter awakened in Coleridge regretful memories as to the elusiveness of his poetic genius, which he recorded in the letter itself. "Is the power extinct?" he asked himself, and replied, "No! . . . scarce a week of my life shuffles by that does not at some moment feel the spur of the old genial impulse. . . . But in the same moment there awakes the sense of *Change without*—Life *unendeared*. The tenderest strings no longer thrill'd. In order to [sic] poetic composition I need the *varied* feeling—thought charmed to sleep; and the too great *continuity* of mind broken up, to begin anew, with *new* power seeking and finding *new* themes."

Early in June in a letter of overwhelmingly warm friendship—which strangely contrasted with some of his references to Dyer at other times—Coleridge replied to Dyer's wish to visit him and introduce some friends. He would be happy to see them any time after twelve, he said, but if before four o'clock, they would find him "with unwashed face." In particular, he would like them to come next Thursday, after six o'clock, and spend a long evening. The Gillmans will be delighted and Dyer would probably meet some old friends. "On Thursday evenings indeed, at any time between ½ past 5 and 11," he added, "you may be sure of finding us at home—and with a very fair chance of Basil Montagu's taking you and Mrs Dyer back in their coach."

On June 18, 1828, Coleridge breakfasted at the Aders' with Robinson and Wordsworth. Robinson, says Coleridge, had offended Irving by correcting him about the revelations and prophecies in the Bible, and Irving had remained away for more than a year. Coleridge said he thought Irving was mad, his brain "turned by the shoutings of the mob," yet Coleridge felt "an affection for Irving as a man of great power."

John Sterling, then a Cambridge undergraduate, was introduced to Coleridge by his tutor Julius Hare. Sterling often made references to Coleridge in these last years. But his only record of Coleridge is of their first meeting. It was published in the *Gentleman's Magazine*, under the title "Anecdotes of the Poet Coleridge," May 1838. Coleridge spoke of his admiration of Luther, whose picture he had. He then turned to landscape gardening, but he said that he preferred natural scenery. He next spoke of the evils of commerce and manufacturers and rejected "the nonsense of universal suffrage, but the land proprietors have too great a proportion of power." He wanted more emigration as a remedy for over-population. Coleridge's talk continued for two and three-quarter hours.

Sterling described Coleridge thus:

> Coleridge is not tall, and rather stout; his features, though not regular, are by no means disagreeable; the hair quite grey; the eye and forehead very fine. His appearance is rather old-fashioned and he looks as if he belonged not so much to this, or to any age, as to history. His manner and address struck me as being rather formally courteous. He always speaks in the tone and in the gesture of common conversation, and laughs a good deal, but gently. His emphasis, though not declamatory, is placed with remarkable propriety. He speaks perhaps rather slowly but never stops, and seldom even hesitates. There is the strongest appearance of conviction, without any violence in his manner. His language is sometimes harsh, sometimes careless, often quaint, almost always, I think, drawn from the fresh delicious fountains of our elder eloquence.

Sterling said that Coleridge could as easily have gone on speaking "for the next forty-eight hours."

Leigh Hunt lived in Highgate from 1826 to 1828. Coleridge, on meeting him, often accompanied him in his walks: "the talk being, as usual, chiefly appropriated by himself." Lamb, who often joined them, also frequently visited Leigh Hunt. "Coleridge," Lamb had told Wordsworth a year or two before, "is seen daily trudging on Highgate Hill, and blooming."

One day, when Coleridge had been holding forth about faith, Hunt asked Lamb, "What makes Coleridge talk in that way about heavenly grace, and the Holy Church, and that sort of thing?" Lamb replied with the hearty tone of a man uttering an obvious truism, but struggling with his habitual stammer, "Ah, there is a g-g-great deal of fun in Coleridge!"

On another occasion when Wordsworth and Rogers had listened to Coleridge for two hours, Hunt reported, "Wordsworth listened with profound attention, every now and then nodding his head as if in assent." On leaving, Rogers said to Wordsworth: "Well, for my own part, I could not make head or tail of Coleridge's oration: pray, did you understand it?" Wordsworth's reply was "Not one syllable of it."

Both Hunt and Carlyle noticed independently the same characteristics of Coleridge's tone on particular occasions. "His voice does not always sound very sincere," wrote Hunt, "but perhaps the humble and deprecating tone of it, on those occasions, is out of consideration for his hearer's infirmities, rather than produced by his own."

Carlyle, too, noticed this "humble and deprecating tone" remarked on by Leigh Hunt, and in his *Life of Sterling* he exemplifies it in the following short but convincing scene: " 'Ah, your tea is too cold Mr Coleridge!' mourned the good Mrs Gillman once, in her kind reverential and yet protective manner, handing him a very tolerable though belated cup'—'It's better than I deserve!' snuffled he, in a low hoarse murmur, partly courteous, chiefly pious, the tone of which still abides with me: 'It's better than I deserve!' '' This phrase Coleridge also used in his letters.

On July 28, 1829, a popular American preacher, John Wheeler, thirty-one years of age, called on Coleridge at Highgate and recorded in his diary one of the most interesting descriptions of Coleridge at this time:

> We drove to Highgate to Dr Gillman's and were politely received by a small, active, sensible-looking woman, Mrs Gillman. The view south from the porch, garden and fields is enchanting. She said, "Will you walk in the garden?" I looked for Mr Coleridge as I stepped down the stone steps and soon saw an elderly man come peeping out from the shrubbery on the left—an elderly man scarcely of medium stature, of full habit, white long hair, with full face, full forehead, prominent orbit of eyes—faculties of languages, mathematics, and locality finely developed. His respiration rather hurried and oppressive from taking snuff in great quantities. "Mr Wheeler, do you know Dr Channing? I have seen him. We differ in theological opinions. Dr Channing is wrong. He contradicts himself." And then the floodgates were opened and he went on giving his opinion, not as his own, but as intuitive truth concerning the Trinity.

Charles Cowden Clarke, who had met Coleridge before at Ramsgate, called on him again with his young wife, formerly Mary Novello, at Highgate in March 1830, and they recorded their impressions:

> We found Coleridge, bland, amiable, affably inclined to renew the intercourse of some years previous on the cliff at Ramsgate. As he came into the room, large presenced, ample-countenanced, grand-foreheaded, he seemd to the younger visitor a living and moving impersonation of some antique godlike being shedding a light around him of poetic effulgence and omnipercipience. He bent kindly eyes upon her, when she was introduced to him as Vincent Novello's eldest daughter and the wife of her introducer, and spoke a few words of courteous welcome: then, the musician's name catching his ear and engaging his attention, he immediately launched forth into a noble eulogy of music, speaking of his special admiration for Beethoven as the most poetical of all musical composers;* and from that, went on into a superb dissertation upon an idea he had conceived that the Creation of the Universe must have been achieved during a grand prevailing harmony of spheral music. His elevated tone, as he rolled forth his gorgeous sentences, his lofty look, his sustained flow of language, his sublime utterance, gave the effect of some magnificent organ-peal to our entranced ears.

Only after Coleridge paused, on exhausting his theme, did he come down to earth to learn the object of his hearer's visit, a message from a poetic friend.

---

*On October 5 of the same year, Coleridge explained to Henry Nelson Coleridge in *Table Talk* his feeling for music: "An ear for music is a very different thing from a taste for music," he said. "I have no ear whatever; I could not sing an air to save my life; but I have the intensest delight in music, and can detect good from bad. Naldi, a good fellow, remarked to me once at a concert, that I did not seem much interested in a piece of Rossini's which had jsut been performed. I said it sounded to me like nonsense verses. But I could scarcely contain myself when a thing of Beethoven followed."

In December 1830 on two different occasions Coleridge spoke of Shelley, who had died eight years before. Shelley, in November 1811, had come with his recently married wife to the Lakes District, intent upon absorbing the wisdom of Coleridge and of Southey. But Coleridge was then in London, and Southey was per force Shelley's only adviser. "He is come to the fittest physician in the world," Southey told a friend afterwards. "It has surprised him a good deal to meet, for the first time in his life, with a man who perfectly understands him and does him full justice. . . . Here is a man at Keswick, who acts upon me as my own ghost would do. He is just what I was in 1794. His name is Shelley." Coleridge, on hearing of Shelley's visit to Southey, exclaimed, "I could have been more useful to the young poet and metaphysician than Southey."

To this incident Coleridge now referred near the close of 1830. "I think as highly of Shelley's genius—yea, and of his *heart*—as you can do," Coleridge wrote to a correspondent. "Soon after he left Oxford, he went to the Lakes, poor fellow! and with some wish, I have understood, to see me; but I was absent, and Southey received him instead . . . I *might* have been of use to him, and Southey could not; for I should have sympathised with his poeticometaphysical reveries, (and the very word metaphysics is an abomination to Southey) and Shelley would have felt that I understood him. His atheism would not have scared *me*." Evidently Southey would not have agreed with Coleridge's opinion on this matter.

In the same month, December 1830, in similar terms, Coleridge spoke to John Frere of this same interview between Shelley and Southey at Keswick twenty years before. And once again Coleridge's regret for his own absence found expression: "Poor Shelley . . . I could have sympathised with him and shown him that I did so, and he would have felt that I did so. I could have shown him that I had once been in the same state myself, and I could have guided him through it. I have often bitterly regretted in my heart of hearts that I did never meet with Shelley." He added, "Shelley was a man of great power as a poet, and could he only have had some notion of order, could you only have given him some plane whereon to stand, and look down upon his own mind, he would have succeeded. There are flashes of the true spirit to be met with his works."

Coleridge's hope of influencing Shelley's opinions receives no support in Shelley's references to Coleridge in his verse. In 1819, in "Peter Bell the Third," Shelley presented Coleridge thus:

Among the guests who often stayed
Till the Devil's petits-soupers,
A man there came, fair as a maid,
And Peter noted what he said,
Standing behind his master's chair.

He was a mighty poet—and
A subtle-souled psychologist;
All things he seemed to understand,

Of old or new—of sea or land—
But his own mind—which was a mist.

This was a man might have turned
Hell into Heaven—and so in gladness
A Heaven unto himself have earned;
But he in shadows undiscerned
Trusted,—and damned himself to madness.

He spoke of poetry, and how
"Divine it was—a light—a love—
A spirit which like wind doth blow
As it listeth, to and fro,
A dew rained down from God above;

"A power which comes and goes like dream,
And which none can ever trace—
Heaven's light on earth—Truth's brightest beam."
And when he ceased there lay the gleam
Of those words upon his face.

A year later, in Shelley's "Letter to Maria Gisborne," Coleridge again appears as one of the important persons Maria must see in London:

You will see Coleridge—he who sits obscure
In the exceeding lustre and the pure
Intense irradiation of a mind,
Which, with its own internal lighting blind,
Flags wearily through darkness and despair—
A cloud-encircled meteor of the air,
A hooded eagle among blinking owls.

In November 1830 Wordsworth, then in London, visited Coleridge several times and was sad to find that his health was "much broken up," but said "his mind has lost none of its vigour." The following month, Coleridge's own account of himself to his nephew-son-in-law was no better. "For some years back," he told him, "but more particularly for the last eighteen months, my life has been an ague, counted by days of intermission and paroxysm." To John Frere, in December 1830, he now ominously remarked: "Thursday nights are over now."

8 "Thursday Nights Are Over Now" (1831-32)

> *"I shall be most happy to see you for any night you like to come, and any day before 12 o'clock. Thursday nights are over now, but any night whether Thursday or not I shall be most happy to see you."*
> —Coleridge to John Frere, December 1830

Although "Thursday Nights are over now," many visitors curious to see and hear Coleridge came to Highgate. For Coleridge's fame was still growing. Various editions of his *Poems* and of the *Friend* had already appeared, and the *Aids to Reflection* and "Church and State" added a large religious audience to the romantic one fascinated by the "Ancient Mariner," "Christabel," and "Kubla Khan." In addition, there was also the fame which Coleridge had acquired as "a Talker."

Thus it was that an American, Emma Willard, an enthusiastic advocate of higher education for women, called on Coleridge on May 14, 1831. When Coleridge appeared Emma gladly detected "all the poet in his large dark eye and intellectual face," while his manner seemed "such as suited his portly and dignified person." Having been previously cautioned on arrival that "if he became fairly engaged in conversation he would need but little response," Emma sat, "a delighted auditor while Coleridge held forth on subjects which interested him." These, as Emma recalled them, were "Nature, intellectual and material, the animals and vegetables, the heavens,—and last of all—the angelic figure that took the loveliest light of the picture, was Heaven's best gift—beautiful, refined, intellectual woman." Emma commented with a touch of irony, "How divinely good ought we to become, to deserve all that the poets say of us!" Nevertheless, she thought Coleridge's oration "passing strange and very grand."

Coleridge's attention to women was particularly observed by Henry Nelson Coleridge on one occasion when he accompanied his uncle to an exhibition of ancient masters at the British Gallery in Pall Mall. "In high spirits," wrote

523

Henry, "excited by the pictures ranged along the walls, he nevertheless refused to make an extensive survey, but," said Henry, "anchored himself before some three or four great works, telling me that he saw the rest of the Gallery *potentially*." And here, as at Highgate, he fell into a semipublic explication of the works he chose to consider, pointing out "the remarkable difference between Claude and Teniers in their power of painting vacant space and moralizing over a *Triumph of Silenus*—"the very revelry of Hell . . . Mark the lust, and, hard by, hate"—with much more to the same effect. Standing there, "half-leaning on his old, simple stick," his hat in hand, the fingers of the other making small diagrams in the air as it were, to elucidate his exposition, and revealing his admiration for Rubens "in a sort of joy and brotherly fondness," he inevitably—and surely not unconsciously—soon attracted a small audience, fascinated as usual by "this silver-haired, bright eyed, music-breathing old man." Of his identity probably none knew, but he held them as ever by his incantation, however little understood.

Watching Coleridge as he made his speech in the gallery, Henry acutely observed, and not for the first time, Coleridge's particular attitude toward women. "In the midst of his speech," said Henry "he turned to the right hand, where stood a very lovely young woman, whose attention he had involuntarily arrested; to her, without apparently any consciousness of her being a stranger to him, he addressed many remarks, although I must acknowledge they were couched in a somewhat softer tone, as if he were soliciting her sympathy. I never was in company with him in my life," Henry added, "when the entry of a woman, it mattered not who, did not promote a dim gush of emotion, which passed like an infant's breath over the mirror of his intellect."

On another occasion Henry also said: "With women he frequently did converse in a very winning and popular style, confining them, however, as well as he could, to the detail of facts or of their spontaneous emotions. In general he was certainly otherwise." Once, generalizing upon women, Coleridge asserted: "I have known many, especially women, love the good for the good's sake; but very few, indeed, and scarcely one woman, love the truth for the truth's sake." Generalizing on another occasion, he remarked: "Man's heart must be in his head. Woman's head must be in her heart."

In September 1831 a party consisting of Henry Taylor, John Stewart Mill, James Stephen, and a friend visited Coleridge and recorded their impressions. For the last two months, they learned, Coleridge had been "under the influence of cholera and other extra disorders, which had left him sadly enfeebled and even crippled." Taylor noted the absence of the old "continuous and unintermitted eloquence." But still occasionally "the flash and outbreak of a fiery mind" was visible. Stephen, a man in his early forties, was less enthusiastic than the twenty-four-year-old Taylor, and on the way home he remarked that he regretted that Coleridge had chosen to talk about the national debt: "A man must be quite right or quite wrong, and if he was wrong on such subjects what he said was good for nothing, whereas he might be more or less wrong in discussing the moral and political relations of society and yet be very instructive."

Yet almost to the end, Coleridge's life continued in its monotonous round of frustrations: physical miseries, disappointments and anxieties, confessions of guilt, and outbursts of repentance.

Before the close of 1830, Coleridge suffered a bitter disappointment in the loss of his pension. King William III on his accession to the throne, pleading poverty, refused to renew it from his Privy Purse. Coleridge's friends tried to obtain compensation for him from the Treasury, which offered him a gift of two hundred pounds. This Coleridge proudly refused as too paltry a sum. A letter signed by Mr. Gillman but evidently dictated by Coleridge appeared in the *Times* on June 3, 1831, stating the reasons for this refusal. This letter much displeased Lamb, who had been one of those who had attempted to interest the Treasury in Coleridge's case. Sotheby sympathetically presented Coleridge with fifty pounds, and Frere told Walter Scott in Malta in 1831 that he himself had compensated Coleridge with an annuity of a hundred guineas.

Sotheby's generous sympathy was aroused by a letter that Coleridge had sent him, explaining his public confession of poverty in Gillman's letter to the *Times*. "I avowed it," Coleridge had written,

> because I knew it to have been not only a blameless but an honourable poverty—no consequence or penance of Vice, Extravagance, Improvidence or Idleness—but the effect and result of an entire and faithful dedication of myself to ends and objects, for the realization and attainment of which I was constrained to believe myself *especially* fitted and therefore *called*, in open-eyed and voluntary dereliction of those more lucrative employments, equally, and at many periods of my life in my power, but which hundreds of my contemporaries could fill with equal or perhaps greater probability of success.

Early in the year 1832 Coleridge made a new acquaintance with whom he could discuss his religious ideas. For at this time a young man of twenty-seven, William Rowan Hamilton, professor of astronomy at the University of Dublin, called on him—anxious to absorb his wisdom. Hamilton had read Coleridge's poems and had carefully studied *The Friend* and the *Aids to Reflection* with admiration. He had long wished to meet Coleridge in person. During his first visit, which lasted one and a half hours in Coleridge's bedroom, Coleridge talked while his dinner grew cold on the table, and Mrs. Gillman regarded them "with no satisfied eyes." Although very ill, Coleridge talked "with great vigour and warmth." He spoke of various poems, parts of which he read with enthusiasm, and other parts of which "he recited with much feeling." Hamilton's second interview lasted two hours. Both, he said, "interested me very much, but I shall not attempt to decribe them, because I feel it almost an injury to the sense of grandeur and infinity with which the *whole* impressed me then . . . I seemed rather to listen to an Oracular voice." In conclusion,

Hamilton contrasted this experience with his meeting with Wordsworth, when he seemed "to hold commune with an exalted man."

Robinson, who made regular visits to Coleridge during these months, found him on April 12, 1832, in bed. He looked beautiful—his eye remarkably brilliant—and he talked as eloquently as ever. His declamation was against the Reform Bill. He took strong ground, resting on the deplorable state to which a country is reduced when a measure of vital importance is acceded to "merely from the danger of resistance to the popular opinion." Wordsworth's fears even exceeded Coleridge's at this time. "He talks of leaving the country," wrote Robinson, "on account of the impending ruin to be apprehended form the Reform Bill."

This Reform Bill has been well summarized by a modern writer thus: "Whilst not increasing the total number of members of Parliament, this bill redistributed them in such a way that a fairer representation of the country was ensured." Imporant places, including Birmingham, Leeds, Manchester, Sheffield, etc., were now enfranchised for the first time.

When a young American student, McLellan, called at Highgate on April 27, 1832, he was invited to walk up to Coleridge's room as, although "very poorly," Coleridge would be "happy to see him." McLellan was impressed by his short stature, careless dress, "strength of expression, venerable locks of white, and trembling frame." Coleridge told him that "for some time past" he had "suffered much bodily anguish," for thirteen months he had walked up and down his room seventeen hours each day, but that his mind had not been in the least affected: "my body and head appear to hold no connexion." Then the conversation wandered to Coleridge's disappointment with Irving, who, in disagreement with his London church, was now founding a new one of his own. "So sudden a fall," said Coleridge, "when his mighty energies made him so terrible to sinners."

Next the conversation with McLellan turned to the social-political scene in England, which Coleridge found as disappointing as Irving: "In a dreadful state, care, like a foul hag, sits on us all"; for he feared a revolution of the working class. Nor could Coleridge allow an American to depart without compliments to his country—where, indeed, Coleridge's own reputation was then much higher than in England. "Happy are you," Coleridge told McLellan, "to hold your birthright in a country where things are different." And he went on to praise his own former American friend, Allston, as "almost unrivalled in imagination and colour."

When, during the summer of 1832, a Scottish physician, David Moir, called on Coleridge, he was still confined to bed. Coleridge invited Moir to come up to his room. A "kind and flattering" welcome was followed by "two hours of divine monologue" retailing much of Coleridge's early life and "reciting some of his juvenile compositions, in a manner which was very characteristic and very striking." Regretting that he had thus led Coleridge into the incomprehensible. Moir wrote, "Unfortunately-I put some questions to him relative to his peculiar speculations in philosophy, and shortly found myself lost in intricacies which, although sprinkled with the honey of Hybla, were no more easily threaded than the Cretan labyrinth.''

Harriet Martineau, a well-known writer and critic then thirty years old, called on Coleridge before the close of the year and later recorded her account of the interview in her autobiography. To Highgate Harriet went as "a great admirer of Coleridge's poetry,'' and she was kindly received by the Gillmans and by Coleridge. "A most remarkable looking personage,'' she thought Coleridge when he entered, "looking very old with his rounded shoulders and drooping head and excessively thin limbs. His eyes were—wonderful—light grey, extremely prominent, actually glittering,'' as, Harriet had learned, was common among opium eaters. Coleridge began, of course, with compliments, informing her to her surprise and amusement that he read her tales as they appeared, month by month. He then objected to her considering society as a collection of individuals which he opposed on metaphysical grounds. "After a long flight in survey of society from his own balloon in his own current, he came down again to some considerations of individuals. . . . ending with criticisms of old biographers, whose venerable works he took down from the shelf. No one else spoke of course, except when once or twice I put a question; and when his monologue came to what seemed a natural stop, I rose to go.''

Contemplating the experience many years later, when Cottle's *Early Recollections* had completed Harriet's disillusion as to Coleridge's moral and intellectual eminence, she was still "glad to have seen his weird face, and heard his dreamy voice, and my notion of possession, prophecy,—of involuntary speech from involuntary brain action, has been clearer since.'' She thought his monologues, philosophic and moralizing, "to be much like the action of Babbage's machine.''*

Now, too, Peacock never tired of treating Coleridge ironically in his works. He introduced him in his latest novel *Crotchet Castle* as "Mr. Skionar, a sort of poetical philosopher, a curious compound of the intense and the mystical . . . who settles everything by sentiment and intuition.'' Nor did Peacock forget Coleridge's tendency to trust to others for salvation from the pecuniary troubles of his unworldy existence; so Lady Clarinda remarks: "They say that even Mr. Skionar, though he is a great dreamer, always dreams with his eyes open, or with one eye at any rate, which is an eye to his gain.''

The background to these visits made in 1831 and 1832 by Coleridge's admirers was, as in so many periods of his life, one of intermittent illness and almost unintermittent recourse to opium. Increasingly frequent attacks of illness kept him in his room and often for long periods in his bed. He rejoiced, however, to find that sickness did not affect his mind; he could still read and think, and his equally inextinguishable sociability even welcomed the visitors who still continued to call upon him throughout these years.

---

*Babbage's machine was a kind of early nineteenth-century computer.

In 1831 Coleridge's complaints about his health, though frequent, were somewhat milder than before. "For more than a year past," he told a correspondent on November 20, 1831, "my life has been a rapid succession of sickness, imperfect convalescence, and relapse—the most favourable form of the complaint, whatever it be, being either erysipelatous affection of one or both legs, or sciatic rheumetism." As the year 1831 closed he complained to young James Gillman of "the compulsory egoism of pain." In opium, despite his continual hopes of its abandonment, Coleridge still found a frequent but deceitful refuge from his many troubles, and the little notes to the chemist Dunn went as regularly as before.

Sometimes his suspicion of a syphilitic infection found expression, even if disguised as a joke. In this mood, in mid-May 1832 describing an intended call by his brother James, he told Green:

My poor—or my rich, brother Colonel Coleridge. . . . called in his carriage this morning—but I would not expose him to the fatigue of getting out of his carriage, and climbing 5 flights of stairs, in order to behold a mask of syphilis, as a Venus *sub* Medicis et Mercurio, when he had expected to see the son of his fathr. Poor Harriet, who had been hard at work in scouring the house, and had not attended on me as usual, burst into hysteric weeping as she first fixed her eyes on me—and at last sobbed out—I could not have believed any thing so frightful, in your countenance—Mr G[illman] repeats, over and over, on his now almost daily visit—"Odd!—it is very odd!"

However, on June 10 Samuel could tell Henry Nelson Coleridge that "The head and features are re-appearing—and I no longer behold in my glass a Hottentot Venus."

Early in 1832 Coleridge was taking a daily dose of laudanum divided into three parts, to be taken at different times. Within a month, revolting againt this slavery, he cried to Green: "By the mercy of God I remain quiet; and so far from any craving for the poison that has been the curse of my existence, my shame and my negro-slave inward humiliation and debasement, I feel an aversion, a horror at the imagining: so that I doubt, whether I could swallow a dose without a resiliency, amounting almost to a convulsion." Although Mr. Gillman now thought that Coleridge looked in better health, Coleridge, seeing his face in the mirror, disagreed; but the maid Harriet, who, he said, "has most kindly and christianly tended me during this affliction," now told him: "Sir! your face has not the same expression of pain, anxiety, and the being worn out by pain; but it is yellower, or brown and yellow, more than I have ever seen it."

In the spring of that year Coleridge again tried to abandon opium, though warned by Mr. Gillman that so sudden a change might be harmful. At any rate Coleridge's temper was not improved by the experiment, and he soon quarreled with Mr. Gillman. To Green he complained that Gillman did not think him ill and did not visit him during the five or six days of "moaning and groaning." But he added: "I have felt no craving for the poison, but rather the contrary." His diet, he continued, included at noon a basin of gruel with half-a-glass of brandy in it—and at 5 o'clock a single mutton chop, with a pint of wine—But in addition to this, I take in the course of the 24 hours two grains of acetate of morphium, with a small portion of the Tincture of Cardamon, and some of Battley's Liquor Cinchonae with Port Wine. Whether this is more or less than adequate to the abstraction of the ounce of laudanum I cannot say—I mean, the difference between a pint of wine taken while I took the laudanum and brandy, and the pint and ½ I take now without it.

Perhaps it is not suprising that he now detected a "retrogression rather than any however slight progression" towards health, and he feared that "after more than 30 years self-poisoning" he would die of dysentery. "It is now five weeks, since I have taken laudanum," he added. A fortnight before Coleridge had described his state to Green as "hopeless." A week later he had complained to his friend of feeling a "death-grasp," and he wished the law allowed a medical "euthanasia." He also wished for a postmortem examination of his body. By this time Coleridge apparently believed himself free from his drug addiction, as he had told Cary on April 22, believing that God has "worked almost a miracle of grace in and for me."

Coleridge's annoyance with Dr. Gillman in the belief that he neglected him was still evident in May. In the first week, lured by the warmth of this spring of 1832, and driven from his room by chimney sweeps, he told Henry Nelson Coleridge: "I have crawled from my lair, like the *slugs*." The advent of the chimney sweeps led to an altercation with Dr. Gillman, who rejected Coleridge's assertion that on previous occasions they had stolen his books. For Henry Nelson's amusement, Coleridge sent him a dramatized version of the incident in dialogue form. Coleridge's resentment against Gillman a month before had not yet died. At that time he had asked Green to obtain another doctor's opinion of his state, if he could do it "without offending Mr Gillman." Now, a month later, he told Green, sardonically, "Mr Gillman found time to look in on me." In the same letter he continued: "I do not feel the slightest wish or craving for the laudanum"—nor do I believe that it would alleviate my sufferings." Before the close of the month Coleridge clearly explained his state to another friend, emphasizing the physical misery caused by his attempt to abandon opium, which left him now

pacing my room like a leopard in his den to the tune of groans and prayers—praying earnestly for death but likewise for grace to add ever "But thy will not mine be done" . . . . Laudanum, which I had taken in enormous doses for 32 years lost all its anodyne powers and at last I proposed to leave it off. But Dr Prout and my friends Mr Green and Mr Gillman could not give their consent to a step which they regarded as bordering too near on suicidal. Well! I struggled for another month but finding no improvement I resolved on leaving off the laudanum at once.

Mrs. Gillman's attentions to Coleridge were still unremitting. A friend recorded how, "when she noticed Coleridge getting depressed and discouraged, she would put aside her occupations and walk out with him to view the sunset from the Scotch Fir Grove, and thus restore his spirits by her sympathetic attention to his rapturous remarks."

Mrs. Coleridge told Poole on August 16, 1832: "You have probably heard that S.T.C. has entirely left off the use of Laudanum. He has suffered greatly by the effort, and has been confined, almost exclusively to his room ever since; but since he has resumed the use of the sulphur-bath he has rallied somewhat, and is at present in less pain and less sick than usual, and able to walk up and down the garden once a day."

Samuel's friends heard of his illnesses with deep concern. "He and my beloved sister," Wordsworth told a friend in June, "are the two beings to whom my intellect is most indebted, and they are now proceeding *pari passu*, along the path of sickness, I will not say towards the grave, but I trust towards a blessed immortality." A week later Lamb, answering a letter from Allsop, wrote: "How you frightened me! Never write again 'Coleridge is dead' at the end of a line, and tamely come in with 'to his friends', at the beginning of another. Love is quicker, and fear from love, than the transition ocular from line to line."

Immediately afterward, in declining health which ever intensified his religious meditations, Coleridge complained to Hamilton, "I am much weaker . . . but God's will be done." With this prelude, he proceeded to give Hamilton a brief outline of his religious beliefs, which were essentially metaphysical. The God who heard his prayers, he explained, was "the Finite in the form of the Indefinite" along with "the Absolute Will," and a long string of increasing abstractions, leading to the "Incomprehensible Ground of all."

As religious emotion more intensively entered into Coleridge's thoughts and feelings during these last years, he became increasingly conscious of his drug addiction as a moral evil—a sin. In this spring of 1832 he cried to Green out of his misery: "Through God's mercy" he was still

> without any craving for the poison which for more than 30 years has been the guilt, debasement, and misery of my existence. I pray that God may have mercy on me—tho' through unmanly impatiency of wretched sensations, that produced a disruption of my mental continuity of productive action I have for the better part of my life yearned towards God, yet having recourse to the evil Being—i.e. a continued act of thirty year's self-poisoning thro' cowardice of pain and without other motive—say rather without *motive* but solely through the goad *a tergo* of unmanly and unchristian fear—God knows! I in my inmost soul acknowledge all my sufferings as the necessary effects of his Wisdom, and all the alleviations as the unmerited graces of his Goodness.

Coleridge's religious thought and emotion were not solely associated with his sense of guilt in regard to opium. His academic attitude toward theology and religious belief was not to be eliminated by his sense of sin.

To Green, who, he feared, was changing his opinions and no longer accepted Coleridge's philosophy, he now expressed his concern. Green must not doubt Coleridge's principle "that Reason is *subjective* Revelation, Revelation *objective* reason. . . . If I lose my faith in *Reason*, as the perpetual revelation, I lose my faith altogether. I must deduce the objective from the subjective Revelation, or it is no longer a revelation for me, but a beastly fear, and superstition." Thus, despite his frequent support of the church—which meant *his* church—Coleridge was far from orthodox, and consequently unpopular with some strict Anglicans.

9 "The End of the Journey" (1833-34)

"Heaven knows that many and many and many a time I have regarded my talents and acquirements as a Porter's Burthen, imposing on me the duty of going on to the end of the journey."
—*Coleridge to Robert Southey, December 31, 1801*

Coleridge's life was now approaching its close; increasing illness with an occasional remission dogged him to the end. In January 1833 he described himself as "a bed-stricken cripple."

The toll of time was also now evident in the lives of those who, thirty-five years before, had been happy with Coleridge at Stowey. For Dorothy Wordsworth, whose long suppressed passion for her brother had caused a mental breakdown, there was no hope of improvement. Wordsworth, increasingly troubled by his old eye weakness, spoke of her with undying affection: her "tenderness of heart," he declared, "was never exceeded by any of God's creatures. Her loving kindness has no bounds. God bless her for ever and ever."

In February Wordsworth refused to believe that Coleridge had been ill in bed, as he had recently attended the consecration of Highgate Church and had had a long conversation with the bishop of London who officiated. However, Wordsworth no longer doubted Coleridge's bed-ridden state in May, but he rejoiced that his mind was unaffected by illness. This month of May 1833 was also a sad time for poor Lamb. His sister Mary was again in a mental home, and Lamb, all his prospects of a happy retirement abandoned, was living near her. "I see little of her; alas! I too often hear her. Sunt Lachrymae rerum—and you and I must bear it," he told Wordsworth. Now, too, writing to young James Gillman, Lamb, who had recently sent Coleridge a copy of his *Essays of Elia*, sent his love to "glorious S.T.C."

Evidently, Coleridge's health soon improved, for in June he suddenly departed for Cambridge in Green's carriage with Green and with Gillman as medical bodyguard. The reason was a meeting there of the British Association.

Coleridge does not appear to have participated in the proceedings of the society, but he was much interested in talk with the scientist Michael Faraday, formerly Davy's assistant. As Faraday's views on religion were somewhat peculiar, Coleridge may have found more satisfaction in discussing them than in learning of Faraday's experiments in electricity.

At Cambridge—where Coleridge as usual remained in bed until the afternoons, although he complained that the bed itself felt like a sack of potatoes—his vanity must have been gratified by the levees of distinguished persons who daily crowded his room. Derwent also came to Cambridge and was delighted to find his father there. Nor was Coleridge's visit to remain unrecorded by others, including his friend Hamilton, who exclaimed during one of Coleridge's discourses that, although he had read most of Coleridge's works, "I am not sure that I understand them all." To this Coleridge urbanely replied: "The question is Sir, whether I understand them all myself."

Coleridge's visit to Cambridge after so many years' absence aroused strong emotions, somewhat different from those which Cambridge had evoked in him in his undergraduate years. To his nephew Henry Nelson Coleridge he later exclaimed: "My emotions at revisiting the university were at first overwhelming. I could not speak for an hour; yet my feelings were upon the whole very pleasurable, and I have not passed, of late years at least, three days of such great enjoyment and healthful excitement of mind and body."

Although Coleridge on his arrival at Cambridge "could not speak for an hour," he certainly soon recovered from that inhibition and talked and orated with his customary fluency. William Jerdan, editor of the *Literary Gazette*, saw Coleridge during this visit standing in admiration before the statue of the once abused Newton in Trinity College Chapel. "He appeared," wrote Jerdan, "to be much moved by the contemplation of it, and all at once his noble ambition burst forth in words: 'Oh that I might deserve an honour like this, in these halls where I have been blessed so much!' and the expression of his countenance was piteous to behold." However, Coleridge quickly recovered and told Jerdan of how a workman had thanked him that morning for a lecture he had given there twenty years ago, which had included such helpful advice that it had not been forgotten.

Despite Samuel's emotional outburst in Trinity Chapel, his real opinion of Newton had little changed, as he revealed later to Henry Nelson Coleridge: "Galileo was a great genius, and so was Newton; but it would take two or three Galileos and Newtons to make one Kepler . . . Newton *was* a great man, but you must excuse me if I think that it would take many Newtons to make one Milton." Nor was Jerdan the only recorder of Coleridge's talk at Cambridge. A young Harrovian, Robert Willmott, then an undergraduate at Trinity, also observed and described Coleridge at this time and later recorded his impressions with admiration and reverence. To Willmott, Coleridge was "the venerable sage" whom he heard in the mood of Bagehot's most hypnotised and dazed auditors. "Who that was present will ever forget that evening under the clock at Trinity," Willmott cried, "which witnessed a symposium from which Plato himself might have carried something away! The remembrance even now creeps over the mind like a Summer Night's Dream.''

Exhilarated by his recent experiences at Cambridge, Coleridge immediately set off at the beginning of July for Ramsgate with the intention of continuing his *Logosophia*. As usual, this good intention was frustrated by many happenings during his stay there. Coleridge came by steamboat and found Mr. Gillman and his son Henry awaiting him on the pier. Mrs. Gillman arrived a little later, having, like Coleridge, come alone except for the companionship of Harriet, the servant. From this time Coleridge was much engaged at Ramsgate writing (for Mrs. Gillman) replies to invitations to himself and the Gillmans from his friends. These included the Lockhart family. Mrs. Lockhart was Walter Scott's favorite daughter, whom Coleridge found "truly an interesting and love-compelling Woman.'' Mr. Gillman was still far from well, and one of Coleridge's anxieties was the difficulty of finding a medical assistant for him. Coleridge now felt much benefited by an enthusiastic resort to "warm salt Shower Baths—standing with my legs in a Tub at the temperature of nearly a 100, and receiving from 30 to 40 gallons of salt water of from 90 to 100.''

At Ramsgate Coleridge's affection for his Jewish friends found a focus in the local synagogue. Years had passed since Coleridge's unpleasant reference to a fellow traveller in the stagecoach as a "stinking Jew.'' This hardly prepares us for the Jewish friendships that Coleridge made in later days in Highgate. One of these was Hyman Hurwitz, director of a Jewish academy there. With Hurwitz Coleridge enjoyed discussions on Biblical interpretations, which Hurwitz elucidated to Coleridge's admiration. When on November 19, 1817, Princess Charlotte Augusta died, Hurwitz composed a Hebrew dirge which was chanted at the Great Synagogue in St. James Place, Aldgate. Coleridge made an English verse translation of it entitled "Israel's Lament.'' Hurwitz's "Dirge'' and Coleridge's translation were published together before the end of the year.

In 1828 Hurwitz, stronly recommended by Coleridge, was elected to the chair of Hebrew in the newly founded University College of the University of London. Hurwitz's gratitude to Coleridge for his assistance found public expression in his inaugural lecture, when he said: "Above all, it will be my most anxious wish to direct the students' attention to what the author of *The Friend* and of the *Aids to Reflection*—a gentleman whom I am both happy and proud to call my friend—and where is the man who knowing his vast learning, genuine piety, and goodness of heart, that would not be proud of his friendship!—so justly calls the Science of Words.''

Another of these Jewish friends of Coleridge was a young neighbor, Adam Steinmetz, who, when he died in 1832, left Coleridge a legacy of £300. In a note to Mrs. Gillman Coleridge spoke of Steinmetz's death as "a loss too great, too awful, for common grief, or for any of its ordinary forms; a state of deepest mental silence, neither prayer nor thanksgiving, but with my whole mind soul and spirit fixed on God.'' Nevertheless, Coleridge, of course, continued to expatiate upon his loss, incidentally recalling how often on

Steinmetz's departure he had remarked, "Alas! there is death in that hand!" The same much advertised remark by Coleridge about Keats' hand suggests that this prophecy—if not in both cases actually *post-factum*—was a cliché to impress hearers. And after all, given time, it must prove true of any hand. As a living memorial to Steinmetz Coleridge invited the dead man's friend John Peirse Kennard to visit him regularly and at any time—"at whatever time he comes, the fraternal friend of Adam Steinmetz will ever be dear and most welcome."

Coleridge's appreciation of the Jews in these days found full and fervent expression to Hurwitz and others. In 1820 he had asked Hurwitz to inform his friends of Coleridge's sympathy with Hurwitz's "complaints against the Anti-mosaic and Anti-christian schism." In the same letter he wrote, "I never read the speach of Shylock without a glow of indignant brotherly love towards the persecuted race." At the same time Coleridge told Hurwitz how, at Malta, by reading a chapter of St. Paul's Epistle to the Romans, he had so influenced a wicked Catholic judge as to prevent an anti-Jewish riot; or in his own words to Hurwitz: "at Malta, and at the time when the God of your Fathers vouchsafed to make me the poor instrument of preventing an intended massacre of your (and my) unoffending brethren." It is regrettable that nowhere else in Coleridge's published writings,—including the *Note Books*—do we find any other allusion to this exciting incident.

So now, vacationing at Ramsgate in 1833, Coleridge took great interest in the local synagogue, "which not Jewish, but Christian ignorance had named the Temple," as he told Mrs. Lockhart when inviting her family to join him in a visit. "If you would further like to see the placed lighted up," he continued,

and their ceremonial service, on Friday evening, of course I should be happy to accompany you. . . . I happen to be a favourite among the descendants of Abraham, and Mr. Montefiore, the munficent founder of this synagogue, has expressed a strong wish to be introduced to the author of *The Friend*. His father, lately deceased, was without exception the most beautiful old man I ever saw—beauty in the form of nobleness and venerableness—I therefore intend to be at the Synagogue on Friday.

As usual during his visits to Ramsgate, Coleridge was occupied in receiving and returning social calls, visits which now included one or two members of the House of Commons. Day after day he pored over "the four folios of Bingham's *Antiquities of the Christian Church*,* which had convinced him, as he told Green, "of the truth of my convictions." Coleridge had also made friends of the brother of Southey and his family and hoped that "the feelings I have left behind with them may perhaps be a means, with God's influence, of

---

*Joseph Bingham (1668-1723) published *Origines Ecclesiasticae* or *Antiquities of the Christian Church.*

making Southey feel his unkind neglect of me—and God knows! it is wholly and exclusively from my persistent regard for *him* and *his* better being that I desire it."

To Green on July 26, the day before their return to Highgate, Coleridge described his condition as "progression in health and countenance, tho' not much in diminished decrepitude. All that I have done," he added, "is to have attained a younger and healthier face, and a less uncomfortable state of bodily sensations."

A week later Mrs. Coleridge told Poole, "S.T.C. is ten years younger in spirit: the tepid-salt-water-shower-bath has done wonders! Now, too, Hartley, engaged in literary work at Leeds, had just completed his *Poems*, which the friendly Murray was about to publish, and Coleridge "is pleased, and much affected *at the dedication to* himself.* So Mrs. Coleridge informed Poole, adding on the subject of Hartley, "He has not seen him for ten years!" Derwent also appeared in his mother's news to Poole: "He has left a great pile of Sermons for his father to criticise"—which must have pleased Coleridge as much as the dedication. In mid-August Coleridge sent one of his little notes to Dunn, promising immediate payment of his account and regretting his delay, but, significantly perhaps, this time there was no request, as in the past, to fill the bottle.

Now, too, Emerson, a distinguished American Unitarian and philosopher, arrived in England intent upon meeting Coleridge, Wordsworth, and Carlyle. Emerson found Coleridge on August 5, 1833, the afternoon of his call, "a short, thick old man, with bright blue eyes and fine clear complexion, leaning on his cane." Emerson noted Coleridge's continual taking of snuff, which soon soiled his tie and black clothes. From the genius of Allston—Coleridge's frequent subject with Americans—he turned to denounce "the folly and ignorance of Unitarianism." When Emerson interjected that he was "born and

---

*Dedicatory Sonnet to S. T. Coleridge
   Father, and Bard revered! to whom I owe,
   Whate'er it be, my little art of numbers,
   Thou, in thy night-watch o'er my cradled slumbers,
   Didst meditate the verse that lives to shew,
   (And long shall live, when we alike are low)
   Thy prayer how ardent, and thy hope how strong,
   That I should learn of Nature's self the song,
   The lore which none but Nature's pupils know.

   The prayer was heard! I 'wander'd like a breeze,'
   By mountain brooks and solitary meres,
   And gather'd there the shapes and phantasies
   Which, mixt with passions of my sadder years,
   Compose this book. If good therein there be,
   That good, My Sire, I dedicate to thee.

This sonnet formed the dedication of Hartley Coleridge to his father, in the 1833 edition of Hartley Coleridge's *Poems*.

bred a Unitarian,'' Coleridge, with none of his usual urbanity, and evidently disliking Emerson, coolly replied: "I supposed so." He himself, Coleridge explained to the silent Emerson, had once been a Unitarian; indeed, he had once been called its "rising star," and so he "knew what quackery it was." And so he continued, with much argumentation often learnedly theological, but not always convincing, while Emerson merely listened, still in silence. Probably Coleridge resented the intuitive perception of Emerson's critical, inquiring mind, and he appreciated the evident although silent disagreement instead of the usual admiration.

When at last Emerson rose to depart, Coleridge began to declaim his recent verses "My Baptismal Birthday." He then went on to speak of Malta and Sicily, which Emerson had lately visited, and of what he had said to the bishop of London about them. But what he now told Emerson he probably did not tell the bishop of London. "There were," he said speaking of Sicily, "only three things which the government had brought into that garden of delights, namely, itch, pox and famine." Emerson's stay, a mere hour, was shorter than usual for Coleridge's visitors, but as he was about to leave, Coleridge showed him a painting by Allston, telling him how a dealer had mistaken it for a Titian.

Emerson's comments afterwards on his visit to Coleridge were far from enthusiastic. He "found it impossible to recall the largest part of his discourse, which was often like so many printed paragraphs in his book,—perhaps the same—so readily did he fall into certain commonplaces. As I might have foreseen, the visit was rather a spectacle than a conversation, of no use beyond the satisfaction of my curiosity. He was old and preoccupied, and could not bend to a new companion and think with him."

Emerson next called on Carlyle and then made a pilgrimage to see Wordsworth in the North, which proved even more disappointing for him than his visit to Coleridge. Emerson's first tentative morning call on Coleridge had been untimely: for Coleridge, still in bed, had told him to call again in the afternoon—an inconvenience for Emerson, which probably had its effect upon the ensuing interview. Most unfortunately, Emerson's call on Wordsworth was even more untimely. For Wordsworth was then writing sonnets—and consequently, in his annoyance at the interruption, he attacked America and all things American with an energy which left Coleridge's diatribe against Unitarianism a mere compliment in comparison. Wordsworth's dislike of America, it appeared, included its "vulgarity in manner," its love of money-making, and its politics. Nor was this all. "they lacked men of leisure—in short, gentlemen,—to give a tone of honour to the community," he told Emerson and—a cheering comparison for Emerson—they also boasted of things that although "done in England every day, should never be spoken of." Besides, Wordsworth had heard that American newspapers were "atrocious, and accuse members of Congress of stealing spoons." When, to turn the conversation, Emerson praised Carlyle, Wordsworth remarked that he "thought him sometimes insane" and complained of his obscurity. For, said Wordsworth, "Even Mr. Coleridge wrote more clearly." Then, like Coleridge, Wordsworth finished by declaiming his own verses as they paced the garden walk at Rydal Mount. Emerson found something comic on seeing "the old Wordsworth, standing apart and reciting to me in a garden-walk, like a school-boy declaiming," Emerson's final memory of Wordsworth was of "a plain, elderly, white-haired man, not prepossessing, and disfigured by green goggles," who had recently "broken a tooth by a fall"—"the impression of a narrow and very English mind."

Coleridge's widening reputation, largely due to these last years of "Conversations" at Highgate, now brought him more requests for sittings from etchers and portrait painters. It was thus in November 1833 that, sending proofs of a drawing of himself made by Abraham Wyville to various friends, including Mr. Aders, he asked Mrs. Aders, "Is one of Wyville's proofs of my face worth Mr Aders acceptance?" And he went on to quote Ovid with his own translation:

> In truth, he's no beauty! cry'd Moll, Poll and Tab,
> But they all of them own'd He'd the gift of the Gab.

A year before Coleridge had given sittings in London to a well-known miniature painter and engraver, Moses Haughton the younger. That portrait is now in Christ's Hospital.

In October 1833 Lamb wrote to Coleridge: "Mr Finden, an artist of some celebrity, is desirous of publishing an engraving of you, as he has done of Southey—Can you lend him your head? I dare say 'tis better than his own—but I say this at a venture." The following month Coleridge invited William Finden to come and see his pencil portrait by Leslie, and another, made recently by a young German artist, J. Kayser. Kayser's portrait did not entirely please Coleridge. "A likeness, certainly," he told Finden, "but with such unhappy density of the nose and idiotic dropping of the lip, with a certain pervading woodenness of the whole countenance, that it has not been thought guilty of any great flattery by Mr Coleridge's friends." Coleridge, in fact, preferred Kayser himself, a handsome young man, who evidently appealed to Coleridge's subconscious homosexual tendency. Some years before Coleridge had written: "I believe it possible that a man may, under certain states of moral feeling, entertain something deserving the name of love towards a male object—an affection beyond friendship, and wholly aloof from appetite." This "state of feeling" induced by Kayser inspired Coleridge's lines "To the Young Artist":

> Kayser! to whom, as to a second self,
> Nature, or Nature's next-of-kin, the Elf
> Hight Genius, hath dispensed the happy skill
> To cheer or soothe the parting friend's 'Alas!'
> Turning the blank scroll to a magic glass,
> That makes the absent present at our will;
> And to the shadowing of thy pencil gives
> Such seeming substance, that it almost lives.

Well hast thou given the thoughtful Poet's face!
Yet hast thou on the tablet of his mind
A more delightful portrait left behind—
Even thy own youthful beauty, and artless grace,
Thy natural gladness and eyes bright with glee!
Kayser! farewell!

Be wise! be happy! and forget not me.

Finden chose neither Leslie's nor Kayser's portrait to copy, but one by Thomas Phillips, the well-known academician. In this same year, 1833, Daniel Maclise added Coleridge to his then famous galley of celebrities for *Fraser's Magazine*.

In the autumn of 1833 Coleridge, despite his visits to Cambridge and Ramsgate, declared to an acquaintance: "I have, till of late, been a prisoner for nearly 3 years to my bedroom and for the far larger portion to my bed—hourly praying against the Desire of Death, which thro' constant Pain and Miserableness I was unable to suppress." Dr. Gillman was just recovering from "a seizure," and his wife was confined to bed, having seriously damaged her leg by another fall caused by a ruck in the carpet. Coleridge's anxiety about Mrs. Gillman's state increased as a more serious injury to her was feared. To Green, who was apparently attending her, Coleridge wrote, "I am very low and disquieted about her;" and he requested Green's opinion of her condition. Two more days passed without any alleviation of Coleridge's fears for Mrs. Gillman. To Lockhart, after speaking of her illness, he added a eulogy of her only less fervent than the one that he had written some two years before: "She is the Life, Love and sactifying spirit of this Household."

Green attended Coleridge, not only as his doctor, for he still continued to help him with the *Logosophia*, which he was to edit—Coleridge had decided—after Coleridge's own death. So now, in this last full year of Coleridge's life, he discussed with Green, in letter after letter, the difficulties of the magnum opus—the problem "of reconciling with right reason . . . the essential Belief of the Christian Church." The following month Coleridge asked Green to transcribe a passage from the manuscript "on Pantheism as the only *speculative* Atheism; and that Socinianism stops short of it, only because it is lazy, and lily-livered." Within a week Coleridge was asking Green to find out the cost of an interleaved Bible which contained the Apocrypha to be specially made for himself.

Sterling, Coleridge had hoped, would come and live with him at the Gillmans' and also help in the great work, which was to begin with the treatment of words for "power and use" continue with Logic, leading to a "disquisition on God, Nature and Man—the two first great divisions of which from the Ens super Ens to the Fall, or from God to Hades; and then from Chaos to the commencement of living Organization—containing the whole scheme of the Dynamic Philosophy." Although Coleridge's interest in his academic and religious theory continued to the end, it was accompanied with increasing frequency by the simpler piety of the orthodox church. This pious Christian attitude inspired a note that Coleridge sent in November 1833 to his daughter Sara. She was ill and soon to give birth to twins, who did not live long. "Night after night," he told Sara, "has my last and most fervent prayer been that of humble intercession for you and for my other suffering friend, Mrs Gillman. I thank God who has thus far given ear to my prayers, and trust to his Mercy."

In July 1833 Coleridge declared that he could write as good verses as ever "if perfectly free from vexations and in the ad libitum hearing of good music." His reason for not finishing "Christabel," he also said, was not the want of a plan, but the inevitable failure of any continuation. In fact, the few verses he wrote in this year were his last. They, like his hundred dream volumes and *Logosophia*, suggest the influence of opium, not in the creation of grandiose plans impossible of achievements, as with these, but in the depressive influence of the drug evident in these last verses. The theme of the best of these late verses was one that haunted Coleridge's thoughts and feelings throughout his life—Love.

In "Love's Apparition and Evanishment," his hopes and disappointments found expression in the description of himself musing in his garden:

I watch'd the sickly calm with aimless scope
In my own heart;

Then in his daydream he cried:

. . . thee, o genial Hope,
Love's elder sister! thee did I behold,
Drest as a bridesmaid, but all pale and cold,
With roseless cheek, all pale and cold and dim,
Lie lifeless at my feet!
And then came Love, a sylph in bridal trim,
And stood beside my seat;
She bent, and kiss'd her sister's lips,
as she was wont to do;—
Alas! 'twas but a chilling breath
Woke just enough of Life in death
To make Hope die anew.

In vain we supplicate the Powers above;
There is no resurrection for the Love
That, bursed in tenderest care, yet fades away
In the chill'd heart of gradual self-decay.

His disappointment with Sara Hutchinson haunted Coleridge's mind to the last.

In mid-March 1834 Harriet noticed on Coleridge's cheek "a peculiar red streak." It indicated another outbreak of the erysipelas from which Coleridge had suffered a year or two before and which had already killed Sir George

Beaumont. In this emergency Coleridge immediately called Green to his aid. Nevertheless, as ever with Coleridge, alternations of recovery and relapse soon followed and continued throughout the remaining four months until his death.

In April he was concerned about the fate of his works. He ordered a copy of his *Poems* to be sent to a friend, and he wrote to Hurst who was now, like his earlier publishers, bankrupt. This attempt to save something from Hurst's failure was unsuccessful. Such, for the time being, was the situation of the *Aids to Reflection* and of "Church and State." In these circumstances Coleridge again reflected sadly upon the loss of his pension. Apparently forgetting his friends' recent gifts and legacies he wailed, "I can truly say I am not worth a shilling of my own since King William the Fourth took my poor gold chain of a hundred links . . . to emblazon d'or the black bar across the Royal arms of the Fitzclarences." The following month he tried to help young James Gillman obtain a curacy, but he was unsuccessful despite his eulogy of James as the worthy son of "dear and exemplary parents."

Two friends of earlier years now called on Coleridge. Poole came during May to Highgate and found Coleridge's mind "as strong as ever, seeming impatient to take leave of its encumbrance"—a delicate allusion to Coleridge's physical infirmities. Memories of the past rather than the devoted friendship of earlier days were now all that remained for Poole: separation over many years could not be overcome.

Similar circumstances also affected the former "friendship" between Coleridge and Sara Hutchinson. She visited him at Highgate on May 8, 1834, and on several other occasions, before returning to the North in June. Coleridge's idealistic feeling for Sara had gradually disintegrated during years of separation and divergent interests, and Sara now copied Wordsworth's poems as devotedly as she had once copied those of Coleridge. Living with the Wordsworths for many years at Rydal Mount, Sara had gradually taken a permanent place in their domestic life, helping Dorothy and Mrs. Wordsworth in household tasks. Of this decline in Sara Hutchinson's "love" into friendship Coleridge had in later years been very conscious.

Coleridge received his admirers to the very last. On June 30, 1834, a young man of twenty-two called at Highgate and was admitted. He was an archeologist and a student and a friend of Hamilton in Dublin, who had given him a letter of introduction. He later became the third Earl of Dunraven.

The young man, Edwin Wyndham Quinn, sent Hamilton an account of the interview on the same day. Entering Coleridge's room, "feeling a mixture of pleasure and awe," he found

a small room, half full of books in great confusion, and in one corner was a small bed, looking mor like a couch, upon which lay certainly the most remarkable looking man I ever saw . . . he was pale and worn when I first entered, but very soon the colour came into his cheeks and his eye brightened, and such an eye as it is! such animation and acuteness! so piercing! . . . His head is finer than I had expected, and his eye different. I supposed it black and rather soft, instead of being grey and penetrating. He laughed a good deal when he alluded to some comparison, I believe he said in the *Friend*, about little toads, and the Emancipation Bill, and the Reform Bill.

Coleridge, Quinn said, had been very ill for three months, but

religion had alleviated very much his hours of pain, and given him fortitude and resignation. He talked about the Chruch, but really I found it so difficult to follow him, that I cannot recollect what he said, but even less can I remember what I should say were the subjects of his conversation: this I think arises from a great want of method; but I say this, feeling I do him injustice: still it strikes me [sic] he rambled on; but I remarked how, when once or twice he was interrupted by people coming into the room and speaking to them, he resumed at the very word he left off at.

The "Conversation" of nearly an hour followed the usual pattern: contemporary political errors re dissenters, his *Logosophia*, and also the introduction to it, which was all ready and

would have been out were it not for his illness. . . . He gave me the plan of the book, but really he got so deep, using words in a sense not familiar to me, that I could not follow him, and I gazed on his ancient and venerable countenance as he went on describing the results of his thoughts. All I can tell you is that his book is on *logic* of some particular kind, and is a sort of introduction to his great work, as he calls the one which Aubrey says exists only in his brain. He gave me a sketch of this also, very brief: the title I thought beautiful and would have given anything to have written it down for you.

Coleridge went on "to speak beautifully about Kant and Bacon, as Aristotelians. Now and then he said something very droll which made us laugh; and he conversed with so much vigour and animation, though he had difficulty in *speaking* at all." Quinn added that he could "willingly have stayed all day. . . . I must say, since I came to London I have not felt so happy as this day; and I consider the visit to Coleridge has been productive of complete pleasure, unmixed with disappointment of any kind."

About this time, on "a lovely afternoon in early summer," Stuart with his teenage daughter Mary rode over to see Coleridge on what proved their last meeting with him. After a quarter of an hour's wait in the dining room, wrote Mary, "the door opened and the old poet (old! he was but sixty-two!) appeared, clad in black, leaning on his staff; much bent, his hair snow white, his face pale; but his eyes, those wondrous eyes! large, lustrous, beaming with intelligence and kindness." Greetings, followed by politics—Disestablishment, which Coleridge opposed with many Biblical quotations especially from Ezekiel—who seemed to Mary "his especial favourite." She had heard him discourse on Ezekiel at a dinner party, but his quotations now were to her "a most bewildering maze." She explained, "Profound as were his arguments, yet the tone, the earnestness, above all the constantly appealing expression of that inspired countenance, fascinated me, and I followed the thread of his discourse delighted, trusting to chance for what I might retain."

"When we rose to depart," she continued,

Coleridge took us into the drawing room to show us a portrait which had lately been taken of himself. He was much dissatisfied with it, and appealed to my father and me that it had not taken his *expression*. But what portrait ever did? He showed us several others, and we stood criticising rather to my amusement, being but in my teens! But his vanity, if such it might be called, had in it such a mixture of benevolence and fun, that one seemd to love him the better for it. At last we went back through the dining-room into Mr Gillman's hall, where he took an affectionate leave of me, and stood talking to my father while I mounted my horse. I think the two old friends of nearly forty years' standing had each a feeling that it might be the last adieu. So loth did they seem to part, Coleridge coming out of the door and shaking hands with my father repeatedly. There he stood while my father mounted! We took our last look, exchanged the last farewell, and rode off. My father was very silent all the way back—while my young brain was busy arranging into order the conversation I had listened to and which I noted down immediately on my return home.

Henry Nelson Coleridge's description of his uncle in 1834 testifies not only to the unique impression made upon him by Coleridge's conversations in the past, but also to his mental vigour almost to the end:

Those who remember him in his more vigorous days can bear withness to the peculiarity and transcendent power of his conversational eloquence. It was unlike anything that could be heard elsewhere; the kind was different, the degree was different, the manner was different. The boundless range of scientific knowledge, the brilliancy and exquisite nicety of illustration, the deep and ready reasoning, the strangeness and immensity of bookish lore—were not all; the dramatic story, the joke, the pun, the festivity, must be added—and with these the clerical-looking dress, the thick waving silver hair, the youthful-coloured cheek, the indefinable mouth, and lips, the quick yet steady and penetrating greenish grey eye, the slow and continuous enunciation, and the everlasting music of his tones,—all went to make up the image and to constitute the living presence of the man. He is now no longer young, and bodily infirmities, we regret to know, have pressed heavily upon him. His natural force is indeed abated; but his eye is not dim, neither is his mind yet enfeebled.

Coleridge's mental vitality, despite illness and pain, impressed all beholders; and the variety of his moods and interests at this time was also noticeable. In the reading of novels, despite his former condemnation of them, he now found an escape from the realities of the sick room, and Marryat's *Peter Simple* was followed by Theodore Hook's *Love and Pride* and by Maria Edgeworth's *Helen*. For a change, he also read Matthew Gregory Lewis's *Journal of a West Indian Proprietor*, which described the life of the Negroes in Jamaica. Shortly afterwards he read with deep interest a life of Bishop Sanford.

Coleridge obtained the novels from the local library at Highgate. Their guardian, Eliza Nixon, sent him flowers as well as books. She received from him kind and flowery letters in return. His last letter to her was written sixteen days before his death. Yet on this very day he expressed to her his belief that he was now convalescent. At other times, too, he told her of his condition. "To be forced in upon *myself*," he wrote, "to be compelled to think about myself, I regard among the saddest aggravations of sickness." In mid-July Coleridge described himself as writing "from a sick-bed, hopeless of recovery, yet without prospect of a speedy removal."

Only a week before, a new generous feminine admirer had appeared and had sent Coleridge the first installment of an annuity. Fate, it seemed—though now with a touch of irony—must send Coleridge annuities to the last moment of his life. In a graceful letter of acceptance, Coleridge described to his benefactress his present state, both physical, mental, and spiritual, and praised the devoted attentions of his two medical friends, Gillman and Green. At the same time he modestly disclaimed "Your too favourable expressions, your too exalted estimate of my moral and intellectual Being . . . I was assured that they proceeded from your love and inward honoring of a Light not mine, but of which you believed yourself to see the translucence thro' the earthly Vessel, the fragile and clouded Lamp vase thro' which the Light gleamed."

So far Coleridge's state, his talk, and his mental clarity all led Gillman to believe the end was far off. But from July 19 Coleridge's health declined so much that the family at Hampstead were informed of his danger and Henry Nelson Coleridge acted to the end as their messenger. Lost in religious meditations, Coleridge sent his blessing to his wife and Sara; but they did not visit him because by this time it seemed that all distrubance must be avoided. Gillman's assistant, Taylor, said a visit from the family would so upset him as to be fatal. It was on this occasion that Henry Nelson saw Samuel for the last time, although he paid regular visits to Highgate until his uncle's death.

But again life revived in Coleridge. Mrs. Gillman, in deep distress and hitherto unable to visit him because of the serious injury to her leg, was carried up to his room on July 22, when all hope was over, to bid him farewell. Gillman was now too ill himself—overwhelmed by the realization of Coleridge's impending death—to visit him. Green and Gillman's assistant, Taylor, were now Coleridge's only medical attendants. Mrs. Gillman, shortly before his death, sent Coleridge a note of gratitude for the blessing he had been to them all.

During a period of recovery Coleridge discussed his philosophy with Green, and the day before his death he repeated his formula of the Trinity to him.* Sara, describing her father's death to Hartley, wrote: "His utterance was difficult but his mind in perfect vigour and clearness—he remarked that his intellect was quite unclouded and he said, 'I could even be witty.' " Coleridge

---

*He sent for Green to whom he wished to dictate some final words for the *Opus Maximum* (*The Logosophia*). J. A. Heraud quoted them in a funeral oration at the Russell Institution. "And be thou sure in whatever may be published of my posthumous works to remember that first of all is the Absolute Good whose self-affirmation is the (I am), as the eternal reality in itself, and the ground and source of all other reality. And next that in this idea nevertheless a distinctivity [sic] is to be carefully preserved, as manifested in the person of the Logos by whom that reality is communicated to all other beings." Green worked on the *Opus Maximum* during the rest of his life, but was unable to coordinate its fragments into any coherent whole. There are some who still think this task may one day be accomplished.

had been given an injection of laudanum, besides doses of the drug along with arrowroot and brandy. Only a few hours before his death his last thought before losing consciousness was for his faithful servant Harriet. It was then that on July 24 he wrote his last letter addressed to Mrs. Gillman and Green, exhorting them to raise funds from friends and relatives to make a "handsome legacy" for Harriet:

> Most dear Mr Green, most dear Mrs Gillman my especial friends, Do impress it on my nephew and son-in-law, Henry Nelson Coleridge, and through him on all who bear my name, that I beg, expect and would fain hope of them according to their means, such a contribution as may suffice collectively for a handsome Legacy for that most faithful, affectionate and disinterested servant Harriet Macklin. Henry can explain. I have never asked for myself.

> S. T. Coleridge

Shortly afterwards Coleridge lost consciousness and remained in that state until his death on the following day, July 25, 1834. He was nearly sixty-two years of age.

The day after Coleridge's death Crabb Robinson, on hearing the news from Mrs. Aders, entered in his diary: "Hear with sorrow of the death of a great man, COLERIDGE." Writing to Wordsworth on the same day, Robinson thus described Coleridge's death: "He died with great composure and fully sensible of his condition. One of the last words that he uttered was a request to Gillman that he would convey to his brothers, the Bishop [doubtless Coleridge's nephew, William Hart Coleridge, bishop of Barbados, 1824–41]—and the Colonel, the assurance that he died with perfect forgiveness towards them, tho' he had felt deeply their ingratitude and unkindness towards him."

On the eleventh day after her father's death Sara Coleridge told Hartley: "The agitation of nerves at the sight of those dear to him disturbed his meditations on his Redeemer to whose bosom he was hastening and he then said that he wished to evince in the manner of his death the depth and sincerity of his faith in Christ." By this time Hartley, on hearing of his father's death, had written to Derwent: "I lived in hopes of seeing our dear departed Parent . . . I might have seen him, might have comforted him, might have been enriched with the fulness of his wisdom; of which, alas, some fragments only abide in my memory."

10   Post Mortem (1834)

Shortly before Coleridge's death he asked Dr. Gillman and Green to make a postmortem examination of his body, which they did. Dr. Gillman did not conduct the examination; it was done by his assistant Taylor and another nameless surgeon. Dr. Gillman's report of it later declared: "The left side of the chest was nearly occupied by the heart which was immensely enlarged. . . . The right side of the chest was filled with fluid enclosed in a membrane having the appearance of a cyst."

This description was sent to the *Times* in 1895 by Dr. Gillman's granddaughter, to refute suggestions that opium and spirits had caused Coleridge's illness. "This will sufficiently account for his bodily sufferings," Dr. Gillman had written, "which were almost without intermission during the progress of the disease, and will explain to you the necessity of subduing these sufferings by narcotics, and of driving on a most feeble circulation by stimulants which his case had imperatively demanded."

Upon the publication of this letter the *Lancet* on June 15, 1895, remarked that Dr. Gillman's account was "not so precise and definite as to be quite clearly interpreted," and objected to some of it as evidently inaccurate. The *Lancet*'s interpretation of Coleridge's condition was that it was probably "dropsical in character, occurring towards the close of life in a subject of chronic cardiac dilation." Nevertheless, despite differences of medical opinions, the *Lancet* agreed with Gillman as to Coleridge's justification for his use of opium and brandy. "This record suffices to prove," it declared, "that this intellectual giant must have suffered more than the world was aware of, and it can be understood that his 'indolence' as well as his opium habit had a physical basis! It can only add to the marvel with which his achievements are justly regarded, that one so physically disabled should have made such extensive and profound contributions to philosophy and literature. It is one more instance of the *triumph of mind* over body."

Yet Sara's account of the postmortem described in a letter to her brother Hartley is interesting, particularly as it is based upon information that her husband brought home from Highgate. Although her summary of the medical details was evidently Gillman's and she accepted the assertion that laudanum could not have been the cause of her father's illness, nevertheless, she had evidently been told that it "is supposed to have been some sympathetic nervous affection." However, she added, "that my father's sufferings were on the whole greatly aggravated by laudanum I have no doubt—but this I firmly believe, that he would have been an invalid and a sufferer all his life if he had never been supplied with this injurious palliative, nor do I believe that it shortened his days."*

Coleridge's funeral took place on August 2 with the usual pomp of the period. Sara described it to her brother Hartley three days afterward as "handsome—a hearse and four—abundance of plumes—two mourning carriages etc." Thus, with all dignity Coleridge was interred in Highgate Cemetery. His grave was on the site of the demolished chapel, which had been the object of dispute both in Highgate and in Parliament.**

Both Lamb and Dr. Gillman, who was ill in bed, were too overcome to attend. Lamb's sorrow found expression to young James Gillman on August 5: "The sad week being over, I must write to you to say that I was glad of being spared from attending; I have no words to express my feeling with you all."

But Coleridge's disciples came, Sara reported: "Green, young James Gillman, Mr. Kinnaird, Mr. Steinmetz, (father of the youth who left my father a legacy), Mr. Stirling, (a young clergyman, a disciple of my father—who begged to be allowed to follow him to the grave, and came from Cambridge on

---

*For further details of the results of the autopsy, see Walter Jackson Bates, *Coleridge* (Lauda, 1969), pp. 103-6.

**Various circumstances led to changes being made in Coleridge's place of burial. Upon her husband's death in 1843 Sara had her father's remains "placed in a new outer coffin and reinterred in what was now the family vault" in Highgate Cemetery. There Mrs. Coleridge was buried upon her death in 1845. In 1866 a school chapel was built over the ground which included Coleridge's grave. Almost a century later a writer of the day visiting Coleridge's grave found the vault so neglected that it had become "a dump for discarded iron, a receptacle for blown litter and leaves and a convenient place for tramps to sleep in." This part of the graveyard so long a subject of discord in Highgate was, it now appears, noone's responsibility. As a result of this discovery an influential committee was created for the removal of the grave to St. Michael's Church in The Grove on March 29, 1961. The fund raised for this purpose was large enough to allow not only care of the church and the grave but also an annual lecture in honor of Coleridge's memory. A dignified ceremony at which the memorial stone to Coleridge was dedicated was held on June 6, 1961, in the presence of a distinguished audience of writers, poets, and members of the Coleridge family, and at which the bishop of London officiated. Although the fund created for memorial lectures on Coleridge proved inadequate for yearly lectures, the lectures were given at longer intervals by leading English poets of the day.

purpose.'' For even after death, Coleridge's magnetism retained its force. The service was read by the Highgate minister, Mr. Mence.

Coleridge's magnetism was still very strong upon Heraud, who, when orating on Coleridge to the Russell Institution on August 8, said: "O what a voice is silent. To that Voice when living I hearkened more than once in admiration and delight—yet to me were permitted but few opportunities of experiencing its fascination. Such was the seduction of his rhetoric, such the magic of his intonation, one was fearful, if resigned, too often to the enchantment of surrendering the independence of one's modes of thought and of submitting to his, without will or power of extrication.''

After the burial Green, "greatly overcome," read the will which had been made on September 27, 1829—a fortnight after Sara's marriage. Green was the sole executor and was instructed to sell Coleridge's effects, consisting chiefly of his books and MSS, which realized less than £3000. This was to be invested by Green on behalf of Mrs. Coleridge, who was to receive the dividends. Coleridge directed that after Mrs. Coleridge's death Sara, if unmarried or widowed without means, should receive the whole bequest, which otherwise should be equally divided between herself and her two brothers. Coleridge's pictures and engravings at the Gillmans' house were left to Mrs. Gillman, "my love for whom, and my sense of her unremitted goodness, tenderness, and never wearied kindness to me, I hope and humbly trust, will follow me, as a part of my abiding Being, into that state into which I hope to rise.''

At the same time he exhorted his children that, although he had "but little to leave them," they would "regard it as part of their inheritance, when I thus bequeath to them my affection and gratitude to Mr. and Mrs. Gillman, and to the dear friend, companion, partner and help-mate of my worthiest studies, Mr. Joseph Henry Green." Nor was Dr. Gillman forgotten. To him was left a manuscript translation of Frere's *Aristophanes*, with an injunction to retain it as a family heirloom. To Frere he left "a continuation" of his prayers. To Green, with a word of appreciation for his assistance as executor, he left "the reverential sense which all my children entertain" of him. Also as an heirloom Coleridge left a book to Sara, "a blessing to both her parents and to her mother the rich reward." To Derwent's wife, "whom I bless God that I have been permitted to see, and to have seen and to esteem and love on my own judgement and to be grateful for her on my own account, as well as on behalf of my dear son," he left an interleaved copy of *The Friend*, with notes by himself, also as an heirloom.

Mourning rings were bequeathed to Lamb (shared with Mary), Basil Montagu, Thomas Poole, and Josiah and Launcelot Wade of Bristol for their help in the past, and to Sara Hutchinson. As for Southey and Wordsworth, who got no rings, he felt that "my children have a debt of gratitude and reverential affection on their own account; and the sentiments I have left on record in my *Literary Life* and in my *Poems*, and which are the convictions of the present moment, supersede the necessity of any other memorial of my regard and respect.''

The will concluded:

> There is one thing yet on my heart to say, as far as it may consist with entire submission to the Divine Will, namely that I have perhaps too little proposed to myself any temporal interests either of fortune or literary reputation, and that the sole regret I now feel at the scantiness of my means arises out of my inability to make such provision for my dear Hartley, my first-born, as might set his feelings at ease, and his mind at liberty from the depressing anxieties of the To-day, and exempt him from the necessity of diverting the talents with which it has pleased God to entrust him, to subjects of temporary interests: knowing that it is with him, as it ever has been with myself, that his powers and the ability and disposition to exert them are greatest when the motives from without are least or of least urgency. But with earnest prayer, and through faith in Jesus the Mediator, I commit him, with his dear Brother and Sister, to the care and providence of the Father in Heaven, and affectionately leave this my last injunction—My dear children *love* one another.

Nearly a year after writing the will, in this same mood, Coleridge had added a codicil, giving Green, Henry Nelson Coleridge, and Dr. Gillman the management of Hartley's possible inheritance, the dividends of which they were to pay to him regularly, but with a proviso that he should be left entirely free to choose his own place of residence at any time, and to bequeath in his will, to whomever he wished, this inheritance.

The reactions of Coleridge's oldest friends to the news of his death were not identical. "He had long been dead to me," said Southey, so long the mainstay of Coelridge's wife and family; "but his decease has naturally wakened up old recollections. . . . All who were of his blood were in the highest degree proud of his reputation, but this was their only feeling concerning him." To the poet Bowles Southey said of Coleridge: "Living wholly to himself as he had so long done, his death has brought with it little grief and no loss to any of them."

Nevertheless, both Sara Coleridge and Hartley were certainly saddened by their father's death. Sara on August 5 sent a long account of it to Hartley in which, after repeating her father's injunction to them "to love one another," she continued with a rhapsodical appreciation of his virtues, which included his complaints against his detractors who left him "misunderstood and misrepresented by many, and grossly calumniated by some." But inevitably, Sara's letter could not reveal a close and personal intimate affection for a father who had so seldom entered her life. Thus, even Sara's passionate letter did not disprove the truth of Southey's assertion. Certainly, Mrs. Coleridge's temperament and marital experience must have modified her grief at the loss of her truant husband. It is typical of her practicality that when Sara, overcome by emotion, was unable to finish her letter to Hartley, her mother took the pen and, in conclusion, promised to send him later full details of the will. At the same time she asked him to pass on Sara's letter "to our dear friends at Rydal." Similarly practical was her wish that Hartley had got "mourning hat, etc." for which "Mrs. Wordsworth will lend the money to pay for it."

Wordsworth, on hearing the news of Coleridge's death (from Henry Nelson Coleridge), an event for which letters from Sara Hutchinson had prepared him, spoke in a formal, almost impersonal manner, of the "great shock the announcement of his dissolution" had given him and the Wordsworth family. For informing them "of our ever-to-be lamented friend's decease" he expressed his thanks. Next, Wordsworth congratulated the family "upon the calmness of mind, and the firm faith in his Redeemer, which supported him through his painful bodily and mental trials, and which we hope and trust have enrolled his spirit among those of the blessed." But apparently realizing the personal aloofness of his letter, he concluded; "I cannot give way to the expression of my feelings upon this mournful occasion. I have not strength of mind to do so." Indeed, he continued, he had lost so many friends in recent years and had had so many anxieties "that it would be no kindness to you were I to yield to the solemn and sad thoughts and remembrances which press upon me."

It was a year later that Wordsworth gave poetic expression, in some of the finest verses of his last years, to the deeper emotions which Coleridge's death, along with that of other friends, including Lamb, awoke in him. But the Coleridge who now inspired Wordsworth was the early Coleridge, the poet:

Nor has the rolling year twice measured
From sign to sign, its steadfast course,
Since every mortal power of Coleridge
Was frozen at its marvellous source;

The rapt One, of the godlike forehead,
The heaven-eyed creature sleeps in earth;
And Lamb, the frolic and the gentle,
Has vanished from his lonely Hearth.

Like clouds that rake the mountain-summits,
or waves that own no curing hand,
How fast has brother followed brother,
From sunshine to the sunless land!

Apart from poetic licence Wordsworth some months later made to Robinson a less exalted comment in sober prose. "In Coleridge," he said, "there was a sort of dreaminess which would not let him see things as they were. He would talk about his own feelings and recollections and intentions in a way that deceived others, but he was first deceived himself." And when, two years later, the first and only volume of Dr. Gillman's eulogistic *Life of Coleridge* appeared, Wordsworth made a similar criticism of Coleridge to a now unknown correspondent. "Mr. Gillman's book," he wrote, "is not better than I feared I should find it. It is full of mistakes as to facts, and misrepresentations concerning facts. Poor dear Coleridge, from a hundred causes, many of them unhappy ones, was not to be trusted in his account either of particular occurrences, or the general tenor of his engagements and occupations. Of idolatrous biography I think very lightly." Wordsworth's repeated accusation of Coleridge's inaccuracies was also, in fact, identical with Lamb's criticism of Coleridge made many years before, but of which Wordworth was ignorant.

Poor Lamb—who died five months after Coleridge—had felt the passing of Coleridge much more keenly than Wordsworth. "Totally incapable," he described himself in a brief reply to a request for letters of Coleridge, of supplying such. As to an article on his friend's death, also suggested: "It would shock me, who am shocked enough already, to sit down to *write* about it." Four months later, in reply to a request for an inscription in a friend's autograph album, Lamb in prose soared far beyond the poetic licence of Wordsworth in his memorial verse. "When I heard of the death of Coleridge it was without grief. It seemed to me that he long had been on the confines of the next world,—that he had a hunger for eternity. I grieved," he continued, "that I could not grieve. But since, I feel how great a part he was of me. His great and dear spirit haunts me. I cannot think a thought, I cannot make a criticism on men or books, without an ineffectual turning and reference to him." Lamb then proceeded to praise Coleridge as an unrivaled conversationalist, and next—for the moment as inaccurate as Coleridge himself—declared: "He was my fifty years old friend without a dissension. Never saw I his likeness, nor probably the world can see again." In this mood even Lamb's dyspathy toward the Gillmans changed to passionate affection. "I love the faithful Gillmans," he cried in a final ecstasy, "more than while they exercised their virtues towards him living. What was his mansion is consecrated to me a chapel." When Lamb visited the Gillmans and heard from Harriet an affecting account of Coleridge's death, he presented her with five guineas as a reward for her devotion to him. During the few months of life that remained for Lamb, he is said to have been haunted by memories of Coleridge and was often heard to exclaim during conversations with others, "Coleridge is dead!" as if forcing himself to believe it.

Unfortunately there is no published letter by Mrs. Coleridge on her husband's death. But in November of the same year she visited the Gillmans and reported to Poole: "They are both in indifferent health and bad spirits; they find it difficult to reconcile themselves to their loss; Nineteen years, they say, in the daily habit of seeing and conversing with such a being as he whom they deplore, cannot be easily forgotten. They have erected a tablet in Highgate Church expressive of their love and reverence for the departed."

Certainly the Gillmans were most sincerely affected by Coleridge's death, and their sorrow found public expression in an epitaph engraved on a marble tablet and placed in the church:

E P I T A P H

Sacred to the memory

of

SAMUEL TAYLOR COLERIDGE

Poet, Philosopher, Theologian.
This truly great and good man rested for the
    Last nineteen years of his life
       in this hamlet.
He quitted the body of this death
      July 25th, 1834.
In the sixty second year of his age.
Of his profound learning and discursive genius
his literary works are an imperishable record.
      To his private worth
      His social and Christian virtues,
      James and Anne Gillman
the friends with whom he resided
during the above period, dedicate this tablet.
      Under the pressure of a long
      and most painful disease,
his disposition was unalterably sweet and angelic

He was an ever-enduring, ever-loving friend
      the gentlest and kindest teacher,
      the most engaging home companion.
"O framed for calmer times and nobler hearts!
O studious poet, eloquent for truth!
Philosopher contemning wealth and death:
Yet docile, child-like, full of life and love.
Here on thy monumental stone thy friends
Inscribe thy worth.*

      Reader, for the world mourn
      A light has passed from the earth,
But for this pious and exalted Christian
      Rejoice, and again I say unto you rejoice!''

To Sara Coleridge Mrs. Gillman expatiated upon Coleridge's qualities which had so dominated the Gillmans' home: "The influence of his beautiful nature on our domestics, so often set down by friends or neighbours to my good management, his forgiving nature, his heavenly-mindedness, his care not to give offence unless duty called on him to tell home truth; his sweet and cheerful temper, and so many moral qualities of more or less value, and all adorned by his Christian principles. His was indeed Christianity.''

*This quotation is *mutatis mutandis* from Coleridge's verses entitled "A Tombless Epitaph" (1809).

Mrs. Gillman described her husband immediately after Coleridge's death as "heart-stricken, and yet determined to conceal his feelings if possible." Later Mrs. Gillman said, "My beloved husband never recovered from his [Coleridge's] death."

Young Caroline Fox, whom Coleridge some years before in her babyhood had fondled on his knee, wrote: "The Gillmans have appeared quite different since the departure of the Bard—their *spirits broken*—and everything testifying that Coleridge is dead."

One friend of Coleridge who did not share the undiluted enthusiasm for Coleridge's memory experienced by the Gillmans and by Sara Coleridge, was De Quincey. His realistic attitude toward Coleridge was shown in a series of articles on him published before the close of the year 1834 in *Tait's Magazine*. There, mingled with much admiration and praise of Coleridge's genius, were indiscreet references to his addiction to opium along with other references to his temperament, which were well below idolatry. Sara Coleridge, though of course appreciating De Quincey's praise, was greatly shocked and indignant at his having publicly exposed her father's weaknesses. So, too, was Sara Hutchinson, who, after reading the articles, described them to Quillinan as "a series of infamous articles on poor Coleridge by his friend the Opium Eater."

Sara Hutchinson's reaction to the death of Coleridge was, nevertheless, unemotional.

> Poor dear Coleridge is gone! He died a most calm and happy death. . . . Tho' he had suffered great pain for some time previous—he was opened—the disease was at his heart. . . . We have not heard *direct* from any of them since the first announcement by Henry. . . . Poor Mr. and Mrs. Gillman will be true mourners—His own relations had more pride in him than Love for him—at least Pride was the foundation of their Love—and even their Pride did not serve to prevent his being dependent upon the Gillmans for his support since the time when his Pension was withdrawn.

How far Sara Hutchinson's affection for Coleridge had been superseded during the long years of devotion to Wordsworth and Southey her letters clearly, though unintentionally, reveal. Only two months after Coleridge's death Sara Hutchinson wrote to Mrs. Coleridge, evidently as to a sympathetic friend, expressing great admiration for Southey himself: "If any man ever deserved the Title of *Christian* Philosopher it is he," she wrote: "so much feeling with so much power to overcome I never before saw exemplified." For Coleridge her letters showed no such enthusiasm.

Some four months later, writing on behalf of Wordsworth in reply to a request from Green for Coleridge's letters, Sara Hutchinson said: "Mr. Wordsworth does not find any among them which could be interesting to the public—as they mostly relate to domestic matters." At the same time she requested the return of a copy of Chapman's *Homer*, which had been sent to Green along with other books of Coleridge. It had been included by mistake as Coleridge had given the book to Sara Hutchinson. "You will observe," she continued, "by one extract from a Letter to me that Chapman's *Homer* was a gift of our dear Friend to me—and therefore will not wonder that I am desirous of re-possessing it." She concluded by expressing her disgust for De Quincey's "infamous articles."

On June 23, 1835, Sara Hutchinson died suddenly after an attack of rheumatic fever. Wordsworth, writing to Southey immediately after Sara's death, was deeply moved:

> O my dear Southey, we have lost a precious friend; of the strength of her attachment to you and yours you can but imperfectly judge. It was deep in her heart. I saw her within an hour after her decease, in the silence and peace of death, with as heavenly an expression on her countenance as ever human creature had. Surely there is food for faith in these appearances; for myself, I can say that I have passed a wakeful night, more in joy than sorrow, with that blessed face before my eyes perpetually as I lay in bed.

Shortly afterward, in a letter to Mrs. Clarkson speaking of Sara Hutchinson's death, Wordsworth added: "She is, we trust, among the blessed. But to us the loss upon earth is irreparable."

Coleridge's death by no means ended his influence upon the Gillmans. Mr. Gillman soon began to write Coleridge's life as a solace to his irremediable sorrow and failing health, and he had completed only the first volume when a paralytic stroke prevented the completion of the second, which at his death he ordered to be destroyed. In the spring of 1843 Mrs. Gillman, now a widow, sorrowfully left the house in the Grove, which had so many memories. Ten years later, when her granddaughter Mrs. Watson regularly visited her, her talk was almost wholly of Coleridge, and the granddaughter on arriving would bring happiness to her almost-blind grandmother by reading Coleridge's writings, both published and in manuscripts—still Mrs. Gillman's chief interest in life.

Mrs. Watson has left us an intimate picture of her grandmother's behavior during these visits:

> At intervals she would comment on various portions from remembrance of his spoken words; sometimes it seemed to me imagining herself back in the old days when his works were despised or unappreciated both by the critics and the public. Then she would reiterate the opinions of her husband and of literary friends, repeating with some emphasis, "These words *must* live, and the day must *come* when the world will acknowledge their truth!" At times when I was reading aloud favourite passages from the Poet's works, some agitation appeared to come over her, she would sigh—and there was a change in the tone of her voice as she would murmur, "Ah! my dear, if only . . . " then after a pause, "Well! let us continue," soon recovering her accustomed calm and gracious manner, she bade me resume the reading, and again spoke hopefully of the poet and his work.

Mrs. Gillman would stress the harmony between herself and her husband who, she said, "never recovered" from Coleridge's death, which was immediately followed by the failure of Mr. Gillman's health, "several slight seizures" which killed him at the age of fifty-seven, some five years after the death of Coleridge. Mrs. Gillman at other times saw reviews of Coleridge and wrote angry comments upon what seemed to her derogatory. "Coleridge," she said, "made no *demands* on others; if love and kind attention followed him, they were the spontaneous offerings of those who thus gratified themselves."

To earnest, idealizing Americans who in these later years came to Mrs. Gillman as to a High-priestess of Coleridge to worship, she discoursed to them as if to her granddaughter of Coleridge's moral and intellectual superiority above all other men:

> He was the same kindly affectionate being from morning till evening—from January to December. He delighted to reconcile little differences, and to make all things go smoothly and happily. He was always teaching "the Beautiful and the Good," while his own daily life was the best illustration of the good and beautiful which he taught. You know how the world sometimes misrepresented him and ill treated him, and he felt it now and then very keenly, but he bore it all with the sweetest patience. As I have said, I never saw him in what could be called an ill temper during the nineteen years he was under our roof. The servants in the house idolised him and when he died it seemed as if their hearts would break. We all had one feeling towards him: we all loved him alike, each in our own way, and we all alike wept when he died. Love was the law of his nature. He clothed his friends, to be sure, in the colours of his own fancy and sometimes perhaps the colours were too bright, but it was his goodness of heart quite as much as his imagination, that was at fault.

Another American visitor who called on Mrs. Gillman at Highgate shortly after her husband's death left a vivid impression of the scene: "I was shown into a back drawing-room where sat an elderly lady in deep mourning. . . . She made a sign to the servant to withdraw, and then gave way to her emotion—'All gone, all Gone!' were the only words she could at first utter. . . . She showed me several of Mr. Gillman's books filled with notes in Coleridge's handwriting. . . . In another room was his bust and in another a fine picture by Allston." She showed him Allston's poem on Coleridge. Shown Coleridge's room, the American gazed at "the bed whereon he died," gazed through the window at Caen wood where

> his lustrous eyes fixed in devout meditation, Coleridge was wont to behold the sunset. Mrs. Gillman tired not of talking of him nor I of listening. . . . To me it was a bright hour, and with feelings of more than esteem for its lonely inmate I quitted the roof where in his afflicted old age, the author of "Christabel" had found a loving shelter. In a few moments I was away again in the whirl of the vast metropolis.

Wordsworth was not the only poet to lament in verse Coleridge's death. The devoted Allston, now back in his native land, deserted the paintbrush momentarily on hearing of Coleridge's death and, inspired by the Muses, sang:

> But he who mourns is not as one bereft
> Of all he lov'd: thy living Truths are left.

So his sonnet continued expressing a fervid devotion to the memory of Coleridge, sailing on

> some starless Sea—all dark above
> All dark below—

Index